TEMPLE AND COSMOS

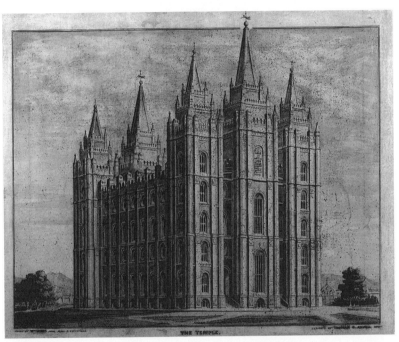

This 1850 drawing of the Salt Lake Temple by William Ward, an assistant to the temple architect Truman Angell, was completed before the first stones were laid. Though some details were later modified, such as the two angel windvanes, it shows the completeness of their conception of the temple. Like its ancient predecessors, it is an enduring monument in stone, a model of the cosmos, that points us toward eternity.

The Collected Works of Hugh Nibley: Volume 12
Ancient History

TEMPLE AND COSMOS
Beyond This Ignorant Present

Hugh Nibley

Edited by
Don E. Norton

Illustrations directed by
Michael P. Lyon

Deseret Book Company
Salt Lake City, Utah
and
Foundation for Ancient Research and Mormon Studies
Provo, Utah

The Collected Works of Hugh Nibley

Volumes published to date:

Old Testament and Related Studies
Enoch the Prophet
The World and the Prophets
Mormonism and Early Christianity
Lehi in the Desert/The World of the Jaredites/There Were Jaredites
An Approach to the Book of Mormon
Since Cumorah
The Prophetic Book of Mormon
Approaching Zion
The Ancient State
Tinkling Cymbals and Sounding Brass
Temple and Cosmos

Library of Congress Cataloging-in-Publication Data

Nibley, Hugh, 1910–
    Temple and cosmos : beyond this ignorant present / Hugh Nibley ; edited by Don Norton.
        p.   cm. — (The collected works of Hugh Nibley ; v. 12)
    Includes bibliographical references and index.
    ISBN 0-87579-523-4
    1. Temples. 2. Temples, Mormon. 3. Middle East—Religion.
4. North America—Religion. 5. Church of Jesus Christ of Latter-day Saints—Doctrines. 6. Mormon Church—Doctrines. 7. Bible. O.T. Apocrypha—Criticism, interpretation, etc. 8. Dead Sea scrolls—Criticism, interpretation, etc. 9. Hermetism. I. Norton, Don E. II. Title. III. Series: Nibley, Hugh, 1910–   Works. 1986 ; v. 12.
BX8643.T4N53   1992
246'.95893—dc20   91-33320
                                                    CIP

Printed in the United States of America   18961-4591A

10   9   8   7

Contents

Illustrations

Temple Articles in Other Volumes of the *Collected Works of Hugh Nibley*

Key to Abbreviations

ANT	Montague R. James, *The Apocryphal New Testament* (Oxford: Clarendon, 1975)
APOT	R. H. Charles, ed., *The Apocrypha and Pseudepigrapha of the Old Testament in English*, 2 vols. (Oxford: Clarendon, 1913)
ASAE	*Annales du Service des Antiquités de l'Égypte*
BYUS	*Brigham Young University Studies*
CWHN	*Collected Works of Hugh Nibley*
DJMT	*Dialogue: A Journal of Mormon Thought*
HC	*History of the Church*
IE	*Improvement Era*
JD	*Journal of Discourses*
LIMC	*Lexicon Iconographicum Mythologiae Classicae*
MS	*Millennial Star*
NHLE	James M. Robinson, ed., *Nag Hammadi Library in English* (New York: Harper and Row, 1977)
OTP	James H. Charlesworth, ed., *Old Testament Pseudepigrapha*, 2 vols. (Garden City, NY: Doubleday, 1983, 1985)
PG	J.-P. Migne, ed., *Patrologiae Cursus Completus . . . Series Graeca* (Paris: Migne, 1857–66), 161 vols.
PL	J.-P. Migne, ed., *Patrologiae Cursus Completus . . . Series Latina* (Paris: Migne, 1844–64), 221 vols.

PO	R. Graffin and F. Nau, eds., *Patrologia Orientalis* (Paris: Firmin-Didot, 1907–)
PT	Pyramid Text
TB	Babylonian Talmud
TPJS	Joseph Smith, *Teachings of the Prophet Joseph Smith,* selected by Joseph Fielding Smith (Salt Lake City: Deseret Book, 1938)
WPQ	*Western Political Quarterly*

Foreword

The words *temple* and *cosmos* appear together in the title of this volume because the "temple is a scale model of the universe" (p. 15). Participation in the instruction and ordinances of the temple enables "one to get one's bearings from the universe." The temple is the link between the seeming chaos and dissolution of this temporal world and the beautiful configuration (cosmos) and permanence of the eternal order. "The mystique of the temple lies in its extension to other worlds; it is the reflection on earth of the heavenly order, and the power that fills it comes from above."

Except among Latter-day Saints, the notion of temple had been all but lost to the world until early in this century, when scholars rediscovered (or perhaps simply began to acknowledge) the richly consistent stories (myths) and practices (rituals) in nearly all cultures (but in particular the ancient Near East) that take place in sacred structures. One can now safely say that the temple is "the source of all civilization" (p. 22): "there is no aspect of our civilization which doesn't have its rise in the temple" (p. 25) — all the arts, government, commerce, the traditional academic disciplines (mathematics, astronomy, history, architecture, philosophy), writing (and hence libraries), athletic competition, judicial systems, our festivals, the patterns of our celebrations, and so on. In fact, many of the accouterments and much of the aura of our contemporary institutions yet resemble what went on in ancient temples.

Latter-day Saints will welcome these "notes" on

temples. In acknowledging the temple as a high expression
of godliness, a place where some of the most vital work
of our dispensation takes place, Latter-day Saints have
suffered some abuse. Outsiders find and remind members
of the Church (sometimes to the point of ridicule) that
temple worship is strange by the standards of the secular
world and most modern religious communities. The
temple is indeed a very "different" experience—as well it
ought to be, reflecting, as it does, the realities of another
world. Nibley most helpfully delineates the flatness of human attempts to avoid the big questions that all humanity
poses—the "terrible questions," as he calls them: Where
did we come from? What is the purpose of life? What
happens to us after death? These are questions the temple
answers.

An interesting dimension to the notion of temple is the
fact that many leading scientists now talk openly about an
"organizing, ordering force" (p. 8) in the universe that
creates and maintains order and stability—this in contradiction to the traditionally conceived "laws of nature,"
according to which everything tends to "corruption and
disintegration" (p. 10). While this occurs on the physical
level, the temple is the school of the mind, producing a
stable cosmic *mental* state: "bringing anything back to its
original state in at-one-ment" (p. 10).

The present book naturally divides into two sections:

1. Articles 1–4: "The Meaning of the Temple" through
"The Circle and the Square." The chapters in this section
focus on the nature, meaning, and history of the temple.

2. The remaining articles: These emphasize the cosmic
context of the temple. A short review of each of the pieces
in this latter section may be helpful.

The temple presents a view of human existence as a
progression toward godhood. "The Expanding Gospel"
emphasizes the dynamic quality of the gospel message, in
contrast to the traditionally static view held by scholars

and clergy, most evident in their restrictive views of the scriptures — an uninspired or closed canon. The discovery of numerous new manuscripts (and these shed new light on long-known apocryphal documents) has led to a reconsideration of "many . . . areas of doctrine and important rites and ordinances" (p. 199). Nibley outlines broadly the documents and principal themes that have emerged — the general features of the plan of salvation (the premortal existence, the process of the creation, the doctrine of the two ways, and many others).

"Rediscovery of the Apocrypha and the Book of Mormon" also rehearses the main themes of the gospel "plan," in particular as set forth in the Book of Mormon — which turns out to be a genuinely cosmic (hence temple) document. The "Apocryphal Writings and Teachings of the Dead Sea Scrolls," along with the Book of Mormon, takes up the persistent themes of creation: again, the process of the creation itself, relationships among the many worlds, the place of ordinances in the cosmic plan, and the role of messengers in communicating the plan to humankind.

"The terrible questions are terrible because they can't be answered. . . . Few people will touch them, or even think about them" (pp. 351, 371): Who are we? What is real? Joseph Smith certainly did not flinch from these questions; and it is the temple that faces them most directly.

"*Hermetism* . . . is the label for a body of knowledge resembling that of the gospel which has been circulated among mankind for a very long time" (p. 389) — knowledge of the primal world, as expressed in countless cultures in sacred myth and ritual from time's beginning. Such knowledge — touching on things "beyond this ignorant present" (William Shakespeare, *Macbeth*, act I, scene v, lines 57–58) — has a way of surfacing from time to time, always contradicting the prevailing practical pursuits of academics, business, and consumerism — the comfortable lifestyle. While Joseph Smith did not draw directly on the Hermetic tradition, much that was revealed to him relates to it and is implicit in temple worship; hence the connections are instructive.

A prevailing modern view is that the facts of history contradict the claims of religionists. In "Do Religion and History Conflict?" Nibley asks, Whose history? And whose religion? He goes on to track the popular heresies of history and traditional religion, inviting readers to view history in a more complete perspective, one that considers open-mindedly the large ancient corpus of primary records; the ancients viewed the world much differently than we do, and in a manner very consonant with the tenets of a revealed religion.

The alphabet, which makes possible writing (the "miracle of miracles" [p. 458]), was a gift of heaven, appearing first in the decor and archives of ancient temples. In "Genesis of the Written Word," Nibley reviews evidence that writing was not, as most scholars believe, the end product of a long, evolutionary process (evidence of intermediary stages is lacking), but a skill we humans have enjoyed from our beginnings.

Nibley calls science fiction "folk scripture" because its authors unoriginally draw their best themes and plots (and sometimes even titles) from the Bible or apocryphal literature. In fact, scripture itself, in its treatment of these themes and plots, is more mind-boggling; and its cosmic content is authentic.

The eternal perspective fostered by the temple provides answers to contemporary issues. "The Best Possible Test" discusses the now largely irrelevant question of why blacks did not hold the priesthood. It approaches this difficult subject in an other-world context: "The greater the tribulation here, the greater the glory hereafter." "Some Notes on Cultural Diversity in the Univeral Church" describes the "Zion culture" and the expression of this culture in various world civilizations.

The book concludes with two reviews: the first, "From the Earth upon Which Thou Standest," of artist Wulf Barsch's paintings; and the second, "Foreword to Eugene England's Book," a review of England's essays *Why the Church Is As True As the Gospel*. In both, Nibley emphasizes the advantage of an other-world perspective, which both England and Barsch reflect in their work.

Indeed, it is in the temple where "time, space, and lives are extended" (p. 83); where men and women are invited to step beyond "this ignorant present" and gain clear perspective of the great plan of the eternities.

This volume, like the other volumes in the *Collected Works of Hugh Nibley*, is the result of countless hours of selfless work by many individuals. The energy and skill they have devotedly given has made this book possible: Glen Cooper, James Fleugel, John Gee, Fran Hafen, William Hamblin, Daniel McKinlay, Tyler Moulton, Phyllis Nibley, Art Pollard, Shirley Ricks, Stephen Ricks, Matthew Roper, Barbara Schmidt, James Tredway, and John Welch. Michael Lyon has directed the production and research on the illustrations, aided by Tyler Moulton, Mark Clifford, and Philip Lyon. Jack Lyon, Shauna Gibby, Patricia Parkinson, and Emily Watts at Deseret Book have been most helpful in the production of this volume. We also wish to thank those whose generous contributions have facilitated the preparation of this and other volumes in the *Collected Works of Hugh Nibley*.

DON E. NORTON

Temple

The Meaning of the Temple

Recently in our family night, I was supposed to talk about the meaning of the temple in light of the gospel. One of the many distinguishing features of our time is the availability of really good popular science summaries written by top men in various fields; and none of us should neglect these, no matter what our own fields are. Any field of serious study today is necessarily highly specialized, and at the same time it calls for branching out into related fields. These summaries go far beyond the popularizing of another day. Because of our marvelous processes of photographic reproduction, magnificently illustrated books on every branch of science are now available.

For example, recently I looked at P. T. Matthews's *The Nuclear Apple*, and before that, it was the biologist Lyall Watson's book *Supernature*, and before that, Nigel Calder's broad survey of recent studies of the brain called *The Mind of Man*. That same Nigel Calder, who works for the British Broadcasting Corporation, goes all around the world getting up television programs of very high caliber. Thus, while surveying recent astronomical developments, he consulted with major astronomers in every part of the world and so built up the programs. The last one was called the *Violent Universe*. It was required reading in our Honors Program (and probably still is), and he recently has put out one on the new geology, plate techtonics, which he

This lecture, originally delivered at Aspen Grove, Utah, on September 1, 1973, was given in this longer version in 1975.

calls the *Restless Earth*. The data of these books is significant. The *Violent Universe, Restless Earth,* and *Supernature*—that is not the way I heard it when I went to school.

In my day, everything was pretty well under control. At best we had a tolerant scientific smile for anything suggesting catastrophism or any dramatic or spectacular event in history or in nature; this kind of stuff smacked of the apocalyptic visions of Mormonism, things classed in the lunatic fringe, apocalyptic sensationalism. There was no place in modern thinking for that sort of thing. Yet in all these books, regardless of the fields, authors today seem to be saying much the same thing. They all come to one very interesting conclusion, which a few quotations will make clear.

First, one basic proposition receives particular attention in all of them, the well-known second law of thermodynamics: everything runs down.[1] And it is stated with strong and bemused reservations, because there is something wrong with it. Let us quote Watson, the biologist (and I understand he has a great reputation in England):

> Left to itself, everything tends to become more and more disorderly, until the final and natural state of things is a completely random distribution of matter. Any kind of order . . . is unnatural, and happens only by chance encounters. . . . These events are statistically unlikely and the further combination of molecules into anything as highly organized as a living organism is wildly improbable. Life is a rare and unreasonable thing. [He belabors the point]: Life occurs by chance, and . . . the probability of its occurring and continuing is infinitesimal.[2]

There is no chance of us being here at all. Furthermore, "the cosmos itself is patternless, being a jumble of random and disordered events."[3] It is not just life that is improbable, but the fabric of life itself—matter. The nuclear physicist P. T. Matthews asks,

> Why is the proton stable, . . . since this is clearly crucial to the world as we know it? From the atomic point of view, the proton is one of the basic building blocks. Yet from the behavior of the other hadrons, . . . there is no obvious reason why it should not disintegrate into, say, a positive pion and neutrino, which is not forbidden by any conservation law.[4]

(The only two stable hadrons are the neutron [n^0] and the proton [p^+]. The neutron has a mean life span of 3×10^3 sec [about 50 minutes]. All other hadrons have mean life spans of from 10^{-8} to 10^{-18} seconds). Matthews goes on to explain the factors that determine the stability of the proton: "The rate of decay of any particle depends partly on the strength of the interaction and partly on the 'amount of room' it has into which it can decay."[5] To describe what he means by "amount of room," Matthews draws an analogy of a room full of objects: "For every object in the room, there are, of course, vastly many more positions in which it would be considered out of place. When these possibilities for all the objects in the room are multiplied together, the number of untidy or disordered states exceeds the ordered ones by some enormous factor."[6]

Then he moves into the domain of the second law of thermodynamics and a mathematical description of this concept. Matthews continues, "The logarithm of the number of different states in which a system can be found is called the *entropy*. Thus the entropy of tidy or ordered states is very much less than that of untidy or disordered ones."[7] To give us an idea about the magnitudes of the numbers we are dealing with, he presents the analogy of a deck of cards:

> The rate at which numbers build up in the Second Law situation can be illustrated by considering a pack of playing cards. We can define an ordered, or tidy, state to be one in which the cards are arranged by value in successive suits. There are just twenty-four such config-

urations which arise from the different possible order-
ings of suits. This is itself a surprisingly large number,
but the number of different ways the fifty-two cards can
be arranged is about ten thousand million, million, mil-
lion, million, million, million, million, million (10^{52}). The
chance of finding a shuffled pack in an ordered state is
the ratio of these two numbers [$24/10^{52}$].[8]

Matthews continues:

The relevance of this to our problem is that one may
think of a proton at rest as a very highly ordered condition of a certain amount of energy—the rest energy of
the proton—which can exist in just one state (strictly two
if we allow for two possible orientations of the proton
spin). If the proton can decay by any mechanism into
two or more lighter particles, these serve to define an
alternative condition of the system which is relatively
highly *disordered,* since it can exist with all conceivable
orientations. The number of allowed states depends on
the relative momentum of the decay products much as
the number of points on the circumference of a circle
depends on its radius. *The decay interaction is the shuffling
agent.* . . . If it exists and operates on a time scale com-
parable with the age of the universe, then by relentless
operation of the Second Law, essentially every proton
would by now have decayed into lighter particles. . . .
Clearly the opposite is the case, and there must be some
very exact law which is preventing this from happening.[9]

Had all the protons decayed, there would be no stable
atoms, no elements, no compounds, no earth, no life.
When the biologist said that life was wildly improbable, a
rare unreasonable event, who would have guessed how
improbable it really was? "A human being," writes
Matthews, "is at very best, an assembly of chemicals constructed and maintained in a state of fantastically complicated organization of quite unimaginable improbability."[10]
So improbable that you can't even imagine it. So "wildly

improbable" that even to mention it is ridiculous.[11] So we
have no business being here. That is not the natural order
of things. In fact, he says that "the sorting process—the
creation of order out of chaos—against the natural flow of
physical events is something which is essential to life."[12]
So the physical scientists and the naturalists agree that if
nature has anything to say about it, we wouldn't be here.
This is the paradox of which Professor Wald of Harvard
says, "The spontaneous generation of a living organism is
impossible. . . . In this colloquial, practical sense I concede
the spontaneous origin of life to be 'impossible.' "[13] The
chances of our being here are not even to be thought of,
yet here we are.

So as I say, in my school days it was fashionable to
brush aside Paley's watch argument with a snort of im-
patience. If you're walking on the beach and find a beautifully made Swiss watch, you should not with Archdeacon
Paley conclude that some intelligent mind has produced
the watch. It proves nothing of the sort. Finding the watch
only proves, quite seriously, that mere chance at work, if
given enough time, can indeed produce a fine Swiss watch
or anything else. Indeed, when you come right down to
it, the fact that Swiss watches exist in a world created and
governed entirely by chance *proves* that blind chance can
produce watches. There is no escaping this circular argument, and some people use it. Today Professor Matthews states the same problem more simply:

> If, after seeing a room in chaos, it is subsequently
> found in good order, the sensible inference is not that
> time is running backwards, but that some intelligent
> person has been in to tidy it up. If you find the letters
> of the alphabet ordered on a piece of paper to form a
> beautiful sonnet, you do not deduce that teams of mon-
> keys have been kept for millions of years strumming on
> typewriters, but rather that Shakespeare has passed this
> way.[14]

But to Professor Huxley or Professor Simpson this is sheer heresy or folly. It was the evolutionist who seriously put forth the claim that an ape strumming on a typewriter for a long enough time *could* produce, by mere blind chance, all the books in the British Museum, but did any religionist ever express such boundless faith? I don't know any religious person who ever had greater faith than that. Yet serious minds actually believed such an impossibility. They say it is impossible, but then it happens.

Remember, "the decay interaction is the shuffling agent [and] . . . by the relentless operation of the Second Law, essentially every proton would by now have decayed into lighter particles. . . . Clearly the opposite is the case." Now "there must be some very exact law which is preventing this from happening."[15]

Kammerer's new law of seriality is in direct opposition to the second law: there is "a force that tends toward symmetry and coherence by bringing like and like together."[16] That is a very interesting point. We say that light cleaves unto light, etc. What is that force? Nobody knows. They say it is there because you see it working. Buckminster Fuller calls it *syntropy*.[17] The greatest Soviet astrophysicist today, the Soviets' foremost man in that field, Nikolai Kozyrev, has been working for years on this question. He claims that the second law of thermodynamics is all right, but it doesn't work. Something works against it, something stronger. He says,

> Some processes unobserved by mechanics and preventing the death of the world are at work everywhere, maintaining the variety of life. These processes must be similar to biological processes maintaining organic life. Therefore, they may be called vital processes and the life of cosmic bodies or other physical systems can be referred to as vital processes in this sense.[18]

We are beginning to realize with the Egyptians and the

Jews that when we speak of everything, we must consider what we are not aware of, along with what we are aware of. We recognize in that principle the overwhelming rate of quantity. What we are not aware of is part of the calculation which must be used; but we've never used it before. We've just heard that anything you haven't experienced doesn't exist. Gertrude doesn't see the ghost of the King standing there. Hamlet does, yet she says she sees "nothing at all; yet all that is I see."[19] Granted, she doesn't see anything, but she has no right to add, "but all that is I see": if I don't see it, it is not there, because I see everything that is there. How does one know if someone else is seeing something else? The Egyptian word for everything is *ntt iwtt*: everything I know and everything I don't know. Everything we are aware of and everything we are not aware of makes up everything. So you can't say "everything," just "everything I happen to know."

Calder says in the *Restless Earth*, "For all who inhabit this planet, the earth sciences now supply a new enlightenment, tantamount to a rediscovery of the earth."[20] And this new knowledge has all come forth since the mid-1960s, as a result of which "suddenly geology makes sense."[21] Then what did geology make all these other years I have been at the BYU? The mid-1960s is not so far away. Calder says it is like the discovery of a new world,[22] something completely different. And finally we are told by the brain specialists that "in our own time, the first attempts at . . . using computers for the translation of foreign language texts, have been an expensive failure."[23] Noam Chomsky played an important part in stopping the computer people and their patrons from wasting more effort on this hopeless task. (I used to share an office with a professor who had worked on a Russian translating machine, way back in the 1940s. He took over the project at Georgetown University, where he worked at it for thirty years and then gave it up. It just wouldn't go. Yet they were all enthusiastic: "There is no problem we cannot solve. The computer is going to solve everything for us." This hope has now gone down the drain.) We are now assured that it is only a working assumption that the mind and the brain are inseparable. Ralph Sperry, who has been doing a lot with this, says, "The brain . . . transcend[s] . . . the properties of its cells."[24] There is something up and above and beyond the brain, and this is what is having a very important influence today. And now the chaos factor makes our uncertainty certain!

The nuclear physicists, speaking on the same subject, say, "Between the electrical signals coming through the eye to the brain and our reaction to a tree in blossom on a fresh spring day, there is a vast gap which physics shows no signs of ever being able to bridge. . . . It may even be that whatever it is that is peculiar to life and particular to thought lies outside the scope of physical concepts."[25] I was also surprised to learn that in the field of the relationship of the particles within the nucleus (nuclear physics), no problem is exactly soluble: "With the present mathematical techniques, we have no idea of how to cope with this problem."[26] In mathematics there is no sign that we will ever be able to solve many of these problems. We just do it by approximations—that is as near as we can get to solving them.

Two things stand out in all this. First is the awareness of an organizing, ordering force in the universe that is very active and runs counter to all we know of the laws of science. The second is the awareness of great gaps in our knowledge that may account for our failure to discover the source of that force. This takes us directly to the subject of the temple—though you would never have guessed this from what I have said so far.

We talk a lot about the second law, but what about the first law—the law about the conservation of energy,[27] which is the conservation of mass and matter, in all their forms. It is important too. With that law, the Latter-day

Saints have never had any quarrel. We have always believed it. By contrast, the Christian world has its doctrine of creation out of nothing—*creatio ex nihilo*. Recently David Winston and Jonathan Goldstein, writing on Jewish Hellenistic thought, have shown at great length that the idea of creation out of nothing was totally unknown to the Christian or the Jewish Doctors before the fourth century A.D.[28] It had no place in their doctrines. It was always taught in the early church, as the Jews teach yet, that the world was organized out of matter that was already there. This Mormon teaching was greatly offensive to the standard Christian doctrine that God created the world out of nothing. We Latter-day Saints don't quarrel with the first law of conservation of energy.

Surprisingly, we also accept the second law. In the course of nature, that law takes its relentless course. Jacob says, "This corruption [could not] put on incorruption" (2 Nephi 9:7; cf. Mosiah 16:10). There is no chance of it. As he put it, corruption is a one-way process that is irreversible: "This corruption could not put on incorruption. Wherefore, the first judgment which came upon man must needs have remained to endless duration" (2 Nephi 9:7). It could not be reversed. Incorruption can put on corruption—something can decay and break down, particles breaking down into smaller and lighter particles—but you can never reverse the process. Nevertheless, something is making it reverse. (This is what the scientists talk about. It is baffling everybody. In fact, Henry Eyring, at the University of Utah, talked about it years ago. The theory is that the universe is exploding, because it was wound up tight. But what wound it up? You have to start out with that.) "This corruption could not put on incorruption," wherefore this death and decay "which came upon man must needs have remained to an endless duration." And notice how he rubs it in: "If so, this flesh must have laid down to rot and to crumble"—that is, to disintegrate into

mother earth—"to rise no more" (2 Nephi 9:7). That is the
second law of nature, but according to Jacob, it is the first
to which nature is subjected—the inexorable and irreversible trend toward corruption and disintegration; it can't be
reversed. It rises no more, crumbles, rots, and remains
that way endlessly, for an endless duration.

This would spell an end to everything, were it not that
another force works against it. "Wherefore, it must needs
be an infinite atonement" (2 Nephi 9:7), he says—in effect,
a principle of unlimited application. An infinite principle
is at work here. "It should be infinite"—Jacob insists on
that. It can't be limited, it can't be provisional, it can't be
a mere expediency; it is an infinite principle, just as much
as the other principle is. Without an infinite atonement,
"this corruption could not put on incorruption." We could
not save ourselves from entropy. Someone else must be
there to do it. Notice what atonement means: reversal of
the degradative process, a returning to its former state,
being integrated or united again—"at-one." What results
when particles break down? They separate. Decay is always from heavier to lighter particles. But "atonement"
brings particles back together again. Bringing anything
back to its original state is at-one-ment. According to the
law of nature (those are Jacob's words—according to the
first principle), that could never happen.

We noted that both the physicist and the biologist were
aware of an ordering and organizing agent that opposes
the second law. Matthews pays tribute to the Pythagoreans: "Why is it then that when we come to examine the
inanimate world we find it controlled by laws which can
only be put in mathematical terms?"[29] For that matter, what
do *I* know about it? Yet all inanimate nature conducts itself
according to mathematical principles conceived of as pure
theory by the human mind. Somebody must be working
things out. And so we begin with the creation story.

There is matter. That is the first law: matter was always

there. There is unorganized matter. Or as Lyall Watson says, "The normal state of matter is chaos."[30] It always is and it always will be. The normal state of matter is to be unorganized. There is unorganized matter; let us go down and organize it into a world. That mysterious somebody is at work, bringing order from chaos. It would be easy to say we were making up a story, if we didn't have a world to prove it. Somebody went down and organized it. Matter was always there, always in its normal state of chaos; and long ago the protons should have all broken down, yet here is the world. Matter is unorganized. The temple represents that organizing principle in the universe which brings all things together. It is the school where we learn about these things.

Why did the Egyptians build temples? Recently, Philippe Derchain has rediscovered a very important Egyptian temple document, the Salt Papyrus 825 (fig. 1).[31] Though known for a hundred years, no one realized what it was until he discovered it again. He begins by noting that the Egyptians felt themselves surrounded by an omnipresent and ever-threatening chaos. They were intensely conscious of the second law of breaking down—it haunted them. They were hypnotized, almost paralyzed, by the terror of that breaking down; and of course you will find in no place more dramatic and uncompromising descriptions of the processes of decay and the evil of death than in the Egyptian funerary texts. They hated death, they loathed it, but they looked it in the eye anyway.

Order and security are the exception in this world. It would seem the Egyptians entered the land in a time of great world upheavals. Their own accounts are full of it; they always talked about it. They had seen nature on the rampage, and they knew man hangs by the skin of his teeth.

Scientists now tell us about the great "Permo-Triassic catastrophe."[32] The great German biologist Otto H. Schin-

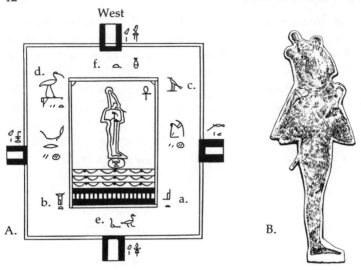

Figure 1. From Salt Papyrus 825, c. 360 B.C. (A), "The House of Life . . . shall be in Abydos. . . . As for the four ⊏⊐'s, . . . Isis [a] being on one side and Nephthys [b] on the other; Horus [c] on one and Thoth [d] on the other. These are the four sides. Geb [e] is its ground and Nut [f] its heaven. The hidden one who rests within it is the Great God. . . . It shall be very hidden and very large. It shall not be known, nor shall it be seen; but the sun shall look upon its mystery [an open-air court protected by walls]. The people who enter into it are the staff of Re and the scribes of the House of Life. . . . They are the followers of Re protecting his son Osiris every day."

The theme is protection with gods and goddesses encircling the center of the House of Life 🜔 , where the figure of Osiris holds the scepter of dominion (cf. Abraham, fac. 2:3, P. of G. P.). He stands on the Nine Bows, the traditional foreign enemies of Egypt, but here a symbol of putting all opposition under his feet. His form echoes the shape of the earlier tradition of Osiris "seed beds" such as this wooden one found in the tomb of Tutankhamun, d. 1323 B.C. (B). In the rich black Nile silt, the green seeds would sprout in the darkness of the tomb, in earnest of the power of resurrection to overcome death.

dewolf calls the movement neocatastrophism, and it is indeed a different picture.[33] How un-Victorian it is to give to books titles like the *Violent Universe*, or the *Restless Earth*.

The earth is stability itself, as lasting and unshaken as the hills. If you but look at the daily paper, you realize that that is not the case at all.

It was the same in Babylonia. We read in the Abraham traditions that the prototemple of Babylonia, the tower of Babel, was built as a place in which to accumulate data and master the knowledge necessary to counteract—to meet, to check, to soften—any major world catastrophe. The Babylonians were scared to death—they had vivid memories of the flood—and desperately determined to avoid involvement in another debacle; they thought that technical know-how could save them.

The Egyptians believed that by the mind alone, chaos is kept at a distance. This implies that the cessation of thought would *ipso facto* mark the end of the universe. This was the great fear of the Egyptians: the most constant preoccupation of endlessly repeated rites was to achieve unlimited, everlasting stability. It was not the earthly temple, which one could pretend to be built for eternity; eternity was static time, *hierophantic time* which could be attained only by constant effort of the mind. You have to work at it all the time. It was by the operation of the spirit alone that things could be effectively preserved from annihilation. I am reminded here of the marvelous book of Fourth Nephi, which describes the model society and how it disintegrated. And you retort, "My land, they lived in a happy time, didn't they?" And, of course, happy are the people whose annals are blank. Nephi doesn't tell us anything about it, because there was nothing to report. It wasn't catastrophic; there were no crimes, no wars. But why did they lose it all? Because it was too strenuous; it required great mental exertion: they spent their time constantly in meetings and prayer and fasting—in concentrating on things (4 Nephi 1:12). The exercise of the mind was simply too exhausting. It was less wearying just to give up and let things drift, to go back to the old ways.

They had to work hard to preserve that marvelous order of things.

Between the forces that create and the forces that destroy, the Egyptian saw himself as a third force, in between the other two. His business was to conserve, to preserve, to keep things as much as possible as they were. There is a force that creates and a force that destroys; humans are in between. But he could conserve only by *la pensée*, thought actualized by symbolic words or gestures. Along with this urgency went a feeling of total responsibility, which in return called for action.

The basic rite of the temple was sacrifice. The point that interests us here is just how the Egyptians thought they could contribute to upholding the physical world order by purely symbolic indications of thought. It was thought that really counted after all. Yet the symbols are important. They direct, concentrate, discipline, and inform the thought. To be effective, thought must be so motivated and directed. Watson's *Supernature* has a great deal to say on this subject.[34] The one thing that all the experimenters in psychokinesis, telepathy, and ESP, and all the borderline probings into the workings of the mind (which in our day are being undertaken with such astonishing results by the most skeptical people on earth—mostly Soviets) agree on is that whenever the task is set, successful performance is directly related to the power of concentration, to the will, to the desire, to total interest and involvement. The person has to be excited; then he can do amazing things. But if the interest and concentration are not kept at a high level, nothing much goes on. When the level is high, the mind actually has a direct effect on things. The mind can do astonishing things just by thought. It is a matter of concentrating and ordering it.

This principle is illustrated in the ancient prayer circle in the temples.[35] Concentration of thoughts in a single structure has a definite significance. (Much could be said about this.) For the Egyptians and the Babylonians, as for us, the temple represents the principle of ordering the universe. It is the hierocentric point around which all things are organized. It is the *omphalos* ("navel") around which the earth was organized (cf. fig. 39, p. 160). The temple is a scale model of the universe, boxed to the compass, a very important feature of every town in our contemporary civilization, as in the ancient world.[36] (Years ago, Sir James George Frazer noticed a definite pattern among ancient religious cult practices: they all followed the same patterns throughout the whole world.[37] He explained that as representing certain stages of evolution in which the mind naturally expressed itself in those forms. But since then the gaps between these various cultures have been filled in, to show that civilization was far more connected.) Civilization is hierocentric, centered around the holy point of the temple. The temple was certainly the center of things in Babylonia, in Egypt, in Greece — wherever you go. This was certainly so in pioneer Utah. This pattern descended, of course, from ancient times to the Latter-day Saint church. The pioneer Saints throughout the half-explored wastes of "Deseret" oriented their streets with reference to the temple. The street is designated first, second, third, east, west, north, or south, depending on its orientation to the temple. The temple is boxed to the compass. On the west end of the Salt Lake Temple you see the Big Dipper represented, a very important feature (fig. 2). Like the Egyptian temple at Dendera, you had to have the Big Dipper there, representing the North Star, around which all things pivot (fig. 3).[38] The main gate must face east. The sun, the moon, and the stars — the three degrees — are represented there. It is a scale model of the universe, for teaching purposes and for the purpose of taking our bearings on the universe and in the eternities, both in time and in space. And of course as far as time is concerned, we take our center there. We are in the middle

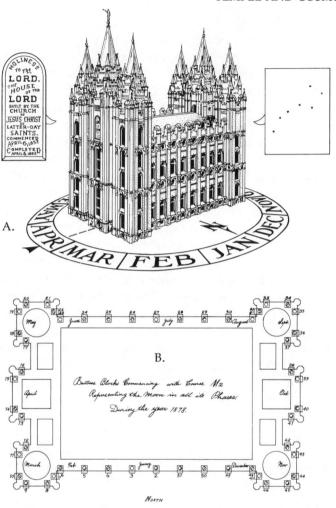

Figure 2. The Salt Lake Temple is a magnificent example of the ancient tradition of representing the universe in miniature. From the foundation of four cornerstones laid in a sunwise (clockwise) rotation (A) and the fifty earthstones designed to show the earth's globe rotating through the seven days of the week, we stand on the earth, as did Abraham, looking up into the heavens. For the moonstones, Orson Pratt designed this arrangement of the lunar phases (B). Above them, the sunstones and moonstones were originally designed to have faces like their thirty

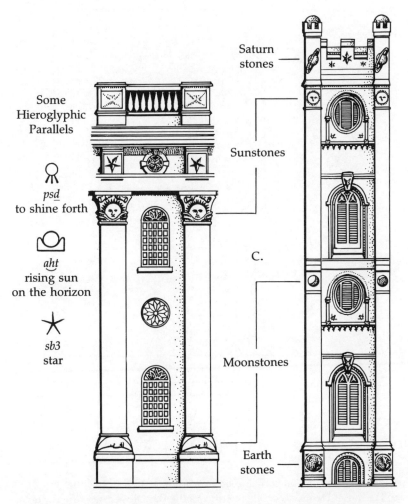

Some
Hieroglyphic
Parallels

psd
to shine forth

aht
rising sun
on the horizon

sb3
star

Saturn
stones

Sunstones

C.

Moonstones

Earth
stones

Nauvoo predecessors (C). The curious Saturn stones may refer to the unlimited glories awaiting worthy Saints. Stars of six and five points are scattered over the entire surface of the temple, representing the glory of the heavens. Truman Angell, the temple architect, interpreted the Big Dipper, "Moral: the lost may find themselves by the Priesthood," just as the ancients used it to find the still center of the turning heavens. Though planned, some details were not carried out, showing us that there is great flexibility in arranging these symbols.

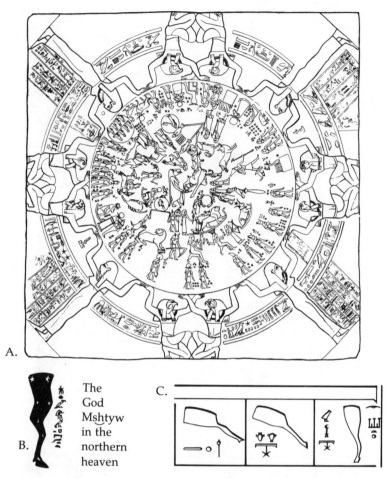

A.

B. The God Mshtyw in the northern heaven

C.

Figure 3. The famous zodiac relief from the roof chapel of the temple of Hathor at Dendera, c. 30 B.C., shows the Big Dipper near the center as Mshtyw, the Foreleg of the Ox. Though impressive in its apparent complexity, it is a late borrowing of Greek and Babylonian astronomy; however, a thousand years earlier, the interior of a Middle Kingdom coffin shows the seven stars arranged as the Foreleg. On the underside of the stone sarcophagus lid of a sacred bull, c. 350 B.C., the Foreleg moves through three different positions within the season Aht. These symbols were placed there to help the deceased join the "Unwearying Ones," the circumpolar stars that never sink below the horizon.

world, working for those who have been before and who will come after. We are, so to speak, "transferring" our ancestors (we have their records—all quite recent; and let us remember that the genealogy records were kept in the basement of the Salt Lake Temple, where they belong) in the sense that the work for people who lived long ago makes it possible for them to project their existences into what is to come in the future.

We stand in the middle position. This earth is the Old English *middan-(g)eard*, the middle-earth. The *markas šamê u erṣeti* of the Babylonians means the knot that ties heaven to earth, the knot that ties all horizontal distances together (cf. fig. 37H, p. 151), and all up and down, the meeting point of the heavens and the earth. It is the middle point at which the worlds above and the worlds below join. This scale model of the universe is the temple. Of course, the word for temple in Latin, *templum*, means the same thing as *template*: a plan marked out on the ground by the augur's staff, to help him determine the exact direction of the prophetic flight of birds. He sat at the *cardo*, the hinge or pivot around which all things turn, where the north-south line crossed the east-west line or *decumanus* (fig. 4). The person who was going to receive divination either by the birds or by the heavens, would sit in the center and take his bearings with regard to his carefully laid-out observatory. This was represented in the ancient stone circles. You find most of them to be of great antiquity—there are over 200 of them in England and in France, in the form and model of the ancient Egyptian temple. The temple is also an observatory (fig. 5). That is what a *templum* is—a place where you take your bearings on things. More than that, it is a working model, a laboratory for demonstrating basic principles by use of figures and symbols, which convey to finite minds things beyond their immediate experience. There the man Adam first sought further light and knowledge. His zeal was rewarded by bestowal from above of principles and

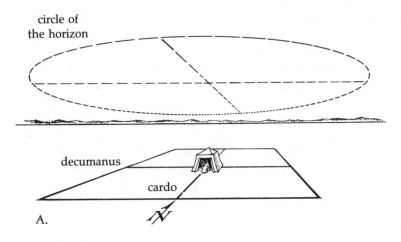

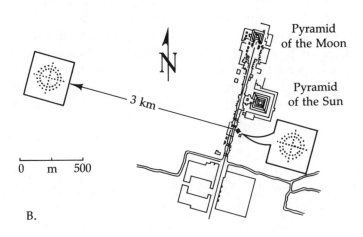

Figure 4. The Roman augur sits in the center of the *urbs quadrata* ⊕ , facing south in his *tabernaculum* and holding the *lituus* (A). When birds and other heavenly phenomena enter the *templum* above, it is recorded and interpreted as the will of heaven. In Teotihuacan the city planners made use of elaborate "pecked crosses" in carefully laying out the orientation of the sacred city (B).

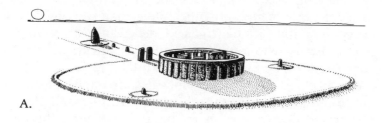

A.

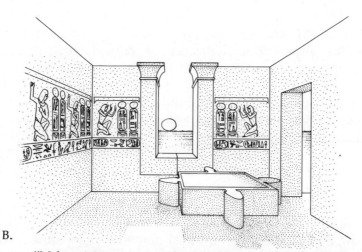

B.

"Make rejoicings to your beautiful face, Lord of the Gods,
Ammon Re," Thutmosis III, c. 1420 B.C.

Figure 5. At Stonehenge, the summer solstice sun arose between two
massive uprights (A), while in this second-story chamber of the Karnak
temple (B), the winter solstice sunrise was observed through a carefully
oriented window (cf. fig. 37, pp. 150–51). As in so many other cultures,
these two widely separated civilizations received their measure of time
from the heavens.

ordinances that he was to study and transmit to his children.

The temple is the great teaching institution of the human race; universities are much older than we might ever expect. A university began as a Greek *Mouseion,* a temple of the Muses, who represented all departments of knowledge (fig. 6). The Egyptians called it the "House of Life." It was an observatory, a great megalithic complex of standing stones (later columns and pylons), with amazingly sophisticated devices for observing and recording the motions of the heavens. A study of Stonehenge shows that it was a computer of great accuracy,[39] a university set in the midst of sacred groves—botanical and geological gardens and groves; it was a "paradise," a Garden of Eden, where all life is sacrosanct. It has often been said the temple is the source of all civilization. A brief statement from a recent article explains that the House of Life in Egypt, where books (which contained some of the earliest poetry) were copied and studied from early times, was a sort of super graduate school. It was here in this part of the temple that all questions relating to learned matters were settled.

The word for poetry, *poiēma,* means "creation of the world."[40] The business of the Muses at the temple was to sing the creation song with the morning stars. Naturally, because they were dramatizing the story of the creation, too, the hymn was sung to music (some scholars derive the first writing from musical notation). The singing was performed in a sacred circle or chorus, so that poetry, music and dance go together.[41] (Lucian's famous essay on the ancient dance, among the earliest accounts, takes it back to the round dance in the temple,[42] like the prayer circle that Jesus used to hold with the apostles and their wives— Jesus standing at the altar in the arms of Adam, and the apostles' wives standing in the circle with them. Some have referred to this as a dance; it is definitely a chorus.)[43] So poetry, music, and dance go out to the world from the temple—called by the Greeks the *Mouseion*, the shrine of the Muses.

The creation hymn was part of the great dramatic presentation that took place yearly at the temple; it dealt with the fall and redemption of man, represented by various forms of combat, making the place a scene of ritual athletic contests that were sacred throughout the world. The victor in the contest was the father of the race—the priest king himself, whose triumphant procession, coronation, and marriage took place on the occasion, making this the seat and source of government. The temple, not the palace, is the source of all government. Since the entire race was expected to be present for the event, a busy exchange of goods from various distant regions took place. (This was what the Greeks called a *panegyris*—an assembly of the entire human race in a circle.) The booths of pilgrims served as market booths for great fairs, while the need to convert various and bizarre forms of wealth into acceptable offerings for the temple led to an active banking and exchange in the temple court. The earliest money from Juno Moneta, which had the temple on the hill in the capital, portrays the defending Juno on the coins (fig. 7). You had to bring an offering to the temple; no one came empty-handed (Deuteronomy 16:16). Coming from a great distance, you couldn't bring a pure dove, so you would exchange a token for one when you got to the temple, then make your offering. Jesus drove out of the temple the moneychangers in the courts who were changing the various monies and also dealing in goods (Matthew 21:12), as well as lambs and doves. It was the center of banking and all exchange.

Since the place served as an observatory, all things there tied to the calendar and the stars. Mathematics flourished; astronomy was a Muse. History was another Muse, for the rites were meant for the dead as well as the living. Memorials to former great ones believed to be in attendance encouraged the production of art of portraiture, sculpture,

Figure 6. The nine Muses and their arts are depicted on this late Roman sarcophagus with their traditional attributes, e.g., Urania with her compass and globe, representing astronomy.

Figure 7. Juno Moneta appears on this Roman coin; the tools of coin manufacture are depicted on the reverse.

Figure 8. In this Old Kingdom tomb, c. 2260 B.C., the royal scribe Idu rises from the dust of the netherworld, his hands ready to receive the offerings brought by his family (A). This dignified Roman marble depicts a husband and wife with their right hands joined in the *dextrarum coniuncto,* the symbol of a marriage that transcends the grave (B).

and painting. The Romans had no art, except the marvelous art of portraiture. Their ancestral busts were amazingly lifelike (fig. 8). They were cut off at the upper chest to represent the person as emerging from the earth, being rescued or redeemed from death. (It was an Egyptian custom taken over, but would have flourished anyway.) In architectural adornments, the design, the measurements, the *middot* of the temple structure were very significant. As a scale model of the universe, a cosmic computer, the measurements were all very important; they had to be correct. The architecture of the hierocentric structures was of prime concern.

Since from that central point all the earth was measured and all the lands distributed, geometry was essential. The writings produced and copied in the House of Life were also discussed there, giving rise to that aspect of philosophy concerned largely with cosmology and natural science. In short, there is no part of our civilization which doesn't have its rise in the temple. Thanks to the power of the written word, records were kept. And in the all-embracing relationship to the divine book, everything is relevant; nothing is really dead or forgotten. In the time of the gathering of all things together, we gather everything good that ever was — not just people — that nothing be lost but everything be restored in this last dispensation. In an all-embracing relationship, nothing is ever really dead or forgotten. Every detail belongs in the picture, which would be incomplete without it. Lacking such a synthesizing principle, our present-day knowledge becomes ever more fragmented; our libraries and universities crumble and disintegrate as they expand. Where the temple that gave us birth is missing, civilization itself becomes a hollow shell.

The temple must be there. It is not just a myth, it is the core of all of our civilization. In 1930 this concept began to reemerge at Cambridge. The Cambridge School began calling what they taught there *patternism*, because they saw the ancient teachings all falling into the same pattern, which I have just described.

In the temple we are taught by symbols and examples; but that is not the fullness of the gospel. One very popular argument today says, "Look, you say the Book of Mormon contains the fullness of the gospel, but it doesn't contain any of the temple ordinances in it, does it?" Ordinances are not the fullness of the gospel. Going to the temple is like entering into a laboratory to confirm what you have already learned in the classroom and from the text. The fullness of the gospel is the understanding of what the plan is all about—the knowledge necessary to salvation. You know the whys and wherefores; for the fullness of the gospel you go to Nephi, to Alma, to Moroni. Then you will enter into the lab, but not in total ignorance. The ordinances are mere forms. They do not exalt us; they merely prepare us to be ready in case we ever become eligible.

We have been assuming almost unconsciously, note well, that our temple is of the same class as the temples of the Egyptians. Let me explain that. The ordinances of the Egyptian temple were essentially the same as those performed in ours. And that can be explained very simply: they have a common origin. The clue is given in Abraham 1:26: "Pharaoh, being a righteous man, established his kingdom and judged his people wisely and justly all his days, seeking earnestly to imitate that order established by the fathers in the first generations, in the days of the first patriarchal reign, even in the reign of Adam, and also of Noah, his father, who blessed him with the blessings of the earth" (Abraham 1:26). He sought diligently, he sought earnestly, to imitate the order that went back to the fathers of the first generation in the first patriarchal reign. The Egyptian ordinance also always had one purpose—to go back to the *sp tpy*—the First Time, the time of the first man, who was Adam. The Egyptians didn't have

it, and they knew it. So they sought to imitate it. Interestingly, Pharaoh was worried sick about this problem.
Pharaoh spent his days in the archives in the House of
Life, searching through the genealogical records with the
nobles of the court turning over the records, looking for
some genealogical proof that he really had authority. He
never found it, and it broke his heart. And "Pharaoh, being
of that lineage whereby he could not have the right of
Priesthood, notwithstanding the Pharaohs would fain
claim it from Noah" (Abraham 1:27) — made a very good
imitation, seeking very earnestly to imitate that order
which went back to the beginning.

So the Egyptian result is a very good imitation of our
temple ordinances (I have just finished a very large book
on that particular subject).[44] My book *The Message of the
Joseph Smith Papyri: An Egyptian Endowment* takes you
through the Egyptian temple without any mention of the
Latter-day Saint temple at all. The latter is not necessary.
It's easy to see what is going on. And all this is an open
secret among scholars today, so we are not giving anything
away. The ordinances do have a common origin; Abraham's comment is the clue. He said the Egyptians did
imitate them. The rites of the Joseph Smith Papyri 10 and
11, known as the *Book of Breathings*, follow a familiar pattern. And to show that I am not reading the pattern into
it, I included in the appendix of my book a number of early
Jewish and Christian writings, each dealing with orthodox
Jewish and Christian texts as if they were the very same
ordinances, which were since lost. The ancient temple ordinances, called mysteries, are found in various degrees
of preservation. If you ask what Joseph Smith knew about
real temples, I reply, everything.

In this connection, there is an interesting sidelight to
the word *telestial,* a word long considered as one of Joseph
Smith's more glaring indiscretions. We know now that
there are three worlds: the telestial, in which we live; the

celestial, to which we aspire; and in between them another world, called the terrestrial. It is of neither the celestial nor the telestial. According to the ancients, this world is represented by the temple, the in-between world where the rites of passage take place. Indeed the root *telos* is a very rich word in this regard and has been treated a lot recently. It deals with the mysteries. *Telos* means initiation.[45] *Teleiomai* means to be introduced into the mysteries.[46] Professor Werner Jaeger of Harvard, a close friend of mine who wrote *Paideia*, was much exercised with that word *teleiōtēs* when he was editing Gregory of Nyssa. He claimed that Gregory was talking about the mysteries. A *teleiōtēs* is a person who has been initiated into some degree or other of the mysteries, and the completion of the degree qualifies him as complete or "perfect."[47]

This word root first appears as indicating various steps from beginning to end of the initiation ordinances of the mysteries. In a recent book, just out this year (1973), Morton Smith has shown at great length that the word "mystery," as used by the early Jews and Christians (taught in secret to the apostles), was nothing else than a series of initiatory ordinances for achieving the highest salvation which today are lost and unknown to the Christian world. He says we don't know what they are; but that is what Christ meant by the mysteries of the kingdom. He meant ordinances, which were necessary; and these he revealed to the apostles during his very confidential teachings of the forty days after the resurrection.[48] The purpose of such ordinances is to bridge the space between the world in which we now live, the telestial world, and that to which we aspire, the celestial world. Therefore, the events of the temple were thought to take place in the terrestrial sphere. Recall that you leave the creation, and you end up at the celestial; but nothing happens in the celestial. Everything happens in the telestial and terrestrial, but not until after you leave the garden. Then the fun begins, until you arrive at your celestial rest. The whole temple represents *teleiōtēs*. It is also *in* the "telestial" world below, a word that nobody used but Joseph Smith. And it means that very thing—the lowest world, the world in which we are placed below the other two. Because the ordinances bridge the two worlds—the telestial and the celestial—the events of the temple were thought to take place in both terrestrial and telestial spheres, the world of the mysteries or ordinances. But the Coptic Text called the in-between world the world of transition. This is a beautiful score for Joseph Smith.

One of the most famous of all temples was that at Jerusalem. In our day there are strange stirrings as Jews and Christians begin speculating (you would be surprised by its seriousness) on the advisability of reintroducing some form of temple activity, though they are embarrassed by such basic questions as "What would we do with a temple, and who should be in charge?" But because of these new texts coming out, apocalyptic texts, all zeroing in on temples, the temple becomes the center. In Christianity and Judaism, the temple played a strangely ambivalent role; the Judaic ties have been the focus of a number of studies. The Jews like the theme, but they are afraid of it; they don't know what to do about it. They needed to exalt the temple, or else minimize it as a mere building. When the temple stood, it was the *palladium* of the nation, and it came to be sort of a fetish—something that we learn from Josephus. This led to the dangerous concept that as long as the people had the temple and its rites, they could consider themselves righteous and infallible; nothing would happen to them. *Templum Dei, Templum Dei, Templum Dei*: it is the temple of God, nothing can hurt us.

The same natural error hangs over the Latter-day Saints, incidentally, who often regard the temple as a kind of fetish. Sister Eve Nielsen, who works in the library at

BYU, specializes in genealogy. She tells that when she was a small girl, she and her brothers and sisters stood at the door of their house in Manti, clinging to their mother's skirts during a terrible thunderstorm and looking at the temple. They said to their mother, "God will not let lightning strike the temple, will he?" And just as her mother was assuring them that he would not, bang! – lightning struck the east tower, which began to burn briskly.

Sister Nielsen's father was in the crew that rushed up and soon put out the fire. When he came home, the children asked him what went wrong. What gives here? He explained to them that the installation of lightning rods had been discussed but not carried out. He said that God had given the means to protect the temple against lightning, and the workers neglected to use those means; they thus had no right to expect miraculous interventions. God expects us to go on the same as ever. The temple itself is not a fetish – it is not a *palladium* (*aegis;* cf. fig. 30, p. 125); because the Jews attached their hopes in the end to a building, its destruction had the most crushing effect on them. The Christians exulted, but the Jews thought they would never be restored again because the temple had been destroyed and the Jews themselves felt utterly discouraged with the passing of the temple – it was all over with.

Everything was based on a building. Indeed, the Lord pointed this out more than once. "Destroy this temple, and in three days I will raise it up" (John 2:14). The Christian Doctors never tired of the old rhetorical clichés that discoursed on the vanity of putting one's faith in a building. Christ, we are told, destroyed the temple of stone, but the church is a spiritual temple, the only kind of temple that really counts. Do you have to have a physical temple? There we see the ambivalence of the argument. The very Fathers – Gregory of Nyssa and John Chrysostom – who in-

veighed against the folly and idolatry of attributing sanctity
to a mere place, a mere building, were the first ones to
join in the pious pilgrimage to go back to the ruins of the
holy building. The church never gave sanction to pilgrimages to the Holy Land. Its leaders did not like them, but
always opposed them. In no instance did the church en-
courage pilgrimages, but rather actually opposed them.
Some people actually insisted on going back to the old
order of things because they thought they could find the
gospel there.

This was the sense of the Crusades: the Crusaders
going back to the temple to the Holy of Holies. This was
in fact the project of Columbus: he wished to discover the
Indies to get enough money to rebuild the temple. The
Protestant pilgrims, of course, denounced the folly of going
to Jerusalem, yet they have been engaged with unsurpassed vigor and passion in doing just that, especially the
less ritually bound Christians, like the Quakers. They are
the ones who love to make such pilgrimages. The first
great modern war, the Crimean, was fought over the protection of the holy places in Jerusalem. Everybody was
concerned. World history actually pivots around the
temple. James T. Lowe's *Geopolitics and War*,[49] a discussion
of Halford J. Mackinder's theory, is geographically centered in that part of the world (that part of the earth where
the sea penetrates the world land mass to a great distance,
which makes it the geopolitical center of the world—the
most strategic point for dominating the whole world by
sea or by land). But not only that, it was the ideological
center. Everybody in the great seventeenth century had
great schemes and plans for getting the temple back. It
has been an obsession with the Christian world, and many
Jews contemplate a forthcoming rebuilding of the temple.

The modern world asks with lofty superiority, Why a
building? Why not a spiritual edifice? Does God need gad-

gets? We are here in the world to familiarize ourselves with a new medium. We may neither deny the reality of solid things nor be taken up too much with them. We shouldn't become hypnotized by them. The Oriental monks went to both extremes: they utterly denied the flesh, and so as a result became obsessed with it.

We Mormons have gone all out in the past to build temples, making great sacrifices of our means. Yet we have not been attached to the buildings as such. Brigham Young nearly worked himself to death getting the Nauvoo Temple built on time. But he did not "again want to see [a temple] built to go into the hands of the wicked." After learning of the destruction of the Nauvoo Temple by fire, he said, " 'Good, Father, if you want it to be burned up.' I hoped to see it burned before I left, but I did not. I was glad when I heard of its being destroyed by fire, and of the walls having fallen in, and said, 'Hell, you cannot now occupy it.' "[50] It was just a building after all. Why then should he knock himself out? We strive to make our temples beautiful, but if in the eyes of many of us some turn out to be something less than breathtaking, that doesn't dampen our enthusiasm for what goes on in them. My favorite temple is certainly the Provo Temple, though as a building I give it very low marks indeed. We are not attached to the building as such (it is but an endowment house). Basic to all temples is their exclusiveness and isolation. The temple is something set apart.

Each dispensation is marked by the return of the temple and its ordinances. The temple lies at the center of apocalyptic literature. Without a temple, there is no true Israel. For there alone is the priesthood; with the destruction of the temple, the Jews also lost the priesthood. And the rabbis rejoiced. We are told that as the temple was burning, the rabbis went to Vespasian and asked (Titus was doing the job) for permission to build the first rabbinical school at Jamnia, and they got it. They actually rejoiced in the fall of the temple.

The Christian Doctors also rejoiced over the destruction of the temple, gloating over it because it meant the end of the Jews. Without the temple, there could be no Judaism; it could never come back again. This theme very much concerns them now. In 1948 President Truman's emissary had a long discussion with the Pope, who was very emphatic when he said that whatever happens, the Jews must never again build a temple. It was very important; they must never go back to Jerusalem, because the prophecy is that they can never go back. The prospect alarmed and annoyed the Christians, but it also fascinated them; they couldn't leave it alone.

The basic institutions of civilization were defined ultimately in the temple or derived from the temple. Many of those institutions became rivals—bitter rivals—of the temple, effectively displacing it. Thus the ancient Sophists took over education. When they did so, the university became an anti-temple, which it has remained ever since, adopting the forms of the temple to discredit its teachings and doctrines.

In our day, as in various other times in history, the sanctity and the authority of the temple have been preempted in the religion of mammon, for example. Our banks are designed after the manner of ancient temples, with imposing fronts, ceremonial gates and courts, the onyx, the marble, the bronze—all are the substances of ancient temples. The sacred hush that prevails, the air of propriety, decorum, and dedication; the pious inscriptions on Zions Bank's walls are quotations from Brigham Young (the one man who really had it in for business). The massive vault door, through which only the initiated may pass, gleams chastely in immaculate metal. The symbol makes the reality of all that is safe and secure—that is, the Holy of Holies. For where your treasure is, there will your heart

be also. This is the Lord speaking. We declare that our
trust is in God, and we give ourselves away by stamping
that declaration where it belongs — on our coins and bills.

As it comes and goes through the dispensations, the
temple is the bridgehead for Zion — preparing the way, a
sort of outpost or outland. It is an alien thing in the world
and as such it is resented. It is feared and envied; it lies
as an intruder, the dread and envy of the world, an invader
in a wicked and adulterous world. Zion is on the defensive.
Our early Latter-day Saint temples were all designed as
fortresses, with their buttresses, their battlements, their
gates, their walls — always the surrounding wall. If the
temple represents the principle of order in chaos, it also
represents the foothold, you might say, of righteousness
in a wicked world. Someone once asked me concerning
the Egyptian ordinances contained in the Joseph Smith
manuscripts, Is this stuff relevant to the modern world?
My answer is no. It is relevant to the eternities. The modern
world is as unstable as a decaying isotope, but the temple
has always been the same. The ordinances are those taught
by an angel to Adam.

The bringing of the temple into the world was a reminder in the days of Enoch, Noah, Abraham, Moses,
Christ, and Joseph Smith that the world as a going concern
is coming to a close. That little phase of human existence
was about to pass away and give place to another. One of
the lessons of the recent scientific research in these many
fields is that the course of history and geology — thinking
of that "Permo-Triassic catastrophe" now — is not one of
slow, infinitely gradual, salutary evolution.[51] The Lord told
the Prophet Joseph Smith in the first vision that he was
fed up with the world: "There is none that doeth good,
no not one."[52] And he was about to remove it. We are told
that the sudden, catastrophic housecleaning is to take place
when the condition of saturation has been reached — when
the people are ripe in iniquity.

The name of the Church will not let us forget that these are the last days. The last days of what? Of the rule of Belial, of the reign of Satan on this earth. In the temple, we first learn by what means Satan has ruled the world, and how it came about, and how he has ruled over the world these many years. Then we proceed to lay the foundation for that order of existence which God intends his children to have here. In both lessons, we deal with specifics. We are given a choice between them — to that degree we live up to the principles and laws of the temple. If we don't live up to them, we are in the power of the other kingdom. It is in the temple that God puts the proposition on the line, and he will not be mocked. The temple is there to call us back to our senses, to tell us where our real existence lies, to save us from ourselves. So let us go there often and face the reality, brethren and sisters.

We testify to the truth of the existence of these things. We ask, What did Joseph Smith know about the temple? He knew everything about it. He gave us the complete thing. So we know that the gospel has been restored, and that the temple is the center of things. So we must repair there often. I have gotten so I am almost an addict. I cannot keep away from the temple. I revel in it, the building I call an endowment house, lacking as it does in so many aspects — but that doesn't make any difference. We can see the ordinances and the endowments. It was built for practical purposes.

In a speech in the 1880s in St. George, Brother Erastus Snow said that every temple has a slightly different design, because it performs a different purpose (fig. 9). The St. George Temple was built after the pattern of the Kirtland Temple, to emphasize certain things. Our Provo Temple is built in a different way entirely. It functions with a different thing in mind — efficiency in getting a lot of work done in a hurry, but also as a teaching tool. In 1897, scholars discovered a marvelous document called the *Apocalypse of*

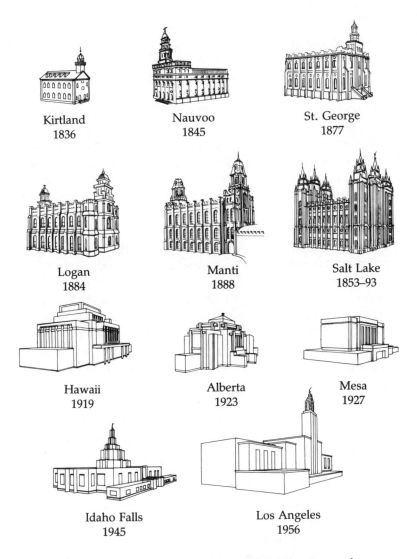

Kirtland
1836

Nauvoo
1845

St. George
1877

Logan
1884

Manti
1888

Salt Lake
1853–93

Hawaii
1919

Alberta
1923

Mesa
1927

Idaho Falls
1945

Los Angeles
1956

Figure 9. The wide variety of architectural design among the many Latter-day Saint temples is seen here in relative scale. Though temples generally face east, Joseph built the Nauvoo temple facing west, where it would be seen to its best advantage from the river. And just as

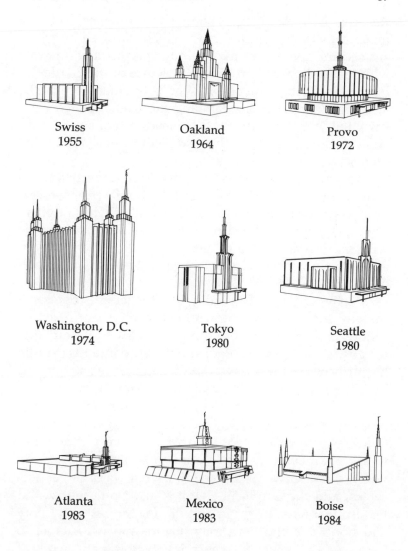

Swiss
1955

Oakland
1964

Provo
1972

Washington, D.C.
1974

Tokyo
1980

Seattle
1980

Atlanta
1983

Mexico
1983

Boise
1984

Solomon's temple resembled its Canaanite neighbors, these modern temples reflect their own time and place. What makes them the "House of the Lord" is not visible to the casual observer or art historian; it cannot be found in their outer appearance.

Abraham. In it, Abraham is shown an ordinance, as if in a moving picture projected on a screen. And an angel instructs him: "Now see this, . . . now this picture. You walk with me in the Garden. This is a picture of the Garden of Eden." And Abraham asks, "Who is the man here?" The angel replies, "That is Adam and the woman is Eve, and I will tell you about them."[53] He leads Abraham through and then he takes him to the next picture, as it is projected on a screen.

Any means we can use to convey the information, to convey the knowledge, will fulfill the Lord's purposes. So no two temples are built alike. Remember what Brigham Young said when they started to build the Salt Lake Temple with six towers instead of one? "Now do not any of you apostatize because . . . it will have six towers, and Joseph only built one."[54]

We live in Vanity Fair today, and the temple represents the one sober spot in the world where we can really be serious and consider these things. It is my testimony that the gospel has been restored, and the Lord intends to fulfill his purposes in these days. And whatever we ask him for, he will give us. This I tell my family without any reservation whatever. I have never asked the Lord for anything that he didn't give to me. Well, you say, in that case, you surely didn't ask for much. No, I didn't; I was very careful not to ask for much. We don't want to be spoiled brats, do we? We ask for what we need, for what we can't get ourselves, and the Lord will give it to us. Don't worry. But he also wants us to get in and dig for the rest. So I pray and hope that the Lord may inspire and help us all to become more engaged—more involved—in the work of these latter-days and visit the temple often and become wiser all the time, because he intends to give us more revelations through that instrumentality. I pray for this in the name of Jesus Christ, amen.

Notes

1. Albert L. Lehninger, *Principles of Biochemistry* (New York: Worth, 1982), 362. *First Law of Thermodynamics*: In any physical or chemical change the total amount of energy in the universe remains constant; *Second Law of Thermodynamics*: All physical or chemical changes tend to proceed in such a direction that useful energy undergoes irreversible degradation into a randomized form called *entropy*. They come to stop at an equilibrium point, at which the entropy formed is the maximum possible under the existing conditions.

2. Lyall Watson, *Supernature* (New York: Anchor, 1973), 8.

3. Ibid.

4. P. T. Matthews, *The Nuclear Apple* (London: Chatto and Windus, 1971), 69.

5. Ibid., 68.

6. Ibid., 69–70.

7. Ibid., 70 (see footnote).

8. Matthews, *Nuclear Apple*, 70; the numerator (24) is calculated from the formula $P(n, k) = n!/(n-k)!$, where P = permutations, n = number of items involved, and k = the number of ways in which the items (suits) can be taken. Here we assume that the suits are already ordered from the highest to the lowest card, and we wish to calculate the permutations of the four suits (hearts, clubs, diamonds, and spades) taken four ways. Substituting into the equation we get $P = 4!/(4-4)! = 4!/0! = 24$. The denominator is calculated similarly: $P = 52!/(52-52)! = 52!/0! = 8.066 \times 10^{67}$. (Note that Matthews underestimates the permutations of all 52 cards taken 52 ways by 15 orders of magnitude [subtracting the exponents, we get $67-52 = 15$]. The ratio of numerator to denominator gives the following: $24/8.066 \times 10^{67} = 2.975 \times 10^{-67}$. Taking the reciprocal, we get: 1 to 3.361×10^{66}, or one chance in 3.36×10^{66} of getting the ordered suit from a randomly ordered deck of 52 cards.)

9. Ibid., 71.

10. Ibid., 142.

11. Watson, *Supernature*, 5.

12. Matthews, *Nuclear Apple*, 143.

13. George Wald, "The Origin of Life," *Scientific American* (August 1954): 4–5.

14. Matthews, *Nuclear Apple*, 143–44.

15. Ibid., 71.

16. P. Kammerer, cited in Watson, *Supernature*, 109–10.

17. Richard Buckminster Fuller, *Intuition* (New York: Doubleday, 1972), 82, 84, 110–11.

18. Nikolai Kozyrev, "An Unexplored World," *Soviet Life* (November 1965): 27.

19. William Shakespeare, *Hamlet*, act III, scene iv, line 133.

20. Nigel Calder, *The Restless Earth* (New York: Viking, 1972), 19, 21.

21. Ibid., 21.

22. Ibid.

23. Noam Chomsky quoted in Nigel Calder, *The Mind of Man* (London: British Broadcasting, 1970), 197.

24. Ralph Sperry, quoted in ibid., 260.

25. Matthews, *Nuclear Apple*, 141–42.

26. Ibid., 64.

27. For definition, see n. 1.

28. David Winston, "The Book of Wisdom's Theory of Cosmogony," *History of Religions* 11 (1971): 191–92; Jonathan Goldstein, "The Origins of the Doctrine of Creation Ex Nihilo," *Journal of Jewish Studies* 35 (1984): 127–35; and David Winston, "Creation *Ex Nihilo* Revisited: A Reply to Jonathan Goldstein," *Journal of Jewish Studies* 37 (1986): 88–91. See also Gerhard May, *Schöpfung aus dem Nichts* (Berlin: de Gruyter, 1978).

29. Matthews, *Nuclear Apple*, 144.

30. Watson, *Supernature*, 3.

31. Philippe Derchain, *Le Papyrus Salt 825* (Bruxelles: Palais des Académie, 1965).

32. Nigel Calder, *The Restless Earth* (New York: Viking, 1972), 122.

33. Otto H. Schindewolf, "Neokatastrophismus," *Zeitschrift der deutschen geologischen Gesellschaft* 114 (1963): 430.

34. Watson, *Supernature*, 128–41, 273, 276–79.

35. Hugh W. Nibley, "The Early Christian Prayer Circle," *BYUS* 19 (Fall 1978): 41–78; reprinted in *CWHN* 4:45–99.

36. Mircea Eliade, *The Myth of the Eternal Return* (Princeton: Princeton University Press, 1974), 6–8; cf. I. E. S. Edwards, *The Pyramids of Egypt* (New York: Penguin, 1961), 256, 287, 290–96. Cf. Hugh W. Nibley, "Comments," in *Mormonism, a Faith for All Cultures* ed. F. LaMond Tullis (Provo: BYU Press, 1978), 22–28; reprinted as "Some Notes on Cultural Diversity in the Universal Church" in this volume, pages 541–49.

37. Sir James Frazer, *The Golden Bough*, 12 vols. (New York: Macmillan, 1935).

38. Edwards, *The Pyramids of Egypt*, 256–57, 259. See the comments by Truman O. Angell (temple architect), in "The Temple," *MS* (1854): 754.

39. Fred Hoyle, *From Stonehenge to Modern Cosmology* (San Francisco: Freemen, 1972); cf. Gerald S. Hawkins, "Appendix B—Stonehenge: A Neolithic Computer," in *Stonehenge Decoded* (New York: Doubleday, 1965), 174–81. [For a review of more recent scholarship on Stonehenge as an astronomical computer, cf. Christopher Chippindale, *Stonehenge Complete* (Ithaca, NY: Cornell University Press, 1983), 216–36.]

40. See *Oxford English Dictionary*, s.v. "poem."

41. See Nibley, "Early Christian Prayer Circle," 48–50; in *CWHN* 4:53–54.

42. Lucian, *Dance* 15 and 23; for an English translation, see A. M. Harmon, tr., *Lucian*, 8 vols. (Cambridge: Harvard University Press, 1936), 5:229, 235.

43. 2 *Jeu* 54 [40], in Schmidt, *Gnostische Schriften in koptischer Sprache*, 99, 193; cf. Carl Schmidt, ed., *The Books of Jeu and the Untitled Text in the Bruce Codex* (Leiden: Brill, 1978), 127, 147.

44. Hugh W. Nibley, *The Message of the Joseph Smith Papyri: An Egyptian Endowment* (Salt Lake City: Deseret Book, 1975).

45. Henry G. Liddell and Robert Scott, *A Greek-English Lexicon*, 9th ed. (Oxford: Clarendon, 1940; with supplement, 1968), 1773.

46. Ibid., 1772.

47. Werner Jaeger, *Paideia*, tr. Gilbert Highet, 3 vols. (New York: Oxford, 1944).

48. Morton Smith, *The Secret Gospel* (New York: Harper and Row, 1973), 16–17, 102–3, 140.

49. James T. Lowe, *Geopolitics and War* (Lanham, MD: University Press of America, 1981), 49–50, 65.

50. *JD* 8:203.

51. Calder, *Restless Earth*, 122.

52. The 1832 recital of the First Vision as dictated by Joseph Smith to Frederick G. Williams. See Dean C. Jessee, *The Personal Writings of Joseph Smith* (Salt Lake City: Deseret Book, 1984), 3–8; Milton V. Backman, *Joseph Smith's First Vision* (Salt Lake City: Bookcraft, 1971), Appendix A; cf. Dean C. Jessee, ed., "The Early Accounts of Joseph Smith's First Vision," *BYUS* 9 (1969): 280.

53. *Apocalypse of Abraham* 23:9–11, in *OTP* 1:700.

54. *JD* 1:133.

Return to the Temple

When the time came for fulfillment of the prophecies of the coming Messiah, heavenly activity was concentrated vigorously on the temple. Granted, it was Herod's temple, which many Jews considered a mere parody of Solomon's and which the pious sectaries claimed to be defiled; still it was there that the angel Gabriel came "from the presence of God" to "preach the gospel" in a long discourse to Zacharias before the veil. This first chapter in Luke is peculiarly relevant to the study of the temple. Zacharias was a priest, and his wife a direct descendant of Aaron (Luke 1:5). Their condition is described in very un-Greek terms that seem to come right out of the Dead Sea Scrolls in bold relief. They were both "upright before the Lord" (yəšārîm lipnê ădōnai), "walking in all the commandments" (mizwôṯ) and judgments (mišpāṭîm) of the Lord, observing the law flawlessly in every respect. It had nothing to do with moral turpitude. Like Job, they were "upright and perfect." The Greek word amemptoi, "perfect" (Luke 1:6), is equivalent to the Hebrew tāmîm.

You would think them the last people in the world to need more religion; yet it was expressly to them that the gospel was given (Luke 1:9). Zacharias's activity during his turn of duty entailed making the incense sacrifice, when he would go before the veil in the Holy of Holies while the multitude stood outside in the court in prayer (Luke

---

This previously unpublished and undated manuscript was originally entitled "Temple."

1:10). What happened is described by Luke with clinical precision (Luke 1:14), matched only by the story of Moroni's visit to Joseph Smith.

Why did the angel make his special appearance? Explicitly to announce the birth of John the Baptist, which was to bring great joy to the world; John would be filled with the Holy Ghost from the womb and observe a way of life strictly withdrawn from worldly practices (Luke 1:15). This was to be a *restoration*: "He would bring back many of the children to the Lord their God" (Luke 1:16); he would precede the Lord in the spirit and power of Elijah, fulfilling the promise made long before: "to turn the hearts of the fathers to the children, and the disobedient" spirits to the way of righteousness (Luke 1:17; cf. Malachi 4:6). (This plainly deals with those who had passed on and looks to a reconstruction of the family.) As to the present generation, the coming prophet was sent to prepare for the Lord a qualified people (Luke 1:16–17). The angel then stated his own role: "I am Gabriel, and am sent to speak unto thee, and to shew thee these glad tidings" (Luke 1:19). Again, just like Moroni.

Next the angel went to Mary, and again, the exact circumstances of the visit are given. She will have a child, and he shall rule and reign in the house of the Lord forever (Luke 1:26–55). Mary burst into a song, declaring that the promises to the fathers were about to be fulfilled (Luke 1:46–55). On the eighth day, John's parents brought him to the temple, where Zacharias, filled with the Holy Ghost (Luke 1:67), proclaimed the restoration of the glories and offices of the temple, culminating with work for the dead: He has taken pity on our *fathers*, "to give light to them that sit in darkness and in the shadow of death" (Luke 1:79). All this had to do with great benefits for those who had died, to be effected specifically by one whose office was to baptize (Luke 2:76–79).

Like John, Jesus too was brought to the temple when

he was eight days old; and there Simeon, being filled with
the Holy Ghost (which had, we are expressly told, brought
him to the temple for that purpose; cf. Luke 2:27), took
the babe in his arms and proceeded to recite from Isaiah
the restoration of that which had been prepared as a glory
to the people of Israel as well as to the nations (Luke 2:28–
32). The next blessing was bestowed by the prophetess
Anna, who never left the temple, where she engaged in
fasting and prayer day and night.

One cannot help but wonder what those people did
who spent all their time in the temple. Fasting and prayer
were not full-time activities, and much in the early Jewish
and Christian literature indicates that there was much more
to be done. Specifically what it was we are never told, for
these things were not divulged to the world.

What is to be noted is how all this activity centers in
the temple. In October 1983, I attended a conference of
Jews and Christians on Holy Land studies in Washington,
D.C. The subject was the restoration of the temple, and
the three words constantly discussed — which would have
been taboo just ten years before — were *restoration* [not ref-
ormation], *dispensation*, and *revelation*. Some of the clergy
are beginning to want the temple back. It was at the temple
that Simeon and Anna gave their prophetic blessings about
Jesus, and that Gabriel hailed the work of John the Baptist,
this babe who was surprisingly "to turn the hearts of the
fathers to the children" (Luke 1:17) (instead of the other
way around), and to bring a great light to them who sat
in darkness — plainly his ministry of baptism was to apply
to the dead as well as the living; and it was the same in
the Dead Sea Scrolls. It was at the temple that Jesus as a
child revealed his special calling to do his Father's business
(Luke 2:46–49). And it was there that he made a general
announcement of his messianic calling. After he had gone,
the saints spent their days, Luke tells us, constantly meeting and praising God in the temple (Luke 24:53). The early

church, in fact, was built around the temple, a thing which many new in-depth studies are bringing to light for the first time.[1]

The primacy of the temple as that appointed place through which God dealt with Israel, both Jewish and Christian, was never revoked. Since both Jews and Christians were without the temple after A.D. 70, both attempted to dismiss it as no longer necessary. Some rabbis disliked and denounced it, discouraging any discussion of its teachings and ordinances.[2] The Christians, of course, claimed, in the spirit of Alexandrian intellectualism, that the crass, physical temple of old had been replaced by a more splendid spiritual structure in the heart of man. But for all the philosophizing, rationalizing, allegorizing, moralizing, and abstracting, both sides missed the temple sorely. Frequent attempts were made to reclaim it, to restore it, to copy it.[3] "We are the heirs to that consecutive imagery. . . . While it is more directly observable in synagogues, churches too in some way or other are likely to express some reminiscence of the biblical shrines."[4] About 200 B.C. a circle of pious priests full of zeal for "the dignity of the temple worship . . . adopted the title of the sons of Zadok," from whom are descended the Sadducees.[5] The people of the scrolls were devoted to the temple and, like the Essenes,[6] "sent offerings to the temple without, however, participating in its cult, for they regarded the priests at Jerusalem as usurpers of the priesthood." The rites of the synagogue were meant to be a reflection of the temple,[7] and churches and cathedrals were designed with their Holy of Holies, their veils, and their ministers, who were even referred to as Levites (cf. fig. 13, p. 68).

But in reading the Bible, one can only ask all denominations today, Where is your temple? Wouldn't you like to have it?[8] S. Brandon answers, "Now in all that we otherwise know from the earliest New Testament sources, . . . there had been no repudiation of the Temple cultus either by Jesus or by his original followers; indeed the evidence is all to the contrary."[9] "There is an abundance of evidence that the Jerusalem Christians continued faithful in their reverence for the temple and in their observance of its cultus; indeed even Paul himself outwardly conformed to the ritual requirements of Judaism and . . . never critized the Temple and the services performed there."[10] "Even the Pharisaic Paul," writes M. Black, "turns again and again to the language of the temple and the altar."[11] Acts 2:46, 5:42, and 21:20–26 show that "the church at Jerusalem . . . adhered to temple worship from the beginning."[12] And Luke 24:53 shows that "Jesus' Messiahship . . . made no breach in the continuity of their Jewish faith and practice. It rather revealed to their minds a new wealth of meaning in the old ritual."[13] Indeed, "the first rallying point of Jewish Christianity was the courts of the holy Temple," for all Jews "looked toward Jerusalem as the rightful center of their activities, and the place at which the returning Messiah would establish his final reign upon the earth."[14] This would seem to give the Mormons an edge, but that depends on what kind of temple we have.

Granted that many Jews want to rebuild the temple, and many Christians would apply the word freely and quite incorrectly to their church buildings, still the question remains: Once you have a structure, a temple, unique and strikingly different from synagogue and church, what do you do in it that makes it different? Here we can take the Bible for our guide. Certain well-known rites, ordinances, and fixtures can be easily copied. In temples and mysteries throughout the ancient world we find washing and anointing — types of ritual purification and healing — a special garment, prayer circles, veils, etc. But these are mere fixtures and properties. The ancient Roman word for rites to be visibly performed (whose Greek equivalent is *drama*, "actions carried out") is the *actio*.

Temples in General

Hundreds of books and articles written since the beginning of the century draw attention to certain basic aspects common to temples throughout the world at all times.[15] The temple is an imposing structure, the place where one gets one's bearings from the universe, a place for the gathering of the entire race at an appointed time, namely the new year, to celebrate the beginning of a new age, the common birthday of mankind, i.e., the begetting of the race in a sacred marriage in which the king takes the role of the first ancestor. It is the "hierocentric point,"[16] the place where all time, space, and humanity come together.[17] The word *templum* not only designates the template, the point of cutting between the *cardo* and *decumanus* from which the observer of the heavens makes his viewing, it is also the diminutive of the word *tempus*, denoting that it measures the divisions of time and space in a single pattern (cf. fig. 4, p. 20).[18] There, all the records of the past are kept and all the prophecies for the future are divined.[19] G. A. Ahlstrom concludes that the two basic symbols of the temple are in general (1) its *cosmic* symbolism, and (2) the *paradise* motif, setting it aside as a sort of halfway-house between heaven and earth.[20] One center would establish others in distant places in the manner, as Augustine says,[21] of a central fire that sends out sparks, each one of these setting a new fire to scatter new centers, etc., so that the whole world is embraced in a common unity around a common center.[22] This idea is reflected in concern with *cosmology*, a theme dominant in the Jewish and Christian writings until the schools of rhetoric took over. "The earthly shrine [is] a microcosm of the cosmic shrine, . . . conceived as preserving the proportions of the cosmic abode of deity in reduced measure."[23] "The *temples*," writes Hrozný, "were not only centers of religious life, they were also centers of cultural, economic, and even political life of Babylonia." They were also schools and universities somewhat like medieval cloisters.[24]

Albright notes that the original temple of Solomon as a point of contact with the other world presented a "rich cosmic symbolism which was *largely lost* in the later Israelite and Jewish tradition."[25] Since the beginning of the century, widespread comparative studies have shown the uniformity and antiquity of this institution as well as its worldwide contamination and decay, so that not a single example remains in its purity, and yet by virtue of comparing hundreds of imperfect and fragmentary institutions, the original can be reconstructed with great confidence and clarity. In 1930 the so-called Cambridge School gave this doctrine the label of "patternism."[26] Scholars avoided it until after World War II; since that time it has been accepted as standard by many.

But it was Joseph Smith who first pointed this out, recalling a common heritage from what he calls the archaic religion, coming down from Adam in such institutions as Freemasonry, and clearly pointing out their defects as time produced its inevitable corruption. What he himself supplied single-handedly is the original article in all its splendor and complexity: *quod erat demonstrandum* ("that which had to be proven"). The cosmic pattern is presented in every external aspect of the Salt Lake Temple. At the dedication of that temple, Brigham Young explained to the people, "So we commence by laying the stone on the south-*east corner* because, *there* is the most *light*."[27] And at the dedication of the St. George Temple, "Precisely at 12 m President Brigham Young, at whose side stood Presidents John W. Young and Daniel H. Wells, broke ground at the south-east corner, and, kneeling on that particular spot, he offered the dedicatory prayer."[28]

The Covenant and the Gathering

God made his covenant with Israel both individually and collectively; he required everyone to repair to a certain place at an appointed time to enter a covenant with him. The names by which the Jews designated the temples are House of the King, House of God (fig. 10); the temple at Jerusalem was called specifically the Dwelling, *ha-bayit,* which does not mean that God dwelt there all the time, for the other name for it was *'ulām,* meaning vestibule or passage. It was also the *miqdāsh,* or place sanctified or set apart; the *naos* or *heykāl,* meaning shrine or sanctuary; *to hieron,* the holy. The most common word with the Jews today is the *House,* Herod's temple being "the Second House." "Josephus calls it the Deuteron Hieron."[29]

"All this must be done at a certain place" he tells Israel; "and I will send an angel to direct you to it. Behave yourselves and pay attention to his voice, because he is acting in my name" (cf. Exodus 23:20–21). They come together as equals, camp in families, follow the directions, note the functions of the appointed priesthood, and hearken to the voice of their prophet and leader when he shows his face after conversing with the Lord. The appointed place always had some structure, even if it was only a tent or stone (usually a ring of standing stones). This structure was considered sacred and was preserved in the building of the temple, which was built to house the original structures.

What Was Done in the Temple?

The central rite of the temple was certainly the offering of sacrifice—the slaughtering of beasts; yet the activities we read about in the Bible simply take that for granted and tell us of preaching, of feasting, and of music. The place seemed to be a general center of activity. The huge outer court allowed for this; the inner court was limited to Jews over twenty who had paid their tax for instruction or teaching, for the temple was a school. In fact, it was all those things for which the Kirtland Temple was dedicated in D&C 109. However, through the years both the structure and the uses to which it was put have remained completely

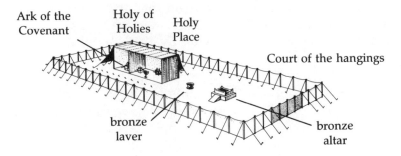

A. The Tabernacle of Moses, the Tent of the Congregation

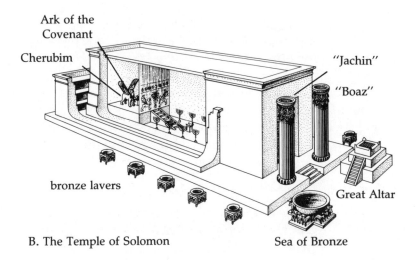

B. The Temple of Solomon   Sea of Bronze

Figure 10. Moses constructed the earthly tabernacle (A) "according to the pattern shewed to thee in the mount" (Hebrews 8:5). The perfect cube of the Holy of Holies with the two cubes of the Holy Place were doubled in dimensions when Solomon fixed the temple in stone (B) according to his father's instruction: "All this, said David, the Lord made me understand in writing by his hand upon me, even all the works of this pattern" (1 Chronicles 28:19). Herod enlarged the temple courts of the Second House (C) by building massive retaining walls on

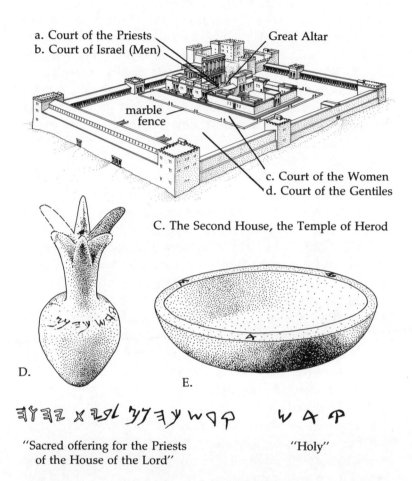

a. Court of the Priests
b. Court of Israel (Men)

Great Altar

marble fence

c. Court of the Women
d. Court of the Gentiles

C. The Second House, the Temple of Herod

D.

E.

"Sacred offering for the Priests
of the House of the Lord"

"Holy"

the temple mount, which can be seen today at the Western Wall. Thus we see over time the temple increasing in size but not in sanctity. The only surviving artifact of Solomon's Temple may be this ivory pomegranate from a priest's walking stick (D) bearing the earliest surviving example of the name of God. This common earthenware cultic bowl (E) found at Megiddo is set apart (qādôš) by the inscribed letters. Bowls like this would have been used in the temple (cf. Isaiah 22:24).

baffling to scholars.[30] What the temple really looked like remains today as puzzling as ever.[31] Welcome light has finally come with the discovery of the great *Temple Scroll* from Qumran (fig. 11). This, as Yadin noted, was not a spiritual temple or an ideal model of a heavenly temple, but the temple which these people actually intended to rebuild as soon as the Lord would command them — a more perfect temple than that which the men at Jerusalem had defiled.[32] Its purpose was the renewal of the covenant made at Sinai, i.e., the temple ordinances that were present before; from the beginning, the building was merely to accommodate them. This temple was to be in three levels, in three concentric squares or in three cubes, as Frank Cross sees it, the *tabnît* being "a model of the cosmic Tabernacle of Yahweh."[33] Joseph Smith takes it back to "the three principal rounds of Jacob's ladder — the telestial, the terrestrial, and the celestial glories or kingdoms,"[34] the highest level being an assembly hall facing a veil that ran from one side of the room to the other. According to Cross, the place behind the veil was reached by workers who would ascend a winding staircase in a tower or "house of the winding stair," which stood ten feet free of the building and was connected with the top story by a little bridge. In the Holy Place, for the priesthood, was the table of the "presence-bread" (i.e., shewbread).[35] Every morning in the temple, twelve loaves were spread out for the twelve tribes, and the workers took the sacrament (Leviticus 24:5–9; cf. Exodus 25:23–30; 29:33–34). The most impressive rite of the temple was the "drinking of the new wine by the entire assembly," which was to symbolize a ransom or redemption.

A stairway led to an upper story connected to the temple attic; equally impressive was the House of the Laver, containing a great bronze tank located in a separate building a few feet from the main temple, with dressing

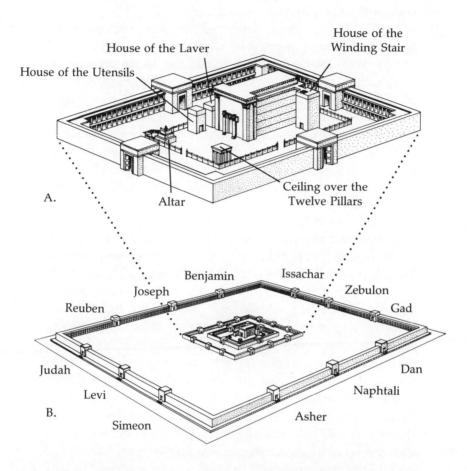

Figure 11. The *Temple Scroll* of the enigmatic Qumran community gives a meticulous description of the purified temple (A) which they believed would replace the defiled Temple of Herod. All Israel was to obey the Mosaic law to come to the great courts surrounding the temple (B) to see the "face of the Lord." To honor the priestly tribe of Levi, the Qumran covenanters placed his name on the eastern gate rather than Benjamin of Ezekiel's order (Ezekiel 48:30).

rooms at hand, emptying into a drain which carried the water off to be absorbed into the ground.

In the far northeast corner of the great enclosure is a roofed building supported by twelve columns with chains and pulleys; this is the place where the sacrificial animals were killed, far removed from the sacred precincts. From all this we see that the sacrificing of animals was only a part of the ritual activities that went on in the temple.[36] According to Milgrom, "The entire scroll is the revealed word of God,"[37] and it begins with the covenant with Moses and a section on the Holy of Holies, which unfortunately is the one part of the scroll which has been completely destroyed.

In both Jewish and Christian sources, one often reads of the five things — five covenants, five tokens, etc. — which are an organic part of the temple: When "prophecy ceased. The Urim and Thummim fell into disuse. . . . Corruption spread among the priesthood. . . . Was this God's holy Temple?" asks S. J. D. Cohen.[38] "Even the high priests were no longer legitimate high priests; they were regular priests who usurped the leadership"; the five things were gone, i.e., the sacred fire, the ark, the Urim and Thummim, the oil of anointing, and the holy spirit (prophecy). These five are the typical list of the schoolmen. According to the *Gospel of Philip,* the five secret ordinances of the Lord are (1) baptism, (2) chrism (anointing), (3) the eucharist, (4) the ordinance of salvation (*sote* — unexplained), and (5) the bridal chamber or highest ordinance.[39] In a very old Manichaean manuscript recently discovered we read, "These five things [ordinances] about which you asked me," says the Lord, addressing the apostles after the resurrection, "appear to the world to be small and foolish things, and yet they are great and honorable or exalted (*eutaiait*). I am he who will reveal to you its ordinances [mysteries]. These five tokens are the mystery of the first man Adam."[40]

Substitutes and Proxies

In the temple, and in other structures, the sacrifices could be substituted (the tent, standing stones, the enclosure, the mountain, all stood for the same appointed and sequestered spot, depending on which structure was the most convenient, and it was the same with the sacrifices). The beasts whose blood was shed were only incidental; they stood for something much more. Already in Exodus when Aaron is crowned with his cap or turban, the crown of sanctification (cf. fig. 17C, p. 98) is added (the round linen cap was to act as a cushion for a metal crown during a long ceremony). Later the cap alone would suffice, since it showed that the owner was qualified to wear the "crown of justification." Aaron's sons, arrayed in their holy garments, then appeared and put their hands on the head of a bullock before the tabernacle; it was killed at the door. Moses, dipping his finger in the blood, put it on the horns of the altar (Exodus 29:5–12). The same thing is done with a ram (Exodus 29:15–18). The same men then lay their hands upon the head of another ram, kill the ram, and put some of its blood on the right ear of Aaron and his sons (Exodus 29:19–20). This recalls the rite of nailing the right ear of a servant to a door (there are only three nerves in the lobe of the ear) to signify an everlasting bond or covenant between the Lord and his servant (Exodus 21:6; Deuteronomy 15:16–17). Moses also marks with blood the thumb of the right hand of Aaron and his sons, as well as the big toe of the right foot (Exodus 29:20). In the *Temple Scroll* the bloody spot is placed in the palm of the right hand, whereupon the priest sprinkles the blood all around the altar to signify that this is the blood of sacrifice. It takes no great mental effort to see that the slaying of the ram is the same as the slaying of the ram which represents Isaac in the *akedah*, or "binding," for Israel, an assurance of the resurrection, a similitude of a great and last sacrifice.[41]

Today for the first time, Jewish scholars have become greatly concerned with this question: Did Isaac make the atoning sacrifice?[42] But Isaac was not put to death! If not he, who then? What is being recognized is that there was much more to the ordinances than the scholars have been aware of. Thus H. G. May tells us that the "tabernacle ('ōhēl), the ark ('ārôn), [and] the ephod ('ēpôd) . . . may be closely related institutions."[43] "The ephod was a portable instrument of divination. . . . One suspects that it was the same instrument . . . [as the] urim and thummim."[44] Are all these things the same? How were they really used? Morton Smith has recently caused a sensation by calling attention to a thing deliberately bypassed by Jewish and Christian scholars alike, namely that for the temple the ancient saints always designated a mystery as an ordinance, and vice versa. He notes that Judaism itself was considered a "mystery religion" and that the rites of circumcision and passover were mysteries;[45] that such early and orthodox Christian writers as Clement of Alexandria "think of Jesus as a 'hierophant,' a teacher of the mysteries."[46] As Dr. Smith sums it up, *"This was the mystery of the kingdom — the mystery rite by which the kingdom was entered,"* i.e., the ordinances of initiation.[47] In Paul, he finds, this is "a preparatory purification," followed "by unknown ceremonies" by which one became "united with Jesus," and so ascended with him and "entered the kingdom of God."[48] The teaching was very secret and was limited to an "inner circle."[49]

After administering the blood, Moses then took the oil of anointing and sprinkled it over Aaron and his sons, clothed in their garments; thereby they became sanctified (cf. Exodus 29:21). This is the oil of healing, which reverses the blows of death. The sons of Aaron were made bloody, as if they had been sacrificed, and then cleansed, as if cleared of their sins. Being "washed in the blood of the lamb" is thus no paradox — the blood actually cleanses them of what most needs cleansing by transferring their sins to another. Leviticus deals with the matter in detail. It begins with every man in Israel who is for Jehovah bringing his offering from the herd, a male animal without blemish, as a personal, voluntary offering. He, not the priest, lays his hand on the animal's head, after which it represents him as an offering and a ransom for his sins (Leviticus 1:2–4). The conditions of the atoning sacrifice are given; all follow the same pattern, and the feast that goes with it is eaten in humility—"and ye shall eat in sorrow" (cf. Genesis 3:17). The principle of proxy continues as we read that the priest is to serve as a substitute or proxy for the king or the people (Leviticus 4:10, 13). He in turn avoided being sacrificed by being bought off (redeemed) by another substitute, a bullock whose blood is sprinkled before the veil while some of it is put on the horns of the altar. This bull is not eaten; the whole animal is burned in the ash-dump outside the camp to eliminate completely all the sins of the people (Leviticus 4:1–12).

And so anciently the principle of proxy was carried out: a goat for a prince who has unwittingly sinned (Leviticus 4:22), a bullock for all the unwitting sins of Israel (Leviticus 4:13–14), a female kid as ransom for any commoner for his unintentional trespasses, a lamb or a kid; or if you could not afford that, two turtle doves; or if you could not afford them, two young pigeons (one for a sin offering and one for burning); if you could not afford that, one tenth of an ephah of flour would do (Leviticus 1:2–2:1). The bread and wine in the temple represent sacrifice and atonement. For sins against holy things, a perfect ram must be brought, or its equivalent in shekels (i.e., by weight of pieces of silver; Leviticus 5:15). A clear case comes from Leviticus 8:12–15: First, oil is poured on Aaron's head to sanctify him; then his sons are brought in, properly attired, leading a bullock. They lay their hands upon its head, for it is to atone for their sins. Aaron kills the bullock, puts the blood on the altar, lǝ-kappēr, to make atonement for them. The

rites with the Levites are the same. Thus the sacrifices are
carried out in the temple without the shedding of human
blood, but if human blood can be spared, why not all blood?
Because this was the similitude of the shedding of blood
for the atonement of sin. Properly, of course, the sinner's
own blood must be used, unless a *gō'ēl*, a representative
substitute advocate or redeemer, could be found to take
one's place. The willingness of the candidate to sacrifice
his own life (the *ʿăkēdāh*) is symbolized by the blood on the
right thumb and right earlobe, where the blood would be
if the throat had been cut.

Symbolic Representations

Great emphasis is laid on the assembly of the people,
both in the Old Testament and the *Temple Scroll*, as the
camp of Israel in the wilderness—an armed, walled camp,
the image vividly depicted in the appointments of the
Temple Scroll. One of the most baffling titles connected with
the temple is that of Metatron, the title normally reserved
to Enoch as the guide of the initiates through the temple.
After much argument and research, it is widely agreed
now that the root of the word is *metator*—the *metator* being
one who goes ahead of the host to set up the camp and
supervise operations. This is also indicated in the name of
Enoch, which signifies a guide or instructor of initiates into
the temple—the *hekaloth*. Anyone approaching the holy
enclosure must identify himself in three steps—the admission of initiates is the central theme of the *Manual of
Discipline*.[50] First, at a distance, he seeks admission, giving
a visible sign by raising his arms (a greeting that can be
seen from afar and is a sign, among other things, that he
is unarmed); approaching closer for inspection, he gives
his name; then approaching for the final test, he actually
makes physical contacts with certain grips, which are the
most secret and decisive. His final acceptance is by the
most intimate tokens of all, including an embrace, or a *unio*

mystica (mystic union), in which the candidate becomes not only identified, but identical, with the perfect model.[51]

The Arrested Sacrifice

The gospel is more than a catalogue of moral platitudes; these are matters of either eternal life or nothing. Nothing less than the sacrifice of Abraham is demanded of us (D&C 101:4). But how do we make it? In the way Abraham, Isaac, and Sarah all did.[52] Each was willing and each expected to be sacrificed, and each committed his or her all to prove it. In each case the sacrifice was interrupted at the last moment and a substitute provided: to their relief, someone else had been willing to pay the price, but not until after they had shown their good faith and willingness to go all the way—"lay not thy hand on the lad, . . . for now I know" (Genesis 22:12). Abraham had gone far enough; he had proven to himself and the angels who stood witness (we are told) that he was actually willing to perform the act. Therefore the Lord was satisfied with the token then, for he knew the heart of Abraham. This is the same for Isaac and Sarah and for us. And whoever is willing to make the sacrifice of Abraham to receive eternal life will show it by the same signs and tokens as Abraham, but he or she must do it in good faith and with real intent. Circumcision is another form of arrested sacrifice in which the victim's own blood was shed and a permanent mark was left. It represents the sacrifice of Abraham, who initiated it (Genesis 17:10–14; cf. Exodus 21:6–7). It was the misunderstanding of both the seriousness of temple ordinances and their symbolic nature that gave rise to all the horror tales about temple ordinances in anti-Mormon literature of the nineteenth and early twentieth centuries.[53]

The Force of the Name

Anciently, the signs and tokens were accompanied by words, the most important being certain names.[54] The epoch-making discoveries from Ebla put great emphasis on the primacy of the name in the rites of the temple and all its activities showing "local[ized] veneration of the divinised *Name* that corresponds to the veneration manifest in the personal names."[55] They are for identification, but they are more than that. Why is it necessary that all be done "in the *name* of the Son?" There is no mystic or esoteric allure to the *logos*, or spoken word. Like the other elements of ordinance, it is a means of communication. God says there is "no end to my works, neither to my words" (Moses 1:38), explaining in the same passage that his work and his glory is to "bring to pass the immortality and eternal life of man" (Moses 1:39). His whole concern, then, is to pass on to others what he has. The glory of God is intelligence, which he wishes to share with all others. Glory is shared intelligence. Hence his works always go along with his words. They are the means by which his thoughts are communicated to other beings and made intelligible to his children. Without works, words would be a futile exercise in a vacuum, the subject of endless and perplexed speculation by the Doctors of the Middle Ages, the Reformation, and the Enlightenment. According to the oldest of all temple documents, the Shabako Stone, and the *Sefer Yetzira*, the way one becomes a member of the universe is through one's sensory perceptors. Whatever gets to us from out there must come through "the seven gateways" of the eyes, ears, nose, and mouth.[56] These are the avenues made functional by the initiatory rite of the Egyptian temples. The Opening of the Mouth, in which the organs of the senses are first washed and then anointed, is to make the organs efficient conveyors to a clear and active brain, by which the mind evaluates, structures, and comprehends reality. But the receptors work only one way: the eyes, ears, nose, and taste buds do not broadcast what they receive. There is only one way that all those impressions — unified, structured, and enjoyed by the mind—can be conveyed to others, and that is by speech, by the word alone. It is the word alone that releases us and opens up a common universe of discourse. If we are full of grace and truth, we have the desire to seek truth and the grace to share what we have so that all can rejoice together. This can only be done through the word. "There is no end to my works, neither to my words" (Moses 1:38; cf. 1:4). The two are inseparable, and all is made intelligible through that one circuit—the voice, the word, the name.

Secrecy

The ordinances are not deep, dark secrets to be kept as such from the world. It is easy to get a temple recommend and then later apostatize and spread abroad the so-called secrets of the temple. The basic idea of the ordinances from Moses back to Adam is separation from the world. The endowment represents steps by which one disengages from a corrupt, secular, imprisoned environment. Segregation is the first step in the law of Moses. The people must give up their worldly practices and avoid contamination. The Mosaic rites and especially the *Temple Scroll* show an almost fanatical preoccupation with being *qādôš*, "sanctified" (cf. Gk. *hagios*, Lat. *purus*)—all of these words for *holiness* mean specifically "set apart," "cut off," not mingled to any degree, because we are dealing with two worlds, the one eternal and incorruptible, the other corruptible and temporal. The slightest taint of corruption means that the other world would be neither incorruptible nor eternal. The tiniest flaw in a building, institution, code, or character will inevitably prove fatal in the long run of eternity. The object of the rules laid down in Leviticus 10:10–12 is to make a sharp distinction *ləhabdîl* (between what is holy and unholy, clean and unclean). Chapters 11 and 12 give a detailed catalog of what is clean and what is unclean, with the strictest rules for keeping the two absolutely separate. The lesson of absolute separation is

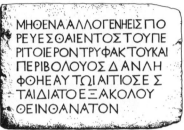

MHΘENAAΛΛOΓENHEIΣ ΠO
PEYEΣΘAIENTOΣTOYΠE
PITOIEPONTPYΦAKTOYKAI
ΠEPIBOΛOYOΣ Δ ANΛH
ΦOHEAY TΩIAITIOΣ E Σ
TAIΔIATOE Ξ AKOΛOY
ΘEINΘANATON

No Gentile shall enter
inward of the partition
and barrier around the Temple,
and whoever is caught
shall be responsible
to himself for his
subsequent death.

Figure 12. A rare fragment of the marble warning fence surrounding
the Second Temple reminds us of the same prohibition given by Moses
more than a thousand years earlier. This severe warning was seen as
a protection for the worshipers, who believed it was physically dangerous to approach the holy place without sufficient purification (cf.
Uzzah in 2 Samuel 6:6–7).

forcefully brought home to Israel in the beginning of Exodus 19, where certain fences are set up at the foot of Mt.
Sinai, with death the fate of any who cross the line (fig.
12). The teachings of Moses begin with a warning to make
the people keep their distance (Exodus 19:21). The priests
are authorized to approach more closely. Why? Because
they are willing to take things more seriously. They are
required to sanctify themselves, and Jehovah will come to
them as a special group (Exodus 19:22). The priests themselves, however, must keep their proper distance: "They
must not try to ascend any nearer to Jehovah or they will
be overpowered"—blown up, $yipr\bar{a}z$ (cf. Exodus 19:24).

Purification is the beginning and end of the *Temple
Scroll*, and it goes back to Adam (Moses 6:8). Temple work
began among Adam's children when God set them apart,
gave them a blessing, gave them a new name, registered
them in the new Book of the Generations of Adam (Genesis
5:1–2), setting the true family of Adam on its course be-

ginning with Seth (whose name means "second, substitute, equal"—he was the living image of Adam [D&C 107:48], and his name shows that), followed by his son, Enos (meaning "man," exactly the same as Adam and Enoch)—the line of patriarchs being carried down in the record.

The ordinances are not secret, and yet they are, so to speak, automatically scrambled for those not authorized to have them. Satan disobeyed orders when he revealed certain secrets to Adam and Eve, not because they were not known and done in other worlds, but because he was not authorized in that time and place to convey them. Likewise he conveyed certain secrets to Cain, who became Master Mahan, and to Lamech, who achieved the same degree of negative glory (Moses 5:29–31, 49–52). Lamech's wives in turn "had not compassion" and spread the secret things abroad (Moses 5:47–48, 53). This is the classical account of the *Watchers*, angels who came to call the human race to repentance, but who, being tempted by the daughters of men, fell and gave away the covenants and the knowledge they possessed.[57] This was their undoing, and was always treated as the most monstrous of crimes, divulging the pure ordinances of heaven to people unworthy to receive them, who then proceeded to exercise them in unrighteousness while proclaiming their own righteousness on the grounds of possessing them (cf. Genesis 6:4–6).

The oldest tradition common to many ancient people is that of the woman who got the secret name from the most high god. It is the Egyptian story of Re and the Son's Eye. Isis, wishing to found the Egyptian Dynasty along matriarchal lines by endowing her sons with the priesthood, begged Re, their father, to tell her his secret name. It is the story of Epimetheus, who loosed all evils upon mankind when he deferred to Pandora's request. Recently that story has turned up in the early Coptic Christian *Third*

Apocryphon of John. Moreover, a two-volume work by Ludwig Laistner traces the Sphinx motif through ancient times. In the Bible it is Samson and Delilah. But the most significant telling of the story is in Moses 5:47–55, the story of Lamech, which reports how this pattern was spread throughout the entire world in the abominations of the ancients. This opens up a whole world of comparative studies telling us how it is that ceremonies resembling those of the temple are found throughout the ancient world.[58]

Why are these temple ordinances guarded with such secrecy when anyone who really wants to can find out what goes on? Even though everyone may discover what goes on in the temple, and many have already revealed it, the important thing is that *I* do not reveal these things; they must remain sacred to *me*. I must preserve a zone of sanctity which cannot be violated whether or not anyone else in the room has the remotest idea what the situation really is. For my covenants are all between me and my Heavenly Father, all others being present only as witnesses. Why witnesses, if this must be so intimate and private? Plainly others are involved in it, too. God's work and his glory is to share that work and glory with others. Abraham said he sought diligently for these ordinances that he might administer them to others (Abraham 1:2). It is because others are engaged in the work that we know that we are not just imagining it. On the other hand I can never share my understanding of them completely with anyone but the Lord. No matter what happens, it will, then, always remain secret: only I know exactly the weight and force of the covenants I have made — I and the Lord with whom I have made them — *unless* I choose to reveal them. If I do not, then they are secret and sacred no matter what others may say or do. Anyone who would reveal these things has not understood them, and therefore that person has not given them away. You cannot reveal what

you do not know! The constant concern is to keep Israel
out of contact with the profane things of the world; the
reason given is not absolute secrecy, but to keep these
sacred things from becoming *ḥālāl*, that is, vulgar, popular,
the subject of everyday discussion, in a word, trivia. This
is what is meant by blasphemy, which signifies not some
awful and horrible commitment to evil but simply taking
holy things lightly. And what is wrong with being *ḥālāl*?
What is evil in innocent everyday conversation about the
temple? Even at its most innocuous, the bringing up of
such matters in public can only lead to their cheapening,
but, worst of all, to all manner of misunderstanding, mis-
representation, disputation, contention, contamination,
and corruption.[59] This is exactly what has happened
throughout history—the possession of God's secrets was
a cause for vanity and self-congratulation. In some parts
of the world where the greatest secrecy was observed—as
at Eleusis and in Egypt, and it would appear that some of
the secrets never leaked out—scholars marveled at how
well those secrets were kept; the rites appear today surprisingly like those in the real temple.

When the Lord speaks of giving precious things to the
dogs and pearls to the swine, it is not with contempt for
those creatures, but with the futility of such a thing for all
concerned—the dogs would find no value in precious
things, which would be thrown away into dirt and trodden
under foot.

With the sectaries of the second century and following,
secrecy becomes a subject of great fascination; it tickles
vanity and gives even the lowliest a feeling of superiority.
It was not so with the early Christians: "Everyone should
be given the highest mystery which he is worthy to receive.
For if ye hide any mystery from a worthy person ye may
be guilty of great condemnation." Whoever asks and
knocks should be given the benefit of the doubt, but we
must not forget that it is very dangerous to give mysteries

to the unworthy—it will harm them and everyone else.[60] The mischief resulting from secrecy has been apparent throughout the history of religion.

There is no doubt at all that the early Christians were not only concerned with the temple but kept their knowledge of it and its ordinances secret.[61] The Roman Catholics have always denied this, claiming that everything Christ taught was to be "preached from the house tops." Roman Catholics are also very uncomfortable with the traditions of the temple. George MacRae goes so far as to assert that Luke gives a completely warped view in his attempt "to show that the primitive Christian community in Jerusalem focused its life around the temple. . . . I don't think Luke had any acquaintance with Jerusalem itself," he writes, "and how the temple actually functioned in the lives of people."[62] The Christian temple ordinances emerge in the forty-day teachings of the Lord to the apostles, which MacRae calls the "revelation-discourse[s]."[63] He considers them based on a complete misunderstanding perpetrated by the Gnostics.[64] In all of his works to disqualify the teachings of the Lord after the resurrection, MacRae never gives the slightest hint that there might *really* have been a forty-day ministry.

Are the Conventional Ordinances Enough?

The ordinances of some Christian churches today are Baptism, Confirmation, Communion (sacrament), Penance, Anointing of the Sick (Extreme Unction), Holy Order, and Matrimony. All of these have come in for examination, and some of them recently for drastic revision. The ancient records show that what corresponds to these rites today is complex and conflicting. Nobody really understands them. The discovery of early records has required constant reappraisal. The Reformation got rid of much ritual and liturgy of patently non-Christian origin, but as a result the liturgical poverty of Protestantism is one of its serious failings. How can such a defect be corrected? Can we trust to the taste and judgment of self-certifying institutions to impart sanctity to forms and observances? An example is the academic caps and gowns. Whether the design is by committees, synods, conventicles, or individuals, by what authority do they act? Wherein does the sanctity of these costumes reside?

The Catholic case is even more dubious. When at the monastery of Solesmnes in 1830 the serious study of old and forgotten manuscripts dealing with the mass was undertaken, it became apparent that there was nothing particularly ancient or Christian in the rites.[65] Today the standard work on the mass is that of Eisenhofer and Lechner, who trace the origin of the Holy Office to four sources—and if there is one thing in which one is not lacking for evidence it is in the ritual of the church, attested in thousands of documents all over Europe.[66] The four sources are as follows:

1. The rites of the *synagogue* consisted of singing, preaching, scripture reading, and prayer. Reminders of the temple are important, but they didn't make it a temple or transfer any of the ordinances.[67]

2. The adoption of antique cult practices, for example the practice of the *annona,* are clearly present in the mass. The word mass, *messis,* is in fact the Latin word for harvest ceremony. The council of Elvira in A.D. 444 forbade the use of candles and incense in churches, since they were a basic pagan practice everywhere. Parts of the mass thought by the apologists of the nineteenth century (such as the naive G. K. Chesterton) to go back to the days of the apostles are no later than the sixteenth century in origin. Such are the epiclesis and the monstrance, that climactic elevation of the host which has become the high point of the mass (fig. 13). The core of the Western rite was the Milanese order brought by Ambrose, a convert when he came from Antioch, via Ephesus and Lyons, while the

Figure 13. An anonymous master painted "The Mass of St. Giles" in 1495, depicting the high altar of the royal chapel of Saint-Denis outside Paris. The veil-like curtain is drawn back, allowing the king to view the sacred mystery of the elevation of the host, a ceremony introduced in the fourteenth century.

foundation of the present Roman mass is the rite established at Aachen in the days of Charlemagne.

3. Much of the splendor of the mass may be attributed
to the Roman Imperial cult, as Andreas Alföldi has shown
at length.[68]

4. The Germanic and Celtic courts of the North contributed some of the most venerated rites of Christian
churches. Henry St. John Feasey's studies on the English
Holy Week's Ceremony show how deeply rooted in pagan
antiquity these rites are.[69]

For years it was accepted doctrine that the early Christians had a choice between *Amt* and *Geist* ("office" and
"spirit"), the two being mutually exclusive. Rudolph Sohm
made this into an article of faith: Whereas the old Jewish
religion was steeped in hierarchy, form, and authority, the
early Christians relinquished all that to be governed by
nothing but a spirit of love—no organization of any kind,
no offices, no orders, no structure, just the spirit that blow-
eth as it listeth. But then there was a reaction. It was easy
for Adolf von Harnack to show how involved the Christians were in an ordinance such as the laying on of hands,
on which they were absolutely insistent and which served,
as the earliest writings make clear, as an ordinance of
initiation, which would necessarily be initiation into an
organization.[70]

More recently the coming forth of the Dead Sea Scrolls
and the early Coptic Christian texts, as well as the rediscovery of a mass of apocalyptic writings, such as the books
of Enoch and Abraham, bring out an intense concern with
the ordinances of the temple. But this is the ideal temple,
the heavenly temple after which the earthly temple is mod-
eled. Needless to say, it is a very different structure from
that which scholars have tried to construct through the
years: To this day no one is sure what the temple was like
or what was done in it. But the *Temple Scroll* is a link
between the two; that document shows how the earthly

temple insensibly fuses with the holy city and eventually embraces all the spirits in the world.[71] The numerous accounts of the heavenly temple are found in a multitude of Ascension texts.[72] These might appear as altogether fanciful were it not that they show a consistent picture of the temple and are supported by numerous points of contact with actual practices. We must not forget the forty-day literature, in which the Lord instructs the apostles in great secrecy after his resurrection in the rites and ordinances of a higher order, such as the prayer circle and "the bridal chamber."[73]

The Terrible Questions

Since the 1950s there has been a revival of the liturgical movement—as if there was merit in liturgy itself—with an inevitable drift to pomp and ceremony. But if there is anything that sets the Mormon temple apart, it is the total lack of display, pomp, or ceremony within its precinct. It is amusing that after the many books written in the nineteenth and early twentieth centuries describing the temple rites as a carnival of glamorous and occult shenanigans in the manner of Aleister Crowley, it should turn out that the Mormons have actually fewer ceremonial doings than almost any other church, including even the Quakers and Baptists, who make a conscious effort to put on some kind of show, even if it is only a show of austerity; for example, the severe eighteenth-century guise of the Mennonites at this late date seems to me to be pure theater. But no such pretense is necessary for the Latter-day Saints, because for them the temple should be a place for serious concern, with no place for pretense or show, no musical chants, bells, gorgeous vestments, processions, declamation, recitatives, trumpets, adornments, color, resounding intonements, nor incense—it is the temple work alone that counts. It should show soberness and austerity, and yet not show severity. It is there that one comes to grips with what the Doctors of the synagogue and the church have banned as "the Terrible Questions," which deal with the fundamental questions of existence, and not in a philosophical, allegorical, or abstract manner. The rabbis and the fathers alike forbade discussion of these issues. Various Gnostic sects tried to keep reviving them, but to do that they had to resort to all manner of contrivance and fakery, mingling scripture with rumors and some authentic traditions.

How do we explain this vacuum? When the apostles met with the Lord behind closed doors, they asked the Lord why he always spoke to the people in parables. "Because," he said, "to you it is given to understand the mysteries of the kingdom of heaven, but to them, it is not given" (cf. Mark 4:11). By the mysteries of heaven he meant "the mysteries of godliness," those ordinances which were closely guarded by the early saints, even at the risk of misunderstanding, scandal, and persecution. At a very early time, Origen, in his work on the first principles of the gospel, regretted that the church did not have clear information on any one of them. Thus, he says, the Bible tells us that there are angels but does not give us the slightest indication of what they were like (did they have wings?).[74] In the same way Basil, in the fourth century, regrets the same lack of specific information about any of the ordinances.[75] We know that the Christians baptized and married, he says, but we haven't the slightest instruction as to how they did it. Was the Lord's supper distributed in the same manner as the loaves and fishes? Were they the same ordinances?

The Creation Motif

According to the eminent N. A. Dahl, "most important has been the discovery of the importance of the worship of the temple, especially the great festivals [i.e., the rites in which all participate] as a common point of departure and coincidence. In the common worship, the *creation* was commemorated and *re-enacted*, and the future renewal for which Israel hoped, was prefigured."[76] M. Dahood sees the closest association between the name and the creation motif in the earliest temples, in such names as "the Voice has Created" — Creation by the Word.[77] Where did the creation begin? The answer for the Jews was in the temple: "The first thing which emerged from the primordial waters was the temple," from which point creation spread in all directions, specifically this earthly creation, for the temple was actually transplanted from a preexistent world created long before.[78] The ancient temple drama begins with the council in heaven when the creation is being planned.[79]

Many features of the Latter-day Saint version of creation are sound and scientific. First of all, this earth was part of a system of worlds made of the same elements and subject to the same physical laws. The creation was neither instantaneous nor simultaneous, as Aquinas describes it.[80] The latter have become the fundamental ideas behind the word *creation* as it is used by scientists and religionists alike. All are agreed today that the word *creation* implies bringing something out of nothing instantaneously and completely. On the contrary, creation is a process in which one step leads to another over an indefinite period of time. The "episodic" nature of life is essential in this version. What we have is one ever ongoing play divided into distinct acts and scenes. Since there is no point at which everything emerges from nothing, we begin with an act and a scene in a play that has already been going on for untold ages and has already seen countless worlds come and go. Our story opens with unorganized matter, then an earth which is "only" earth, then a globe completely invested with water, then a division of the waters, causing the upthrust of earth by plate techtonics, which proceeds to form mountains and hills, down from which rush great rivers and small streams, supplied by the torrential rains that fall from the darkness that covers the face of the deep—the dense cloud-cover which begins to break up as first the sun, then the moon, then the stars appear. They were not created at that time; they were already there. Human history is not primarily concerned with the creatures of other ages or of other planets; its proper beginning is placed at that momentous period of transition between the Cretaceous and the Tertiary when the first angiosperms appeared as grass, flowers, shrubs, and trees, supplying sustenance for the elephant, the lion, and other large mammals. The mammoths were the first to appear of those herds of grazing animals, the herd which emerged as soon as the grass was provided—a very sudden event in the course of nature, "an explosion," Loren Eiseley calls it.[81] They supplied a livelihood for the predators—the lion, the tiger, and the bear, which preyed upon the herds. All these were in preparation for man. If the above rules out the whole fundamentalist picture of creation, Darwinism is no less rejected by the basic doctrine that the creation was both directed and planned. The planning began long before the actual operation was carried out, and the process required constant oversight and direction.

The Temple Drama

The principal recorded activity which took place at the ancient temples on the occasion of the great assembly was the temple drama, a ritual combat, a showdown between good and evil. Before the world could be safely launched on a new age or cycle of existence, the problem of evil had to be settled, for a faulted world could not be a safe or enduring one.

The drama began with a prologue in heaven. The premortal council, as well as good and evil, are the subjects of the discussion. The argument is that an eternal, spiritual being is to be subjected to temptation, to which, in fact, it must yield if it is to experience a part of existence which must be taken into account; for sooner or later there must be opposition in all things, and the new world is to be set apart as a special place for testing.[82] For that purpose it must be quarantined. Man must be temporarily cut off from the presence of God and angels, that he might demonstrate to himself his capacity or incapacity for coping with evil. By yielding to temptation, man loses his immunity and innocence as the price of gaining knowledge. But since he cannot return to God in his fatally flawed condition, a Savior will be provided on certain conditions of obedience. The situation, and indeed the whole plot of the temple drama, is vividly set forth in the book of Moses, way back in 1830, before anyone ever thought of serious study of ancient temples except on a mystic or occult basis. The fourth chapter contains the provisions for Adam's redemption, but first comes a matchless presentation of man's condition. Moses' situation is that of a man trapped in a sewer. The only way for him to escape is for someone to go beneath him so that he can stand on his shoulders and climb out. He must recognize the situation and make an effort to respond: the whole plan is one of repentance — the man must "repent and call upon God . . . forevermore" (Moses 5:8) in the name of the Son, who is to help him. He is, as it were, calling upon God to send the Son to his aid. *Inter finitum et infinitum non est proportio,* which means that all are equally in need of repentance. Ten miles falls as far short of infinity as 10,000 miles, and I am just as far from being *"full* of grace and truth" today as I ever was or will be.

The Combat

Every drama must have a conflict, and nothing is more impressive than the manner in which the problem of evil was treated in the temple. The showdown is of course between good and evil; and these, following the usual temple practice, are represented figuratively or by proxy.

Before the altar in Jerusalem all the sins and vices of the people were shifted to the figure of a scapegoat, which thereby became an object of utter loathing, a *pharmakos*, an embodiment of all evil, driven out into the wilderness to perish, taking all the sins of the people with him. Elsewhere in the ancient world the combat is between the holy king and Mot or Seth, who is everything that is evil—the good guy versus the bad guy. But the God of Moses was wiser than that. In the scapegoat, Israel recognized that the enemy they were driving with stones and curses was the evil that was in themselves. They were the bad guys. In the Songs of David composed for the temple drama, the king cries out *de profundis*, from the depths; he is in utter despair, overwhelmed by the waters of darkness, overpowered and beaten by the evil one; yet the cause of it all, as he recognizes, is the king's own guilt. That is the evil he is combatting: his psalms are penitential. By contrast, the ancient Greek choruses at the temple mourn for their afflictions but never for their sins—the characters in the play seek for the guilty parties but, like Oedipus, they absolutely refuse to recognize the guilt in themselves.[83]

Satan cannot force us to sin, in which case we would be helpless (innocent—no contest!); but he can *bribe* us to sin, in which case we are guilty and follow him on our own free will. We make covenants with the understanding that we mean to keep them, and the alternative is to place ourselves in Satan's power (Moses 4:4; 5:23). We are placed here expressly to be proven herewith whether we will be true and faithful to our understanding with God, while Satan is allowed to try us and to tempt us, to invite and to entice, to see how far he can shake us.

In a direct frontal attack, as Moses discovers, Satan is stronger than mere mortals, and, for that reason, Satan is not permitted to make such frontal attacks. God has placed enmity, a wall of first defense, between the seed of the woman and the serpent; the first reaction to sin is one of

loathing and revulsion, which is the safest protection one
can possibly have against evil. Satan, however, knows how
to overcome that, and God allows him to play his own
game, which is to break down our resistance and win us
to his side with money. There is no more impressive aspect
to the ancient temple drama than dealing with the problem
of evil, which philosophers and theologians to this day
consider ultimately insoluble. It is by using money as bait
that Satan leaves it up to us to decide whether we will
follow him or not, and God permits that arrangement, since
that is the very purpose of the test. His maxim is a true
one: "money answereth all things" (Ecclesiastes 10:19),
which means that in this world money is the name of most
every game going; and anyone who would play any other
game must pay a heavy penalty for what Stuart Chase
called the "the luxury of integrity." In Satan's world, "he
who turneth away from sin maketh himself a prey" — you
must play this game merely to survive.

The existence of this primordial temple drama has long
been recognized. It is vividly set forth in the Memphite
Theology, the oldest written record known — whether or
not it began in Egypt; and the Shabako Stone makes it clear
that the drama was already very old when it was performed
to celebrate the dedication of the temple and the founding
of the first dynasty of Egypt (cf. fig. 43, pp. 180–81). It
spread from there to Greece, where we have a collection
of horrendous tragedies dealing with the subjects of good
and evil, and in terms of power and gain.[84] Not only
Greece, however, but the rest of the world sooner or later
adapted the same standard temple drama.[85] It should be
noted that this drama in its oldest and purest form was
not meant to be a spectacle but an instructive demonstration.[86] The theme is fully developed throughout the ancient
world in all its detail, which can't be treated here, though
it should be noted that the purpose of it is a participation

of mankind in rites and in seeking the assurance of resurrection.[87]

There is an instructive parallel between the loss of the First Temple and the Second Temple by the Jews, and the loss of the Kirtland and Nauvoo temples. In every case, it was for the same reason—the covetousness of the people. The temple doesn't need to be protected; it doesn't need security, since it *is* the only security. The positive side of the injunction to live up to every covenant made is that it will absolutely guarantee prosperity—the law of consecration being the most difficult of the tests. We have been repeatedly assured that if the Saints observe that law, they will never suffer by privation or persecution.

The Archaic Background

The greatest of Jewish philosophers, Maimonides, says that the altar in the temple was where Adam offered a sacrifice after he was created. Indeed, Adam was created from the very ground; as the Sages taught, Adam was created from the place where he made the atonement offering. In 2 *Baruch* we read, "This building . . . is not that . . . which was prepared beforehand here from the time when I took counsel to make Paradise, and showed it to Adam before he sinned." Adam was shown the heavenly temple. "After these things I showed it to my servant Abraham by night among the portions of the victims, and again also I showed it to Moses on Mount Sinai when I showed him the likeness of the tabernacle and all its vessels. And now behold it is preserved with me, as also Paradise"[88] (this was written just after the destruction of the temple in Jerusalem). At the dedication of the St. George temple in 1877, Brigham Young said, "It is true that Solomon built a temple for the purpose of giving endowments, but . . . they gave very few if any endowments. . . . I will not say but what Enoch had temples and officiated therein, but we have no account of it";[89] but today we have a great amount of ancient material concerning Enoch, and much of it centers in the temple. Indeed, the principal Hebrew record of Enoch's doings is called the *Hekhalot*, or chambers of the temple, indicating the steps in initiation to which Enoch introduced his people as the guide or teacher of the ordinances. "The first man brought the five ordinances with him when he came out of the aeon of light," says a newly discovered Mandaean manuscript; and "having completed his testing [*agōn*] he ascended again with these good tokens and was received into the aeons of light."[90] Today much is being made of Abraham as the restorer rather than the initiator of the knowledge of God, recapitulating what had been given to Adam. This is symbolized by his rebuilding of the ancient altar of the first fathers, last used by Noah. Abraham, according to Maimonides, dedicated the spot on Mount Moriah where the future temple was to stand, and "God also showed him the future temple service and the law."[91] There is a wealth of tradition now being zealously studied to show that the temple ordinances really go back to the beginning, as Joseph Smith declared. The four names associated with the tradition are those of Adam, Enoch, Abraham, and Elijah. The main concern is salvation for the dead, as is brought forth repeatedly in the so-called ascension literature. It is here that we find the significant equation of John the Baptist and Elijah. We recall that when Dives, the rich man, looked up to see Lazarus in heaven, he beheld him resting in Abraham's bosom (Luke 16:22). Abraham, according to tradition, cooperates with Michael in interceding with God for sinners who have died. In fact, as K. Kohler observes, "The main power of Abraham is his constant intercession for spirits awaiting judgment in the other world." This idea is expressed in the *Kaddish*, or prayers for the dead, in which Abraham seeks to bring about their salvation in the temple.[92]

Work for the Dead

At the time of the Crusades the orders of the Hospitalers and Templars were founded to provide protection
and hospitality for those coming to the temple at Jerusalem.
No one has the vaguest idea how it all began, writes a
contemporary, and there are all sorts of wild stories going
around.[93] The accepted account was that such hospitality
went back to the time when the temple was retaken by
the Jews and Judas Maccabeus, when he "rescued the
temple from profane hands" and found in the holy place
great amounts of gold and silver. This money Judas dedicated for the salvation of the dead.[94] To explain this activity
we are told that when the Jewish casualties of the war were
being collected and buried, it was found that many of them
were wearing pagan charms around their necks. For this
they would be condemned to hell. "When Judas Maccabeus saw and understood that it was a good and proper
practice to pray for the dead he sent twelve pieces of silver
to Jerusalem to be used for the building of a hospice for
the poor who would be asked to pray for the dead, and
Melchiar established the practice as a regular order of appointed brethren. Then Christ appeared to Zacharias while
he was sacrificing and told him to go to the house in Jerusalem where John the Baptist was born."[95] Here we have
garbled accounts connecting the work of John the Baptist
to turn the hearts of the dead fathers to the children, a
work for the dead which survived in the temple till the
time of the Maccabees. Today some Roman Catholics see
in Matthew 16:18, in the mention of the keys and the stone,
the much desired admission to or exclusion from the
temple, the gates in question being expressly the gates of
the temple. The keys are the keys that open the gates that
hold back (katischuō) those who are being retained in the
other world. Along with this, the Rock is now identified
with Abraham as well as with Peter, particularly in his
capacity as the champion for simple mortals.[96]

The Ancient Significance of the Veil

A study of the earliest Jewish shrines and monuments has pointed out the importance of the veil and its identity with the mantle worn by the high priest.[97] It is at one and the same time the veil that hangs between the worlds (his "curtains are stretched out still" [Moses 7:30]), bearing on it the cosmic marks of the compass, the square, the *omphalos* or universal center, and the *eben shǝtiyyāh* or solid earth on which a man kneels to praise God. In the temple these marks are clearly shown in the Astana examples (Taoist-Buddhist-Nestorian veils from the sixth to seventh centuries A.D.; cf. fig. 28, pp. 114–15). It is, according to the Talmud, at the veil that information is exchanged between the worlds.[98] "For the man who is privileged to have children in this world will through them be worthy to enter," according to the *Zohar*, " 'behind the partition [veil]' in the world to come."[99] In the *Testament of Levi* the garment of the priesthood "refers to the garment of the angel or of the personified temple itself."[100] The mysteries of the marriage covenant, according to the *Gospel of Philip*, are hidden in types and images behind the veil.[101] These symbols, it notes, are despised and misunderstood by the world.[102] *Second Jeu* is one of those baffling documents conveniently and loosely designated as Gnostic. The Gnostics were numerous sectarians who copied the secrets of the early church, claiming to have received them secretly from one of the apostles or other disciples. They waited, says Hegesippus, until the last apostle or eyewitness was dead before they came out of the woodwork, each claiming that he had the true gnosis.[103] What they pretended to have was a catalogue mixing traditions and customs from various sources but always including some authentic teaching by which they could claim the allegiance of Christians. One of the most remarkable of these is 2 *Jeu*. It tells how one approaches through the stages, passwords, and mysteries in a process which alone qualifies one to return to the Father. These ordinances cannot be obtained until one first receives baptism.[104] "There are three stages to be passed through and at each one a password or name is required."[105] "There is a series of veils that are drawn before the great king. When you come to this barrier you must recite the mystery and give the proper answer."[106]

The final stage is the complete Adam or Jeu (the name is a form of Jehovah). There Christ checks to make sure that everything has been done correctly; he questions everyone at the veil personally.[107] All who pass through are in a world surrounded by light. This whole thing, says one of the most recent and thorough students of the subject, "introduces us into a world of the most mystifying speculation: the Temple is here considered as a person and the veil of the temple as a garment that is worn, as a personification of the sanctuary itself."[108] Theophylactus, commenting in the eleventh century on Hebrews 9:3, says the veil is of course the entrance to the tent. "The first veil divided the court of the people and the bronze altar from the tent where only the priests could enter. Next there was another veil to the holy of holies and through this veil only the high priest could go once a year. It was called the tent"[109] because it was the place where one entered into the presence of God or was allowed to get a glimpse of him. Somewhat later, Simplicius describes the inner shrine rather as an *anapausis* or resting place, where the saints are given rest or, as in the celestial room, may rest awhile on their upward journey to the father.

The Opposition

It has always been a well-known principle among the Jews and Christians that Satan's tactic is not the frontal attack but the clever counterfeit. The devil inverts the truth and imitates the divine ordinances, writes Tertullian,[110] exactly as the Lord does them: "He baptizes the faithful,

he promises by the bath the expiation of sins; in the rites
of Mithra he marks the forehead of the soldiers. He has
his ritual oblation of bread, he presents the image of a
resurrection, and he crowns you with a throne under the
blade"; it is all corruption and contamination.

But Is It Real?

If the gospel is more than a catalogue of moral platitudes, if we are really dealing with the things of eternity,
it cannot be practiced on an everyday level. Joseph Smith
has given us the temple ordinances, but are they real? As
the *Temple Scroll* tells us, these ordinances can only be had
by revelation, and therefore they lie beyond the pale of
ordinary discussion. It was Descartes who insisted that we
are wasting our time trying to talk of eternal and infinite
things in an everyday idiom. But Descartes also realized
that there are certain tests which justify taking propositions
seriously and pursuing further investigation.[111] In the case
of Joseph Smith we have to consider that (1) what he has
given us is the only thing of its kind—true, there are resemblances everywhere but always they are speculative,
fragmentary, uncertain, and conflicting; (2) there was in
ancient times such an institution as he has given us; it is
found at various levels of splendor or decay, but in the
early days men were working hard to bring heaven down
to earth; (3) this unifying and teaching institution was the
core of every civilization; and (4) Joseph Smith brought
forth the whole vast complex in a perfectly consistent and
coordinated form, a work totally without parallel in the
world today.[112]

The study of world religions and comparative religions
which has exploded since the beginning of this century
shows that Joseph Smith was right on target; moreover,
he recognized a primal archaic order which had produced
all manner of broken fragments and scattered traditions.
The reality of this archaic order has been emerging only

in the last two decades through the insight of men like de Santillana, who bring a scientific knowledge to a serious contemplation of the ancient heritage.[113] The supreme issue remains today as then ever the same: Is this life everything? Is that all there is? Is there another dimension? In the temple, time, space, and lives are extended; everything there is "as in other worlds." No matter how men try, they have never been able to liberate themselves from that question. The only alternative to eternal life remains, as the foremost artists and scientists of our time emphatically declare, an existence of absurdity. Between the temple and the absurd we are given no other choice.

To Prove Him Herewith

The supreme test was, in ancient as in modern times, an economic one. Every Israelite made his token sacrifice at the temple once a year, but at the same time he brought his basket, and consecrated all his property. The bulk of the old law is taken up with the economic obligations of the individual. The beginning and ending of the law is not legalism or ritualism but grace and truth; the whole teaching of the law is to be fair, compassionate, magnanimous, with heavy emphasis on equality. The first two commandments tell it all: If you really love God and your neighbor, there is no need to be commanded not to steal or lie, or do any contemptible thing. Yet they enter their covenants with the understanding that unless they fulfill rigorously and completely *every* covenant they make in the temple, Satan will have power over them. We are also told by the prophet that the ordinances are the same in every dispensation. Yet attempts have been made to mitigate and qualify the law of consecration, which, said Brigham Young, was easier to understand and more unequivocally clear than any other commandment. Unless the ordinances are observed exactly as prescribed, they will be a curse and not a blessing. And this is where Israel fails: The last of the covenants and promises is fittingly the hardest. The story of the rich young man shows that this is the breaking point: he was faithful in his prayers, tithes, and alms, but when the Lord said, "There is yet one thing remaining" (cf. Mark 10:21), namely the law of consecration, the young man could not take it. Many Latter-day Saints, also, are pure Teflon where this principle is concerned.

Notes

1. Discussed in Hugh W. Nibley, "The Idea of the Temple in History," *MS* 120 (1958): 228–37, 247–49; Hugh W. Nibley, *What Is a Temple? The Idea of the Temple in History* (Provo: Brigham Young University Press, 1963); reprinted as "What Is a Temple?" in *CWHN* 4:357–61, esp. n. 13; cf. Eusebius, *Historia Ecclesiastica (Ecclesiastical History)* X, 4, in *PG* 20:848–80.

2. See Shaye J. D. Cohen, "The Temple and the Synagogue," in Truman G. Madsen, ed., *The Temple in Antiquity* (Provo: Religious Studies Center, 1984), 152–74.

3. Discussed in Hugh W. Nibley, "Christian Envy of the Temple," *Jewish Quarterly Review* 50 (1959–60): 97–123, 229– 40; reprinted in *CWHN* 4:391–434.

4. Carol L. Meyers, "The Elusive Temple," *Biblical Archaeologist* 45 (Winter 1982): 41.

5. A. Dupont-Sommer, *The Jewish Sect of Qumran and the Essenes* (New York: Macmillan, 1956), 69–70.

6. Josephus, *Antiquities of the Jews* XVIII, 1, 5.

7. Cohen, "The Temple and the Synagogue," 169.

8. Nibley, "Christian Envy of the Temple," 97–123, 229–40; in *CWHN* 4:391–434; cf. S. G. F. Brandon, *The Fall of Jerusalem and the Christian Church* (London: SPCK, 1951), 120–21; James Hastings, ed., *Dictionary of the Apostolic Church*, 2 vols. (New York: Scribner, 1918), 2:556–57.

9. Brandon, *Fall of Jerusalem and the Christian Church*, 127.

10. Ibid., 263.

11. Matthew Black, *The Dead Sea Scrolls and Christian Doctrine* (London: Athone, 1966), 80–81.

12. Samuel Davidson, *An Introduction to the Study of the New Testament*, 2 vols. (London: Longmans and Green, 1868), 1:264.

13. Hastings, *Dictionary of the Apostolic Church*, 2:556.

14. H. E. Dana, *Jewish Christianity* (New Orleans: Bible Institute Memorial, 1937), 18.

15. Nibley, "What Is a Temple?" in *CWHN* 4:357–61.

16. Hugh W. Nibley, "The Hierocentric State," *WPQ* 4 (1951): 226–53; reprinted in *CWHN* 10:99–147. Varro, *De Lingua Latina* VII, 6–9.

17. Stefan Weinstock, "Templum," *Römische Mittheilungen* 47 (1932): 100–101. Cf. Alfred Jeremias, *Handbuch der altorientalischen Geisteskultur* (Berlin: de Gruyter, 1929), 146, 185. Eric Burrows, "Some Cosmological Patterns in Babylonian Religion," in Samuel Hooke, ed., *The Labyrinth* (London: SPCK, 1935), 45–70.

18. Weinstock, "Templum," 102–3.

19. G. W. Ahlstrom, "Heaven on Earth—At Hazor and Arad," in Birger A. Pearson, ed., *Religious Syncretism in Antiquity, Essays in Conversation with Geo Widengren* (Missoula, MT: Scholars, 1975), 67–71.

20. Ibid., 67–69.

21. Cf. Hugh W. Nibley, "Unrolling the Scrolls," in *CWHN* 1:131–70; Hugh W. Nibley, "Treasures in the Heavens: Some Early Christian Insights into the Organizing of Worlds," *DJMT* 8 (Autumn/ Winter 1973): 76–98; reprinted as "Treasures in the Heavens," in *CWHN* 1:171–214.

22. Cf. Frank M. Cross, "The Priestly Tabernacle in the Light of Recent Research," in Madsen, ed., *The Temple in Antiquity*, 94; William F. Albright, *Archaeology and the Religion of Israel* (Baltimore: Johns Hopkins University Press, 1942), 103–5; cf. *CWHN* 1:210.

23. Cross, "Priestly Tabernacle in the Light of Recent Research," 94.

24. Bedřich Hrozný, *Ancient History of Western Asia, India and Crete*, tr. J. Prochazka (New York: Philosophical Library, 1953), 93.

25. Albright, *Archaeology and the Religion of Israel*, 154 (emphasis added).

26. See Hugh W. Nibley, *An Approach to the Book of Mormon* (Salt Lake City: Deseret Book, 1976), x, 243; reprinted in *CWHN* 6:xv, 295.

27. Brigham Young, *MS* 15 (1853): 488 (emphasis added).

28. *Deseret News*, May 2, 1877.

29. Paul Jouön, "Les mots employés pour désigner 'le Temple' dans l'Ancien Testament, le Nouveau Testament et Josèphe," *Recherches de science religieuse* 25 (1935): 329–43.

30. Carol L. Meyers, "Jachin and Boaz in Religious and Political Perspective," in Madsen, ed., *Temple in Antiquity*, 136, notes that "countless attempts have been made to explain, describe, and otherwise comprehend . . . the twin pillars flanking [Solomon's temple] entrance."

31. Meyers, "Elusive Temple," 33–41.

32. Yigael Yadin, *The Temple Scroll* (New York: Random House, 1985), 112–15.

33. Cross, "Priestly Tabernacle in the Light of Recent Research," 93.

34. *TPJS*, 305.

35. Cf. Cross, "Priestly Tabernacle in the Light of Recent Research," 93; Yadin, *Temple Scroll*, 122–46.

36. *Gospel of Philip* 115:27–29; Carl Schmidt, ed. and tr., *Kephalaia* (Stuttgart: Kohlhammer, 1940), 33–38; Cohen, "Temple and the Synagogue," 158.

37. Jacob Milgrom, "The Temple Scroll," *Bibilical Archaeologist* 41 (1978): 119.

38. Cohen, "Temple and the Synagogue," 157–58.

39. *Gospel of Philip* 115:27–29.

40. Schmidt, *Kephalaia*, 38.

41. Hugh W. Nibley, "The Sacrifice of Isaac," *IE* 73 (March 1970): 88.

42. Ibid., 84–93.

43. Herbert G. May, "*Ephod* and *Ariel*," *American Journal of Semitic Languages and Literatures* 56 (1939): 44.

44. Ibid., 51.

45. Morton Smith, *The Secret Gospel* (New York: Harper and Row, 1972), 83.

46. Ibid., 28.

47. Ibid., 96.

48. Ibid., 113–14.

49. Ibid., 141.

50. Hugh W. Nibley, *The Message of the Joseph Smith Papyri: An Egyptian Endowment* (Salt Lake City: Deseret Book, 1975), 255–62. Brigham Young says that "they have been fully acquainted with every password, token and sign which have enabled them to pass by the porters through the doors into the celestial kingdom," *JD* 10:172. Associated with these signs are the pilgrim signs of antiquity and the Middle Ages, badges of marks borne by pilgrims to various holy shrines. Thus in *Piers Plowman* we read, "On his hat were the signs of Sinai and the Shells of Galicha [the shrine of St. James of Compostella; they are the Western equivalent of the Jerusalem Temple], and the keys of Rome, . . . for men should know and see by his signs whom he hath sought," Thomas Hugo, "Notes on a Collection of Pilgrims' Signs, of the Thirteenth, Fourteenth, and Fifteenth Centuries, found in Thames," *Archaeologia* 38 (1860): 130.

Also related to these signs were the *tesserae hospitales,* which figure so largely in ancient rites; see Hugh W. Nibley, "Sparsiones," *Classical Journal* 40 (1945): 538–43; reprinted in *CWHN* 10:162–65. Those who are finally saved, says the *Pistis Sophia,* will not hereafter "have to give answer at the *topos* (station or place) nor apologies nor tokens, for they are without tokens and have not receivers (*paralemptores,* guides through the temple) but penetrate through all the kingdoms until they reach the highest level to which they have received the ordinances. They cannot put on the orders of the inheritance unless a sign and seal of the ineffable is placed upon them. . . . Then the veils will be parted to souls purified anew and they will receive new mysteries of the ultimate order." *Pistis Sophia* II, 98, in Carl Schmidt, *Pistis Sophia,* tr. Violet McDermot (Leiden: Brill, 1978), 243.

51. Cf. Nibley, *Message of the Joseph Smith Papyri,* 266, 278.

52. Nibley, "Sacrifice of Isaac," 84–93.

53. See for example, Bruce Kinney, *Mormonism: The Islam of America* (New York: Revell, 1912), 123–27, and N. W. Green, *Mormonism: Its Rise, Progress, and Present Condition* (Hartford, CN: Belknap and Bliss, 1870), 41–53.

54. Nibley, *Message of the Joseph Smith Papyri,* 250–53, 271–72.

55. Mitchell J. Dahood, "The Temple and Other Sacred Places in the Ebla Tablets," in Madsen, ed., *The Temple in Antiquity,* 85–86.

56. Knut Stenring, tr., *The Book of Formation (Sefer Yetzirah)* (London: Rider and Son, 1923), 27–28. Shabako Stone, line 56; cf. Kurt Sethe, *Das "Denkmal memphitischer Theologie": Der Shabakostein des Britischen Museums* (Hildesheim: Olms, 1964), 59.

57. See Hugh W. Nibley, "Enoch the Prophet," in *Pearl of Great Price Symposium* (Provo: Brigham Young University, 1975), 78–87; reprinted in *CWHN* 2:3–18.

58. Ludwig Laistner, *Das Rätsel der Sphinx* (Berlin: Hertz, 1885).

59. 2 *Jeu* 43, in Carl Schmidt, *The Books of Jeu and the Untitled Text in the Bruce Codex,* tr. Violet McDermot (Leiden: Brill, 1978), 100–101.

60. *Pistis Sophia* III, 105–6, in Schmidt, *Pistis Sophia,* 268–70.

61. Cf. Hugh W. Nibley, "Evangelium Quadraginta Dierum," *Vigiliae Christianae* 20 (1966): 1–24; reprinted as "Evangelium Quadraginta Dierum: The Forty-day Mission of Christ—The Forgotten Heritage," in *CWHN* 4:10–44.

62. George MacRae, "The Temple as a House of Revelation in the Nag Hammadi Texts," in Madsen, ed., *The Temple in Antiquity,* 186–87.

63. Ibid., 188.

64. Ibid., 187.

65. Hugh W. Nibley, *Since Cumorah* (Salt Lake City: Deseret Book, 1970), 14; reprinted in *CWHN* 7:12–13.

66. Ludwig Eisenhofer and Joseph Lechner, *The Liturgy of the Roman Rite* (Freiburg: Herder and Herder, 1961).

67. Cohen, "Temple and the Synagogue," 152–53.

68. Andreas Alföldi, *Studien zur Geschichte der Weltkrise des 3. Jahrhunderts nach Christus* (Darmstadt: Wissenschaftliche Buchgesellschaft, 1967), 297–301.

69. Henry J. Feasey, *Ancient English Holy Week Ceremonial* (London: Baker, 1897), passim.

70. Adolf von Harnack, *The Constitution and Law of the Church in the First Two Centuries* (New York: Williams and Norgate, 1910), 26.

71. Yadin, *Temple Scroll*, 112–15.

72. Cf. Martha Himmelfarb, "Apocalyptic Ascent and the Heavenly Temple," *Society of Biblical Literature 1987 Seminar Papers* (Atlanta: Scholars, 1987), 210–17.

73. See n. 61.

74. Origen, *Peri Archon (De Principiis)* I, 9, in *PG* 11:120.

75. Basil, *Letters 363, 265, 266,* in *PG* 32:976–81, 984–96.

76. N. A. Dahl, cited in W. D. Davies and D. Daube, eds., *The Background of the New Testament and Its Eschatology* (Cambridge: Cambridge University Press, 1956), 424 (emphasis added).

77. Dahood, "Temple and Other Sacred Places in the Ebla Tablets," 85–86.

78. Philo, *Questions and Answers on Genesis* IV, 151; *Questions and Answers on Exodus* II, 83; Eusebius, *Ecclesiastical History* X, 4, in *PG* 20:848–80. Alfred Jeremias, *Das alte Testament im Lichte des alten Orients* (Leipzig: Hinrichs, 1916), 49–51.

79. Hugh W. Nibley, "The Expanding Gospel," in *Nibley on the Timely and the Timeless* (Provo: Religious Studies Center, 1978), 24–34; reprinted in this volume, pages 179–95.

80. Thomas Aquinas, *Summa Theologica* q. 44–45, 65–66, 71 (New York: McGraw-Hill, 1964), 426–57, 609–28, 662–64.

81. Loren Eiseley, *The Star Thrower* (New York: Times Books, 1978), 67.

82. Nibley, "The Expanding Gospel," 34–37; reprinted in this volume, pages 195–99.

83. Cf. Hugh W. Nibley, "Three Shrines: Mantic, Sophic, and Sophistic," in *The Ancient State, CWHN* 10 (Salt Lake City: Deseret Book and F.A.R.M.S.), 343–51.

84. B. H. Stricker, "The Origin of the Greek Theatre," *Journal of Egyptian Archaeology* 40 (December 1954): 34–47.

85. Jean Capart, Review of A. Rosenvasser, *Nuevas textos literarios del antigio Egipto*, in *Chronique d'Égypte* 13 (July 1937): 202.

86. Étienne Drioton, *Le Texte Dramatique d'Edfou* (Cairo: Imprimerie de l'Institut Français d'Archéologie Orientale, 1948), 7–8.

87. Jan Zandee, Review of Siegfried Morenz, *Ägyptische Religion*, in *Bibliotheca Orientalis* 19 (1962): 40.

88. 2 Baruch 4:3–6, in *APOT* 2:482.

89. *JD* 18:303.

90. Schmidt, *Kephalaia*, 38, lines 8–13.

91. Moses Maimonides, *The Guide for the Perplexed* III, 45 (New York: Dover, 1955), 355.

92. K. Kohler, "The Pre-Talmudic Haggada," *Jewish Quarterly Review* 7 (July 1985): 603–4; cf. Nibley, "Sacrifice of Isaac," 58.

93. *De Primordiis et Inventione Sacrae Religionis Jerosolymorum (On the Origin and Discovery of the Holy Religion of Jerusalem)*, in *Monumenta de Bello Sacro (Memorials of the Holy War)*, Appendix II to Godfrey of Bouillon, in *PL* 155:1097.

94. Ibid., in *PL* 155:1098.

95. Ibid., in *PL* 155:1101.

96. Hugh W. Nibley, "Setting the Stage—The World of Abraham," *IE* 73 (January 1970): 58.

97. J. Massyngberde Ford, "Thou Art 'Abraham' and upon This Rock . . . ," *Heythrop Journal* 6 (1965): 289–301.

98. TB *Hagigah* 16a, in Goldschmidt, *Babylonian Talmud*, 3:839.

99. *Vayera* 115a, in Harry Sperling and Maurice Simon, trs., *The Zohar*, 5 vols. (New York: Soncino, 1984), 1:361.

100. *Testament of Levi* 10:3, in M. de Jonge, ed., *Testamenta XII Patriarchum* (Leiden: Brill, 1970), 16.

101. Cf. *Gospel of Philip* 84:21–30, in *NHLE*, 150.

102. *Gospel of Philip* 85:10–18, in ibid., 150.

103. Hegesippus in Eusebius, *Ecclesiastical History* IV, 8, 103, in *PG* 5:1319–20; 20:321–24.

104. 2 Jeu 45, in Schmidt, *Books of Jeu and the Untitled Text*, 108.

105. 2 Jeu 44, ibid., 104.

106. 2 Jeu 44; 1 Jeu 33–38, in ibid., 105, 83–87.

107. 1 Jeu 41, in ibid., 97–98; cf. 2 Nephi 9:41.

108. Marc Philonenko, *Les interpolations chrétiennes des Testaments des Douze Patriarches et les manuscrits de Qoumrân* (Paris: Presses universitaires de France, 1960), 18.

109. Theophylactus, *Expositio in Epistolam ad Hebraeos (Exposition on the Epistle to the Hebrews)*, in *PG* 125:297–98.

110. Tertullian, *De Praescriptionibus adversus Haereticos (The Prescription against Heretics)* I, 9, in *PL* 2:66–67.

111. Cf. René Descartes, "Discours de la méthode," in Charles Adam and Paul Tannery, eds., *Oeuvres de Descartes*, 10 vols. (Paris: Vrin, 1973), 6:4–5, 31–40; René Descartes, "Meditationes de Prima Philosophia," in ibid., 7:36–37; René Descartes, "Principia Philosophiae," in ibid., 8:14–15.

112. Hugh W. Nibley, "Looking Backward," in Madsen, ed., *The Temple in Antiquity*, 51; reprinted in *CWHN* 4:383.

113. Giorgio de Santillana and Hertha von Dechend, *Hamlet's Mill* (Boston: Gambit, 1969).

Sacred Vestments

The conventional vestments of Christian clergy won't concern us here, because all authorities agree that they were adopted late by the church (fourth century at best) and that they are of pagan origin.

The basic equipment of the early Christian (fig. 14), for example, is a dark brown or purplish-brown *cassock*. It appears to have been a dark brown dress for the ordinary Roman day worker, the ordinary clothes of a Roman citizen, not the clothes of the nobility. In fact, the early Christians used to be made fun of because their leaders did not wear special clothes in public. The special vestments were inherited at a later time.

The *stolē* goes with the later priestly *surplice*. It was strictly a gift given by the emperor, first by Constantine to Pope Sylvester as a personal gift, following the old Persian custom. The king gave a congratulatory robe, the *stolē*, and he gave it to other bishops too, who started passing it around after the fourth century. But it is admitted by everyone to be of purely pagan origin. So is the *cappachon* (*cope*), the ancient *amice* or *amictus* (an archaic *pallium*), which went with it, as well as the cap (the *camelaucum*). When Constantine offered Sylvester the imperial crown to wear, Sylvester refused. Constantine did give him a white cap formed like a Phrygian cap, which he put on Sylvester's head with his own hands, and which the bishop and his

---

This previously unpublished lecture, originally accompanied by slides, was given in 1975.

Figure 14. From a third-century papyrus, we see a man with uplifted
arms, an image so common in early Christian art that historians have
given them the name *orantes,* "the praying ones," and speculate that
they stood in this position in imitation of their crucified Lord, though
Jewish artists used the gesture as well (cf. fig. 26A, p. 110). This particular figure is identified by one scholar as Christ and by another as
just a Christian; such confusion is possible because both would be shown
wearing everyday clothes.

successors wore in procession as a mark of royal favor (fig. 15). A similar accoutrement is a *pileus,* which later on became the bishop's mitre. But none of this really applies to our discussion here (fig. 16).[1]

The liturgical colors are first given significance in the ninth century. The Roman clerics say, the devout Catholics say, and the great authorities on this concede that they have absolutely no antique or sacred Christian background. In themselves, the colors are not ancient, and they are not at all sacred in the church. The first explanation of them was given by William Durandus (following Pope Innocent III), who died in the beginning of the thirteenth century. In attempting to discover a reason for the colors, Jungmann says, in his most recent book on the Roman rite, that "white [is] . . . festive, . . . red [is] for martyrs' days, . . . black for days [of] penance, and . . . green for days without a festal character"[2]—all of which is logical enough, but the point is that the ignorant must work out the answers for themselves. The key to the practice has been lost.

So the conventional Christian robes needn't concern us. But the Jewish and Christian apocalyptic, which scholars such as Klaus Koch and Pierre Grelot only began to take seriously around 1960, and which was substantially ignored before 1948,[3] tells a different story. These writings have a great deal to say about certain holy garments and their nature and significance. What they say is in closest agreement with the oldest writings of the Egyptians and Babylonians, for that matter, taking us into a world which has been completely forgotten until our own day and introducing us to concepts in modern times first made known to the world by Joseph Smith.

In the appendix to my book on the Egyptian endowment, I cite the *Pistis Sophia,*[4] a very early Christian writing, written in the third century but sounding as if it belongs to the forty-day literature.[5] When the Lord spoke to the

a. The *nimbus* or halo indicates the Emperor's more-than-human status, although he was still alive at the time.

b. The *chlamys,* at first a simple cloak, became the imperial purple robe fastened with an ornate pearl clasp.

c. The *tablion* was an elaborate brocade square sewn into the robe to further enrich it.

d. The episcopal *pallium* is draped around the neck and hangs from the left shoulder.

e. The *phelonion,* like its counterpart the *chlamys,* became the later *chasuble.*

f. A full-length white *dalmatic* with *clavi,* two purple vertical stripes, originally indicated high rank on the Roman tunic.

Figure 15. In the famous mosaics in Ravenna, c. 545, the haloed Emperor Justinian is depicted in the usual gaudy Byzantine "imperial purple." He is holding a golden *paten* or communion plate, while his Archbishop Maximianus holds a jeweled cross. The similarity of their pose and specialized garments demonstrates the close interdependence and importance of possessing at least the appearance of authority.

a. The *pileus,* a white linen cap, later became the mitre.
b. "The *amice,* a square or oblong piece of linen worn over the shoulders, was originally a hood."
c. The *pallium* is here a circular yoke with pendant bands of white wool, symbolizing episcopal authority.
d. "The *chasuble,* the outermost garment worn by the priest, is usually richly ornamented."
e. "The *maniple,* a long silk band looped over the arm of the priest, symbolizes work and service."
f. "The narrow scarf-like *stole* is placed around the neck and then crossed over the chest."
g. "The *alb* is a long white gown symbolic of the soul's purity."

Figure 16. This German manuscript of c. 1120 shows another example of the constant tension between church and state. A seemingly demure Henry V bows his head as he receives the orb of kingship from Pope Paschal II, who was actually his prisoner in Rome at the time. The explanatory quotations are from a modern Catholic source.

disciples after the resurrection, he formed a prayer circle: his disciples, men and women, stood around behind Jesus, who himself stood at the altar, thus facing, as it were, the four corners of the world, with his disciples who were all clothed in garments of linen (quoting the disciples). Jesus proceeded to give the prayer.[6] The *Pistis Sophia* claims to be derived from 2 *Jeu*, a book allegedly written by Enoch and then hidden up in the cleft of a rock.[7] *Second Jeu* says: "All the apostles were clothed in linen garments, . . . their feet were placed together and they turned themselves to the four corners of the world."[8] And Jesus, taking the place of Adam, proceeded to instruct them in all the necessary ordinances. The point is that when they formed a prayer circle, they always mentioned "clothed in their garments" or "clothed in white linen." Next comes the passage I cited from Cyril of Jerusalem;[9] it is the fullest description we have, the only definite mention of particular garments. We see why it was not well known and was not followed through: "Yesterday, . . . immediately upon entering you removed your street clothes. And that was the image of putting off the old man and his works. . . . And may that garment, once put off, never be put on again!"[10] "As Christ after his baptism . . . went forth to confront the Adversary, so you after your holy baptism and mystic anointing [the washing and anointing] were clothed in the armor of the Holy Ghost [a protective garment], to stand against the opposing . . . power."[11] "Having put off the old man's garment of sorrow, you now celebrate as you put on the garment of the Lord Jesus Christ."[12] "Having been baptized in Christ and having put on Christ (cf. Galatians 3:27)[13] [notice the imagery that follows: you put on Christ, you put on the new man, you put on the new body; this is very closely connected with the putting on of clothes], like a garment, you come to resemble (*symmorphoi gegonate*) the Son of God."[14]

The next day Cyril continues, "After you have put off

the old garments and put on those of spiritual white, you should keep them always thus spotless white. This is not to say you must always go around in white clothes [these clothes were real; futhermore, we know of the baptismal garments, for we have references to them], but rather that you should always [be] clothed in what is really white and glorious." Then he cites Isaiah 61:10: "Let my soul exult in the Lord, for he hath clothed me in a robe of salvation and clothing of rejoicing."[15]

This is the fullest of early Christian references to the vestments. But these are not vestments in the modern sense at all. They are worn by all Christians—but not all the time, not as a sign of clerical vocation within the church, and not as a public sign.

The combination of the items that make up the full clothing comes from the description of the high priestly garments at the beginning of Exodus 28. Very recently in Jerusalem, a magnificent book was published based on an attempt to reconstruct the kēlîm, the supellectila, the implements and equipment of the temple, and the priestly garments (fig. 17). A section at the end of the book describes them in detail.[16] In this particular passage there is general assemblage, a listing, and then a description of what the articles are.

"Thou shalt make holy garments for Aaron thy brother," the Lord tells Moses (cf. Exodus 28:2), ləkābōd ultip'eret, "both for glory and for magnificence"—to give an impression, to fill one with awe. And the Lord instructed Moses to say to all the people of "thoughtful-mindedness" and intelligence "that they shall do so, and make such garments for Aaron, for holiness, and for his priesthood, to represent his priesthood to me" (cf. Exodus 28:3). "And these are the garments which they shall make; a breastplate, and an 'epod [the much disputed ephod!], and the məᶜîl," a "cloak, a covering, a long garment"; "a kətōnet," the "shirt"; "a tashbēts," a thing elaborately woven

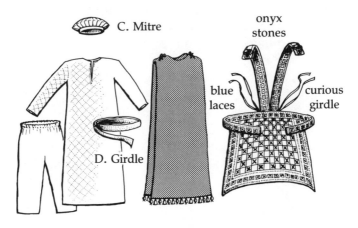

A. Breeches   B. Coat   E. Robe of Blue   F. Ephod

Figure 17. While all priests wore the basic garments (A, B, C) of white linen, the "broidered coat" (B) being of a curiously woven plaid or checker pattern (cf. fig. 20 p. 104), the high priest wore all the vestments (A–H). The names of the twelve tribes are inscribed on the two onyx

in a checkerboard pattern, or something similar; "a mitre," *miznepet,* "a turban," "a round cap"; "and a girdle" or "sash"; "and these garments they shall make holy for Aaron, thy brother, and for his sons, to serve me in the priesthood" (Exodus 28:4).

Here is the *shesh,* "white linen," a necessity to both the *kətōnet,* or "shirt, coat," which is of white linen, and the pants that go along with it (Exodus 39:28). What is the ephod? According to our source, it is worn on the two shoulders and tied around the waist with knots—everything tied, never any buttons. This shows the latest speculative reconstruction of the ephod. The ephod is best rendered "apron," and it wraps around the *məʿîl,* or blue robe. The word *sabib* (Exodus 28:31–34) suggests it must be somehow embroidered. The high priest is shown in the full outfit; not so full either. And here is a view from the back. And then the breastplate is tied on, and that is dif-

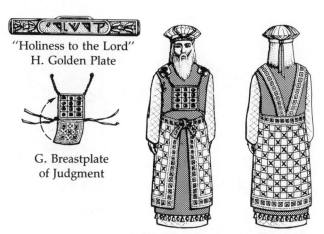

"Holiness to the Lord"
H. Golden Plate

G. Breastplate
of Judgment

I. "Golden Garments" of the High Priest

stones of the shoulder bands of the ephod (F) as well as on the twelve
stones of the breastplate (G); thus the high priest "bears" all Israel when
he stands before the Lord (I). The Urim and Thummim are kept in the
pouch formed by folding up the embroidered panel behind the breastplate stones.

ferent from the ephod. As Rashi describes it, "the fabric
[of the ephod] was the same as the fabric of the veil and
the screen of the Tabernacle. . . . The ephod . . . was like
a sash to the robe; it was girt around the robe as the girdle
was girt around the tunic."[17]

The book gives a description of the cap: "And you shall
make a *miznepet shesh*" — of white linen (Exodus 28:39).
Miznepet means a "turban," or something wrapped around
with white linen, worn by every priest. "This gold band
shall be of pure gold" (Exodus 28:36); this is worn only by
the high priest, and he wears it on top of the regular priest's
mitre. The book has a note which tells us that there are
three levels at which the garment is worn: one, the high
priest, one, on the Day of Atonement, and one, the ordinary.[18]

These are speculative reconstructions, the best scholars
can do. We do have fuller descriptions in combinations.

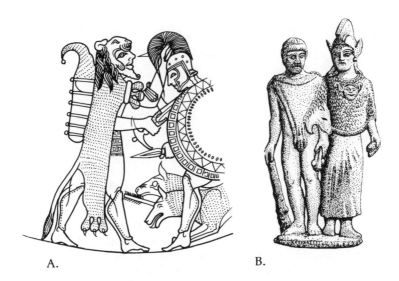

A.   B.

Figure 18. In this earliest surviving representation of Heracles, c. 620
B.C. (A), he dispatches the giant Geryon, an inhospitable ruler of what
is now Cadiz. Our wandering hero wears the trophy of his first labor,
the impervious skin of the Nemean lion, just as Menerva (Athena) wears
the protective goat-skin *aegis* adorned with the Gorgon's head in an
Etruscan bronze of the fourth century (B). In each case, the leather
garment is both sign and protection.

The fullest, and one of the most instructive, is from the
Testament of Levi from the *Testaments of the Twelve Patriarchs*.
In it, Levi goes to *Beit-el* (the house of God, the place of
the temple),[19] after he has received his trials and test; he
goes to receive the ordinances. This is the temple, the same
place where Joseph Smith saw the ladder representing the
three degrees of glory.[20] Rendered very literally, the story
is as follows: Levi goes to *Beit-el*, where he says, "And I
saw seven men, clothed in white, who said to me, 'arise
and put on the garment (*endusai*),' "[21] a holy, protective
leather garment. Originally it had to be leather; it is as-

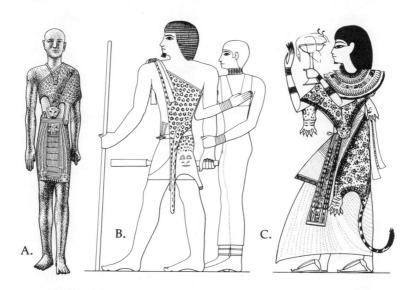

Figure 19. As an example of how these things get around, this Egyptian votive bronze (A), c. 600 B.C., was found in the Greek city of Ephesus located in Turkey. The priest displays the ancient sign of authority, an entire leopard skin worn over the shoulder with his Pharaoh's name and authorization inscribed down the center. Two thousand years earlier, in a bas-relief (B) from the tomb of the son of the builder of the great pyramid, Khufu-khaf and his wife Nefert-kau move gracefully into eternity. He wears the same sacred badge of office; even the knot over his shoulder is recognizable as the loop amulet *st̠* ⤶ . His elegantly coifed wife holds his arm in a gesture suggesting the "delicate intimation that married love endures after death, that it actually conquers death." Evidently the leopard can change his spots, as when later priests identified them with the stars in the heavens and marked them accordingly on special robes such as those worn by astronomer priests of Heliopolis. This example (C), from the tomb of Userhet, c. 1300 B.C., goes one step further and uses the sign for the Duat ⊗ , the place of the next life, thus making the ancient symbol of the leopard skin a true heavenly garment.

sociated with the lion skin Heracles always wore[22] (fig. 18)
and also the leopard skin that an Egyptian priest must
wear over one shoulder (fig. 19).[23] It protected Heracles
when he went through the world on his twelve labors as
the benefactor of the human race; there was a lot of risk,
and he needed protection, which the *stolē* gave him. This
later became the imperial *stolē* which the emperor gave to
Pope Sylvester; earlier it was the holy protective leather
garment of the priesthood.[24]

There were additional items. First, there was the *stephanos* that surrounds or encircles the head—a crown,
wreath, or chaplet (following the form used here). The
main emphasis of the word implies that it crowned the
head and was round, surrounding or encircling it.[25] Then
there was the *logion tēs syneseōs*, that is, the oracle-breast-
plate—the Urim and Thummim of understanding. There
was the *podērēs*, a long, overall robe that hung down to
the feet and went over one shoulder. It was the basic robe
of truth. There was the *petalon*, some kind of garment made
of wild olive leaves, signifying faithfulness. Next came the
zonē, or "girdle," also called *mitra*, as worn by a wrestler—
a band of *sindōn*, of *echema*, "firmness," a symbol of
strengthening. Last of all, Levi received the *'epod* of prophecy.[26]

Each of the seven angels, the seven men in white, as
he placed an item of clothing upon Levi, said:

> From this time, thou art a high priest of the Lord,
> thou and thy seed after thee, for all eternity. The first
> anointed me with holy oil and gave me the staff of judg-
> ment. The second washed me with pure water and gave
> me bread and wine in the Holy of Holies, and placed
> upon me the holy and glorious garment [the leather *stolē*,
> the protective garment]. The third placed about me a
> linen robe like an ephod.[27]

This mention of a linen robe shows that the ephod is
not the little, brightly colored, plaid thing beneath the

breastplate (though the plaid apron, the first *tunica*, is universal).[28] The Scotch plaid is the same item as the Arabic *qumaṣ* (*qamiṣ*) — a sacred tribal garment, a garment of identification. The tribe of Levi used it, but like the Scottish clans, the traditional plaid is the crest on the arrow, woven two ways. Your plaid identifies you: your tribe, your arrow after you have shot it. Thus, you can get your arrow back again so you can claim that you have shot your victim. Otherwise there would be a lot of arguing.[29]

This very same archaic plaid was worn by the early Greeks and is found all around the Mediterranean; the plaid and bagpipes go together among the Scots, the Irish, the Minoans, and the Egyptians who all had them (fig. 20). It is a very ancient dress. The *kaunakēs* of the earliest Sumerian priests was first made of the leaves of the *ficus religiosus*, the fig tree (fig. 21).[30]

When Levi received the glorious garment,

> the third angel put on the linen robe like an ephod, and the fourth put a girdle or sash about me like [resembling] purple [*homoian porphurā*]. And the fifth gave me the olive branch of prosperity, a flourishing state of the body (*piotētos*), and the sixth placed a *stephanos* around my head. The seventh tied on the *stephanos* (the priestly diadem), and he filled my hands with incense material (*thumiamatos*) [fig. 22] to show that I was to serve as a priest of the Lord. And he said to me, Levi, thy seed is chosen to have authority in three things, in similitude of a *semeion* [sign, miracle] of the glory of the Lord to come: (1) [he who first believeth, Adam, who was the first to hold the priesthood, in degree, love, and ministry,] and there shall be no greater than he, (2) the priesthood of Aaron or Levi, and (3) the priesthood to come, bringing a new name. For a king shall arise out of Judah and establish a new priesthood after the manner of the Gentiles which shall be unto all nations. His *parousia*, his

Figure 20. From the First Dynasty, c. 2900 B.C., a small ivory pharaoh (A), wearing the white crown, wears a cloak in a diamond-shaped plaid; the design reappears in the mummy wrappings of the Late Period (cf. fig. 26B, p. 110). This widespread pattern shows up in a seated figure from Italy, c. 600 B.C. (B), and in a bronze statuette of a Gaul from France, c. 200 B.C. (C).

glorious coming, cannot be told; it is secret, as an exalted prophet of the seed of our Father Abraham.[31]

When Jacob awoke, he said, "I hid these things in my heart and told them to no man."[32] They were very secret, things not communicated to us in the Old Testament. This is a fuller description of the garments than we find in Exodus 28. The significance and the symbolism of some of these things is explained in the *Testament of Levi*, but it was top secret.

Jerome, who lived fifteen years in Palestine, and who was more acquainted with the early church than any other man of his time, said that the priestly garments are full of

Figure 21. This Sumerian priest (A), c. 3000 B.C., wears a checkered apron, either a woven plaid or a stylized sheepskin. On this Neo-Sumerian limestone stele (B), c. 2200 B.C., the crowned gods wear the sacred fleece garment, the *kaunakēs*, over their shoulders; Ningizzida holds Gudea by the wrist and leads him into the presence of the gods.

cosmic symbolism. But we don't know what they were. They have some celestial and divine meaning.[33]

The Wisdom of Solomon takes up this same theme: "For upon Aaron's long high-priestly robe was the whole world pictured, and the glories of the Father were engraved upon the four rows of precious stones."[34] The *Zohar* explains that the same marks were on the mantle of the temple. We have a recent discovery regarding these marks: in 1966, in the Bar Kokhba Cave, on the Dead Sea, was found a cave of scrolls, and also many old garments, remarkably well preserved. Some of them bore the *gamma* patterns. Here is one of them with the *gamma* pattern (fig. 23).[35] This is evidence that these patterns stay around and

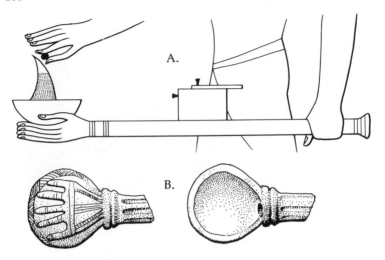

Figure 22. Incense was often burned in special holders made in the form of a cupped hand, the "golden spoons" of Exodus 25:29. From the Egyptian version (A) at Beni Hasan, c. 1100 B.C., to an actual steatite example (B) found at Meggido, the "filled hand" (the Hebrew letter kāp̄ כ means "palm") is the widespread sign of offering sacrifice.

are interpreted in various ways. These date from the time of Bar Kokhba, the early part of the second century. The discoverer of these garments, Professor Yadin, writes about them: "An amusing development in early Christian art can now be better explained: in many of the famous mosaics in Rome, Ravenna, and Naples, especially from the fifth century A.D. and later [but earlier also], one can see that all the mantles of the biblical figures are depicted with a single pattern similar to the Greek letter *gamma*"[36] — a little more like a right angle — a square. The most famous examples come from the fifth century, from Ravenna. The pattern is on the edges of the robe, but it is quite common (fig. 24). There are many examples of it in the earliest Christian representations, but not later, because by then they had been transferred to the altar cloth (fig. 25). Originally they belonged to the veil of the temple.[37]

Yadin continues, "It is known that Christian artists

Figure 23. The largest surviving example, 1.4×2.7 m, of a fine woolen *tallit* or mantle with purple *gammadia* woven in the corners, c. A.D. 130, was found in the Cave of the Letters. Roman-style tunics with *clavi* (cf. fig. 26A, p. 110) worn by these Jewish survivors were also found.

used earlier Jewish illustrations and particularly illuminated Bibles in order to emulate their motifs. By that time the differences between the two types of mantles had been forgotten, and the *gammas* appeared in full; . . . they may have assumed that all patterns were *gammas*."[38] But all we find are these marks. An especially holy person will have this mark on him. "The pattern ultimately became the most popular in the altar-cloth of the Christian church, and even the altar-cloth itself came to be known as the *gammadia*."[39] There are two types of early Jewish garments. Yadin finds them amusing because, he explains, the Christians didn't understand them. But what was the original Jewish usage? Do we have earlier examples than those of the first centuries? Yes, the garment was an "amusing" Jewish development from much earlier forms. The Egyptian garments were similar, and we have interesting examples (fig. 26).

There are certain marks on the garment, certain marks of recognition for the initiated, and the marks themselves always have cosmic symbolism. The *Pistis Sophia* makes a

Figure 24. A youthful Christ dressed in the royal purple blesses the loaves and fishes, reverently held by his disciples, who wear white *dalmatic* with *clavi* and mantle. Unlike the preceding example, these *gammadia* are oriented differently in the corners of their mantles.

great many references to these. For example: "I found an ordinance inscribed upon my garment (*enduma*)," says the hero, "written in five words. . . . It is the garment which belonged to you in the pre-existence, from the beginning, and when your time is come on the earth, you will put it on and return home to us." He adds, "In this garment, it has the five marks," which he calls *charagmē*, meaning "cuts" or "marks."[40] The second garment has the marks and all the glory of the name; the third garment has all the mysteries of the ordinances. This is the doctrine of the three garments of Jesus, and of the five *charagmē*. In the Manichaean *Kephalaia* (written in Coptic), there are five mysteries; the strings—which later become the *tzitzit*—were considered the fifth sign or mark, because they were

Figure 25. Another Ravenna mosaic, c. A.D. 520, shows the priest-king Melchizedek in a purple cloak, offering bread and wine at the altar (Genesis 14:18–20). The white altar cloth is decorated with two sets of *gammadia*, as well as the so-called "seal of Melchizedek," two interlocked squares in gold. Abel offers his lamb as Abraham gently pushes Isaac forward. The hand of God reaches down to this sacred meeting through the red veils adorned with golden *gammadia* on either side. The theme is the great sacrifice of Christ, which brings together the righteous prophets from the past as well as the four corners of the present world, thereby uniting all time and space.

special. These five mysteries, the five tokens, first originated among the Godhead. The mysteries were brought to this world, being preached by an apostle. Men learned them and established them in their midst. These five tokens are the marks of the church. The first is the greeting of peace, by which one becomes a son of peace. The second is the grasp of the right hand, by which he is brought into the church. The third is the embrace, by which he becomes "a son" (editors assume that means "of the church").

A.

B.

Figure 26. Here are more examples of *gammadia*. From the Dura Europos synagogue, c. A.D. 245, we see a large checkered version on the robes of Moses as he creates the well of living water at the door of the Tabernacle (A). A symbol of the Divine Law, it flows to each of the tents of the Twelve Tribes, where praying figures receive it with joy (cf. fig. 14, p. 92, also Mosiah 2:5–6). This burial shroud is a meeting of East and West — "modern" Hellenistic art and ancient Egyptian mysteries. A priest wearing the Anubis mask guides the initiate forward into the presence of the god Osiris. The priest wears the archaic robe ornamented with checkerboard patterns, as well as symbols of Isis and Osiris. The Roman toga of the initiate bears a carefully painted *gammadion,* outlined in white and projecting past the edge of his mantle so we can see it clearly (B).

The *Odes of Solomon,* discovered in 1906, say, "Thy seal is known, and all thy creatures know it, and thy hosts possess it, and the elect angels are clad with it." Being clad with certain signs are the five archons.[41] Discovered around 1913, the Coptic *Bartholomew* says that Adam and Eve had written upon their garments certain characters or marks, as signs of the Holy Ghost, written in seven places.[42] The Pastor of Hermas[43] mentions it, as does the *Pistis Sophia.*[44]

In the 1800s in Egypt, Petrie excavated numerous mummies with amulets arranged in the wrappings. Figure 27A shows, as Petrie describes it, the compass-like level and the square on the breast. He was able to generalize that the square probably means "rectitude," uprightness, and that the other tool (which is hung in that position, they assume, because it has a mark on the top of it) means "making equilibrium, . . . evenly balanced mind," or measure in all things.[45] Schäfer discovered some among other amulets, and here are pictures of what they were like (fig. 27B, C).[46] Thus the Egyptians also used *gammadia* marks, sometimes located on either breast. Some garments bearing *gammadia* have been found in graves in Palestine. Are all instances of *gammadia* of Egyptian origin? Not necessarily. These things do get around. They become lost; they become simply designs; nobody understands what they are; nobody understands any more the meaning of the words. Thus we speculate as we try to reconstruct them.

Most challenging are the veils from Taoist-Buddhist tombs at Astana, in Central Asia, originally Nestorian (Christian) country, discovered by Sir Aurel Stein in 1925 (fig. 28). We see the king and queen embracing at their wedding, the king holding the square on high, the queen a compass. As it is explained, the instruments are taking the measurements of the universe, at the founding of a new world and a new age.[48] Above the couple's head is the sun surrounded by twelve disks, meaning the circle of the year or the navel of the universe. Among the stars depicted, Stein and his assistant identified the Big Dipper

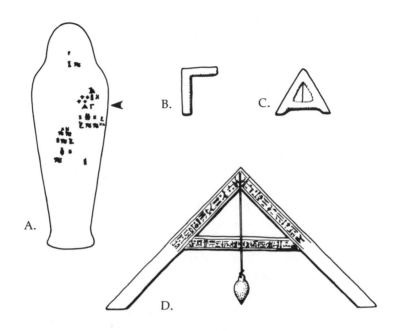

Figure 27. When the Egyptian embalming priests of the 30th Dynasty wrapped the corpse in the many yards of linen cloth, they included various amulets (A) to protect and strengthen the deceased. Located over the heart were two miniature tools, the square (B) and the compass-alone as clearly discernable.[47] As noted above, the garment draped over the coffin and the veil hung on the wall had the same marks; they were placed on the garment as reminders of personal commitment, while on the veil they represent man's place in the cosmos.[48]

When the temple was destroyed, the priesthood was lost and the robes of the priesthood or their ministrations disappeared. Churches do not bother about these anymore. When the ordinances were lost, the garment became purely allegorical. In the famous literature of Mozarabic Spain, and even earlier, there is the Latin poem called "The Lorica,"[49] *lorica* being the garment described as a protective apron. Its meaning was purely allegorical, its whole func-

E.

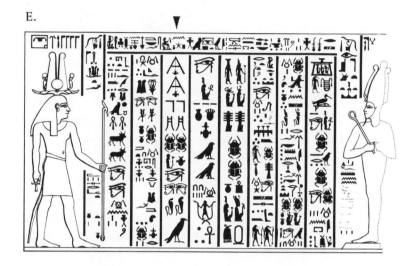

like horizontal level (C). An actual working example of a wooden A-frame with a plumb bob suspended from its apex (D) was found in the tomb of Sennedjem, c. 1200 B.C. About the time of Christ, these same symbolic tools were included in the list of amulets carved in the Osiris chapel on the temple roof at Dendera (E).

tion theatrical. It became a showpiece — clumsy, costly, ornate, and impractical. Constantine at Nicea is a good example. His garments were completely encrusted with jewels. Eusebius says when sunlight hit him (it was carefully prearranged that sunlight would hit him when he stepped out before the assembly), one would have thought he was an angel of heaven. He moved like an Egyptian pharaoh (fig. 29).[50]

At the other extreme, one might say that the garment is unique, the real thing, magical. If you had the garment, it was all you needed. But the magic is not the garment; the garment is not magic. Later, it was said that all you needed in order to have Moses' divine power was the staff

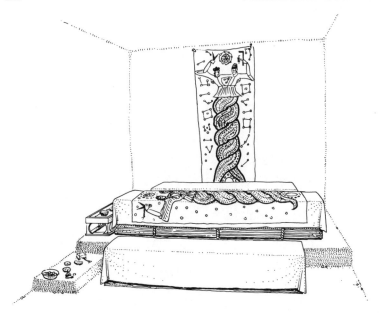

of Aaron. Or if you could find the Seal of Solomon, then you would have the power. We know that these things work only according to faith. Israel, like the Nephites and Lamanites, sinned at both extremes, the esoteric and exoteric. The Israelites were either overdressed in fine clothes and all manner of costly apparel or went about as the Nephites and Lamanites did in their times of degeneracy, without anything on at all. Both extremes are equally offensive: in either case, it is a vulgar display of one's person. If you overdress or underdress, you are just showing yourself off, and that distracts from the real purpose of dress.

The putting on of the body is compared not only with the putting on of the garment; it is accompanied by an act. A newborn babe receives his swaddling clothes in a ritual — the baptismal garment of the new Christian, which was regarded as an extension of the body, an aura. It is an

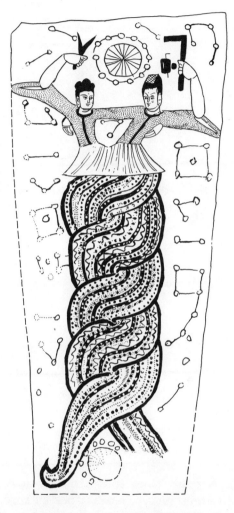

Figure 28. In the underground tomb of Fan Yen-Shih, d. A.D. 689, two painted silk veils show the First Ancestors of the Chinese, their entwined serpent bodies rotating around the invisible vertical *axis mundi*. Fu Hsi holds the set-square and plumb bob (cf. fig. 27D) as he rules the four-cornered earth, while his sister-wife Nü-wa holds the compass pointing up, as she rules the circling heavens. The phrase 規矩 *kuei chü* is used by modern Chinese to signify "the way things should be, the moral standard"; it literally means the compass and the square.

Figure 29. The curtains have parted to reveal the Consul Gallus, c. A.D. 350, in all his Byzantine gaudiness—halo around his head, *victoriola* in one hand, scepter of Mars in the other, and a bag of gold at his feet. His stiff robe is heavily embroidered with images of the gods.

expression of personality and a necessary protection. Garments belong to that type of symbols that are more than symbols, like water and food. Just as water cleanses symbolically, it cleanses, revives, and purifies literally; water can also be a death—overwhelming; you must pass through it. It really does those things—it really does refresh, really does revive, really does cleanse, really does soothe, and really can drown. Likewise a garment is a sign of protection, of dignity, of modesty; it is not just a sign of those things—it actually does impart them.

A very early Syrian hymn on baptism, for example, says that though you strip off the garment outside you, you do not put off the garment within you when you have been baptized. For if you continue to be clad in it, the storms and trials of life will not prevail against you. Beware of the enemy, lest he strip you as he did Adam, and make you an alien to the kingdom. Like many similar passages it propounds the idea of a protection necessary in this world. Here is a famous passage from the *Odes of Solomon:* "I stripped it off and cast it [the earthly garment] from me, and the Lord renewed me with His garment, and he possessed me by His light; and from above, he gave me immortal rest."[51] Another from the *Odes of Solomon:* "I put off darkness and clothed myself in light, and even I myself acquired a body, free from sorrow or pain,"[52] for the passing from one state of existence, one body to another, is always compared to and accompanied by the putting on and putting off of garments. In the newly discovered *Papyrus Bodmer* is an interesting comment: the garment is as necessary and therefore as real a part of the body as food is. Food is a symbol; it is not really a part of the body, yet when you eat it, it does become so. It gives you strength; the garment is like food—it is extraneous; it is out there, you can acquire it and put it away, if you want. But at the same time, it is a real part of you, very intimate. The belief used to be that the contact with it had definite significance. We could have discussed specific aspects of the garments, but it has been safer to generalize.

The Mandaeans had a lot to say about the heavenly garment. When you left the world above, and each time you passed from one state of initiation to another, you changed garments (cf. fig. 50, p. 300). We likewise make some change or alteration in the garment, at each state of initiation. In a wonderful passage in the Mandaean hymn of *The Pearl,*[53] the hero returns to heaven. In this old doctrine—which you meet quite often—he, like all of us, left his garment—his spotless garment—there. He yearned to return to it, to be able to wear it again. It is now being kept for us in reserve up there, and one of the great tragedies of messing things up in this life is that we will not be able to go back and wear it. Of course it stands for other things, too. In *The Pearl*, the prince hurries homeward, back to his garment laid up in heaven, the garment and the toga are wrapped and sent down by his parents. He puts them on halfway—he is so eager—and suddenly he says, as if in a mirror, "The garment was my very first. It fitted me; it would fit no one else." All of a sudden it glitters, recalling to his mind all his former glory, because there are signs on it. He returns to his garment.[54]

The garment motif is almost an obsession in the literature of Christ's forty-day ministry after the resurrection. Christ, sitting with the apostles, says, "Do not touch me. I am not in the right garments yet." He had left his garment in the tomb. The disciples had found an angel sitting at the foot of the couch on which Christ had been lying, on which the garment lay neatly folded. He was gone, and he had put on another garment, the one he was wearing when Mary met him. (According to a very old account, he told her not to touch him: "I'm going to my father and receive the garment that is waiting for me." He talked to the apostles a lot saying, "When I have finished my work here, and have had my last meeting with you, then I will put on that other garment. I cannot until I am finished with my earthly mission here." Then he will go back and put on his garment, returning to his robes of glory, as each of us will.)

The theme is clearly reflected, incidentally, in the book of Moses in the expression "clothed upon with glory" (Moses 7:3). Why the insistence on that particular word? Enoch says, "I was clothed upon with glory. Therefore I could stand in the presence of God" (cf. Moses 1:2, 31).[55] Otherwise he could not. It is the garment that gives confidence in the presence of God; one does not feel too exposed (2 Nephi 9:14). That garment is the garment that awaits us above, the official garment of heaven, the garment of divinity. So as Enoch says, "I was clothed upon

with glory, and I saw the Lord" (Moses 7:3–4), just as
Moses saw Him "face to face, . . . and the glory of God
was upon Moses; therefore Moses could endure his presence" (Moses 1:2). In 2 *Enoch,* discovered in 1892, we read,
"The Lord spoke to me with his own mouth: . . . 'Take
Enoch and remove his earthly garments and anoint him
with holy oil and clothe him in his garment of
glory.' . . . And I looked at myself, and I looked like one
of the glorious ones."[56] Being no different from him in
appearance, he is qualified now, in the manner of initiation. He can go back and join them because he has received
a particular garment of glory.

In the *Apocalypse of Moses,* another recent discovery,
Adam, after being washed three times in the Acherusian
Lake, is conducted back to the third heaven. Then he is
clothed in linen garments and anointed with oil, and prepared to go into the presence of the Father.[57] In the *Apocalypse of Elijah* too, we read, "Then will Gabriel and Uriel
portray the fiery columns. They will come down as in a
column from heaven, and they will lead them into the holy
land. And they will settle them there so that they may eat
of the tree of life and wear a white garment, . . . and there
they will not thirst."[58] The motif is common.

The *Acts of Thomas,* still another recent discovery, contains the famous psalm of Judas Thomas: "They shall be
in the glory, and they shall be in the joy into which some
enter. And they shall put on shining garments and shall
be clothed with the glory of the Lord, and they shall praise
the living Father of whose food they have received which
never has any impurity in it, and they will drink of eternal
life."[59] The food and your garment go together.

A puzzling passage in the Coptic *Gospel of Philip,* found
in the 1950s, says that in this world our garments are
inferior—inferior to the person.[60] Let us hope they are.
That is why we should not try to boost ourselves too much
by putting on fine apparel. In the next world, there won't

be the distinction of dress and person. The garment will be so much a part of us, we won't think of it. People wonder why, when the Angel Moroni came, Joseph Smith said, "I could see into his bosom"; Joseph saw that Moroni was wearing only a very white cloak over him (JS–H 1:31). That is all that was necessary. First, he was not coming to minister in the ordinances. Second, Joseph Smith had not yet been introduced to the garments; he had not received his endowments. There was no reason why Moroni should not come to Joseph informally, in a very easy and relaxed outfit.

Much is now being written about garments. Hugo Gressmann, who dealt with Hebrew literature, says the garment of linen is the cultic representation of the body of life. The reason why the early Egyptians adopted linen was that linen was derived from plants and did not attract bugs and maggots, whereas wool, being of animal origin, did. Leather and wool decay and smell, they attract bugs. Linen remains relatively white and clean. Although it turns yellow, we have in beautiful condition thousands of pieces of magnificent linen from the first dynasty of Egypt, beautifully made, the equal, as Drioton says, to any linen that could be made in France today.

All the saints looked forward to the time when this garment would be removed and the heavenly garment resumed. Also, no unclean person can be clothed in the garments of glory. The investiture is always preceded by a washing, purification, and anointing—the bestowal of the special status; and the garment should be white linen. Part of the purification is the removal and discarding of all previous garments. The interesting rite of trampling on the old garment has recently been discovered.[61] When you renew a covenant or turn aside and leave your old life, you take off your old clothes, trample them, and put on new ones. This may be what the Nephites did around the title of liberty, when "they cast their garments at the feet of Moroni, saying: We covenant with our God, that . . . he may cast us at the feet of our enemies, even as we have cast our garments at thy feet to be trodden under foot, if we shall fall into transgression" (Alma 46:22). Leading the people, Moroni virtually says, "This was the garment of our father Joseph." It was a double garment, part of which had decayed and part not (a story not known in the West until recently, through Thaᶜlabi). The people trample on them, while taking an oath: "May we be trampled on as we trample on these garments, if we break our covenants — if we break our oath."[62] This practice is well attested to now. It happened in some other cases too.

In 2 *Jeu*, a very important Coptic writing (in fact, Carl Schmidt thinks it is one of the most important of all early Christian writings), the Lord, after the resurrection, orders the apostles to clothe themselves in white linen robes, then orders them to be washed again; he seals them, after which they receive fire in the spirit at their spiritual baptism.[63] An interesting note also occurs in the Elephantine writings. A Jewish community in Elephantine dates back to the sixth century B.C. These Jews, who perhaps left Jerusalem at the time Lehi did in the sixth century, got permission to build a temple there, far up on the first cataract of the Nile. A priest or an officer of the temple had left his garment in the temple annex. He left a note, asking his friend to please be good enough to pick it up for him and bring it home. Thus, he wore a special garment when he went into the temple.[64]

An Oxyrhynchus fragment from the third to fifth century has received a good deal of notice. It is a story about Jesus, regarded as authentic. One of the high priests, a Pharisee who meets him in the court of the temple, takes him to task, saying, "What is this talk about being pure? I am pure. I am pure, for I have washed in the pool of David and I have changed my old clothes and put on the white garments; and being thus purified, I proceeded and participated in the holy ordinances and handled the holy vessels." Jesus replies to him, "The dogs and the pigs have bathed upstream from the pool of David where you bathed. You anointed yourself, but the whore and the tax collectors do that. They bathe and anoint themselves and put on fair garments, but does that cause them to be pure?"[65] This is an important point. Jesus is not making fun of the purification and anointing, but is saying that the garment is inadequate without the thing that it signifies. It will not protect you unless you are true and faithful to your covenant, and only to the degree to which you do not dishonor your garment has it any significance at all.

On the other hand, you say, "Well, if you have these virtues, what do you need the garment for anyway?" It has been commanded, and this is an important principle, because it works both ways. The garment will teach you sobriety, and sobriety will sanctify the garment and make it meaningful.

A Coptic missal published in 1915 says in effect: "Let us put on splendid apparel, suitable to the honor that befits this great event this day [that is to say, righteousness and charity and judgment and every good quality, for this is the apparel that pleases God]. Let us never permit ourselves to be stripped bare through carelessness. Woe unto those whom the bridegroom shall see without the wedding garment when he comes."[66]

In the *Acts of Thomas:* "To the wedding feast I have been invited, and I have put on white garments. May I be worthy of them. May I remember to keep my light bright that I may keep its oil," etc.[67] Another very important writing is the so-called *Gospel of Truth*, discovered in Egypt, one of the Nag Hammadi papyri: "The word of the Father clothes everyone from top to bottom, purifies, and makes them fit to come back into the presence of their Father and their heavenly mother."[68] And there are many other examples.

Jerome explains:

> No one can receive the vestments who has not first been cleansed, washed of all uncleanliness, all impurity, nor had been first ordained and received a priesthood. And except he has been reborn as a new man in Christ [in other words, he received baptism], he may not put on the linen vestments, which have nothing of death in them but are entirely the garment of life. As we see when the initiates come out of the baptism: the first thing we do to those that come out of the water, we clothe them round about, we cover them properly with truth, having washed away all their previous sins.

The reason for white is explained (Plato expresses this also)[69] in numerous references, among them also Plutarch and Hesiod, who said the Egyptians used this rationale.[70] Thomas the Dyer seems to contradict himself: "Are you washed white in the blood of the lamb?" Since when can anyone be washed white in blood? The rationale expressed in these documents is that if you mix all colors together, you have a garment that is perfectly white, meaning that it can take any color. If you combine all colors, all experience, all knowledge, you will get (if there is any light at all) white. Of course if you turn off the light, all will be black. But it is the light, and the garment of white, in which all colors of the spectrum are contained.

As Jerome says, the linen garments of the Egyptian priests were worn both as undergarments (*intrinsecus*, "inside, inwardly") and as outer garments (*extrinsecus*, "from without, outside").[71] Many examples of that have been found.

Notably, one receives the garment always when passing from one stage of existence to another. It marks the condition one is in. To change the garment is to change one's condition, to perform a passage of initiation. Secrecy is important.

The fate of the garment of the priesthood — the garment

of Adam—is quite an epic. Adam, when he came to earth, had a garment. He received a garment of light, when, in the Garden of Eden, he was gloriously clothed in 'ur (he changed it for ᶜor). The fact that ᶜor and 'ur are so similar has led to a great deal of controversy. 'Ur is "light"; ᶜor is "skin." So Adam lost his garment of light at the Fall and had to clothe himself in a garment of skin, a reversal of the process. His new leather garment was nonetheless a glorious one, a sign of authority. Eisler calls it the garment of protection.[72] It was necessary to protect Adam in his exposed and fallen state. Because he had gotten himself into a dangerous position in which he needed assurance and protection, he received this kind of garment. He could no longer wear his glorious one; it was up above, waiting for him.

"Any of you who will put me on," says the *Odes of Solomon*, "shall not be injured. You shall possess a new world that is incorrupt."[73] The garment is for special protection when one visits other worlds. Much is recorded about Jesus going from world to world, how he changed for each one—"when in Rome, do as the Romans do" (that's the explanation given). Christ is not to be recognized except by the faithful and the righteous to whom he gives the tokens. Others are not supposed to know them. Thus he puts on the garment of the world he is visiting—an interesting concept.

Philo, a Jewish writer at the time of Christ, tries to explain the leather garment, then gives up. He says, in effect, that the tunic of skin is the natural skin of the body. There are many passages on this particular leather clothing and protection. It becomes the *aegis;* it becomes the golden fleece (which is a skin garment, which protects you from all ill, if you wear it). The *aegis* is held on the arm—Pallas Athena holds it there (fig. 30), as the leather garment that will protect. She is the overseeing, the protecting one, and

A.   B.

Figure 30. In this classical marble statue of c. 200 B.C. (A), Athena holds
up the *aegis* fringed with serpents, a sign of authority from her father
Zeus, which he made from the skin of the goat that nursed him. She
later adorned it with the apotropaic Gorgon's head (cf. fig. 18B, p. 102).
This same image carved in wood was the *palladium* of the Trojans, their
guarantee of divine protection until its theft by the wily Odysseus (B).

she protects Athens with the symbol of the *aegis,* which
she holds up. And it is of leather.

John Chrysostom says that this garment of Adam signifies at the same time both kingship and repentance.[74]
Many texts about John the Baptist describe him as going
around dressed in skins, in camel's hair, in other various
things — always in garments of skin, or of light. He
preaches repentance because he is the voice in the wilderness, representing Adam in the dark and dreary world.
John Chrysostom talks about the tradition, and so does
the Slavic *Halosis* of Josephus,[75] as well as others. The Slavic
Halosis says, "At the time there was a most wonderful man
who wandered around in an uncanny sort of way."[76]

People did not understand him—he was like a man cast out. He compared himself to Adam in the wilderness, wore a garment of skin, and called upon all people to repent. Furthermore, he lived on a primal diet of locusts and honey. "He lived like a spirit without flesh. His mouth knew no bread, not even at the Passover. Wine and strong drink he would not allow in his presence. He went about exposing every form of iniquity." That was his calling, and it represents here the garment of repentance. As a result, you find it being worn by the earliest monks everywhere. The Syrian monks still wear the leather garment, which they call "the garment of repentance."[77]

Clement of Rome's *First Epistle to the Corinthians*, the earliest Christian writing known for a long time after the New Testament, says, "Let us be imitators of those who in goatskins and sheepskins went about proclaiming the coming of Christ. I mean the prophets Elijah, Elisha, and even Ezekiel."[78] So John the Baptist was just following type—following the men who went around in goatskins and sheepskins proclaiming the coming of Christ, i.e., in a state of humility and repentance.

Another new discovery, the Armenian *Revelation to Peter*,[79] talks about a community of saints up in the mountains that he visited. A community of them was transfigured, but they all wore sheepskins and coats of skin, which signified that they were already dead to things of this world. Theophylactus says that James the brother of the Lord wore only one garment all his life, and it was a garment of repentance. Also a very strict Nazarite, he never cut his hair, even when he was a very, very old man. He wore no wool, but only linen. "Why did you come to the desert?" (Jesus had said the same thing about John the Baptist). Was it to see a man in soft garments? No. Kings and the great ones wear soft garments, and they will not be able to know the truth (cf. Luke 7:24–25). It is the raiment of repentance.

Figure 31. When the devout Muslim begins the *hajj*, the required pilgrimage to Mecca, he wraps the *iḥrām*, the white garments of purity,
around his waist and over his shoulder and prays, "Here I am, O God,
in obedience to thy will." He stands with uplifted hands, like his early
Christian counterpart (cf. fig. 14, p. 92). Upon his return home, he will
preserve these robes; and when he dies, his family will bury him in
them.

Noah exhorted the righteous, says the book of *Jubilees*,
to cover their shame.[80] According to the *Book of Adam*, it
was commanded that they hide the shame of their flesh,
for it had been so commanded in the heavenly tablets.[81]
In order to do this, Adam had what is called "the garment
of mortification," like the *iḥrām*, which Muslims use in the
same way (fig. 31). Being very valuable, Adam's garment
was handed down from father to son.

In an interesting account in a very small but important
work called the *Combat of Adam*, Satan is always trying to
get the garment. It starts out with Satan trying to get it

from Adam. There are a number of very old versions of
the way in which the garment was stolen and faked by
kings — this among other vicissitudes of the garment. In
this particular one, we are told that Satan sent one of his
five friends back to Jared's cave to get the garment of Adam.
He did not get it, but he faked it, put on a mask, then
returned, wearing the mask of great beauty, which fooled
Jared and the people into thinking that he had the real
thing. Although he got the people to follow him, it was a
fraud. For this reason, as Basil the Great recalls the tradition, the garments of Adam were not immediately forthcoming, because they were prizes reserved only for the
man who could escape Satan's fraud, whom Satan was
constantly trying to get. Because of that particular danger,
Adam did not receive permission to make these public.
Furthermore, the *Pistis Sophia* tells of a fight for possession
of the garment in heaven. The rebels sinned against the
light, and everything was shifted to another frame of reference. Trying to stay in power as long as they could, they
tried to grab the garments, but the new order came suddenly. Unable to use their own contaminated stuff, they
tried to get new garments before they were kicked out.[82]
These are very dramatic stories.

The *Psalm of Thomas* says that "those who were not of
my Father's house took up arms against me. They fought
me for my holy garment, my light garment, which lightens
the darkness. They tried to take it from me."[83] The *Book of
Jasher* tells us that "after the death of Adam, the garments
were given to Enoch, the son of Jared, and when Enoch
was taken up to God, he gave them to Methuselah, his
son. And at the death of Methuselah, Noah took them
with him in the ark. And as they were leaving [the ark],
Ham stole those garments from Noah his father, and he
took them and hid them from his brothers." Then Ham
secretly gave the garments to his favorite son, Cush, who
handed them down in the royal line.[84] We meet this idea

of the stolen garment often. We are told in one document that the garment of Adam was owned also by Noah and Ram, the brother of the biblical Jared; but the tradition is that Ham, the father of Cainan, saw the skin garment of his father, showed it to his brothers outside, made copies of it, and claimed it for himself.[85] According to Rabbi Eliezer, Noah came to himself and saw what had happened — that Ham had stolen his garments. (The world used "nakedness" as the word; "skin garment," the same word, is simply a derived or secondary meaning. The word means "skin covering.") When Noah found out what he had done, he cursed Ham and said, "Because you grabbed it ahead of time, Ham, you cannot have the priesthood until the end of time. Meanwhile, I will give the garment to Shem, and part of it to Japheth, but you cannot have it." Why? Because Noah had anticipated that Ham would get it illegally. To show that he was justified, Ham tried to fake it and caused a great deal of confusion thereby. In the Midrash *Genesis Rabbah,* Rabbi Johanan says, "Shem began the good deed [they returned the garment to their father], and then Japheth came and hearkened to him; therefore, Shem was granted the *tallit* and Japheth the *pallium*" — the large cover,[86] a cloak with clasps and buttons on the shoulder. *Tallit* here means a fringed garment; Rabbi Johanan means that the reward of Shem, the ancestor of the Jews, "was the precept of the fringes" in the garment, "while that of Japheth," representing the Greeks, "was the *pallium*," the "cloak, betokening his dignity."[87]

The Midrash goes on to tell us that as a reward they received from God prayer cloaks (others say it was robes of state), while Ham was denied the protection of the garment, because he had stolen it. This was the priesthood that he was trying to get illegally. And Rabbi Jehudah says in the *Pirkê de Rabbi Eliezer,*

The coats which the Holy One . . . made for Adam

and his wife were with Noah in the ark. . . . When they
went forth from the ark, Ham, the son of Noah, brought
them forth with him, and gave them as an inheritance
to Nimrod. When he put them on, all the beasts, . . .
came and prostrated themselves before him [because this
was the garment which Adam wore in the Garden, and
the beasts all reverenced him because he had dominion
over them as long as he acted as God would act]. Therefore, [the sons of man] made him king over themselves.[88]

He fooled everybody into thinking he had the priesthood
because he had the garment. The *Apocalypse of Abraham*
says, "Cush loved Nimrod, the son of his old age [Cush
got it from Ham], and gave him that garment in which
God had once clothed Adam as he was forced to leave
paradise."[89] This garment passed from Adam to Enoch to
Methuselah to Noah, who took it into the ark. Here Ham
misused it and secretly handed it to his son Cush, whose
son Nimrod, while wearing this garment, was invincible
and irresistible. The garments enabled him to conquer the
world and proclaim himself its ruler, so that mankind offered him worship. (There is a profound mystery concerning these garments, which is one of the secrets the
ancients kept to themselves.) Then what happened? According to Jewish lore, Nimrod had it; then Esau was jealous of Nimrod, who was another great hunter. He lay in
ambush, slew Nimrod, took the garment from him, and
brought it home. This garment was the birthright which
Jacob got from Esau, who got it back again. This was the
garment of Jacob, the garment of Ham. "Nimrod, Amra-
phel, king of Babel, went forth with his people on a great
hunt. At that time he was jealous of the great hunter Esau.
As Nimrod approached with two attendants, Esau hid and
cut off Nimrod's head before the other two. Esau then fled
with the valuable garment of Nimrod, which had made
him victorious over the entire world. Then he ran exhausted to Jacob, after hiding the garment."[90] That was

the deal: he was willing to sell it in a financial sense. In another account, "Nimrod, the king of Babel, went hunting in the field; Esau was observing Nimrod all the day, for jealousy had formed in his heart, Esau against Nimrod. Esau lay in ambush and cut off his head and then he took the valuable garment of Nimrod because Nimrod prevailed over the land, and ran and concealed it in his house."[91] This was the birthright which he sold to Jacob, and there are other versions of the same thing.[92]

The *Pirkê de Rabbi Eliezer* says,

> Esau, the brother of Jacob, saw the coats of Nimrod, and in his heart he coveted them, and he slew him, and took them from him. . . . When he [Esau] put them on he also became, by means of them, a mighty hero. . . . And when Jacob went forth from the presence of Isaac his father [after receiving the blessing from Isaac] he said: Esau, the wicked one, is not worthy to wear these coats. So Jacob stole the garment from [Esau's] tent and he dug in the earth and hid [the garments] there.[93]

Somebody is always trying to steal the garment; somebody is always trying to fake it. It reminds one of "The King's Ankus," the story by Kipling.[94] But always there is the false version of the garment going around: Then Jacob buried the garment. It was this garment in which the first-born of Israel performed the priestly functions of Mt. Sinai. It was the priestly garment of Adam.

Another version says the same thing. There is a great deal said about stealing. Ham, Cush, Nimrod, Esau—all are accused of it. Finally, there is the garment that came to Joseph. Thaᶜlabi tells the marvelous story about the two garments.[95] When Jacob gets the garment from his sons, who had taken it from Joseph to prove to Jacob that his son Joseph was dead, Jacob delivers a very interesting speech on the garment. He is blind, and he knows there are two garments. He weeps for the part that has rotted away (this is the story that Moroni tells), showing that

Israel will fall away, but rejoices because of the part that hasn't, and therefore has joy and weeps at the same time. He recognized it, Thaᶜlabi says (Thaᶜlabi picked up these stories from the Jews living in Persian villages of the ninth century), by the smell of the garment of paradise, because it was the garment that Adam had worn in paradise. Moreover, Abraham says there was no other garment like it in the whole world, and Jacob knew it was the garment of Abraham. Above all, he recognized it because of certain marks or cuts in it. He felt the marks and knew that it was *the* garment—there was none other like it in the world. It was the one that Adam had in paradise, and the one that Abraham had, too. The stealing of Joseph's garment by his brethren shows Joseph to be the type of the Savior. This is exactly what Moroni says: we are the outcasts of Joseph—despised, rejected, acquainted with grief. In the *Testaments of the Twelve Patriarchs,* we are told many particulars about the figure of Joseph and his garment; the story is of two garments, of the good one and of the bad one, which we find in Alma 46:24–25. The *Testament of Benjamin* tells about an Ishmaelite who tried to fake the garment and was smitten for it.[96]

So these various stories go around; breaking them down is very confusing. I myself always get confused, but some notes are too good to miss.[97]

Notes

1. In general, see Ferdinand Cabrol and Henri Leclercq, eds., *Relliquiae Liturgicae Vestustissimae,* Monumenta Ecclesiae Liturgicae I (Paris: Firmin-Didot, 1913).

2. Josef A. Jungmann, *The Mass of the Roman Rite: Its Origins and Development (Missarum Sollemnia),* ed. C. K. Reipe, tr. F. A. Brunner (New York: Benziger Brothers, 1961), 84, 195–97.

3. See Klaus Koch, *The Rediscovery of Apocalyptic,* tr. M. Kohl (London: SCM, 1972).

4. Hugh Nibley, *Message of the Joseph Smith Papyri: An Egyptian Endowment* (Salt Lake City: Deseret Book, 1975), 273–78.

5. For a full discussion of the literature, see Hugh W. Nibley,

"Evangelium Quadraginta Dierum," *Vigiliae Christianae* 20 (1966): 1–24; reprinted as "Evangelium Quadraginta Dierum: The Forty-Day Mission of Christ—The Forgotten Heritage," in *CWHN* 4:10–44.

6. *Pistis Sophia* IV, 136, lines 16–22, in Carl Schmidt, ed., *Pistis Sophia*, tr. Violet MacDermot (Leiden: Brill, 1978), 353; 2 *Jeu* 42, in Carl Schmidt, ed., *The Books of Jeu and the Untitled Text in the Bruce Codex*, tr. Violet MacDermot (Leiden: Brill, 1978), 99.

7. *Pistis Sophia* III, 134; II, 99, in Schmidt, *Pistis Sophia*, 349; 247, lines 4–7.

8. 2 *Jeu* 47, in Schmidt, *Books of Jeu and the Untitled Text*, 114. Cited in Hugh W. Nibley, "The Early Christian Prayer Circle," *BYUS* 19 (1978): 46–47; reprinted in *CWHN* 4:51.

9. Nibley, *Message of the Joseph Smith Papyri*, 280, referring to the "First Lesson on the Initiatory Ordinances," *mystagogikē protē katechesis*; cf. Hugh W. Nibley, "The Idea of the Temple in History," *MS* 120 (1958): 228–37, 247–49; reprinted in *CWHN* 4:364.

10. Cyril of Jerusalem, *Catecheses (Instructions)* XX [II], 2, in *PG* 33:1077–79.

11. Ibid., XXI [III], 4, in *PG* 33:1092.

12. Ibid., XIX [I], 10, in *PG* 33:1073–76.

13. With regard to Paul's phrase of "putting on Christ," see Hans Dieter Betz, *Galatians* (Philadelphia: Fortress, 1979), 187, which notes: "This concept, which has a powerful and long tradition in ancient religions, describes the Christian's incorporation into the 'body of Christ' as an act of 'clothing,' whereby Christ is understood as the garment. . . . This phrase presupposes the christological-soteriological concept of Christ as a heavenly garment by which the Christian is enwrapped and transformed into a new being. The language is certainly figurative, but it goes beyond the dimension of merely social and ethical inclusion in a religious community; it suggests an event of divine transformation."

14. Cyril of Jerusalem, *Instructions* XXI [III], 1, in *PG* 33:1087–89.

15. Ibid., XXII [IV], 8, in *PG* 33:1104–5.

16. Moshe Levine, *The Tabernacle: Its Structure and Utensils*, tr. Esther J. Ehrmann (Tel Aviv: Melekhet ha-Mishkan, 1969), 124–31, from the 1968 Hebrew *Mele'khet ha-Mishkan: Tabnit ha-Mishkan ve-Kelav*.

17. Ibid., 130.

18. Ibid., 124, 141.

19. *Testament of Levi* 7:4, in *OTP* 1:790.

20. *TPJS*, 304–5; 12–13; cf. *Evening and Morning Star* 1 (August 1832): 3; *HC* 1:283.

21. *Testament of Levi* 8:2, in *OTP* 1:791.

22. Apollodorus, *The Library* II, 4, 10; cf. James G. Frazer, tr., 2 vols. (Cambridge: Harvard University Press, 1921/1967), 1:179.

23. [Cf. I. E. S. Edwards, *Treasures of Tutankhamun* (New York: Metropolitan Museum of Art, 1976), 104–5.]

24. See also Hugh W. Nibley, *Lehi in the Desert and the World of the Jaredites* (Salt Lake City: Bookcraft, 1952), 160–64; reprinted in *CWHN* 5:168–71 and notes.

25. Levine, *Tabernacle*, 141.

26. *Testament of Levi* 8:2, in *OTP* 1:791.

27. *Testament of Levi* 8:3–6; in ibid.

28. Francis Boucher, *20,000 Year of Fashion* (New York: Abrams, 1967), 81.

29. Hugh W. Nibley, "The Arrow, the Hunter, and the State," *WPQ* 2/3 (1949): 328–29; reprinted in *CWHN* 10:1–2.

30. Robert Eisler, *Iēsous Basileus ou Basileusas*, 2 vols. (Heidelberg: Winter, 1930), 2:33–38; cf. Hebrews 11:37–38.

31. *Testament of Levi* 8:6–15, in *OTP* 1:791.

32. *Testament of Levi* 8:18–19, in ibid.

33. Jerome, *Epistolae (Epistles)* 64, in *PL* 22:607–22.

34. Wisdom of Solomon 18:24.

35. Yigael Yadin, *Bar-Kokhba: The Rediscovery of the Legendary Hero of the Second Jewish Revolt against Rome* (New York: Random House, 1971), 76–77, 79, and the accompanying plates.

36. Ibid., 76, 79.

37. Ibid.; cf. *Untitled Text* 12, in Schmidt, *Books of Jeu and the Untitled Text*, 251, lines 7–16.

38. Yadin, *Bar-Kokhba*, 79.

39. Ibid.

40. *Pistis Sophia* I, 10; in Schmidt, *Pistis Sophia*, 16–18.

41. *Odes of Solomon* 4:7–8, in *OTP* 2:736.

42. E. A. W. Budge, *Coptic Apocrypha in the Dialect of Upper Egypt* (London: British Museum, 1913), xxiv. Nibley, "Early Christian Prayer Circle," 45–47, 58; in *CWHN* 4:49–51. Cf. summary and bibliography in *ANT*, 181–86; on Adam and Eve, see ibid., 184.

43. Pastor of Hermas, *Similitudo (Similitudes)* III, 9, 8, in *PG* 2:987.

44. *Pistis Sophia* I, 10, in Schmidt, *Pistis Sophia*, 18.

45. W. M. Flinders Petrie, *Amulets* (Warminster, England: Aris & Phillips, 1972; reprint of 1914 ed.), 16.

46. Heinrich Schäfer, "Die Entstehung einiger Mumienamulette," *Zeitschrift für ägyptische Sprache und Altertumskunde* 43 (1906): 67. Discussing the level and the square, he says, "Im einzelnen aber

kann uns jeder neu auftretende Sarg ein neues Gerät zeigen." Of all workman's tools, only the compass or level and the square are found as amulets.

47. Sir Mark Aurel Stein, *Innermost Asia*, 3 vols. (Oxford: Clarendon, 1928), 2:707.

48. Ibid., 2:665–67, 707; cf. Nibley, "Early Christian Prayer Circle," 66–67; in *CWHN* 4:73–74.

49. Leo Wiener, *Contributions toward a History of Arabico-Gothic Culture*, 4 vols. (New York: Neale, 1917), 1:60–73.

50. Eusebius, *De Vita Constantini (Life of Constantine)* III, 10, in *PG* 20:1063–66 (A.D. 325); note the similar appearance of King Agrippa I at Caesarea (A.D. 44), also described by Eusebius, *Historia Ecclesiastica (Ecclesiastical History)* II, 10, 1–5, in *PG* 20:157–60; following Josephus, *Antiquities of the Jews* XIX, 8, 2, and Herod in Acts 12:19–23.

51. *Odes of Solomon* 11:10–12, in *OTP* 2:745.

52. Ibid., 21:3–4; cf. 25:8, "And I was covered with the covering of your spirit, and I removed from me my garments of skin."

53. Nibley, *Message of the Joseph Smith Papyri*, 267–72; cf. "Hymn of the Soul," in *ANT*, 411–15. Edgar Hennecke and William Schneemelcher, *New Testament Apocrypha*, 2 vols. (London: Lutterworth, 1963), 2:498–504. Hans Jonas, *The Gnostic Religion* (Boston: Beacon, 1958), 112–29.

54. *Acts of Thomas* 112 [76] – 113 [99], in *ANT*, 414–15.

55. For some comparisons on this theme in the Enoch literature, see Hugh W. Nibley, "A Strange Thing in the Land: The Return of the Book of Enoch," *Ensign* 7 (April 1977): 82–83; reprinted in *CWHN* 2:228–32.

56. *2 Enoch* 22:5, 8–10, in *OTP* 1:137–38.

57. Moses Gaster, *The Asatir: The Samaritan Book of the "Secrets of Moses"* (London: Royal Asiatic Society, 1927). Compare the Coptic *Bartholomew* in *ANT*, 185, and the ending of the *Apocalypse of Paul*, summarized in ibid., 554 (excerpting the *Apocalypse of Elijah*). *Life of Adam and Eve* 37:3–5, 40:1–2, in *OTP* 2:289–91.

58. *Apocalypse of Elijah* 5:5–6, in *OTP* 1:750.

59. Cf. William Wright, *Apocryphal Acts of the Apostles*, 2 vols. (London: n.p., 1871; reprinted in 1 volume, Amsterdam: Philo, 1968), 2:246–47.

60. *Gospel of Philip* 57:19–22, in *NHLE*, 135.

61. Jonathan Z. Smith, "The Garments of Shame," *History of Religions* 5 (1965): 217–38; cf. Hugh W. Nibley, "Since Cumorah," *IE* 69 (August 1966): 711–12; reprinted in *CWHN* 7:243.

62. Thaʿlabī, *Qiṣaṣ al-Anbiyāʾ*, cited in Hugh W. Nibley, *An Approach to the Book of Mormon* (Salt Lake City: Deseret Book, 1957), 178–89; reprinted in *CWHN* 6:209–21. Cf. Hugh W. Nibley, *Since Cumorah* (Salt Lake City: Deseret Book, 1970), 227, 274; reprinted in *CWHN* 7:199, 243; Hugh W. Nibley, "New Approaches to Book of Mormon Study," *IE* (November 1953–July 1954): 56–57; reprinted in *CWHN* 8:94–95; Hugh W. Nibley, "Howlers in the Book of Mormon," *MS* 125 (February 1963): 28–34; reprinted in *CWHN* 8:249–50; Hugh W. Nibley, "Bar Kochba and Book of Mormon Backgrounds," *BYUS* 14 (Autumn 1973): 115–26; reprinted in *CWHN* 8:280–81; Hugh W. Nibley, "Freemen and Kingmen in the Book of Mormon," in *CWHN* 8:335–36.

63. 2 *Jeu* 46–47, in Schmidt, *Books of Jeu and the Untitled Text*, 109–12; cf. Nibley, "Early Christian Prayer Circle," 46–47, in *CWHN* 4:51.

64. Ostracon, Cairo 48, 624, in N. Aimé-Giron, "Trois ostraca araméens d'Éléphantine," *Annales du Service des Antiquités de l'Égypte* 26 (1926): 27. Cf. Bezalel Porten, *Archives from Elephantine: The Life of an Ancient Jewish Military Colony* (Berkeley: University of California Press, 1968), 277.

65. For a fuller account, see *ANT*, 29–30.

66. Cf. Encomium of Theodosius, Archbishop of Alexandria, Egypt (British Museum Oriental Manuscript 7021), in E. A. Wallis Budge, *Miscellaneous Coptic Texts* (Oxford: Oxford University Press, 1915/1977), 914–17.

67. Cf. *Acts of Thomas* 5–6 and 26, in *ANT*, 366–67, 375; W. Wright, *Apocryphal Acts of the Apostles*, 2:245–51.

68. *Gospel of Truth* 23:33, 24:7, in *NHLE*, 41.

69. Plato, *Republic* IV, 429D-430C.

70. Plutarch, *Isis and Osiris* 382B-C; Plutarch, *Oracles at Delphi* 393C-D.

71. Jerome, *Commentarius in Ezechielem (Commentary on Ezekiel)* XIII, 44, in *PL* 25:437, and in Theodor Hopfner, *Fontes Historiae Religionis Aegyptiacae*, 5 vols. in 1 (Bonn: Marx and Weber, 1922–25), 642.

72. Eisler, *Iēsous Basileus ou Basileusas*, 2:33–38.

73. *Odes of Solomon* 33:12, in *OTP* 2:764.

74. John Chrysostom says that this garment of Adam signifies at the same time both kingship and repentance, because he is in a fallen state. John Chrysostom, *Commentarius in Sanctum Matthaeum Evangelistam (Commentary on Matthew)* X, 4, in *PG* 57:188–89. Cf. Nibley, *Lehi in the Desert and the World of the Jaredites*, 161; in *CWHN*

5:169, 266, n. 39; Nibley, "Evangelium Quadraginta Dierum," 1–24; in CWHN 4:38, n. 78.

75. Eisler, Iēsous Basileus ou Basileusas, 2:6–8, 16.

76. Ibid., 2:6.

77. Ibid., 2:30–38. Cf. Hebrews 11:37–38.

78. Clement, Epistola I ad Corinthios (First Epistle to the Corinthians) 17, in PG 1:241–44.

79. Revelation to Peter 238, in E. Verdapet, "The Revelation of the Lord to Peter," tr. F. C. Conybeare, Zeitschrift für die neutestamentliche Wissenschaft 23 (1924): 17.

80. Jubilees 7:20, in OTP 2:70.

81. In J.-P. Migne, Dictionnaire des apocryphes, 2 vols. (Paris: Migne, 1856), 1:87–88 (volumes 23–24 of Troisième et dernière encyclopédie théologique).

82. Pistis Sophia I, 55; II, 71, in Schmidt, Pistis Sophia, 104; 160.

83. Psalms of Thomas 2; cf. C. R. C. Allberry, A Manichaean Psalm Book, 2 vols. (Stuttgart: Kohlhammer, 1938), 2:205.

84. Book of Jasher 7:25–29.

85. See Tha'labī, Qiṣaṣ al-Anbiyā', 96.

86. Jacob Neusner, Genesis Rabbah, 3 vols. (Atlanta: Scholars, 1985), 2:31.

87. Ibid.

88. Gerald Friedlander, Pirkê de Rabbi Eliezer (New York: Hermon, 1965), 175; cf. 144, 178.

89. Angelo S. Rappoport, Myth and Legend of Ancient Israel, 3 vols. (London: Gresham, 1928), 1:234–35.

90. Book of Jasher 27:2–12.

91. Louis Ginzberg, The Legends of the Jews, 7 vols. (Philadelphia: Jewish Publication Society of America, 1937), 1:318–19.

92. Neusner, Genesis Rabbah, 3:364.

93. Friedlander, Pirkê de Rabbi Eliezer, 178.

94. Kipling, "The King's Ankus," in The Jungle Book (Garden City, NY: Doubleday, 1945), 125–48.

95. Tha'labī, Qiṣaṣ al-Anbiyā', cited in Nibley, Approach to the Book of Mormon, 209–21; in CWHN 6:218–21; cf. Alma 46:24–25.

96. Testament of Benjamin 2–3, in OTP 1:825–26.

97. For additional information, see Percy Dearmer, "Church Vestments," Essays on Ceremonial, ed. Vernon Stanley (London: De la More, 1904), 177–92; D. Duret, Mobilier: Vases, objets et vêtements liturgiques (Paris: Letouzey and Ane, 1932); Ludwig Eisenhofer and Joseph Lechner, The Liturgy of the Roman Rite, tr. A. J. and E. R. Peeler (Freiburg: Herder, 1961), from the 1953 Liturgik des römischen

Ritus; Josef A. Jungmann, *The Early Liturgy, to the Time of Gregory the Great*, tr. F. A. Brunner, *Notre Dame University Liturgical Studies* 6 (South Bend: Notre Dame, 1959); Robert Lesage, ed., *The Twentieth Century Encyclopedia of Catholicism, Vestments and Church Furniture* (New York: Hawthorn, 1960); Herbert Norris, *Church Vestments: Their Origin and Development* (London: Dent, 1949); Marcus von Wellnitz, "The Catholic Liturgy and the Mormon Temple," *BYUS* 21 (1981): 3–35; John E. W. Wallis, *The Church Vestments* (London: SPCK, 1924).

The Circle and the Square

What exists on the earth's surface is supported, much like a troupe of actors, by countless backstage assistants. I've often referred to the earth as a stage, to which Joseph Smith gives us the scenario. He talked about the stagehands, forming a network that extends far behind and beyond the theater walls. The props and the stage are there, along with the stagehands. The big question is, Is there a play? Is there a plot? Is there a meaning to it all?

Surprisingly, since ancient times, only Joseph Smith has come up with any kind of a plot. When he faced the world he had nothing to go on, and everything against him; he couldn't lose. He had something concrete to put up, while the rest of the world had none. They had the abstract, the moralistic, etc., but nothing in the way of the infinities, of the realities of the next world. Only Brother Joseph had something to offer.

Certainly the earth is not the center of the universe. This illusion has been discarded forever. Still, this crowded earth is one of those perhaps innumerable places in the cosmos where both life and consciousness flourish. Many factors united to produce and maintain the right conditions where life was generated by a concentration of mighty forces upon one relatively tiny point.

This is the center I am talking about, and it's exactly what we read in the book of Abraham, where he says that everything is relative to the individual: the individual is

---

This is a previously unpublished and undated manuscript.

the center. All distances, all times, all places are measured
in terms of the "[earth] upon which *thou* standest" (Abraham 3:5). Its distances, its motions, etc., are not the center
of anything. Moses says the same thing: "Tell me, I pray
thee, why these things are so" (Moses 1:30). The Lord
replies: I'm not going to. "Only an account of *this*
earth . . . give I unto you" (Moses 1:35). You must be content with that, but remember that there are others: "Worlds
without number have I created" (Moses 1:33).

"Tell me concerning *this* earth," Moses returns. "Then
thy servant will be content" (Moses 1:36).

So for us, the earth is the center of things, so long as
we're here.

There arises the question of whether we need a psychological center—some kind of center we can refer to.
Thus we frequently quote Yeats's famous lines: "Things
fall apart; the center cannot hold; mere anarchy is loosed
upon the world."[1] Our civilization is collapsing, falling
apart, because there is no center; everything is loosened.

In the opening lines of the famous first of modern
geography books, Ratzel begins, "Every man regards himself as the center of the universe around him." There is a
real center, but it is also relative. There is also each person's
awareness that other people have their centers too, unless
you're a solipsist, or something similar. Since there are
other people, there must be other centers. For the purposes
of getting together, can we agree on one center—a fictitious
center, a model of some sort, and act as if that were the
center?

Actually we don't have to do that, because we have
one very real center. If you traveled over the entire earth
viewing the heavens, you wouldn't come to a center, but
you would find two places that looked very much alike:
the center polestars, of course. They stay fixed, while all
else revolves around them. Thus on the west tower of the
Salt Lake Temple there is the Big Dipper (cf. fig. 2, pp. 16–

17), pointing up — to the polestar.[2] The temple is a point of reference, a place where you take your bearings on the universe.

That's what the word *templum* means. Everyone knows what a template is that you put over a map. It's as if we put a template over the temple in Salt Lake City; most every street in the city, and every city in the state, is measured east, west, north, and south from that arbitrary point. (Certain points on the earth do seem to be particularly suited as central points — they have a special power, charm, or attraction about them.)

So are we there among the stars, or are we not? Giorgio de Santillana said we should not be too sure we aren't.[3]

Our present tradition comes from the great migrations, after some kind of Golden Age, which broke up around 3500 to 3000 B.C. This was a horrible time; everything went to smash. Everything was uprooted; everyone became migrants. And, obsessed with the idea of the temple, they took it with them — though it was a different concept from the older, permanent one. When people are uprooted, they develop two yearnings: a passion for permanence, and a zest for distance and adventure.

As we see in the *Odyssey*, Odysseus, who wandered for ten years, enjoyed his journey, at least with Calypso. She twitted him about it. Still he blubbered all day long to be home with his dear wife. He loved to travel, but he couldn't wait to get home. He had to have both. It is like a French geographer's description of the mad force of the sun and the wise force of the earth. The latter pulls you back, although you want both. This is what our ancestors documented in the great migrations.

Ancient tribal shrines of the Near East are known variously as the Arabic ʿutfa ("the standing place"), the *maḥmal* ("a wagon, or something you ride in"; fig. 32), the *markab* ("a camping place"), a *qubba* ("dome, or navel center —

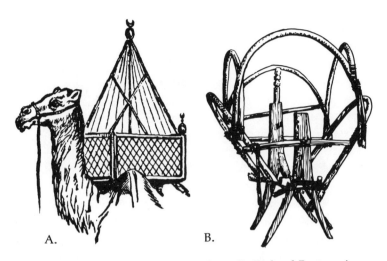

A.   B.

Figure 32. The intrepid Victorian explorer Sir Richard Burton gives us
a view of the undraped camel shrine, the *mahmal,* which he encountered
on his visit to Mecca in 1853 (A). A modern *haūdaj,* or woman's enclosed
saddle of the Al-Murrah Bedouin, shows the simple but efficient dome-
like form these structures could take (B).

something that doesn't move, like a Navajo hogan"), a *bayt*
(a place where you spend the night only — our words *booth,*
abide, etc.), a Hebrew *'ărôn* ("an ark or vessel, like the ark
of the covenant"), and an Arabic *tābūt* (borrowed from the
Egyptian word for "chest, coffin") — all these words des-
ignate the ancient tribal shrines.[4] And they have two char-
acteristics in common: they are dome-shaped, and they
are mounted on a boxlike frame; the two come together in
a substructure, *merkābāh,* a vessel or wagon (something
you ride on). The word has a great mystical meaning in
the Jewish cabbalistic literature. The *merkābāh* is the vessel
by which God conveys his wisdom, whatever it might be,
to whomever. Whatever its precise meaning, it was meant
to provide mobility.

    Two recent studies discuss the cosmic nature of the
wheel, the dome-shaped shrine, or royal *balde, baldekin* or
baldaekin, or, paradoxical as it may seem, such a symbol of

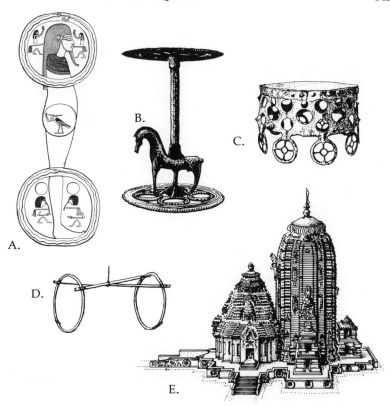

Figure 33. From one of his golden shrines, the enigmatic figure of Tutankhamun as Osiris stands with his head and feet encircled by the protective serpent *Mḥn,* shown twice (A). This is an early depiction of the *ouroboros,* the World-Serpent who endlessly wheels about, growing by devouring itself. The design resembles a near contemporary bronze lampstand from Celtic Spain, with its two sun-wheels and axle, yet designed to be set vertically, as shown by the horse centered on the *axis mundi* (B; cf. fig. 28, pp. 114–15). The much later Swedish bronze altar also "revolves" on ten sun-wheels that encircle it, shedding light on the fairy-tale accounts of mysterious bronze castles and beds revolving in circles (C). The Kogi Indians of Northern Colombia, who have little use for the wheel, still describe the circular crossing path of the sun in terms of this wheel-like calendar model hung in their thatch-roofed temples (D). The great Sun Temple at Konarak, India, c. A.D. 1200, has 24 ten-foot stone wheels encircling its world mountain (E).

supreme stability as the throne, temple, holy city, and even
sacred mountain. World mountains are often depicted as
revolving wheels or as mounted on wheels (fig. 33).

That's a strange thing. The Roman *quadrata* represents
the four corners of the earth, and the center of everything;
the Romans always drew it this way: $\oplus$. But it's also the
picture of a wheel. The Babylonians combined the two very
neatly in their cosmic design. It's the wheel that goes round
and round but never moves.

For the nomads, it's a *qubba* – a dome; the Latin word
is *cupola*: a cap, cup. It represents the dome of the heavens,
and you find it everywhere as the common shape of
churches. And the square church accompanies it. The
dome, like a *stupa* in India, is mounted over a perfect cube
(fig. 34). To the nomads the *qubay*, or domed red leather
tent of the chief, is the *qubba*.

The Islamic *qibla* derives from a root meaning "to face,
to receive, to look toward." When a Muslim prays five
times a day, what direction does he face? To Mecca – the
center of the world. How does he know where the center
is? In his house he has a *qibla*, a marker that tells the
direction he must face, "by which the tribe when it camps,
takes its bearings in space; the *qibla* itself is oriented with
reference to the heavenly bodies (fig. 35). For the Asiatics
as well as the Romans, the Royal Tent is a *templum* or
tabernaculum."[5]

The word *tabernaculum* is the Roman name for a quickly
made booth, a "little house of boards," something thrown
up very quickly of brush, boards, blankets, or anything
you might happen to have.[6] The Feast of Tabernacles is
the *sukkôt* of the Hebrew, which is the *sh* of the Egyptians.

It's the same thing as the outer court of the Greek
temple, the *temenos*, which means "temple," "to cut" – the
point at which the two lines, the *cardo* and the *decumanus*,
intersect (the *axis mundi*; cf. fig. 4, p. 20).[7] All space comes
together at this absolute, theoretical, perfect point. It is the

center of everything, which doesn't exist. It's like the singularity that physicists talk about today — things that are real and conceivable, but not describable. Thus it's a device for taking our bearings on wherever we are. That's precisely what a temple does: it puts us into the picture of time and space. It's a sort of sacred observatory, like the tabernacle or the camp of Israel, and at the same time a kind of planetarium, a model of the cosmos.[8]

The temple at Jerusalem was built to accommodate the ark of the covenant. The ark, *'ărôn,* could travel in a tent, because it does travel. Even when housed in Solomon's temple, the ark had the carrying poles on it, so it could be carried around. It resembles an archaic Egyptian shrine, even to the details (fig. 36).

This double quality (the ever-moving center) caused much dispute among the Doctors of the Jews. Some said that a stone temple that tied down the ark, and hence the chosen people, was an abomination; others said it was the very symbol of endurance and everlasting assurance.[9]

The central pole of the tent (see Eliade's work on Shamanism)[10] is often identified with the pole (the polestar) of the heavens. "The tent itself is the *Weltenmantel,* the expanse of the firmament. Other tent poles sometimes represent the four cardinal points or the two turning points of the sun in the summer and winter solstice."[11] The tent pole theme is carried over into the pillars of the temples and palaces, even into the columns of medieval churches and the stately façades of our own public buildings.[12] Thus we all are familiar with the idea (fig. 37).

There are two kinds of temple architecture — the circle and the square. The earliest nine pyramids along the Nile were perfectly square. When I checked this in my pyramid texts, the symbol was drawn thus: $\triangle$. At Gilgal twelve stones stand in a circle. Generally, the rites are said to be in the form of a circumambulation. The king goes through the land in a great circle, in his Royal Progress, the "king's

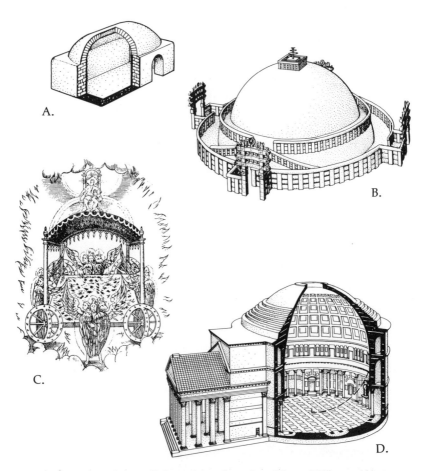

Figure 34. From the small domed royal tomb at Ur, c. 3000 B.C. (A), to
the Buddhist relic mound of the Great Stupa at Sanchi, c. 250 B.C., the
dome has been a perennial symbol of the heavens (B). In this seventeenth-century English Bear's Bible, the artist attempts to show the
wheeled vehicle, called the *merkābāh*, which Ezekiel saw in vision (Ezekiel 1), with God seated on the rainbow over the "firmament" or dome
of the heavens (C). For six hundred years, Hadrian's Pantheon, A.D.
124, was the world's largest dome (D). Imperial audiences and religious
rites were held in the marble interior, which encloses a perfect sphere,
the symbol of its central importance.

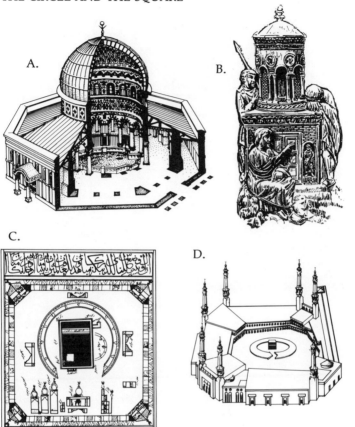

Figure 35. Mohammed originally instructed his followers to pray toward Jerusalem, where they erected Islam's earliest dome, replacing Justinian's domed church, which itself was built on the site of the Roman domed temple of Jupiter Aelia (A). Even the tomb of Christ on an ivory panel, c. A.D. 400, has the typical dome of a Roman hero shrine (B). When Mecca became the Muslim center, helpful tourist maps such as this one of the fifteenth century (C) showed the square of the black-draped Ka'ba within its circular wall. The newly expanded mosque (D) can hold a quarter of the two million pilgrims who make the annual *hajj,* in which they perform the *ṭawāf,* or circumambulation of seven circuits, as Muslims once did in Jerusalem. The Buddhists call their encircling movement *pradakṣiṇā* and go clockwise (cf. fig. 34B); regardless of the direction, both rituals point to the same divine center.

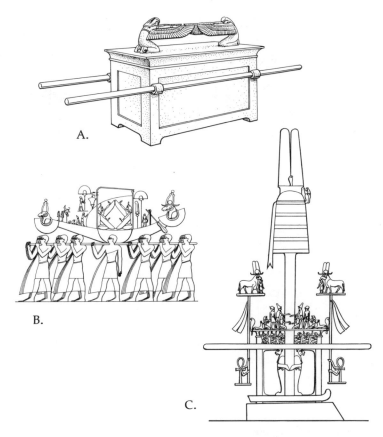

A.

B.

C.

Figure 36. When the Lord commanded Moses to build a gold-covered portable wooden chest (A) to hold the Tablets of the Law, his covenant with Israel was made even more tangible. He promised to speak with Moses from the Mercy Seat between the cherubim. The Egyptians also made use of special portable shrines, such as this one of Thutmosis II, c. 1480 B.C. (B); the two winged Maat goddesses represent truth and justice. From the temple of Ramses I at Abydos, we see the abstract symbol of the god Osiris (C), in the form of his stylized head on the world pillar, flanked by two lion-headed winged figures; the entire shrine is plated with gold and rests on the Maat stone of truth, just as the Ark was thought to rest on the *eben shetiyah,* the Stone of Foundation.

tour." He visits one by one each holy place, to take possession of his land, something he has to do every year. When he arrives at each, he circumambulates it three times. That's the combination: the circle and square.[13]

To the Pythagorean mystic, the cube represents perfect solidity; the sphere is perfect continual motion (cf. fig. 55, p. 413). The two must always be together; thus we find them so combined in ancient temples, and in our temple too. The Manti Temple features the square building, but it has a circular staircase. The Provo Temple has a square bottom, but is rounded off (it would have been nice had they made up their minds whether they wanted it square or round). It looks like a typical "stupa" (cf. fig. 34, p. 146). And of course it has a tall, round ornament at the top. There is always motion around, but also always stability in the center. It is satisfying to have it both ways.

For this reason, the temple lends itself to duplication, an important principle. The ancients often referred to it as "the spark." We are now into the mechanics of the creation process.

All ancient temples rehearsed the story of the creation, and the establishment of mankind and the royal government of God upon this earth. Then they moved into the heavenly sphere and the theology associated with the worlds beyond.

The order and stability of a foundation are achieved through the operation of a "spark." The spark is sometimes defined as "a small idea."[14] This is interesting, because it reminds us of the contemporary anthropic idea. "That comes forth from God and makes all the difference between what lives and what does not."[15] This spark must go from world to world, and wherever it goes, it sets up a new center; this center in turn goes out and sets up other new centers.[16]

St. Augustine uses this image, interestingly, when he refers to Jerusalem. The church always fought pilgrimages

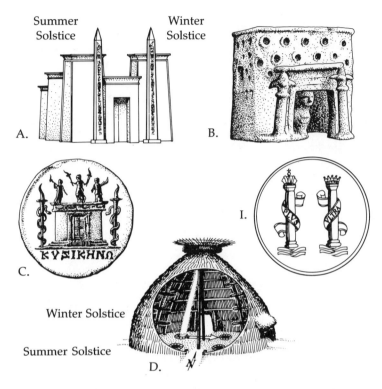

Figure 37. The pillars of the temple have always been more than mere decoration. As late as the fourteenth century, the Arab chronicler Maqrizī could describe the solstice suns "crowning" the copper-capped obelisks of Senwsret I, c. 1940 B.C., at Heliopolis, "so marvelous that no one has ever seen anything as wonderful or significant" (A). A modern scholar has even described them as petrified sunbeams. This clay model of a temple in Cyprus, c. 600 B.C. (B), shows two floral-capped pillars flanking the entrance. Robertson Smith believed Solomon's pillars were immense lampstands, such as the bronze serpent-wrapped torches outside the sanctuary of Demeter at Cyzicus, Turkey, c. A.D. 120 (C). The Kogi Indians continue to build sophisticated models of their universe (D) in which the four pillars of their "world house" support a small woven aperture, which allows the sun to penetrate the darkness. This shaft of light becomes a sun pillar, successively touching one of the four fireplaces, which mark the four corners of the year, "weaving" the fabric of time and space. The pillars of the temple that

Jesus saw were probably adorned with spiral garlands of gold, such as can be seen in the Torah shrine painting at Dura Europos (E). The pillars flanking the niche closely resemble the pillars supporting the star-decked vault over the baptistry in the nearby Christian house-church (F). Herod's Temple inspired the twisted pillars of Constantine's Basilica (G), which were carted off to St. Peter's in Rome and were called pillars "Salomónica." The "square knot" pillars of Justinian's church (H) tied heaven and earth together. Charles I of Spain depicted his Pillars of Hercules at Gibraltar with wrapped scrolls (I), which in shorthand may have been the source of our dollar symbol: $. Even the niche facing Mecca in the al-Aqsa Mosque on the Temple Mount has two thirteenth-century Byzantine entwined columns (J). On this silver plaque from a synagogue in Lithuania (K), the sacred pillars are combined with the ancient symbol of the entwined serpents of the caduceus (cf. fig. 28, p. 114). The Freemasons picked up on Solomon's pillars and combined them with the tradition of Enoch's pillars and the hidden wisdom of the ancients (cf. fig. 58, pp. 422–23).

to Jerusalem, because it was a vote of no confidence for
Rome. There must be more than one center in the world,
Augustine argued. Just as a fire sends forth sparks, and
each new spark lands somewhere and starts a new fire,
so did Jerusalem. Despite the fact that there were many
centers, they were all one. There is no need to be disturbed
by the existence of multiple centers. Compared with it all,
the worlds are but as a shadow, since it is the Spark whose
light moves all material things.[17]

The Latin word *fundamentum* refers to the lump of butter in the cream you are churning.[18] At first there is nothing
hard, nothing firm. There's matter out there, but it's very
thin.[19] So the frog starts to churn, starts to work at it, and
in time a lump forms, quite mysteriously—as anyone
knows who has ever churned butter (fig. 38). This text
reads, "The *fundamentum* of the world begins to take form
when it is touched by a *scintilla*; the spark ceases and the
fountain is stopped when the inhabitants transgress."[20] We
find this in the vision of Zenez (Kenaz), a record discovered
long after Joseph Smith wrote about a Zenos in the Book
of Mormon.[21]

"Matter without light is inert and helpless," says the
Pistis Sophia.[22] "It is the first light which reproduces the
pattern of the heavenly model, wherever it touches";[23]
"when the rays from the worlds of light stream down to
the earthly world, for awakening mortals."[24] Sometimes
the column of light joins heaven to earth, as in our Facsimile
No. 2 (a very important principle), even as the divine plan
is communicated to distant worlds by a spark. According
to Carl Schmidt, it is the dynamics of light from one world
that animates another.[25] "God's assistants, the faithful servants of Melchizedek, rescue and preserve the light particles, lest any be lost in space."[26] The spark is also called
"the drop"; the Egyptians call it the *prt* ("drop"). It is the
divine drop of light that man brought forth with him from
above, the spark that reactivates bodies that have become

inert by the loss of former light.[27] It's like a tiny bit of God himself. Christ calls upon the Father to send light to the apostles.

It is the ultimate particle, the *ennas*, which came from the Father, of those who are without beginning, emanating from the treasure house of light from which all life and power is ultimately derived. Thanks to the vivifying and organizing power of the Spark, we find throughout the cosmos an infinity of dwelling places, other worlds, *kosmoi* (*topoi* is the word always used — the "places"), either occupied or awaiting tenants. These are colonized by migrants from previously established *topoi* or worlds, all going back ultimately to a single original center.[28]

The colonizing process is called "planting," and those spirits which bring their treasures to a new world are called "plants," more rarely "seeds," of their father, or "planters" in another world. For every planting goes out from a Treasure House, either as the essential material elements or as the colonizers themselves, who come from a sort of mustering-area called the "Treasure-House of Souls." (These early Christians had quite a system.)[29]

With its "planting" completed, a new world is in business. A new treasury has been established from which new sparks may go forth in all directions to start the process anew in ever new spaces; God wants every man to "plant a planting," nay, he has promised that those who keep his law may also become creators of worlds. Thus you can say there is indeed but one God who fills the immensity of space, yet we are in the act too, as potential creators of worlds.

The idea of the universal center of the race is found throughout the ancient world. It's the scene of great events.[30]

At hundreds of holy shrines, each believed to mark the exact center of the universe and represented as the

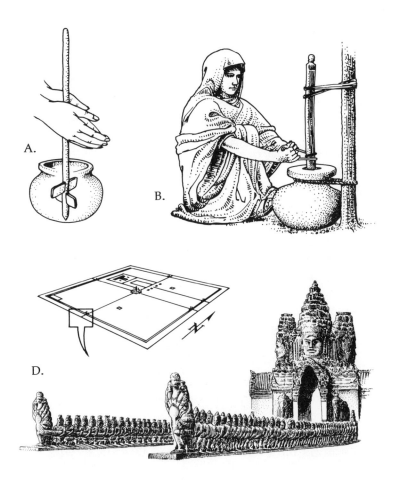

Figure 38. The tools that make possible the everyday miracle of creating a solid from a liquid, i.e., butter from milk, have ancient roots. From the Egyptian butter stirrer (A), which descends from the twirled fire-drill, to the Pakistani woman who efficiently churns by alternating pulls on a cord wrapped around the stirrer (B), we see this practical idea becoming increasingly widespread. In early India, this mundane device was seen as a type of the cosmic creation, where gods and demons joined in a tug-of-war to churn the Milky Ocean and create the universe (C). The most spectacular example is Angkor Thom in Cambodia, c.

A.D. 1200 (D), where the railings of the causeways leading to the central quincunx world mountain are stone versions of the gods pulling on the cosmic serpent. As the worshipers walked past, they assisted the gods in the primeval act of creation. From churning butter to kindling fire may seem quite a jump, but Shinto priests still kindle sacred fire by pressing down on the bar of the reciprocating fire-drill (E). The cosmic tug-of-war to create light and heat was reenacted yearly by German peasants as they kindled the Need-Fire, as seen in this 1900 depiction (F).

point at which the four corners of the earth converged [the middle *omphalos*] — "the navel of the earth" [the *umbilicus*] — one might have seen assembled at the New Year — the moment of creation, the beginning and ending of time — vast concourses of people, each thought to represent the entire human race in the presence of all its ancestors and gods.[31]

Time and place are always coordinated. After all, if you are going to have a universal meeting of people scattered all over the realm, what do you do? You appoint a particular place for them to come to. But if they are to assemble, they must come at a particular time, in a face-to-face meeting. That's the function of the great assembly at the New Year, the best time, because there's no planting or reaping going on. But most dramatically, it's when the sun reaches its lowest point and must be renewed. And we must all participate in the revival of a new year, and a new age, in bringing things to life again, and make our new oaths and covenants for a new time.

> A visitor to any of these festivals would have found a market or fair in progress, the natural outcome of bringing people together from wide areas in large numbers, and the temple of the place functioning as an exchange or bank. He could have witnessed ritual contests: foot, horse, and wagon races, odd kinds of wrestling.[32]

The Icelandic colony in Spanish Fork, Utah, used to celebrate Icelandic Day in that fashion, at which there was ritual wrestling. It was a type of belt wrestling that is beautifully depicted in some ancient pictures from Egypt. At such festivals there was a Troy Game, beauty contests to choose the queen, etc.[33] "All came to the celebration as pilgrims, often traversing immense distances over prehistoric sacred roads."[34]

During this time, the King's Highway was sacred, and to break the peace there was a capital offense. On that free and open passage, the king's peace prevailed, for anyone who wanted to come to the king's presence for any purpose. And during the festival, they naturally dwelt "in booths of green boughs," to protect them from both the heat of the sun and from showers.[35] They can have no houses: it's not a place where the living dwell. When you leave it, as we learn in Exodus and again in Leviticus, you must eat the Passover with your staff in your hand and your shoes on your feet; and there must not be any of the food left by morning. Then you must hasten away and not look back (Exodus 12:11). It's a holy place, and when the sun rises, the holy time is over. You no longer belong there. It's *maktos*, the place of the spirits, because you had been there with the spirits and others.

"What would most command a visitor's attention to the great assembly would be the main event, the now famous ritual year-drama for the glorification of the king. In most versions of the year-drama, the king wages combat with his dark adversary of the underworld, emerging victorious after a temporary defeat from his duel with death."[36] This is beautifully set forth in the first chapter of the book of Moses. Moses is proclaimed king after he has overcome many waters of Meribah—death; therefore, God says, "I shall make you king in my place, and you shall rule over my people as if you were God." Moses is put in God's place. "Blessed art thou, Moses, because thou hast overcome" (cf. Exodus 7:1; Moses 1:25–26).

So it was with the devil—up and down, up and down. Satan got Moses down, but in his last breath, Moses appealed to God and was rescued. When he saw the bitterness of hell, then it was that he went down (Moses 1:12–22). But he was rescued and became the victor, and it was declared, "He shall rule my people and be to them as if he were God. And they shall follow him."

Everything comes together at a particular time and place, at the center of the universe. "The New Year was

the birthday of the human race and its rites dramatized
the creation of the world; all who would be found in the
'Book of Life opened at the creation of the World' must
necessarily attend."[37] You have always had the *incisi* in
Rome, or among our ancestors you had to have your *herör*,
and if you were touched by the king's arrow, you had to
come to the king's presence; anyone who didn't come to
the New Year's celebration within three days—whether at
Swansea, or at Lund, or at the great Thing in Iceland, or
in a hundred different places in England—would be banished from the kingdom for three years. You were considered to be in a state of rebellion, because you didn't come
to acclaim the king. You refused to give him your voice,
your acclaim.[38] This was all very important. In Rome, during the time of the Republic, you had to come with your
family from great distances, even from Sicily, so they could
be registered again and receive the *annona*,[39] the yearly gift,
a guarantee of prosperity for the new year. If you didn't
come, your name would be struck from the list of the *incisi*,
the huge lead tablets that swung on great, wooden poles
in the temple in the capital. If your name was not on that,
you were *hosticus*, an outlaw of the state.

That's where the word *outlaw* comes from. If you did
not come to the king's presence when he summoned you,
you were outside of the law, because you would not acknowledge the law. That was the case with Cain, who was
thrown out.

So if you are not there, you are not found in the Book
of Life, which is

> opened at the creation of the World. . . . There were
> coronation and royal marriage rites, accompanied by a
> ritual representing the sowing or begetting of the human
> race; and the whole celebration wound up in a mighty
> feast in which the king as lord of abundance gave earnest
> of his capacity to supply his children with all the good
> things of the earth. The stuff for the feast was supplied

by the feasters themselves, for no one came "to worship
the king" without bringing his tithes and firstfruits.[40]

No one comes to the presence of the king empty-handed.
So here they are, all coming together.

And the *omphalos* is a three-dimensional center (fig. 39),
the origin of the "hierocentric idea," coined by Eric Burrows,[41] the Assyriologist who pointed out in such writings
as the poem *Enuma Elish* what happened on the new year
when all the people came together. *Enuma elish* means "as
once above," "as it once happened above,"[42] in the beginning at the creation, when the Lord of life was challenged
by the powers of darkness; and in order for the trinity to
combat it, the Father begat Marduk in his own image. First
Marduk slew the monster Tiamat and made the material
world out of its body.[43] Tiamat was the great matriarch
who plotted to put her son Kingu (who is Satan) on the
throne.[44] They were overcome and cast out. Then Marduk
placed part of the material above, part below. Between
these three levels he placed a barrier — a bolt.[45] "Then he
went the rounds of the heavens ("around them") and inspected the various holy places, in order to establish there
an exact replica of the Apsu, the dwelling of Ea.[46] So the
Apsu (the abyss) is what is above, and what is below. Ea
is water; the Sumerian word for temple is Esagil (Babylonian: Esagila), which is over the waters of the underworld. The idea is that he traced an exact replica of each
world on the other (the Egyptian rule of three, which Gardiner tells us about). Whatever happens in this world happens above and happens below. The three levels are related.

Then the Great Lord measured the dimensions of the
Apsu and established his own dwelling, his image, Ešarra,
which shall be his temple on *this* earth — as Ea is below,
and the Apsu is above.[47] On this earth is the Esagil (the
great palace at Babylon), which has the same dimensions

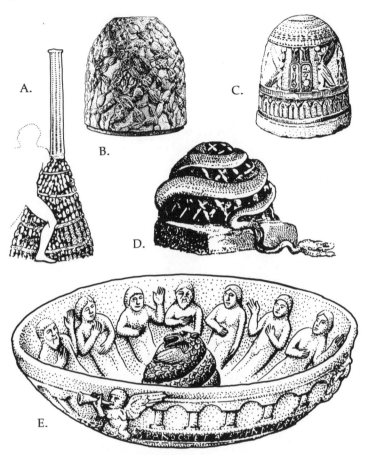

Figure 39. The *omphalos* or navel of the world at Delphi took many
forms, from the world pillar atop the net-covered mound, c. 340 B.C.
(A), to the late Roman marble example actually found there (B). The
idea was transmitted to surrounding cultures as far away as Nubia, for
the oracle of Ammon at Gebel Barkal, c. A.D. 1 (C). Though Apollo had
slain the Python, the serpent remained a powerful element of this image,
as seen in the Pompeian mural, c. A.D. 100 (D). This alabaster Orphic
bowl shows the god Phanes (cf. fig. 54, p. 404) as a winged serpent
coiled around the World Egg. The praying figures encircling it are
witnessing the miracle of creation (E). Whatever the form, the powerful
idea of a tangible sacred center to the cosmos always fascinated the
ancient world.

as the Apsu — and Anu, Enlil, and Ea (the great trinity) then occupy their dwellings.[48]

The Anunnaki, the spirit children who come down to earth, built the great temple of Esagil, a replica of the great abyss, the temple at the Apsu. They represented it by the *ziggurat*, which is over the Apsu.[49]

Now Enlil, Ea, and Marduk founded his dwelling, his house. After that, the Anunnaki traced for themselves their sanctuaries upon the earth at Esagil, the great temple, which is the vault of the Apsu — the dome — at which point they would come together and unite themselves. There they received their orders from the gods.[50]

This is the Babylonian hymn of the creation. The king of Babylon had to disappear each year, in order to show that he could overcome death. He would disappear in an underground vault, where he would be humiliated. A priest would slap his face until the tears ran down; he would be clothed in a mock robe and crowned with a crown of weeds. A reed would be put in his hand. Then the lord of misrule, the false king, took his place for three days.[51]

At the end of three days, the king emerged from the tomb triumphant to show that he had overcome death and to rule for a new year. As he came forth, a great hymn, the *Enuma Elish,* was intoned by all the people. In other words, they were repeating what had happened elsewhere, before — the pattern on which this particular earth was founded: "This is Babylon, the place upon this earth where you shall dwell."[52] (The same thing happened at the beginning of Egypt, much earlier.) The *Enuma Elish* was written about 1700 B.C., though the rites were much earlier.[53]

"Come here and rejoice in this play, and celebrate his festival."[54] That sounds exactly like Deuteronomy. "They served the Zarbabu and inaugurated the festival. In the *Esagil* . . . all the laws were fixed, and all the destinies were determined."[55] The king would go up to the top of the ziggurat (of seven levels), to a round table which represented four possibilities (fig. 40).

He would cast the dice, which bore 36 possibilities, to find out what would happen each day of the year—to determine the destinies of the year, according to which quarter of the table the dice landed on.

> The stations of the heavens and the earth were fixed at this place. [All time and space shall meet here.] The laws were fixed here. [Everything is determined here.] And his fathers exalted the work which he had done [and celebrated God].[56]

> Let the son be exalted, . . . may his power be almighty, may he impose his yoke upon his enemies. Let him exercise his pastorate upon the black heads [which is what they called themselves: the true people]. Let them come to this place under his protection throughout the years. Let them repeat these rituals without ever forgetting any of his exploits [or any of his great deeds for them].[57]

These deeds were repeated in Rome—*non rite non recte minus solemniter*. In the Roman year rites, if there was anything—*non rite non recte parum solemnitatis,* i.e., that had not been done correctly, or without sufficient solemnity, the whole seven-day festival had to be run over again. It could be done as many as seven times over. Remarkably, you find the same pattern pervasively, and it's very old.

"And let them here burn incense and receive guarantee of nourishment for the year."[58] The Arabic *mathal* could be translated as "a likeness" in the heavens of that which is done on the earth. What interests me now is how old this stuff is.

I spent eight months in 1943 and 1944 preparing for the invasion of Europe, at Grenham Lodge, not far from Avebury, near Marlborough, on the plains of England. This is one of the oldest (2600 B.C.) and largest monuments of

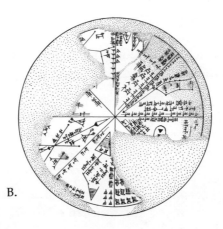

Figure 40. The ziggurat is the mountain of God throughout Mesopo-tamia. This is Parrot's reconstruction of the seven-tiered Tower of Bab-ylon, called E-temen-an-ki, "House of the Foundation of Heaven and Earth" (A). Now almost completely obliterated, it originally was de-signed to fit within a 300-foot cube. The circle of the heavens is shown on this clay planisphere inscribed with stars (B).

Europe, 500 years older than Stonehenge. It's enormous.
Much excavating has been done there. On days off, I had
a chance to inspect it, and I was electrified by it. I had a
lot of guesses about what had happened there. Silbury Hill
(Wiltshire), an artificial mound, was set up there in the
place of the assembly, for the mountain of the law (fig.
41).

Excavations have revealed that originally it was a sevenfold tower, like the towers in Babylon, or like the original
pyramids (step pyramids) of Egypt, rising in seven stages.[59]
The author of *Prehistoric Avebury*, Burl, is a very conserv-
ative scholar. He abhors anything sensational. So his conclusions are very interesting. At this same time "in other
parts of the British Isles people were already putting up
great stone circles for ceremonies. At Stennes in the Ork-
neys [in Scotland halfway to the North Pole] twelve stee-
pling columns stood in a ring"[60] — as Jacob did in Israel,
whenever he made a covenant (Genesis 31:45–46).

> Twelve steepling columns stood in a ring. . . . In
> Ireland the chambered round cairn of New Grange with
> its quartz walls with a passage aligned towards the mid-
> winter sunrise was placed inside a circle of over thirty
> massive blocks of stone. In the Lake District, source of
> many stone axes, people were going to splendid stone
> circles with names that peal like a prehistoric role of
> honour: Long Meg and Her Daughters, the Carles at
> Castlerigg, Sunken Kirk, the Grey Horses. Rites inside
> these sacred rings differed but in every region where
> there was a fair-sized population circular enclosures
> were the foci [notice the focus, the center points] of
> ceremonies, megalithic rings in the north and west,
> henges of earth or chalk in the stoneless areas of lowland
> Britain.[61]

That is how they differed in form, but they always have
the ring, and they always do the same thing when they
come together. It is vastly older than the pyramids, is

beautifully done, and contains magnificent things. These did not necessarily originate from the Near East, as once was thought. Ideas worked both ways.

The point is that our ancestors were doing all this far back in time. The Beaker people didn't come until 2100 B.C. They were the ones that built Stonehenge, though they hooked into the existing traditions while bringing their own. In the earliest times, everybody seemed to be doing the same sort of thing, building the same kinds of structures.

Burl is very fond of comparing these things with the "Hopewell Indians of the Ohio," a good three thousand years after (fig. 42). Why should this be, he asks, that they should be doing the same thing?[62]

"Avebury became almost a metropolitan centre to which people came from miles around to trade and to settle disputes, to worship in the marvelous stone rings that expressed the barbaric pride of the natives."[63] And the remains are not a few. There are piles of stuff to show what was going on at these places. They were all doing the same sort of thing.

More to the point:

> Death and regeneration are the themes of Avebury. The presence of human bones, the pieces of stone, the red ochre, the pockets of fertile earth, the antlers, the shapes of the sarsens, the architecture of the avenues and circles, all are consistent with the belief that Avebury was intended as a temple in which, at various times of the year, the large population could gather to watch and take part in ceremonies of magic and evocation that would safeguard their lives.[64]

Less than a year ago I received a report from the University of Chicago, in cooperation with a university in Spain, of an excavation of the most ancient of these foundations in the world, very accurately dated to about 13,920 B.C., give or take two hundred years.[65] Fourteen thousand

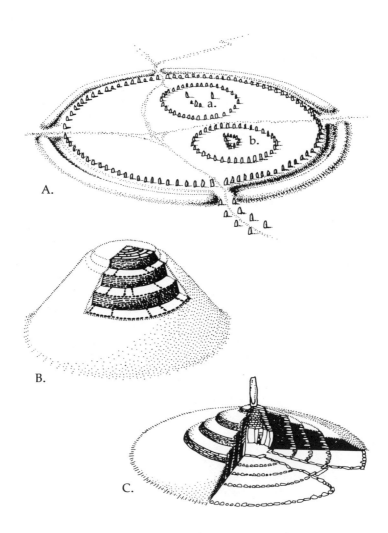

Figure 41. The gigantic size of Avebury (A) awes the modern visitor
with its northern (a) and southern (b) circles. Silbury Hill (B), a mile
away, is the largest man-made mound in Europe. Its symmetrical cone
conceals multiple sloping tiers. An early megalithic beehive tomb in
Brittany shows a similar tier arrangement (C). In Egypt, the Old Kingdom temple-tomb of Osiris at Medamud was an oval mound enclosing

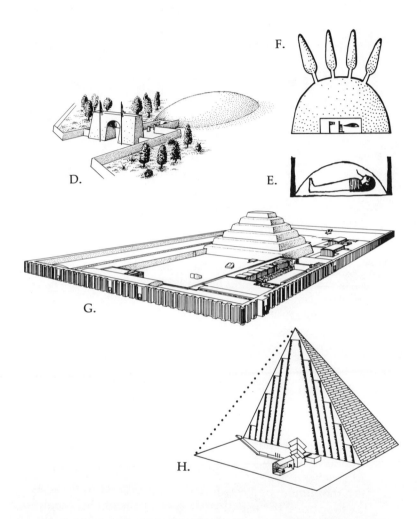

a sacred chamber (D). The idea was preserved in the hieroglyph for the tomb of Osiris (E) and in this Late Period sarcophagus drawing showing the mound with trees growing on it (F). Imhotep, architect to Pharaoh Djoser, created the earliest cut-stone monument in the world when he built the Step Pyramid at Saqqara, c. 2630 B.C. (G). Even the later smooth-sided pyramid of Unas (H), with the famous Pyramid Texts inscribed on its tomb walls, shows the same stepped design within its structure.

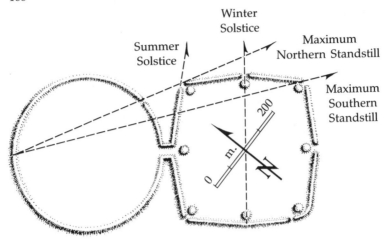

Figure 42. The Hopewell culture of the Ohio river valleys, c. A.D. 1–500, erected elegant earthwork constructions that continue to intrigue scholars. The giant circle and square at the High Bank Works, c. A.D. 400, show various solar and lunar alignments.

years ago is a long time; Avebury is only 2600 B.C. And would you believe it, excavators are finding the same stuff—the same combination of stuff way back then? You can't get away from it. Primitive man was really up to something; he had a definite idea behind what he was doing.

Gordon Childe [the great Scottish prehistorian] thought of Avebury as a cathedral, Stuart Piggot as an open sanctuary associated with a sky-god, Isobel Smith as a monument dedicated to a fertility cult whose practices included the use of stone discs, balls of chalk and human bones. Jacquetta Hawkes wrote of fertility rites involving the earth and the sun although "what those mysteries were we shall never know." However generalised these observations there is agreement about a religious centre for fertility cults linked with the earth, the sun [the heavenly bodies in their motions], ritual objects and dead bones [i.e., with the ancestors, and scholars all agree on that]. Not many years ago Patrick Crampton went further, suggesting that Avebury was not only a temple of the powerful Earth Goddess but also a "city," the first "capital—religious, cultural, commercial—of most of southern Britain."[66]

So these concepts are very old. I myself was enormously impressed by the size of the stones, weighing sixty tons, set in a great circle 350 yards across. It was an amazing accomplishment that they dragged them to the site. It required great work, concentration, and leadership. Burl says the population of all Western Europe couldn't have been more than forty-eight thousand people at the time. But there must have been many more than that.[67]

The enormous ditch around the stones is thirty feet deep, dug out by use of only deer horns.[68] For ritual reasons, they could not use anything else.

I used to fly over the area frequently. You could see radiating from the site great table stones, and the great prehistoric roads that led to the site, from hundreds of miles to the north. From everywhere, people came to Avebury, nearly five thousand years ago, to celebrate the very thing we do in our temples today—the continuity of life.

We do have from this same time the actual full pyramid texts, from the tomb of Unas, who ended his rule in 2524 B.C. The Egyptians did the same things when they met at the sacred points. The reading begins with the council in heaven, followed by a dramatization; from that to the creation of the world and the coming of man; then to the fall and the redemption—all accompanied by ordinances. At that time, only the king received them, but very soon after, the nobility also did, and eventually all the people. They received their washings and anointings, their names, and the whole initiation. As the end of the Shabako Stone says, "to become glorified, a king for eternal exaltation."[69] All were supposed to do that.

The temple as the center of the universe may be a myth,

but it is the most powerful myth that ever possessed the human race. Mircea Eliade has written a book on that topic, *Cosmos and History: The Myth of Eternal Return,* in which he deplores the fact that contemporary man has completely cut that tradition off. He says,

> The chief difference between the man of the archaic and traditional societies and the man of modern societies [with reference to the place he assumes in the cosmos] with their strong imprint of Judaeo-Christianity lies in the fact that the former feels himself indissolutely connected with the Cosmos and the cosmic rhythms, whereas the latter insists that he is connected only with History.[70]

We now live in a technological world; let us not worry about other problems. Technology will solve all those. The other stuff is outdated. But for thousands and thousands of years, our ancestors went through those things. So let us think about it all for five minutes.

Notes

1. William Butler Yeats, "Second Coming," stanza 1, lines 14–16; in Joseph Hone, *W. B. Yeats* (New York: Macmillan, 1943), 351.

2. James E. Talmage, *The House of the Lord* (Salt Lake City: Deseret Book, 1912), 178.

3. Giorgio de Santillana and Hertha von Dechend, *Hamlet's Mill* (Boston: Gambit, 1969), 383–86, 306–7.

4. Cf. Hugh W. Nibley, "Tenting, Toll, and Taxing," *WPQ* 19 (1966): 602; reprinted in *CWHN* 10:35; 74, n. 15.

5. Cf. Werner Müller, *Die heilige Stadt: Roma quadrata, himmlisches Jerusalem und die Mythe vom Weltnabel* (Stuttgart: Kohlhammer, 1961); and Werner Müller, *Kreis und Kreuz: Untersuchungen zur sakralen Siedlung bei Italikern und Germanen* (Berlin: Widukind, 1938).

6. Charlton T. Lewis, *A Latin Dictionary* (Oxford: Clarendon, 1969), 1831.

7. Mircea Eliade, *Cosmos and History: The Myth of Eternal Return* (New York: Princeton University Press, 1974), 12.

8. Cf. Nibley, "Tenting, Toll, and Taxing," 603–4; in *CWHN* 10:41; 76, nn. 25–26.

9. Hugh W. Nibley, "The Hierocentric State," *WPQ* 4 (1951): 226–53; reprinted in *CWHN* 10:99–147.

10. Mircea Eliade, *Le Chamanisme et les techniques archaïques de l'extase* (Paris: Librairie Payot, 1951); for translation, see Willard R. Trask, tr., *Shamanism: Archaic Techniques of Ecstacy* (New York: Pantheon, 1964).

11. Cf. Nibley, "Tenting, Toll, and Taxing," 604; in *CWHN* 10:41; 76–77, nn. 27–29.

12. Eliade, *Le Chamanisme et les techniques archaïques de l'extase;* for translation, see Trask, tr., *Shamanism: Archaic Techniques of Ecstacy,* 260–61.

13. Nibley, "Hierocentric State," 226–53; in *CWHN* 10:99–147. Cf. Eric Uphill, "Egyptian Sed-Festival Rites," *Journal of Near Eastern Studies* 24 (1965): 365–83.

14. *1 Jeu* 39, in Carl Schmidt, ed., *The Books of Jeu and the Untitled Text in the Bruce Codex,* tr. Violet MacDermot (Leiden: Brill, 1978), 88, lines 13–22.

15. *Second Gnostic Work* 2a-3s, 18a; see *Untitled Text* 1–3, in Schmidt, *Books of Jeu and the Untitled Text,* 226–30; cf. Hugh W. Nibley, "Treasures in the Heavens: Some Early Christian Insights into the Organizing of Worlds" *DJMT* 8 (Autumn/Winter 1973): 83; reprinted in *CWHN* 1:184.

16. *Pistis Sophia* I, 58, in Carl Schmidt, ed., *Pistis Sophia* (Leiden: Brill, 1978), 112, lines 4–25.

17. *Untitled Text* 2, in Schmidt, *Books of Jeu and the Untitled Text,* 227.

18. Cf. Lewis, *Latin Dictionary,* 792.

19. De Santillana and von Dechend, *Hamlet's Mill,* 383; see the discussion on Amritamanthana.

20. *The Vision of Kenaz,* which appears in M. R. James, *Apocrypha Anecdota, Texts and Studies,* ed. J. A. Robinson, 10 vols. (Cambridge: Cambridge University Press, 1893), 2:3:179; cf. *OTP* 2:342.

21. James, *Apocrypha Anecdota Texts and Studies,* 174–77; cf. Hugh W. Nibley, *Since Cumorah* (Salt Lake City: Deseret Book, 1967), 322–27; reprinted in *CWHN* 7:286–90; cf. *OTP* 2:341–42.

22. *Pistis Sophia* I, 55, in Schmidt, *Pistis Sophia,* 107.

23. Text 146:14–16, in Alexander Böhlig and Pahor Labib, *Die koptisch-gnostische Schrift ohne Titel aus Codex II von Nag Hammadi* (Berlin: Akademie-Verlag, 1962), 39; cf. *On the Origin of the World* II, 98, 14–15, in *NHLE,* 162.

24. Ethel S. Drower, *The Thousand and Twelve Questions* (Berlin: Akademie, 1960), 99–100.

25. Carl Schmidt, *Gnostische Schriften in koptischer Sprache aus dem Codex Brucianus,* in *Texte und Untersuchungen* 8/1–2 (Leipzig: Hinrichs, 1892), 331.

26. *Pistis Sophia* I, 25, in Schmidt, *Pistis Sophia,* 34–35.

27. *Sophia Christi* 104:4–6; 119:1.

28. *Untitled Text* 19–20, in Schmidt, *Books of Jeu and the Untitled Text,* 261–63.

29. Mark Lidzbarski, *Das Johannesbuch der Mandäer* (Giessen: Töpelmann 1915), 60, n. 6; cf. *CWHN* 1:209, n. 98.

30. Nibley, "Hierocentric State," 226–53; in *CWHN* 10:99–147.

31. Ibid., 226; in *CWHN* 10:99.

32. Ibid.

33. Ibid.

34. Ibid., 226; in *CWHN* 10:99–100.

35. Ibid., 226; in *CWHN* 10:100.

36. Ibid.

37. Ibid.

38. Hugh W. Nibley, "The Arrow, the Hunter, and the State," *WPQ* 2/3 (September 1949): 330–31; reprinted in *CWHN* 10:4–5.

39. Cf. fig. 15 in *CWHN* 10:159.

40. Nibley, "Hierocentric State," 226–27; in *CWHN* 10:99–101.

41. Eric Burrows, "Some Cosmological Patterns in Babylonian Religion," *The Labyrinth,* ed. Samuel H. Hooke (London: SPCK, 1935), 46–48; Nibley, "Hierocentric State," 226–27; in *CWHN* 10:99–101.

42. *Enuma Elish* I, 1.

43. *Enuma Elish* IV, 133–40.

44. *Enuma Elish* V, 146–55.

45. *Enuma Elish* IV, 138–46.

46. *Enuma Elish* IV, 138–42.

47. *Enuma Elish* IV, 142–44.

48. *Enuma Elish* IV, 145–46.

49. *Enuma Elish* VI, 62–64.

50. *Enuma Elish* VI, 68–70.

51. François Thureau-Dangin, *Rituals Accadiens* (Paris: Leroux, 1921).

52. *Enuma Elish* VI, 72.

53. Henri Frankfort, *Kingship and the Gods* (Chicago: University of Chicago Press, 1971), 319.

54. *Enuma Elish* VI, 77–78.

55. *Enuma Elish* VI, 77–78.

56. *Enuma Elish* VI, 85.

57. *Enuma Elish* VI, 106–9.

58. *Enuma Elish* VI, 112–13.

59. Aubrey Burl, *Prehistoric Avebury* (London: Yale University Press, 1979), 131; cf. Burrows, "Some Cosmological Patterns," 68–69.

60. Burl, *Prehistoric Avebury*, 140.

61. Ibid.

62. Ibid.

63. Ibid.

64. Ibid., 200.

65. L. G. Freeman and J. González Echegaray, "El Juyo: A 14,000-Year-Old Sanctuary from Northern Spain," *History of Religions* 21 (August 1981): 1–19.

66. Ibid., 202.

67. Ibid., 178.

68. Ibid., 175–76.

69. Cf. *Shabako Stone,* line 64, in Miriam Lichtheim, *Ancient Egyptian Literature,* 3 vols. (Berkeley: University of California Press, 1943), 1:56.

70. Eliade, *Cosmos and History,* xiii–iv; cf. de Santillana and von Dechend, *Hamlet's Mill.*

Cosmos

The Expanding Gospel

The expression "expanding gospel" is not a contradiction in terms. Even the Roman Catholic authorities concluded after much thought that the proper business of theology and philosophy is to expand men's *knowledge* of the gospel while leaving the scriptures, the sacred deposit and source of that knowledge, untouched by the addition or subtraction of so much as a syllable.[1] Thus men, by the exercise of their intellects, may add to the gospel, but God may not. But this puts the thunder before the lightning: where has God imposed any limits on his own prerogative of imparting his word to man? The scriptural warnings against adding or subtracting, aside from being limited to specific individual books, are addressed specifically to men—no *man* may add to the scriptures. That imposes no restriction on God. But it is men who have expanded and contracted the scope of the holy writ to conform to their broad or narrow views of the gospel; it is men who have selected the books that make up the word of God, and these men have not been in agreement. The debate has raged for centuries about certain well-known writings, and still remains undecided.[2]

Now we are faced by a new and important development. A sizable number of writings have recently been

This address was given as the Second Annual BYU Faculty Lecture on March 17, 1965, and appeared in Brigham Young University Studies 7 *(1965): 3–27; it was reprinted in* Truman G. Madsen, ed., Nibley on the Timely and the Timeless *(Provo: Brigham Young University Religious Studies Center, 1978), 21–47.*

discovered claiming apostolic or otherwise inspired authorship and enjoying unprecedented antiquity. What is
to be done with them? Of the author of some of the prophecies in the Dead Sea Scrolls, Father Daniélou writes:

> A revelation was made known to him . . . that the
> Messiah was near. . . . Now what is amazing is that this
> prophecy was verified exactly. Thus between the great
> prophets of the Old Testament and John the Baptist he
> emerges as a new link in the preparation for the Advent
> of Christ: he is, as Michaud writes, one of the great
> figures of Israel's prophetic tradition. It is amazing that
> he remained so unknown for so long. Now that he is
> known the question arises as to what we are going to
> do about this knowledge. . . . Why does not this mes-
> sage, then, form part of inspired Scripture?[3]

This question, says Daniélou, now confronts equally
the Jewish and the Christian world. How can they expand
their gospel to include the words of a newly found prophet?
If the new discoveries only contained exactly what was
already known and accepted, there would be no objection
to admitting them to the canon; but neither would they
have any message for us, save to confirm what is already
known. But what makes the documents so exciting is that
they follow along familiar grooves to the end and then
continue onward into new territory, expanding the confines of the gospel. Are we to assume that their writers,
so strict and upright in their ways and so conscientious in
their teachings, are saints as far as we can follow them,
only to become deluded purveyors of fraud and falsehood
the moment they step beyond territory familiar to us?

Before reaching a decision on this important head, our
first obligation is to inform ourselves as to what it is that
these writings teach over and above conventional Jewish
and Christian doctrine. What they teach, that is, seriously
and as a whole. Speculative flights and picturesque odd-
ities can be expected in any sizable apocryphal writing,

and when such are confined to one or two texts, they can be ruled out as serious doctrine. But in working through the newly found documents, one soon becomes aware of certain themes that receive overwhelming emphasis and appear not only in a few texts but in many or most of them. Such deserve our serious attention. Among the most conspicuous of these is the matter of a certain council held in heaven "at the foundation of the world" where the divine plan of salvation was presented and received with acclamations of joy; joined to this we are presented almost invariably with some account of the opposition to that plan and the results of that opposition. Around these two themes of the plan and the opposition a great deal of the old apocryphal writing revolves.

But it is in the very oldest records of the race that we find some of the clearest statements of the doctrines, which in the oldest fragment of all, actually goes under a recognized label as "the Memphite theology." The antiquity of the material contained in the so-called Shabako Stone of the British Museum has been fully demonstrated and is today not seriously questioned (fig. 43).[4] The only puzzle to scholars has been how anything so completely thought-out and sophisticated could turn up in what may well be the oldest known religious text in existence. There is nothing "primitive" in this dramatic presentation which was to mark the founding of the First Dynasty of Egypt. It is divided into two parts — historical and theological — the former explaining how the kingdom came to be established and organized after its peculiar fashion, and the latter how and why the world itself was created. The beholder of the drama, which was enacted by the priests with the king taking the leading role, is never allowed to forget that what is ritually done on earth is but the faithful reflection of what was once done in heaven.[5] Since a number of scholars today see an unbroken line of succession between the "Memphite theology" and the Logos-theology of John, the

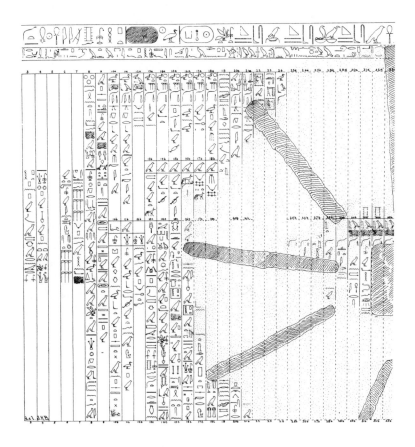

Figure 43. When the Nubian Pharaoh Shabako, c. 700 B.C., began to build his dynastic temple, his workmen found a worm-eaten scroll containing the theology of the priests of Ptah at Memphis in the form of a drama complete with stage directions. Recognizing its great importance and desiring to preserve it for all time, he had a copy carefully inscribed on this highly polished granite slab and installed deep within

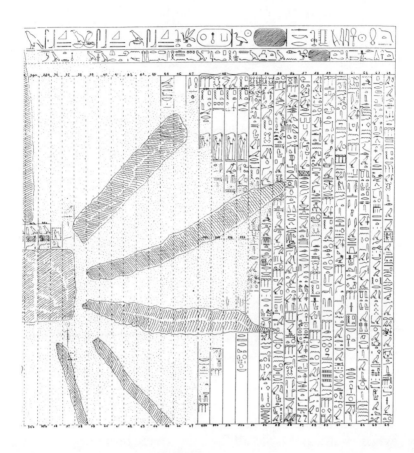

his temple. Though slightly defaced by later Seth-hating Egyptians, it was the practical Romans, unconcerned with its message, who used it as a millstone and ground out the center of the text, like using the Great Seal of England to crack nuts. It languished unrecognized in the British Museum basement until Breasted discovered its value and published this copy in 1901.

Shabako Stone may not be out of place as the starting point in a study of the expanding gospel.[6] But quite aside from that, it deserves mention as the earliest and one of the best descriptions of the council in heaven.

In the beginning, we are told, "all the gods assembled in the presence" of Geb, who "made a division between Horus and Seth, and forbade them to quarrel," giving each his assigned portion.[7] Then for some reason Geb decided that Horus should be his unique heir and solemnly announced to the assembled gods, pointing to Horus, "I have chosen thee to be the first, thee alone; my inheritance shall be to this my heir, the son of my son, . . . the first-born, opener of the ways, a son born of the birthday of Wepwawet," that is, on the New Year, the Day of Creation.[8] Thus, instead of being two portions, they were both united for the duration of the festival.[9] The middle portion of the Shabako Text is obliterated, but from countless other Egyptian sources, we know that the conflict between Horus and Seth never ceased on this earth, the combat and victory of Horus being ritually repeated at every coronation.[10] After rites dealing with a baptism, resurrection, and the building of the temple at Memphis, the text breaks off completely to resume with a catalogue of Ptah's titles such as "he who sitteth upon the great throne, Heavenly Father who begot Atum, Heavenly Mother who bore Atum, the Great One, the Mind and Mouth [heart and tongue] of the Council of the Gods [the Ennead]."[11] "In the heart [of Ptah] through whose mind and word all the spirits were brought forth."[12]

> And through whose mind and word [of God] all physical members were invested with power, according to the doctrine that He [God] is as that which is in every body [i.e., the heart] and in every mouth [i.e., the tongue] of every god, of every human, of every animal, of every creeping thing, of whatsoever possessed life; for whatever is thought and whatever is uttered is according to his will. . . . The council of the gods brought

forth the seeing of the eyes, the hearing of the ears, the breathing of the nose, that these might convey information to the heart, which in turn became aware of things, to which awareness the tongue gives expression, giving utterance to the mind. In such a way were all the gods brought forth — Atum and the council of Nine. But the word of God was first that which was conceived in his mind and then what was commanded by his tongue. In such a way were the spirits brought forth and the ḥmśwt-spirits elected, for the provision of all nourishment and food, according to the mind and word of God.[13]

The best interpretation of ḥmśwt-spirits, following Sethe's long discussion of the word, would seem to be spirits chosen for specially high callings, in particular to have progeny.[14] The spirits having been thus created and a physical basis for life supplied, a law was laid down,

that he who does what is good [lovable, desirable] shall be given life to be in a state of peace [or salvation], while he who does evil [that which is hateful] shall be given death to be in a state of punishment [or condemnation]. All the works [of men], all the arts and crafts, the labors of the arms and the goings of the legs, the motion of all the members are subject to this law, conceived in the mind and declared by the tongue [of God], which law shall be the measure [yimakh] of all things.[15]

All this was done and nourishment and food and all other good things provided by God alone and he saw that his work was good.[16] "And thus it was that all the gods and all the spirits assembled" before the throne of God, the source of all life and joy.[17] The king, representing Osiris, who is the dead king, his own predecessor, "goes through the secret gates in the splendor of the lord of Eternity, . . . in the footsteps of Re of the great throne, to enter the courts on high and become united with the gods and with Ptah, the ancient of days [lord of years]." In the concluding scene the earthly king publicly embraces his

son and heir, declaring his calling and succession, even as
the god did in the beginning.[18]

That the picture actually goes back to Menes, the
founder of the First Dynasty, is confirmed right at the
beginning of the Pyramid Texts in a writing for Teti, the
second king of the dynasty and immediate successor of
Menes:

> Spoken by the great heavens in the midst of the lower
> hall of Geb [i.e., the temple of Memphis as the earthly
> counterpart of the heavenly court]. This is Teti, my be-
> loved son, who sits upon the throne of Geb [the principle
> of patriarchal succession], who is well pleased with him;
> he hath declared him to be his heir in the presence of
> the great assembly of all the gods; every god hath ac-
> claimed him joyfully with upraised hands, saying, Wor-
> thy is Teti with whom his father Geb is well pleased![19]

In the Coffin Texts the theme is carried on as Ptah
summons the Great Assembly, "they who share the secrets," gives them formal greeting, and introduces his son
and heir to them, who, shouting for joy, acclaim him as
the earthly Prince of Peace and Righteousness.[20] The
earthly rites reflect the heavenly, and the king (or noble)
announces in his Coffin Text, "I am in the human assembly
what he is in heaven. I am . . . the seed of Atum, the issue
of him who gives the names in the day when Atum discussed it with the gods."[21]

The great Babylonian creation text, the *Enuma Elish*,
begins and ends with the great assembly in heaven. "As
once above," it starts out, "when the heavens had not yet
received their name and the earth below was not known, . . .
the Creator, he of vast intelligence, omniscience, omni-
potence," presided over "a great assembly among his
brethren the gods."[22] Since the purpose of this version of
the hymn is to exalt Marduk of Babylon, he takes over the
principal functions of creating man and settling the score
with the adversary. The most concise statement is on tablet

VI: "Then Marduk resolved upon a wondrous work. He opened his mouth and addressed Ea [his father], and told him of what he had conceived in his heart: 'I wish to bring blood and bone together and to organize them into a human being, whose name shall be man; let it be his duty to serve the gods and satisfy them.' "[23] To provide satisfaction, however, was beyond the power of man, and "Marduk, in order that there be satisfaction, proposed a plan to the gods: 'Let one of their race be put to death that humanity might be. Let one of the assembled gods be delivered up as a guilty one, that they might subsist.' "[24] But Kingu opposed the plan; it was he who made Tiamat rebel and caused the war. But he was defeated and cast down by Marduk, and the great assembly gave all the power of heaven and earth to Anu and through him to Marduk for carrying out the execution of the plan.[25] Throughout, the earthly rites are a ritual repetition of what was done (in the opening words and title of the hymn) "Once above" (*enuma elish*); and the affair ends with the admonition that the rites be repeated at the same place from year to year forever:

> Let them rehearse throughout the ages to come at this spot what God has done, that they may never forget it. . . . For this is the earthly image of that which is done in the heavens. . . . Great planner, full of loving-kindness, may he forgive their sins and deliver them by his grace. . . . Let us praise his name. They who have taken their places in the assembly to declare his name, in the holy place let them all together proclaim his name.[26]

Though the texts are full of repetitions, contamination, overlapping of different versions coming from different times and places, the main themes of the council and the plan recur consistently.[27]

We know today that the religion of Israel cannot be studied in isolation from that of its neighbors, and for many years the experts have recognized affinities between the documents just cited and certain biblical texts. We have referred to them here, however, primarily to forestall the claim commonly made that the doctrines we are considering are of late, even Gnostic origin. The newly discovered Jewish and Christian apocrypha have so much to say about the council in heaven and the plan laid down at the foundation of the world that every student should be aware of the very great antiquity and wide ramifications of the idea. According to Ben Sira, the great assemblies of Israel were the ritual repetition not merely of the gathering at the foot of Sinai but specifically of the great assembly at the creation of the world, when "God set before them [the human race-to-be] a covenant, the Law of Life . . . and showed them his judgments. Their eyes beheld his glorious majesty and their ears heard his voice."[28] According to 2 Baruch the whole plan of the history of the world was set forth in detail "when the Mighty One took counsel to create the world."[29] According to the book of Enoch, in the beginning "the Head of Days, his head like white wool, sat with the Son of Man beside him upon the throne of His glory, and the books of the living were opened before Him," the books of the living being the register of names of those who were to live upon the earth.[30] Then the calling or mission of the Son and the plan, both of which had been kept secret until then, were "revealed to the Elect."[31] It is not too much to say that the dominant theme of the Thanksgiving Hymns of the Dead Sea Scrolls is an ecstatic contemplation of the wonder of man's participation in heavenly affairs going back to the beginning. Consider a few lines from Hymn 6 (or F):

> Thou hast caused me to mount up to an eternal height and to walk in an inconceivable exaltation. And I know that there is a hope for everyone whom thou didst form of dust in the presence of the eternal assembly; and that the sinful spirit whom thou hast purified of great sin may be counted with the host of the saints

and enter the society of the congregation of the Sons of
Heaven. Thou didst appoint unto man an eternal share
with the Spirits that Know, they praise thy name in joyful
unison with them and to recount thy wondrous works
in the presence thereof.[32]

The whole point of this is that man actually belongs
by prior appointment to that community of the Elect who
share in the knowledge of the plan and who shouted for
joy at the foundation of the world. In the preceding hymn,
God is hailed as "Prince of the Gods and King of the
Venerable Ones": and we must remind ourselves that this
is neither a Gnostic nor a pagan production.[33] The baffling
tenth and eleventh pages of the *Manual of Discipline* come
to life in light of this imagery. To refer their message to
prayers at various times of day makes good sense, since,
as we have noted, earthly rites are but the reflection of
heavenly events; but if we leave it there much is left unexplained. "He has placed them as an eternal treasure, and
established for them a share with the saints, and has joined
their society to the family of the sons of Heaven, the council
of the Church, and the assembly of the Temple, an establishment [literally, 'planting'] which reaches forever into
the future and the past."[34] The word that we have translated as "share" above is usually rendered as "lot" (it occurs seventy-six times in the Old Testament), but it is not
the gift of chance, but is rather one's "lot" in the sense of
having been appointed by God ahead of time. If we turn
back to the opening lines of the preceding section of the
hymn (plate X), we may see in the prayers at dawn a
conscious counterpart of the celestial drama: we are told
of God's blessing "at the times which he fixed at the beginning of the rule of light, along with his cycles, and in
the assembly at the place appointed by him, when the
Watchers of Darkness also began." The Watchers, as is
well known, were fallen angels, here the equivalent of
those who first opposed the Rule of Light. At that time,

the text continues, God "opens his treasury and shows his plan." The treasury is referred to many times in the apocrypha, especially in the *Hodayot Scroll,* as that knowledge which was with God in the beginning, and which he imparted to his Elect.[35] The last word of the phrase is in code — a plain indication that the text does indeed have a double meaning, as it goes on to tell us in terms of lamps in a shrine, of the shining ones being received in the mansion of glory. We are even told that the great light of the Holy of Holies here actually signifies something else.[36]

This interpretation is borne out at the beginning of the *Clementine Recognitions,* a work having close affinities to the Dead Sea Scrolls, in which Peter tells of "the plan [*definitio*] of God which he announced [*promisit*] as his own will and desire in the presence of the First Angels, and which he established as an eternal law for all."[37] This is from a very early and strongly anti-Gnostic work, but the Gnostics have preserved the teaching and given it a characteristic Gnostic twist: "My Father, the joyful glorious light," says the *Psalm of Thomas,* "summoned all the Aeons of Peace [the First Angels have here become mere abstractions], . . . all his sons and all the angels, [and] . . . established them that they might rejoice in his greatness [i.e., share it]."[38] "All bowed the knee before him and . . . sang his praises together, . . . hailing him as the Illuminator of the Worlds."[39] The newly discovered *Creation Apocryphon,* another "Gnostic" interpretation, tells us that this earth is the result of a discussion in heaven: "On that day began the discussion in which gods, angels, and men participated. And the decisions of the discussion were then carried out by gods, angels, and men. But the Prince Jaldabaoth did not understand the power of faith," and so was denied "the authority over matter" which the others shared.[40] The power of faith, it will be recalled, was the power "by which the worlds were created" (cf. Hebrews 11:3).

THE EXPANDING GOSPEL 189

The unimpeachably orthodox Pastor of Hermas is quite as specific: "Behold God, constructing the world in accordance with the great council [in some manuscripts, 'the most honored council'], . . . creating the beautiful world and turning it over to his chosen ones, that he might carry out his promise to them, which he gave in the midst of great glory and rejoicing, that is, if they keep his laws (*legitima*) which they accepted in great faith."[41] The Mandaean version is interesting because it calls the Creator Ptah-il, combining the archaic Egyptian and Semitic names,[42] and, while giving the familiar account of the great council, adds the important detail that three messengers were sent down to supervise the world and to instruct Adam, these three being glorious angels who were later to live upon the earth as ordinary mortals and prophets.[43]

So far we have only mentioned the bare fact of an assembly in the presence of God at the foundation of the world, but even so it has not been possible to do so without giving some indication of what the business of the meeting was, namely, the agreement upon the great *plan* which is to be "the measure of all things" for those who live upon the earth. Recently J. Fichtner has pointed out that the preoccupation with "Yahweh's *plan*" is the very core and center of Isaiah's thinking, and scholars are now noting that the presence of a heavenly council from the beginning has been part and parcel of Jewish thought from the earliest times.[44] In fact, it was concentration on God's preexistent plan, Seligmann avers, which freed the Jews from the danger of falling into the "naturalistic fatalism" that engulfed the religions of their neighbors. Before the creation, according to 4 *Ezra*, "even then I [God] had these things in mind . . . as also the end";[45] and at the Creation itself "when the Most High made the world, and Adam, . . . he first [of all] prepared the Judgment, and the things that pertain unto the Judgment."[46] Where there is a purpose there is a plan; where there is neither, there is only chaos and change, leading to the "naturalistic fatalism" of the pagans and the philosophers. God knew, Enoch tells us, "before the world was created what is forever and what will be from generation to generation."[47] Or, in the words of Ben Sira,

> When God created His works from the beginning, after making them he assigned them their portions. He set in order his works for all time, and their authority unto their generations; . . . and after this God filled the earth with good things, . . . and then finally created man, . . . and gave him a fixed number of days, and gave him authority over all the earth.[48]

When the plan is discussed, we usually hear of a definite time schedule as part of it, with set ages, dispensations, and ends carefully worked out and determined ahead of time, along with a definite and fixed number of spirits appointed to go to the earth in each of those dispensations. The so-called *Manual of Discipline* has a positive obsession with times and periods as part of God's plan: "From God is the knowledge of all that is and all that will be; and before they existed he established their whole plan [*maḥăšebtām*], and when they exist [upon the earth] he prescribes the conditions of their existence according to his glorious plan."[49] Since God created man "according to his own plan [or purpose]," says a *Thanksgiving Hymn*, "before thou didst create them, thou didst know all their doings from eternity to eternity."[50] This writer often reminds us that man was allowed to share in the plan: "In the wisdom of thy knowledge thou didst establish their knowledge before they existed . . . and without thy knowing nothing was done."[51] The *War Scroll* reminds us that both blessing and cursing are but the faithful working out of God's plan, that a definite day "has been appointed for the overthrow and humbling of the rule of Wickedness," and that the saints should never despair in their time of probation "until

God gives the sign that he has completed his test."[52] The Zadokite documents teach that the wicked on this earth were those who were not chosen and called up in the preexistence; thus Rabin translated a key passage on the subject:

> For God has not chosen them "from of old, ⟨from the days of⟩ eternity," and before they were established He knew their works and abhorred the generations [when they arose], and He hid His face from the land from [their arising] (or: and from Israel) until their being consumed. And He knows (or: knew) the years of their existence and the number (or: set times) and exact epochs of all them that come into being in eternity (or: in the worlds) [and past events], even unto that which will befall in the epochs of all the years of eternity (or: the world). And in all of them He raised for Himself "men called by name," in order "[to leave] a remnant" for the land and to fill the face of the universe of their seed, and to make (or: and He made) known to them by the hand of His anointed ones His holy spirit and shew *them* (or: [demonstration of]) truth. And with exactitude He [set out] their names; but those whom He hated He caused to stray.[53]

Rabin has taken liberties with the next-to-last sentence which, as many have pointed out, states as clearly as possible that God has made known the truth to chosen spirits, called up in the premortal existence, through the Holy Ghost, bestowed "by the hand of His Messiah."[54]

Almost always when the plan is mentioned something is said about its glad reception, "when the morning stars sang together, and all the sons of God shouted for joy" (Job 38:7). The great year-rites, common to all ancient societies, are a rehearsal of the Creation, usually presented in dramatic form; invariably the rites end with a great and joyful acclamation.[55] Thus the concluding lines of the Shabako Stone, with which we began our story: "so all the

gods and all the spirits came together to hail God upon
his throne . . . and they rejoiced before him in his temple,
the source of all good things."[56] And the Mesopotamian
Enuma Elish ends with an exhortation to all men to "come
to this place and rejoice and celebrate the festival," hailing
God for his wonderful deeds and his loving kindness, even
as was done "once above" [Akkadian: *enuma elish*].[57] In the
rites of the *aśvemedha*, the king is joyfully hailed at the
Creation as a reminder that the question put to Job, "Where
wast thou when I laid the foundations of the earth, when
the morning stars sang together and all the sons of God
shouted for joy?" was not a rhetorical question at all, for
Job is expected to give the right answer — "answer for thou
knowest!" This is confirmed in the *Testament of Job,* where
that prophet says, "the Lord spake with me in power, and
showed me the past and future."[58] The same writing recommends study of the hymns of Job's daughter, designating them as inspired poems. The word *poema,* meaning
literally creation, owes its prominence, as Walter Otto has
shown, to the circumstance that the first poets were all
inspired people who sang one and the same song, namely
the Song of Creation: that was the standard ritual hymn
at all the ancient cult centers where the Muses were housed
and the royal year-rites rehearsed and performed.[59]

The whole purpose of the book of *Jubilees* is to show
that the great rites of Israel, centering about the temple
and the throne, are a celebration "which had been observed
in heaven since the creation."[60] All who were present on
that occasion, according to *1 Enoch,* took an oath to abide
by the proposed order and then burst forth into a mighty
spontaneous shout of joy.[61] Like Job, the psalmist of the
Thanksgiving Hymns is frightfully downcast until he is reminded that "the humble bless thee, while the Sons of
Heaven jubilate in eternal glory."[62] "Thou hast placed the
lot of man eternally with the eternal spirits to shout for
joy and to tell thy wonders."[63] The thing to notice here is

that man shares fully in these heavenly jubilations; the poet is simply intoxicated with the assurance that man, a mere speck of "wet dust," is allowed not only to know about the secret councils of the beginning, but actually to share in them, not only as a participant but as one of the directors! The words *marvellous, knowledge, treasures, secrets, counsel, intelligence, understanding,* etc., occur in constant and varied association in the scrolls. "Mere man is to be raised up to join the heavenly hosts . . . and be among Those Who Know in the great choir of jubilation."[64] "Who is man that God gives him intelligence to share in such marvels and let him know his true secrets?"[65] "Thou hast given to thy children a rich portion of the knowledge of thy Truth, and to the degree of a man's knowledge will he be glorified."[66]

This equating of knowledge with glory may lie at the root of the unique Jewish reverence for things of the mind: "Endowed with intelligence, O Lord, I have known thee. . . . I have learned sure and certain things regarding thy marvellous secrets, thanks to thy Holy Spirit."[67] And "in the wisdom of thy knowledge didst thou establish their knowledge before they existed."[68] The same thoughts preoccupy the author of the *Manual of Discipline,* who also asks, "Who is man . . . that he should take place before thy face. . . . How can the clay and the potter sit together; or who understands thy wonderful plan of God?"[69] The *War Scroll* supplies the answer: "For eternal glory he has chosen me, and for that he teaches me."[70] The Way of Light itself is "the spirit of the understanding of all the Plan. . . . Without thee nothing came into existence — and he instructed me in all knowledge."[71] Even the *War Scroll* recurs to the theme: "Thou hast engraven them," speaking of the elect of Israel, "on the Tablets of Life for Kingship . . . in all the promised ages of the eternities."[72] Hence if it should happen that the hosts of Israel are defeated in battle, one seeks the explanation where Job found it, in

the economy of heaven; the ultimate victory of the earthly
hosts is assured by their close cooperation with the heavenly hosts, of which they are but a local extension:

> He hath magnified the authority of Michael through
> eternal light, . . . so as to raise amongst the angels the
> authority of Michael and the dominion of Israel amongst
> all flesh. And righteousness shall flourish in heaven
> while all those who embrace God's truth [on earth], shall
> have joy in the knowledge of eternal things. So, Sons
> of the Covenant of God, be ye strong in God's crucible,
> until He shall lift up His hand and shall complete His
> testings [through] His mysteries with regard to your
> existence.[73]

This was the answer that Job received.

The oft-recurring statement that nothing exists whatever except in the will and plan of God has led scholars
to see a connection not only of the Dead Sea Scrolls but
of the Shabako Stone itself with the Gospel of John.[74] One
scholar's suggestion, that the *logos* may sometimes be
translated "council," deserves closer consideration.[75] If applied to the beginning verses of the Gospel of John, the
passage would read: "In the beginning was the logos
[council, discussion] and the logos was in the presence of
God, and God *was* the logos. This was in the beginning in
his presence. Everything was done [determined] by it, and
without it not a single thing was created" (cf. John 1:1–3).
Recently N. A. Dahl has shown that the early Christian
conceived of salvation "as a counterpart to the beginnings
of the world. . . . As a divine act of creation, conforming
to the creation of the world, eschatology and creation can
be linked up with one another even in this way."[76] Eschatology, that is, cannot be understood without protology
(Dahl uses the word), or an understanding of what took
place in the beginning before the foundation of the world.
The words of the early Christian Barnabas might have been
taken right out of the Dead Sea Scrolls: "Praise the Lord

who put wisdom and intelligence (*nous*) in us for the understanding of his secrets. . . . Who understands the Plan
(*parabolen*: project) of the Lord save the wise one who
knows and loves his Lord?"[77] We have seen in the Pastor
of Hermas that God's plan was "promised in the midst of
great glory and rejoicing."[78] The theme is as conspicuous
in the earliest Christian writings as in the Jewish, but after
the fourth century the Doctors of both religions rejected it
completely.[79]

The early Christian apocrypha are especially concerned
with the *opposition* to the plan, which was also initiated at
the foundation of the world. The combat between the powers of light and darkness enjoys a very conspicuous place
in ritual, being one of the essential episodes of the world-
wide creation drama of ancient times.[80] In the scroll entitled
The War between the Sons of Light and the Sons of Darkness,
we have ample illustration of the ritual and doctrinal concern of the Jews for this motif, and the quotation just cited
from that work shows that the embattled hosts on earth
were but a local version of the war in heaven.[81] Satan, who
opposed the plan, led a rebellion and was cast out of
heaven with his followers, to become an unwilling agent
in the carrying out of the plan upon the earth. The name
Mephistopheles, "der stets das Böse will, und stets das
Gute schafft," denotes the ultimate frustration of the Evil
One, who with the worst intent in the world, can only
contribute to the exaltation of man by providing the opposition necessary for testing him in the time of probation
upon the earth.[82] In the early Christian apocrypha, Satan's
rebellion in heaven begins not with a refusal to worship
God, but with his refusal to bow down to *Adam*. "I have
no need to worship Adam," he says in one early writing,
"I will not worship an inferior and younger being. I am
his senior in the Creation; before he was made I was already
made. It is rather his duty to worship me! When the angels
who were under me heard this, they refused to worship

him also," and so the revolt was on.[83] "Now, the Prince,"
says the recently discovered *Papyrus Bodmer X,* "not being
righteous wanted to be God"; he had his own counterplan
to propose, and the apostates of the Church "actually accept the plan of the serpent whenever they reject God's
plan."[84] The two plans represent the two ways that confront us in life, the devil himself having a definite mission
on earth. "If I am a fisherman of men," says the Lord in
the *Gospel of the Twelve Apostles* (a writing which Origen
says is older than the Gospel of Luke),[85] "the Devil is also
a fisherman, who catches many in his nets. . . . If I have
come to take for my kingdom those who are mine, why
should not he do the same?"[86] The Evil One, upon meeting
Adam out in the dreary world after the Fall, cries out:

> O Adam, I was cast forth from my glory because of
> thee, and behold I have caused thee to be expelled from
> paradise . . . because thou didst cause me to become a
> stranger to my home in heaven. Know thou that I shall
> never cease to contend against thee and all those who
> shall come after thee . . . until I have taken them all
> down into Amente with me![87]

The contrast and choice between the Way of Light and
the Way of Darkness is made possible by Satan's presence
upon the earth. "Horus has two heads," says the famous
seventeenth chapter of the *Book of the Dead,* "the one is
truth, the other is sin; . . . he gives truth to whoever brings
truth to him, and sin he gives to whoever sins."[88] The
concept of this world as a double sphere of light and darkness, good and evil, war and peace, meets us in the earliest
meaningful human documents, the prehistoric palette,
seals, "standards," reliefs on temples, and designs on clay
vessels. On these we find in dramatic opposition to the
happy and orderly banquet scenes, rural charm and religious processions opposing scenes of conflict, rapine, and
military aggression.[89] The contrast is shown on the shield

of Achilles in the eighteenth book of the *Iliad*,[90] and Hesiod
in the eighth century B.C. reminds his wayward brother
that two ways are always open to man: "O Perses, the
better road of the two is that of Righteousness," the hard
and narrow one.[91] Evil upon the earth is not a dreadful
mistake, as St. Augustine thought,[92] for, as the *Zohar* says,
"if God had not given men a double inclination to both
good and bad, he would have been incapable either of
virtue or of vice; but as it is he is endowed with a capacity
for both."[93] "All things have their opposites," says the old
and mysterious *Sefer Yetzira*, "good and evil." It is "the
good" which "marks out the evil," and vice versa.[94] Hence
in this world "we may live either by the Law of the Lord
or the Law of Belial," according to the *Testament of Naphthali*,[95] and though the *Testament of Abraham* announces the
alarming news that for "seven thousand that walk on the
road of perdition, there is hardly one soul that walks on
the path of righteousness . . . to find salvation."[96] The
presence of the two ways is a blessing, giving man a freedom of choice and opportunity for exaltation that makes
him "envied of the angels."[97] "Happy is the man," says
Ben Sira, "who could have fallen away and did not fall
away; who could have inflicted injury but did not do
so. . . . Poured out before thee are fire and water, stretch
forth thy hand and take thy choice. . . . Life and death are
before man, and that which he desireth shall be given
him."[98] This state of things, according to *4 Ezra*, was established when the Most High made the world and Adam,
and is "the condition of the contest which every man who
is born upon the earth must wage."[99] The *Manual of Discipline* takes up the theme with zeal: "To these two ways
all the children of men are born, and to these two divisions
they are heirs; every one of them each in his generation,
and in his time every man shares more or less in both of
them."[100] The whole human race, "all kinds of their spirits
and their natures," are put to the same test, each in his

own dispensation, "until the final appointed end-time." The real issue is never lost from sight, for Satan himself remains actively engaged:

> And all the blows that smite them, (and) all the times of their distress, are because of the dominion of *his* malevolence [Angel of darkness: *mastemah*]. And all the spirits of his lot cause the sons of light to stumble; but the God of Israel and His Angel of truth succour all the sons of light. Truly, the spirits of light and darkness were made by Him; upon these (spirits) He has founded every work, upon their [counsels] every service, and upon their ways [every visit]ation. [Him] God loves everlastingly, and delights in all his deeds forever.[101]

The main idea of "the plan which God laid down . . . in the presence of the First Angels for an eternal universal law," according to the *Clementine Recognitions,* is that "there shall be two kingdoms placed upon the earth to stay there until judgment day, . . . and when the world was prepared for man it was so devised that . . . he would be free to exercise his own will, to turn to good things if he wanted them, or if not to turn to bad things."[102] In the Dead Sea Scrolls and the earliest Christian writings this is expressly designated as "the ancient Law of Liberty."[103]

The *Didache,* one of the oldest (discovered in 1873) Christian writings known, begins with the words, "There are two roads, one of life and the other of death, and there is a great difference between the two," which difference it then proceeds to describe.[104] All the other so-called apostolic fathers are concerned with this doctrine, but one of the most striking expositions is in the newly found *Gospel of Philip,* a strongly *anti*-Gnostic work: "Light and Darkness, life and death, right and left, are brothers to one another. It is not possible to separate them from one another," in this world, that is, though in the next world where only the good is eternal this will not be so.[105] This is the doctrine of "the Wintertime of the Just," i.e., that while we are in this world men cannot really distinguish the righteous from the unrighteous, since in the wintertime all trees are bare and look equally dead, "but when the Summertime of the Just shall come, then the righteous shall bear their leaves and fruit while the dead limbs of evil trees shall be cast into the fire."[106] It is another aspect of the plan. "We believe that God organized all things in the beginning out of unformed matter," says Justin Martyr, "for the sake of the human race, that they, if they prove themselves by their works to be worthy of his plan, having been judged worthy to return to his presence [so we believe], shall reign with him, having been made immortal and incorruptible. At the creation they themselves made the choice . . . and so were deemed worthy to live with him in immortality."[107]

There are many other areas of doctrine and important rites and ordinances set forth in the newly found writings and in the longer known texts which must now be reread and reconsidered in the light of recent discoveries. In time these are bound to exert some pressure to push out the walls of conventional Christian doctrine. But before the student gets involved in them it would be well to consider one issue which forces itself on the attention of every serious student of early Christianity and Judaism. We mean the problem of literalism. Just how literal are all these things supposed to be? What we have been talking about implies a different view of reality from that of conventional Christianity; it introduces as it were a third dimension into the purely two-dimensional pictures given us by scholastic philosophy and naturalism. The great difference between the Primitive Church and conventional Christianity is that the two take different things literally.[108] The history of Christian dogma has been one long process of accommodation and deeschatologizing by which one body of belief has been completely displaced by another, eschatological reality being supplanted by sacramental piety.

The teachings with which we have been dealing in this
paper definitely imply a level of reality above that of the
allegory and symbolism of the schools of rhetoric which
became the official teachers of Christianity. The early Christian literalism was an *horrendum* to the schoolmen, but the
more we learn about the early church, the clearer it becomes that that very literalism is the distinctive stamp not
only of the Christian religion but of the Jewish as well.[109]
Today scholars are being forced into a compromise. A recent study of Christ's forty-day ministry concludes: "What
happened after our Lord's resurrection was that He moved
constantly back and forth between these two 'spaces' or
worlds — the seen and the unseen. There *is* another world
than this. It is not at some remote point in outer space. It
exists side by side with this; . . . it is the world of the spirit,
and this is the world of matter."[110] Here a rather surprising
concession to literalism is made only to be promptly withdrawn as the "other world" turns out to be only the im-
material "spirit" world after all, in spite of all the pains to
which the Lord went as he "moved continually back and
forth" between the two worlds to make perfectly clear that
he was *not* a spirit.

The earliest Christian apologist, Aristides, rejects spiritual or allegorical interpretations outright when his col-
leagues at Athens want to introduce them into their religious discussions. If religious stories are "mythical," he
insists, "they are nothing but just so many words . . . but
if they are allegorical they are simply myths and nothing
else."[111] Early Christians were not interested in myths or
allegories. The youthful Clement leaves the schools of the
philosophers in distress because they cannot answer what
he considers the important questions of life: When was the
world created? What was before that? Will a man really
continue to live after death?[112] Only Peter could answer
such questions, and Peter opens his discourse by saying,
"To begin with, we say unequivocally that there is nothing

bad about material substance."[113] This was the absolute
antithesis of the teachings of the schools; it was the Gnostic
intellectuals who first insisted on dematerializing Christian
doctrine, followed by the Neoplatonists. Between those
two the attitude of Christian theology to literalism was
given its fixed and permanent form. The *Papyrus Bodmer
X* shows how early they attacked with their basic weapons:
"They deny the resurrection, they are ashamed of the physical birth and death of the Lord."[114] The charge is repeated
by all the apostolic fathers and in all the oldest Christian
apocrypha. "Christianity," wrote Schopenhauer, "has this
peculiar disadvantage, that, unlike other religions, it is not
a pure system of doctrine: its chief and essential feature is
that it is a history, a series of events, a collection of facts."[115]

If the eschatological drama deals with real rather than
allegorical events, part of those real events took place long
ago and far away, but part of them are actually being acted
out here upon the earth. If the saints were taught to think
of themselves as outcasts in a hostile world, it just so
happened that they *were* outcasts in a hostile world; one
had only to look around to see that the pitfalls and dangers
were real and physical as well as "spiritual." The faithful
actually have found themselves more often than not holing
up in the desert places of the world—Ernst Käsemann's
"Wanderndes Gottesvolk"—and when they talked of
being gathered out of the world and taking leave of it, they
were thinking in the most factual and spatial terms.[116] Even
those learned Doctors of the church who utterly deplored
the old-fashioned literalistic ways of thinking constantly
slip back to those ways themselves, especially in times of
crisis; and the spiritual miracles, spiritual parousia, spiritual pilgrimage, spiritual temple, and spiritual Jerusalem,
etc., of the schoolmen never proved very satisfying to the
Christian mind, which displays a constant tendency to
revert to the tangible article whenever possible—even the
great Doctors prefer the dinner to the menu, when they

can get it!¹¹⁷ Today a return to literalism is part of the
expanding gospel.

But there is ambiguity here. Take for example the business of light and darkness. In the thousands of passages
contrasting the two they are most of the time quite plainly
figurative. Yet the shining garments of heavenly beings,
as of Jesus at the Transfiguration, are real; and so is the
darkness: "As every man's nature in this life is dark," says
Enoch, "so are also his conception, birth, and departure
from life."¹¹⁸ When in the Pastor of Hermas, the church is
described as a tower built above the water, we are told
that the tower is a symbol, but that the water is very real:
no one can enter the topological tower without passing
through real water.¹¹⁹ From this we see that rites and ordinances present an ambiguous situation, with some
things to be taken literally and done literally and others
figuratively. But in our ancient texts the reader is rarely
left in doubt as to which is which; it is only the Doctors
of the church, all men of the schools, who insist on min-
imizing the literal at the expense of the allegorical. Once
one comes to understand, Origen assures us, that the historical parts of the Bible are to be understood symbolically,
the historical interpretation of the whole becomes not only
expendable but actually misleading, and should be abandoned altogether!¹²⁰

The mixing of types and images with reality is of the
very essence of our life upon the earth, where we see
through a glass but darkly. In the scriptures and the Apocrypha we are told of things that are real and yet too wonderful for us even to imagine here, let alone describe; we
simply can't conceive them: "Eye hath not seen, nor ear
heard, neither have entered into the heart of man, the
things which God hath prepared" (1 Corinthians 2:9). Consequently, if these things are to be mentioned at all, it must
be in terms of types and images which are not real. Yet
the types and images are not for that reason to be despised.

A valuable commentary on this theme is supplied in the newly discovered *Gospel of Philip:* "Truth did not come into the world naked, but she came clothed in types and images. One cannot receive the truth in any other way."[121] The solid reality behind the images can only be known through *apocatastasis,* or restoration to a former state.[122] If people do not receive the ordinances here, we are told, they will not enjoy the real thing hereafter.[123] Marriage, for example, has a different form in the next world to what it has here;[124] but only by entering it *here* will one be allowed to enter it there: "If anyone does not receive it while he is in this world, he will not receive it in the other place."[125] So it is with all the ordinances: he who has not mastered "the places" here "will not be able to be master of that place."[126] "The mysteries of the truth are revealed as types and images" here, while "the veil conceals how God really governs the physical creation."[127] The rending of the veil is not the abolition but the revelation of what is behind it, "in order that we might enter into the truth of it. . . . We enter in our weakness through despised symbols,"[128] but enter we must, for who does not "receive the light" through these ordinances "will not receive it in the other place," while he who does receive it "cannot be held back, and will be beyond the reach of all his enemies even in this world. And when the time comes for him to go out of this world he has already received the truth in the images."[129]

If one makes a sketch of a mountain, what is it? A few lines on a piece of paper. But there is a solid reality behind this poor composition; even if the tattered scrap is picked up later in a street in Tokyo or a gutter in Madrid, it still attests to the artist's experience of the mountain as a reality. If the sketch should be copied by others who have never seen the original mountain, it still bears witness to its reality. So it is with the apocryphal writings: most of them are pretty poor stuff, and all of them are copies of copies. But when we compare them we cannot escape the impression that they have a real model behind them, more faithfully represented in some than in others. All we ever get on this earth, Paul reminds us, is a distorted reflection, but it is a reflection of things that really are. Since we are dealing with derivative evidence only, we are not only justified but required to listen to all the witnesses, no matter how shoddy some of them may be. For years the evidence of the Egyptians, Greeks, Babylonians, etc., has been brought into court as a powerful refutation of the Bible's claims to originality and inspiration. Their voices do indeed refute the claim of conventional Christianity to the absolute originality and exclusive inspiration of the Bible, but the Bible itself never made such claims.[130] What the outside texts prove is the antiquity and universality of the gospel and its central position in the whole history of civilization. It is not a local or tribal tradition on the one hand, nor is it the spontaneous expression of evolving human intelligence on the other, but is the common heritage of all ancient civilizations, battered, corrupted, and distorted in most cases, to be sure, but always recognizable in its main features and much too ingenious and elaborate to be the product of independent discovery.[131]

But what are we to make of pagans possessing the gospel, and that from the most ancient times? We did not say they had it, but only that their records testify to it. If we examine those records we soon discover that all that their authors possess are mere fragments which they do not pretend to understand. For them all those elements of the gospel which fit so perfectly into the account of things given in the story of the redemption are but distant traditions, shattered remnants of a forgotten structure, completely mystifying odds and ends that once meant something but whose meaning can now only be guessed at. This attitude to the heritage of the past may fairly be called the basic mood of Egyptian religion. In the seventeenth chapter of the *Book of the Dead,* to which we have already referred, the question is regularly asked, "What does this mean?" and fourteen times when an answer is supplied, it is with the reservation that "others say" it means something else. From the earliest times, "the impression made on the modern mind" by the Egyptians, according to I. E. S. Edwards, "is that of a people searching in the dark for a key to truth . . . retaining all lest perchance the appropriate one should be lost."[132] They know there is a key, that is, but they also know they do not have it. It would be easy to show that the keynote of the literature and religion of all ancient people who have left us their records, with the exception of Israel, is one of pessimism and despair. We would only have to quote the authors of the standard literary histories of the various nations to make that clear. Israel escaped both that pessimism and fatalism by being constantly reminded by the prophets of the great preexistent plan that lies behind everything that happens. This we believe to be the most significant element in the expanding gospel.

Notes

1. Martin Grabmann, *Die Geschichte der scholastischen Methode,* 2 vols. (Graz: Akademische Druck- und Verlagsanstalt, 1957), 1:1–37; Owen Chadwick, *From Bousset to Newman* (Cambridge: Cambridge University Press, 1959), chapters 1–3.

2. For recent treatment of this much-treated theme, see Otto Eissfeldt, *Einleitung in das Alte Testament* (Tübingen: Mohr, 1964), 2–9.

3. Jean Daniélou, *The Dead Sea Scrolls and Primitive Christianity* (Baltimore, MD: Helicon, 1958), 83–84.

4. Kurt Sethe, *Das "Denkmal memphitischer Theologie": Der Schabakostein des Britischen Museums,* part 1 of *Dramatische Texte zu altaegyptischen Mysterienspielen* (Leipzig: Hinrichs, 1928), 1–5.

5. In this, as in the Pyramid Texts, it is often impossible to tell whether a given scene is laid in heaven, on earth, or in both places. Louis Speleers, *Textes des Cercueils* (Brussels: n.p., 1947), xlv-xlix.

6. See for example Louis V. Žabkar, "The Theocracy of Amarna and the Doctrine of the Ba," *Journal of Near Eastern Studies* 13 (1954):

87; Helmuth Jacobsohn, *Die dogmatische Stellung des Königs in der Theologie der alten Ägypter* (New York: Augustin, 1939).

7. Shabako Stone, lines 7–8, in Sethe, *"Denkmal memphitischer Theologie,"* 23–26.

8. Ibid., lines 10c–18b, in Sethe, *"Denkmal memphitischer Theologie,"* 27–32.

9. Ibid., lines 13c–14c, in Sethe, *"Denkmal memphitischer Theologie,"* 27–32.

10. Kurt Sethe, *Der dramatische Ramesseumpapyrus: Ein Spiel zur Thronbesteigung des Königs,* part 2 of *Dramatische Texte zu Altaegyptischen Mysterienspielen* (Leipzig: Hinrichs, 1928), 95–96; cf. the *Victory over Seth* (Louvre 3129; British Museum 10252, 13).

11. Shabako Stone, lines 48–52a, in Sethe, *"Denkmal memphitischer Theologie,"* 46–50.

12. Ibid., lines 53–54, in Sethe, *"Denkmal memphitischer Theologie,"* 50–56. On the nature of Ptah as Father, Begetter, Opener, etc., see Maj S. Holmberg, *The God Ptah* (Lund: Gleerup, 1946), 258–71.

13. Shabako Stone, lines 56–57, in Sethe, *"Denkmal memphitischer Theologie,"* 59–64.

14. Ibid., line 57, in Sethe, *"Denkmal memphitischer Theologie,"* 62–64.

15. Ibid., lines 57–58, in Sethe, *"Denkmal memphitischer Theologie,"* 65, renders *imakh* as "der die Bedeutung aller Dinge macht."

16. Ibid., lines 58–60, in Sethe, *"Denkmal memphitischer Theologie,"* 66–68, notes that the passage "vividly recalls the Biblical Creation story."

17. Ibid., line 61, in Sethe, *"Denkmal memphitischer Theologie,"* 70–72.

18. Ibid., lines 63–65, in Sethe, *"Denkmal memphitischer Theologie,"* 73–77.

19. Pyramid Texts 1:3; for an English translation, see Samuel A. B. Mercer, *The Pyramid Text in Translation and Commentary* (New York: Longmans and Green, 1952), 20.

20. Adriaan deBuck, *The Coffin Texts,* 7 vols. (Chicago: University of Chicago Press, 1935–61), 1:111–13 (spell 33); cf. 2:6–7 (spell 76), 24–26 (spell 79), etc. In the Coffin Texts the theme is carried on as Ptah summons the Great Assembly, "they who share the secrets," gives them formal greeting, and introduces his son and heir to them, who acclaim him as the earthly Prince of Peace and Righteouness, shouting for joy.

21. Ibid., 1:167–69; 171–73 (spell 39–40); 2:7 (spell 76). On the possible identity of Atum with Adam, see E. Lefébure, "Le Cham et l'Adam égyptiens," *Bibliotheque égyptologique* 35 (1913): 16–21.

22. *Enuma Elish* I, 21, in René Labat, *Le Poème babylonien de la création* (Paris: Maisonneuve, 1935), 76–77. The same situation, a great earthly assembly representing the divine council at the creation of the world, is described in early Sumerian texts supplied by Edward Chiera, *Sumerian Religious Texts* (Upland, PA: Crozer Theological Seminary, 1924), 1:27–31. For an Old Babylonian parallel, see W. G. Lambert, *Babylonian Wisdom Literature* (Oxford: Clarendon, 1960), 163. Hittite ritual texts contain "obvious allusion to an assembly of the gods for the purpose of 'fixing the fates'; the scene is laid in heaven . . . but the inference that such a gathering of gods was actually enacted in ritual form, as in the Babylonian festival, can hardly be evaded," O. R. Gurney, "Hittite Kingship," in Samuel H. Hooke, *Myth, Ritual, and Kingship* (Oxford: Clarendon, 1958), 108.

23. *Enuma Elish* VI, 1–8, in Labat, *Le Poème babylonien de la création*, 143; cf. VI, 143.

24. *Enuma Elish* VI, 13–16, in ibid., 145.

25. *Enuma Elish* VI, 29–30, in ibid., 147. The authority is bestowed in tablet IV.

26. *Enuma Elish* VI, 115–23, 135, 165, in ibid., 155, 157, 159, from which we have selected typical expressions.

27. The mixed and derivative nature of the text is clear from the declaration in *Enuma Elish* VI, 121–22, 155, and VII, 140–44, in ibid., 173, that "for us, whatever name we call him by, he is indeed our god, though we have called him by fifty names."

28. Wisdom of Ben Sira 17:11–13.

29. *2 Baruch* 56:3.

30. *1 Enoch* 46:1–2; 47:3, on the nature of the Book of the Living.

31. *1 Enoch* 62:7.

32. *Thanksgiving Hymn* 6.

33. This rendering is that of A. Dupont-Sommer, *The Dead Sea Scrolls* (New York: Macmillan, 1956), 77.

34. *1QS* 11:7–9.

35. The treasures of wisdom are kept beneath God's throne on high, *2 Baruch* 54:13; this is the treasury of life on which all the heavenly hosts depend, *Psalms of Thomas* I, 9–13; from this chest God took the elements in the presence of the hosts when the creation of the world was being discussed in ibid.; it is "the treasure-chamber of the light," *Odes of Solomon* 16:16; Wisdom of Ben Sira 39:17; from it the worthy take the riches of knowledge, *1QS* 10:2; *Thanksgiving Hymn* 10:23–24, 29. Cf. Carl Schmidt, *The Books of Jeu and the Untitled Text in the Bruce Codex*, tr. Violet MacDermot (Leiden: Brill, 1978),

102–5; and Johannes Leipoldt, ed., *Religionsgeschichte des Orients in der Zeit der Weltreligionen* (Leiden: Brill, 1961), 86, 109–10.

36. *1QS* 10:1–3.

37. *Clementine Recognitions* I, 24, in *PG* 1:1220–21.

38. *Psalm of Thomas* I, 6–12.

39. Ibid., VIII, 9–14.

40. *Creation Apocryphon* 148:17, rendered by Hans M. Schenke, "Vom Ursprung der Welt," *Theologische Literaturzeitung* 84 (1959): 249.

41. Pastor of Hermas, *Visio (Visions)* I, 3, in *PG* 2:893–96.

42. Geo Widengren, "Die Mandäer," in Leipoldt, *Religionsgeschichte des Orients in der Zeit der Weltreligionen*, 86.

43. Ibid.

44. Johannes Fichtner, "Jahves Plan in der Botschaft des Jesaja," *Zeitschrift für alttestamentliche Wissenschaft* 63 (1951): 16–33.

45. *4 Ezra* 6:1–6, in *APOT* 2:574–75.

46. *4 Ezra* 7:70, in *APOT* 2:586.

47. *1 Enoch* 39:11.

48. Wisdom of Ben Sira 16:26–30; 17:1–2.

49. *1QS* 3:15.

50. *Thanksgiving Hymn* 1:7–13. The whole passage is relevant.

51. Ibid.

52. *The War of the Sons of Light with the Sons of Darkness* 17:7–9, in Yagael Yadin, *The Scroll of the War of the Sons of Light against the Sons of Darkness* (Oxford: Oxford University Press, 1962), 8.

53. *Zadokite Document* 2:7–13, in Chaim Rabin, *The Zadokite Documents* (Oxford: Clarendon, 1954), 6–8.

54. Dupont-Sommer, *The Dead Sea Scrolls*, 65, points out that in this passage we are dealing with "three great divine entities." To escape such a conclusion, Rabin, *Zadokite Documents*, 8, n. 4, puts *messiah*, "anointed ones," in the plural and then explains in a footnote that such a plural form may refer to prophets.

55. We have described the situation in Hugh W. Nibley, "The Hierocentric State," *WPQ* 4 (1951), 226–28; reprinted in *CWHN* 10:99–102, and Hugh W. Nibley, "Sparsiones," *Classical Journal* 40 (1945), 521–23; reprinted in *CWHN* 10:151–52.

56. Shabako Stone, line 61, in Sethe, *"Denkmal memphitischer Theologie,"* 70–72.

57. *Enuma Elish* VI, 73; VII, 32–33; VII, 146–50; VI, 72–81; VI, 108–13, in Labat, *Le Poème babylonien de la création*, 151, 165, 173, 151, 153, respectively.

58. F. C. Conybeare, "The Testament of Job and the Testaments of the XII Patriarchs," *Jewish Quarterly Review* 13 (1901): 112.

59. Walter F. Otto, *Die Musen und der göttliche Ursprung des Singens und Sagens* (Darmstadt: Wissenshaftliche Buchgesellschaft, 1961).

60. See the discussion by R. H. Charles, *The Book of Jubilees* (Jerusalem: Makor, 1972), lii.

61. *1 Enoch* 61:6–10; 69:25–27.

62. *Thanksgiving Hymn* 11:25, 61.

63. *Thanksgiving Hymn* 3:22–24.

64. *Thanksgiving Hymn* 3:22–24.

65. *Thanksgiving Hymn* 10:4–5.

66. *Thanksgiving Hymn* 10:28.

67. *Thanksgiving Hymn* 12:11–12.

68. *Thanksgiving Hymn* 12:19.

69. *1QS* 11:18.

70. *War Scroll* 10:9–12, in Yadin, *Scroll of the War of the Sons of Light*, 304–7.

71. *1QS* 11:17–18.

72. *War Scroll* 12:3–4, in Yadin, *Scroll of the War of the Sons of Light*, 314–15.

73. *War Scroll* 17:6–9, in ibid., 340–41.

74. Žabkar, "The Theocracy of Amarna and the Doctrine of the Ba," 87.

75. Henry G. Liddell and Robert Scott, *A Greek-English Lexicon* (Oxford: Clarendon, 1968), 1057–59.

76. In W. D. Davies and David Daube, eds., *The Background of the New Testament and Its Eschatology* (Cambridge: Cambridge University Press, 1956), 424–25.

77. Barnabas, *Epistola Catholica* 6–7, in *PG* 2:740–41.

78. Pastor of Hermas, *Visions* I, 3, in *PG* 2:893–96.

79. See *PG* 1:1222–23, n. 20.

80. Hooke, *Myth, Ritual, and Kingship*, 8.

81. Discussed by Yadin, *Scroll of the War of the Sons of Light*, 229–42.

82. Ibid., 232–33: "The Lord placed Belial to carry out his specific task"; this doctrine of the Dead Sea Scrolls being "in complete agreement with the statements about Belial (or *Beliar*) in the Apocrypha and Pseudepigrapha."

83. *Life of Adam and Eve* 14:2–3; 15:1.

84. *Papyrus Bodmer X*, 54:12.

85. See E. Revillout's discussion in *PO* 2:126–29.

86. Ibid., 2:154.

87. Timothy of Alexandria, "Discourse on Abbatôn," folio 21a, in E. A. W. Budge, *Coptic Martyrdoms*, 5 vols. (London: British Museum: 1914), 4:240–41.

88. Hermann Grapow, *Das 17. Kapitel des ägyptischen Totenbuches und seine religionsgeschichtliche Bedeutung* (Berlin: Paul, 1912), 43.

89. Anton Moortgat, *Tammuz* (Berlin: de Gruyter, 1949), treats the theme at length.

90. Homer, *Iliad* 18:480–90.

91. Hesiod, *Works and Days* 214–16.

92. Irenaeus, *Contra Haereses (Against Heresies)* IV, 37, 1, in *PG* 7:1099: "Misera necessitas non pose non peccandi," this being the exact opposite of the early Christian teaching that men's freedom to choose their own way makes them envied by the angels.

93. *Zohar, Bereshith* 23a.

94. *The Book of Formation (Sefer Yetzira)* 6:9.

95. *Testament of Naphthali* 2:6.

96. *Testament of Abraham*, cited by K. Kohler, "The Pre-Talmudic Haggada," *Jewish Quarterly Review* 7 (1895): 586.

97. Irenaeus, *Against Heresies* IV, 37, 1–6, in *PG* 7:1101–3.

98. Wisdom of Ben Sira 31:8–10; 15:14–17.

99. *4 Ezra* 7:127.

100. *1QS* 4:15.

101. *1QS* 3:23–4:1.

102. *Clementine Recognitions* I, 24, in *PG* 1:1220–21. See Hugh W. Nibley, *The World and the Prophets* (Salt Lake City: Deseret Book, 1974), 166–73; reprinted in *CWHN* 3:182–83.

103. The Law of Liberty (*khoq kherut*) of the Dead Sea Scrolls (e.g., *1QS* 10:1, 6, 8, 11), can only be the Christian "*ancient* Law of Liberty" discussed in the references in the preceding note.

104. *Didache* I, 1. The *Epistle of Barnabas* after a brief introduction begins almost the same way.

105. *Gospel of Philip* 53:14–17.

106. The classic statement of the doctrine, which is very often met with slightly altered form through the Apocrypha, is in the *Pastor of Hermas, Similitudo (Similitudes)* 3–4, in *PG* 2:959–62.

107. Justin Martyr, *First Apology* 10, in *PG* 6:340–41.

108. This is seen in the fourth-century description of a typical old-fashioned Christian, in Sozomen, *Ecclesiastical History* I, 10–11, in *PG* 65:885–89.

109. Hugh W. Nibley, "Christian Envy of the Temple," *Jewish Quarterly Review* 50 (1959–60): 98–100; reprinted in *CWHN* 4:391–434.

110. B. Holt, "Realities of the Ascension," *Encounter* 24 (1963): 89.

111. Aristides, *Apology* XIII, 7.

112. *Clementine Recognitions* I, 1, 1–2, in *PG* 1:1207–8.

113. Ibid., IV, 23, in *PG* 1:1324.

114. *Papyrus Bodmer X,* 51:10–15.

115. Arthur Schopenhauer, "Essay on the Christian System," in *Religion: A Dialogue, and Other Essays,* tr. T. B. Sanders (London: Sonnenschein, 1893), 111.

116. This theme is treated extensively in Hugh W. Nibley, *An Approach to the Book of Mormon,* 2nd ed. (Salt Lake City: Deseret Book, 1976), 106–34; in *CWHN* 7:135–67; cf. Hugh W. Nibley, *Nibley on the Timely and the Timeless* (Provo: Religious Studies Center, 1978), 155–86; reprinted in *CWHN* 8:326, n. 1.

117. Hugh W. Nibley, "Christian Envy of the Temple," *Jewish Quarterly Review* 50 (1960): 230–32; reprinted in *CWHN* 4:408–9.

118. *Secrets of Enoch* 68:4.

119. Pastor of Hermas, *Visions* III, 3–5, in *PG* 2:901–4. In the same way the hero stands "sentry duty" not only symbolically but literally, see Pastor of Hermas, *Similitudes* V, 1, in *PG* 2:957.

120. Jean Daniélou, *Origen,* tr. Walter Mitchell (New York: Sheed and Ward, 1955), 155–57; cf. 119, 141–44, 152.

121. *Gospel of Philip* 67:10–12.

122. *Gospel of Philip* 67:15–18.

123. *Gospel of Philip* 86:3–8.

124. *Gospel of Philip* 76:7–9.

125. *Gospel of Philip* 86:3–7.

126. *Gospel of Philip* 76:33–36.

127. *Gospel of Philip* 84:24–25.

128. *Gospel of Philip* 85:1–16.

129. *Gospel of Philip* 86:5–10.

130. As discussed in Hugh W. Nibley, *Since Cumorah* (Salt Lake City: Deseret Book, 1970), 24–25; reprinted in *CWHN* 7:21–23.

131. Lord Raglan, *The Origins of Religion* (London: Thinker's Library, 1949); chapters 7–8 develop this theme.

132. I. E. S. Edwards, *The Pyramids of Egypt* (Baltimore: Penguin, 1964), 29–30.

Rediscovery of the Apocrypha and the Book of Mormon

The Open Scriptures

The world today has forgotten that the most shocking and offensive thing about the Book of Mormon was what? For years and years, nobody could find any objectionable teachings in it. So what were they so upset about? It was this: It presented a completely unfamiliar set of scripture and revelation — a completely new idea of scripture. Nobody had ever thought of the scriptures being open like that. They said, "Now look, we have the Bible, and this Bible was a concrete, monolithic block written by the hand of God, and there is nothing else." Then came the Book of Mormon, not only butting into the picture, but giving a whole new conception of what scripture was, how it had been composed, and how it had been made, how things built up; it tells us a lot about writing, about recording, about handing down traditions, about how the people thought of the book. If we go into all the early criticism of Mormonism, this is the thing people resented. They couldn't understand anything like it. But this is exactly what we run into in the newly discovered apocryphal texts.

We have in the Book of Mormon a unique treatise on how men receive revelation from above; we find there a

---

This previously unpublished lecture was given on a Sunday evening in the Smith Fieldhouse at Brigham Young University in the 1960s.

great deal on the subject of revelation. The Book of Mormon is much preoccupied with the physical transmission of records, as well as with visitations of angels. We are told that there exist records that reveal all things from the foundation of the world unto the end thereof — there are records that contain all basic knowledge (2 Nephi 27:7, 10–11). The mysteries of God are to be had on ancient plates and ancient records. There is a basic body of knowledge around which history pivots, and this is recorded knowledge, sometimes hidden away, and sometimes available — in libraries here and corpuses there. That is, the books have been "kicking around," often concealed, but kept and transmitted; they possess a tremendous amount of information if men could only get hold of them. And now some of those books are here upon the earth. Again, this was a new concept, and it comes up a great deal in the Book of Mormon.

These documents are an indispensable aid to the knowledge of things as they are. This is what the Book of Mormon is! I've mentioned the third dimension. The other churches live in a two-dimensional world. But our gospel adds a third dimension, so to speak. We think of the other world as being a reality, and so we actually live in another dimension. That's a nice thing, theoretically, but what we have got to show is more than theory. We have the Book of Mormon; it cuts a furrow through everything that's been done before. It plows right through all our old concepts, upsetting things! It breaks the circle, the age-old argument of the scripture and the apocrypha. The world says that the documents of the Bible, properly selected and evaluated, are the word of God. But they select the documents! So we go around in a circle, declaring these to be the word of God, insomuch as they're properly selected and evaluated. But who selects and evaluates? Oh, we do! We make our own word of God. That is what it amounts to. And that's all we can do — just run around in a circle. The Book of Mormon breaks right into that — coming in from the outside, having nothing to do with any of the formal concepts of scripture. It's a completely jarring note, and so it's a remarkable document.

The apocryphal writings, especially those recently discovered, pay the same careful attention to bookkeeping that the authors of the Book of Mormon do. They represent a tradition handed down at all times, the idea that a particular volume or volumes are hidden, and thus transmitted. It is an old story, and we run into it frequently. The Egyptians are especially full of the idea; the Dead Sea Scrolls are completely caught up in it.

The Egyptians, from the earliest to the latest times, frequently refer to a mysterious box that contains a record of the race. It has been hidden, and if they could only get to it, they would have something. An Egyptian noble of the old kingdom boasts that he has seen the box, the ephod of *sia* ("wisdom"), and he knows what is in it. Many a noble Egyptian, many a pharaoh, and many a king spent all his days reading the tablets and writings in the House of Life, above all seeking for *the* book. The House of Life was a very important institution in Egypt, a magnificent building, a library; and it contained mostly genealogical records.[1] That's what the great Gardiner, just before he died, found out. The Egyptians used to spend their days in the House of Life, looking for something they felt was lost—especially *the* book. Somewhere in these treasures was *the* book, the book written by the hand of Thoth himself, Dhwty, or whatever name we want to give him. It would contain all knowledge—certain secrets, secrets of life.

A New Kingdom writing: "It is in the midst of the Sea of Coptos, in a box of iron, in a box of bronze, which is in a box of kita wood, which is in a box of ivory and ebony, which is in a box of silver, which is in a box of gold, in which is the book"—if we could only get into it! This account says the story can only be read once we've found the book by the inspiration of Ammon.

The Babylonians were, if anything, even more taken with the *Book of Life* than the Egyptians, and indeed (we should read something from the Gilgamesh epic here), the legends in both countries reflected real practices throughout the Near East of recent years. Piggott tells us that "the whole business archives of a single family have sometimes been recovered from the ruins of a single house."[2] Throughout the Near East—Asia Minor, Mesopotamia, or Egypt—it is not uncommon to discover the business archives and histories in private libraries. We realize that most of the great libraries of antiquity were private libraries, kept in people's houses. This came as a surprise too; they are not even temple libraries.

Again, we find a good Book of Mormon custom, according to which Laban had the archives, and it was there he kept the plates. Why? Because it was a private record; he was directly descended from Joseph, and the family kept the genealogy there, in their house of life. Lehi had to get the records from Laban, and we can see why Laban was in no mood to part with them!

The idea that a king, a near contemporary of Lehi, should cause transcriptions and translations to be made of a royal speech and sent to various parts of his dominion, so a copy of it should turn up in the ruins of a Jewish community far up the Nile in Elephantine (among Jewish refugees from Lehi's Jerusalem), would not have occurred to anyone before 1906, unless one happened to have read about such things in the Book of Mormon. Yet another, even better example has recently turned up in Egypt, in the form of the royal speech. The king at his coronation gave a speech, and since the speech could not be heard by everyone, he had brochures made of it and circulated, as Benjamin did in the Book of Mormon.

Among the Jewish apocrypha, Baruch is particularly

concerned with a guiding book. Baruch read this book in the hearing of the king's son, and in the hearing of all the people that came to hear it in Babylon; then they had a copy made and sent to Jerusalem. Baruch was the secretary of Jeremiah, the friend of Lehi, and so all these customs were familiar—we see why the Book of Mormon people would take them with them. And "this is the Book of the Commandments," says Baruch; "the Book of the Commandments of God. . . . All they that hold it fast are appointed to life; But such as leave it shall die. Turn thee, O Jacob, and take hold of it: Walk towards her shining in the presence of the light thereof."[3] This is the idea of taking hold of things, the motif of grabbing the iron rod. Baruch comments on the custom of hiding the book, a theme often mentioned in the apocrypha: the holy book has to be hidden. All the treasures of Israel, he says, must be hid up unto the Lord, "so that strangers may not get possession of them. For the time comes when Jerusalem also will be delivered for a time, until it is said that it is again restored forever. And the earth opened its mouth and swallowed [the records] up."[4]

In 2 *Baruch* we read an interesting thing. All the treasures of Israel, he says, must be hid up unto the Lord so that strangers may not get possession of them. And in Helaman, where people are rebuked for hiding their private treasures, we read, "They shall hide up treasures unto [the Lord]" (Helaman 13:19). It's a commandment. We usually think of this as denouncing people for hiding up treasures. It's Samuel the Lamanite who says their treasures are going to become slippery because they did not hide them up to the Lord when they fled from their enemies; when we do flee from the enemy we must hide up our treasure to the Lord (cf. Helaman 13:31, 20).

Later Baruch tells us how "they hid all the vessels of the sanctuary, lest the enemy should get possession of them."[5] Though this writing was published only since Cu-

morah, a more recent find gives it solid historical dimensions—the famous *Copper Scroll*, found in Cave Four at
Qumran. The significance of this, an important record written on copper alloy sheets and hidden up, is that it was
in fact written and prepared with the express purpose of
its being hidden up. That's why it was written, for it contains a record of all the other treasures hidden up to the
Lord.

Here we have a concrete and indisputable example of
an ancient Israelite practice: "For I will, saith the Lord,
that they shall hide up their treasures unto me; and cursed
be they who hide not up their treasures unto me" (Helaman
13:19). If we hide them unto the Lord, that's a good thing;
he wants us to hide treasures to him, in regular old Jewish
fashion. Again, Baruch, the secretary of Jeremiah, writes
that when Jerusalem was destroyed (referring to the destruction of Jerusalem at the time of Lehi), the Lord wanted
the treasures to be buried up unto him. It's a rule, and
now we know from the *Copper Scroll* that it was actually
done.[6] And this is the way it was done. And then Baruch
says, "And none shall redeem it. . . . And the day shall
come that they shall hide up their treasures, because they
have set their hearts upon their riches. . . . When they
shall flee before their enemies; because they will not hide
them up unto me" (Helaman 13:19–20). When we flee before our enemies, we hide our treasure up unto the Lord;
it's a commandment.

Let me say a word about reformed Egyptian here. It
was demotic, learned by Lehi in the Old World. Spiegelberg defines demotic as the cursive form of writing developed between the eighth and fourth centuries B.C., an
abbreviation of the hieratic.[7] So we start out with the hieroglyphic; then came the hieratic, which was, in turn, a
short form of hieroglyphic. As a shorthand of a shorthand,
demotic was the best shorthand ever invented. It was ideal
for saving space, putting a great deal of writing into a small

amount of space. It became the dominant type of writing in Egypt about Lehi's time. About 600 B.C., everyone turned to it; it became *the* way of doing things, and the script really was reformed.

Figure 44. The god "Ammon," in increasingly abbreviated script.

Here's one way the name Ammon is written in Egyptian. Next it was written more rapidly in hieratic, but by the time of the demotic representation, the name Ammon is simply this. You can recognize the hieratic, but the demotic form is reformed Egyptian. We can see what economy they would enjoy in writing documents that way. It's strange that people made so much fun about Joseph Smith and his "reformed Egyptian"; what other name could he possibly give it? It was Champollion who first gave it the name of demotic. In 1828 he published his first work on the subject, about the same time the Book of Mormon appeared. Nobody had ever given any name to this before, and what better name could we give it than reformed Egyptian? Hebrew writing, on the other hand, has always been singularly clumsy from this point of view. It's quite correct to call the last of these forms reformed Egyptian, reformed beyond recognition by anyone but an expert.

In the old apocrypha, both Jewish and Christian, we find certain favorite images and expressions. This is mostly what I will talk about now, because there are some very nice ones. I have talked about doctrines, the same doctrines emphasized in the Book of Mormon, but now I will talk about images, because they're more concrete. Again, if we arrange these types and images in order of frequency, they are as distinctive as fingerprints. First consider the images, which are peculiar and characteristic; they also reflect the peculiar cultural background of the people. I could talk about the geographical, physical, and cultural background, but instead I will speak about the images as they appear in both the Book of Mormon and the apocryphal writings. Their literary occurrence is a different thing, a comparison that hasn't been done before. What we didn't fully appreciate was their literary and scriptural importance, and that's not surprising, since it was the Dead Sea Scrolls that first brought those to light, and the scrolls were first discovered in the very same year that I wrote my series on "Lehi in the Desert," though nobody even knew about any Dead Sea Scrolls then.

Desert Imagery

Desert imagery has been shown to be vivid in the writings of the Jewish sectary. For example, a wealth of expressions refers to travel in the desert—the desert road that is so dangerous to leave. "That I may walk in the path of the low valley, that I may be strict in the plain road!" (2 Nephi 4:32). This prayer of Nephi, the desert traveler, sounds like stilted English until we take it in a literal sense. "The mists of darkness," says Lehi, explaining this image, "are the temptations of the devil. . . . [He] leadeth them away into broad roads, that they perish and are lost" (1 Nephi 12:17). In *our* civilization, the broadest roads are the safest; in the desert, they are the most confusing and dangerous. "Walk in the strait path," says good old Nephi—in true desert style—"which leads to life, and continue in the path until the end of the day of probation" (2 Nephi 33:9). It is not the geographical, but the apocryphal reference that interests us now. In the late Egyptian period (the Egyptian of Lehi's day), according to Grapow, it became a very common teaching that a man should never depart from the right road, but be righteous, not associate his heart with the wicked, nor walk in the path of unrighteousness. This had actually become a literary convention in Lehi's day; and in his culture, it is very closely connected with the Israelite use of it.

That's not accidental at all. It is an early appearance of
the Doctrine of Two Ways: the road of safety and the road
of danger; the road of life and the road of death. Couroyer
shows a definite connection between the Egyptian and the
Israelite teachings on the way of life.[8] The Wisdom of Ben
Sira, from the early second century B.C., says, "the paths
are plain for the blameless, even so they offer stumbling
blocks to the presumptuous."[9] Compare this with Nephi's
plain road: "Oh Lord, . . . wilt thou make my path straight
before me! Wilt thou not place a stumbling block in my
way, . . . and hedge not up my way, but the ways of mine
enemy" (2 Nephi 4:33) — the same image, praying that his
enemies may get the stumbling block, and that he may
have the plain road.[10]

Ben Sira accords the desert traveler "the image of the
man most dependent upon God."[11] So he refers to the
traveler again and again, and to life as a journey through
the desert, where man is most dependent upon God; and
this is the lesson of 1 Nephi. The Wisdom of Solomon says,
"We went astray from the way of truth, . . . [and] we jour-
neyed through trackless deserts. But the way of the Lord
we knew not."[12] This expression is of the very same type
the Book of Mormon uses. This is what Lehi dreams about,
what terrifies him — getting lost. "The eternal being," says
the *Manual of Discipline*, "is the rock which supports my
right hand, the road to my feet."[13] Notable here is the
common practice of mixing metaphors, especially in enthusiastic passages. The metaphors are closely parallel, and
sometimes they appear in rather tasteless profusion.
Helaman 3:29–30 is a classic instance, so thoroughly typical
that anyone reading much of the Dead Sea Scrolls would
notice how much alike they sound. "Yea, we see that whosoever will may lay hold . . . " (Helaman 3:29). Helaman
has just spoken about support for his hand and laying hold
of the way of truth — "he is the rock that supports my hand,

the road to my feet." These expressions are like finger-prints; they crop up in abundance:

> Whosoever will may lay hold upon the word of God, which is quick and powerful, which shall divide asunder [it's now a two-edged sword] all the cunning and the snares and the wiles of the devil [now we've got the image of a trap], and lead the man of Christ in a strait and narrow course [now we get the road] across that everlasting gulf of misery which is prepared to engulf the wicked [it is the road across the gulf] — And land their souls [now they're crossing some water], yea, their immortal souls, . . . in the kingdom of heaven [even more imagery], to sit down with Abraham, and Isaac, and with Jacob, and with all our holy fathers, to go no more out. (Helaman 3:29–30)

Such a mixture of familiar metaphors is fairly characteristic of this type of literature.

Another favorite desert image is the great castle in the desert, which, as Nephi tells us, represents "the pride of the world; and it fell, and the fall thereof was exceeding great" (1 Nephi 11:36). Consider the castle of Agormi, from the time of Nectanebos the Second (from the time of Lehi); it was indeed a great and lofty building, with date trees growing at the foot of it and a big fruit tree in the court-yard — reminiscent of Lehi's description. The archetype of the great building that falls and slays its wicked owner is the house of Cain; we can trace this to the work called the *al-Iklīl*, the crown. The castle of Ghumdan is described by al-Hamdānī as the "great and spacious building" which "stood as it were in the air, high above the earth," with the finely dressed people (fig. 45).[14] It falls, representing the destruction of the wicked, the vanity of the world — and it's overwhelming. The Jewish legend goes back to the house of Cain, the first house to be built of stone. It was a very splendid house, and the way Cain died was that the house fell on him and killed him. The book of *Jubilees*

Figure 45. This mud-brick Bedouin fortress has staggered overhanging layers which, like our shingles, allow the rain to sheet off more quickly. They reach surprising heights for such simple constructions but can collapse unexpectedly. In Yemen, stories are still told of the huge tower built by a vain king, with a roof of translucent alabaster as his penthouse skylight.

reports that Cain was killed when his stone house fell on him: "For with a stone he had killed Abel, and by a stone was he killed in righteous judgment."[15] We have cited the Arabic versions of the tradition of the great house, but this text shows that it's also among the oldest of Hebrew traditions. The book of *Jubilees* itself is relatively old. Cain built the first great house of vanity, and it fell upon him and killed him.

The Plan

When I recently collected, sorted, and classified many doctrinal elements in the early apocrypha, the most conspicuous was the plan laid from the foundation of the world. The idea has been suppressed by the editors and translators of the Bible, but it breaks out repeatedly in the apocrypha, and it is nowhere more succinctly and emphatically stated than in the Book of Mormon: "The way is prepared for all men from the foundation of the world" (1 Nephi 10:18). It provided every man with a choice throughout his life, by placing not one but two ways before him. "It must needs be that there was an opposition," as Nephi says, "even the forbidden fruit in opposition to the tree of life [there was a tree of life and a tree of death; there was fruit to eat, and a fruit forbidden], the one being sweet and the other bitter. Wherefore, the Lord God gave unto man that he should act for himself" (2 Nephi 2:15–16). Accordingly, "if ye have sought to do wickedly in the days of your probation, then ye are found unclean" (1 Nephi 10:21). "And the days of the children of men were prolonged, according to the will of God" (2 Nephi 2:21).

Sometimes the way is called the plan, sometimes the will of God, sometimes both. That's what the "will of God" means—what he gave in the beginning, what was agreed on then. "The days of the children . . . were prolonged, according to the will of God, that they might repent while in the flesh; wherefore their state became a state of probation" (2 Nephi 2:21). "Because . . . they are redeemed from the fall they have become free forever, knowing good from evil; to act for themselves and not to be acted upon" (2 Nephi 2:26). "O how great the plan of our God" (2 Nephi 9:13), exclaims Nephi, using the word "plan." The plan was laid in the premortal existence through worlds already provided; the righteous shall inherit the kingdom of God, which was "prepared . . . from the foundation of the world" (1 Nephi 10:18). The plan laid at the foundation of the world was met by a counterplan of the devil—"O that cunning plan of the evil one!" (2 Nephi 9:28).

Centuries after Nephi, Alma summarized the doctrine: "There was a space granted unto man in which he might repent; therefore this life became a probationary state" (Alma 12:24). "If it had not been for the plan of redemption, which was laid from the foundation of the world, there could have been no resurrection of the dead" (Alma 12:25); and all things trace back to this plan of redemption. "There-fore, [God] sent angels to converse with [men], . . . and made known unto them the plan of redemption, which has been prepared from the foundation of the world; . . . [so they could become] as Gods, knowing good from evil, placing themselves in a state to act" (Alma 12:29–31). No-tice, "to act for themselves and not to be acted upon" (2 Nephi 2:26). The fact that that reference to the plan occurs forty-seven times in the Book of Mormon shows the ex-treme prominence of the idea.

The concept receives the same emphasis and expres-sion in the newly found apocrypha as in the Book of Mor-mon, though it's minimized by the editors of the Bible. Let me add a few points. "Let us prepare our soul," says Baruch, "that we may possess and not be taken possession of."[16] Ours is the active, not the passive part; man is "to act, . . . and not to be acted upon." We are to take pos-session, and not to be taken possession of. The notion of opposition is the same, the antithesis that Alma and Nephi, Book of Mormon writers, use.

Speaking of mankind in general, the Wisdom of Solomon remarks, "by judging them by little and little," the plan extends mankind's means; it extends the day of probation: "Thou gavest them a place of repentance, though thou knewest their nature."[17] His judging them little by little prolongs the day of their repentance (cf. 2 Nephi 2:21). Of the righteous, the Wisdom of Solomon says, "God tested them, and found them worthy of himself. As gold in the furnace he proved them; . . . in the time of their visitation they shall shine forth."[18]

This passage appeared almost verbatim on the first page of the first Dead Sea Scroll discovered (the *Serekh Scroll*). The *Zadokite Fragment*, the oldest of the Dead Sea Scrolls, says that "the righteous person who fails to follow the command is one that has failed his testing in the furnace" (the citing of the place being a test).[19] One of the most striking statements of Lehi's principle is that there "must needs be, that there is an opposition in all things; . . . all things must needs be a compound in one" (2 Nephi 2:11). Sometimes these expressions in the Book of Mormon make us look twice; could they have used language so sophisticated to express the idea so perfectly?

The newly found *Gospel of Philip* starts out in the best vein of the apostolic Fathers, denouncing those members of the church who desert the doctrine of the resurrection of the flesh. The work is strictly orthodox, and very strongly anti-gnostic, although some people try to explain it away by saying it *is* gnostic. The same idea occurs exactly: "In this world, the right and the left, the light and the dark, the good and the evil are twins, and they cannot be separated." They are compounded in one; they belong right together. "And this is according to the Lord's plan," that there should be one.[20] The Lord intends it that way.

The Book of Mormon begins with a report of a vision,

which Lehi has of affairs in heaven. He goes out in the desert, where he sees a light. He goes home and throws himself on his bed. There he has a vision. He's carried away into the court in heaven, where he attends a great meeting and sees the great assembly, the great council, held at the foundation of the world, where the gospel plan was explained.

When the people in the assembly were very downcast, like Job, or the Hodayot singer in the *Milhāmāh (War) Scroll,* after the army was beaten, they are all taken back and reminded of the council in heaven, and told, so to speak, "Now don't be worried—this is all going according to plan." This is exactly what happens to Lehi. He sees the council at the foundation of the world, the Lord's way of explaining to him the gospel plan. Everything actually begins with that council. A very large portion, the majority, in fact, of early Christian and Jewish apocrypha belonged to a type of literature designated as the *testaments* (testamentary literature), which I have treated elsewhere.[21] The genre is typical of the great patriarchs—there are testaments of Noah, Abraham, Isaac, Jacob, the Twelve Patriarchs, and Job. Some of these, such as the testaments of Isaac and Job, have been discovered fairly recently. There are all sorts of testaments, all basically telling the same thing. There are testaments because the man is talking to one or two of his children or to one of his new disciples. He names them in order, then gives them instructions; often the author tells that he's been to heaven and seen a vision—God on his throne, being acclaimed.

This is the way Lehi starts out in 2 Nephi 1–4. Lehi gives advice to his sons—Nephi, Laman, Lemuel, Sam, Jacob, and Joseph; the sons of Ishmael; and even Zoram and his descendants, giving each one a prophecy, a promise, a warning, a little history of the past. In each instance he refers to the story of the heavenly vision, because it has

changed his view of everything. This is the main characteristic of the testamentary literature.

"It is only natural," explains a modern commentator,
"that the last words of a dying patriarch [the testamentary
literature in general] contain the predictions of the future
as well as reminiscences of the past, and exhortations for
the present." Each of Lehi's speeches is the same. To each
of his sons in the wilderness, he tells the past trials, trib-
ulations, temptations, and sins of their ancestors; he tells
of his present danger, gives a warning, tells what the situation is, why he named each as he did, and then prophesies the future. So the Book of Mormon is strictly in the
authentic tradition.

One striking image that meets us in this account of
Lehi's heavenly vision is that of a meeting breaking up.
Lehi sees God on his throne, the people are singing the
hymn; but then the hymn stops, the meeting breaks up,
and everyone goes about his business (1 Nephi 1). One of
the newly discovered apocrypha, the so-called *Creation
Apocryphon,* also describes such a situation. And what was
decided on in the heavenly council is now being carried
out by Gods, angels, and men. This concept of heaven is
alien to conventional Judaism and Christianity, in which
the chief characteristic of the heavenly order, conforming
to the teachings of Athanasius, is absolutely motionless
stability. Heaven is complete fulfillment, static permanence, a meeting in the presence of God where the opening
hymn is sung forever and ever and ever. Christians can't
think of anything else to do, just go on singing that hymn.
This is why the Christian heaven is such a bore. When
Athanasius was asked, "What do we do?" he replied, "If
we read in the Bible that people sing hymns, I guess that's
all we ever do!"[22] What he didn't know was that these
scenes are merely a flashback to the great conference in
the premortal existence.

The meeting that Lehi sees breaks up; it's apparently

the meeting where the great plan was approved. It could
have been the later one, when Christ's mission was confirmed and more local arrangements made, but it looks
like the first one, where all present shouted for joy, because
they were all singing to and acclaiming the One on the
throne. Other prophets have seen the same vision, as a
means to explain to them why we have to go through with
what we do here on the earth.

When the meeting breaks up, twelve particular persons
descend to the earth. And yet another: Nephi saw one
descend out of the midst of heaven (cf. 1 Nephi 12:6); "he
also saw twelve others following him, and their brightness
did exceed that of the stars in the firmament. And they
came down and went forth upon the face of the earth" (1
Nephi 1:10–11). It is the image of the descending stars to
which I draw attention, for the correct and conventional
way of designating holy persons who descend to earth to
carry out assignments among men is to call them stars, or
the stars that shine above the stars.

There are some interesting references to that. In the
Coffin Texts, the Pharaoh coming to earth is referred to as
the unique star, as he comes forth through the gates of
heaven to circulate among men. The gatekeeper hails him
as the unique, the only, the unequalled star; the indestructible stars—the other stars—turn aside for him.[23] Of
course the seven moving heavenly bodies, the planets, are
the origin of the idea of the seven wise men, who circulate
constantly among the children of men. The seven wise
men must lay the foundations of Uruk, the oldest city in
the world, for all sacred foundations have to be established
with direct reference to the stars. In an Egyptian building,
palace, or temple, the foundation had to be laid by the
Pharaoh, and it had to be laid at night. He would go out
at night with his chief astronomer, and they would take
very careful observations. The Pharaoh would drive the
pegs (fig. 46). It had to be done at night, because reference

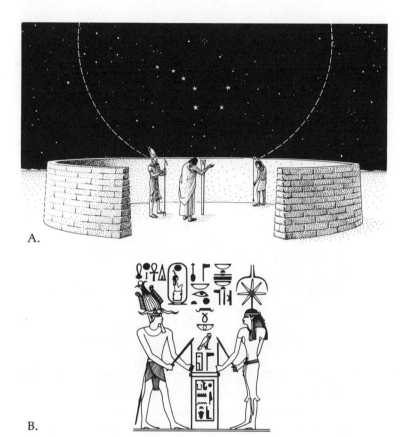

A.

B.

Figure 46. I. E. S. Edwards proposes a plausible method of how the
Egyptians may have determined true north based on the observation
of a specific circumpolar star (A). They would mark its rising on an
artificial circular horizon and at the end of the night indicate its setting.
Bisecting the angle formed with the astronomer-priest at the center
gives the north-south baseline from which every other measure of the
pyramid or temple is derived. In this bas-relief of 1100 B.C. (B), Queen
Hatshepsut, dressed in masculine garb and wearing the crown of Osiris,
lays out the groundplan of her temple at Karnak by driving stakes with
the assistance of the goddess Seshat, who wears a seven-pointed star
on her head. The boundaries of the temple are determined by a stretched
loop of rope around the stakes.

had to be made to the stars. We are told that the hero,
Enkidu (a friend of Gilgamesh), in this very archaic, prehistoric epic of the Babylonians, is equal to the star of
heaven who came down to him. In the beginning, according to the *Enuma Elish*, the creator created the stations and
established the stars in their places, especially the star
Nibiru, who represents the Savior with them, shining forth
to all who see in him their beginning and their end.[24] Nibiru
alone abides in his place. When the God descends to earth
from the holy mountain in the *Ras Shamra Texts,* from the
Palace of Baal, he is preceded by Qodesh, the Holy One,
carrying a torch to light the way.[25] Even Amrur, coming
down like a star from the heights, from the heights of
Saphon to move among men, bears a torch like the star.
In the same work the hero is called the Man of Hermi,
with the specification that the offering of Hermi is the
offering of the stars.[26] According to the Mandaeans (theirs
was the cult of Venus), the morning star, Lucifer, brings
great sin into the world. There is a negative star, a bad
star, as well as the good. According to the Mayas, Venus
is the morning star, the bringer of all evil, a very dreaded
thing. Enoch reports that he "saw many stars descend and
cast themselves down from heaven to that first star" which
had come down. Later, God summoned the first star, who
led away all the other stars and cast him into an abyss.[27]
But the idea of coming and going is represented by circulating stars, and this first comes out in Lehi's vision, in
which he sees the meeting break up in heaven. Then some
individuals descend like stars. One comes down, and
twelve others like him, he being brighter than any of the
others. The Lord says in a work called the *Secrets of Enoch,*
"I appointed for him four special stars, and called his name
Adam, and I showed him the two ways."[28]

After apostasy, the time will come to restore things. In
the very important, old Jewish *Testament of Levi,* he prophesies to his sons, "Then shall the Lord raise up a new

priest. And to him all the words of the Lord shall be revealed. . . . His star shall rise in heaven as of a king. The
heavens shall be opened. . . . And in his priesthood the
Gentiles shall be multiplied in knowledge upon the
earth."[29] One thinks immediately of the star of Bethlehem,
of course, and few Christians would deny it some element
of reality, if only on the charts of the magi. It was in the
form of a star, according to an early apocryphon, that
Michael led the magi to Christ.[30] Judah, in the *Testament
of Judah,* tells the same sort of thing. After long ages of
darkness and captivity, "after these things shall a star arise
to you from Jacob, in peace, and a man shall arise [from
my seed] like the Sun of Righteousness, . . . and the heavens shall be opened unto him."[31] The righteous, according
to *4 Ezra,* "are destined to be made like the light of the
stars, henceforth incorruptible." Their faces "shall shine
above the stars," while the faces of the wicked are "blacker
than the darkness."[32] Again we have the faces shining
above stars — as in Lehi's vision. "The stars shined in their
watches, and were glad," says the book of Baruch, which
again reminds us of the designation of the watchers as
stars. When he called, they said, "We are here" (the stars
all called out together). They shined with gladness unto
him that made them.[33] We are reminded of the morning
stars shouting for joy at the creation. In the *War Scroll* of
the Dead Sea Scrolls, the deliverer, the leader of the sects
of that time, a prophet who led them in the desert, was
called the Star from Jacob— reference to the older writing,
in which a star is said to arise from Jacob. Sometimes he's
referred to just as "the Star," the name for the leader of
the community.[34]

In the *Zadokite Fragment,* the Star is the searcher of the
law, a real person who came to Damascus, as it is written.[35]
The Star is specifically an inspired lawgiver to the order.
The mystery of Christ's birth was made known to the
Aeons, says Ignatius, speaking in what some would call

the purest gnostic theme, by a star — a completely new star. All the other stars and the sun and the moon made a chorus to *the* star, while it cast its radiance over all.[36] Clement, in his *Recognitions*, describes the pirating of Christian ideas by the Zoroastrians, and he resents it: "They call their prophet the 'living star,' whereas that name is what we really give to Christ, calling him the friend of God, and saying that He too was taken up to heaven in a chariot."[37]

The star image had nothing to do with the worship of stars. When Lehi goes home, convinced he has had a vision in which he saw the stars coming down, he prophesies. He feels good about it; everything is strictly in order with his soul. The visions just cited — from Baruch, Enoch, and others — were also writings from Lehi's culture.

Heavenly Treasures

Another image of great importance in the Book of Mormon is treasure. The Book of Mormon has much to say about earthly and heavenly treasures, in the same sense in which the newly found apocrypha do. Of course the image is also found in the New Testament. The Book of Mormon prophets explain many references to heavenly treasures in the Bible. Helaman is fondest of treasures. "And even at this time, instead of laying up for yourselves treasures in heaven, where nothing doth corrupt, . . . ye are heaping up for yourselves wrath against the day of judgment" (Helaman 8:25). This is the correct concept of what is meant by a treasure; it is a very common idea in the early apocrypha. We find in the many treasure passages that the treasure is the wisdom and knowledge we left behind us when we came down to this earth. In the premortal existence, we left our treasure in God's treasury, in his keeping. There it is, and by our good works here we can add to it; more will be waiting for us when we go back. So let us not try to pile up wealth and possessions on earth. They're not going to do us any good; we can't

take them back there. Let us lay up our treasures there—
add to our treasure store. We really do have one there,
because we had one before we came. We left it behind,
and we're going back to it. It's a very vivid concept, and
basic to it is the doctrine of the premortal existence.[38]
There's a great treasury in heaven which contains all good
things; it is to share in this treasury that all seek. But in
the Jewish apocrypha, in the Wisdom of Ben Sira, God
orders, by his word, the lights in the heavenly height, and
by the utterance of his mouth he opens the treasury, where
the righteous have a store of good works preserved.[39] These
are good works preserved, already done. And they're
being preserved; everything we add to our credit is being
preserved in God's treasury.

"At that time," says 2 *Baruch*, "the treasuries will be
opened in which is preserved the number of the souls of
the righteous."[40] *Second Enoch* puts another unpopular
interpretation on the heavenly treasury. It is the treasure
house of the various elements.[41] We're told, in a recently
discovered writing, the Syriac writing called *The Pearl*, how
the prince is completely outfitted by his heavenly parents
to come down to this earth. He's warned and given final
instructions; then with a heavy heart they send him forth.
They know he's going to be tested, but it's quite a happy
event nevertheless. He's left his treasure behind, and also
his special garment, which he will resume when he comes
back if he's worthy. So he goes down and lives in the
wicked world in Egypt, becomes defiled, forgets his treasure, and has to have a special messenger sent to remind
him that he has a treasure, and that he's going to lose it
if he doesn't behave himself. So he reforms his ways and
works hard, trying to gain the pearl again so he can bring
it back, to put it into the treasury, where his garment is
waiting for him.[42]

This idea of a waiting garment occurs many times—
about a hundred times—in the newly discovered texts. The

righteous are completely outfitted by the treasurers with the garments and jewels from the royal treasury, and those God returns. "God has hidden the kingdom as a treasure," says Peter in the *Clementine Recognitions*, "burying it under mountains, where it can only be reached by zealous work. The righteous attain to it, enjoy the treasure, and want to give it to others."[43] In another text, the Lord commands at the creation, "Bring out all the knowledge, bring the books from my storehouse, bring the necessary equipment from my laboratory and my treasury, and bring a reed of quick writing, and give it to Enoch and let's get to work here."[44] These things are in storage. The *Zadokite Fragment* explains that God laid open his hidden things before them, as well as knowledge of the times and the seasons which is kept in his treasury.[45]

According to the *Serekh Scroll,* or the *Manual of Discipline,* God in the beginning opened his treasury and poured out his knowledge. That knowledge is being kept there. He poured out his knowledge before the first angels.[46] (This is the time when the world was created in the presence of the first angels.) The writer of the *Thanksgiving Hymns* rejoices constantly in being able to receive from the treasury of God's secret knowledge. This is what *2 Jeu* calls "the great mystery of the treasury of light," which can be approached only by those who have passed through all the eons and all the places of the invisible God.[47] We return to obtain it, bringing a lot of experience.

"The treasury of the heavenly king is open," says the *Acts of Thomas;* "and everyone who is worthy takes and finds rest, and when he has found rest he becomes a king."[48] The *Gospel of Thomas* counsels us to "search for the treasure which fails not," and tells us that the kingdom is like a treasure hidden in a field; someone bought the field, found it there, and began lending money to everyone. So also we want to share the treasure.[49] In the *Psalms of Thomas* the evil one and his robbers attack and plunder the great treasure ship and carry off the booty to other worlds, using it to adorn and furbish their own planets. God has vivid things in this treasury, and he sends out various issues from it; one of these is raided by a band of the evil ones, who carry off the stuff. And when they get it they use it to make their own worlds and fit them out. Anything they happen to have on their planet has been stolen from people going and coming. It's something for a science fiction writer, a vivid picture drawn in the *Psalms of Thomas*. It goes on: Hearing that this stuff has been plundered, has been taken away, and is being falsely used by people who aren't qualified to use it, the Lord calls his treasurer, namely Reason (this is a gnostic work, which rationalizes the doctrine), and finally gets back the treasure — the treasure of life, which the thieves have hidden under a black mountain. Then, having summoned all the heavenly host, the father establishes a treasure house of life containing living images that do not perish. Moreover, in the presence of the first angel, he opens his treasure chest and takes from it the elements from which he is to organize another world.[50] So there are great supplies, in large supply houses.

Apocalyptic Imagery

Another image is interesting because it comes out in the Book of Mormon, the first source we have that talks about it. Apocalyptic imagery is not missing from the Book of Mormon, though it's not nearly as prominent as one would expect if the book had actually been composed in the world of Joseph Smith, because this was the one kind of doctrine that did have popular reception — the apocalyptic destruction. End-of-the-world sects were very common in Joseph Smith's time; the forerunners of the Seventh-Day Adventists were expecting the end of the world in 1843 or 1844, as were many people. The Book of Mormon avoids this image. The fire and smoke of hell, and other apocalyptic images, are clearly stated to be types, rather than realities, as is the monster death and hell. This practice agrees with the old apocrypha. Typical is the phrase of Alma: "I was in the darkest abyss; but now I behold the marvelous light of God" (Mosiah 27:29). "He has freed us from the darkness to prepare himself a holy people," says Barnabas.[51] To the image of the diggers of the pit who themselves fall into it, there are many parallels. Nephi mentions it twice (cf. 1 Nephi 14:3; 22:14). Ben Sira says, "He that diggeth a pit shall fall into it; and he that setteth a snare shall be taken therein."[52]

The solemn and impassioned outbursts of prophets and patriarchs, appealing to their sons and followers in this testamentary literature, come from this same mold. Where does the following passage come from? "And now, my children, . . . how terrible and awful it is to come before the face of the ruler of heaven. . . . Who can endure that endless pain?" This sounds like Alma talking to his sons, or like Nephi; or compare it with Alma 36:21. It's actually from the *Secrets of Enoch*,[53] discovered in 1828, shortly after Joseph Smith received the plates of Mormon, though in 1820 a text had already been made available in England, an Ethiopian text, from the sixteenth century (it would be interesting to know if it made it to New York State). Compare Alma 36:21 with this statement by Enoch: "And now my children, how awful it is to come before the face of the ruler of heaven. Who can endure that endless pain?" This is a translation by R. H. Charles. The Book of Mormon says, "Yea, I say unto you, my son [not my children], that there could be nothing so exquisite and so bitter as were my pains" (Alma 36:21). "The very thought of coming into the presence of my God did rack my soul with inexpressible horror" (Alma 36:14). My sons, how terrible, how awful, it is to come before the face of the Ruler; that was what "racked his soul with horror." And who can endure that endless pain, as he puts it, "so exquisite and so bitter were my pains" — the same ideas, presented in the same ways.

In one verse, Alma 19:6, the word *light* occurs six times, in every one of the familiar senses in which it meets us in the Nag Hammadi texts and in the Dead Sea Scrolls:

> Now, this was what Ammon desired, for he knew that King Lamoni was under the power of God; he knew that the dark veil of unbelief was being cast away from his mind, and the *light* which did *light* up his mind, which was the *light* of the glory of God, which was a marvelous *light* of his goodness — yea, this *light* had infused such joy into his soul, the cloud of darkness having been dispelled, and that the *light* of everlasting life was lit up in his soul, yea, he knew that this had overcome his natural frame, and he was carried away in God. (Alma 19:6)

Mohlin's book on the Dead Sea Scrolls, *Die Söhne des Lichtes*, deals extensively with the images of light and darkness;[54] the images are so constant that the Dead Sea Scrolls people are today called the "Sons of Light." The title to the second of the great scrolls is in fact *The War of the Sons of Light with the Sons of Darkness*. It is exactly the same light and darkness of which Alma speaks, in the same sense, when talking about King Lamoni, who was overcome in this struggle.

The Right and Left Hand of God

The ritual significance of the right and left hand of God receives far more emphasis in the apocrypha than in the Bible. It's a very old theme. Siegfried Morenz has recently written a study on the right and left hand, and on the judgment of the dead.[55] Right and left always refer to a position near the throne of God, in the sense that Mosiah uses it in a solemn ritual text (Mosiah 5:9–10). Whoever accepts the name and covenant will be on the right hand of God, and whoever rejects it will be on the left hand. It is a common image.

The White Garment

The image of the white garment is interesting, and
Erwin Goodenough has made a study of it. It appears in
the earliest Jewish art, among the earliest Jewish expressions he could find anywhere.[56] Alma is obsessed with the
image of the white garment: "There can no man be saved
except his garments are washed white" (Alma 5:21); "therefore they were called after this holy order, and were sanctified, and their garments were washed white through the
blood of the Lamb" (Alma 13:11). "Now they, . . . having
their garments made white, being pure and spotless before
God, could not look upon sin" (Alma 13:12). "May the
Lord bless you, and keep your garments spotless," Alma
says to his sons, "that ye may at last be brought to sit
down with Abraham, Isaac, and Jacob, and the holy prophets [the "big three"], . . . having your garments spotless
even as their garments are spotless, in the kingdom of
heaven, to go no more out" (Alma 7:25).

Such expressions forcibly call to mind the work of Professor Goodenough, in which he shows that the white
garment had a special significance for the early Jews. God
himself may be represented in the earliest Jewish art as
one of three men clothed in white (fig. 47). The three men
have a very special significance. Sometimes they are
Moses, with Hur and Joshua; sometimes they are Abraham, Isaac, and Jacob—but always three men clothed in
white, and sometimes the Godhead itself. We may sit down
with Abraham, Isaac, and Jacob, having our garments spotless as their garments are spotless. This image wasn't even
known to exist until 1958, but every time Goodenough
goes back into the earliest Jewish pictorial representations
he can find, there are the three men in white, or a single
figure, the prophet in white. The symbol of the chosen
prophet, an emissary from God, is always the white robe,
which is reserved for heavenly beings. Nephi says that

Figure 47. This scene from the Dura Europos synagogue, c. A.D. 245, shows the canopied Ark of the Covenant in an oxcart returning to Israel after having vanquished the Philistine idols (1 Samuel 5–6). The three men in white robes standing behind the departing wagon direct the oxen with their fingers. Goodenough calls this the "Triumph over Paganism" and cautiously identifies the three men as those who appeared to Abraham and therefore represent God himself.

the righteous shall be "clothed with purity, yea, even with the robe of righteousness" (2 Nephi 9:14).

The Strait Way; the Filthy and Pure Waters

When Lehi had a vision of a fountain, he failed to notice, according to his son who had the same vision, that the water of the fountain was filthy water; it swept people away to their destruction, because they weren't faithful. "The fountain of filthy water, . . . and the depths thereof are the depths of hell" (1 Nephi 12:16). Though a queer and unpleasant image, we meet it a number of times in the newly discovered apocrypha. Remembering that this flood of filthy water swept many away to destruction, as 1 Nephi 8:32 says, we turn to the *Odes of Solomon*, discovered in 1906: "Great rivers are the power of the Lord: and they carry head-long those who despise Him and entangle their paths: and they sweep away their fords, and catch their bodies and destroy their lives."[57] This is exactly the picture of the wild desert sail or *sayl*, sweeping away the unwary, as the Book of Mormon describes, the thing that Lehi dreaded. In another of the same *Odes of Solomon* there is an impassioned invitation, such as Lehi gave his family, to "Fill ye waters for yourselves from the living fountain of the Lord. . . . Come all ye thirsty, and take the draught; and rest by the fountain of the Lord."[58] This is like Lehi's beckoning to his family in the vision: Lehi saw that Sariah, Nephi, and Sam rested by the fountain and drank of the water, but he couldn't get his other sons to do this, though he invited them to do the same thing. "Blessed are they who have drunk therefrom and have found rest thereby," the same ode continues.[59] The poet plays freely with the same ideas. The wild desert torrent, which is the power of God sweeping the wicked to destruction, in a mass of wreckage, is described in the *Odes*.[60] In a *Thanksgiving Hymn* of the Dead Sea Scrolls, we read of the same wild torrent, but this time it's the way of the princes of this world.[61] They go forth suddenly, with a great rush and a fuss, sweeping all things away, only to dry up just as suddenly, while the spring of life flows pure and even forever. "It is the sweet spring that never faileth," says the *Acts of Thomas*, "and the clear fountain that is never polluted."[62] Never filthy, never polluted. In other words, they see the filthy fountain, and the pure fountain; the family of Lehi drank from the pure fountain, as he wanted them to. The others were swept away in the filthy fountain. Notice how the metaphors mix all the time, though the basic ideas remain. The filthy water sweeps them away, or it is the dirty water we don't want to drink. On the other hand, both the *Zadokite Fragment* and the *Habakkuk Commentary* speak of the false teachers of Israel as "drenching the people with waters of falsehood" — evil water, filthy waters, which cause the people to go astray in a wilderness without a way.[63] This is because of the pride of the world, which causes them to turn aside from the low way, the path of righteousness.

But aren't we lifting all this from the Book of Mormon? No, this is from the Dead Sea Scrolls. Notable are the connections between the water which they refuse and the desert road—all in the same sentence. Nephi says, "May I be true in the low way," not only in the plain way, but in the low path, the path of righteousness. The foul waters and the straying in the desert are part of the same verse and sentence in the *Zadokite Fragment*, as they are also in 1 Nephi 8:32: "Many were drowned; . . . and many were lost from his view, wandering in strange roads."[64] The fountains and the road are not only related images, but they also occur in the same peculiar combination in these earliest Jewish apocrypha and the Book of Mormon. The apocryphal Baruch says, "Thou hast forsaken the fountain of wisdom" and wandered away from the "way of God."[65] Forsake the fountain and wander away on the false road— the same combination.

Looking beyond the Mark

One of the most powerful verses in the Book of Mormon says, "Jews . . . despised the words of plainness, and killed the prophets, and sought for things they could not understand. Wherefore, because of their blindness, which blindness came by looking beyond the mark, they must needs fall" (Jacob 4:14). This "looking beyond the mark" now occurs with surprising frequency. The Jews usually moved the mark, or went beyond the bounds, or crossed the mark; that is the difference (cf. Deuteronomy 19:14; 27:17; Proverbs 22:28; 23:10). But in the *Zadokite Fragment*, they're the false teachers of Israel, the very types of Jews of whom Jacob is speaking: You have removed "the land-mark which our forefathers had set up in their inheritance." All those who entered the covenant have broken out of the boundary of the law of God, and have stepped over the line and gone beyond the mark.[66] This was the sin of the false teachers of the Jews.

Jacob talks about the wise ones, the intellectuals, the Jews who wanted to be so smart, and for that reason they overlooked the simple things and went beyond the mark. This is exactly the charge the *Zadokite Fragment* brings against the false teachers who had been teaching the Jews at this time, the very same smart-alecks, in the very same sort of way. Interestingly, the writer uses that point.

The reason the people receive error, according to the so-called *Gospel of Truth*, is that they insist on looking for a God who is so far beyond the mark.[67] This passage from the early Christian library in Egypt uses the same expression. Bright minds insist on looking for a God who is far beyond the mark, far beyond any place we can measure. When they expect that kind of God, they're not going to find him.

Most conspicuous among false teachers in the Dead Sea Scrolls is the "man of the lie," a theme that goes back to a very early time, the time of Jeremiah. The account is of Belchir, a false prophet, from the *Ascension of Isaiah*. "He was found," says this writing, "in the days of Hezekiah, speaking words of lawlessness in Jerusalem." He accused Isaiah the prophet and those who were with him, saying, "Isaiah himself has said [notice how clever he is in his arguments, arguing exactly as the opponents of the prophets argue in the Book of Mormon]: 'I see more than Moses the prophet,' but Moses said, 'No man can see God and live.' And Isaiah hath said: 'I have seen God and behold I live.' . . . Isaiah and those who are with him prophesy against Jerusalem and against the cities of Judah that they shall be laid waste."[68] This is the typical Book of Mormon false prophet who goes around using clever arguments, flattering words, and contradictions to tie people up. Belchir led most of the people astray, and he definitely got the edge on Isaiah.

Flight into the Wilderness

The idea of quarantine, the lone prophet, is interesting. The way they observe the law of Moses is unique. The flight into the desert is very important. The Book of Mormon begins with the flight of Lehi; and the righteous keep fleeing forever after. In this they consciously compare themselves to the movement of Israel in the desert. Lehi fled into the wilderness from his brethren, he said, so he could observe to keep the judgments, statutes, and commandments of the Lord in all things according to the law of Moses — this almost directly parallels the opening first two lines of the Dead Sea Scrolls. And the redundance of expression is very characteristic. What's the difference between a statute, a commandment, a judgment, and a law? They're all basically the same. The redundance is necessary — though it would be very tasteless in our way of writing. But the Dead Sea Scrolls writers never say just one thing, always three, as if there were some charm connected with it.

"Keep[ing] the law . . . [thus]," says Jacob, "it is sanctified unto us for righteousness, even as it was accounted unto Abraham in the wilderness" (Jacob 4:5). The Nephites compare themselves to Abraham in the wilderness: "Wherefore, we search the prophets, and we have many revelations and the spirit of prophecy" (Jacob 4:6). They had the spirit of prophecy, as an inspired, charismatic group, searching the prophets and having their own revelations. It was with us, says Jacob, even as it was "in the provocation in the days of temptation while the children of Israel were in the wilderness" (Jacob 1:7).

Now he compares the Nephites to the children of Israel in the wilderness at the time of Moses. Every phase of Israel's wandering in the wilderness is compared in 1 Ne-

phi to that of his own people, including their rebellion,
"and notwithstanding they being led, the Lord their God,
their Redeemer, going before them, . . . they hardened
their hearts, . . . and reviled against Moses," says Nephi
(1 Nephi 17:30).

The Tree of Life

The tree of life is a very common image, but I won't
go into it at length. The idea of its being white is not
common. The perfect whiteness of the tree is an odd twist.
Nephi says, "the whiteness [of the tree] thereof did exceed
the whiteness of the driven snow" (1 Nephi 11:8); and "the
fruit thereof was white, to exceed all the whiteness that I
had ever seen" (Nephi 8:11). White is not an appetizing
quality in trees or fruit; I would not like to eat perfectly
white fruit, and we do not think of perfectly white trees
as particularly charming, unless they're covered with blos-
soms. Yet the whiteness of trees and the fruit is a strong
image. In the *Creation Apocryphon*, the tree of life is
described as a cypress that has fruit that is perfectly white.
Incidentally, in the newly discovered *Genesis Apocryphon*,
Abraham compares himself in a dream to the cedar tree.
Nephi makes much of those lost souls who refused to eat
the fruit of the tree, which reminds us of a newly discovered logion of Jesus: "You do not know who I am, you
who have become as the Jews who love the tree but hate
its fruit." It's the story of the olive tree.

Zenos/Zenez

The prophet Zenos, who lived long ago in Palestine,
gives us a particularly valuable clue; more common than
the image of the water or the tree alone are those pictures
in which they appear together—the tree growing by the
water of life. Again, it's a natural combination. So I'll turn
to a specialized instance: the story of the olive tree, a particularly valuable clue, since the Book of Mormon author,

Jacob, gives his source. It is the prophet Zenos, who lived long ago in Palestine, not in the new world. He is introduced in the Book of Mormon a number of times as representative of the long line of messianic prophets who suffered persecution for his messianic teachings. He was no minor prophet; he's cited in the Book of Mormon more than any other prophet but Isaiah. His name, along with the names of other prophets — Zenock, Ezias, Neum — has disappeared without a trace. The Book of Mormon explains why they disappeared: Their messianic doctrine was highly offensive to the leaders of the Jews. Is the existence of such a line plausible? It's not only plausible, today it's demonstrable. In the Dead Sea Scrolls, forgotten prophets of major stature now emerge. Speaking of one of these, Father Daniélou writes,

> Between the great prophets of the Old Testament and John the Baptist, he emerges as a new link in the preparation for the Advent of Christ: "He is," as Michaud writes, "one of the great figures of Israel's prophetic tradition." "It is amazing," he says, "that he remained so unknown for so long. Now that he is known, the question arises as to what we are to do about this knowledge. It is a question that is posed to the Jews. . . . Furthermore, the question is put to the Christians: . . . Why does not this message, then, form part of the inspired scripture?"[69]

The Book of Mormon gives the answer clearly. We are actually given a brief biography of Zenos, and a very precious one, in Alma 33. We get his life's history; his written records were in the possession of the Nephites, who brought them across the water. Alma reminds them, 550 years later, "Don't you remember to have read . . . ?" So Zenos was popular; people were expected to have read him. "Do ye remember to have read what Zenos, the prophet of old, has said concerning prayer or worship? . . . Thou art merciful, O God, for thou hast heard my

prayer, even when I was in the wilderness" (Alma 33:3–
4) — it starts right out like a *Thanksgiving Hymn* from the
Dead Sea Scrolls, and the man who wrote these hymns
talks just like Zenos. In fact, it sounds much like Zenos;
both write the same type of hymns in the same way, and
both also tell us about the olive trees. Furthermore, in 1893,
some other fragments of an old Hebrew prophet Zenez
were discovered — sometimes Zenez, sometimes Kenaz.
They were published in Cambridge and edited by Montague Rhodes himself.

From the Book of Mormon, we know the following
about Zenos. He wrote: "Yea, thou wast merciful when I
prayed concerning those who were mine enemies." He
had enemies, who were making trouble for him. "And
thou didst turn them to me" (Alma 33:4). But they turned
to him again; he won them back. These are the troubles
we usually encounter. Then what happened? "Yea, O God,
and thou wast merciful unto me when I did cry unto thee
in my field" (Alma 33:5). He also worked in the fields.
"When I did cry unto thee in my prayer, and thou didst
hear me. And again, O God, when I did turn to my house
thou didst hear me in my prayer" (Alma 33:5–6). Then he
continues, "Yea, O God, thou hast been merciful unto me,
and heard my cries in the midst of thy congregations"
(Alma 33:9). "Congregations" occurs only thrice in the Old
Testament, in particular in the Psalms (Psalm 89:5).[70] Yet
"the midst of the congregations" occurs repeatedly in the
Dead Sea Scrolls, and these are the communities out in
the desert. So he lives in the wilderness, is rejected, people
take him back again, praise him, and then he is accepted.
His voice is heard in the midst of the congregations — that
is, he is taken in by some of the desert communities. But
he has a rough time: "Yea, and thou hast also heard me
when I have been cast out and have been despised by mine
enemies; yea, thou didst hear my cries, and wast angry
with mine enemies [the tables were turned against them],

and thou didst visit them in thine anger with speedy destruction" (Alma 33:10). Something calamitous happened to them. "And thou didst hear me because of mine afflictions and my sincerity; and it is because of thy Son that thou hast been thus merciful unto me, therefore I will cry unto thee in all mine afflictions, for in thee is my joy; for thou hast turned thy judgments away from me, because of thy Son" (Alma 33:11).

Alma continues: "Do ye believe those scriptures which have been written by them of old?" (Alma 33:12). He's reading from the scriptures, the writings of Zenos. Then he goes on to tell them about Zenock, who was put to death. We learn from Alma 33:3 that even the Zoramites know about Zenos. According to Alma, they actually had read Zenos's words, from which it is clear that his writings were among those contained in records brought from Jerusalem by Lehi and his family. This being so, it becomes clearer yet how intimate Lehi's people were with that outcast desert branch of Judaism, of which this man is so representative, to which they constantly refer, and with which they constantly associate themselves.

Hymn 14 of the wonderful *Thanksgiving Hymns* of the Dead Sea Scrolls is the writer's own biography; in *Hymn* 14, the writer talks about the trees, particularly the olive tree, though the references are scattered. *Hymn* 8 starts out, "I thank thee O my Lord," exactly as Alma does in quoting Zenos. It continues, "those who have led thy people away, those false prophets who by their flattering words . . . "[71] The false prophets in the Book of Mormon — the Sherems, the Nehors, the Zeezroms, and the Korihors — also always use "flattering words."

I have mentioned above the writing of Belchir, a false prophet who made a lot of trouble for Isaiah, who gained the ear of the king, and who was responsible for having Isaiah thrown out. Such false prophets were an institution in Israel; people fled to the desert mostly because of threats that drove them out. There was much tension between the two, and this is part of the tradition carried across the water by these people; specifically, Laman and Lemuel favored the other faction in Israel. They liked to go along with such people and accused Lehi and Nephi of being the visionary type of prophet they didn't like; they preferred the other school of prophets. This old feud carried right over to the new world, as did the same type of prophecy: "Those false prophets who have seduced thy people by their flattering words, and have by their tricks and their falsehood wrested the scripture. And I was despised by them"; "they held me in no esteem whatever; they caused me to be cast out"; "they drove me out of their country and out of their communities like a bird from his nest. All my companions, all those who were my followers and friends were turned against me," just as Lehi says his people turned against him right at the beginning (1 Nephi 1:20); then as the scrolls say, they turned back to him again: "They turned against me, they considered me of no more use. While they, those false interpreters, those liars, they formed against me a clever plan, plots of Belial, and by twisting the law, which thou hast engraved in my heart, they by their flattering words led thy people astray. And they have forbidden those who were thirsting from going and drinking of the water of life and of knowledge."[72] (The Book of Mormon imagery of the early period always comes back, when those memories were yet so vivid.) The false prophets forbade the people from partaking of the waters of life: They have locked them out from it. "They have kept the thirsty from drinking, even when they had thirst. They made them drink vinegar [not filthy water, but vinegar], and we have seen their distress." They have been caught in their nets, tricked in their dismay, "and O, and they, those who are hypocrites, those whose projects were those of Belial, those who conceived evil and sought for my undoing, being double-hearted; those who were not firm in the way of truth, their work has produced a bitter fruit." This is the bitter fruit of the olives, which the scrolls also liked to talk about.

> And their obstinate hearts are now seeking after idols, for thou hast caused them to stumble [compare the stumbling block of Nephi], caused them to stumble in their sins, and they have fallen on their face, they have not been able to oppose me, they have not been able to achieve their aims. For they did not hearken to thy voice, they did not lend an ear to thy word, for they have said of the vision and the revelation, "there is no more vision, there is no more revelation," and this way they led this people astray from the ways of thy heart, and then that they may be taken in their own plots and lead many away from thy covenants. But thou, O Lord, will affirm thy judgments and will reveal the trickery, the wickedness of all men, and they will not find themselves successful.[73]

He goes on to talk about how they will be overthrown:

> As for me, because I have leaned on thee, I will arise, I will be victorious again. I will arise again and will return to those people, will preach to them again; I will go again to those who despised me, who turned their hand against me because they had been led astray by false teachers, false traditions [compare the Book of Mormon missionary stories] and had me as a thing of nought. For thou didst appear to me in a vision, just at dawn, and my face was not covered with shame, and all those who had sought after me have now come back again and joined into thy alliance, and are now listening to my word. And those are now walking in a way which is dear to thy heart. They have raised themselves on my side, they have again joined the assembly of the saints. Thou hast made triumph their cause, through truth and through justice, and thou hast given no concern for those miserable ones who have gone astray.[74]

This is the way the scrolls read—the same story as

Zenos, who is driven out like a bird from its nest and turns
back victorious (notice the sudden overthrow of his enemies). And then the scrolls talk about the trees, describing
Israel as God's plantation, in which he plants trees in various parts of the world; the fruit shouldn't be bitter:

> Thou hast planted precious trees, cypresses and
> elms, mixed with all sorts for thy glory. [These are trees
> of life.] Throughout secret places, in unknown places
> [again, they were planted in secret places in Zenos's
> story in Jacob; Jacob was just quoting Zenos] these are
> planted for an eternal planting, and they shall take root
> in the various places where they have been set up, in
> many places, and they shall send out their roots toward
> the waters, even toward the waters of life. . . . And
> those that don't send out their roots won't have the
> waters of life. . . . And, from these trees which partake
> of the water, they shall raise up their branches because
> of their planting, they shall grow and they shall flour-
> ish. . . . And thou, O God, thou hast shut in thy vine-
> yard [notice he's calling the orchards vineyards] in the
> mystery of those who are valiant in thy service, who
> come to work in the vineyard, and the spirits of the
> saints that work for thee. . . . And with ancient and
> withered trees they do not drink the water, even the
> water of holiness, therefore they wither up and are lost.[75]

It's the same imagery of the withered trees that don't
partake of the water, trees being cultivated by God, but
some will bear good fruit and others will not; and the trees
get old and die and are weak. This would have been written
many hundreds of years after Zenez, and handed down
in this form to these people who preserved it. These hymns
are very valuable because they are beautiful. Whether Alma
would have a better text, I don't know, but we certainly
have the same type of men, doing the same type of thing,
writing the same type of scripture.

We should note here that aside from literary parallels,

Jacob's treatment of olive culture in the Book of Mormon shows a remarkable grasp of the business. Jacob 5 is a long, long discourse, one that always stops the little kids who start reading the Book of Mormon. Everything goes lovely until they get to Jacob and the olive tree. Then they grind to a halt; it's like walking through sand. That's as far as I ever got for years—I'd start out with high resolve, but as soon as I got to the olive part, I'd bog down. Joseph Fielding Smith says it's the best part of the Book of Mormon, the most powerful part.[76] And there *is* a lot to it.

Olive Culture

Jacob knows much about olive culture! Olive trees *do* have to be pruned and cultivated diligently, they *were* commonly planted in vineyard areas in the old world. In fact, the word *carmel*, in one early text, means either olive orchard or vineyard; and these two words are used interchangeably in Jacob's account. The tops do perish first, the good stalk is greatly cherished, and if you get a good olive tree, it's rarer than fine gold; many things must be done to preserve it. Some have been preserved for as long as thirty-five hundred years! Trees that old are still alive today—the stalk is so rare, so important. The common way to strengthen the old trees was, indeed, and it still is in Greece, to graft in the shoots of the wild olive, the oleaster, when the tree starts to get weak. Olive shoots from valuable old trees were often transplanted to keep the stalk alive, as the Lord does here. The best trees do grow, surprisingly, in the poorest and the rockiest ground, whereas very rich soil produces inferior fruit. Nevertheless, the plant must be very diligently fertilized, dug about, and especially dunged—since ancient times this has been the fertilizing practice in olive orchards.

Again, this is the very expression of the Book of Mormon. The grafting of shoots does lead to a cluttered variety of fruit and is considered a risky business. Our tree is encumbered with all sorts of fruit because we did too much grafting, he says. The top branches, if they are allowed to grow, as they are in Spain and France, to provide shade trees along the roads, make a picturesque tree, but they completely sap the strength of the trees, as they are said to do in the Book of Mormon. The tall branches take away the strength of the tree and get too high. The thing most to be guarded against in the fruit, of course, is bitterness. And so all these things are casually included in Jacob's story of the olive culture. This is just a lesson in agriculture, but who would know anything about olive culture in upstate New York in 1829? Today we find it all quite accurate; it follows the ancient method, not the way it's done today, necessarily, but of course olive culture is very ancient. All this is very authentic.

Redeemer of Israel; Likening the Scriptures

Reference to the Redeemer is very significant — the Lord their God, the Redeemer, going before them. Studies are now being done on the patriarchal tradition in Moses and the great emphasis on the *gō'ēl,* the doctrine of the Redeemer — a new thing in Old Testament study. It was the Redeemer who led them. And this applies to us all. For example, the *Habakkuk Commentary* compares the things described in Habakkuk with other battles that Israel has had to fight. Who were the Kittim, for example? Were they the Romans? The Greeks? The Babylonians? The Assyrians? The Persians? The Philistines? Various scholars say it was one, others say it was another; suddenly there was a big fight, and it occurred to them that the comparison applied to all these peoples. They were comparing all the scriptures to themselves, to their own fight. Israel had done it before. So today, scholars are no longer thrashing that out as they used to. Isaac Rabinowitz was the one who started it going. We were at school together in a Hebrew class from Professor Popper; it was he who first suggested that the Kittim were the Romans, and speculated on various other things. There was in the 1950s very active discussion. All that has been put to bed now, because of this principle Lehi teaches us: We "did liken all scriptures unto us, that it might be for our profit and learning" (1 Nephi 19:23). When the *Zadokite Fragment* deplores the apostasy of Israel in its own time,[77] it reminds us this is the very thing that Jeremiah said to Baruch (Jeremiah 36:1–32), and which Elisha, long before, had said to his servant Gehazi: "All of them have forsaken the well of living water" (cf. 2 Kings 4–5). It's the same combination of ideas — "all of them have forsaken" — referred to in the *Zadokite Fragment*. The Jews had forsaken it, just as Jeremiah said to Baruch in the time of Lehi, just as Elisha has said to his servant Gehazi long before that (2 Kings 5:26). They compare the scriptures to themselves.

The Rekhabites, as early as the time of Lehi, observed this principle; they called themselves the "ones who had kept the covenants of their fathers." One peculiarity of the apocrypha is their description of the righteous as the poor. This is very striking in the *Milḥāmāh (War) Scroll*. The people arrange themselves for battle and go forth in their might. It's a very elaborate arrangement of things, skillfully ordered, with strict ritual accompaniments. Yet after all this has been done, they know they don't have a chance. If they win at all, it will be in the same way that David beat Goliath — because the Lord helped them.

And they are the poor; the host of Israel are always described as being the poor, the down-trodden, those cast out from the world, as against the world, which are the mighty and the powerful. The issue is always drawn between the rich and the poor. However correct this may be, it's strictly in the tradition of the Book of Mormon, where the poor are mentioned no fewer than thirty times. H. J. Schoeps says the proper designation for these people in the Dead Sea Scrolls should be *ebyônîm*, the poor. They always talked of themselves as being the poor, as against the rest of the world, and the rest of Israel.

The organization of the church is rather elaborate. The keeping of the books and reading of the records is also striking. The people are always reading out of the scriptures; as Nephi said, "I did rehearse unto them the words of Isaiah, who spake concerning the restoration of . . . the house of Israel" (1 Nephi 15:20); "wherefore they may be likened unto you, because ye are of the house of Israel" (2 Nephi 6:5). Then he says a remarkable thing: "I have read these things that ye might know concerning the covenants, . . . that he has covenanted with . . . the Jews, . . . from generation to generation, until the time comes that they shall be restored to the true church and fold of God" (2 Nephi 9:1–2).

The *Manual of Discipline* likewise begins by instructing the people that these things shall be read to them from generation to generation until the restoration of Israel— the very same thing. Alma had to get permission from king Mosiah to found churches; "therefore they did assemble themselves together in different bodies, being called churches; every church having their priests and their teachers. . . . And they were called the people of God" (Mosiah 25:21, 24)—which is what the Jewish sectaries called themselves, the *Bene El*.

Then Limhi wanted to found a community along these lines, but he couldn't because he lacked the authority: "Therefore they did not at that time form themselves into a church, waiting upon the Spirit of the Lord" (Mosiah 21:34). The tradition goes right back to Jerusalem, when Zoram thought that Nephi "spake of the brethren of the church" (1 Nephi 4:26).

The waiting upon the spirit of the Lord is very common. The word *El* is used a great deal. In the Dead Sea Scrolls, everything exists only until there shall come a Messiah of Aaron and Israel. All is temporary; the community are simply waiting upon the Lord. They describe themselves as the remnant, and those who are waiting as the church of anticipation.

Ritual War

Another characteristic of the Book of Mormon is the ritual nature of war. In Alma 44:5, we have what can be called a "Rule of Battle for the Sons of Light." War is highly ritualized in the Book of Mormon. It is one thing that used to excite derision from Book of Mormon critics. What could be more silly, they used to ask, than a general who would give away his plan of battle to the enemy, or allow him to choose the time and the terrain? Yet this is very particular and strictly in order. In a study by Gardiner, he himself refers to "Piankhi's Instructions to His Army." That is a peculiar name, a pure Egyptian name, and one odd enough that no one could have possibly invented it in the Book of Mormon. Piankhi was a general before the time of Lehi, was very famous, became king of Egypt, and the name became quite popular afterwards. Piankhi-meri-amen has a very "Book of Mormon" sound. But of course the name occurs in the Book of Mormon (Helaman 1:3). It was this name, I strongly suspect, that first put Professor Albright on the track of the Book of Mormon. He recognized that it couldn't possibly have been faked or forged. Here's Piankhi, and there are the instructions. "Piankhi commands his generals to give the enemy choice of time and place for fight."[78] This is the way it was usually done, arranging battles ahead of time, just as the Book of Mormon people used to.

Kings and Covenants

I've already written somewhat about patternism and royal cult in the Book of Mormon and in the Near East.[79] Some points have recently arisen since then which deserve notice. In 1959, a study was published called "Der Vertrag

zwischen König und Volk in Israel" ("The Contract between the King and the People in Israel").[80] This is exactly
what we find in Mosiah 5, of course, a formal contract
entered by the king and the people. According to the Talmud, when Josiah invoked all the priests and prophets
and the people of Jerusalem and read its contents to them
from a platform erected in the court of the temple (the way
Benjamin does), the people enthusiastically entered into a
new covenant, "to walk after the Lord, and keep his commandments and his testimonies and his statutes" (2 Kings
23:3; cf. 2 Chronicles 34:31). Notice the three—commandments, testimonies, and statutes. The king reads the covenant to them; they enter into the contract, the covenant,
exactly as we find it in the book of Mosiah in the Book of
Mormon.

The tower is also interesting. The best description of
that is in Nathan the Babylonian, who is a tenth-century
writer who witnessed it with his own eyes, in the ninth-
century coronation of the Exilarch, the Hebrew king in
exile.[81] The most striking thing is Benjamin's oration. A
very Book of Mormon character was King Horemhab of
Egypt, a philanthropic, idealistic, religious man who had
a dream and founded a dynasty. But in Israel these were
not merely individual but formalized qualities. J. K. Bernhardt has recently shown that the sacral kingship in Israel,
the priesthood of Melchizedek transferred to David, goes
back indeed to the common great year festival—as I have
said it does, but with a difference. In Israel it got a peculiar
twist. There is, he notes, a marked tendency to democ-
ratization which receives its most striking expression in an
oration the king is expected to give on the occasion of his
coronation. Bernhardt says,

> The characteristic feature of the Israelitic concept of
> kingship is the formal refusal of the office of king with
> explanatory arguments. The custom of a royal polemic
> on the subject of kingship is among the oldest utterances

about monarchy in the Old Testament. The king formally refuses the office and accepts it on other grounds.[82]

Benjamin formally refuses in a set oration to accept the kingly office in its standard Near Eastern form. He says you accept the office, but you do it to the Father, not for me; he has never asked the people to bring the treasures to him as you do to a king; he has never asked for offerings, has never imposed taxes; has never asked them to bow down to him. They claim him; he's been elected. He gives himself and the setting a human and a much broader twist and democratic turn. At the end of his speech, Benjamin has the people formally enter into a covenant, with the statement: "This day he hath spiritually begotten you; . . . therefore, ye are born of him and have become his sons and his daughters" (Mosiah 5:7).

In the newly found sayings of Moses from the Dead Sea Scrolls, we are taken back to the occasion on which the state of Israel was founded by Moses. Moses announces it with a formal statement: "This day you have become the people of God." Then follows a list of all the good things God has given them—the vineyards and the olive trees, which they did not plant, of which they can eat and be filled, for God had given them victory over their enemies.[83] Need I discuss Benjamin's oration? Victory, plenty, and sharing with one's neighbor are the themes. Benjamin formally renounces kingship; as Bernhardt puts it, "the characteristic feature is the formal refusal of the office of king with explanatory arguments."[84]

Benjamin does—he refuses it in the old sense and gives his explanatory arguments, his speech on government. He gives them a royal polemic on the subject of kingship, which is among the oldest practices of the Israelite nation. It's not a recent thing; it always went with kingship. But most of the royal rites have been lost—they're not in the Bible, they're not in the prophetic writings, except in the

Psalms, which deal a lot with the coronation. This stuff is now meeting us exactly as it is in the Book of Mormon.

Even in Egypt something similar happens. Here is a typical description of an Egyptian coronation: as Moret has revived it, the king introduces his son and announces his name, declaring him to be his successor on the throne. All present then acclaim him in a single voice, at the invitation of the king, who then gives an oration. "This speech of the king is received with an acclamation, which proclaims the name of the new king. Then all smell the earth at his feet, prostrating themselves at the royal command."[84] Notice that Benjamin accepts the prostration, only on the condition that it is for the heavenly king. "I know you've fallen down. That's the thing you should always do on this occasion, but remember, you're falling down for God, your heavenly king, and not for me." "For the absent ones, a copy of a circular," as Moret puts it, "is sent around the land, telling of the coronation." This was all strictly understood by the Egyptians to correspond to the assembly in heaven. After the acclamation, the king receives a crown from God, is purified and clothed in the holy garment, and takes his place in the double divine pavilion (ḥeb-sed) with a priest on either side of him, who represent Seth and Horus (fig. 48); they usually wear masks, and there he's crowned on his throne, always with the three.[85] And this is exactly the way the Jews do it in the writings of Nathan the Babylonian. The ceremony ends with the dancing maidens, followed by the coronation, and a thunderous acclamation.

Conclusions

In 1816, the apocrypha were outlawed by the American Bible Society (which had great influence). They were regarded as devilish works, not to be used at all. So they came to have no prestige, were not read, were not known at all. They were not published in this country; little was

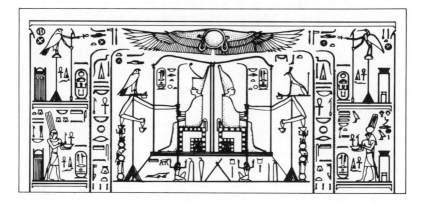

Figure 48. This elegant stone lintel from the temple of Senwsret III at Medamud, c. 1860 B.C., shows the king twice, each figure wearing a crown of Upper or Lower Egypt, being given the palm rib symbol of "millions of years" by the divine standards of Horus and Seth. The king sits on the Maat stone of truth under the double canopy, which became the hieroglyphic symbol of the *heb-sed* 𓊹

known about them. The apocrypha sank to their lowest level in 1945, when H. H. Rowley, the last surviving person to study the apocrypha, said, "We'll just close the door now and forget about these. Nobody's reading them anymore. It is so." And then, bingo, next year the whole thing broke loose again, and everyone was embarrassed, because no one knew anything about apocrypha. The new discoveries caught them completely off guard.

A study should be made of exactly what books were available to Joseph Smith in his time. Wilford Poulson has compiled a bibliography of works available in libraries in Palmyra in Joseph Smith's time; from it, we can see what books Joseph Smith could have read, but it is very doubtful that he read many, because he was very busy. He was very hard pressed by poverty; what could he have had at his disposal? Very little. Allowing the maximum, if he'd spent *all* his free time studying and had people going around the countryside bringing these books to him, he still wouldn't have had much to go on. Yet again and again we see in the Book of Mormon the world of ideas and images now unveiled by the rediscovery of the apocrypha.

Notes

1. Bob Brier, *Ancient Egyptian Magic* (New York: Quill, 1981), 41–45.

2. Stuart Piggott, *The Dawn of Civilization* (New York: McGraw-Hill, 1961), 188.

3. 1 Baruch 4:1–3, in *APOT* 1:591.

4. *2 Baruch* 6:7–10, in ibid., 2:484.

5. *2 Baruch* 80:2–3, in ibid., 2:522.

6. John M. Allegro, *The Treasure of the Copper Scroll* (Garden City: Doubleday, 1960), 61–62.

7. William Spiegelberg, *Demotische Grammatik* (Heidelberg: Winter, 1925), 1.

8. B. Couroyer, "Le chemin de vie en Égypte et en Israël," *Revue biblique* 56 (1949): 412–32.

9. Wisdom of Ben Sira 32:15, in Patrick W. Skehan, tr., *The Wisdom of Ben Sira* (New York: Doubleday, 1987), 34.

10. Wisdom of Ben Sira 32:15, in ibid.

11. Wisdom of Ben Sira 42:17–26, in ibid., 486.

12. Wisdom of Ben Sira 5:6–7, in *APOT* 1:542.

13. Millar Burrows, tr., *The Dead Sea Scrolls* (New York: Viking, 1955), 387.

14. Al-Hamdānī, *Al-Iklīl* VIII (Baghdad: Syrian Catholic Press, 1931), 15–16; cf. Hugh W. Nibley, *An Approach to the Book of Mormon* (Salt Lake City: Deseret Book, 1976), 211–12; reprinted in *CWHN* 6:257–58.

15. *Jubilees* 4:31, in *APOT* 2:19.

16. *2 Baruch* 85:9, in ibid., 2:525.

17. Wisdom of Solomon 12:10, in ibid., 1:554.

18. Wisdom of Solomon 3:5–7, in ibid., 1:539.

19. *Zadokite Fragment* 9:31, in *APOT* 2:820.

20. *Gospel of Philip* 101:10, in R. McL. Wilson, tr., *The Gospel of Philip* (New York: Harper and Row, 1962), 29.

21. Hugh W. Nibley, *Since Cumorah*, 2nd ed., *CWHN* 7 (Salt Lake City: Deseret Book and F.A.R.M.S., 1988), 37–38.

22. Cf. Athanasius, *Oratio Contra Gentes* (*Oration against the*

Heathen) 2–3, 22, 27–30, 38, in *PG* 25:5–9, 44–45, 52–61, 76–77; also see Athanasius, *Oratio de Incarnatione Verbi (Oration on the Incarnation of the Word)* 6–7, 15–19, 42–43, 45, in *PG* 25:105–9, 121–29, 169–73, 176–77.

23. Coffin Texts, spells 722, 724, and 443.

24. *Enuma Elish* V, 1, 6.

25. *Ras Shamra Texts from the Palace of Baal* 4:16–17, in J. C. L. Gibson, tr., *Canaanite Myths and Legends* (Edinburgh: Clark, 1977), 59.

26. Ibid.

27. *1 Enoch* 86:1, 3; 88:1, 3, in *APOT* 2:250–51.

28. *Secrets of Enoch* 30:14–15, in ibid., 2:449.

29. *Testament of Levi* 18:1–3, 6, 9, in ibid., 2:314–15.

30. *The Gospel of the Hebrews*, fragment 1; cf. Edgar Hennecke and William Schneemelcher, *New Testament Apocrypha*, 2 vols. (Philadelphia: Westminster, 1963), 1:137, 163.

31. *Testament of Judah* 24:1–2, in Hennecke and Schneemelcher, *New Testament Apocrypha*, 2:323–24.

32. *4 Ezra* 7:97, 125, in ibid., 2:589, 591.

33. 1 Baruch 3:34, in ibid., 1:590.

34. Cf. Millar Burrows, *More Light on the Dead Sea Scrolls* (New York: Viking, 1958), 224, 335.

35. *Zadokite Fragment* 9:8, in *APOT* 2:816.

36. Ignatius, *Epistola ad Ephesios (Epistle to the Ephesians)*, in *PG* 5:659–60.

37. *Clementine Recognitions* IV, 28, in *PG* 1:1327; cf. Alexander Roberts and James Donaldson, trs., *Ante-Nicene Fathers*, 10 vols. (Grand Rapids, MI: Eerdmans, 1981), 8:141.

38. This theme is treated at length in Hugh W. Nibley, "Treasures in the Heavens: Some Early Christian Insights into the Organizing of Worlds," *DJMT* 8/3–4 (1974), 76–98; reprinted in *CWHN* 1:171–214.

39. Wisdom of Ben Sira 39:17, in *APOT* 1:457.

40. *2 Baruch* 30:2, in ibid., 2:498.

41. *2 Enoch*, ch. 5–21.

42. Hugh W. Nibley, *Message of the Joseph Smith Papyri: An Egyptian Endowment* (Salt Lake City: Deseret Book, 1975), 267–72.

43. *Clementine Recognitions* III, 53, 58, in *PG* 1:1305–7; see Roberts and Donaldson, *Ante-Nicene Fathers*, 8:128–29.

44. *2 Enoch* 22:11; in *OTP* 1:140–41.

45. *Zadokite Fragment* 2:3–8, in *APOT* 2:807.

46. *1QS* 3:13–4:26.

47. *2 Jeu* 42, in Carl Schmidt, *The Books of Jeu and the Untitled Text in the Bruce Codex*, tr. Violet MacDermot (Leiden: Brill, 1978), 99–100.

48. *Acts of Thomas* 136, in *ANT*, 424.

49. *Gospel of Thomas* 50:109, in *NHLE*, 129.

50. *Psalms of Thomas* 3; cf. C. R. C. Allberry, ed., *A Manichaean Psalm-Book*, 2 vols. (Stuttgart: Kohlhammer, 1938), 2:207–9.

51. Barnabas, *Epistola Catholica (Catholic Epistle)* 17–21, in *PG* 776–81.

52. Wisdom of Ben Sira 27:26, in *APOT* 1:408.

53. *Secrets of Enoch* 39:8, in ibid., 2:454.

54. Georg Mohlin, *Die Söhne des Lichtes* (Vienna: Herold, 1954), 21–23, 31, 33, 43, 98, 129, 151, 160, 169, 178, 182, 185.

55. Siegfried Morenz, "Rechts und Links in Totengericht," *Zeitschrift für ägyptische Sprache und Altertumskunde* 82 (1958): 62–71; reprinted in Siegfried Morenz, *Religion und Geschichte des alten Ägypten: Gesammelte Aufsätze* (Cologne: Böhlav, 1975), 281–94.

56. Erwin Goodenough, *Jewish Symbols in the Greco-Roman Period*, 13 vols. (New York: Pantheon, 1964), 9:165–74; 10:95–97.

57. *Odes of Solomon* 39:1–3, in J. Rendel Harris, ed., *The Odes and Psalms of Solomon* (Cambridge: Cambridge University Press, 1909), 134.

58. *Odes of Solomon* 30:1–2, in ibid., 128.

59. *Odes of Solomon* 30:7, in ibid., 128.

60. *Odes of Solomon* 39:1–3, in ibid., 134.

61. *Thanksgiving Hymn* 2; cf. Geza Vermes, *The Dead Sea Scrolls in English* (New York: Penguin, 1975), 155–56.

62. *Acts of Thomas* 39; cf. *ANT*, 384.

63. *Zadokite Fragment* 1:10–17, in *APOT* 2:801–2; *Habakkuk Commentaries* 1–2.

64. *Zadokite Fragment* 1:10–17, in *APOT* 2:801–2.

65. 1 Baruch 3:12, in ibid., 1:588.

66. *Zadokite Fragment* 1:11, in ibid., 2:801.

67. *Gospel of Truth* 17:10–20, in *NHLE*, 38; cf. *Gospel of Truth* 22:20–34, in ibid., 40.

68. *The Martyrdom of Isaiah* 3:6–11, in *APOT* 2:161–62.

69. Jean Daniélou, *The Dead Sea Scrolls and Primitive Christianity*, tr. Salvator Attanasio (Baltimore: Helicon, 1958), 83–84.

70. [The Topical Guide lists the word "congregation" as appearing eight times in the Old Testament.]

71. Cf. *Hymn* 8, in Theodor H. Gaster, *The Dead Sea Scriptures in English Translation*, 3rd ed. (Garden City, NY: Anchor/Doubleday, 1976), 157.

72. *Hymn 8,* in ibid., 157–58.

73. *Hymn 8,* in ibid., 157–59.

74. *Hymn 8,* in ibid., 159.

75. Cf. *Hymn 14,* in ibid., 175–76.

76. Cf. Joseph Fielding Smith, *Answers to Gospel Questions,* 5 vols. (Salt Lake City: Deseret Book, 1957), 1:150–53.

77. *Zadokite Fragment* 1:9–17, in *APOT* 2:800–802.

78. Alan H. Gardiner, "Piankhi's Instructions to His Army," *Journal of Egyptian Archaeology* 21 (1935): 219–23.

79. Nibley, *Approach to the Book of Mormon,* x, 243; in *CWHN* 6:v, 295.

80. Georg Fohrer, "Der Vertrag zwischen König und Volk in Israel," *Zeitschrift für die alttestamentliche Wissenschaft* 71 (1959): 1–22.

81. Nathan Ha Babli (Nathan the Babylonian), "The Installation of an Exilarch," ch. 10, in Benzion Halper, *Post-Biblical Hebrew Literature* (Philadelphia: Jewish Public Society of America, 1943), 64–68. Adolf Neubauer, *Medieval Jewish Chronicles and Chronological Notes* (Anecdota Oxoniensia IV and VI), 2 vols. (Oxford: Clarendon, 1887–1895), 2:77–88.

82. Karl-Heinz Bernhardt, *Das Problem der altorientalischen Königsideologie im alten Testament* (Leiden: Brill, 1961).

83. *The Oration of Moses,* in Gaster, *Dead Sea Scriptures in English Translation,* 374.

84. Bernhardt, *Das Problem der altorientalischen Königsideologie.*

85. Alexander Moret, "Du caractère religieux de la royauté pharaonique," *Annales du Museé Guimet* 15 (1902): 82.

86. Ibid., 84.

Apocryphal Writings and Teachings of the Dead Sea Scrolls

I shall probably bore you tonight, but the subject shouldn't, because it's a very good one. I am not going to be bored at all. I love to talk about this stuff! I will get all excited, so don't pay any attention to me! Since World War II tremendous discoveries have been made. Certain ancient libraries have been discovered: the Dead Sea Scrolls; Chenoboskion (Nag Hammadi), the earliest Christian library discovered the same year, under much the same circumstances, but a thousand miles away from the Dead Sea Scrolls; and then the Papyri Bodmer, which includes the *Letters of Paul,* far older than anything we have ever known about before. Then there are the Manichaean and Mandaean discoveries; and earlier than them, the Chester Beatty Papyri; and also the *Odes of Solomon.* We can go back to the Oxyrhynchus and the Bryennios Papyrus (the *Didache*), and finally to the big libraries of the nineteenth century. These sensational finds have completely changed our picture of the early Christian and Jewish world.

Simply to describe these finds and where they are found, under what circumstances, how old they are, how we know they are that old, etc., would be very interesting

This previously unpublished talk was given at a Long Beach, California, seminary graduation, in 1967. It has circulated under the title "Teachings from the Dead Sea Scrolls."

and quite relevant, but we can't do it, because that would take up a great deal of time.[1] We can mention, however, that the documents are found in batches — not a scrap here and a scrap there, but whole libraries, complete. But why do we find them now?

These are not like other libraries that have been found, because these were buried for the purpose of being found in the later dispensation, the later generation. The people who sealed them up sealed them up to come forth in a later time, "when men would be more worthy to receive them," as they put it. That is remarkable — they have been preserved in their purity. As the Book of Mormon tells us, the only way to preserve a record in its purity is to bury it. Because just as surely as you copy a document, you will make mistakes; and just as surely as the next person comes along and copies your mistakes, he will try to correct them; and just as surely as he tries to correct them, he will make new mistakes. The next person will come along and try to correct him, and before you know it, the document is a mass of corruption, whether deliberate or not. But no document can ever escape these basic distortions and corruptions, except if buried to come forth in its purity at a later time. And so now we find a library buried and sealed in jars. The Dead Sea Scrolls were first written on nice, newly prepared leather, then rolled up and wrapped carefully, and covered with linen; then the linen was covered with pitch, just as if one was laying a mummy away. Then they were put in specially made cylindrical jars, sealed with lead and pitch on top with caps that fit on tightly. Then they were arranged neatly in a cave and covered with nice, dry sand so there would be no corruption; everything was hermetically sealed. Then the cave was cemented up so you couldn't see a thing; you're not coming back next week to get them. That's not merely a guess, because the documents themselves tell us why they were buried in this way and what the owners had in mind.

Whenever you find a new batch of records, the value or significance can only be gradually appreciated, because the picture they give is so shocking, so different from any ideas we had before about the early church. They call not only for a reevaluation of our ideas, but for rereading all the stuff we have already. But who is going to do that? It is embarrassing to have to reevaluate the whole of our literature, the entire field. That's hardly the work for narrow specialists, and yet narrow specialists are the only people who ever read any of these documents at all. So it's not an exaggeration — it's quite probable, in fact, almost certain — to say that many great treasures are lying about us and around us, undiscovered and ignored.

I do not suppress the wild rumors that go around about these documents. Anytime you talk about such things, you get wild rumors, completely irresponsible and greatly exaggerated; but on these particular matters, for example, the Gnostic and Coptic Texts, I don't think rumors should be suppressed; no matter how wild your story is, it can't be more fantastic than the truth. It is better to be ignorant and interested than ignorant and not interested, and there's no third alternative here. We're ignorant in any case, so you might as well be ignorant and interested in these things.

Gardiner always said that the first rule for an Egyptologist is always to have an idea, always to make a suggestion. If it's a wrong idea, it is better than no idea. A wrong translation is better than no translation.[2] You will at least have something to shoot at, something to work on. A wrong theory is better than no theory, and there is no such thing as a right theory. Theories are always changing, and in science, as well. This is what men like Thomas Kuhn[3] and Karl Popper[4] tell us today. A theory is something to work on. So is a wrong rumor, a wrong idea. At least a rumor gets around when something has been found and that's important; there emerges a big picture, which changes everything. You can't exaggerate that.

A description of the contents of one or two of these new documents, or pictures of it, would miss the cumulative impact. When just one document, like the one in the first cave at Qumran, was found by the shepherd boy Mohammed Dhib, lots of people, like Professor Solomon Zeitlin, who edited for so many years the *Jewish Quarterly Review,* said that it was a fraud; these things were a plant, not real documents, all faked.[5] (Mohammed's uncle was sort of a majordomo in the house of President Barnes at the American University of Beirut. He spoke Aramaic— one of a few people left who spoke the language of Jesus. It was this nephew who discovered the Dead Sea Scrolls, the shepherd boy who threw the rock into the cave. He was very much interested in the Book of Mormon, and especially in the Pearl of Great Price; he could see the significance of the Dead Sea Scrolls, and the way these things hang together.) Zeitlin started a lively discussion. Then another cave opened, and another, and another, and another—two hundred and thirty new caves discovered, many with documents in them! It had to be some forgery job to produce that! When the documents were first discovered, Father de Vaux went out, and then soldiers; the King sent Jordanian soldiers to see that there was no hanky-panky.

The Arabs around were mostly illiterate; they couldn't have forged the stuff. Still they were bringing documents in from the caves, so the archaeologists went out to see if they couldn't discover some of their own, and they did discover some of the most important caves: Nos. 4 through 13—all discovered by scholars and men who couldn't be fooled. The Arabs didn't tell them where they were or anything else. The archaeologists found them themselves; they shaved the wall of the cliff right off, and there underneath were the documents, perfectly preserved. What's on them is the important thing.

We'd miss the cumulative impact of the hundreds and hundreds of caves if we just talked about a document here, a document there. Each would be very important; it would change your ideas. The hundred give a full picture; and not only is there a library at Qumran, but thousands of miles away another was being kept by Christians—the same sort of thing. The best we can do is to indicate some of the teachings and some of the information common to all, or nearly all, of the major documents, whether from Syria (east of the Tigris), or at the south end of Mesopotamia, in Qumran in Palestine, or in southern Egypt, sixty miles north of Thebes at Nag Hammadi; or whether the documents be Mandaean or Manichaean (the early Syriac). The Nag Hammadi is a great Christian library, in about thirteen codices—nice, beautifully bound books in jars in their original leather bindings that hadn't been touched, from the fourth century, in perfect condition, just as if they had been written yesterday, buried by a little Christian church before the apostasy hit it, before Gnosticism hit it. They represent the earliest level, the earliest teachings of the church, a totally different picture from what anybody had imagined it would be like. And the extent of these things is remarkable.

So the next thing will be to indicate some of the teachings and some of the information that all these have in common, because these sources are new and unspoiled, and we have been willing to accept from them what we have never been willing to accept from previously discovered documents. Lots of other documents have been hanging around for a long time and have been trying to tell us the same things, but we wouldn't listen to them because they were just a "late corruption," "Gnostic nonsense," "Medieval forgeries," and the like. You can't say that anymore, because there are so many recent discoveries, and they are so much older than any other documents known before — both Jewish and Christian — that you have to treat these with respect. Men are being forced to receive these new teachings, which before they had been able to combat successfully. And it is these new documentary findings which are behind the ecumenical reforms today — changes in the ordinances of both the Catholics and the Protestants today. Christians are discovering that if this is the way it was in the early church (there was no mass, or anything like that), they have to change things to conform to the new doctrines. There is lots of information.

A good example of the teachings propounded in the early Jewish and Christian documents, now being forced on us, is "cosmism." The word was used by Carl Schmidt (the great document man of that time) at the turn of the century. A very important Christian document discovered in 1897 is called the *Epistle of the Apostles*[6] — an old, very long, and vitally important document of the early church. It opened our eyes to a lot of this. Schmidt edited it, and although he didn't coin the term, he was the one who pointed out that this is what makes the difference between the early church and the later church. The early church accepts "cosmism": Somehow the physical cosmos is involved in the plan of salvation. We say "naturally," and Fred Hoyle says, "You can't make three meaningful sentences about anything without some reference to the physical world." But that's not what was thought in Alexandria. In the third and fourth centuries, it was very fashionable at the university of Alexandria to allegorize and spiritualize everything. Everything had to be spiritual, and the Doctors converted the Jews (e.g., Philo) and the Christians. All eight early Christian Doctors of the church were students at the university of Alexandria, and they followed the party line. Talk of physical, tangible things was crass, vulgar, nonintellectual. When the Doctors of the third and fourth centuries adopted the attitudes and teachings of the university of Alexandria, they turned their backs on what they called the "old wives' tales" of the early church.

It was Jerome who coined the term "Primitive Church," to him a term of contempt. The early Christians were primitive. They didn't have the education the Doctors had, and so the Doctors got rid of all the offensive ideas; and it wasn't too hard, because they had all the learning of the day on their side. They denounced and renounced most passionately what was called "cosmism" as being the crassest literalism and materialism, the complete antithesis of everything that was intellectual and spiritual.

But they were stuck with three doctrines they didn't like at all, and this unsettled them, because they couldn't find a way to get around them. The first was creation. After all, the physical world is a terrible mistake. According to Neo-Platonism, God is essence and spirit and is pure, and all matter is bad. As Iamblichus says, "Any contact with matter corrupts even God Himself."[7] But who created this physical world? According to them, God did, and such a creation by God stumped them. They couldn't understand how God could actually create a physical world, for he was pure spirit, pure essence; and all physical things are a vile corruption. Why would he make a physical universe?

But even worse was the incarnation, the second point. Origen said, "I don't think the apostles could understand that; I don't think even the angels could understand that. How could God be born into a little child and have a body?" Origen works on this dilemma: He had to be fed when he cried and had to have his change of diapers.[8] Such is unthinkable. There can't be such a thing. Imagine how the schoolmen at the university of Alexandria would go for that.

After you've accounted for the physical things with some kind of argument, the third and worst of all things is for the Lord to resurrect us all with these physical bodies after we have finally sloughed off the mortal coil and gotten rid of the vile material connection. After returning to pure essence, to the nothingness from which we came, we are then stuck with a physical body forever! They didn't like that at all.

Yet these were the teachings of the early church, which couldn't get away from such "cosmism." Justin Martyr, the first apologist of the church, in the middle of the second century (300 years before Jerome tore his hair out over these things), said, "We Christians do not believe in creation out of nothing"[9] — emphatically not, as a number of recent studies have pointed out.[10] Both Catholics and Protestants point out that not until the time of the Doctors of the church (the first Latin Doctor was Ambrose, and the first Greek Doctor Athanasius, both in the fourth century) does the church became wholly committed to the teachings of the schools. There was no early Christian doctrine of creation out of nothing at all. Yet it became the official teaching of the church after the fourth century. For the early Christians, matter — creation and how it was done — was important. The *Clementine Recognitions* is a key text. You can always go back to the *Recognitions* to get your bearings. It is a very useful guide, whether you use the Dead Sea Scrolls, Nag Hammadi, or the Mandaean texts; they all tie up in the *Clementines,* where Peter says, "There is absolutely no evil in matter, as such."[11] Eusebius himself stated in the *Preparation of the Gospel* that matter is not the cause of evil. "I cannot explain it," says Origen, "but it is important nonetheless to understand that this world is not pure incorporeal idea."[12] "God is the Father of all our eternal bodies," says an important Coptic work discovered just three or four years ago, "bringing about the resurrection of the flesh through a member of the Godhead. Do not be afraid of the physical universe."[13] "The living spirit clothes itself in a body of elements," says the *Berlin Papyrus,* "through which it is able to carry out its works in the world."[14] The spirit has to have a body of element if it is going to work at all. Creation means organizing of elements;[15] Justin Martyr also says the same thing.[16] Matter is a difficult and recalcitrant medium for the spirit to work with. But it's supposed to be. For all that, God is aware of it and makes good use of it. His activity and concern are everywhere evident in number and in measure, as evidence that he is organizing things.

The Cosmos does form a pattern. *Cosmos* means "organization, order." *Cosmetic, cosmology,* means "putting things in order." With cosmetics, you put your face in order—your eyes up where they belong, your nose approximately in between them, etc. Roughly, you push things around and get some sort of order in your face. Typical is the *Pistis Sophia,* a very important Coptic work. "There is an appointed place for everything in the Cosmos," it says. There is a numbering of souls for each world: and a dispensation is not completed until the *teleos* ("completed") number has been fulfilled for that dispensation. Every soul stays in its appointed place until it has fulfilled the task for the *topos,* for that place.[17] "God plans times and seasons for all things," says the newly discovered and very important work, the *Apocryphon of John.*[18] The Dead Sea Scrolls are full of set times: a time for iniquity, the time allotted for Satan to tempt mankind, and a time of suffering and a time for punishment—all exactly prescribed from the beginning. The Archons wanted to check Adam's power by limiting his time (on earth), but they couldn't, "because all times were fixed by God's plan in the premortal existence." "For the *kairos* is fixed, and the limit set for every individual according to the way prescribed for the 'Sons of Light,' " according to the Scrolls.[19]

It is well understood that all of this setting of times is constructed according to our nature, not according to God's nature. Time is for our testing—like holding a stop watch on a particular process to see how things have been going. All this time and place business is characteristic of this particular world. "For [God], there of course is not time," says the *Apocryphon of John;*[20] Alma says the same thing (Alma 40:8).

"If you ever set yourself to build," advises the newly discovered *Manichaean Songbook,* "let the measuring come first for you. If you build without a measuring device in your hand, your building will be crooked. Measurement is the very essence of construction."[21] "The whole creation," says Clement of Alexandria, "is to be understood as a synthesis: the imposing of inner order on outer material." It's a progressive organizing of materials from the center out. You first organize a center, and that structure becomes firm enough to organize more onto it. "And so this synthesis," continues Clement of Alexandria, "is building from the center out, and organizing that way"[22] — from an inner order to an outer material. This is the background material; more and more of it is absorbed into the system — all is organization and synthesis.

In the *Apocalypse of Abraham,* a very important Jewish discovery, Abraham hails God: "God! Thou who dost bring order into the confusion of the universe, ever preparing and renewing worlds for the righteous."[23] The *Codex Brucianus* (a new document) says the same thing: Creation is organization, and God is ever bringing order into the universe and is progressively ever preparing and renewing worlds for the righteous.[24]

But it is not enough to arrange matter in order and system. Such matter remains, for all its pretty patterns, inert. If you organize it, you've just got a geometrical structure or something similar, but it's still inert. It's only background stuff. The *Pistis Sophia* says that, without light, matter is inert and helpless.[25] It must be improved by the action of light; according to these texts, you've got to put into it some animating principle. Whenever that active

principle is withdrawn, the matter at once falls back into
its original lifeless, inert condition. It's like removing an
electric current from a tube of one of the inert gases—the
tube shines as long as the charge goes through it; remove
the charge, and it becomes just nothing again. "Matter
must be improved by the action of light," and whenever
the active principle is withdrawn, it at once falls back into
its original lifeless, inert condition (like the inert gas argon).
This vitalizing principle is referred to everywhere as "the
spark," which you must have if anything is to happen.
"Without this spark," says a very important new work
called the *Second Coptic Gnostic Work,* "there is no awareness,"[26] no consciousness. The electric eye that opens the
door for you when you go into the supermarket is not
conscious of you; that is, it's not thinking at all. It's purely
automatic. An awareness, a consciousness, must be added
to the electric eye, or it has no mind at all. That is the
difference: things just automatically reacting, or, having a
mind.

There are cabalistic teachings about how God's intelligence unites with matter to form light or life. This is called
a unity—except that it goes by a concept of cabalism (medieval Jewish mysticism),[27] for which reason we say that God
is in everything because he animates everything. The Coptic *Gospel of Truth,* discovered in 1956 (one of the most
sensational discoveries of our time, a tremendously important document, which caused enormous excitement
when it was discovered; but then it started telling too
much, so it got swept under the rug, though much has
come to support it), says much the same thing: "Unity
engulfs matter within itself like a flame."[28] This contrasts
with the absolute separation of matter and spirit in an all-
or-nothing arrangement like that of the Gnostics and Neo-
platonists whom the church Fathers followed—matter as
either inert and wicked, or divine pure spirit, with no
choice in between; it was corrupting to try to bring the two

together. Later Christian theology has never been able to reconcile the two.

The early Christian apologist Aristides explains everything in terms of a "divine mixture," which produces the new type of life in the manner of the original creation.[29] Melito of Sardis, one of the earliest Fathers of the church, referring to the physical universe, says, "By the power of God, all the world is moved and animated as the body is moved by the spirit."[30] "When this vitalizing principle touches matter," according to the *Psalm of Thomas* (a very important Syriac text, recently discovered), "consciousness is expanded. The worlds of darkness gathered and beheld his brightness. They breathed his fragrance and orbited about him and bowed anew and worshipped him."[31] They came into organization and started to orbit about him as he had determined. This is the "thought of life," working with the elements, which brings about creation, according to the *Berlin Papyrus:* "At the time of the creation, the great thought came to the elements, united with them, spirit joining with matter."[32] Though now joined with spirit, matter is not spirit. It is still itself and is constantly undergoing a processing. Matter at every stage is in some form of processing. The way these writings talk about these matters is extremely interesting; it certainly beats science fiction.

Speaking of science fiction, I went to the bookstore and looked at some titles on the shelf. Do these ancient books sound like a lot of science fiction? They do. These were some of the titles I found on the shelves — *Bow Down to Null, Ten Years to Doomsday, The End of Eternity, The Second Foundation* (the names of main top sellers today), *Billennium, The Burning World, The Passport to Eternity, Worlds for the Taking, Budrys' Inferno, Beyond the Galactic Rim, Possible Worlds, The Three Stigmata of Palmer Eldritch* ("three stigmata" — a Christian reference), *Transfinite Man, Stranger in a Strange Land, Zolan's World, Earth Abides, Those Who Walk,*

Recalled to Life, and so forth. So we ask this question: Since the ideas are nothing but conscious or unconscious plagiarism of biblical and apocryphal ideas (all these themes go back to the old plan of salvation — scriptural and apocryphal ideas), why do these works have so much greater appeal than the originals? Because the originals, as they are given in the Bible and the apocrypha, have been systematically denatured. That was the policy at the university of Alexandria: to spiritualize everything — to cut out anything that was material, real, tangible, or literal. The schoolmen didn't like the literalness; that was for children. We want the purely spiritual, symbolic, allegorical, but nothing real, nothing tangible. So they robbed the scriptures of the one thing that made them interesting. All the original force was destroyed. Thus science fiction — "folk-scripture" — has taken the place of real scripture. We retain the idea of the possibility that such a thing is actually conceivable. But the Christian world says, "No, this is not actually conceivable in the literal sense. It is to be understood spiritually; it can never happen." So Christianity becomes an anemic, bloodless, meaningless sort of thing, because there's no real doctrine, nothing you can get your teeth into. The doctrines are all pretty, aesthetic, and moral, but still dime-a-dozen. Anybody can have that sort of thing, as the philosophers do. A world is interesting only when it's a real possibility. Maybe there *is* "Budrys' World." Maybe there *is* something beyond "The Rim of Eternity." That is the appeal of science fiction. But of course it has become a horror in our day, because as far as the writers can figure out, there is nothing beyond.

I will return to that a little later. The processing of matter got us into science fiction, because it beats science fiction — how matter is processed from other worlds to make it serviceable for the needs of spirits. Of course, the Pearl of Great Price says that as one world comes into existence another passes away (cf. Moses 1:38); "Worlds without number have I created" (Moses 1:33).

The *Gospel of Thomas* enjoyed a big sale, and so out came the *Gospel of Philip*, its twin, available in rather ambitious translation at the request of the Protestant ministers. But it was quickly suppressed. It became hard to obtain, because the clergy didn't like what it said. When we had a hard time trying to buy a few copies, Harper's explained that that's what had gone wrong.

As the *Gospel of Philip* puts it, "There is no permanence in matter, which is always undergoing change as worlds come into existence and pass away. Only progeny is eternal."[33] This world is just a background for our goings-on; we will have to have new worlds or worlds refurbished, cleared out by a melting down and "decontamination." The writers like that word. The creators decontaminate so they can use the matter again in other worlds. But we ourselves don't get reused. We go on: "Only progeny is eternal"; only sons are eternal. Other worlds change as they must from time to time in order to adapt themselves to new types of beings, if you will. But progeny — sonship — goes on forever and ever. All *physis* — all physical universe, all nature, all plasma, all things that are made of material, all *ktisis* (construction, all structural work), all physical work — is interdependent, says the newly discovered *Gospel of Mary*, a very interesting work. (Although it has very little to do with Mary, it was given that title.) "These will return to their own root." But the root is not destroyed.[34] Matter is indestructible, whatever its root.

A passage in the *Apocalypse of Abraham* reads like a modern description of the seething, ever-changing elements within a star. Abraham was shown the stars. An angel comes and takes him on a journey, during which Abraham goes into a trance (fig. 49). His spirit leaves his body, for when he comes back, it enters his body again and he has to be raised onto his feet. His spirit leaves his

Figure 49. In this illustration from a Slavonic *Apocalypse of Abraham,* c.
A.D. 1300, the angel Yahoel (Metatron or Enoch) gestures to the heavens
above as he leads a hesitant Abraham by the wrist. They ascend on the
wings of eagles (cf. Exodus 19:4).

body, and the angel takes him to watch a star in the process of transformation. What an effect it has on him! He says he sees an indescribably mighty light, and within the light a vast fire in which there is a host of tremendous forms, which are always changing and exchanging with each other, constantly changing their shape as they move and consume each other and alter themselves.[35] First, the hydrogen goes into a helium cycle, then to the next cycle, the main phase within a star. According to Abraham, it's quite a thing to see the stars always altering themselves. He frankly does not know what is going on. "I've never seen anything like this," he says. But of course he's not supposed to have, so he asks the angel, "Why have you brought me here? I've become weak, I can't see a thing, and I think I'm out of my mind."[36] The angel tells him to stick close to him and not be afraid. But later they are both wrapped in something like flame, and the noise is as the voice of many rushing waters.[37] (This was long before the time of Christ and the day of Pentecost—and we hear much of it in the Kirtland Temple.)[38] Then even the angel takes precautions. Abraham wants to fall on his face, but he cannot, "because there was no earth or ground anywhere to fall on."[39] Abraham is awfully glad to get back into his body again and feel solid earth under his feet. What a terrifying experience—to see this transmutation of elements within the fire within the body of a star, constantly changing from one element to the next. Very impressive!

The documents talk a good deal about decontaminating matter and then putting it into orbit, so to speak, where it will circle around a center until someone uses it again. Then the creators draw off various elements as they need them, according to specific gravity and all the certain, specific temperatures necessary for their fusion, and so forth. They had it all worked out, way back then.

The most useful property of matter seems to be its

plasticity—its ease of adaptability. It submits readily to handling. Eusebius himself points this out.[40] So matter cannot itself be the cause of evil, because you can control it. Lehi said that man is here "to act . . . and not to be acted upon" (2 Nephi 2:26). Matter is to be acted upon. You can't blame it for making you sin, as many of the Christian world in the Middle Ages thought—blaming our physical bodies, our nature, for sinning. Matter is inert. We make the matter act; it doesn't make us act. Eusebius, as I said, points that out in the *Preparation of the Gospel.* Matter is always being reformed, reorganized, reused, according to the law of plenitude, which the scriptures teach. Nothing is wasted. There's no space without something in it. Nothing is wasted; nothing is duplicated. Matter is to be reused, so to speak—melted down and then purified, and definitely decontaminated. In this decontaminating process, the action of the light on matter is always important. It has a purifying effect, whether for the first time or for reuse. Indeed, strictly speaking, there is no reuse, no old matter, since the action of the spark or light upon the matter always makes it renewed matter. "Let matter rejoice in the light," says the *Pistis Sophia,* "for the light will leave no matter unpurified."[41]

"The treasure or physical substance used by each spark must be taken from other treasures," says the *Kephalaia,* "and before it can be used it must first be purified."[42] You can't create matter out of nothing; it must always be taken from some other treasure. But before it can be used, if it has been used before, it must be purified; that is, "the various elements must be separated, cleansed, and reclassified for reuse."[43] The *Gospel of Thomas* describes it as sort of a junkyard process—the idea of reuse. The word used is "trough":[44] the matter is put into a trough, a sort of a circular trough in orbit. From this melting-down trough comes all the nondescript, used matter. Then you sort it out: "But we separate it out when we reclassify it."[45] When the flame engulfs the substance to form a new unity, then obscurity becomes light, death becomes life, and old jars are broken to make new jars (cf. Jeremiah 18:1–6), says the *Gospel of Truth*.[46] You don't make new jars out of nothing; you break the old jars, then use that matter over again. That expression is used a lot. Peter uses a like figure in the *Clementine Recognitions*, where he tells Clement that "the universe is like an egg shell which exists only for its inside — only to be broken and thrown away, that greater things may come."[47]

The *Odes of Solomon* has a wonderful passage on the theme of dissolution and then renewal (the *Odes of Solomon*, just discovered, were the earliest hymns of the church): "God took dead bones and covered them with bodies. They were inert and he gave them energy for life. Things were brought to corruption by God that everything might be dissolved and then renewed, and so founded again on a rock."[48] The author is talking about the resurrection in terms of the remaking of the worlds too.[49] God furnished the spark, the living principle.

Every new creation, according to the *Kephalaia*, leaves behind the matter of its old ages (its old *aeons*). "From the beginning, the elements were purified by the holy, living bearers of light. And from the first context, they were mixed with the background material and have remained so ever since." (Those are the actual words used in the *Berlin Papyrus*[50] — "background material" — as if its authors had been reading Fred Hoyle back in the fourth century!) The same text explains that when the poison or contamination of old matter has been removed, that matter becomes sterile. It's pure, but it's sterile; you can't do anything with it. It has to be reenergized. In fact, the Greek word used is "receives" — *energia*; i.e., it must receive new energy to get going again.

In the *Apocalypse of Abraham*, Abraham addresses God, "Oh thou who abolishest the confusion [or mix-up] of the

universe" — the confusion that follows the disintegration
of the world of both evil and righteous alike; "for thou
renewest the world of the righteous."[51] After this disintegration, after the falling away, God is the one who abol-
ishes the confusion and reorganizes it. When the worlds
reach a certain point, they disintegrate. Then they are organized again: God "reneweth the world of the righteous."
From this last statement, it would appear that the spirits
are involved in the process; this is the doctrine of man's
body being actually a microcosm, following the pattern of
Adam.

One thing Origen couldn't get out of his system was
the idea of real space. There is a lot of study about space
today, because the Bible is taken up with the idea. A Lu-
theran, recently writing on this subject, examined these
passages in the Bible. He argues that expressions like "to
visit the earth" and "he went and preached to the spirits
in prison," etc., cannot be taken in any but the most literal
sense.[52] When Christ visits, he goes somewhere; when he
went and preached, he went to another place to do the
preaching (cf. 1 Peter 3:19). A Catholic writing of just a
few months ago says, "We are never allowed to forget in
the early church what we have forgotten today; that heaven
is not only a state but a place."[53] There really is such a
place. Catholics have always thought — Thomas Aquinas
and others like him — that heaven is just a state of mind.
But the early Christians believed that heaven is a place.

According to the *Pistis Sophia*, every creation seeks a
more roomy place in chaos.[54] Every creation is always pushing, wanting more space. This is the idea of the expanding
universe, a basic principle. The *Second Coptic Gnostic Work*
says, "Every kingdom requires a space and will need more,
but by the law of plenitude, or perfect economy, no space
should be wasted and none should be crowded."[55] The
Odes of Solomon explains, "There is abundant room in thy
paradise, and nothing is useless therein; there is no waste,

but neither is there any crowding."[56] Nothing is useless. Everything performs a function. That is the law of perfect economy, the law of plenitude. Nothing is wasted, nothing is duplicated; nothing is just there to be there.

In the *Ginza*, Father Uthra (cf. Jesus) is told, "Go down to that place where there is no occupied place, where there is no world, and create for us another world after the fashion of the Sons of Salvation."[57] Go down to that place where there are no occupied *topoi*, no worlds, etc. The same writing explains that when the mass and number of the world are filled, a squeeze begins, and it is time for expansion. "All spaces come" from the Father, says the *Gospel of Truth*, but first, they have neither form nor names.[58] When they are organized and become the scenes of activity, then you have a feeling of space awareness. The concept of space comes into the picture. The idea of pure space, of absolute space, of empty space, totally void without even chaotic matter in it, is abhorrent to these writers. They cannot conceive of such a thing. Even if there is one atom to a thousand cubic miles, it is still not empty space.

The ultimate form of damnation is "to be like the demons of the air." Satan is the prince of the air (Ephesians 2:2–3), because he has no place for his foot — no sure footing, no base of operations anywhere. As the *Pistis Sophia* says, "To be deprived of the ordinances is like being suspended in air, having no place for his foot."[59]

"All spaces were broken and confused" at the time of the transition from old worlds to new,[60] the *Gospel of Truth* tells us. At the time of breaking up in this transition, the scene becomes rather terrifying. In quite a number of these writings, the apostles ask the Lord if they can see such things, and he replies, "Don't ask. It's not a healthy thing. It would upset you; it would disturb your thinking and everything else if you saw too much of these things."[61] You're not equipped to go out and stare at such things.

They would drive you mad (it would be like taking some LSD or other mind-altering drugs)—you'd see in other dimensions, which is not a healthy thing if you're not ready for it. Live in the world in which you belong. In passing from old worlds to new, all space is broken and confused, for they have no fixity or stability during that time. That's a time to avoid.

In *1 Enoch*, the ultimate horror is "a place without firmament above or foundation below," a place kept as a "prison for the stars . . . that transgressed."[62] Note the great emphasis on the foundation—the rock, the cornerstone, the place to start from. You must have some firm footing in space in order to begin your building. The concept of the temple in the hundreds of legends, stories, and ideas connects it with the idea of the rock. You must have something unshaken to start; otherwise there is no confidence in anything. All creation must have as its first step a base or foothold in the void to start with. Without that, there can be no structure, no organization, as is well known. It was always believed that in the beginning, the temple provided that foothold. It was the beginning place of the world, the rock where other things are founded. All of the texts are very fond of the word *topos*. All the texts, no matter what language they were written in, use the word *topos*—the beginning place or the rock—as a specific place, not just space, but a special space marked off and set apart for a special activity, a dedicated piece of space. The *topos* is a useful space (cf. John 11:48), just as a *kairos* is a useful period of time for carrying out some specific task.

Thus we are also told that the Lord, having accomplished his mission on earth, returned to the *topos* from which he came. John tells us that (John 14:2–3). It also occurs in the *Gospel of Peter.*[63] God started out by creating a *topos* where his children could settle, there to recognize and to serve him as their Father, according to one of the manuscripts. In the *Ginza*, God tells Adam, "Adam, this is the place where you are going to live; your wife Eve will come and join you here, and here your progeny will thrive."[64]

The idea of distances is very real. A very early Christian writing says, "From the place (*topos*) which the righteous soul will inherit, our sun, because of its great distance, will look like a tiny grain of flour, a mere speck."[65] It is a real place, but a very great distance away. These terms are common in the documents.

We have been talking in terms of multiplicities of worlds almost as a matter of course. Here are a few typical quotations on that theme. The *Askew Manuscript* says that after the plan of creation was accepted, it was communicated to all the other worlds, and they approved and rejoiced. For the worlds exist, says the *Second Coptic Gnostic Work*, so that intelligent spirits might come and inhabit them.[66] "In the limited confines of the flesh, which condition all our thinking," says the Lord in the *First Apocalypse of James* (a very important work, recently discovered), "we mortals can't possibly count or reckon the heavens."[67] "The Lord revealed all to me," James says, "He who has moved among worlds. Not only are they countless, but they have been going on forever and ever."[68] Father Adam's holy angels inhabit many worlds, says the *Sophia Christi*[69] (another important work I haven't yet mentioned). "Thou, light of our world," they say to the Lord, "come and be king in our land, our Holy City."[70] "No words can describe Thy power over all Thy worlds," says the *Ginza*. "The Father taught me about the worlds of the Lord and the Glory that abides in them. The Adam of light treads upon the earth's trembling foundation, which is laid in the midst of the worlds."[71] "To the Christians," said the impeccable Justin Martyr, "is promised endless worlds, endless cosmoses."[72] Jedaiah ben Abraham Bedersi (a Jewish writer writing after the New Testament times) says: "Man is nothing in the midst of the worlds. This world is but a speck among the worlds, of which man is nothing."[73] "It was the degenerate Minaeans that first taught that this is the only world," says the Talmud—which says this is the teaching of the devil, to believe that there are not any other worlds.[74] A Dutch scholar, van der Meer, has recently written a monograph in which he points out that the Roman Catholic and the Protestant view of man is not the biblical one. And recently, a Catholic study in the *New Scholastic* points out that "the heavy, sluggish earth must be the center of everything," the only world, so there can be no other but this one. That is from Aristotle, not from the Bible, and was not taught by the early Christians. They believed in many, many worlds, of course. That was part of their teachings. Over against this, our older Christian sources often remind us that in the great scheme of things, everything is plural—worlds, universes, plans, gods, places (*topoi*), saviors, etc.

All the worlds are organized on a common pattern, we are told, which isn't surprising. For example, we are told in the important *First Apocalypse of James*, in the *Second Coptic Gnostic Work*, and in the *Apocryphon of John*, that in all the worlds you will find God alone rules, but with a presidency of three and through a council of twelve.[75] This is the rule of all the worlds. The repetitions are infinite in number and scope. "In any world," say *1 Jeu* and *2 Jeu* (incidentally, *2 Jeu* appears to be one of the most important early Christian manuscripts ever discovered, older than anything we have in the New Testament), "as a Jeu becomes a Father in a new world, the Fathers then appoint new Jeus [Jehovahs] for new worlds, who in turn will become Fathers," etc., *ad infinitum*.[76] "Each Jeu has created for its hosts ten thousand times ten thousand." In the *Sefer Yetzira* (some think this is the oldest Jewish work in existence), "the earth and planets are but atoms in an infinity of like systems."

This is a very old, orthodox Jewish work, a great and mysterious work.[77]

Origen, the first and by far the greatest of all Christian theologians, had a lot of intellectual problems because he was born and brought up at the university of Alexandria, where he saw that what was taught wasn't what the early Christians preached; he became a church theologian to try to reconcile these teachings. He does not give his personal opinion, but the teachings of the early church—and our Church—when he states that "there will be another world after this one."[78] We thus share a common nature with other worlds. Or, as Methodius puts it, "Christ came down from his vast rules and kingdoms in other worlds to save one percent of those on this evil earth, and to enroll the human race in the Heavenly Register."[79]

What does this do to the oneness of God? It doesn't do anything at all to it. In nothing is the idea of the real oneness of God more convincingly apparent than in the contemplation of the real cosmos. "There are many mansions," says the *Second Coptic Gnostic Work*, "regions, spaces, heavens, degrees, and worlds, and they all have but one law. If you keep that law you too can become a creator of worlds."[80] "It is the perfect Father who produced the all, in Whom the all is, and in Whom the all will rule," says the *Gospel of Truth*.[81] "Out of the One come countless multitudes which yet remain in the One," says the *Sophia Christi*.[82] But the one God always remains in control. For only on condition of being exactly like him can souls take the next step. God will trust you to represent him, to act for him, only if he knows that you will do exactly what he would do in all circumstances. Then he can leave you alone. He trusts you. You're like him—a perfect identity, as far as your function is concerned. You can just carry on his work. It's like arriving at the same answer to a problem. He will trust you only if he is sure you will come out with the same answer as he did. "All other worlds look to the same God, also to the common Son," says the *Untitled Gnostic Text*.[83] The crucifixion is effective in other worlds, as it is in this one. "All the cosmoses follow the pattern of a single world (called the *topos*)," says the *Sophia Christi*.[84] "Ever since the beginning this has been so. This pattern keeps the entire *physis* (physical universe) in a state of joy and rejoicing,"[85] being dominated by one mind, by one great plan.

"The worlds exchange wisdom with each other because they are equally dependent upon the Most High," say the *Odes of Solomon*. "They are the heralds of his thoughts. By his word, they communicate with each other. They knew him who made them because they were in converse" (they all have the same Maker, so they're all playing the same tune); "for the mouth of the Most High spake to them. The worlds are made by his word and the thoughts of his heart, so they are all as one."[86] "There is no rivalry or competition among them," says the *Ginza*, "but they are glorious in their firmaments, and there is agreement among them, fitting together like the lashes to the eye. All rejoice in each other, each being more glorious and bright than the other" (meaning that there is a hierarchy among them, forever and ever; they just get greater and greater).[87] Indeed, according to the *Kephalaia* (another important writing I haven't yet mentioned), all the gates of the firmament were opened to assist when this world was made. Everyone wanted to contribute. "When beings from different worlds meet, they exchange garments and treasures as a sign of mutual esteem and identification," says the *Ginza*.[88] "For the creation of endless worlds follows a single pattern—that laid down by God the creator. The planets say, 'Come Lord of the gods, Lord of the entire cosmos.' [They rejoice and say], 'Come be our head, be the head of our whole world.' "[89] The Lord lets his countenance shine in one world and then in another (as it tells us in D&C 88:51–61), and they wanted him to stay as long as possible, of course. "Christ sounded with a trump in the worlds far and near alike. He roused them all alike," says the *Manichaean Psalm-Book*. "For he is the Savior of the worlds. The worlds will come before him in order and in shining oath."[90] "God is the Father of all the worlds," says Clement. "He knows them. They keep their courses in covenant to him."[91] "He calls them by name and they answer him from eternity to eternity," says the *Ethiopic Enoch*.[92] "As the Father of greatness is in the glorious worlds, so his Son rules among those cosmoses as the first Chief Lord of all the powers."[93] Thus one recent study observed that the multiplicity of successive worlds tends towards unity. The cosmos is not simply a oneness and nothing else, but rather a multiplicity comprised in a oneness.

So there is a vast monotony. But is it just a repetition, more of the same thing, when you get into another world? "Only little minds are impressed by size and number," said Sir Isaac Newton. What's the point to endless repetitions of the same? That's what makes science fiction so depressing. Characters arrive in another world in the usual boy-meets-girl sequence. They have an exotic background. Things are a little different, but, after all, it's just the same old stuff. So the science fiction becomes very depressing. Most of its writers have become very negative, even terrifying, in that picture of hopelessness. You're not going anywhere; it's all just more of the same when you get out into another world—people rending and tearing each other, strange monsters, etc.

One of the nicest things about the early Christian cosmology is that it is not a repetition of sameness. The types are there, but always expressed in individuals who never express the type in exactly the same way. What could be more monotonous than the design of the six-pointed snowflake? No two snowflakes are the same, yet they must all conform. In these writings, those who have seen other worlds in visions (and it is a very common thing) say that

you simply cannot imagine what they are like. They are
not like this world at all. In 2 Corinthians 12:2, Paul says
he "knew a man . . . caught up to the third heaven." And
in 1 Corinthians 2:9, "Eye hath not seen, nor ear heard,
neither have entered into the heart of man." We cannot
begin to imagine what it is like. So don't try to get a picture
of heaven. Whatever it may be like, what we find beyond
is not just more of the same. "Other worlds cannot be
described in terms of this one," says the *Pistis Sophia*.[94]
"Not only is there nothing common between other worlds
and this world, they are as different from each other as
any of them is from us." "In the limited confines of the
flesh [James again] which condition our thinking, we can't
possibly grasp the nature of other existences, or even begin
to count the number of worlds."[95] We are necessarily prone
to think in terms of our world, the *Gospel of Philip* explains;
but when we are talking about the other worlds, this is
completely misleading. We haven't the remotest idea of
what it is like there. We use the words we do because we
know no others.[96] When we say "light," the *Sophia Christi*
says, we think of our kind of light. But that's wrong. There
are all sorts of ranges in the spectrum of which we know
nothing. Marriage, for example, would be entirely different
there from what marriage is here, though we must des-
ignate earthly and heavenly marriage by the same name.
Even though the spirits may be eternal and thus equal in
age, says this writing, they differ in intelligence, appearance, and in other things. These differences are primary.
They are as unbegotten as the spirits themselves.[97] They
are just different, and that's that. "Where my Father is,"
the Lord tells the apostles in the *Epistle of the Apostles* (an
authentic early work—everyone as far as I know has accepted this as one of the very earliest records we have from
the church and the writings of the apostles), "it is entirely
different from this world. There you will see light which
is nobler than your kind of light."[98] "In the millions of

worlds that God has made for his sons," says the *Ginza*, "every world is different from the other and wonderful in its own radiance."[99] Hence, one of the joys of existence is that the worlds constantly exchange with each other what they have, each possessing something different and peculiar to itself. "There is nothing superfluous anywhere" (which means that nothing is a mere duplication of something else), says the *Odes of Solomon*.[100]

In the *Berlin Papyrus*, we are told how every world breaks down into five spirits or bodies, just as there are five tastes and senses, etc.; and they are not alike anywhere. They are in different combinations. An interesting passage explains that "there are literally all kinds of strange beasts on other worlds [a teaching of Joseph Smith, incidentally][101] that we can't even imagine,"[102] because they adapt themselves to other conditions and other worlds. When we go back to other geological ages, we find very odd and strange creatures. They pass away; they change themselves to different environments. They adapt themselves, and so these are odd-looking creatures. "In some worlds, reproduction is carried out differently from here."[103] "There are all sorts of creatures," the *Zohar* says (it and the *Sefer Yetzira* are the two oldest Jewish works), "for there are all sorts of environments—except one for man. He is the same everywhere. If you go to any other world he will be the same, and yet he's the most individual of all." He doesn't have to change, adapt himself, like these other creatures; instead, he protects himself against these environments and changes them to suit himself. He is the same everywhere, and yet he is the most different.

The vast variety exists wherever you go. Tyrannosaurs and dinosaurs and other odd creatures adapt themselves, but man doesn't have to. He's the immortal, the only one that goes on and on. "Everything else changes, but only progeny is eternal," the *Gospel of Philip* says.[104] "Among ten thousand times ten thousand worlds," says the *Ginza*,

"you will find no two alike." Before this world, there had
already been a thousand thousand mysteries and a myriad
myriad of planets, each with its own mysteries or ordinances.[105] Athanasius says, "The multiplicity of worlds
forms a perfect unity as the strings of the lyre do. Each
plays a different note [that's why their difference is jus-
tified], and together they make marvelous harmony."[106]
They don't all play the same note—there's no duplication.
Each has a contribution to make to the magnificent, organic
whole. This is a common idea among the ancients. Plotinus
taught that each star existed for the sake of the whole to
which it contributed its individuality. Each had its particular part to play, and, thus, by being unique within itself,
could make a contribution of maximum value,[107] which it
couldn't make if it were just like every other star. Don't
be like anybody else. Be different. Then you can make a
contribution. Otherwise, you just echo something; you're
just a reflection.

This is the principle of subordination, a very important
point. Among lights, none are identical; there is a hierarchy
(there is a greater and a greater and a greater). There is a
hierarchy among the many worlds, says the *Pistis Sophia*.[108]
Many of these documents are concerned with the elaborate
theoretical breakdown of this hierarchy, a favorite theme
of the Gnostics: dividing it up into how it broke down,
what power was above what, which angel was superior
to which—like our friends the Seventh-Day Adventists,
who argue as to who has five stars in his crown and who
will have six. The hierarchy among the many worlds is
part of a tradition, a good illustration of the individual
variations on a general theme.

One of the many points of difference between the
Gnostics and their rivals was the different way they would
put in order and arrange the cosmic hierarchy. All of them,
however, share the idea of three main degrees of glory.
The *Pistis Sophia* says, "You can visit the order below you,

but not the levels or orders above you."[109] This is the rule in all worlds: you can go to the lower ones, but not to the ones above you. The degrees are described in many of these writings. In his early *Epistle to the Trallians*, Ignatius (the second earliest Christian writer we have who is accepted by everyone as authentic) says, "I could write you about the mysteries of the heavens, but I am afraid to, for it would do you harm. . . . But I am able to understand the orders of the heavens, the degrees of the angels, the variations among them, the differences of dominions, of thrones, of powers—of the Holy Ghost, and of the kingdom of the Lord, and the highest of all—the rule of God over everything else."[110] "There's an infinite hierarchy in the worlds," says the *Sefer Yetzira*.[111] "Christ rules in the second place, his rule exactly duplicating the Father's, but over a more limited number of cosmoses." Methodius explains, "If other stars are greater than our world, then it is necessary that they contain life greater than ours, and greater peace, and greater justice, and greater virtue than ours."[112] Of course we think of Abraham: If there is one, there shall be a greater one, and "I am more intelligent than they all" (Abraham 3:16–19). The hierarchy goes on and on until there's no place to end it, except when it reaches the Father himself.

These writers were aware of the fact that these doctrines carried over, but they couldn't understand them anymore, so the church Fathers got rid of them in the fourth century.

The church Fathers called them "the teachings of the elders" and considered them great mysteries, because they didn't know what to do with them. Methodius says that the spirits are equal in age, but different in power, intelligence, and appearance. They have been so throughout all time. Why should one be greater than another? This is one of the things the fathers liked to talk about. Origen was greatly intrigued and exercised by the diversity, and especially by the inequality among God's creatures. "Such an inequality," he says, "could not have been arbitrary, or else the Creator would be unjust. He couldn't create a thing small with another great over it — would that be just?" So he concludes that the levels on which we all find ourselves in this world must somehow have been merited in a former life.[113] However, the later schoolmen, following Aquinas, said that "there is indeed a hierarchy and a diversity simply because God wants it to be that way, and for no other reason."[114] They gave the idea up.

Aquinas had his ideas of the multiplicity of worlds, and the great differences among them, and the hierarchy of worlds. What next? The idea that they are all moving forward. It is not a static system; every world is progressing. "Until Christ opened the way," says the *Gospel of Philip*, "it was impossible to go from one level to another [death and resurrection]. He is the great opener of the way because he gave us the plan by which we can progress. He is the way."[115] That's why we call him "the way, the road, or the gate." The false progress of this world he compared to the ass turning a wheel, going around and around, turning the wheel and getting nowhere at all.[116] But being the "way," the Lord himself also advances. The *Gospel of Truth* says, "Thus the Word of the Father advances in the cosmos, being the fruit of his heart and the expression of his will." Through the ordinances, one makes progress in knowledge, and the ordinances go on and on.[117] "There are mysteries so much greater than these," says the *Pistis Sophia*, "that they make these look like a grain of flour, just as the sun looks like a grain of flour from distant worlds."[118] That's in an old Jewish source too. "Everyone here on this earth descends, as it were, to the dregs [earth or dirt] and shares a common substance with all living things." We are the same matter as the oyster, the cockroach, etc. They will be resurrected too, for they have a spiritual side — another very common teaching. "We share a common substance with all living things, and from here on out we begin to work our way up, step by step, to a knowledge of all things, ever seeking for instruction and carrying out the required ordinances that will lead us to more," says the *Epistle of the Apostles*. This is the idea of progress.

"Thus we move," says *1 Jeu*, "from truth to truth." The farther advanced one is, the faster one moves.[119] The gap broadens as you move in a progression. The more advanced you are, the faster you go, and the more advanced you get in relation to each other — a principle Latter-day Saints also teach. "To them that have shall be given." With exaltation comes an increase and acceleration of exaltation. Thus "we are passed on from hand to hand, from degree to degree!" Our example is Adam, who, having been established in Christ and God, next established his son Seth in the second order, which was to follow him on up, says the *Pistis Sophia*.[120]

"He who has fulfilled all the ordinances and has done good work cannot be held back," says the *Ginza*. "We are taught the principles of salvation, so that we cannot be held back in this world. Those who receive certain teachings and carry out their instructions in this world cannot be held back in this world or the next." "Those who shut the doors against me will be held back in the abode of darkness. Those that open the doors to me will advance in the place of light." The great blessings pronounced on Adam, according to the same source, say, "Thou shalt have progress onward."

Let us talk a little about ordinances. Very nearly all of the early Christian documents (and there are over 200 of them) have to do with what the Lord taught the apostles after the resurrection. What was said in the forty days? The New Testament does not tell us.[121] What did he tell the apostles? According to these documents, he gave them the ordinances of the temple — but only to the apostles, to be held in secret. They would last only two generations, he explains, then they would be taken away. So they were not to pass beyond the general authorities, but were given to them as a special blessing to make that dispensation complete. They would be restored later on (in our dispensation). The ordinances are described in great detail. You could almost go through the temple using just these documents, for so much is there. Now it is public property; anyone can use it. However, the authority remains in one church.

That's why we're finding the libraries today—they were all buried on purpose. They were not to be read by just anyone; the records weren't to be sent abroad; the world wasn't to receive them. They were regarded as very secret. Because this was a very important part of the plan, it was easy for them to get lost. And after they were lost, people could pretend they had them. Hence the false Gnosticism, and all sorts of other phonies and quacks. There were at least eighty-eight different sects in the church, each claiming it had the secret teachings the Lord gave the apostles after the resurrection.

That's what gnosis is: the knowledge of what the Lord taught the apostles after the resurrection.[122] When he came back, he found the apostles not believing; they all took to their heels and ran away. When Mary and Joanna told them that they had actually seen their living Lord, they said, "You're crazy" ("nonsense" is the actual word used in Luke 24:11); "You're very foolish and unbalanced; you're out of your mind." Then they saw the Lord, but Thomas wasn't there. "I won't believe it," Thomas said, though all the apostles testified they had seen the Lord. Thomas (and he was a good apostle—the firmest of the lot) persisted, "No, I can't believe it until I've seen for myself" (cf. John 20:25). They didn't understand or invent the resurrection story, as the theory goes. It wasn't their idea at all. They actually fought the precept. When somebody told them the Lord was resurrected, they didn't say, "Hooray! It was just as we thought. We knew it would happen!" It was the last thing in the world they would have invented.

This is when the Lord gave them the special teachings. It says, "Then they were able to go out and preach the gospel." Before then they weren't ready to. But we don't have anything that the Lord taught them. At the end of Luke, we learn that he came to them behind locked doors, and when he did, he rebuked them for their unbelief and their hardness of heart. He gave them the opening words of the plea, "O fools, and slow of heart" (Luke 24:25, 27, 44–45). That is about all we have in the New Testament of what he taught them during the forty days. Now what about these forty days? Isn't this the most important teaching of them all? We have one-half hour of reading time of what the Lord taught the apostles during the three years that he was with them, and that was not enough to convert them. They just did not understand what the resurrection was all about during that time. Yet that's all *we* have. Can we understand so much better than the apostles? We say, oh yes, in light of the resurrection. But, oh no! The Lord had to stay with them; he had to teach them time after time.

We have sixteen accounts of his returns and teachings. We also have the marvelous account in 3 Nephi of the Lord coming and teaching the apostles after the resurrection. But what did he teach them? That is the point. He must have given them something extremely important to change their whole view of everything, because then they were ready to go into the world and preach the gospel.

The forty-day documents have four things in common. First of all, they were *secret*—for the apostles only, not for general knowledge. They were not handed down; that is why they could be faked later on. Of course, people knew the sort of thing the Lord taught, and consequently the sort of thing to fake — so everybody pretended to have the knowledge, but nobody did.

Second, they paint a very *gloomy picture*. In all of these accounts, the apostles ask the Lord, "What's going to happen to us now? What's going to happen to the church? Why are we going to all this trouble in this dispensation if it's all going to be taken away?" The Lord tells them, This is for two generations now, then it's going to be taken away; a lesser church will be left in its place; it will be kept on the fire, so to speak; the true church will return later when I return with my Father. This of course was a doctrine the Christians didn't like. It was very bad news for the later church to have the Lord telling the apostles that all these things were going to be taken away. Yet he had said the same thing in several places in the New Testament.[123] The documents make this very clear; thus these teachings were unpopular.

Third, the Lord taught them *strange doctrines*, and the Christian world didn't like that sort of thing at all. The churches liked spiritual things, the things that came out of the university of Alexandria.

Fourth (the main thing), the Lord gave the apostles the *ordinances*. We can't speak about these ordinances specifically, only in general.

There is the doctrine of the "Sent One" — somebody who is sent. Recently, a great deal of attention is being paid to this doctrine of the "Sent One." Geo Widengren, a Swede, has written a book on the subject of "The One Who Is Sent"[124] — the one who is sent from one world to another with a message and instructions. In fact, the word *apostle* means "sent one." Instead of personally intervening by direct methods into the affairs of men, God sends his agents to act for him. The purpose of the Sent Ones, all agree, is to help the struggling lower creatures out, by instructing them in what they have to do to survive here and hereafter, and where necessary to show them how to go about following instructions. Their great work is, thus, to uplift and to give help to those beneath them. The greatest of the Sent Ones is, of course, the Savior himself. "The Lord brings earth up to Heaven," as *1 Jeu* says.[125]

During the forty days the Lord said in the *Epistle of the Apostles* (its proper title is *What the Lord Told the Apostles in Secret Conversations after the Resurrection*), "I have been sent with all authority from my Father to lead all those in darkness into the light."[126] He promises the apostles, "I will send Gabriel to visit you in your prison and to represent me."[127] This follows the principle of the spark: one Sent One represents another. The apostles are sent out in the same way: "I have the word of the Father, and the Father is in me . . . and I send you out as guides to others."[128] These exact same things happen in John 14:16 and in 3 Nephi 11:12: you represent me as I represent the Father.

The Sent Ones emerge most frequently and most dramatically in the apocryphal literature in the story of Adam. "After the physical Adam was created," says the new apocryphal *Book of John*, "a messenger was sent to the head of all creations, Adam, and at his call Adam awoke and said, 'How the precious, beautiful life has been planted in this place. But it is hard on me down here.' Then the Sent One reminded Adam and said, 'But your beautiful throne awaits you, Adam. Why then do you, the image of God, sit here complaining? All this is being done for your good. I have been sent to teach you, Adam, and to free you from this world. Listen and return to the light.' " Then the messenger gives him instructions.[129] The *Ginza* (which means "a treasure, mystery, what is hidden and precious") tells us, "when Adam stood praying for light and knowledge, a helper came to him, gave him a garment, and told him, 'Those men who gave you the garment will assist you throughout your life until you are ready to leave earth.' "[130] The commonest account, also found in the *Ginza*, is that "When Adam was created, he was found in a deep sleep,

Figure 50. From a 1934 copy of an old Mandaean magic scroll, Adam, Šitil, and other perfected souls in priestly dress give the *kušṭa,* or ritual hand-grasp, to each other.

from which he was awakened by a helper, who forthwith began to instruct him. And at his death also, the Sent Ones came to take Adam back to the great first Paternal House and to the places in which he formerly dwelt."[131]

It describes how he went back: "First—he was taken to a place of detention, a *shomai* [a treasure place]—where he meets the one who holds the nails of glory and the signs in the hands, and the key of the *kushta* of both arms."[132] That is the code for the signs that Adam had to receive—his instructions. The one who holds the nails of glory, and the signs in the hands, and the key to the initiation rites is the master of the Treasure House (fig. 50). "Hither a messenger from the house of light was sent to fetch Adam farther when he was ready."[133] The reason it is so often the Adam of Light, the premortal Adam, who is sent to help suffering humanity (he's our great helper), is that he, as our first Father, was himself thus helped in the beginning. He couldn't have helped himself out of things had not a Savior been provided.

"When Adam awoke," we are told in the *Ginza,* "he faced the light and called for help. The Lord Himself approached him, in glory, and took him by the palm of the right hand and calmed him and instructed him. Then he comforted Eve. In this way, I have brought joy and aid to his descendants."[134] "The Sent Ones came to bring hope to Adam, who was in the image of God."[135]

This "Adam incident" is repeated in the case of Abraham, who took a trip to heaven, to the stars, and when his spirit came back to his body, he awoke as if from sleep or a daze. After he had first spoken with the Lord, he fell to earth, for his spirit had left his body, which "became as a stone." "Then the angel who had been sent to me took me by the right hand and said, 'Abraham, awake and arise! I have been sent to you to strengthen you and bless you in the name of the Creator.' " Then the angel instructed him.[136]

In the vast majority of accounts, it is three Sent Ones who instruct Adam. There is no conflict, since the Sent Ones are many. They come whenever they are needed. Indeed, according to sources, Adam himself was one of the three great Sent Ones who created the world in the beginning. The *Berlin Papyrus* says, "The first man was the third of the Sent Ones—the Father, the Son, and Adam"— when they came down to create the world. According to the *Apocryphon of Adam*, Adam was awakened from a deep sleep by three men from on high, who said to him, "Adam arise and hear the teachings of the Savior."[137] "It was through a team of three," according to the *Sophia Christi*, "that God created everything, employing them as his agents."[138] As the *Abbatôn* puts it, "The Father instructed the Son, who in turn instructed that first angel to go down and form a new world." But they didn't merely delegate the work, they worked together. "The three," says our source, "stretched forth their hands, took clay, and made man. And many expeditions were sent to the earth before things were ready to receive Adam."[139] "Whenever that life-giving spark is sent to initiate a first step of creation in the material world, it is always followed by three Sent Ones who come down to give proper instructions. So in any world, those that receive the spark (the word sent from God) will also find three helpers sent to instruct them."[140]

At the creation, says the *Ginza*, God gave orders that the angels should come to keep Adam company. At the beginning, it was the Lord himself and two companions who instructed Adam and Eve in everything.[141] "When Adam was placed on earth, three messengers were sent to oversee him, with myself at their head," says the Lord to the apostles during the forty days.[142] "I taught Adam and Eve the hymns, and the order of prayer, and the ordinances which would help one to return to the presence of the Father."[143] "I'm sending three, God says to them, giving them instructions. He said to the pure Sent One, his Son, 'Go call Adam and Eve and all their posterity and teach them concerning everything about the Kingdom of Light and the Worlds of Light. Be friendly with Adam and keep him company, you and the two angels which will be with you. Warn them against Satan; also, teach them chastity.' "[144]

Because the three were always there to supervise, the evil spirits protested. They didn't like the interruption. A very interesting passage from the *Ginza* says, "The evil spirits, who claim this world for their own, resent the Sent Ones' instructions. These three men are in the world," they say, "but they are not really men. They are light and glory, and they have come down to little 'Enosh' [physical man—Adam] who is helpless and alone in the world. They are intruding on our world. The children of men have taken over the earth. They are really strangers who speak the language of the three men. They have accepted the teachings of the three men and rejected us in our own world. They refuse to acknowledge our kingdom and our glory." The devils don't like the three men interrupting their program and spoiling things. "Thus, the evil ones plotted to overthrow Adam, who was hoping for *Mandadihaya*

(Teacher of Life), the messenger from the Father, to come and give him aid and support."[145]

We read also of another team of three men: When Adam called upon God, the Great Spirit sent them from the land of brightness, those who would belong to the twelve. So at one time three of the apostles were sent down. These were the three, the pillars of the Church as described later in the New Testament in Galatians 2:9 — Peter, James, and John (cf. Matthew 17:1). Whenever that expression is used — "The three who belonged to the twelve" — it means Peter, James, and John, who were hidden then within the veil of light (Goodenough shows who they were). The three Sent Ones in another account are Michael, Raphael, and Gabriel. But if you go to the same account in the earlier Greek version, they are the Father, Michael and the angels, when Jesus says, "I will come, and my Father, and Michael." So it's Elohim, Jehovah, and Michael (and all the angels); this is the highest committee (cf. fig. 47, p. 239).

Throughout Christian literature, going to heaven is consistently described as a return to an old home, which raises the notion of premortal existence. In the *First Apocalypse of James*, the Lord says to the apostles, "They will ask you where you are going. Your answer: The place from which I came. I return to that place."[146] "The elect are those individuals," says the *Gospel of Thomas*, "who shall find the Kingdom, because they came from it in the first place."[147] The *Gospel of Truth* dwells at length on the theme of the return:

> Whoever has this knowledge is a being from on high. When he is called, he hears, answers, and turns toward him who calls and reascends to him. He knows when he is called; he knows whence he has come, and where he is going. He has turned many from error and proceeded unto places which belong to them, but from which they have strayed. Joy to the man who has rediscovered himself, awakened, and has helped others to wake up.[148]

Just so, according to the *Manichaean Psalm-Book* (a marvelous book), Adam is received by a happy family when he dies and goes back to the other side. We are told that on the other side they have been awaiting him in high expectation. They have been awaiting the return of the first man and news from him. They eagerly await the news of his victory, the success of his mission. And they want to hear it from his own mouth when he returns.[149] On his part, Adam, being away from home, asked the news-bearer who comes down to visit him after his death (he's called "the news-bearer of the skies"), "How is my Father, the Father of Light? How is my Mother, the Mother of the Living, whom I left, and her brethren also? Rejoice with me, ye Holy Ones, for I have returned to my original state again, my archaic, my original rule, and place."[150] And again, in leaving the earth, he says, "My hour is come; they summon me. I will go from your midst and return to my true home."[151] Accordingly, the Sent One comes to take the soul of Adam back to the great first house of the Father, to the place where he formerly lived.[152] And so his children are admonished, "Arise, oh soul, return to your original home, to the place from which you were planted. Put on your garment of glory, sit down upon your throne, and dwell in the dwellings among thy brethren."[153] Again, the *Ginza* says, "Now, arise and return to the place of your true family."[154] "I came from the house of my father," says the *Psalm of Thomas*, "from a far land. I shall mount up until I return to the land of the pure."[155] In a moving scene at the end of *The Pearl* (an early Christian hymn), the hero finally returns to his home, his mission accomplished. He is met at the "gate of greeting and honor" (as it's called) by his entire family. He bows and worships his Father, and the Christ and the Father, the Eldest Son who is with him, "who has sent him the garments and given him the orders of what he should do to get back. All the princes of the house were gathered at the gate. All embraced me with tears of joy." And as the organ played, they all walked back into the house together.[156]

Commenting on this, Gregory of Nyssa, one of the great Doctors of the fourth century, observes: Christians are all confused about the premortal existence (he refers to the state of things in his church in Palestine). Some say we lived in families there, and in tribes, just as we do here, and that we lost our wings when we came down here, and that we'll get them back again upon returning.[157] The Christians mixed up tenable and untenable, and all sorts of other teachings. The church was in great confusion on this doctrine in the fourth century. Regardless of what the true explanation might have been, it is clear by such remarks from the early Fathers that the early church did preach the premortal existence, the idea of coming from heaven and returning. Pope Paul VI is preaching that, referring to life as a short pilgrimage away from home, etc. These ideas are coming back. Talk of returning to heaven as a return home does away with creation from nothing (*creatio ex nihilo*). If we just came into existence here—if this is the only place we've ever lived—why are we homesick? Why aren't we properly adjusted here? Why does everybody suffer a nostalgia and want to return to their heavenly home? Thus the Pope talks about being strangers here; this is a wayfaring church; we are lost here, wandering, looking for a return to our heavenly home, etc.[158] He himself has been reading these early writings. The decline of the idea of creation *ex nihilo* of course necessitates our existence in some sort of a spiritual state before our coming here.

Back to the theme of the Sent Ones, which is behind these ideas: the Sent Ones came down and taught Adam certain ordinances by which he was supposed to return to the presence of the Father. I have hundreds of pages on this point—the great council in heaven, the plan of salvation with everything being planned and worked out, the discussion in heaven of the new plan. That discussion did

not go over easily. Not only were there the interruptions
of Satan, there were a lot of objections because it was a
little too hard, too risky a thing; it introduced too much
suffering, etc.

> Adam was active in the council of the creation, and
> was one of the three who participated in directing the
> whole operation. When the plan was made known,
> Adam fell down at the feet of the Father and worshipped
> him, saying, "My Lord and my God, thou hast caused
> the thing to be done which was not before." God then
> appointed a crown of glory and a throne for Adam, and
> a diadem of kingdoms and the entire hosts of Heaven
> to honor Adam, crying, "Hail, Thou form and image of
> God!"

This is from the *Kephalaia*, and from the *Berlin Papyrus*,
and from the *Gospel of Bartholomew*. "As he left Heaven to
come down and undergo his earthly trials, Adam received
affectionate farewell embraces from all his faithful children.
He put on his physical body and went forth to oppose the
primal enemy. Before the creation of this world, the third
Sent One (as Adam is called) came into the free space and
began to organize this world." Before he ever came down
to be tested, he was one of the three who organized the
world. "This third Sent One was Christ's great co-worker
in the Plan of Salvation, but in all things he has precedence."[159] "This was Adam," says the Lord in the *Gospel
of Bartholomew*, "for the sake of whose posterity I descended
from Heaven."[160]

Adam, finding himself alone in the dreary world, knew
that he could not save himself. So he called mightily upon
God for a helper. It is because Adam received power to
call upon the holy and perfect name that he was able to
establish the plan of life in the new world, says the *Second
Coptic Gnostic Work*.[161]

This source gives the secret words of prayer (they differ
from text to text): *I-oy-el I-oy-el Io-i-a*, which is interpreted

as "God is with us forever and ever, and through the power of revelation."[162] This prayer of Adam when he calls upon the Lord has different interpretations in different works, but it's always recorded in a special code, and it's mentioned many times. One of the first things the Lord told Adam and Eve was that they should always call upon God, in whatever they did, in the name of the Son. In the same way, Abraham, in the *Apocalypse of Abraham*, when he makes the first offering, called upon God, saying, "*El, El, El! El Ya-O-El!*," meaning, "God receive my prayer! Let my offering be acceptable!"[163] The angel came and taught him the proper order of prayer, which was made according to the command "that I should sacrifice and seek thee." "Show me, teach me, give light and knowledge to thy servant according as thou hast promised." So Abraham called upon God as Adam did, and as a result an angel visited him and gave him knowledge. Then we're told what he received.[164]

When Adam, being greatly downcast, appeals for aid against Satan (who is more than a match for him), God tells the angel Muriel, "Go down to the man Adam and instruct him in my doctrine." The *Apocryphon of John* says, "A messenger went down and awakened Adam and showed him how to keep himself pure against the day of another visitation."[165] In some versions, Adam is awakened from his sleep by three men whom he does not recognize. As he is talking to them, the Lord himself appears and asks Adam, "Why are you so sorrowful?" He is sorrowful because he is doomed, he says. The Lord promises him that "if he hearkens to the angels, they will teach him and his posterity the Gospel."

It was by establishing ordinances, says the *Gospel of Philip*, that Christ completed what Adam began. Adam and others prayed to God and asked him to give them the rules to attain the promises. So he gave them ordinances, decrees, commandments, and instructions, establishing

places of preparation and transition, etc.[166] Adam received
the teachings, the ordinances, and the seals of all the powers above and below, the *Kephalaia* says. The *Berlin Papyrus*
says that at their new birth, Adam and Eve received the
seals and the tokens. As Adam stood praying and sup-
plicating, God sent someone who came and gave him a
greeting of peace (*shalom*), embraced him, and preached
the gospel to him.[167] The helper came and awakened the
Lord of Mysteries, who is Adam. For Adam went through
all the ordinances, including baptism, washings, and
anointings, says the *Mandaean Prayerbook*. According to the
Ginza, the Lord and two companions taught Adam and
Eve all the ordinances and blessed them. "The Great Light
planted us here and gave us helpers who taught us the
prayer of Adam in the world." Three angels were sent to
teach Adam and Eve the law of chastity, to instruct them
to be true and faithful when misfortune came upon them,
and to dedicate all of their property to the needy and the
poor—the rule which is binding upon all the elect. They
were to call upon God without ceasing, in the name of the
Son, and not to trust in the things of this world.[168]

One text says that these ordinances which Adam received in his dispensation have always been the same.
They were taught to Adam and his posterity by three angels. His descendants were required to call upon God even
as he had, and thereafter to do everything as he had done.
Their treasure must be their good works, not gold and
silver. They must teach the law of chastity to their children.
The true baptism is the baptism of Adam, which was
preached by John the Baptist. The three who were sent to
Adam were called "the three who belong to the twelve,
who were hidden within the veil of light." And in the
Apocalypse of Abraham, Abraham is awakened by the Sent
Ones, and their instructions to him and the ordinances
exactly parallel those of Adam. Abraham says, "I arose
and looked upon him that had taken me by the right hand,

and he set me on my feet. . . . The hair of his head was like snow."[169] It was the Savior himself.

Adam, you recall, had lost memory of his former existence. "I have caused a sleep to come over Adam," says the *Abbatôn* (a significant early writing of the apostles), "and a forgetting."[170] Adam's sleep was the putting of a veil between him and his former knowledge. It enveloped him like a garment, and, while his memory was shut off by it, his *epinoia* (intelligence) retained its force. He remained smart, but he forgot everything. In fact, during the episode of the creation, Eve was made (not from a literal rib, according to this source) while Adam was in sort of a drugged stupor, his mind separated by a veil from what was really going on.[171] He is aroused, then, and taught ordinances. He is the double for Michael, for Adam is Michael. Adam is Michael throughout these writings; it's a common theme.

For some reason, the ordinances are vital. They are not mere forms or symbols, they are analogues. Standing with the apostles in the prayer circle, the Lord tells them, "I will teach you all the ordinances necessary that you may be purged by degrees and progress in the next life."[172] In many of these forty-day stories (and there are several), after the Lord is about to leave the apostles, he says, "I have taught you all these things. Now we will stand in a circle, and you will repeat after me this prayer, and we will go through all the ordinances again."[173] This is repeated in 2 *Jeu*, which, as I say, Carl Schmidt regarded as the most important of all the early Christian writings. But standing with the apostles in the prayer circle, the Lord tells them, "I will teach you all of the ordinances necessary, that you might be purged by degrees and progress in the next life. These things," he further explains, "make it possible for you to achieve other places (*topoi*), but they must be performed in this life. Unless one performs them here, he cannot become a 'Son of Light.' "[174] All the texts, whether Syriac, Hebrew, Coptic, or Greek, always like the title "Sons of Light," meaning those who have received the ordinances of the temple. That's what the code name "Sons of Light" means, and it's used a great deal. The Lord explains in 2 *Jeu* what that name means: "By very definition, the 'Sons of Light' are those that are perfect in the ordinances."[175] It is interesting that this same definition applies to the mysterious title *Nazorean*, which means the same thing. "Until Christ came," the *Pistis Sophia* explains, "no soul had gone through the ordinances in their completeness. It was he who opened the gates and the way of life."[176] Those who received these ordinances are in the dispensations of the "Sons of Light" in whatever age they lived, and they receive whatever they desire. They are those upon the right hand of the Father, for it is by their faithfulness in these things that they show they are worthy to return and inherit the kingdom. Without the ordinances, therefore, there is no foothold or foundation to anything in this life. If you want to go to the Father, says 1 *Jeu*, you must pass through the veil.[177]

These five things you have asked me about (the Lord tells the apostles after his resurrection, in the *Kephalaia*) appear very small and unimportant to the world, but they are really a very great and holy thing. I will teach you the mysteries now. These tokens (*semeia*) go back to the ordinances of the first man, Adam himself. He brought them with him when he came out of the garden of Eden, and having completed his struggle upon the earth, he mounted up by these very same signs and was received again into the Aeons of Light. The person who receives these becomes a Son. He both gives and receives the signs and the tokens of the God of truth, while demonstrating the same to the Church—all in hopes that some day these things may become a reality. So the apostles realized that these things are but forms and types, yet you can't do without them. You cannot do without analogues. For us they may only be symbols, but they must be done here, the Lord says. They may be but symbols here, but they are indispensable steps to the attainment of real power. "In fact," says the *Pistis Sophia*, "without the mysteries one loses one's power. Without the ordinances, one has no way of controlling matter, for such control begins with the control of one's self. The ordinances provide the very means and the discipline by which light operates on material things. You don't understand this now," it continues, "but your level, or *taxis*, in the next world will depend on the ordinances you receive in this world. Whoever receives the highest here will understand the whys and the wherefores of the great plan." "You can't understand it now, but you will. Your faith is being tested here. It is through the ordinances that one makes this progress in knowledge, so that those who receive all available ordinances and teachings here shall pass by all the intermediate *topoi* and shall not have to give the answers and signs, nor stand certain tests hereafter."[178]

John the Baptist, who performed the ordinances with which he was entrusted, foretold in a special language that Christ would bring the ordinances of the higher priesthood after him, because John the Baptist had only the ordinances of the Aaronic, or lesser priesthood, the *Pistis Sophia* tells us.[179] And in the *Epistle of the Apostles*: Indeed, it was the Lord who, during the forty days, finally revealed all the ordinances in full. To repeat, "Everyone goes to the place indicated by the ordinances he has received. Even a sinless person," the Lord tells them, "cannot save others without these ordinances."[180] Let us not think this trivial because these things should be given to all who ask for them. If they are not worthy, the risk is theirs. For everyone should be given the highest ordinance he is capable of receiving at any time. No one is to be refused, for the risk is theirs, the ordinances are so important to have.

"The all important thing is that the ordinances must

be received in this world," says the *Pistis Sophia,* for we
may never get another chance.[181] "It is here that one must
look upon the Living One; for if he does not, he will seek
him in vain after death," says the *Gospel of Thomas.*[182] He
reveals the gate to those who are willing to enter. Each of
us will receive his reward. For us, God has provided a
Savior and helper. You, James, will be the enlightener and
redeemer of those who are mine. You will become a Savior
to them, he tells James, and they will be thine also.
Whoever receives these ordinances, signs, and tokens will
be added upon and have true increase forever and ever,
says the *Kephalaia.* By means of these good signs and tokens, such shall enter into the light and shall become
perfect men, and give honor and praise to the God of
truth.

The ordinances are indeed but "types and images,"
says the *Gospel of Philip.*[183] One must not think that they
are completion or fulfillment. For example, you cannot
send up a rocket into space without types and images.
Rockets are just as physical as anything, yet they are just
drawings on a board, abstractions, marks on a graph, etc.
The ordinances are indeed but "types and images," says
the *Gospel of Philip,* "but if you do not receive them here,
you will lose them. They are the steps of salvation. The
Lord required each of the apostles to go through them all.
Above all, if you do not receive them in this life, you will
never receive them at all. Here is where all of the work
[and it says, specifically, the baptism] must be done. In
short, you must be perfect in this life, for if you have not
mastered the places in this world, you will not be able to
master them in the next world, but must settle for the
middle kingdom" (as he calls it).[184]

The instruction is given to Adam and Eve in the beginning: Go down into the world, Adam, and grow up in
the body, in that garment which has been assigned to you.
Go down and grow up in the ordinances, that the ordi-

nances may be magnified by you, that your progeny may thereby be firmly established. The Man that taught the elect righteous and the Nazoreans, who were to exist upon the earth in the premortal existence, said, "When you beget generations, and when you teach them their knowledge, explain to them, show them, and tell them about the rites which you have performed." The wholesome things were transplanted from the world above.

The early church placed tremendous emphasis on doing certain rites and ordinances which the later Christian world lost entirely. The greatest weakness in the Christian world today (and both Catholic and Protestant churches confess it) is a matter of rites and ordinances, because the Catholics realize that the mass isn't ancient at all. When monks at the Solesmes Monastery started working on the problems again at the end of the nineteenth century, they hit upon eighth- and ninth-century manuscripts which they thought were the old Roman mass, but they discovered that the old Roman mass isn't Roman at all — it's the old Gallican mass, invented in the court of Charlemagne. They had been following late versions from pagan sources. The mass introduced into the church in the ninth century had virtually nothing to do with the early Christian church at all. Those early ordinances had been lost, taken away, as it was predicted they should be.[185]

Several of the manuscripts end by telling us about the prayer circle. In most of these sources, the Lord gives to the apostles, as they stand in a prayer circle, a complete summary of all the rites, with an explanation of their meaning. In the *Pistis Sophia*, for example, at the end of the teaching and the performing of the ordinances, the Lord ordered the apostles and their wives to form a circle. (The apostles' wives are in on all this.) He stands at an altar on one side, and then all recapitulate the ordinances after him. He opens with prayer, raises his hands, and gives it in code — "*YAO, AOI, OIA*" — which is explained in other

writings as meaning, "Hear me Father, hear me Father."[186]
In *1 Jeu*, the Lord calls upon the Father in different words,
also cryptic (these words are always in a special language),
"*IE, IE, IE.*"[187] We are told that in every world there is a
twelve that officiates under the direction of a three (a presidency). They always form the circle, without a lower or
higher, says *1 Jeu*, for there is no head of the table in the
circle[188] — no idea of rank or precedence, or beginning or
ending, as a circle indicates. And all are instructed, and
they are instructed in all things. It was in such a circle, we
are told in this interesting writing, that God in the premortal existence said, standing and looking around the
circle, "These I will make my rulers at the creation of the
world" — and Abraham was one of them. Of course that's
just like our book of Abraham.[189]

Before forming the circle, the Lord has them sing a
hymn, and, when it is finished, the apostles and their wives
all form a circle standing around the Lord, who tells them
that he will lead them through the ordinances of eternal
progression. Clothed in their holy garments, they form a
circle, foot to foot, arm resting upon arm, and Jesus says
that he will take the part of Adam and lead them all. They
are to say "Amen" to each of the phrases of the prayer;
then he gives the prayer.[190]

In another recently found text, the *Qaṣr el-Wazz Text*,
Jesus gives this same prayer. I got hold of this text within
a week after it was discovered in Egypt just last year (1966),
as the waters of the Nile were just flooding, about a mile
and a half north of the Aswan Dam on the Egyptian-Su-
danese border, almost in the Sudan. It would have been
lost within a few hours in the back-up waters of the Aswan
Dam if it hadn't been found in time. The photographs of
it came from Chicago. The discoverer, G. A. Hughes, was
probably the only person working in that particular area.
I asked him if there were anything on the forty days. "Yes,"
he said, "take these." So I immediately had duplicates

made. This is one of the forty-day texts in which the Lord leads the apostles out in the prayer. It says, "We made a circle around him, and he said, 'I am in your midst in the manner of little children.' And when they finished the hymn, they all said, 'Amen.' " This tradition is recalled a number of times in the earliest Christian literature.[191] For example — as mentioned in many of the early writings — the Lord is said to have held it with the apostles in the upper chamber of the Last Supper.

The *Acts of John* says,

> Before he was taken by lawless men, he gathered us all together and said, "Before I am delivered up unto them, let us sing a hymn to the Father." Then he commanded us to make, as it were, a ring, holding each other's hand, with Himself standing in the middle. He said, "Respond 'Amen' to me." Then he began to sing a hymn, "Glory to Thee Father," and we would say "Amen" to that. And the other phrases to which the apostles pronounced "Amen": "We praise Thee our Father; we give thanks to Thee. I would be saved and I would save. I would be loosed and I would loosen." "Amen" they said to that. "I would be born and I would bear others." [Another text says, "I would be washed and I would wash others"].[192] "I have no temples, I would have temples." Then the Lord commands, "Thou seest thyself in Me, who is speaking; and when thou hast seen what I do, keep silent about the mysteries. You must see Me as I suffer, what I suffer, who I am, and then ye shall know that I go hence." Then he gave them certain signs, and he took their hands and said, "Know my suffering and thou shalt have the power not to suffer. I will be crucified so that you won't have to be. You will merely be in token," he says. "That which thou knowest I Myself will teach thee."[193]

The prayer circle is mentioned not only in the *Acts of Peter,* but also by Irenaeus, Augustine, and Commodian, in *1 Jeu* and *2 Jeu,* the *Testament of Our Lord and Savior Jesus*

Christ, the *Second Coptic Gnostic Work*, the *Pistis Sophia*, in the Council of Ephesus, and in other places. Augustine, in reporting the episode of the prayer circle, says the whole thing was always kept most secret by the early Christians.[194] Epiphanius, the Bishop of Sardinia, at the Second Council of Nicea in A.D. 787, reported on it and included it in the list of blessings; then the churches decided to do away with it because they could not understand it anymore. So they got rid of this very important ordinance.[195]

The earliest (Melkite) Syriac text we have (discovered in 1899, but not brought out until recently), called the *Testament of Our Lord and Savior Jesus Christ*, mentions that the bishop in the church, one day each year, would form a prayer circle with the deacons, and this is the way they would do it: he would first address those in the circle and say, "If anyone has any ill feeling towards anyone in the circle, let him be reconciled, or if any feels himself unworthy, let him withdraw. For God is witness of these ordinances, and his Son and the Holy angels."[196]

In a new text, though, in which the apostles celebrate this ordinance after the Lord had left them, Mary tells them a story. She says she wants to take the place of Jesus at the altar. There is some discussion whether she should be allowed to do it; they had rather an argument. "Well, I will lead you out anyway, because I will tell you something," she says. She begins by calling upon God, raising her hands three times and speaking in an unknown language, a code. "El O . . . ," etc. Having finished the prayer, Mary then asks President Peter (he is called "president") to support her right hand while Andrew supports her on the other side, and then she tells them how it was at the birth of Christ. She was in the temple,

> and the veil was rent before the birth of Christ, and she saw an angel [*mal'āk*] in the temple at the veil. He took her by the right hand, and after she had been washed and anointed and wiped off and clothed in a garment

by one who hailed me as a "blessed vessel," took me by the right hand and took me through the veil. And there was bread on the altar in the temple, and he took some and he ate of it and then gave me some, and we drank wine together, and I saw the bread and wine had not diminished.[197]

According to this, she was married in the temple. At this point, the Lord himself appeared and forbade Mary to tell them any more: "You've told them all that you can tell them now." It was all actually very secret. Some of the apostles rebuked Mary for having told them too much anyway.

The *Apocalypse of Abraham* tells us that "Abraham, on Mt. Horeb, had his people stand around in a ring to learn the ordinances and to sacrifice unto the Lord."[198] In 2 *Jeu,* the Lord says to the apostles, "I will teach you all of the ordinances necessary that you may be purged by degrees and progress in the next life."[199] He warns them first that "these ordinances are very secret."[200] He leads them through all the *topoi,* and explains that "all these things must be done in this life, since to be a 'Son of Light' one must be perfect in the ordinances." The prayer is the same prayer that Adam pronounced. "The Great Light planted us here and taught us about the prayers which Adam prayed in this world." "Teach the saints these things, give them the grips of the right hand; lead them to the Light. Teach the prayers, the hymns, the order of prayer so that they can behold the Father hereafter."[201] And the Lord reports that when Adam called upon him for help in his distress, "I approached him in glory, I took him by the palm of the right hand, I calmed him, and instructed him. In this manner I visited all his sons. Abel rejoiced in my glory, and Seth called aloud upon the name of his helper, just as Adam had, and after I visited Adam, he comforted Eve." "Abraham went with the Lord, and fasted for forty days, and God took him to Mt. Horeb; and there was an

altar, but no offering. The animals being miraculously provided, Abraham was commanded to make offerings [the
old Law of Sacrifice was being taught him] and share the
meat in a sacramental meal with his followers, after the
manner of the Only Begotten who was to come. They were
taught to stand in a ring and were instructed in the proper
manner of sacrifice," says the *Apocalypse of Abraham*.[202]

You see what these manuscripts deal with, the sort of
things they talk about, the sort of doors these are now
opening. It is surprising. Just since I first began to write
these notes down, I've collected ten times as much,
hundreds of pages. It is very difficult to present it all. But
as you can see, we have the same rites and ordinances that
the Lord taught the apostles. Catholics have been told that
their masses were in the order of the old gospel (compare
Justin Martyr), but these newly discovered papyri do not
support those claims. The Pope today recognizes that what
Catholics do today is nothing like what the apostles did.
The other churches will have to consider introducing these
things gradually, if they want to be like early Christianity.
There are groups who want to restore twelve apostles and
claim various charismatic gifts—speaking in tongues, and
also certain ordinances. The Catholics have changed such
ordinances as Extreme Unction; it is now Anointing of the
Sick. They realize now that this was the practice of the
early church; that's the track they should have been on all
the time. Of course, it's a strange time to lock the barn
door after the horse has been stolen for over a thousand
years! These things suddenly occur to them now, and primarily because of these documents. Of course the churches
don't give these documents as much credit as they might,
but they do admit to what is behind the reforms. They are
discovering now what the old order is—what Christians
used to do—and it's quite different.

This applies to the Jews too. Just the day before yesterday, I was visited by a Jew from Ohio State University,

who is extremely interested in the gospel. What he asked me had to do with the temple. The Jews, of course, have gotten the old temple place back, and some are thinking about building a temple. "But what did they used to do in the temple?" I asked him. "Do you think all they used to do was slaughter beasts in the outer court of the temple and call that their holy ordinances?" He answered, "No, but that's all we know about. We do know they did a lot of other things that had to do with the creation and salvation." "All right, you'll have to wait until you get the ordinances, and you'll have to have the authority along with them." A rabbi isn't a priest.

Questions and Answers

Question: Where did the Masons get the ceremonies they have today? Did they come from these documents?

Answer: Their ceremonies didn't come from these documents. Nobody had the texts until recently. They do give us an interesting check. The Masonic rites have a lot in common with ours. Of course in part they do have the same source, if you trace them way back. But what a different picture you see. The Masons don't give any religious meaning to them. They think of them as symbolic, as abstract. They don't see any particular realities behind them. The rites have nothing to do with salvation, but consist only of broken fragments. This is obvious if you've seen the Masonic rites and ordinances; they don't hang together. They have been picked up from various times and places, and you can trace them back. Actually, they go back to very early times. These are the ordinances of the Knights Templar and the Hospitalers—two early secret orders imported into Europe at the time of the Crusades. But these were actually based on Solomon's temple and on work for the dead. Read St. Bernard (he wrote both the prologue and the constitution for the Hospitalers, which we have still), who shows that they go back to the time of the Maccabees. At the time of the Maccabees, many of the Jews went off and worshiped false gods; and when they lost the battle, many of the dead were found with pagan amulets around their necks, showing that they had apostatized from the God of Israel. Still they had died as heroes for the cause, and they wondered what they might do to get them saved.

They decided to do their work in the temple by proxy. A vast fund of money was provided to have sacrifices and sin offerings made in the temple in their behalf so that these could be saved in the resurrection.[203] This is the tradition carried on by the Knights Templars and Hospitalers — actual work for the dead. But all this was covered up and lost later on.

Lots of people have fragments of these things. The Egyptians had many of them. You can reconstruct from the funerary literature most of the temple ordinances. But you will also find the question, What does this mean? (E.g., in the *Book of the Dead* 17 and 125.) Some say it means this. Others say it means that. Others say we don't know what it means. It is just a tradition.

So the remnants of these rites and ordinances are found throughout the whole world. But nowhere out there do you find an organic whole in which they fit together and make sense and belong to the plan of salvation. We're the only people that have anything like that.

Question: You mentioned the resurrection of the animal world — will they be associated with the world of man?

Answer: Aquinas used to talk about that. This idea (and it's a rather good idea) is discussed in a famous book on the subject by Lovejoy, called *The Great Chain of Being*.[204] He had the theory that variety is a good thing in itself. It's more interesting to have a world made of angels and devils than a world made just of angels alone. It's better actually to have bad people along with the good people, because the more variety the better. Variety is a good thing in itself, because in just repetition, once you've seen one, you've seen them all; there is nothing more. But when you have infinite variety, all these creatures get into the picture. The more the merrier. You can't get too many. I rather like the idea.

Question: How authentic are the titles of these documents you have been quoting from? Are these just titles given them today, or are they their ancient titles? Were these documents actually written by the original apostles whose names they bear?

Answer: Some of these titles are written on the documents themselves, titles they bore anciently to identify them. The Lord said there had to be three record keepers to write down everything he did. Remember, when he came to the Nephites he made a big thing about keeping records. He went through the records himself and made sure that all the prophecies were mentioned. Samuel the Lamanite had prophesied something that was fulfilled. You didn't put it down here, he says to Nephi. Nephi's face turned red and he said, Well, we'll see that it gets put down! (cf. 3 Nephi 23:6–13). It was very embarrassing, believe me, when the Lord himself was there! But he wants those records complete. These newly discovered records say the same thing: the Lord appointed three apostles to keep a careful record of everything; but these records were not to go forth until the proper time. They were buried, and now they come out.

Are these really the documents? We have one by Thomas, one by Philip, one by Andrew, and especially many writings of John. Just how authentic are they? Are they just a copy of a copy, or do they really go back to one of the apostles? Well, they are the earliest Christian documents we have; they contain the sort of thing the apostles talked about—we know that. You see, it is an advantage to have so many of them—you can check one against another. You're not limited to just one library in Egypt, or to one library up in the Delta, or to one library over in Syria, or to one library up in Iran, or to one in Palestine, or to one in Constantinople. You can check them against each other.

I mentioned the story told in the *Abbatôn*. The Bishop of Alexandria (a very important man) in the year 381 had to go to a conference at Jerusalem. He had heard that the apostles left some old documents there, and he wanted very much to get into those documents, so he undertook a very diligent search.

He went to where they kept an old iron chest in which they preserved the records under lock and key and persuaded the keeper to show him a particularly valuable book, a "Discourse of Abbatôn," a record of teachings of the Lord after the Ressurection that was supposed to have been left behind by Thomas.

How genuine is it? Remember, no one would fake these documents. What these things talk about are not only unpopular today, they were extremely unpopular with the Fathers of the church from the third, fourth, and fifth centuries on. They hated this stuff. They would have been the last people in the world to forge it or make it up. Nobody wanted it. Nobody was interested in it. These teachings upset them greatly. They gave a negative message—that the church was going to be taken away, and the usurpers wouldn't have the real records. And it told them doctrines they didn't like and described ordinances they didn't know anything about. So it was very easy to shove these aside.

There grew quite an accumulation of this stuff, building up through the years, and nobody paying much attention to it, until by 1947, as Torrey said, there was a conspiracy to ignore it completely; nobody was studying any of it anymore. The year 1947 was the great year—the year the Dead Sea Scrolls, the Nag Hammadi texts, and the great Manichaean texts all were discovered. The circumstances of the discoveries are dramatic; they get into the newspapers, so people find themselves stuck with the story. They would be ever so happy if they could sweep it under the rug and just forget it. But it is really building up, and now it's reached the point where it's actually obliging the Christian world to change their ideas about ordinances, about practices, justifying them in making changes they never would have dreamed of making ten years ago, because they can see that it was so different in those days.

Question: Do you feel that the Lord's hand was involved in the discovery of these documents?

Answer: Yes, he said he would bring these things out in his own way and in his own time, and it's really quite miraculous the way these things have happened, when you see the opposition to them. The Lord said he would send his words hissing forth from the dust (cf. 2 Nephi 29:2; Moroni 10:28), and none would be able to stop them; and there *were* conspiracies to stop them. It was touch and go how near the Dead Sea Scrolls came to being destroyed time and time again—the efforts, you might say, that Satan has made to destroy them, the near misses. When the first of the scrolls was first discovered way back in 1897 by Solomon Schechter, he suppressed it for fourteen years. A good orthodox Jew, he didn't like what it taught. He actually refused to publish it. He had the right to first publication, but he just suppressed it. That was the famous Zadokite fragment, the Damascus Covenant, lying around until the other part was discovered among the Dead Sea Scrolls.

Question: Won't these documents prove that the gospel is true?

Answer: No, you'll never prove the gospel. You'll never prove the Book of Mormon or the Bible or anything else. Remember, people have been working on the Bible now for hundreds of years, and do people believe it? When is a thing proven in science or anywhere else? When you have had enough experience, enough observation, enough thinking, enough testing, enough personal impressions to convince *you* that it's so. That might not convince another scientist at all. Equally eminent men may have the same evidence in front of them, and when is it proven to one? When he believes it's so. When is the gospel proven to you or anyone else? At the point at which you personally are convinced. That isn't necessarily the point at which somebody else is convinced. You can't force your testimony onto somebody else — it's nontransferable. You can't get a testimony from anybody else. That is the marvelous thing about it. Remember the first rule the Lord gave the Nephites when he came to them? "There shall be no disputations among you, as there have hitherto been" (3 Nephi 11:28). There shall be no more disputations among you about any points of doctrine or anything else. There shall be no more of this among you. I will not stand for it, he says. It is not of my gospel where there is any contention or any disputation at all. It is of the devil and not of me (cf. 3 Nephi 11:29–30). How can you discuss things if you don't dispute? He goes on to tell them: You know by your own individual testimony. The Holy Ghost speaks to you, and you know, and that's it. Now there's nothing to fight about, is there? If he doesn't speak to you, I might feel that's too bad for you, but I can't bang you over the head and say, "You're so stupid, you can't see it!" That isn't where I got my conviction at all. My conviction is the result of a building up of personal impressions, of storing up experiences and ideas through the years on a particular point, to a point where I am convinced. You haven't had that experience at all. You don't have that background; you have a different one. If I had yours, I wouldn't believe it, or I'd believe something else. That's why we have to have the Holy Ghost and have to listen to the promptings of the Spirit. Otherwise, we're not going to agree on anything.

Question: Does the message of these scrolls provide evidence to support the Book of Mormon?

Answer: Yes, they talk about all sorts of things which are remarkably like the Book of Mormon. What's the situation in the Dead Sea Scrolls? Things go bad in Jerusalem. The Jews at Jerusalem have gone sour. They've corrupted the rites of the temple, and so some righteous people go out into the desert and form the community of Qumran. They feel that the only way they can live the gospel in its purity is to leave Jerusalem, go out and live in the desert, and set up their own colony. So they take their seeds with them, and go out and live there. They practice their baptisms, they have their sacraments, and they look forward to the coming of the Messiah and hope for the restoration of the true temple. This is the pattern.

But if you don't have your own testimony, you're in a bad way. As I said, nothing is proven otherwise. Some ministers in Scotland wrote a letter to President McKay awhile back, which he forwarded down to me. It said, "Can you make us believe the Book of Mormon? Can you provide proof that will twist our arms and make us believe the Book of Mormon?" Since when did the Lord ever twist anybody's arm or force them in anything? What credit would you get for believing something if you were forced to believe it? What kind of evidence is there in the world that can force any scientist to believe in anything he doesn't want to? You don't have to believe in the laws of Newton anymore. For 300 years, they were absolute gospel, which no scientist would dare question. But today, they are just one of a number of competing systems. They are not the only possible explanation of how gravity works. Einstein made Newton's system just one among several competing systems. You can believe it if you want to, but whether you believe it or not depends entirely on you—on the impressions you have had, on your experiences and feelings. You have your own personal testimony of a thing like that and of anything else. If you know it, you know it for yourself. If you ask the Lord, he'll give you knowledge of these things. That's what the gospel is here for. Otherwise, we could go on discussing things forever and ever and never come to a knowledge of the truth. Science is just an open-ended discussion that's always going on. As long as science is progressing, it's changing.[205] The picture is always changing—we haven't the final word. We must have guidance from the Lord. We must receive testimonies, or we won't know where we're going at all.

So I pray that the Lord will give us all testimonies. I wish to bear my own, that I know the gospel is true. Not through what I have discussed here; that has nothing to do with whether I know the gospel is true. It would be in spite of this, as far as I'm concerned.

I know the gospel is true. I rejoice in it. It's marvelous to know the gospel is true. Brothers and sisters, get a testimony, and keep with it. The Lord will give you this knowledge, and he will cause you to rejoice, and he will tell you what you have to do in this world. Many things are to be done. Who knows what we have to do? There's no duplication. He doesn't want any one of us to do exactly what anybody else is doing. The harvest is large and ripe, the workers are few, and time is short. We must have the Spirit to guide us. We must listen to the promptings of the Spirit. Everyone must stand on his own feet and know for himself that the gospel is true, and through no other way.

Notes

1. For a map and description of the major finds, see Hugh Nibley, *Since Cumorah* (Salt Lake City: Deseret Book, 1967), 53–55; reprinted in *CWHN* 7:47–49.

2. Alan H. Gardiner, "The Eloquent Peasant," *Journal of Egyptian Archaeology* 9 (1923): 5–6.

3. Thomas S. Kuhn, *The Structure of Scientific Revolutions*, 2nd ed. (Chicago: University of Chicago Press, 1970).

4. Karl R. Popper, "Science: Problems, Aims, Responsibilities," *Federation Proceedings of the American Societies for Experimental Biology* 22 (1963): 961–72.

5. Solomon Zeitlin, "The Propaganda of the Hebrew Scrolls and the Falsification of History," *Jewish Quarterly Review* 46 (January 1956): 209–58.

6. *Le Testament en Galilée,* in *PO* 9:177–232; Carl Schmidt, "Epistola apostolorum," *Gespräche Jesu mit seinen Jüngern nach der Auferstehung,* in *Texte und Untersuchungen* 43 (Leipzig: Hinrichs, 1919), 25–155. *Le Testament en Galilée* in Ethiopic in ibid., appendix 1–26; Edgar Hennecke and William Schneemelcher, *New Testament Apocrypha,* 2 vols. (London: Lutterworth, 1963), 1:189–226; and in Montague R. James, *The Apocryphal New Testament* (Oxford: Clarendon, 1924), 485–503.

7. Iamblichus, *On the Mysteries* I, 11–16, 19–21, in Edouard des Places, ed., *Iamblique, Les Mystères d'Égypte* (Paris: Belles lettres, 1966), 59–62, 67–68, 71–74, 76–77.

8. Origen, *Peri Archon (De Principiis)* II, 6, 1–2, in *PG* 11:209–11.

9. Justin Martyr, *First Apology* X, 67, and *Second Apology* 5, in *PG* 6:339–42, 429–30, 541–54.

10. For a thorough treatment of the subject, see H. F. Weiss, *Untersuchungen zur Kosmologie des hellenistischen und palästinischen Judentums* (Berlin: Akademie Verlag, 1966), 59–74; Cf. W. Richter, "Urgeschichte und Hoftheologie," *Biblische Zeitschrift* 10 (1966): 97; H. A. Brongers, *De Scheppingstradities bij de Profeten* (Amsterdam: Paris, 1945), 3–18.

11. *Clementine Recognitions* IV, 23, in *PG* 1:1324.

12. See Origen, *De Principiis* II, 1, 4, in *PG* 11:184–86.

13. *Apocryphon of John* 1:20–15:15; 19:10–20:1; 20:30–21:20, in *NHLE*, 106, 109–10.

14. Walter C. Till, "Die gnostischen Schriften des koptischen Papyrus Berolinesis 8502," in *Texte und Untersuchungen* 60 (1955): 52–61, 194–295.

15. *Pistis Sophia* II, 96, in Carl Schmidt, ed., *Pistis Sophia,* tr. Violet MacDermot (Leiden: Brill, 1978), 228.

16. Justin, *Cohortatio ad Graecos (Hortatory Address to the Greeks)* 20, in *PG* 6:276–77.

17. *Pistis Sophia* II, 86, in Schmidt, *Pistis Sophia,* 196–97.

18. *Apocryphon of John* 28:30–32, in *NHLE*, 114; cf. 3:31–32, in *NHLE*, 100.

19. Cf. *War Scroll* 1:4; 13:17; *1QS* 4:18, 20, 25; 9:23; 10:2, 19 (Deuteronomy 32:35); *Ages of Creation* 80:2–4, in John M. Allegro, *Qumrân Cave 4*, vol. 5 of *Discoveries in the Judaean Desert*, 7 vols. (Oxford: Clarendon, 1968), 5:77–78.

20. *Apocryphon of John* 3:31–32, in *NHLE*, 100.

21. C. R. C. Allberry, ed. and tr., *A Manichaean Psalm-Book*, 2 vols. (Stuttgart: Kohlhammer, 1938), 2:189.

22. Cf. *Clementine Recognitions* VIII, 9–16, in *PG* 1:1373–79.

23. *Apocalypse of Abraham* 17:11–13, in *OTP* 1:697; see also *Gospel of Bartholomew* 13:2–5, in Hennecke and Schneemelcher, *New Testament Apocrypha*, 1:493.

24. *Untitled Text*, 7–9 and 17, in Carl Schmidt, ed., *The Books of Jeu and the Untitled Text in the Bruce Codex*, tr. Violet MacDermot (Leiden: Brill, 1978), 238–41, 258–59.

25. *Pistis Sophia* I, 55, in Schmidt, *Pistis Sophia*, 107.

26. *Untitled Text* 2, in Schmidt, *Books of Jeu and the Untitled Text*, 227. *Apocryphon of John* 6:11–13, in *NHLE*, 102; 30:23–32, in ibid., 115.

27. Daniel Matt, tr., *Zohar, The Book of Enlightenment*, selections (New York: Paulist, 1983). Isaac Myer, tr., *Qabbalah: The Philosophical Writings of Solomon Ben Yehudah Ibn Gabriol or Avicebron* (Philadelphia: Myer, 1888). George Sassoon and Rodney Dale, trs. and eds., *The Kabbalah Decoded: A New Translation of the "Ancient of Days" Texts of the Zohar* (London: Duckworth, 1978). Harry Sperling and Maurice Simon, tr., *The Zohar*, 5 vols. (London: Soncino, 1984).

28. *Gospel of Truth* 25:15–17, in *NHLE*, 41.

29. Bernard P. Grenfell and Arthur S. Hunt, *Oxyrhynchus Papyrus XV* (London: Oxford University Press, 1922), n. 1778, for Greek fragments of *Apology;* H. J. M. Milne, "A New Fragment of the Apology of Aristides," *Journal of Theological Studies* 25 (1924): 73–77.

30. Melito of Sardis, *Fragmenta (Fragments)*, in *PG* 5:1229.

31. Cf. *Acts of Thomas* 108 (*Hymn of the Soul* 93–99), in *ANT*, 414–15. *Psalm of Thomas*, in William Wright, *Apocryphal Acts of the Apostles*, 2 vols. (Amsterdam: Philo, 1968), 2:245–51.

32. *Apocryphon of John* 7:4–16; 9:25–27; 10:4, in *NHLE*, 102–4; cf. Papyrus Berolinensis 8502:3; and *Sophia Christi* 111:13–112:4, in Till, "Die gnostischen Schriften," 262–64; in *NHLE*, 222–23.

33. *Gospel of Philip* 75:7–11, in *NHLE*, 145.

34. *Gospel of Mary* 7:5–6, in *NHLE*, 471.

35. *Apocalypse of Abraham* 16:1; 17:1, in *OTP* 1:696–97.

36. *Apocalypse of Abraham* 16:1–4, in ibid., 1:696.

37. *Apocalypse of Abraham* 16:3–4; 17:1, in ibid.

38. *HC* 2:428.

39. *Apocalypse of Abraham* 17:2–3, in *OTP* 1:696.

40. Eusebius, *Preparation for the Gospel* V, 9–10, in *PG* 21:337–46.

41. *Pistis Sophia* I, 32, 32–33, in Schmidt, *Pistis Sophia*, 51, lines 17–23.

42. *Kephalaia* 43–44, 53, in Carl Schmidt, ed. and tr., *Kephalaia* (Stuttgart: Kohlhammer, 1940), 113–14, 130.

43. Ibid.

44. *Gospel of Thomas*, logion 74, in *NHLE*, 126.

45. *Kephalaia* 43–44, 53, in Schmidt, *Kephalaia*, 113–14, 130.

46. *Gospel of Truth* 25:15–35, in *NHLE*, 41.

47. *Clementine Recognitions* III, 27–29, in *PG* 1:1295–96.

48. *Odes of Solomon* 22:9–12, in *OTP* 2:755.

49. *Odes of Solomon* 22:9–10, in ibid.

50. *Kephalaia* 53, in Schmidt, *Kephalaia*, 130.

51. *Apocalypse of Abraham* 17:17 (author's translation), in *OTP* 1:697.

52. Martin H. Scharlemann, " 'He Descended into Hell': An Interpretation of 1 Peter 3:18–20," *Concorda Theological Monthly* 27 (1956): 89–90.

53. Janusz Frankowski, "Requies, Bonum Promissum Populi Dei in VT et in Judaismo," *Verbum Domini* 43 (1965): 149.

54. *Pistis Sophia* I, 47, in Schmidt, *Pistis Sophia*, 84.

55. Cf. Ethel S. Drower, *The Thousand and Twelve Questions* (Berlin: Akademie-Verlag, 1960), 164.

56. *Odes of Solomon* 11:23, in *OTP* 2:746; cf. John 14:2.

57. Mark Lidzbarski, *Ginza: Der Schatz oder das grosse Buch der Mandäer* (Göttingen: Vandenhoeck and Ruprecht, 1925), 98; for an English translation, see Werner Foerster, *Gnosis: A Selection of Gnostic Texts*, 2 vols. (Oxford: Clarendon, 1974), 2:171.

58. *Gospel of Truth* 20:19–22, 21:25, in *NHLE*, 39–40.

59. *Pistis Sophia* I, 56, 22–23, in Schmidt, *Pistis Sophia*, 107.

60. *Gospel of Truth* 26:15–16, in *NHLE*, 42.

61. *Gospel of Bartholomew* III, 1–9, in Hennecke and Schneemelcher, *New Testament Apocrypha*, 1:494–95; cf. D&C 76:46–47.

62. See 1 *Enoch* 18:12, 14–15, in *OTP* 1:23; cf. Jude 13.

63. *Apocryphon of John* 1:12–14, in *NHLE*, 99.

64. Lidzbarski, *Ginza*, 113–19; cf. Foerster, *Gnosis*, 2:194.

65. *Untitled Text* 19–20, in Schmidt, *Books of Jeu and the Untitled Text*, 261–63.

66. Ibid.

67. Cf. *First Apocalypse of James* 27:1–5, in *NHLE*, 243.

68. Cf. *First Apocalypse of James* 26:20–30, in ibid.

69. *Sophia Christi* 100:14–102:1, in Till, "Die gnostischen Schriften," 240–44; cf. *NHLE*, 217–18.

70. Lidzbarski, *Ginza*, 258; *Psalms of Thomas* 8:1–15, in Allberry, *Manichaean Psalm Book*, 2:214.

71. Cf. Foerster, *Gnosis*, 2:149–50.

72. Cf. Justin Martyr, *Dialogus cum Tryphone Judaeo (Dialogue with Trypho)*, in *PG* 6:752–53.

73. Jedaiah ben Abraham Bedersi, *Behinat ʿOlam, or An Investigation of Causes Arising from the Organization of the World, in Which Man Is Particularly Interested* (London: Alexander, 1806). See J. Chotzner, "Yedaya Bejaresi," *Jewish Quarterly Review* 8 (1895/96): 414–25; S. Doniach, "Abraham Bédersi's Purim Letter to David Kaslari," *Jewish Quarterly Review* 23 (1932/33): 63–69, 349–56.

74. TB *Barayta* 54a, in Nicholas Sed, "Une cosmologie juive du haut moyen âge: La berayta di Ma'aseh Breshit," *Revue des études juives* 123 (1964): 259–305.

75. Cf. *Untitled Text* 1; 4; 6, in Schmidt, *Books of Jeu and the Untitled Text*, 226, lines 3–4; 231–32; 233–34; *First Apocalypse of James* 25:26–26:5, 22–23; 36:1–4, in *NHLE*, 243, 247; *Apocryphon of John* 2:1–14; 5:7–9; 8:22–28, in ibid., 99, 101, 103. *Sophia Christi* 107:4–8; 110:2–11, in ibid., 221–22 (cf. the three divine men of the parallel *Eugnostos the Blessed*). 1QS 8:1–3; Theodor H. Gaster, *The Dead Sea Scriptures*, 3rd ed. (Garden City, NY: Doubleday, 1976), 60.

76. *1 Jeu* 5–6, in Schmidt, *Books of Jeu and the Untitled Text*, 48–50.

77. Adolph Franck, *The Kabbalah* (New York: Bell, 1940), 28, noted the absence from the *Sefer Yetzira* of the Greek, Latin, and Arabic expressions common in the later Talmudic and cabalistic material. Franck argued that it was both pre-Christian and Aristotelian.

78. Origen, *De Principiis* III, 5, 3, in *PG* 11:327.

79. Methodius, *Convivium Decem Virginum (Banquet of the Ten Virgins)* III, 6, in *PG* 18:68–69.

80. *Untitled Text* 19, in Schmidt, *Books of Jeu and the Untitled Text*, 261–62.

81. *Gospel of Truth* 18:33–35; 19:7–10, in *NHLE*, 38–39.

82. Cf. *Sophia Christi* 99:13–100:4; 110:10–111:5 [91:17–92:16; 110:10–15]; in Till, "Die gnostischen Schriften," 222–24; 260–62; cf. *NHLE*, 213, 222.

83. *Untitled Text* 2, in Schmidt, *Books of Jeu and the Untitled Text*, 229–30; Lidzbarski, *Ginza*, 258; *Psalms of Thomas* 8:13–15, in Allberry, *Manichaean Psalm-Book*, 2:214.

84. *Sophia Christi* 113:15–19 [116:3–10]; in Till, "Die gnostischen Schriften," 272; cf. *NHLE,* 224.

85. *Sophia Christi* 113:20–22 [116:11–17], in Till, "Die gnostischen Schriften," 272; cf. *NHLE,* 224.

86. *Odes of Solomon* 12:7–9, in *OTP* 2:747. Rutherford H. Platt, ed., *The Forgotten Books of Eden* (Newfoundland: Alpha House, 1927), 126–27.

87. Cf. Foerster, *Gnosis,* 2:151; *Psalms of Thomas* 8:13–15, in Allberry, *Manichaean Psalm-Book,* 2:214.

88. Lidzbarski, *Ginza,* 10–11; Drower, *Thousand and Twelve Questions,* 112.

89. Lidzbarski, *Ginza,* 258; *Psalms of Thomas* 8:9–15, in Allberry, *Manichaean Psalm-Book,* 2:214.

90. Allberry, *Manichaean Psalm-Book,* 2:23.

91. Clement, *Epistola I ad Corinthios (First Epistle to the Corinthians)* 19–20, in *PG* 1:247–54.

92. *1 Enoch* 69:21, in *OTP* 1:48.

93. Cf. *1 Enoch* 62; 69:26–29; 71:14–17, in ibid., 1:43, 49–50.

94. *Pistis Sophia* II, 88; 84, in Schmidt, *Pistis Sophia,* 200–201; 186–89.

95. *First Apocalypse of James* 27:1–7, in *NHLE,* 243.

96. Cf. *Gospel of Philip* 53:23–54:15, in *NHLE,* 132–33.

97. Cf. *Sophia Christi* 103:1–8 [96:19–97:8]; in Till, "Die gnostischen Schriften," 232–34; *NHLE,* 215.

98. *Epistle of the Apostles* 19; in Hennecke and Schneemelcher, *New Testament Apocrypha,* 1:202.

99. Lidzbarski, *Ginza,* 152.

100. *Odes of Solomon* 11:23, in *OTP* 2:746.

101. *TPJS,* 291–92.

102. Cf. *Sophia Christi* 109:4–110:5; 113:1–10, in Till, "Die gnostischen Schriften," 258–60, 270.

103. *Gospel of Philip* 76:6–10, in *NHLE,* 145.

104. *Gospel of Philip* 75:7–11, in ibid.; cf. 81:19–33, in *NHLE,* 148–49.

105. Lidzbarski, *Ginza,* 152.

106. Athanasius, *Oratio Contra Gentes (Orations against the Heathens)* 38, in *PG* 25:76–77.

107. Plotinus, *Enneads* III, 2, 14.

108. Cf. *Pistis Sophia* I, 1, in Schmidt, *Pistis Sophia,* 2.

109. *Pistis Sophia* II, 91, in ibid., 205–7.

110. Ignatius, *Epistola ad Trallianos (Epistle to the Trallians)* 5, in *PG* 5:665–68. See also Hugh W. Nibley, *The Message of the Joseph*

Smith Papyri: An Egyptian Endowment (Salt Lake City: Deseret Book, 1975), 283.

111. *Sefer Yetzira* 1:5, in Akiba ben Joseph, *The Book of Formation: Sepher Yetzirah,* tr. Knut Stenring (London: Rider, 1923), 21.

112. Methodius, *Banquet of the Ten Virgins* VIII, 15, in *PG* 18:165, 168.

113. Origen, *De Principiis* II, 9, 6, in *PG* 11:230–31.

114. See question 47, art. 1, in Thomas Aquinas, *Summa Theologica,* ed. Anton C. Pegis (New York: Random House, 1945), 459.

115. *Gospel of Philip* 68:17–22, in *NHLE,* 141.

116. *Gospel of Philip* 63:11–17, in ibid., 138.

117. *Gospel of Truth* 16:31–17:1, in Harold W. Attridge, ed., *Nag Hammadi Codex I* (Leiden: Brill, 1985), 83.

118. *Pistis Sophia* II, 84, in Schmidt, *Pistis Sophia,* 186–89.

119. *1 Jeu* 33–39, in Schmidt, *Books of Jeu and the Untitled Text,* 83–89.

120. *Pistis Sophia* II, 98, in Schmidt, *Pistis Sophia,* 240.

121. See Hugh W. Nibley, "Evangelium Quadraginta Dierum," *Vigiliae Christianae* 20 (1966): 1–24; reprinted as "Evangelium Quadraginta Dierum: The Forty-Day Mission of Christ—The Forgotten Heritage," in *CWHN* 4:10–44.

122. Irenaeus, *Contra Haereses (Against Heresies)* IV, 33, 8, in *PG* 7:1077, on the "true gnosis" as "the doctrine of the Apostles."

123. These are discussed in Hugh W. Nibley, "The Passing of the Primitive Church: Forty Variations on an Unpopular Theme," *Church History* 20 (June 1961): 131–54; reprinted in *CWHN* 4:168–208.

124. See Geo Widengren, *The Ascension of the Apostle and the Heavenly Book (King and Saviour III),* Uppsala Universitets Årsskrift 7 (Uppsala: Almquist and Wiksells, 1950), 47.

125. *1 Jeu* 3, in Schmidt, *Books of Jeu and the Untitled Text,* 41–42.

126. *Epistles of the Apostles* 39, in Hennecke and Schneemelcher, *New Testament Apocrypha,* 1:199.

127. *Epistles of the Apostles* 39, in ibid.

128. *Epistle of the Apostles* 17, in ibid.

129. Mark Lidzbarski, *Das Johannesbuch der Mandäer* (Giessen: Töpelmann, 1915), 57, no. 13. G. R. S. Mead, *The Gnostic John the Baptizer: Selections from the Mandaean Book of John* (London: Watkins, 1924), 91. See also A. L. B. Hardcastle, "Fragments of the Mandaean Mass for the Souls of the Dead," *Theosophical Review* 29/174 (February 1902): 493; Foerster, *Gnosis,* 2:253–54. Robert Haardt, *Gnosis: Character and Testimony* (Leiden: Brill, 1971), 381.

130. Lidzbarski, *Ginza,* 488.

131. Foerster, *Gnosis*, 2:257–61; Allberry, *Manichaean Psalm-Book*, 2:197–202; Hardcastle, "Fragments of the Mandaean Mass for the Souls of the Dead," 494, 496.

132. Lidzbarski, *Ginza*, 429.

133. Ibid.; cf. Foerster, *Gnosis*, 2:200–202.

134. Lidzbarski, *Ginza*, 101–2; cf. Foerster, *Gnosis*, 2:263.

135. Lidzbarski, *Das Johannesbuch der Mandäer*, 57; cf. Mead, *Gnostic John the Baptizer*, 91.

136. *Apocalypse of Abraham* 10:2–6, in *OTP* 1:693–94.

137. *Apocalypse of Adam* 65:26–66:8, in *NHLE*, 257.

138. Cf. *Sophia Christi* 100:20–102:20, in Till, "Die gnostischen Schriften," 226–32.

139. Timothy Archbishiop of Alexandria, "Discourse on Abbatôn," in E. A. Wallis Budge, *Coptic Martyrdoms etc. in the Dialect of Upper Egypt* (London: British Museum, 1914), 482.

140. *Untitled Text 8*, in Schmidt, *Books of Jeu and the Untitled Text*, 238–39.

141. Lidzbarski, *Ginza*, 15–27.

142. Cf. Foerster, *Gnosis*, 2:197; *Mandaean Prayerbook* No. 379, "And Hibil-Ziwa [Radiant-Abel] came and blessed three 'uthras [Spirits-of-Life], And the three 'uthras blessed Adam and all his descendants" (cf. No. 42). Ethel S. Drower, tr., *The Canonical Prayerbook of the Mandaeans* (Leiden: Brill, 1959), 292; see also Nibley, *Since Cumorah*, 175–77; in *CWHN* 7:155–56.

143. Foerster, *Gnosis*, 2:197.

144. Lidzbarski, *Ginza*, 16.

145. Ibid., 263–64.

146. *First Apocalypse of James* 34:17–19, in *NHLE*, 246.

147. *Gospel of Thomas* 49, in ibid., 123.

148. *Gospel of Truth* 22:2–12, in ibid., 40.

149. Allberry, *Manichaean Psalm-Book*, 2:201–2.

150. Ibid., 2:197–99.

151. Ibid., 2:72.

152. Ibid., 2:197–202.

153. Lidzbarski, *Ginza*, 511–12. Cf. Foerster, *Gnosis*, 2:261–62.

154. Lidzbarski, *Ginza*, 454–56, 461, 463, 465, 499, 511, 513; cf. Foerster, *Gnosis*, 2:254–63.

155. *Psalms of Thomas* 17:3–10, in Allberry, *Manichaean Psalm-Book*, 2:224.

156. *The Pearl* 98–105; *Acts of Thomas* 108–13; cf. Hennecke and Schneemelcher, *New Testament Apocrypha*, 2:503–4.

157. Cf. Gregory of Nyssa, in *PG* 46:108–12.

158. Regarding Paul VI, see *The Pope Speaks* 10 (1965): 365; Nibley, *Since Cumorah*, 17, nn. 25–26; reprinted in *CWHN* 7:16, nn. 32–33.

159. This is discussed in Hugh W. Nibley, "The Expanding Gospel," *BYUS* 7 (1965): 3–27; reprinted in this volume, pages 177–211.

160. *Gospel of Bartholomew* I, 22, in Hennecke and Schneemelcher, *New Testament Apocrypha*, 1:290–91.

161. Cf. *Untitled Text* 13, in Schmidt, *Books of Jeu and the Untitled Text*, 252.

162. *Untitled Text* 4, in ibid., 213; cf. *Gospel of the Egyptians* 3:50, in *NHLE*, 199; *Trimorphic Protennoia* 39, in *NHLE*, 464.

163. *Apocalypse of Abraham* 17:13, 20, in *OTP* 1:693–97.

164. *Apocalypse of Abraham* 17:5–21, in ibid., 1:697; cf. Hugh W. Nibley, "The Early Christian Prayer Circle," *BYUS* 19 (Fall 1978): 52; reprinted in *CWHN* 4:57.

165. *Apocryphon of John* 20:14–25, in *NHLE*, 110.

166. *Gospel of Philip* 55:5–25, in *NHLE*, 133.

167. Cf. *Apocryphon of John* 20:15–25, in *NHLE*, 110.

168. Lidzbarski, *Ginza*, 14–27.

169. *Apocalypse of Abraham* 11:1–2, in *OTP* 1:694.

170. "Discourse on Abbatôn," in Budge, *Coptic Martyrdoms*, 225–249, 474–96.

171. Cf. *Apocryphon of John* 20:14–21:16; 22:20–21; 22:34–23:14, in *NHLE*, 110–11.

172. *2 Jeu* 44, in Schmidt, *Books of Jeu and the Untitled Text*, 105.

173. Cf. *2 Jeu* 42, in ibid., 99; *Pistis Sophia* IV, 136, in Schmidt, *Pistis Sophia*, 353–54.

174. *2 Jeu* 51, in Schmidt, *Books of Jeu and the Untitled Text*, 126; cf. *Pistis Sophia* III, 125, in Schmidt, *Pistis Sophia*, 314–15.

175. *2 Jeu* 51, in Schmidt, *Books of Jeu and the Untitled Text*, 126.

176. *Pistis Sophia* III, 135, in Schmidt, *Pistis Sophia*, 350.

177. Cf. *1 Jeu* 39, in Schmidt, *Books of Jeu and the Untitled Text*, 89. This subject is discussed generally throughout the whole text of the books of Jeu.

178. *Pistis Sophia* II, 97, in Schmidt, *Pistis Sophia*, 234–35.

179. Cf. *Pistis Sophia* III, 132, in ibid., 347–48.

180. *Pistis Sophia* II, 97; III, 133, in Schmidt, *Pistis Sophia*, 234–35; 346–47.

181. *Pistis Sophia* III, 125, in Schmidt, *Pistis Sophia*, 314.

182. *Gospel of Thomas*, logion 59, in *NHLE*, 124.

183. *Gospel of Philip* 85:14–16, in *NHLE*, 150.

184. *Gospel of Philip* 76:27–36, and cf. 72:29–37; 73:1–8, in ibid., 143–44, 146.

185. Romey P. Marshall and Michael J. Taylor, *Liturgy and Christian Unity* (Englewood Cliffs, NJ: Prentice Hall, 1965), 125.

186. *Pistis Sophia* IV, 36, in Schmidt, *Pistis Sophia*, 353; cf. *2 Jeu* 42, in Schmidt, *Books of Jeu and the Untitled Text*, 99.

187. Cf. *1 Jeu* 41; *2 Jeu* 45, in Schmidt, *Books of Jeu and the Untitled Text*, 93; 107.

188. Cf. *1 Jeu* 8, in ibid., 54.

189. Cf. *Apocalypse of Abraham* 22:1–5, in *OTP* 1:700.

190. Cf. *2 Jeu* 45, in Schmidt, *Books of Jeu and the Untitled Text*, 107; cf. *Pistis Sophia* IV, 136, in Schmidt, *Pistis Sophia*, 353.

191. See Nibley, "The Early Christian Prayer Circle," 46–47; in *CWHN* 4:51.

192. Ibid., 4:42.

193. *Acts of John* 94–96, in Hennecke and Schneemelcher, *New Testament Apocrypha*, 2:227–32.

194. Augustine, *Epistola (Letter)* 237, in *PL* 33:1034–38.

195. Johannes Dominicus Mansi, *Sacrorum Conciliorum Nova et Amplissa Collectio*, 53 vols. (Graz: Akademischer Verlag, 1960), 13:168–76.

196. Ignatius Ephraem II Rahmani, ed., *Testamentum Domini Nostri Jesu Christi* (Monguntiae: Kirchheim, 1899), 36–37, cited in Nibley, "The Early Christian Prayer Circle," 43–44, nn. 5–7, in *CWHN* 4:47–48, nn. 5–7.

197. A. Wilmart and E. Tisserant, "Fragments grecs et latins de l'évangile de Barthélemy," *Revue biblique* 22 (1913): 321, cited in Nibley, "The Early Christian Prayer Circle," 45, nn. 11–13; in *CWHN* 4:49–50, nn. 11–13.

198. *Apocalypse of Abraham* 12–17, in *OTP* 1:694–97.

199. Cf. *2 Jeu* 45, in Schmidt, *Books of Jeu and the Untitled Text*, 105.

200. *2 Jeu* 43, in ibid., 100–102.

201. Lidzbarski, *Ginza*, 113–19; cf. Foerster, *Gnosis*, 2:194–98.

202. *Apocalypse of Abraham* 12–17, in *OTP* 1:694–97.

203. 2 Maccabees 12:34–45.

204. Arthur O. Lovejoy, *The Great Chain of Being: A Study of the History of an Idea*, William James Lectures at Harvard, 1933 (Cambridge: Harvard University Press, 1936).

205. Karl R. Popper, *The Logic of Scientific Discovery* (New York: Harper and Row, 1968), 280.

The Terrible Questions

This speech was not my idea, and that's a good thing, because if it was my idea, my talk would be very stiff. I'm supposed to talk about something I've already talked about before, and that I refuse to do. Also, I see the sponsors have stretched the time out to an hour and a half, in a futile attempt to slow me down. That won't succeed. Don't think I don't try to slow down, but things just come out chaotically, in all directions. If I'd talked on this subject before, I wouldn't be interested in talking about it now, and yet you'll excuse me if you recognize a lot of old, familiar territory on the "terrible questions."

Last week I received two letters that introduce us very well to the "terrible questions." One was from a gentleman in Colorado, a long, long, extremely indignant letter with ninety-eight questions. He labored very hard on the letter, copies of which he has sent to the First Presidency and all members of the Council of the Twelve, challenging them to answer him.

He places the questions in various categories. And if the Brethren don't answer these, he writes, it shows that the Mormon Church has no quality at all. "Don't you have any officials that answer these questions?"

He doesn't realize that he has put his finger on one of the greatest strengths of the Church: We don't have a

This talk was given on September 8, 1988, in Riverton, Utah, as part of a lecture series sponsored by Deseret Book and the Foundation for Ancient Research and Mormon Studies.

professional clergy—a paid ministry that gives official interpretations of the scriptures—as we've always said we don't. There's no office in the Church that qualifies the holder to give the official interpretation of the Church. We're to read the scriptures for ourselves, as guided by the Spirit. Joseph Smith himself often disagreed with various of his brethren on different points, yet he never cracked down on them, saying they'd better change this or that, or else. He disagreed with Parley P. Pratt on a number of things, and also with Brigham Young on various things. Brigham said that Joseph didn't know a thing about business.

Joseph rebuked Parley P. Pratt for things said in the newspaper Parley was editing, but he didn't remove him from the editorship. "The paper is not interesting enough. You're not putting the right things in it." Still he left it entirely up to Parley what to do. This has always been the policy in the Church—a lot of degree of differences. It should not worry us.

In questions on epistemology our correspondent asks fifty-four questions. For example, "If God is a junior god in the universe, and there are more senior gods, why shouldn't I put my faith in a senior god?"

Next are questions on ontology, the nature of being. For example, "How is Mormonism different metaphysically from ancient pagan concepts?" (We could write a long book on that question!) "What about autonomy of the human will, and free agency?"

Then come eighteen questions on ethics, or "ethica," as he calls it. "How would you respond to Gordon Clark and his *Religion, Reason, and Revelation*, that such a thing as free will cannot save your God from being responsible?"

The author of the ninety-eight questions concludes with: "And I will be looking for the 'official' response to these questions." I won't read my responses, though I do tell him in answer to his book-length letter that I've already

treated many of these questions in things I've published,
which I recommend to him. "There is much more," I concluded, "for as certain primitive Christians remark during
the preliminaries of the glorious Nicene Council, it's a
question of which is more miraculous, to make a stone
speak or a theologian shut up."[1]

Theologians can talk about these things until the cows
come home. It is inexhaustible; they keep themselves in
work forever talking about these things. If you visit a divinity school, that's what you hear.

The other letter is equally profound. It comes from a
worried inmate at the Point of the Mountain (the Utah
State Penitentiary), who has been having some talks with
Mark Hofmann in the exercise yard of the prison. Hofmann
is out to demolish this man's testimony. You'd think the
smart Mark Hofmann, with all his resources and his know-
how, would be able to come up with something better than
three questions which "absolutely demolish Joseph
Smith": the Kinderhook Plates, no horse bones found in
South America, and Adam-God—the old anti-Mormon
chestnuts. I'm sending the inmate some things on these
topics.

You do see how feeble the approaches of these attacks
are, how irrelevant. What does any of this have to do with
the eternities, with eternal life? What does any of this have
to do with anything that interests me at all? There is only
one question, the sole question for religion, the only reason
for religion existing at all. Religion alone is supposed to
answer it, and if religion can't, then religion can't do anything—let us forget religion. I don't worry about tomor-
row's football scores; I don't worry about all these questions concerning the nature of God. We have at Brigham
Young University literally thousands of volumes of theological discussions on these questions down through the
centuries.

If these questions were the right ones, it would take

but two minutes to answer them. Why the thousands of volumes? Why can't they come up with answers? Are they evading the question? Yes, they are. They only talk all around it.

There is only one justification for religion, one sole question, so let us not talk about the endless, abstract problems (for example, the nature of God) that obsessed the church Fathers, who always come out the same door wherein they entered.[2] It's presumptuous, even wicked, to investigate the nature of God; he is so totally different from us, you can't discuss him at all. So they write hundreds of volumes on the subject. Chrysostom is a good example: he wrote seventeen volumes on the nature of God, after saying it was a crime even to mention the subject.

In the hereafter, what difference will these questions make? The real question, of course, is, Is this all there is? This is what everybody wants to know, the only question that bothers us. If you can answer that definitely, then our troubles are over; there is nothing left to worry about. The person who leads a happy life approaches that question, and it's a question being asked today, in a poignant manner. "Must life end so soon?" the happy person asks. "I've barely started with life. With all this ability, are we going to just cut life off? Why does it have to stop here?" And if you've led a miserable life, you have the same question: "I've not even had a chance yet, and you're going to cut it off here? Don't I get a break? Can't I have a year more or so?" Of course that's the theme of much drama — of *Faust*, of *The Devil and Daniel Webster:* Give me a chance, an extension.

It's the answer to that question that satisfies us, and everything else we can forget about. Who cares about how politics turn out? Or the economy? Or even the military threat? We're going to die anyway; what difference do any of these things make? Religion exists to answer that question, none others. Of course there are side issues—for example, the study of God. But why study him? He is the only one who has the knowledge and power to guarantee that we will go on. But if we exist only to drop into a sea of Nirvana, a sea of nothing—if we are to vanish entirely, we don't care whether there is one god or thousands; whether he's fierce and ferocious, or kind and loving. It makes no difference to you at all; you won't be there. You won't be anything. Yet this is what people commonly believe.

Brigham Young puts it this way: "The greatest gift that God can bestow upon the children of men [you have to admit] is the gift of eternal life; that is, to give mankind power to preserve their identity—to preserve themselves before the Lord."[3] That is what it is.

There's something very much out of kilter in our enormous overkill in our mental capacities. Arthur Henry Wallace used to drive Darwin crazy about becoming bitter over it. Wallace actually did more for evolution than Darwin did, yet he used to needle Darwin with this issue: We have developed our various gifts and capacities and organs and dimensions, etc., as a challenge to survival. When we need a sharp smeller, we develop one; when we need fast legs, we develop them; and so we survive, and the faster we are, the better we survive? All these things are necessary to survival, and we maintain them to the point at which we need them, a point of adequacy. Why on earth did God give us a brain that wasn't necessary for survival at all? Creatures with no mentality at all are very good at surviving, much better than man is, as a matter of fact. Though not particularly bright, they swarm over the earth. And when the climate knocks them out, everybody gets knocked out. (You can't do anything about the dinosaurs, whether it's meteorites[4] or something else. There was nothing we could do about the Yellowstone forest fires. When these times come, they come.)

So why all this overkill? Why do we have a thousand times more brain power than we ever needed to survive? It must have developed in a situation in which we did need such power, Wallace said to Darwin. What could that situation have been when we developed such an enormous mental capacity? At least it must be in reserve for something we can really put to use, because we never develop an organ we're not going to have to use. It would atrophy. Maybe that's why our brains have atrophied. Darwin would simply try to explain it away by saying, because that is how things work.

If we are not using our brain, if we don't need a brain, then why have one? And the fact is, no one is using but a small fraction of the brain. The dilemma has been expressed in various poignant ways; we can quote the poets. It is the issue that gets closest to people, the theme of tragedy—the "black night."

Oedipus is the most tragic figure of all tragedies. In *Oedipus at Colonus*, the chorus asks, What is going to happen to Oedipus? His life is so tragic. He's gone through so much. He's going to die[5] —which fate is going to happen to all of us. What is so tragic about Oedipus? So we come to the big issue: no one can escape Oedipus's fate.

Brigham Young also said that the great and grand secret of salvation, which we should continually seek to understand through our faithfulness, is the continuation of lives—carrying on, going on. If life is not an ongoing thing, if it's going to be cut off, then who cares?

Today we are doing what Catullus described the Romans as doing, in his famous Fifth Ode: "Vivamus, mea Lesbia, atque amemus" (Let's love and live it up, my darling Lesbia); "rumoresque senum severiorum omnes unius aestimemus assis" (and consider all the severe censures of the moralists around us as not worth one penny, because) "soles occidere et redire possunt" (the sun goes down and the sun comes up again) "nobis cum semel occidit brevis

lux" (and once *our* sun goes down) "nox est perpetua una
dormienda" (we have nothing remaining but one long
night). Everybody believed that. So, continues Catullus,
let's get into it. Give me a thousand kisses and a thousand
more. Let's live it up and have sex.[6] What else is there to
look forward to?

Shakespeare takes up the same theme: "The weariest
and most loathed worldly life that age, ache, penury, and
imprisonment can lay on nature is a paradise to what we
fear of death."[7] The worst life is better than anything, even
death. In *Measure for Measure,* when Isabella's brother tries
to avoid being executed for somebody else, he says, "Ay,
but to die, and go we know not where; to lie in cold ob-
struction, and to rot; this sensible warm motion to become
a kneaded clod."[8]

That's it. What else is there? You can't depict anything
worse than death, and you can't escape it. Hence the terrible question, Is there anything more?

Now let us start our story. The situation is best illustrated by a favorite story of mine, the story of young Clement of Rome. Very probably Clement is the first of the
apostolic Fathers. After the New Testament, the oldest
Christian writings we have are the seven apostolic Fathers,
and the first and oldest of them is First Clement, then
Second Clement, Ignatius, etc. This is First Clement.

His autobiography is very interesting. Unlike other
early writings, it contains nothing miraculous, no hokum.
We could call it the first Christian romance;[9] but if it's a
romance, it's very autobiographical; everything in it is
highly veristic — no miracles, no supernaturalism, but containing the very sort of thing that was happening in the
church.

It belongs to the literary genre *recognitiones* (recognitions), the "recognition type." In the Roman empire at that
time, things were very insecure. Things were becoming

desperate. At the great public festivals, children would be
stolen and sold as slaves, as good business, just as children
are often kidnapped today. There's a market for children.
So the theme is this: a child is stolen, then is recognized
later, when the family members are brought together.
Shakespeare uses the theme in *Comedy of Errors*.[10]

Clement's parents had been lost at sea, and the family
were reunited in Palestine at a council of the Church; they
had all joined the Church independently. It's a very happy
ending.

The story of Clement is in the first volume of the *Patrologia*, after the *Apostolic Constitutions*, because it's pre-
sumably the first Christian writing we have after the New
Testament. This is what Clement, residing in Rome, says:
"Ego Clemens in urbe Roma natus, ex prima aetate pud-
icitiae studium gessi" (I Clement was born in Rome, and
from the earliest age, I was devoted to chastity). I was
constantly bothered by one question: "dum me animi in-
tentio velut vinculis quibusdam sollicitudinis et moeroris
a puero innexum teneret" (while the bent of my mind held
me bound from childhood as with chains of care and anxiety), a question that wouldn't let go of me at all. It was
the condition of my mortality. These were the questions
that were constantly going through my mind: "utrumne
sit mihi aliqua vita post mortem an nihil omnino postea
sim futurus" (whether there would be a life for me after
death or whether I wouldn't be anything at all afterward).[11]
He is living in pagan Rome, the center of all studies; he
has a very good education; the chief men and great philosophers all resided there. He had made it a point to visit
all of them.[12] His parents had been very rich.

This led inevitably to the other question that kept turning about in my heart: "si non fuerim antequam nascerer"
(I wondered . . . if I didn't exist before I was born — premortal existence). "Vel si nulla prorsus vitae huius erit post

obitum recordatio, et ita immensitas temporis cuncta ob-
livioni ac silentio dabit, ut non solum non simus, sed neque
quod fuerimus, habeatur in memoria" (or if there won't
be any recollection of this life after death, and the bound-
lessness of time will consign everything to oblivion and
silence, so that we not only will not exist, but also that
which we were, will not be held in memory).[13]

As I've said, this is the question that religion answers,
and which no theologian will touch with a forty-foot pole.
The skill with which they evade it is remarkable. We'll
come back to that point. And then, if we're to live hereafter,
will we have any memory of what we've done here? Of
what we did during our lifetimes? Will we retain that? This
leads to other questions. If I lived before I came here, before
I was born into this world, then there must be this question:
"Quando factus sit mundus vel antequam fieret, quid erat,
aut vero semper fuerit" (when was this world made, or
what was there before it was made, or did it always exist?).
Then he goes into the plurality of worlds, into cosmology,
which you can't avoid. All the early Christian and Jewish
writers go into this, though the Fathers from the third
century on won't approach it at all. They love abstractions
and things like that.

Now to his fifth question: Or, if the world was made
at all, "nam certum videbatur, quod si esset factus, esset
et profecto solvendus, et si solvatur, quid iterum erit?" (for
it appeared certain that it had been made, and if it does
dissolve what will there be afterward?).[14] And if it passes
away completely, then what will be left after that? Will
there be other worlds?

He asks all the basic questions, which everybody
avoids. Scientists, of course, won't touch them. The religious should handle them; that is why they are there, to
give us comfort. But they won't touch the questions either.

And then finally, a very good question, "Nisi forte
oblivio cuncta et silentium teget, aut forte aliquid erit"

(unless by chance all things shall be buried in oblivion and silence, or will there perhaps be something) — could there be something like a singularity? Some condition or state hereafter, "quod nunc sentire mortalium non potest mens" (that mortal minds can't possibly conceive of now?) Which could be real, but we just don't conceive it?[15] That's what black holes and quasar stars are, singularities — real, yet nobody can describe them, or even conceive of what they are like. Still they are there, they are measurable. After all, he leaves the door open to a singularity. There *may* be another explanation after all.

He was a pretty smart kid. So he decided to see if he could find an answer to his questions. He went everywhere. He visited his friends. He visited the many schools in Rome, consulting with top professors. He could afford it. But he got nothing from them but "endless propositions put forth or refuted in clever disputations and skillful syllogisms. They argued and discussed the subject. When one celebrated philosopher would prove definitely that the soul was immortal, I was elated. Then another would come along and prove just as definitely that the soul was not immortal."[16] That would send him into a deep depression. And this went on and on.

"Along with this, I brooded on such things as when the world was made."[17] He claims he was driven nearly crazy by these concerns; in fact, he became physically ill — losing weight, causing concern among his family. They tried to take his mind off things with various pleasures. But he couldn't escape it.[18] "Immortalitatis cupido" (desire of immortality; nothing could satisfy my yearning for life).[19]

"It was all a matter of definitions and opinions," he explains.[20] Remember the ninety-eight questions I just talked about — do we have to answer them? Are they any of our business? Has anybody ever answered any of those to anyone's satisfaction? No, we could debate them forever. It's a philosophical sinecure; you'll never have to worry about answers to those questions. It's a closed shop, like the Bureau of Reclamation, which has built enough dams to dam the Pacific Ocean. It's time to stop, but the bureau has to stay in business, so they go on building dams, which they will probably do forever, in your backyard, before you know it—wherever they can find a place.

So the clergy argue about these things, as is evidenced in the religious journals that come out. The English journal *The Expository Times* reviews all the important articles that come out, so you can keep up to date. The writers simply go round and round. Recently a Swede wrote a resumé of all the great advances that have been made in church history study in the last fifty years (I was teaching at Claremont, Pomona, and Scripps colleges fifty years ago, talking about religion in humanities courses I was teaching, and getting people upset all the time). His conclusion is that the scholars are exactly where they started; there has been no progress whatever.

From time to time there is a review of the literature on New Testament criticism. It's back to the problems and answers of seventy years ago, so here we go again. There will be no answers, and this is what bothered Clement.

"They had nothing tangible to offer," Clement continues.[21] To put his mind at ease, he tried to rationalize to himself about the problems. "I can forget about them. If I am not to exist after death, there is no point in getting all worked up about it. There is nothing I can do about it."[22] One can get drunk and forget about it, but as A. E. Housman says, "The troubles of our proud and angry dust are from eternity, and shall not fail. Bear them we can, and if we can we must. Shoulder the sky, my lad, and drink your ale. Could man be drunk for ever with liquor, love or fights, lief should I rouse at morning and lief lie down of nights. But men at whiles are sober and think by fits and starts and if they think, they fasten their hands upon their hearts."[23] You can't avoid the confrontation; it will catch up with you every time.

This happened to Clement. He tried to have some fun, but of course it's the mummy at the banquet "memento mori" (remember to die). You remember, the emperor at the peak of his triumph had a slave at his right side, whispering in his ear, "Remember, you are human. You are temporary here too." That was to bring him down to earth.

It was part of the Roman temperament (though not of the Italian) to brood on subjects of death. They always celebrated a person's death, not the birth. There is still in Italy a great obsession with graveyards; they are the biggest thing in town, where people go for celebrations. That is why Clement broods on the subject; it's part of the culture. "If there *is* one life, then why should I spend this life worrying about the remote possibility of various hells?"[24]

By going back to tradition, to the poets, to various rites and religions, the doctors of the schools were able to give him all sorts of pictures of the hereafter, for example, the *Phlegethon*, or the *Nekyia*, the eleventh book of the *Odyssey*, where Odysseus goes down to hell.[25] There are all sorts of visits to the underworld, through the gate of ivory, or the gate of horn, of the Aeneid. And of course in the mysteries one was introduced to a foretaste of the other world. It was dramatized; a big thing was made of it. You were to worry about the other world, because that is where you were going.

Clement had gotten a big dose of that: Tartarus, Sisyphus, Tityus, and the tortures hereafter and other horrible things. Why should Clement worry about hell?[26] Long before Christianity, the Romans were worrying about a hell, which is exactly what the Church adopted later on, but it is not found in the scriptures at all. "I decided that all this stuff was only fables of the philosophers, but that didn't relieve my anxiety. If it's all so uncertain, why not live it up and enjoy the pleasures of the flesh?"[27]

None of these arguments pleased him. He got worse and worse. "What should I do?"[28] There was only one way that remained. Since he had never heard of revelation, he told himself, "I will go to Egypt, where I'll gain the confidence of some hierophants, or priests or prophets, administering in one of the temples or shrines there [of which there were many — colleges that engaged in these exercises very diligently], and for a fee get him to bring up a spirit from the other world," and show me, once and for all, that there is an afterlife, no matter how terrible it might be. Just so there's something there. That's all I want to know. Just bring up one ghost.[29]

This is the theme of Banquo's ghost,[30] or of the earliest German opera, *Der Freischütz*.[31] The one thing you must know is that the ghost lives, and he appears. People are desperate about such things.

Clement had a friend who was a philosopher, who warned him not to go to Egypt for two reasons. One, if the spirit doesn't appear, then you'll be in deeper trouble than ever. You'll be in dumps you'll never get over; you'll be sure there is nothing there, yet still go on wondering anyway that perhaps it was a misfire. Second, that thing is *exosum*, something to be avoided.[32] It's morbid, unclean; it doesn't leave you feeling well. It is like our saying, "Don't get yourself psychoanalyzed"; avoid it if you can — as you avoid going to court.

Dallin Oaks was in my priesthood quorum for years, and he always used to tell us that the worst settlement out of court is better than the best settlement in court. So before you go to see a psychoanalyst, or a spiritualist, or to court, look for an alternative. Brother Oaks was very emphatic about avoiding court if at all possible: Stay out of court, whatever you do! You're in trouble if you go to court.

So it is when you start fiddling around with spirits. I myself know people in Hollywood, where I lived many of my days, and still have many friends; among them was the president of the Fortian Society, Fred Keating, a famous high-class magician. When I was at Claremont, the gang would get in a bus and come out for a seance and to get drunk. It isn't a good thing, though it is a way to try to escape reality. These people are afraid. As T. S. Eliot says, "I have seen the eternal footman hold my coat, and snicker, and in short, I was afraid."[33] Eliot was a very calm, sophisticated, well-educated modern man, but he was scared stiff. You can't get away from it.

So Clement decided not to go to Egypt. While he was going down a street in Rome, he heard a street meeting going on. Somebody was speaking in a heavy Levantine accent; it was near the school, and there were many students around, heckling the speaker. It was Barnabas, who had come as a missionary from Palestine, to preach in the streets of Rome. The students were making fun of his accent and were also asking questions: "They wanted to go into syllogisms and questions. If you are so smart in religion, why did God make a little gnat (*culex*) with six legs and wings, and a great big elephant with only four and no wings. That proves there's no god."[34] These are the sort of arguments you get.

Barnabas gives a good answer: "I'd love to argue with you. Being a Jew, I could out-talk you anyway. But I'm not sent here for that. I'm sent here as an ambassador. I have a specific message to deliver, and I must deliver it. That's all. But, what I tell you is this [and this is what stopped Clement cold in his tracks], I can only tell you what I have seen and what I have heard."[35] Clement writes, "The first thing I noticed about him was that there was nothing of the dialectical artifice in the man. He set forth simply and without the slightest rhetorical dramatics, or anything like that, the things which he had seen and heard about the Son of God."[36] And that's what Clement had been looking for, and what none of the Doctors of the schools could give him. This was something specific, the

first time he had an indication that he might get an answer
to the terrible questions.

Things got pretty nasty. The students started throwing
things. Clement ran up and grabbed Barnabas, pulling him
down a side-alley to his home.[37] Barnabas was very de-
pressed. His mission to Rome had not been a success at
all. This story is not your typical Christian myth that starts
emerging in the fifth century, like the infancy gospels and
the Golden Legend. This is the sort of thing that actually
would have happened.

Clement dragged Barnabas to his house. They were
exhausted. Barnabas felt he had failed, but he had to return
to Palestine, because the church was having a general conference and Barnabas had to be in attendance. Clement,
becoming interested, said he would like to go too, but he
had some business affairs to settle. He took Barnabas down
to the harbor in Ostia and saw him off, taking his baggage
aboard the boat, and said that he would follow as soon as
he had settled his own business affairs.[38]

Clement arrived in Caesarea, in the midst of great excitement over the conference. Peter was hard to see, so
Clement met Zacchaeus.[39] Peter was involved in major
preparations, and there was a crowd around him all the
time. Incidentally, the picture of Peter is very appealing:
he has a hot temper, but a terrific sense of humor. As an
ex-fisherman, he loves to go swimming. He jogs on the
beach every morning, takes a cold swim, then gets ready
for breakfast and the conference.

When Barnabas and Clement met, they threw themselves into each other's arms: "You did come after all!"
Barnabas exclaimed. "I can get you an introduction to Peter."[40]

Amid the bustling crowds at the conference, he was
finally able to interview Peter, and the first questions Clement asked are the main and terrible questions he had been
asking himself. "The first and foremost thing I would es-

pecially like to know is if the earth was created, and for what purpose, and whether it will pass away, and whether it will be dissolved or renewed to something better, or if there won't be anything else after this world. And without making a longer list, can you give me a clear answer to those and all sorts of questions like them."[41] "Stop, stop. I get the idea," Peter replied.

That repetition showed that Clement really was sincere, so Peter gave him the answers. And interestingly, they were very different answers from what the schoolmen had given in Rome—and very different, by the way, from what he would have gotten a century later from the Christian schoolmen at Rome, or from the bishops anywhere in the big cities of Christendom. Those bishops had all become orators.

The terrible questions are terrible because they can't be answered. To those whose business it is to give the answers, not having them becomes a terrible dilemma, calling for all kinds of indirection and subterfuge. Here we are referring to the clergy, but it applies to science as well. In the nineteenth century, as Loren Eiseley now writes, "science . . . [itself was beginning] to ask . . . 'the terrible questions.' . . . [The clergy had avoided them, because they were the business of religion, not science.] They had involved the nature of evil, the age of the world, the origins of man, of sex, or even of language itself."[42] Of course the scientists came up with the answers: the answer is no to everything. From the days of the Miletians, Lucretius, Xenophanes, and the Sophists, the object of science was to escape the terrible questions and put the fears and dreams and fancies and childish misgivings of men behind them. This was the idea of Anaxagoras: there are no evil forces out there, no heaven, no hereafter, no goblins, nothing to worry about. Of course, that left people more frightened than ever. I'd sooner think there are goblins out there than nothing at all, "nox est perpetua una dormienda," the "perpetual black night."[43] We learned in high school in my day, from the sophisticate Omar Khayyam, the tent maker who wrote the famous *Rubaiyat*, that this life is it. I memorized the *Rubaiyat* in its entirety (we used to do things like that in high school).

Note, too, the day when H. L. Mencken was really crowing, trying to get rid of all our Christian superstitions and beliefs—heaven and hell, and everything else. It was "hick from the sticks" stuff; we're too sophisticated for that. Of course we know of his own tragic and pathetic last days; he wasn't happy about those at all.

Many verses from the *Rubaiyat* are relevant; "One Moment in Annihilation's Waste"—that's us. Though Fitzgerald didn't translate the poem correctly, he did write good English; the *Rubaiyat* was a good excuse for writing good poetry, and it certainly caught the spirit of the times, the Victorian "enlightenment." "One moment, of the well of Life to taste, The Stars are setting and the Caravan Starts for the dawn of Nothing—Oh, make haste!"[44] You're going nowhere, says the last verse: "And when Thyself with shining Foot shall pass Among the Guest Stars—scatter'd on The Grass, And in thy joyous errand reach the Spot Where I made one—turn down an empty Glass."[45]

It's not because of old age that I'm brooding on these things. I learned them all in high school. I was brought up on those things. These were the terrible questions, and we crowed and laughed about them and made fun of them. Then suddenly things got very serious, because it meant that if there was nothing there, that was more scary than anything else.

If people don't answer the questions, then what happens? Here's how you can avoid the terrible questions.

First, you assume you have the answer, and simply despair. That's what science does. We've had George Gaylord Simpson, the great geologist from Harvard, visit us;

and Shapley, the astronomer; and Röhmer, the geologist. All have come to Brigham Young University to lecture on the same thing. They couldn't leave the topic of religion alone: we should grow up, become mature and adult, leave off these religious superstitions, and be willing to face reality, the truth. They were even evangelistic about it. They didn't come to teach geology or astronomy; we already knew that part of it. They came to tell us—because we were a religious school—to get rid of childish preconceptions and prejudices; and face the cold, scientific facts. But that is the answer of despair.

Here is a marvelous passage from C. P. Snow, who wrote his novels about life in Cambridge, England, in the 1930s—a life he knew very well, because he was himself teaching there. I asked I. E. S. Edwards (who was teaching there at the same time and who was at Brigham Young University recently) about C. P. Snow. Edwards said that Snow was very bitter about everything and everybody, and so turned everyone against him.

In any event, here is how Snow observed science in the 1930s:

> The tone of science at Cambridge in 1932 was the tone of Rutherford. Magniloquently boastful, creatively confident, generous, argumentative and full of hope. Science and Rutherford were on top of the world. Worldly success—he loved every minute of it: flattery, titles, the company of the high official world. He was superbly and magnificently vain as well as wise, and he enjoyed his own personality. He enjoyed a life of miraculous success. But I am sure that even late in life he felt stabs of sickening insecurity. . . . Does anyone really believe that Bertrand Russell, G. H. Hardy [the great mathematician], Rutherford, Blackett, and the rest were bemused by cheerfulness as they faced their own individual state? In the crowd they were leaders; they were worshipped. But by themselves, they believed with the

same certainty that they believed in Rutherford's atom that they were going after this life into annihilation. Against this, they had only to offer the nature of scientific activity, its complete success on its own terms. [You do enjoy it while it's going on—it is invigorating.] In itself it was a source of happiness. But it is whistling in the dark when they are alone.[46]

Snow is talking about the greatest and most successful scientists of our century, but they are "iced," as Raymond Chandler related in the "Big Sleep,"[47] by the thought that "the iceman cometh."[48]

You can avoid the issue by talking about related issues, the way this man wants to—philosophy, ethics, aesthetics, morality, etc. This assures us all along that we are working on the problems. This is what members of the clergy do—they talk about these problems, and the problems are related to the real problem. But to entertain an illusion, after all these centuries, that they are approaching a solution to the problem shouldn't fool us at all.

You can also build a stately institution and barricade the problem, as the Roman Catholic Church has done—with the last rites, etc., since the last Vatican Council. They realize now that the last rites were not a sacrament of the ancient church, though they are pleasing and satisfying to the mind. The forms and observances, for example, the candles, do help (although the Council of Elvira in A.D. 404 forbade the use of candles in the church altogether, because they were nothing but pagan). The candles do build up the feeling that there is something you can lean back on. So people in their old age panic at the thought of death and become Catholic—a common happening.

Wilfred Griggs tells the story of a vicar and archaeologist in England by the name of William H. C. Frend, now retired, who became a Roman Catholic, not because he believes in it, but because the tradition—what's back of it all—gave him some assurance. Such a barricade can make you feel secure and comfortable, but only for a while. You'll panic in the end.

There is also comfort in numbers, as we see in evangelism and mission work. It masks one's emptiness by partisan passion, by building up your faction, by having big arguments, as the TV evangelists do. They talk about success in life, and friendship, and the wickedness of the world, or of this or that politics, and money—around and around it all. But it's just more or less whistling in the dark, working to keep the mind off the real questions. It's an empty sort of thing: the evangelists walk back and forth, they sweat, they work on a sentence for five minutes—yet it means nothing at all.

You can turn to the occult—to UFOs, to space visitors, to other various California fads. They have always flourished there. "There must be something else, or there wouldn't be UFOs."

Or you can emphasize the cosmetic matters.

The Hermetic literature does deal with real issues. That's its great attraction: it got close up to such issues, but just as you get to the edge, it always fizzles out and goes into abstractions—avoidance of any crass physical interpretations, because it claims to be a higher, spiritual, even ghostly, sort of thing. So you are let down gently, and that ends it. The Hermetic tradition does not solve the real problems.

Consider Clement's questions. I have reduced these to five, which I will answer by telling you how the early Christians answered them, and then how the Christian Doctors later shifted their positions and the councils changed things; what the official statements of the churches are today; and finally, the tendency to return to the old literalism. The churches are creeping back to the old interpretations, because they are nervous; they don't feel safe in their views. The new handbooks of the 1980s take up the questions that were always avoided. They have to consider them now since they are essential to religion, even though we've always avoided them.

Clement's first concern was his dissatisfaction with philosophy. He wanted some real answers, not philosophy and allegory. He followed Barnabas because Barnabas said he had "seen." And Peter convinced Clement of many more things. So the first issue is revelation. The early church did insist that there be revelation, and they did have it. Basil, one of the "eight Doctors" of the church (whose philosophy became the foundation of the theology of the church), prayed that they might not lose the power of prophesying "the way the Jews did."[49] Jerome reported that to break the painful lack of revelation, all sorts of fakers and pretenders had begun to appear.[50] Methodius, like Basil, pities the poor, neglected Jews, left with scriptures alone to guide them, "like a moth trying to gather honey from leaves. . . . They weave their airy fantastic structures as if the scriptures belonged and applied to them."[51] They do the best they can, but have no real revelation. "Let's not fall into the same conditions as the Jews," the Doctors said. But that's exactly what happened. When John Chrysostom (one of the Greek Fathers) tells us, "If we no longer have revelation, we have something better, the bodies of the martyrs, which the demons fear."[52] But was that something better?

Chrysostom adds, "Heavenly things, being incorporeal, are seen only by the intellect. The coming of the Lord can never be visible. This whole thing is only to be spiritual from now on."[53]

Thus we have the position of the churches today; for example, this quote from the first volume of *The American Anthropologist* (1899), a scientific analysis of Mormonism, reads: "A portentous danger-sign, . . . [a] monstrosity, born of deceit and bred in falsehood, . . . [a] monster of iniquity and deceit. [Its] teachings and precepts are not in themselves immoral, [we are assured.] . . . There is nothing immoral in the Book [of Mormon, but] . . . its adherents have discovered a most dangerous weapon against the moral world in this doctrine of 'a continuing revelation.' "[54] That was the one thing unforgivable in Joseph Smith. And so the churches stand today: You don't forgive the doctrine of revelation.

In 1897, the League for Social Service, which included some of the most famous of Americans—Jane Addams, the Choate family, Reverend Edward E. Hale, Margaret Sangster, and others—published a Declaration of Ten Reasons why Christians cannot fellowship the Mormon Church.[55] The first three reasons are: First, Mormons teach that they have the only true gospel.[56] Second, revelation is still possible. We cannot fellowship people who believe that—such is the stance of the Christian world.[57] Third, Joseph Smith was a prophet of God.[58]

So the Christians lost revelation, and they regret it now. Paul Tillich has declared, "It is among the tragedies of Christian history that this [prophetic] tradition was actually lost from the time that the official church achieved ascendancy."[59] They admit they lost it, but now they regret it. Others say they are glad they got rid of the tradition, because it was something, according to Augustine, that couldn't be controlled. So ceremonies and ordinances replaced revelation, because they can be controlled, and hence are far superior to revelation for building a church.

We read now in McCasland and others, "The return to ideas of inspiration and revelation may be put down as one of the marked trends of our biblical scholarship of the last decade"[60]—or twenty years. The scholars are beginning to talk about the theme seriously.

The banning of the literal, by people who wanted to be spiritual and not literal about things, began with the first Christian apologist, Aristides, who wrote that the early Christians simply would not accept any allegorical explanations: "They are just myths and nothing else."[61] But he is followed by Justin Martyr, a convert and a Doctor of the schools, who always wore his sophist's robe in school — he had grown up in the schools. He argued that it was not the Christians but the Greeks who tainted their allegory with suggestions of physical reality.

The early apologist Athenagoras insisted that life would be utterly wasted without the resurrection; it is the resurrection which gives everything in human life its meaning.[62] Yet Rufinus tells us that "after the resurrection, all will be spirit — no bodies."[63] But, says Hilary, there must be a physical resurrection. The scriptures say it's so. But it can only be for the wicked. Only they deserve that kind of punishment.[64] That's certainly a desperate twist. Gregory of Nyssa, one of the four great Greek Fathers, said if you must "gape after sensual enjoyment, and ask . . . 'Shall we have teeth and other members [after the resurrection?],' . . . the answer is yes, since the scriptures [won't allow us to deny it — they] are perfectly clear, we shall have all our members — but we will not make use of them."[65] Jerome himself says yes, our bodies will be resurrected, but since we have no further need of bodies, the minute we are resurrected, we will start to dissolve; and "all matter will return to the *nothing* (*nihilum*) from which it was once made" — back to Nirvana.[66] But is that satisfaction? I ask.

Epiphanius says there were actually Christians in the early days who believed that "in his image" actually referred to Adam's body.[67] Eusebius himself applauds the nobility and good taste of the Greeks and Romans for interpreting their own deities allegorically, the way all deities should be interpreted.[68]

There is a lot of talk today about Christ's *descensus* — Christ's descending to the spirits in the underworld. No passage of scripture has been such a riddle and such an annoyance to the Christian mind in general, especially to

Protestants. The policy of the theologians has been a general "hands off."

So the Fathers and the Doctors of the church call the issue both ways. "I believe the resurrection to be the transition from this physical gnosis to incorporeal contemplation (*theoria*)," says Basil.[69]

"The most learned of the Fathers, by a very singular condescension, have imprudently admitted the sophistry of the Gnostics. Acknowledging that the literal sense is repugnant to every principle of faith as well as reason, they deem themselves secure and invulnerable behind the ample veil of allegory," wrote Gibbon.[70]

Classical rhetoric gave a great boost to the Christian mysteries: " 'To be rapt away from matter' — that is the longing of the Christian Greek"; it is Ambrose's "cup of the spirit, 'which from heaven is held out to the earth.' "[71] It becomes all allegory: "If one resorts to that easy, if self-contradictory, expedient of denying that the manifold of finite things has any existence, all problems disappear at a stroke."[72] In other words, just say it is spiritual, and you have explained everything.

One of the first things Peter says to Clement in their conversation is, "We affirm absolutely that there is nothing evil in matter."[73] That's quite a different message from that of the later scholars, for example, Lactantius, the first of the Latin Fathers, and the best Latinist of them all: "Whoever desires the highest good, let him desire to live without a body, for all matter is evil."[74] They shifted completely over to the new notion.

The great Reinhold Niebuhr states the situation neatly when he says that biblical eschatology must be taken "seriously but not literally."[75] For example, M. Jack Suggs contends that we are really resurrected when we believe in the Lord of Life.[76] That's how he defines resurrection. Then after World War II, the theologians discovered that the Jesus of history had nothing of the supernatural about him. That was Albert Schweitzer's *Leben Jesu*.

"Ten years later, [this view] had been not only abandoned but discarded with contempt." Today, only twenty years after that, the doctrine is that "materials in the Gospels had survived only as an expression of faith, not as historical data. . . . [There's nothing historical in the gospel.] Jesus had become 'a mere saving event' and ceased to be a person."[77] This in an article by a devout Protestant minister.

That's how the clergy and scholars speak today, while at the same time they creep back to the literalist view. J. Alberto Soggin takes note of this: "The story of salvation only exists when we are dealing with reality, and not with later artificial workings over. . . . As Hesse says, 'Only what actually happened interests us, everything else not at all or only incidentally.' "[78] Why not be honest about it, he asks. We've got to face the terrible question, so who do we think we're kidding? The other questions interest us not at all, or only incidentally. Such persons as F. Hesse and J. Alberto Soggin, very eminent men, talk that way now.

On the subject of the restoration of visions, among the scholastic philosophers today, a Catholic theologian writes, "Man must be forever grateful to matter[!] and to the cosmos because matter has brought man to the verge of the supernatural. . . . The universe and matter are so sacred thereby, that God must be in and with it through an incarnation."[79] So since Christ was incarnated, then matter must not be damned at all; it must be sacred. This is a new view, in contrast to the assertion that all matter is evil.

The study of cosmology and the stars has connection with the Pearl of Great Price. We Latter-day Saints are involved in such subjects. R. H. Charles was disgusted with Enoch for preferring cosmology to ethics in all Enoch's writings. Ethics is religion, Charles claimed, not cosmology.[80]

The Talmud tells us four things which the Jewish student would never be allowed to think about: What is above, what is below, what is before, and what is behind. In other words, the whole cosmic scenario. Gregorius Thaumaturgus (Gregory the Great) tells how Origen "first taught him rhetoric," then "holy mathematics, incontrovertible geometry and astronomy" — what was taught originally. Origen was the last Father with a foot in the old church, and he was divided between the old and the new. These topics set "us a ladder to the things of Heaven." "When finally by the grace of God the saints shall reach celestial places, then shall they comprehend all the secrets of the stars; God will reveal to them the nature of the Universe."[81] It was for doctrines like this that Origen never became a saint.

Arthur McGiffert in discussing Augustine says, "Astrology he wholly lost confidence in, and his intellectual development reached the point where much of the boasted wisdom of the Manichaeans seemed only folly and pretense. After a protracted period of indecision, he finally broke with them altogether."[82] But later on, he decided that since astronomy could not save a soul, he has nothing but contempt for it.[83] He finally settles for rhetoric, an abstraction, while admitting that what was taught was vain, superstitious, and without content.[84]

The early church was steeped in cosmology. But later, when Origen left Egypt, he set out to achieve "perfect knowledge, purged of all that is physical and corporeal," and recommended Philo of Alexandria to the student since he used the same approach: he spiritualized the entire Old Testament. Everything became symbolic — whether Moses, or the twelve sons of Israel, or whatever. They stand for things of an abstract or philosophical nature. And the Jews went for it, and the Christians went for it. According to

Origen, the scriptures are silent on the exact nature of the heavens.[85]

Thomas Aquinas had a better idea: For him, the "planets were regarded as being composed of a special sort of matter which was radically different from all terrestrial matter."[86] Florovsky today says that Origen's ambivalence "led [him] into insuperable difficulties in Christology. . . . His 'aberrations' were in fact the birth-pangs of the Christian mind. His own system was an abortive birth."[87] The Christian mind he refers to had to give up cosmology. Father Lagrange says all the apocalyptic literature "gives the impression of a gigantic effort in the void, or of a tedious dream, with a few flashes of good sense in this sick man's nightmare."[88] Charles Torrey said in the 1930s that it was "unquestionably a small survival from an extensive literature," well lost, "that product of unbridled imagination called the 'apocalypse.' "

The great W. Bousset said we should counter that opinion. "We must energetically renounce the idea" that the Apocrypha and Pseudepigrapha are an "uncontrolled (freischaltende), wondrous, and grotesque fantasy."[89] It's what the early church actually taught.

The celebrated New Testament scholar Rudolph Bultmann declared the New Testament itself to be nothing else but a blending of two mythologies — gnosticism and Jewish Apocalyptic. Arthur Lovejoy (author of that famous book *The Great Chain of Being*) spiritualized everything in Genesis and called it the pseudo-Dionysius. But *they* will not let us deny a real universe, concluding, "consequently the language of *acosmism* . . . is never to be taken too literally,"[90] although everybody uses it. Forget the cosmos; it has no place in religion. According to G. Van der Leeuw, "A general human inclination, also found in Christianity, is to base trust in salvation on the cosmic. . . . Only when the human suffering of the divine savior has a cosmic background does salvation seem sufficiently assured."[91] It has to be real and solid.

The doctrine of the plurality of worlds was a very basic doctrine in the early church. We can actually begin with the Greek Xenophanes, of the early Milesian school, who found it only reasonable to assume "there are boundless suns and moons, and all of them have the same substance as this earth."[92]

Back to our friend Origen:

> [Some] assert that worlds sometimes come into existence which are not dissimilar to each other, but in all respects equal. . . . If . . . a world [is] similar in all respects (to the present), then it will come to pass that Adam and Eve will do the same things which they did before. . . . It seems to me impossible for a world to be restored for the second time, with the same order and with the same amount of births, and deaths, and actions; but that a diversity of worlds may exist . . . for some unmistakable reasons better (than this), and for others worse, and for others intermediate. But what may be the number or measure of this I confess myself ignorant, although, if any one can tell it, I would gladly learn.[93]

This he said when arguing with the pagan Celsus, who makes fun of Christian beliefs, arguing that there is nothing scientific about them. "Yes," Origen continues, "we might believe two worlds,"[94] but he doesn't know. If Origen didn't know it, then nobody did. It was lost to the early church, yet it was what the brethren taught; but, says Origen, we don't teach those things today.

Jerome said that Origen solved the problem by accepting an infinite number of worlds, but he avoided the pagan cosmology by having them exist not all at once, but in succession, one after another[95] — so there was just one world at a time. That was one way to get around the issue. Plato's idea of perfection led the later Jewish and Christian thinkers to pleniarism (the notion that God, being good, must have done as much good as he possibly can; if the world is a good thing, then there should be as many worlds as possible—God shouldn't stop creating).

In the Lord's statement "I am not of this world," Origen sees a clear implication that there must be other worlds. According to him, it was alien to Christians of his time "to speak of an incorporeal world existing in the imagination alone, or in the fleeting world of thoughts (*mundum incorporeum dicere, in sola mentis phantasia . . . consistentem*). . . . There is no doubt, however, that something more illustrious and excellent than this present world is pointed out by the Saviour." So he has no satisfactory answer. "And I just don't see how we are to explain it, when the Saviour is *inde* (out-there), or the Saints go up hither."[96] They must be going somewhere. Since the scriptures tell us nothing definite about how many heavens there are, Origen recommends consulting Philo on the subject.[97] Of course Philo is not scripture, but that's where the Doctors went for insight.

The common doctrine of the Jews and the Mandaeans, at an early time, was that God creates and destroys worlds, and you too will be able to create worlds and to destroy. So this was a prominent doctrine among the Christians, from which they afterwards shifted, turning to Philo.

Later on, Justin Martyr, the first convert-martyr, said to his students, "If you follow me, I can promise you unlimited and beautiful worlds (*aidiois . . . kosmois*)," but then with him you never know how literally to take it.[98] Later, it was only the heretics who still clung to the old belief "that the worlds (*mundos*) are infinite and innumerable, according to the silly opinions of some philosophers." After all, Genesis 1:1 says plainly "that the world is one, and from one source."[99] Yet Methodius, referring back to the cosmologies of the Egyptians and Chaldaeans, argues that if the sun, moon, and "other stars are divine and greater than man, they must necessarily have better life than ours and greater peace, justice, and virtue."[100]

It was Aristotle who insisted that there could only be one world, and the Doctors had to follow him. It was for the express charge of teaching a plurality of worlds that Giordano Bruno was burned at the stake in Rome.[101] He preached all sorts of things, but the specific doctrine for which Clement VIII put him to death was preaching that there were many worlds.

Later the Church did accept it. In the seventeenth century, P. Borel's idea of "habitable celestial bodies, with creatures more or less like ourselves," enjoyed great popularity. His writings were put on the Index of Forbidden Books. Borel's *Discours nouveau prouvant la pluralité des mondes (New Discourse Proving the Plurality of the Worlds)* called attention to mountains on the moon and recalled that Pythagoras called the earth a moon and that Campanella believed the sun was inhabited by beings far superior to ourselves.[102] By the early sixteenth century, the theory of plurality of systems and inhabited worlds of infinite number and the infinite extent of the universe was already a topic of discussion. Just after his death, Bruno would have been perfectly safe, because it was a popular doctrine. The great Isaac Newton was very strong on that particular subject: "In God's house (which is the universe) are many mansions, and he governs them by agents which can pass through the heavens from one mansion to another. For if all places to which we have access are filled with living creatures, why should all these immense spaces of the heavens above the clouds be incapable of inhabitants?"[103]

By combining Democritus and Newton, the immortal Kant also concluded that the cosmos must be infinite because of the infinite power of God; and he develops it into an infinite hierarchy of island universes—the spiral nebulae.[104]

The atheists fought the idea. Richard Bentley, the famous classical scholar at Oxford who argued with Dr. Arnold, maintained that all bodies were formed for the sake of intelligent minds. The atheists replied, "What indeed can be the usefulness of these innumerable stars that are not even seen by us?"[105] If we don't see them, if they are not known to us, what good can they do? This is similar to Ingersoll's argument: Why does God rain on the seas? That proves there is no God, because it rains on the ocean, where it isn't necessary. If there were a God, he wouldn't waste his rain that way.[106]

In our own times, it has been widely assumed that the discovery of life on other worlds would be an end to a belief in God. Mormons believe just the opposite: such life would be additional evidence for the existence of God. In 1955, one astronomer described the dramatic reversal and outlook on the subject of life outside the earth, and predicted that in the 1960s many astronomers would prove conclusively and to their own satisfaction that inhabited planetary systems are quite common.

In 1964, an astronomer, addressing scientists regarding a project designed to send and receive messages to other worlds, wrote, "This is a subject that we would not have dared discuss on this kind of a platform even as recently as two years ago."[107]

When I myself went to school, if you talked about many worlds, everybody would have laughed at you and thrown you out of the room. The notion was deemed science fiction—romantic and wishful thinking. It had no place in real science. And the astronomers would become very emphatic and angry if you brought the question up.

But consensus was never complete; it shifted back and forth. Leibniz defines "monde" (a world) as one of a system of worlds that *could* exist, but of which only a single one has been effectively realized. There he had to drop the question, because he didn't want to offend official Christian doctrine. He also had to bring it up because "an infinite, immutable, and sempiternal God could not be conceived . . . as limiting His creative action to a small stretch."[108] Descartes said the same thing: "To suppose that the power of the Creator is so imperfect that no such stars can exist"[109] — he could make them, he just didn't want to.

Today, Arthur Clarke (of TV fame) says it will never be possible to converse with anyone on another planet, because of the time lapse between galaxies. The whole business should not concern us at all. "Any form of control or administration over other islands [in space] would be utterly impossible, and all parallels for our own history thus cease to have any meaning."[110]

A statement by Jerome gives us a good idea of how everything was mixed up in a common stew. Jerome asks whether all created things

> have come down from the heaven as the Pythagoreans, all the Platonists, and Origen think; or are all things part of God as the Stoics, Manichaeans, and Priscillians think? Or are they drawn from a treasury once established by God [in the preexistence], as some stupid churchmen think? Or are they created daily and sent into bodies . . . (John 5:17)? Or are our bodies created from other bodies or spirits from other spirits as Tertullian, Appollinaris, and most of the Eastern Christians believe?[111]

These represent quite a roster of eminent early Christian Fathers and saints, and a tremendous spread of opinion as to how to answer the terrible questions—which none were ever able to answer.

With regard to a premortal existence, Clement said, "Well, if I live after, I must have lived before. Doesn't that follow?"[112] The idea of "the memory of all former births" and of "Buddha-lands innumerable"[113] is akin, in its appeal, to the individual ego of Plato's *anamnesis* and its elaboration by Plotinus. They believed in it. In other words, it's an idea older than the Jews and Christians, an ongoing belief from very early times. Iamblichus, commenting on Pythagoras, notes that it was the story of Euphorbus and the Phrygian in Homer which offered a key to the recollection of one's premortal existence; and even finds the genius of Homer to lie in his power to stir such intimations of immortality—a sense of other world, in all of us.[114] Plotinus, one of the greatest of the Christian Neoplatonists, argues that the recognizable differences in children at their very birth shows that each must bring something with him into this life from another one[115] (as anyone who has had a lot of children recognizes).

R. H. Charles, commenting on 2 *Enoch* 23:4, says: "For all souls are prepared to eternity, before the foundation of the world," and he notes that "the Platonic doctrine of the pre-existence of the soul is here taught. We find that it had already made its way into Jewish thought in Egypt. . . . This doctrine was accepted and further developed by Philo [*De Somniis* i:22]. . . . This doctrine of the pre-existence of the soul was, according to Josephus, . . . held by the Essenes. . . . It became a prevailing doctrine in later Judaism,"[116] and is still taught by the Hasidic Jews who join the Church, one of the reasons they accept the gospel. They firmly believe in the doctrine.

Origen, following the teaching of the early brethren (an interesting explanation of why people are born so unequally), explains these inequities on the grounds that the soul had a previous existence in a life of its own, where even as in this life it was given its free agency by the Creator: such souls as grew weary in doing good entered this life at a disadvantage, having passed the test less satisfactorily.[117]

The Pastor of Hermas (c. A.D. 120), in one of the earliest postapostolic writings we have, says, "All flesh which is found undefiled and unspotted, wherein the Holy Spirit dwelt, shall receive a reward."[118] Clement of Alexandria, in the second century, writes, "God knew us before the foundation of the world, and chose us for our faithfulness even at that time. . . . Now we have become babes to fulfill the plan of God."[119]

Clement of Rome, whom Barnabas converted, tells us that "cujus interna species est antiquior," that the Earth was created and prepared for man, whose real nature, though he came last of all, is older than any of it. And Clement's *Second Epistle to the Corinthians* tells us of "the first church, the spiritual [one, (*spiritum*) which] was created before sun and moon." He says he got the doctrine from "The Book of the Apostles."[120] Man existed before the creation of the world — a doctrine that Peter taught him.

The Dead Sea Scrolls bring up much of this creationism material. In the *Odes of Solomon*, for example, one of the early Christian hymns, we read, "For I know them," says the God of the Saints, "and before they came into being I took knowledge of them, and on their faces I set my seal. . . . By my own right hand I set my elect ones."[121] The famous poet of *The Pearl* said the same thing.

Thanks to the *Patrologia*, a collection of the writings of all the Christian Fathers, in chronological order, which grows all the time, we literally have hundreds of volumes of writings; and the first volumes say more on this subject than any others, because the Christians depart from the doctrine after that. In these volumes the editor, J.-P. Migne, speaks of the four different positions on the subject. "For some taught that the spirit was before the body, others that it came after, still others, that they came into existence together, while others are not willing to make any assertion. Along with these opinions should be mentioned the errors of the Pythagoreans, Platonists, Gnostics, and Origenists."[122] The later Doctors still could not make up their minds. "Under the influence of the prevailing philosophy, many Christian thinkers asked themselves," writes H. de Leusse, "in the third and fourth centuries, if it was permissible to think of a pre-existence of souls."[123] Augustine believed the doctrine firmly up until the year A.D. 410; after that, he hesitates, and does not cease to hesitate between traducianism (the idea that the spirit enters the body at the moment of conception, and didn't exist before, but was "traduced" into the body at the moment of conception) and infusionism (the idea that the spirit existed before). He repeats endlessly that he has not made up his mind. In short, Augustine "truly does not know, . . . and it is perhaps temerity to want to penetrate a mystery reserved to God himself."[124] So the first of the great Latin theologians, who got nearly all of his doctrines from Origen, anyway, could never resolve the problem for himself.

In A.D. 523, the African bishops agreed that "we should either leave the question in silence or consider it without contention"; since "the holy scriptures give us no clear statement, it should be investigated with caution. The more so since it's possible for the faithful to ignore it without any particular disadvantage (*detrimento*) to their faith."[125]

Brigham Young said that more Saints apostatized because of the doctrine of premortal existence than any other doctrine—more than polygamy, more than tithing, more than jealousies, or anything else. Over it, people left the Church in droves, yet today, everybody accepts the doctrine as the most natural thing in the world. Eliza R. Snow, as well as Wordsworth, taught it. When Augustine's personal friend Jerome read in Revelation 4:6 about the familiar animals around the throne of God—the same types of beasts found on earth—and asked whether this didn't imply a premortal existence, he rejected the idea, because such literalism destroys the *allegorical* value of the scriptures.[126] If you take it literally, you can't use it as an allegory.

In the interest of time, and my failing voice, my roaring, flaming, flaring peroration will have to be omitted. I apologize that I talked too fast and didn't say very much. Yet a few points should be made: There are the terrible questions, and it's marvelous how few people will touch them, or even think about them. They've been ruled out of Christian theology. And this was what Joseph Smith was put to death for—for bringing these unforgivable questions up, especially the issue of revelation. The learned people of the century could not forgive that—the most dangerous doctrine you could have,[127] according to the one source.

How do I myself find an answer to the terrible questions? Well, many of us have received particular answers, though we don't talk about them. We have seen and heard, and it is that direct impact that counts as testimony. Seeing and hearing short-circuit all the other questions and issues—that enormous computer board with all its relays and smoking wires and the smells of rubber—all the playing around with incidentals, while never addressing the simple, safe question, which is borne from testimony.

I wish to testify that I know that the gospel is true, which I do in the name of Jesus Christ, amen.

Notes

1. Cf. Sozomen, *Ecclesiastical History* I, 18, in *PG* 67:917.

2. *Clementine Recognitions* I, 3, in *PG* 1:1208; cf. Omar Khayyam, *Rubaiyat* XXVII, tr. Edward Fitzgerald (London: Harrap, 1985).

3. *JD* 6:333.

4. Boyce Rensberger, "Death of Dino," *Science Digest* (May 1968): 28–35, 77–78; cf. Kenneth F. Weaver, "Invaders from Space," *National Geographic* (September 1986): 405, 416–18.

5. Sophocles, *Oedipus at Colonus*, 228–550; for a discussion of *Oedipus Tyrannus*, cf. Hugh W. Nibley, "Three Shrines: Mantic, Sophic, and Sophistic," in *The Ancient State, CWHN* 10 (Salt Lake City: Deseret Book and F.A.R.M.S., 1991), 343–51.

6. Catullus, *The Poems of Catullus* V; for an English translation, see F. W. Cornish, tr., *The Poems of Gaius Valerius Catullus* (Cambridge: Harvard University Press, 1950), 6–8.

7. William Shakespeare, *Measure for Measure*, act III, scene i, lines 128–31.

8. Ibid., lines 117–20.

9. See Thomas Smith, "Introductory Notice to the Recognition of Clement," in *Ante-Nicene Fathers*, 10 vols. (Grand Rapids, MI: Eerdmans, 1951), 8:73.

10. William Shakespeare, *The Comedy of Errors*, act I, scene i (the family is split up); act V, scene i (they are reunited).

11. *Clementine Recognitions* I, 1, in *PG* 1:1207.

12. Ibid., I, 3, in *PG* 1:1208.

13. Ibid., I, 1, in *PG* 1:1207.

14. Ibid.

15. Ibid.

16. Ibid., I, 3, in *PG* 1:1208.

17. Ibid., I, 1, in *PG* 1:1207.

18. Ibid., I, 2, in *PG* 1:1207.

19. Ibid.

20. Ibid., I, 3, in *PG* 1:1208.

21. Ibid.

22. Ibid., I, 4, in *PG* 1:1208.

23. A. E. Housman, *Last Poems* IX-X, in *Complete Poems of A. E. Housman* (New York: Holt, 1959), 108–9.

24. *Clementine Recognitions* I, 4, in *PG* 1:1208–9.

25. See J. Edward Zimmerman, *Dictionary of Classical Mythology* (New York: Harper and Row, 1964), 173.

26. *Clementine Recognitions* I, 4, in *PG* 1:1209.

27. Ibid.

28. Ibid., I, 5, in *PG* 1:1209.

29. Ibid.

30. William Shakespeare, *Macbeth*, act III, scene iv; act IV, scene i.

31. Ernest Newman, "Der Freischütz" (act II), in *Stories of the Great Operas and Their Composers* (Philadelphia: Blakiston, 1930), 535–36.

32. *Clementine Recognitions* I, 5, in *PG* 1:1209.

33. T. S. Eliot, "The Love Song of J. Albert Prufrock," in *Complete Poems and Plays* (New York: Harcourt and Brace, 1952), 2, 6.

34. *Clementine Recognitions* I, 8, in *PG* 1:1211.

35. Ibid.

36. Ibid., I, 7, in *PG* 1:1211.

37. Ibid., I, 10, in *PG* 1:1212.

38. Ibid., I, 11, in *PG* 1:1213.

39. Ibid., I, 20, in *PG* 1:1217.

40. Ibid., I, 12, in *PG* 1:1213.

41. Ibid., I, 14, in *PG* 1:1214.

42. Loren Eiseley, *The Unexpected Universe* (New York: Harcourt, Brace, and Jovanovich, 1969), 125.

43. Catullus, *The Poems of Catullus* V, 6.

44. Omar Khayyam, *Rubaiyat* XXXVIII.

45. Ibid., LXXV.

46. [Nibley cites C. P. Snow several times in this volume, but we have been unable to locate the source.]

47. Raymond Chandler, *The Big Sleep* (New York: Alfred Knopf, 1939).

48. Eugene O'Neill, *The Iceman Cometh* (New York: Vintage, 1957). The ice-man represents the termination of life—the animation of death. Curiously, fire and ice often appear together in this context in a physical or psychological setting, see Nigel Calder, *The Restless Earth* (New York: Viking, 1972), 125; scientists acknowledge a destruction by ice: "The ice retreated to its present lairs only 6000 years ago. There is no reason to suppose the series of ice ages has finished; rather, we are in one of the 'interglacial' periods which, on past evidence, last for 100,000 years or more." Cf. Joseph W. Krutch, "If You Don't Mind My Saying So," *American Scholar* 34 (1965): 17: "Consider the case of what might be called the orthodox eschatology of science. . . . Sir James Jeans . . . was making the Second Law of Thermodynamics as fashionable a topic of intellectual conversation as 'alienation' is today, and we all took it as proved fact that increasing entropy would inevitably extinguish all life in a universe where no difference in temperature between one place and another could exist. Yet Jeans was hardly safe in his grave when his biographer, the late Professor E. Milne, ended his book with a beautiful British understatement: '. . . I am now convinced that an unconditional prediction of a heat-death for the universe is an over-statement.' That was published in 1952, and now we are being assured that the real end of our world will be by fire not by ice. . . . The white dwarf stars are now supposed to represent a late stage in the life of a sun that has fallen in on itself. Our own little private sun is still in its youth, but someday it will turn into a white dwarf and be so hot that everything on earth will be quickly consumed. If the literary mind believes incompatible theories simultaneously, the scientific mind accepts them successively, and I am not sure that that is anything to boast about. It was a poet [Robert Frost] who observed: 'Some say the world will end in fire, some say in ice' '': Cf. Robert Frost, "Fire and Ice," *Complete Poems of Robert Frost* (New York: Holt, 1949), 268: "Some say the world will end in fire / Some say in ice. From what I've tasted of desire / I hold with those who favor fire. But if it had to perish twice / I think I know enough of hate / To say that for destruction ice / Is also great / And would suffice." We see this same theme portrayed in other literature—the extremes of

hell. Cf. Dante Alighieri, *Inferno, Canto III: The Vestibule of Hell*, tr. John D. Sinclair (New York: Oxford University Press, 1979), 44; Dante describes hell as "the other shore, into eternal dark into fire and ice," see line 87; or cf. psychological extremes as in A. E. Housman, "A Shropshire Lad XXX," 30, stanza 4, in *Complete Poems of A. E. Housman*, 47: "And fire and ice within me fight beneath the suffocating night." In religion, we have the purification of the earth by fire when it's again raised to its paradisiacal glory. So here we have the two hands of the destroying angel—fire and ice. Annihilation of life as we know it is predicted to occur by the extremes of energy states—either by too little heat or energy, or too much heat or energy.

49. Basil, *Commentarius in Isaiam Prophetam (Commentary on Isaiah)* III, 100, in *PG* 30:281.

50. Jerome, *Liber de Viris Illustribus (Book on Noted Men)* 40, in *PL* 23:690.

51. Methodius, *Convivium Decem Virginum (Banquet of the Ten Virgins)* 36, in *PG* 18:177.

52. Cf. Marc Lods, *Confesseurs et Martyrs; successeurs des prophètes dans l'Èglise des trois premières siècles* (Neuchatel: Delachaux and Niestle, 1958).

53. John Chrysostom, *De Perfecta Caritate, de Mercede Operum pro Merito Tribuenda, deque Compunctione (On Perfect Charity)* 6, in *PG* 56:286–87.

54. Perry B. Pierce, "The Origin of the 'Book of Mormon,' " *American Anthropologist* 1 (1899): 694.

55. A pamphlet entitled "Christian Fellowship: Ten Reasons Why Christians Cannot Fellowship the Mormon Church" (Salt Lake City: League for Social Service, 1897).

56. Ibid., 2–5.

57. Ibid., 5–6.

58. Ibid., 4–6.

59. Paul Tillich, "Die Wiederentdeckung der prophetischen Tradition in der Reformation," *Neue Zeitschrift für systematische Theologie* 3 (1961): 237.

60. S. V. McCasland, "The Unity of the Scriptures," *Journal of Biblical Literature* 73 (1954): 6. Treated at length in Hugh W. Nibley, "The Return of the Prophets," in *The World and the Prophets* (Salt Lake City: Deseret Book, 1974), 258–72; reprinted in *CWHN* 3:284–98.

61. Aristides, *Apologia* 13, in J. Armitage Robinson, ed., *Texts and Studies* (Cambridge: Cambridge University Press, 1967), 1:1:109.

62. Athenagoras, *De Resurrectione Mortuorum (The Resurrection of the Dead)* 19, in *PG* 6:1012–13.

63. Rufinus, *Apologia (Apology)* I, 24, in *PL* 21:562.

64. Hilary, *Tractatus super Psalmos (Tractate on the Psalms)* LV, 7, in *PL* 9:360.

65. Gregory of Nyssa, quoted in *Letters of Severus* 96, in *PO* 14:187–88.

66. Jerome, cited in Origen, *Peri Archon (De Principiis)* II, 3, 2, in *PG* 11:189.

67. Epiphanius, *Adversus Haereses (Against Heresies)* III, 1, 2, in *PG* 42:341.

68. Eusebius, *Praeparatio Evangelica (Preparation for the Gospel)* II, 8; III, intro, in *PG* 21:148–49, 152, 156.

69. Basil, *Epistulae (Letters)* I, 8, 7, in *PG* 32:257.

70. Edward Gibbon, *Decline and Fall of the Roman Empire*, 3 vols. (New York: Heritage, 1946), 1:356.

71. Hugo Rahner, "Earth Spirit and Divine Spirit in Patristic Theology," *Spirit and Nature* (New York: Princeton University Press, 1972), 145–46.

72. Arthur O. Lovejoy, *The Great Chain of Being* (Cambridge: Cambridge University Press, 1942; reprinted in 1978), 92.

73. *Clementine Recognitions* IV, 23, in *PG* 1:1324.

74. Lactantius, *Divinae Institutiones (Divine Institutes)* VII, 5, in *PL* 6:756.

75. M. Jack Suggs, tr., "Biblical Eschatology and the Message of the Church," *Encounter* 24 (1963): 19.

76. Ibid., 30: "[Paul] declares that we have *already* been raised with Christ to a newness of life. It is by Christ's resurrection from the dead that he is designated Lord of life. Therefore, to believe in him is to submit to the lordship of him who has conquered death. And this means that 'I no longer live,' having already died, surrendering the insecure securities of temporal existence; but 'he lives in me,' opening before me a future filled with the 'possibility of newness of life.' "

77. A. W. Hastings and Reverend E. Hastings, eds., "Notes of Recent Exposition," *The Expository Times* 75 (1963): 2.

78. J. Alberto Soggin, "Geschichte, Historie und Heilsgeschichte im Alten Testament," *Theologische Literaturzeitung* 89 (1964): 729.

79. Leo A. Foley, "Cosmos and Ethos," *The New Scholasticism* 41 (Spring 1967): 152.

80. *APOT* 2:169: "The sole aim of his book [*1 Enoch*] is to give

the laws of the heavenly bodies. . . . Through all these chapters
there is not a single ethical reference. The author's interest is scientific."

81. Origen, *De Principiis* II, 11, 7, in *PG* 11:246.

82. Arthur C. McGiffert, *A History of Christian Thought*, 2 vols.
(New York: Scribner, 1933), 2:75.

83. Stillman Drake, tr., *Discoveries and Opinions of Galileo* (New
York: Doubleday/Anchor, 1957), 184–85.

84. Franz X. Eggersdorfer, *Der heilige Augustinus als Pädogoge
und seine Bedeutung für die Geschichte der Bildung* (Freiburg i/B: Herder,
1907), 44, 13.

85. Origen, *Contra Celsum (Against Celsus)* VI, 21, in *PG* 11:1321.

86. John L. Russel, "St. Thomas and the Heavenly Bodies,"
Heythrop Journal 8 (1967): 27–28.

87. G. Florovsky, "Eschatology in the Patristic Age," in *Texte
und Untersuchungen* 64 (1957): 243–44.

88. M. J. Lagrange, *Le Messianisme chez les Juifs* (Paris: Gabalda,
1909), 39.

89. Wilhelm Bousset, "Die Beziehungen der ältesten jüdischen
Sibylle zur chaldäischen Sibylle und einige weitere Beobachtungen
über den synkretistischen Charakter der spätjüdischen Litteratur,"
Zeitschrift für die neutestamentliche Wissenschaft 3 (1902): 49.

90. Lovejoy, *Great Chain of Being*, 93.

91. G. Van der Leeuw, "Zum Mythus und zur Gestalt des
Osiris," *Archiv für Orientforschung* 3 (1926): 11. "Erst wenn die
menschliche Passion des Heilandgottes einen kosmischen Hinter-
grund hat, scheint die Seligkeit genugsam verbürgt."

92. Xenophanes, cited in Heinrich Ritter and Ludwig Preller,
Historia Philosophiae Graecae (Hildesheim: Gerstenberg, 1975), 84. Cf.
Hippolytus, *Refutatio Omnium Haeresium (Refutation of All Heresies)*
I, 14, in *PG* 16:3037–40.

93. Origen, *De Principiis* II, 3, 4, in *PG* 11:193.

94. Ibid.

95. Jerome, *Epistolae (Epistles)* CXXIV, 5, in *PL* 22:1063.

96. Origen, *De Principiis* II, 3, 6, in *PG* 11:195.

97. Origen, *Against Celsus* VI, 21, in *PG* 11:1324.

98. Justin Martyr, *Apology* II, 11, *PG* 6:461. This phrase may also
be rendered "everlasting and precious graces."

99. Philastrius, *Liber de Haeresibus (On Heresies)* 115, in *PL*
12:1239.

100. Methodius, *Banquet of the Ten Virgins* VIII, 15, in *PG* 18:168.

101. Lovejoy, *Great Chain of Being*, 116.

102. J. S. Spink, *French Free Thought from Gassendi to Voltaire* (London: Athlone, 1960), 53–54.

103. Oskar Piest, *Newton's Philosophy of Nature* (New York: Hafner, 1953), 67.

104. William Hastie, ed. and tr., *Kant's Cosmogony* (Glasgow: Maclehose and Sons, 1900), 138–39; and Milton Munitz, "One Universe or Many?" *Journal of the History of Ideas* 12 (1951): 249.

105. Alexandre Koyré, *From the Closed World to an Infinite Universe* (Baltimore: John Hopkins University Press, 1982), 188.

106. Robert G. Ingersoll, *The Works of Robert G. Ingersoll* (New York: Dresden, 1919), 58.

107. Walter Sullivan, "Is There Intelligent Life beyond the Earth?" in *Brigham Young University Speeches of the Year* (20 February 1964), 2.

108. See Koyré, *From the Closed World to an Infinite Universe*, 275.

109. See Lovejoy, *Great Chain of Being*, 123.

110. Arthur Clarke, *Profiles of the Future* (New York: Holt, Rinehart, and Winston, 1984), 131.

111. Jerome, *Epistle* CXXVI, 1, in *PL* 22:1085–86.

112. *Clementine Recognitions* I, 1, in *PG* 1:1207.

113. Joseph Campbell, *Mythic Image* (New Jersey: Princeton University Press, 1974), 222.

114. Iamblichus, *De Vita Phythagorica* 14 (63).

115. Plotinus, *Ennead* II, 3, 10; cf. English translation, in A. H. Armstrong, tr., *Plotinus*, 6 vols. (Cambridge: Harvard University Press, 1966), 2:76.

116. 2 *Enoch* 23:5; see n. 5 in *APOT* 2:444; cf. Wisdom of Solomon 8:19–20, in ibid., 1:549.

117. Origen, *De Principiis* I, 8, 4, in *PG* 11:179; and ibid., II, 9, 6–8, in *PG* 11:230–32.

118. Pastor of Hermas, *Similitudo (Similitudes)* III, 5, 6, in *PG* 2:962–63.

119. Clement of Alexandria, *Paedagogus* I, 7, in *PG* 8:321.

120. Clement, *Epistola II ad Corinthios (Second Epistle to the Corinthians)* 14, in *PG* 1:329.

121. *Odes of Solomon* 8:16, 21; see English translation in J. Rendel Harris, tr., *The Odes and Psalms of Solomon* (Cambridge: Cambridge University Press, 1909), 99–100.

122. *Clementine Recognitions* I, n. 20, in *PG* 1:1222–23.

123. H. de Leusse, "Le Problème de la préexistence des âmes

chez Marius Victorinus Afer," *Recherches de science religeuse* 29 (1939): 197.

    124. Ibid., 236–37.

    125. Ibid., 237.

    126. Jerome, *Epistle* XCVIII, 8, in *PL* 22:798–99.

    127. Pierce, "The Origin of the 'Book of Mormon,' " 694.

One Eternal Round: The Hermetic Version

Primitive Atonement: our theme the last time was atonement, a bringing together of God and man. Those humans, spirits, or angels who are "at one" with God are naturally at one with each other and with all his creatures. We are speaking of a real event, past and future. This great bringing together or gathering in of all things was rehearsed in the grand manner by the earliest people who have left a record, a subject I have been writing on for fifty years. It begins with a survey of those prehistoric ceremonial centers, found throughout the world. The consistency of the pattern by which they are laid out suggests their use as ceremonial centers, and through the years accumulating data has sharpened the picture. Folklore, myth, legend, and custom, along with the geometrical sophistication of the centers and their astronomical correspondences, confirm the impression of something great going on long before anyone had hitherto suspected it.

There are two dominant theories explaining this strange world-wide phenomenon. One is C. J. Jung's: "With primitives . . . nothing alters, except perhaps the language. . . . Religious rites . . . have grown spontaneously out of the basic conditions of human nature, which

"One Eternal Round" was given on January 12, 1989, in Riverton, Utah, as part of a lecture series sponsored by Deseret Book and the Foundation for Ancient Research and Mormon Studies. Nibley's previous lecture, "The Meaning of the Atonement," was published in CWHN 9:554–614.

are never invented and are everywhere the same."[1] The other, which is now generally accepted, is expressed by Lord Raglan: "There is nothing natural in the performance of rites";[2] "all extant rituals are derived from a single ritual system."[3] Moreover, "in all religions the myths, the doctrines, and the rites form a connected whole," including the death and resurrection of the god, a myth of creation, combat with an adversary, a sacred marriage, a triumphant procession.[4] In terms of language, Raglan asks us to envisage a people of great intelligence and sophistication who expressed their ideas in a rich idiom which has left its marks throughout the world among other far simpler languages. "What the evidence suggests is that the originators . . . of all known languages were people of acute and fertile minds who took a pride and a pleasure in working out complex grammatical systems . . . which have been wholly or partly abandoned in all modern language."[5] The labor of the great nineteenth-century philologists was to trace that spread and declension.

I summed up the ritual situation thus in an article thirty-eight years ago:

> At hundreds of holy shrines, each believed to mark the exact center of the universe and represented as the point at which the four quarters of the earth converged — "the navel of the earth" — one might have seen assembled at the New Year — the moment of creation, the beginning and ending of time (that's the eternal round) — vast concourses of people, each thought to represent the entire human race in the presence of all its ancestors and gods.[6]

The picture was confirmed some years later by Mircea Eliade, the foremost student of comparative religion of our time: "By virtue of these paradigmatic models revealed to men in mythical [i.e., prehistoric] times, the Cosmos and society are periodically regenerated."[7] Note that the man said "revealed." "It does not seem that any of them [rites] can be explained," Raglan concludes; there is "no accepted theory of its origin, or of the reason why it is believed to be efficacious."[8] So Eliade gives the logical explanation: "For the man of the traditional and archaic societies, the models . . . [were] 'revealed' at the beginning of time, . . . having a superhuman and 'transcendental' origin."[9] The author puts the words "revealed" and "transcendental" in quotes, because he, of course, does not believe in such revelation (at least in his scholarly writings); yet he must use that explanation because that is the only one given by the ancients or available to moderns. Whether the ancient scenario was spontaneous or whether it was carefully worked out in one place before it spread throughout the world, the phenomenon is equally astounding—tribes and nations around the globe going through the same elaborate rites in the same settings and at the same portentous times—a vast and grandiose spectacle.

The elaborate appointments of the sacred places and the activities they indicate require a rationale, a doctrine. "The temple in particular—preeminently the sacred place—had a celestial prototype."[10] On this I have written a good deal; Eliade goes on to explain that the purpose of the rites, in particular the sacrifice, is "to restore the primordial unity, that which existed before the Creation, . . . to restore the *whole* that preceded the Creation."[11] That primal unity is the one-ness between heaven and earth which we have called atonement. In a recent study Karl Albert views the great feast or common meal as an example of how "cult grows out of a longing for *Daseinsgemeinschaft*, a one-ness with the divine existence." He cites Albrecht Dieterich: "These prehistoric 'mysteries' are to achieve a *Liebesvereinigung*, a return to the primal Father and Mother as a child, a rebirth, a return to celestial company, . . . a yearning for the restoration of a firmly held common existence of man and of the Godhead—*Verlangen nach Wiederherstellung der geglaubten Daseinsgemeinschaft zwischen den Menschen und der Gottheit"* — a perfect definition of atonement.[12] The doctrine is inseparable from the rites; wherever we go, Eliade reminds us, "there is always a central myth which describes the beginnings of the world." The various versions of the story "taken all together . . . constitute a fairly coherent history" everywhere the same.[13] How far back does it go, and how does it concern us? Intensive studies of the British ruins made since World War II have steadily pushed back the dates until now we find the great "henge" monuments appearing around 3400 B.C.[14] Avebury (cf. fig. 41, pp. 166–67), where I spent happy days in utter solitude back in 1942 (it has now become an overrun tourist trap), is dated to 2500 B.C.; but Silbury Hill, which is part of the complex and is the largest artificial mound in Europe, perfectly round in shape, and the work of "a capable and well-organized society which was highly motivated and disciplined," was begun circa 2750 B.C., about the date of the Great Pyramid of Giza.[15] The renowned Stonehenge, instead of 1500 B.C., is now put at 2500.[16] More surprising is the fact that the land was covered with well-kept farms by the middle of the fifth millennium B.C., with "agriculture . . . established on a more permanent basis around 3800 B.C."[17] To this day many farms in nearby Devon have "hedgerows, boundaries and landmarks described in Saxon charters [that] can still be identified."[18]

Studies in "archaeoastronomy," by such researchers as Alexander Thom and Mrs. E. C. Baitty, have put the ball squarely in the western European court after it was so long in the position of the Orientalists. In particular, findings in the lower Balkans of "enormous quantities of ritual vessels, altars, sacrificial equipment, inscribed objects, clay models of temples, actual temples, and pictorial paintings on vases or on the walls of shrines, already attest a genuine civilization," and that not later than the seventh millennium B.C. — an *urban* civilization at least 2,000 years earlier than the first appearance of civilization in Egypt.[19]

Along with magnificent jewelry and the astonishingly deep mines from which the precious metals were taken emerged thousands of figurines and paintings showing "a pantheon of gods, . . . costumes and masks, which throw much light on ritual drama and life as it was then lived, . . . ritual drama involving many actors, both gods and worshippers." This was no isolated and vanishing dream world, but a wellspring of later civilization, for "much the same practice seems to have been current in Anatolia, Syria, Palestine, and Mesopotamia,"[20] while the neighboring "Minoan culture mirrors the same values, . . . [and] aptitude in artistic endeavour[s]."[21] The trappings of true theatre are here common to the "Old European" civilization — Minoan Crete, Ancient Greece, and Rome.[22] The main theme would seem to be "the rite of annual death and resurrection" (we always begin with the terrible questions), while "the central idea of the ritual drama, the 'Sacred Marriage' . . . of the male god and a female goddess" was introduced not "later than c. 6500 B.C.,"[23] when quite possibly "rites similar to the Eleusinian Mysteries were performed."[24] To complete the picture are the paintings, particularly vase paintings which, as with those of the Native Americans, illustrate "the organization of the cosmos."[25]

The wealth of forms and objects which Ms. Gimbutas examines is the special and largely exclusive property of the Hermetic people. What is going on here? I refer to that handbook of the archaic world called the book of Moses, and call attention to the great assembly at Adam-ondi-Ahman for a presentation of the original model (D&C 107:53–57). "Adam-in-the-presence-of-God" is the quintessential atonement. Here we must hasten to point out the intellectual achievement of those forgotten ages which has been the special concern of the eminent scientist and historian Giorgio de Santillana, who finds in that world "vast protohistoric" schemes of thought[26] — a "great world-wide archaic construction," attested by "thousands of clues to the gigantic puzzle which is waiting to be reassembled."[27] In the prologue, which he calls "Of High and Far-off Times," he says, "the colossal intellectual effort [is] worthy of the greatest modern theorists. We must assume every age has minds of the order of Archimedes, Kepler, or Newton."[28]

But alas, Ms. Gimbutas' civilization suddenly disappeared under the onslaught of patriarchal invaders out of Asia. The mass destruction of world civilization has happened more than once in the past — the Bible gives us stunning examples: "As it was in the days of Noah" (JS–M 1:41) — and promises more to come. The world collapse produces the typical "Heroic Age" of the Great Migrations, such as we find in Genesis 14 and the book of Ether — those desperate times which are the background of the "epic milieu" of the great bards.[29] But always something lived on, as Aristotle tells us. We see signs of recovery from such a collapse when Mortimer Wheeler, viewing a vast agglomeration of archaeological sites, tells us how in the third millennium [B.C.] the idea of civilization was in the air in Western Asia and things were looking up, fortified by the consciousness that it had been done before, and in that consciousness they won through.[30] The author is referring to the earlier achievements of Egypt and Mesopotamia, but their makers in turn had suddenly appeared on the scene as migrating hosts in times of world upheaval and turmoil, salvaging and replanting the remnants saved from an earlier debacle. As if he were paraphrasing the inspired insight of Joseph F. Smith, Professor de Santillana notes that "what we observe as 'primitive' conditions are, with very few exceptions, . . . only what is left of the rise and fall of past higher cultures. . . . We uncover in our search what is not [ancient] virgin soil but areas once cul-

tivated and still full of ancient seeds."³¹ He writes as if he
had been studying those amazing air photographs of Britain showing well-cultivated farms in the far north from the
fifth millennium B.C. In an eloquent passage de Santillana
reminds us, "The dust of centuries had settled upon the
remnants of this great world-wide archaic construction
when the Greeks came upon the scene. Yet something of
it survived in traditional rites, in myths and fairy tales no
longer understood. Taken verbally, it matured [in] the
bloody cults."³² Such is the condition we find at the opening of the book of Abraham when things had degenerated
to that stage. More importantly, the original themes could
flash out again, preserved almost intact, in the later
thought of the Pythagoreans and Plato.

This takes us into another stretch of road, usually designated as Hermetic. How did anything happen to survive?
That is the "Hermetic" secret. We all know that what is
hermetically sealed is tightly preserved from the destruc-
tive influence of the atmosphere against a future time when
we open and smell the beans or peaches. Let us recall that
the book of Moses, which tells us about far-off times, was
written by command and sealed up to be "had again among
the children of men—among as many as shall believe. . . . Show them not unto any except them that believe" (Moses 1:41–42). The book of Ether, another record
of archaic times, was "sealed by the hand of Moroni," who
had edited the text hundreds of years later and which by
him was "hid up unto the Lord, to come forth in due time
by way of the Gentile" (Book of Mormon Title Page). And
let us also recall that the book of Abraham was actually
hidden in a crypt which has been described by eyewit-
nesses. Hence the word *Hermetic* lays considerable emphasis on sealing the record.

But why all the hiding? Nothing is more understand-
able, given the conditions. For sadly the enlightened order
of things of the great days, "Adam-ondi-Ahman" or Ar-

cadia, cannot endure the normal rascality of the race. Men
had spoiled it already in Adam's time: "And Adam and
his wife mourned before the Lord, because of Cain and
his brethren" (Moses 5:27). In each dispensation the world
went bad while the prophets united in futile protest, as in
the days of Samuel, Hezekiah, Isaiah, and Jeremiah. In the
powerful phrase of Ether, "the prophets mourned and
withdrew from among the people" (Ether 11:13). The
prophets always tended to form societies of their own for
mutual comfort and security, for they usually appear in
numbers in time of crisis: "And in that same year there
came many prophets, prophesying unto the people that
they must repent" (1 Nephi 1:4). They were not well received. When not preaching it was their custom to keep a
low profile, or simply to depart from the scene in the time-
honored manner of the Rechabites, a pattern we find repeated over and over again in the Book of Mormon and
vividly depicted in the Dead Sea Scrolls. The holy outcasts
would form with their followers a community of saints, a
church, waiting and working for Zion. Zion itself is a model
of such a retreat from the world: "And from thence went
forth the saying, ZION IS FLED" (Moses 7:69). In their
retreat the righteous refugees take particular pains to preserve the sacred records—we think of Moses, of John, of
Ether, of Moroni, etc., preserving, studying, and editing
the sacred writings by special command. Without that protective care, the malice and envy of the wicked or the
carelessness of the stupid would soon distort and mock
the holy books. The righteous recluse—sometimes appointed by God to survival, escaping the persecution,
wars, and natural disasters—is a standard fixture of history: "Come out of her, my people, that ye be not partakers
of her sins, and that ye receive not of her plagues" (Revelation 18:4).

This arrangement divides the world into two camps.
Origen, the first and foremost of Christian theologians,

divided the church itself into two bodies of members—the "esoteric" and the "exoteric"—corresponding to two different ways of comprehending the teachings. The words are his, and they speak volumes. Both societies shared the common membership, but while the exoteric side made up the popular congregations, the esoteric community was limited to those who understood and could be trusted with the deeper meaning of the doctrine.

This division between the people is not a natural one or an inevitable one, for normal human beings are capable of qualifying for either society. Men were not always "carnal, sensual, and devilish" (Moses 5:13), we are told, but only became so when they yielded to the enticings of Satan and were henceforth "shut out from the presence of God" (Moses 6:49)—denying at-one-ment with him. It wasn't until Satan came among Adam's children that the split took place (Moses 5:13). Being carnal, sensual, and devilish is an acquired skill. Nephi gives up on his own people but cannot excuse them: "And now I, Nephi, cannot say more; the Spirit stoppeth mine utterance, and I am left to mourn because of the unbelief, and the wickedness, and the ignorance, and the stiffneckedness of men; for they will not search knowledge, nor understand great knowledge, when it is given unto them in plainness, even as plain as word can be" (2 Nephi 32:7). And these were people whom he had earlier led away from the corrupt society of his own brethren as another of those righteous communities fleeing into the wilderness (2 Nephi 5:5–10). So Mormon laments at the end, "and I have but the strength of a man, and I cannot any longer enforce my commands" (Moroni 9:18). At times we even find all mankind subjecting themselves to the devil (cf. Moses 7:26). It is the same with Israel: when do they ever live up to the law of Moses? Not in his own day, not in the days of the prophets whom they stoned, not in the time of the Lord's mission among them, and not today.

The division between the two societies, cultures, or "worlds" is truly a great and yawning gulf, much greater than we realize. Actually, the meeting between the two worlds produces a severe culture shock if one of them is really holy. The appearance of an angel causes shock and fright to Zacharias (Luke 1:12), to shepherds who were "sore afraid" (Luke 2:9) when the other world moved too near, as were the Apostles on the Mount of Transfiguration (Matthew 17:6), and even Joseph Smith in the presence of Moroni (JS–H 1:32).

Throughout the Book of Mormon the church itself regularly splits into a worldly society, notably the religion of the Nehors, and another consisting of "a few . . . humble followers of Christ" (2 Nephi 28:14) to whom special gifts and revelations were given (Alma 12:9). These were Origen's exoteric and esoteric churches respectively. That is why true Israel was called a peculiar people; people often ask today in what sense the Latter-day Saints are still peculiar, and it is not always easy to find an answer.

The gospel that the retreating wise men take with them into hiding is guarded as a secret, and that by express command. Why seek it? The jealousy and envy of the others can be dangerous; they resent being shut out from something great and mysterious, like boys excluded from the club tree house. They usually take out their wrath and frustration by wrecking the place. A classic instance of that is the destruction of Pythagoras's school in Calabria. The books are protected by sealing and hiding, for which preservation they must be written on enduring tablets and buried in the earth or hidden in crypts. But above all they are protected from dangerous exposure by the cryptic and symbolic signs and language in which they are written; and, even if they could be read, the information is disguised as myths and parables. The Lord said to a small, closed group of disciples,

It is given unto you to know the mysteries of the

> kingdom of heaven, but to them it is not given, . . .
> because they seeing see not; and hearing they hear not,
> neither do they understand, . . . for this people's heart
> is waxed gross, and their ears are dull of hearing, and
> their eyes they have closed; lest at any time they should
> see with their eyes and hear with their ears. (Matthew
> 13:11–15)

The Lord is here observing and preserving the ancient order of things. His mission is directed to two separate societies, those who have heard and received the message, and those who heard but would not accept it.

Hermetism or *Hermeticism* is the label for a body of knowledge resembling that of the gospel which has been circulated among mankind for a very long time. How does it relate to the gospel? That is the question I shall now attempt to answer. It was always claimed by those who accepted the Hermetic message as true that it was knowledge revealed in the beginning to one Hermes Trismegistus (fig. 51). He was a man who became deified only after his death. He was always identified with Thoth, the Egyptian god who presided over all branches of knowledge and the dispensing of such. He was also identified by the learned Egyptians with the famous Imhotep, the great vizier of Djoser, the founder of the Third Dynasty, and one of the great creative geniuses of all time. Imhotep was beyond dispute a real person, and whether he was the thrice-greatest Hermes or not is beside the point, which is that there actually were men living in far distant times of the caliber of the fabulous Trismegistus and the equal of any who have lived since.

Here we are dealing with world-class noodles, who are naturally drawn to each other and excite ever-mounting distrust, suspicion, and envy of those excluded from the magic circle. "I was destined to prove a disturber and an annoyer of his [Satan's] kingdom," said Joseph Smith (JS–H 1:20), whom we can confidently place among the

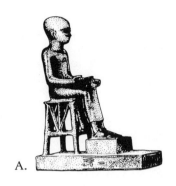

A.

B.

Figure 51. Imhotep, architect to Pharaoh Djoser (cf. fig. 41G, p. 147), was one of only two commoners ever to be deified in ancient Egypt. From this bronze of the Late Period, we see him as patron of medicine and architecture (A). From the floor at the center entrance of the Siena Cathedral, c. 1488, this inlaid marble pavement shows Hermes Trismegistus, "a contemporary of Moses," handing over the mystical teachings to the grateful Egyptians in turbans (B).

few great ones of Hermetic stature. For we are free to use the word in a secular sense, though there is always something transcendental about it. We all know how the public received the prophet Joseph, who was placed in the great-

est danger, not from angry outsiders but from his jealous
followers, like the Higbees and the Laws. The ancient
Ephesians passed a law banishing great achievers from the
city—they were a standing rebuke to the rest: "If they must
excel," they said, "let them go and excel over somebody
else." No Ephesian (and remember it was they who kicked
out Paul) was more illustrious than the great Heraclitus,
whom many consider the most enlightening of ancient
pundits, whose caustic remarks fully explain the behavior
of his fellow citizens: *kynes gar katabauzousin hon an mē
gignoskosin,* which means "dogs bark at anyone they don't
recognize."[33] Anything they don't understand makes dogs
and people uncomfortable, distrusting, and dangerous. As
the immortal Aristophanes shows us, in the simplistic society of the businessman and the farmer, the egghead is
a disquieting intruder—who knows what he might be
thinking? Even if he told us we would not understand,
and that can be dangerous! The one way of not only equal-
izing things but of gaining the upper hand over the smart
guys has ever been to make mediocrity obligatory by the
authority of money—if you are so smart why aren't you
rich? *Fortune Magazine, Forbes, The Wall Street Journal, Bar-
ron's,* and even the *Reader's Digest* are devoted to suffusing
wealth and success with an aura of sanctity, presenting its
achievers surrounded by the skillfully crafted symbols of
ultrarespectability, amounting at times to apotheosis. Even
so the great robber barons surrounded themselves with
the glories of authentic imported Classical and Renaissance
masters. "Business in education" moves in on the scene,
patronizingly offering the wisdom and skill of the successful entrepreneur or stockbroker to the learned community which has become their dependent. To retain its
right to continue operations, the University of Utah must
now justify its existence by advertising how helpful its
discoveries and inventions have been to business. Still,
universities are hardly in a position to complain of such a

comeuppance, since within recent years they have remodeled themselves into full-time business colleges where the MBA has largely supplanted the seven liberal arts, which had become spurious labels anyway. Incidentally the seven arts were introduced by Proclus, a thoroughgoing Hermeticist. The university colleges of the middle ages were direct descendants of the "Hermetic colleges," the most famous of which is that of Pythagoras, burned and stoned out by the mob. Lesser men knew how to adapt themselves and claimed to offer that same recondite learning in less offensive forms with all the trappings and mysteries, uncomplicated by any deeper learning. A. E. Housman used to say of classical scholars, "Among the blind a one-eyed man is king." The one-eyed man is safe in his glory because he presents no real threat to his rivals. Everyone wanted to get in on the act, and this was possible with the ancient sophists as it is in the modern university by putting the emphasis on forms and appearances, titles and degrees. In that way, anybody can be Hermetic.

But there is no reason why the real product shouldn't be made available to one and all. No one has stated the Hermetic ideal more clearly than Brigham Young:

> We have the privilege of becoming classical scholars — of commencing at the rudiments of all knowledge — we might say, of perfection. We might study and add knowledge to knowledge, from the time that we are capable of knowing anything until we go down to the grave. If we enjoy healthy bodies, so as not to wear upon the functions of the mind, there is no end to man's learning.[34]

> We are made expressly to dwell with those who continue to learn.[35]

> [The greatest and] most important labour we have to perform is to cultivate ourselves.[36]

> Every accomplishment, every polished grace, every

useful attainment in mathematics, music, and in all science and art belong to the Saints, and they should avail themselves as expeditiously as possible of the wealth of knowledge the sciences offer to every diligent and persevering scholar.[37]

And that's our duty. "We should cease to be children, and become philosophers, understanding our own existence, its purpose and ultimate design, then our days will not become blank through ignorance."[38] Ever since then *ignorant* has meant "naughty" in the rustic Mormon vocabulary.

Brigham also recognizes that the Hermetic ideal does not last among men, and predicts that the world will lose the height of knowledge it has attained: "The Lord has bestowed great knowledge and wisdom upon the inhabitants of the earth—much truth and knowledge in the arts and sciences."[39] Note that Brigham Young accepts the Hermetic tradition as attendant on the gospel:

> Those nations that deny their God and Saviour will have those principles of intelligence taken from them. . . . This wisdom will be taken from the wicked. Who will receive it? My faith and my desire[s] are that there should be a people upon earth prepared to receive this wisdom. It should not be so forfeited as to be taken from the earth, for I question whether it would return again.[40]

Exactly the same Hermetic idea is expressed by de Santillana, who notes that the most advanced scientific knowledge is grasped only by a handful of savants. As science becomes ever more esoteric and obscure, the chances of that knowledge surviving grow less and less. The only hope, of course, is for it to be passed on to the next generation; and lacking that, to some future generation, by consigning it to varied writings in the earth, trusting its restoration to the same wise providence that gave it to us in the first place—direct revelation.[41]

We may consider the gospel as the most advanced knowledge on earth, known to but a few because it is accepted and believed by but a few and can be understood by no others. After all, it is the simplest ideas that win Nobel prizes. The gospel belongs to that body of knowledge which has been passed down in patriarchal succession, even as the Hermetic knowledge supposedly has been. Are they the same? The first step to answering that is to consider the fatal flaw of Hermetism, i.e., its irresistible appeal to ambitious and weak-headed persons. Where higher knowledge is concerned, a great and yawning gulf lies between it and me; and in a society, nay, in a world that lives by appearances, where the appearance is the reality, you are whatever people think you are. The Hermetic image has never lost its appeal, the thrill and mystery of the unknown and the secret possession of those powers in which Owen Glendower gloried. Today the infection is rampant. What used to be the stock figure of the great scientist of nineteenth-century science fiction is now no less than the master of the universe; dungeons and dragons, wizards and magicians, Spocks and Merlins are the standard fare from the infant's cartoon TV through the orgiastic mysteries of MTV, to the endless mystery and power of the corporate giants—"secret combinations, to get power and gain" (Ether 8:22), and the unfathomable secrets of the stock market. There is something Hermetic about it all. Though the quantum physicist has made awesome nightmares plausible, the same appeal of the marvelous and sinister was exercised by the best-selling novel of the late nineteenth century, Bulwer-Lytton's silly novel *Zanoni*.

There is a legitimate interest in the lost learning of the past; it is a fascinating subject in itself, and all the more interesting as new prospects promise retrieval of ever more of it. In the early days of the Church the mysteries of the past intrigued and aroused the brethren. They were fascinated by the ancient records to which they were being directed (D&C 7–9), and God encouraged them to use their brains in deciphering them. Joseph regretted that the cares of the world kept him from those exercises for which he had such a lively appetite. Even the pioneers, forced to relinquish the luxury of books, discovered new delights and surprises all along their arduous journey; and upon arriving in the valley they scattered in all directions on new adventures. So I was told by all my grandparents, who declared that the interest and excitement of discovering new things more than compensated for the inconvenience of exhaustion and dysentery. "We were like kids let out of school," my grandfather used to say.

Today we use the cares of the world, the imperatives of business, to neglect and condemn serious study. Recently, when a young man who had made a lot of money in a hurry told his stake president that he intended to take off some time to study some of the things that had always been his real interest, the president flew into a rage. "Do you mean to tell me," he said, "that you are going to spin your wheels reading books when you could be making big money?" The gulf between Adam's golden age and our own becomes narrow at those times when the gospel is restored, but presently starts to broaden as the Saints begin to drift away toward the normal human condition. Nephi found this to be a law of nature. In ancient times, apostasy never came by renouncing the gospel but always by corrupting it. No one renounces it today, and so we have the strange paradox of people stoutly proclaiming beliefs and ideals that they have no intention of putting into practice.

1. Every Sunday we thank God for our beautiful surroundings, which in many neighborhoods are being systematically destroyed by developers all around us.

2. We seek knowledge as our greatest treasure, while the poverty of most of our manuals and handbooks defies description.

3. As a Church authority commented to me after the last Conference, the President's keynote address on the Book of Mormon was hardly mentioned during the rest of the Conference.

4. For years we hailed the Welfare Plan as a living demonstration of continued revelation — and then phased it out in deference to the private sector.

5. Since the days of Joseph Smith, presidents of the Church have made resounding pronouncements against the wicked practice of needlessly killing animals and birds for pleasure,[42] and have been unheeded; we have just passed a law permitting fourteen-year-olds the pleasure of killing big game.

6. A great and inspired bicentennial message by one we called our prophet was instantly swept under the rug.[43]

7. The oldest and best testimony to Joseph Smith's first vision has received no attention whatever by the Latter-day Saints since its discovery in 1969, and so it goes.[44]

8. The prophet Joseph studied biblical languages with dedicated zeal to help him understand the scriptures, but such studies are frowned upon by too many in our religious institutions.

Joseph Smith sums up the general situation even as Nephi and Moroni do: "God has instructed man to form wise and wholesome laws, since he had departed from Him and refused to be governed by those laws which God had given."[45] We must always settle for second best, and as men keep drifting away they must periodically be recalled: "From time to time these glad tidings were sounded in the ears of men in different ages of the world down to the time of the Messiah's coming."[46] But always the prize has escaped them. "For our own part," says the Prophet, "we cannot believe that the ancients in all ages were so ignorant of the system of heaven as many suppose."[47] And the loss of great promise is not slow in coming: "How vain and trifling have been our spirits, our conferences, our

councils, our meetings, our private as well as public conversations—too low, too mean, too vulgar, too conde-
scending for the dignified characters of the called and chosen of God, according to the purposes of His will, from
before the foundation of the world!"[48] They still had failed
to get the point: "We are called to hold the keys of the
mysteries of those things that have been kept hid from the
foundation of the world until now."[49] They had been offered the greatest prize of all, yet it is not strange that they
slighted their opportunities, since "it is in the nature and
disposition of almost all men" to turn the knowledge and
power of God to their own interest and vanity "in unrighteous dominion," whereupon that power automatically shuts off and the light is taken away—"Amen to the
priesthood of that man!" (D&C 121:39, 41).

And that has been the way of the world as well as that
of the Church. The great apostasy in the time of the apostles
was not a renouncing of the faith but its corruption and
manipulation. If the gospel light can be redirected for convenience, the Hermetic tradition has also ever been an
invitation to fraud. We have said that something claiming
to be a Hermetic community was allowed to flourish in
the world in the guise of the university. Such sufferance
was possible, however, only because the university itself
was but a charade. Oliver Cromwell's Minister of Education, William Dell, instructed his Roundhead preachers to
displace "the religion of the 'dull and drousie Divinity of
Synods and Schools' buttressed by authority, degrees, and
ceremonies," whose desire was "especially . . . to Preach
to rich men, and great men, and men in place and authority," to get for themselves "favour, preferment, and
a quiet life."[50]

But the appeal of Hermetism is universal. The classic
demonstration is the case of Faust, superscientist and
magician, who, in the opening scene of Goethe's great
play, laments that he has spent all his days putting on an

Figure 52. Dr. Faustus stands in the mystic circle of the zodiac and planets as he summons the devil to do his bidding. Astronomical instruments, such as the planisphere, astrolabe, and Jacob's staff, adorn his office walls.

act; he wants to see what really holds the universe together, as he says, and not have to go on misleading his students with the false display of omniscience. He decides that the only solution is to take a great shortcut and turn to magic, and, in the most drastic step of all, makes a pact with the devil (fig. 52). Thereby he has instant access to the four things which Nephi tells us will destroy us—power, gain, popularity, and the lusts of the flesh (1 Nephi 22:23; 3 Nephi 6:15). Satan promises them all to Faust for a price, and the price is his salvation. What Faust got from him anyway was only bogus, an extravaganza of false Hermetism, make-believe, eyewash, and special effects.

Does the Hermetic tradition begin as a real thing, or

was it always suspect? Its beginnings are out of sight in the prehistoric world. It is convenient but absurd for such historians of science as Mary Hesse to say simply that it all began in the third century A.D. True, that was when most of the very fragmentary corpus of Hermetic literature was produced; that was a time of assimilation, not creation, and so the busy clerks and collectors of the time brought together the accumulated materials of the Hermetic tradition, but they did not create it. It was always associated with the mysteries and lived in a zone of uncertainty, a borderline science, a twilight zone. And indeed, how could that be avoided, considering the abiding need for secrecy, which was a standing invitation for quacks and pretenders to lay claim to it without having to make their claims good? That was the nature of gnosticism.

The great line of pretenders emerges with the Sophists, men like Empedocles and Apollonius of Tyana. They claimed the same wisdom as Plato, but Socrates exposed the false nature of their teachings in his conversation with his Sophist friends Gorgias and Protagoras. Were the Hermetic books, whose remains I have here, the actual source of Hermetic wisdom? For the ancients they contained all essential wisdom and were written by Thoth, the primal custodian and purveyor of all information and at almost all points the equivalent of the Greek Hermes—Plato uses both names in speaking of the hero. There is no shortage of evidence that the Egyptians did keep books from the earliest times, and that those books were meant to contain the sum total of wisdom and knowledge. In the temple library were books on all subjects "to describe the universe and its phenomena."[51] The library itself was called the House of Life, and the building represented a model of the universe—a microcosm.[52] The books were thought to be the actual "Power of Re," i.e., direct revelations from heaven.[53] The aim of the archaic cultic activities not only in Egypt but also everywhere else was, according to Karl

Figure 53. In this Buddhist wall painting from Central Asia, we see the hourglass-shaped World Mountain broken to indicate the passing of a world age. The sun and the moon with its rabbit plummet from the heavens with the other falling stones of the "Broken Frame."

Albert, "to restore the primal community of Gods and men,"[54] or, as we would say, to achieve atonement; and the ordinances were inseparable from the doctrines that went with them. Everywhere we find myths and legends about how the primal bond that existed between heaven and earth in the Golden Age was broken by the wickedness of men (fig. 53); the great common assemblies ceased and the gods departed.[55] But, as Aristotle notes, some bits of the old knowledge always survived to the next age. A study by Fabio Mora on "The Silence of Herodotus" notes that the three things in the mysteries that Herodotus would never talk about were (1) the grand mystery of the true nature and character of God, which could be known only by revelation, (2) the ordinances by which the mysteries were taught and implemented, and (3) the doctrine or rationale of the whole, including that which explained the rites.[56] Plato makes Thoth the inventor of writing and tells us that all wisdom was contained in thirty-six of the Hermetic books,[57] and Plutarch reports that in his day the authentic forty-two books of Hermes were still to be found in temple libraries.[58]

The name Trismegistus means "thrice-greatest" and has naturally led to all sorts of explanations. One of the most learned of ancient astronomers, the renowned Abu Maᶜshar al-Balkhī, like al-Thaᶜlabī, explored ancient legends and traditions all over the Middle East and found that there were indeed three Hermes, all related and united in glory—Thrice-Great indeed! The Persians believed him to be Gayomart, the grandson of Adam. The Hebrews also made him third in descent from Adam and so confused him with Enoch, the son of Cain. "Adam," they say, "taught him the hours of the day and the night," and he first studied the structure of the cosmos and built the first temple. "He wrote many books . . . on the knowledge of things of heaven and earth." This earliest Hermes lived in Upper Egypt, where he enriched the world with scientific schemes and diagrams of all sorts and invented characters for writing the scriptures for "those who would come after him."[59]

The second Hermes, according to al-Balkhī, lived in the land of the Chaldeans and taught the world medicine, philosophy, and the nature of numbers, reviving those studies after their loss in the Flood. The third, like the first, lived in Egypt. He wrote a great book on alchemy and its related crafts, and was the teacher of Aesculapius.

But three is merely a beginning. Hermes Trismegistus has been identified with almost every superwiseman who ever lived, beginning with Noah and the first pharaoh; the list includes Zoroaster, Mithra, Elijah, Pythagoras, Aesculapius, Hesiod, Plato, Aristotle, Buddha, and Zosimus. Originally, Hermetic books copied in the temples were written on tablets, some of which various wise men of old claimed to have discovered at various times and places. When we are told that Geb, the founder of patriarchal rule on earth, had the history of the settling of Egypt by Re and Shu read to him from the Annals which were written down at the time of Atum,[60] we can surmise that the tradition of record keeping was as old as the civilization itself. That impression is confirmed when we discover in the Pyramid Texts extensive reuse and reapplication of much earlier texts. Many have shown that the Pyramid Texts, "the oldest book in the world," the Coffin Texts, and the *Book of the Dead*, each succeeding the other, have, as Lacau puts it, absolutely the same object, and that the fundamental teachings, the language, and the script remain virtually unchanged from beginning to end, one simply continuing the tradition of the others.

What was that tradition? Hornung has recently shown that it is always the same: what the *Book of the Dead* contains, faithfully carrying on the tradition, is nothing less than the complete manual or handbook of all knowledge — the epitome of the Hermetic library.[61]

Alexander Moret, who made a special study of the Egyptian mysteries, concluded that all arts and sciences are mysteries and secrets, which men could learn only by revelation. The secret books of rituals were miraculous things written by the very hand of Thoth.

Eduard Naville, who first edited the complete *Book of the Dead*, stated frankly that the *Book of the Dead* must belong to the books which Clement of Alexandria called Hermetic, being written by Thoth. To indicate how old the records are, we have Otto's recent discovery that the implements of the funerary cults have no recognizably Egyptian names — all are prehistoric, mystic code-names, *Decknamen*. Moreover, he notes that the rituals are almost never depicted, though they were the main activity, and that no ritual is ever presented in its completeness; also, that from what we know we can find no significant variation between the rites of the very earliest and the very latest times. Hornung shows us how in Egypt alone we can see a central perennial tradition handed down for thousands of years, preserving its contents through changing forms.[62] As Iamblichus puts it, the Egyptians ask all the basic questions about God and creation and never cease insisting upon the one universal God and king upon whom all things depend. He assures us that their approach to the interface (*Nahtstelle* or "seam") between the worlds is the one we must follow if we would ever hope to get "a peek through a chink in the wall."[63]

The Egyptians were not the only ones; other mysteries and cults claimed to be every bit as old. The resemblance of these early cults to each other produced a rich mix down through the centuries, and Herodotus reports that the Orphics, Bacchics, Egyptians, and Pythagoreans were all one with the Delphian Apollo.[64] The Hermeticism of Hermes Trismegistus was confused with Egyptomania, Orphism, and Pythagoreanism," according to Derchain.[65] The claims of Orpheus are as venerable as Trismegistus himself. The ancients believed, according to Jacob Burckhardt, that "Orpheus 'was the father of all rites and of all mysticism in general.' "[66] He left the world a body of hymns and rites going back to the prehistoric mysteries of Eleusis, the "very ancient Demeter cult . . . [in which the basic ideas were] purification, fertility, rebirth; [and] . . . striv[ing] toward a luminous 'other world.' "[67] The "Orphic Phanes . . . combined in himself all the gods and cosmic forces" (fig. 54).[68] Orpheus, like Trismegistus, began as a mortal, the prototype of "a long series of 'divine men' " such as Epimenides of Crete, Abaris the Hyperborean, and Zalmoxis of Thrace, who can be "placed at the side of the sages or shamans such as the Seven Sages, who met at Delphi" in periodic sacred conferences.[69]

At this point of my labors I thought it would be well to bring myself up-to-date on the position of the philosophy faculty on these matters, and so I read the recent volumes of Frederick Copleston on *The Philosophy of Greece and Rome*[70] and discovered that there really is no such thing

Figure 54. Within the oval of the zodiac and the four winds, the winged figure of the god Phanes, or Aion, stands on the bottom half of the cosmic egg, its other half above his head, symbolizing the creation of the universe (cf. fig. 39, p. 160). This figure, c. A.D. 125, was developed by a late Roman religious movement that sought to combine elements of Eastern and Western religions.

as being significantly up-to-date on subjects in which we are dealing with opinions.

First and foremost the author finds that Greek philosophy, which after all *is* ancient philosophy, deals primarily with "the theme of the relation between the One and the Many, . . . [which] runs indeed through the whole of philosophy," the perennial problem being "to reduce the Many to the One,"[71] or as we would say, to achieve at-one-ment. It is gratifying to find that we are on the track. The next greatest problem, he says, is "to discover the ultimate cause or causes of the world," another gospel theme.[72] Then there is that great problem, the nature of the soul. "The Pythagorean conception of the soul," our author notes, "exercised a very considerable influence on the thought of Plato,"[73] while "the most important contribution of post-Aristotelian philosophy to psychology . . . was . . . the religious aspect of the human soul."[74]

You will note that these are all terrible questions. In trying to answer them by speculation, we find only a few solutions, and these are repeated over and over again in Copleston's book. This is why there is endless debate over which ancient philosopher or school is borrowing from which, and why their teachings become so easily mixed up. We end the book feeling let down, for all we have read is opinions. The author must repeatedly insist that this is great stuff; the culmination of philosophy in "the system of Plotinian Neo-Platonism [is] one of the supreme achievements of the human race."[75] Thus the devoutly wished consummation of philosophy is in mysticism, little by little opening the door ever wider to the other world. For after a thousand years of pure reason attempting to solve the great questions of existence, it was clear that they were getting nowhere—"Myself when young did eagerly frequent Doctor and Saint, and heard great Argument about it: but evermore came out by the same Door as I went in."[76] The conclusion is that any confirmation of the final answers to the eternal questions can only come from revelation. And so philosophy steadily drifted toward mysticism.

The trouble was that no one could offer anything definite, concrete, and specific beyond his own personal, nontransferable dreams and feelings. In the end even Plato must dig up the case of Er the Armenian, which he assures us was a real happening, to answer the number one terrible question: Is there more to come after this life?[77] And Socrates testified in his last hour to vivid personal experiences that firmly convinced him of a judgment in the hereafter.[78] Our teacher never mentions these things but glories in the ultimate achievement of true philosophy, the doctrine of *creatio ex nihilo,* a teaching which he insists is far loftier

than anything conceived of by the ancients. He appeals to
his readers to recognize in philosophy the equivalent of
the great artistic and literary triumphs contemporary with
its own development. But philosophy is not art or literature—it is a means to an end, while they are the end. Even
mathematics is a "good of first intent."[79] But the student
endures tedious expositions and refutations in an awkward
and unlovely jargon for the sake of discovering new truth.
Philosophy is the road, not the goal, which it never reaches.
If you want answers to the questions which it proposes,
you can get them in the end only by revelation. That is
where the ultimate triumph of Father Copleston's philosophy ends up, with Plotinian Neo-Platonism tottering on
the brink of revelation. So the Neo-Platonists come up with
the right answers without ever having heard of Christ, and
"the Augustinian philosophy was, through Neo-Platonism, strongly impregnated with the thought of Plato,"[80] as
corrected by Aristotle.

Hermetism came to its own when the Greek city-state
passed away with Alexander; all the local cults, like the
local governments, "were merged in a larger whole,"[81] and
religion became eclectic or, as the expression goes, syncretistic. Representative of the times is Poseidonius of Apa-
mea (135–51 B.C.). He has been called the most universal
mind since Aristotle.[82] After visiting Egypt, he founded a
school in Rhodes. He taught stoic monism, "the 'sympa-
thy' that prevails between all parts of the cosmic system,"
in a universal hierarchy of beings. He also taught that man
is both body and spirit, having both an earthly and heavenly home; operating in the interchange between worlds
are angels and devils. "Poseidonius readopted the Platonic
theory of the pre-existence of the soul" as well as its immortality.[83] Bear in mind that he taught all these things
long before the time of Christ. He taught further that there
was once a golden age followed by corruption and a fall,
and that laws were given to bring men back again into the

fold, and that the duty of philosophers was to teach them the saving morality.[84]

What is called Middle Platonism is represented by Plutarch, who, though strongly opposed to superstition, believed in prophecy and revelation.[85] He saw that some pagan rites had been taken over or instituted by evil spirits, but he supported others as sincere attempts at religious behavior.[86]

The Jews were in on such teachings all along. Josephus shows Orphic-Pythagorean traits in Jewish-Hellenistic philosophy, including the Essenes, both in teaching and in practice.[87] Copleston will not allow Philo, the Jew who reconciled Old Testament history with Hermetic philosophy, the decisive influence on Christianity usually attributed to him, for "the Philonic philosophy could never admit the Christian doctrine of the Incarnation," even though "Christianity itself insists on the Divine Transcendence and . . . the Incarnation is a mystery."[88] That seems like some sort of convergence, and the process is all but complete in its triumphant culmination in Plotinus: "In the system, . . . then, the Orphic-Platonic-Pythagorean strain of 'otherworldliness,' intellectual ascent, salvation through assimilation to and knowledge of God, reach their most complete and systematic expression. Philosophy now includes not only logic, cosmology, psychology, metaphysics and ethics, but also the theory of religion and mysticism."[89] Plotinus's confidence lay in his own personal experience "as the Supreme attainment of the true philosopher." With him "philosophy tends to pass into religion."[90] What's the difference? They attempt to answer the same questions, the terrible questions, in fact, but in different ways, philosophy by endless arguments and speculation. Joseph Smith points this out: "As Paul said, 'the world by wisdom know[s] not God,' so the world by speculation [is] destitute of revelation."[91] Religion answers by private but nonnegotiable spiritual experiences. With his usual insight, Plotinus sees atonement as the solution: "The Father Land to us is that place from whence we came; and in that place is the Father."[92] The important addition of Neo-Platonism to Christianity was "that of contributing to the intellectual statement of the revealed religion"; to Plotinus, "the greatest of the Latin Fathers (and so the universal church) owed no inconsiderable debt."[93] Had Jesus done such a poor job, then? Unless he fell short, we are plainly dealing here with something quite different from what he had in mind. At the very least, conventional Christianity contains a strong infusion of Hermetism to take the place of out-and-out revelation.

This is clear in the case of Proclus, the Athenian Scholarch, with his "enthusiasm for all sorts of religious beliefs, superstitions and practices, even believing that he received revelations"; he has been called "the greatest Scholastic of Antiquity."[94] In his Athenian School of Neo-Platonism, we find "agreement between Plato, the Pythagoreans, the Orphics, and the 'Chaldaic' literature."[95] Finally, the Neo-Platonists of the Latin West become mere schoolmen, clerks and compilers rather than independent thinkers, gathering and classifying and especially translating the works of Plato, Aristotle, Themistius's paraphrase of Aristotle, Poseidonius, etc. But the theme of it all remains as ever the One and the Many and how they are brought into union.[96] It is significant that Copleston, in dealing with men who consider themselves in debt to Trismegistus, never mentions Hermetism, while for him Egypt does not even exist. Like all the professors of philosophy I have known, for him philosophy begins with the Greeks, whose own repeated insistence that they are in debt to their Egyptian masters goes unheeded. He recognizes in Alexandria the great philosophical clearinghouse from the fourth century B.C. on, but he ignores the all-important triangle of Egypt, Israel, and Greece, all of which borrow from each other. He also has little to say of the Sophists, who opened the door to pseudo-Hermetic influence on a large scale. That spirit animates those philosophers who play philosophy off against religion while skillfully hinting of dark powers which they rarely offered to demonstrate.

The tradition carries on into the Middle Ages with Averroes (for it was the Arabs who really took over the Hermetic tradition in his time), Albertus Magnus, Aquinas, Roger Bacon, Lully; and so into the Renaissance with such brilliant figures as Marcilio Ficino (who brought Greek Hermetic texts to Europe, fervidly defending their Egyptian origin), Pico della Mirandola, Johann Reuchlin, Philippus Theophrastus Paracelsus, J. V. Andrea, Robert Fludd, Francis Bacon, Giordano Bruno, John Dee, Athanasius Kircher, Cagliostro (Balsamo), Emanuel Swedenborg; and into the nineteenth century (when science broke the spell and a line of quacks and occultists took over) with Anton Mesmer, A. L. Constant (Elephas Levi), Madame Blavatsky, Bulwer-Lytton, Aleister Crowley, etc. (one can look them up in an encyclopedia or in Peter Tompkins). Copleston never once mentions the newly emerging Coptic literature, so full of Hermetism — after all, Plotinus, Ammonius Saccus, and Iamblichus were true native Egyptians, who along with Hermes Trismegistus and Horapollo and the Jewish pseudepigrapha compose, as Derchain puts it, a "bricolage, a new universe of representations containing all the debris of the ancients." Over a vast sweep of time, "the cosmogony of prehistoric Heliopolis has passed into that of the author of the Book of the Secrets of Enoch . . . as part of a vast syncretistic movement at the end of the ancient world with Alexandria as one of the most active centers." Such basic teachings as the journey of the soul through the heavenly spheres was taken over by the Roman Imperial cult in Roman Egypt, by the Gnostics, Jews, and early Christian Apocalyptic, according to Eberhard Otto. Heaven and hell are described in the old Egyptian fashion in the Coptic writers, Bartholomew, Paul,

Elijah, the Greek *Enoch,* the *Apocalypse of Peter,* and the *Gospel of Peter* (found in an Egyptian tomb). All this means, according to Otto, that a new interpretation of Egyptian religion is necessary, soft-pedalling the overworked "mystic" traits. Reexamination of temple and grave reliefs and inscriptions now shows them in an altered context in which we actually discover quotations from Greek tragedies and epics, showing that the classical writers and the Egyptian scribes were well aware of each other's works.

In about 1460 the monk Leonardo da Pistoria brought to Florence fifteen Greek treatises of the *Corpus Hermeticum.* Cosimo de' Medici bought them and gave them to the famous Marsilio Ficino, who translated them. By 1600 the work had run into sixteen editions. Ficino's even more famous pupil, Pico della Mirandola, "was the first to join Hermetism to the Qabbalah." The result was theosophic speculative Pythagoreanism.[97] So the mixing went on. In England, John Colet was the disciple of Ficino; they thought that what they had in the Hermetic books was the *prisca theologia.*[98] More's *Utopia* (1516) shows the influence of Hermetism, and Trismegistus is often cited in Heinrich Cornelius Agrippa's famous work *De occulta philosophia* (1533). The late sixteenth and early seventeenth centuries are the golden age of religious Hermetism. For the great protestant scholar Duplessis-Mornay, Hermes is the source of the *Zohar,* Orpheus, Zarathustra, etc. On the other side, the Counter-Reformation used the Hermetic writings as a weapon against the Protestants. But when Genevan Isaac Casaubon in 1614 claimed the Hermetic texts to be no older than the first century, they suddenly lost authority and their devotees went underground as Rosicrucians.[99] The old excitement of Hermetic writings was continued at a lower level by occultism, spiritualism, theosophy, astrology, etc., with such gifted but imaginative champions as Jesuit Athanasius Kircher, who stirred up that Egyptomania which swept Europe and is still alive.[100]

A key figure in sixteenth-century Hermetism is the renowned Paracelsus, who strove to replace the Aristotelian-Galenic system of chemistry and medicine "by the Christian Neo-Platonic and Hermetic texts." "He should turn first to the book of divine revelation — The Holy Scriptures — and then to the book of divine Creation — Nature."[101] For, to quote the mathematician Morris Kline, "the work of sixteenth-, seventeenth-, and most eighteenth-century mathematicians was . . . a religious quest. The search for the mathematical laws of nature was an act of devotion that would reveal the glory and grandeur of His [God's] handiwork."[102] C. H. Dodd sees in the Hermetic writers a "reaction against the pure rationalism, . . . [a] philosophy . . . of gnosis, which itself was held to come from divine revelation." It was "Platonism with its mystical and theistic elements emphasized. With it was combined a revived Pythagoreanism, and Stoicism," uniting "the mythology and ritual of various religions of the Near East, . . . [believing that] all [was] communicated [as] divinely revealed [*gnosis*]."[103] So it is not surprising that "the priest-physician concept . . . was a fundamental part of Renaissance neo-Platonism, and it is likely that their ultimate source may be found in Ecclesiastes 38:1." As "the *Magus* transfers the powers of a celestial field into a small stone, . . . the physician extracts the hidden virtues of herbs and prepares powerful remedies."[104]

The early Paracelsians turned from Aristotle and Galen to "the recently translated Hermetic Alchemical and Neo-Platonic texts . . . for a new Christian understanding of nature as a whole."[105] Van Helmont's (1597–1644) sensational discovery of gas, though it was a "rather incidental part of a religious and vitalistic system of natural philosophy," nevertheless provided the nearest thing to spirit so far discovered, standing at a sort of interface between the worlds.[106] The aim of science was an "UNIO with 'Deus Sive Natura' "[107] — more "at-one-ment," after the brethren

ran short of patience with the endless *artificiose altercari* or
word-juggling of the Jesuits.[108] Hermetism reached back
"to a secret tradition of knowledge which gave a truer
insight into the basic forces in the universe than the qual-
itative physics of Aristotle."[109] But of course the pretenders
were eager to climb on the wagon with the great ones,
who increasingly resented, as one of them put it, "the
windy impostures of magic and astrology, of signatures
and physiognomy."[110] P. M. Rattansi informs us that there
have been "recent explorations of Renaissance Neo-Platonism and Hermeticism,"[111] imparting a higher importance and dignity to the subject than modern science has
been inclined to accept. For example, "the Neo-Platonic
cosmology is indispensable" in understanding Copernicus's system.[112] In his work *De Revolutionibus*, "Copernicus
appealed to . . . Neo-Platonic tenets: the study of astronomy as the vehicle for drawing the mind to the contemplation of the highest good."[113] Kepler accepted Coperni-
canism in preference to Aristotelianism, since he viewed
God as "an ever-active and an ever-generative God dif-
fusing his power into all things" (fig. 55)[114] ("in all things,
and is through all things, and is round about all things,"
D&C 88:41). Kepler's famous Third Law came from a search
"for the 'music of the spheres.' "[115] "Such harmony is in
immortal souls," wrote Shakespeare, the Hermetist, "but
whilst this muddy vesture of decay doth grossly close it
in, we cannot hear it."[116] His insights into Hermetism appear in *Love's Labours Lost*, lightheartedly presenting the
precious devotees, recalling the Elizabethan Hermetists
that gathered at Sir Walter Raleigh's house.

Rattansi points out that "The Cambridge Platonists
. . . restate classical Neo-Platonist philosophy to safeguard
a *religious* vision of the world."[117] Hence Newton's ab-
sorption in the "literature of alchemy, . . . biblical chro-
nology, and prophecy," which, he assures us, "must have
had some connection with his scientific work."[118] John

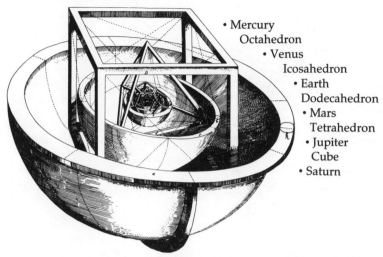

• Mercury
  Octahedron
  • Venus
    Icosahedron
    • Earth
      Dodecahedron
      • Mars
        Tetrahedron
        • Jupiter
          Cube
          • Saturn

Figure 55. On July 9, 1595, while teaching a geometry class, Kepler suddenly felt divinely inspired when he thought he had found a way to reconcile the perfection of the Pythagorean solids with the assumed perfection of the heavenly spheres and their planets. To his credit he abandoned his elegant theory when the observed data did not match his model, as shown in this engraving. It demonstrates the age-old desire to see the universe, the round and the square, from God's viewpoint.

Maynard Keynes shows us just how close the connection was. He tells us how Newton wrote on "the measurements of Solomon's Temple, the Book of Daniel, the Book of Revelations, . . . hundreds of pages of Church History and the like, designed to discover the truth of tradition. . . . The scope and character of these papers have been hushed up, or at least minimized, by nearly all those who have inspected them."[119] How was such stuff related to his scientific work? They were part of it—to him by far the more interesting part; and they "are marked by careful learning, accurate method, and extreme sobriety of statement. They are just as *sane* as the *Principia*, . . . nearly all composed during the same twenty-five years of his mathematical studies" (fig. 56).[120]

"The Philosophers' Stone with its wheels of the elements"

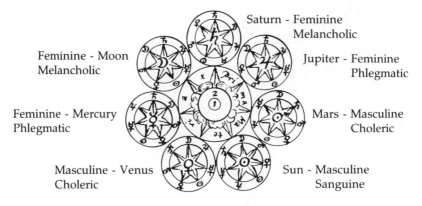

Saturn - Feminine
           Melancholic

Feminine - Moon
Melancholic

Jupiter - Feminine
            Phlegmatic

Feminine - Mercury
Phlegmatic

Mars - Masculine
           Choleric

Masculine - Venus
Choleric

Sun - Masculine
          Sanguine

Figure 56. Newton himself made this copy of an alchemical diagram in
which the sun, moon, and five planets make seven seven-pointed stars,
each revolving around the central "prima materia." It evokes the hex-
agonal benzene ring seen by Kekulé in an 1865 daydream as the *ouroborus*
eating its own tail and circling in the fire (cf. fig. 33, p. 143).

In an arresting passage cited by de Santillana, Keynes
writes:

> Newton was not the first of the age of reason. He
> was the last of the magicians, . . . the last great mind
> which looked out on the visible and intellectual world
> with the same eyes as those who began to build our
> intellectual inheritance rather less than 10,000 years
> ago. . . . His deepest instincts were occult, esoteric, se-
> mantic. . . . Why do I call him a magician? Because he
> looked upon the whole universe and all that is in it *as
> a riddle,* . . . a sort of philosopher's treasure hunt to the
> esoteric brotherhood. He believed that these clues were
> to be found partly in the evidence of the heavens and
> in the constitution of the elements, . . . but also partly
> in certain papers and traditions handed down by the
> brethren in an unbroken chain back to the original cryptic
> revelation in Babylonia.[121]

Or in Egypt, rather, for all of the Hermetic traditions
pointed in that direction. Newton also talked as Joseph

Smith did, that "truth had been given by God in the beginning, but had been fragmented and corrupted in the
course of time; its traces survived in enigmatic form in
these different sorts of literature, but had to be recovered
by a sort of dialectic between hard, disciplined inquiry and
the ancient sources."[122] How could one whom Rattansi calls
"the cold and austere Newton" take such stuff seriously?
It was because the idea of a mechanistic universe gave him
"a chilling sense of its inadequacy as a world-view to live
by."[123]

Egypt or Babylon? That was the ancient controversy.
But in the nineteenth and twentieth centuries the argument
was between three rivals: Greece, Egypt, and Iran. In the
twenties, my friend and teacher Werner Jaeger drew attention to the self-declared indebtedness of Plato and Aristotle to Zoroaster. Richard Reitzenstein, who for years
had insisted on the Egyptian origin of Hermetism as opposed to the stubborn insistence of the Germans that the
Greeks alone invented everything, suddenly shifted his
allegiance to Iran and from then on saw an ancient Persian
background in everything Hermetic. A recent study by
Karl-Wolfgang Troeger discusses the three-corner rivalry
and in the process takes note of the gnostic problem, which
cannot be ignored in any discussion of Hermetism. "The
relationship between the gnosis and the mystery religions," he writes, "often mentioned together in the same
breath has, to the present day, never been properly clar-
ified." That, he says, is because there is no general agreement on just what is meant either by Gnosis or by
Mysteries[124] — so how are they related? If we had some ham,
we would have some ham and eggs, if we had the eggs.

Along with the gnostic problem goes the cabala (fig.
57). "Intimate resemblance" in language and thought between gnostic sects and the cabala proves to some that
"Gnosticism borrowed a great deal if not precisely from
the *Zohar*, at least from its traditions and sources"; and

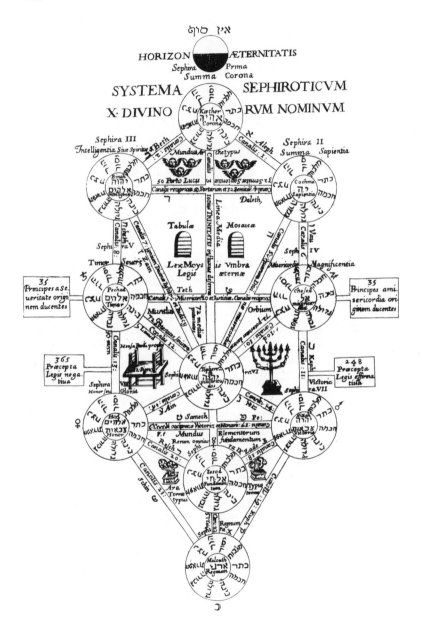

Professor Franck asked, "Could there have existed an older doctrine, from which, unknown to each other, both the kabbalistic system and [the] so-called Alexandrian Platonism" could have borrowed?[125]

Alexander Altmann traces the "impulse for cosmological speculation by the Palestinian rabbis of the first three centuries . . . [to] Plato's *Timaeus,* mediated by Philo of Alexandria, and Gnostic" writers and resulting in a special "rabbinic Gnosis."[126] Yet J. Van der Ploeg finds the cosmological teachings already present in the Psalms.[127] The "mystique cosmologique" of the medieval Jewish *Berayta* is traced by N. Séd to the apocrypha of the first to fifth centuries, when it was shared by Jews and Christians.[128] It is significant that when Origen moved to Palestine he had to give up his use of the Apocrypha, which he had cited freely to his fellow Christians in his native Egypt.[129] He knows that the elders whom he cites were the original Christians, yet he has doubts about them and even about revelation in general. He always remains on the borderline: "When finally by the grace of God the saints shall reach

---

Figure 57. The pedantic Jesuit Athanasius Kircher included this version of the cabalistic Tree of the Sephiroth in his 1652 compendium of Counter-Reformation natural science, obligingly translating much of the information obtained from his Jewish sources. Each of the ten *sephiroth,* from "Kingdom" at the bottom to "Crown" at the top, have the ten attributes arranged like spokes of a wheel, reminding us of its origins in the traditions of the Merkabah, the golden Chariot of the Cherubim (1 Chronicles 28:18; cf. fig. 34C, p. 146). To ensure we don't miss the temple connection, he has inserted pictures of the Tabernacle furniture. We enter from the bottom, past the two altars and between the Table of Shewbread and the Menorah to the Tablets of the Law contained in the Ark surmounted by cherubim (as six cute little Italian *putti*). Predictably, the planets and letters of the alphabet are also identified with the *sephiroth,* showing the desperate attempt to create their own Unified Field Theory by synthesizing the many conflicting strands of Jewish mysticism with the tangible reality of the temple.

celestial places, then shall they comprehend all the secrets
of the stars; God will reveal to them the nature of the
universe, etc."[130] But the Hermetism of the schools breaks
through at the end of the passage when he commends
"perfect knowledge, purged of all that is physical and corporeal," and recommends Philo the Jew to his students,
"since the Scriptures are silent on the exact nature of the
heavens."[131] Having a foot in both camps led "Origen into
insuperable difficulties in Christology; . . . his 'aberrations,' " writes G. Florovsky, "were in fact the birth-pangs
of the Christian mind. His own system was an abortive
birth."[132] The *Third Epistle to the Corinthians* in the recently
discovered Papyrus Bodmer lists as the first and worst
offense of the Gnostics that they would not accept a physical resurrection or even a physical creation, and it is clear
from the famous Tractate XIII of the *Corpus Hermeticum* that
the essence of Gnosticism was that very spiritualizing of
everything. It was a major shift, and Hermeticism is a
transitional phenomenon. Thus, Augustine in the *Horten-
sius* tells us that astronomy was his favorite study, but he
gave it up entirely when he realized it would not save a
soul.

Concerning Tractate XIII that everyone cites, it is
agreed that it contains both gnostic and mystery elements.
Some, like Walter Scott, see in it a lesson in Platonic idealism; for H. Doerrie it was "a transposing of Platonic
philosophy into religious revelations," just as Karl Albert
sees in Plato's idealism a transposition of archaic cult practices into philosophy, taking Hermetism back to the very
beginning of things. For Reitzenstein, Tractate XIII was
indisputably of Iranian origin; H. Jonas said it was Egyptian, Quispel Alexandrian.[133] Recently discovered Coptic
texts are now being read as Hermetic.[134]

The *Sefer Yetzira*, whose author is unknown, is reputed
to be the oldest and most respected book of Jewish mysticism (commonly attributed to Abraham); apart from the

Bible and Talmud, it is probably the most discussed work of the Jewish national literature. To cite Louis Ginzberg, "There is a wide divergence of opinion regarding the age, origin, contents, and value of the book, since it is variously regarded as pre-Christian, Essene, Mishnaic, Talmudic, or geonic."[135]

Of special interest in America is Freemasonry. The most consistent thing about histories of Freemasonry by its most eminent historians is the noncommittal position in the important matter of origins. Freemasons are sure of where things come from. The surest support for their claims is what they call "the doctrine of chance coincidence," which is indeed the basic rule for all conflicting theories about the authenticity and value of Hermetism. In the inaugural address at the opening in 1886 of the famous Quatuor Coronati Lodge in London, dedicated to research in Masonic origins, Reverend Adolphus Woodford expresses it thus:

> To accept for one moment the suggestion that so complex and curious a system, embracing so many archaic remains, and such skilfully adjusted ceremonies, so much connected matter, accompanied by so many striking symbols, could have been the creation of a pious fraud or ingenious conviviality, presses heavily on our powers of belief, and over passes even the normal credulity of our species. It is, no doubt, true, that as the years have run on, this old and quaint ceremonial of ours has been modified, re-arranged, and, perhaps, modernized, here and there; but the traces of antiquity are too many to be overlooked or ignored.[136]

Woodford claims a Hermetic background for his mystery and defines Hermetism as "the profession and study of occult lore by a band of philosophers or adepts, whose last great outcome was the Rosicrucian Brotherhood."[137] He accepts Henry Morley's idea that "Hermetic Societies and notably the Rosicrucians . . . spread over Europe in the 14th and 15th centuries, calling themselves a fraternity, adepts, children of light, brethren."[138] In their secrecy and symbolism we may have a clue to much that seems difficult to account for in the peculiar existence of Freemasonry. "It is just possible," he continues in a highly speculative vein, "that Freemasonry may have been consciously or unconsciously . . . affected by various influences and controlled by various exigencies as time ran on. It may not have always borne the same outward form."[139] All in all, the most he can be sure of is that "there seems to have been a great analogy between hermetic and masonic use and teaching."[140] But then there was, as we have seen, a great analogy between Hermetic use and teaching and almost any other ancient or medieval conclave you choose to name. Woodford ends by noting that "Freemasonry, like everything else, is or has been evolutionary,"[141] and he quotes Gibbon, who refused to commit himself on the subject of ancient Masonry "by the apprehension of discovering [that it] had never existed."[142]

Albert Pike, one of the leading historians of the society, traces the rites to the Aryan mystery, and particularly to the *Zend Avesta,* the Iranian theory of Hermetism which had come into vogue at the time.[143] But Robert R. F. Gould, the principal historian of the order, did not believe the Hermetics and Rosicrucians were closely related at all.[144] On the other hand, Albert G. Mackey, in the *Encyclopedia of Freemasonry* (s.v. "Hermes"), claims that "in all the old manuscript records which contain the Legend of the Craft, mention is made of Hermes as one of the founders of Masonry."[145] As Woodford explains it, "The Hermetic School which passed from the East to the West . . . seems to have flourished from early times, and was in great vogue in the monasteries of medieval days."[146] To Hermes was attributed "the substratum of all occult speculations. . . . At a very early age they added the study of alchemy, . . . the search after the *Aurum Potabile,* Elixir of

Life, [and] . . . the Philosopher's Stone. . . . Astrology . . . became so mixed up with the reveries of the Hermetic School, . . . that it was eventually made a subject for ridicule."[147] Hence since the eighteenth century, discredited by a line of notorious characters such as Lully, St. Germaine, Cagliostro, etc., there has been a severance, so to say, between Freemasonry and Hermeticism.[148]

Freemasonry is defined in the *Coronati* account as "a peculiar system of morality, veiled in allegory and illustrated by symbols [fig. 58]."[149] According to the constitution drafted in 1721 by the Reverend James Anderson, "Masonry is non-sectarian and teaches humanistic morals, fraternity, and deistic beliefs," defining itself as "a secret organization for the erection of a spiritual temple of humanity in the heart of man."[150] "It is so far interwoven with religion, as to lay us under the obligation to pay . . . rational homage to the Deity, . . . to view . . . the glorious works of creation, and [it] inspires him [man] with the most exalted ideas of the perfections of his Divine Creator."[151] This is a poetic but not satisfying answer to the terrible questions. "Whence these doctrines were originally derived," writes A. G. Mackey, "it would be impossible to say—but I am disposed to accept Creuzer's hypothesis of an ancient and highly instructed body of priests, having their origin either in Egypt or in the East, from whom was derived religious, physical, and historical knowledge, under the veil of symbols." All quite romantic and glamorous, but nothing very definite. The *Coronati* statement sums it up in affirming that though all is unproven, "we believe, that in some form or other, some way or other, perhaps as yet hardly clear to the student, perhaps yet to be traced, . . . the old Craft Masons were our forebears,"[152] and that among their legends, that of the "Quatuor Coronati" itself is quite "confused and hazy, . . . adumbrated by no little uncertainty and considerable confusion of facts and names."[153] "As the tendency of masonry is essentially subjective," we read in the *Schaff-Herzog Encyclopedia*, "many internal dissensions arose," as well as "the most varied degrees of fantastic terminology and mysterious ceremonial."[154] Though much is made of Egypt—"much . . . of the present Masonic symbolism] can be traced to Egyptian counterparts and Egypt was the home of the 'Mysteries' " —according to Gould, "we doubt whether any connexion between modern Freemasonry and Egypt can be established."[155]

In all of this I cannot help recalling that for Eduard Meyer, who made by far the profoundest study of Mormonism of any non-Mormon, the most striking thing about Joseph Smith is the uncompromising, unwavering, explicit certainty of the things he taught and especially of the histories he introduced. Everything is concrete and straightforward, Meyer finds; whereas every other major religious founder went through a mandatory period of uncertainty and self-doubt, there is in Joseph Smith's behavior never a moment of doubt or hesitation as to what is what.

In his founding speech in London on January 12, 1886, Woodford challenged Masonic historians to search the

> Aryan sources, . . . the mystic symbolism of the Egyptian Book of the Dead, . . . hieratic *papyri*, . . . the *aporreta* of Greece and Rome, . . . Scandinavian *sagas*, . . . Teutonic mythology, . . . the communities of Greece

---

Figure 58. Called a trestle-board, this 1818 arrangement of symbols could be distributed publicly in books because only instructed Masons would be able to "read" the hidden messages of such common images as the all-seeing eye, the sun, the moon, the stars, etc. The coffin refers to the martyrdom of Hiram Abiff and the death of the initiate himself but also holds forth a promise of resurrection. The initiate ascends the steps, where stand Hiram Abiff, the temple architect; Hiram, king of Tyre; and King Solomon as Master Mason. The bronze pillars, Boaz and Jachin (cf. fig. 10B, p. 50, and fig. 37, pp. 150–51), support an arch from which hangs the letter G, symbolizing both God and the geometry by which he created the universe.

and the *collegia opificum* of Rome. [They must explore] medieval tendencies, Hermeticism, . . . the Craft Guilds [of the Middle Ages, etc.][156]

It is all very stirring, but how do you go about it? The Germans called their method *Wissenschaft*, of course, but it consisted solely of utterly authoritarian scholarly impressions, limited of course to the scope of one's own reading. Everyone decided for himself, and defended against all others his impression of what texts resemble each other, to what degree, and in what order of priority.

Joseph Smith restored what he called "the Ancient Order," the "Patriarchal Priesthood, . . . this 'holy order' of parents and children back to Adam."[157] It is "one eternal order . . . ever the same. The Saints cannot begin to comprehend it now, their minds being dark." With the Priesthood was "instituted the ancient order of things for the first time in these last days, . . . setting forth the order [of things] pertaining to the Ancient of Days."[158] It was the "ancient order" in its full pattern introduced for the first time, the Order of Melchizedek, "after the order of the covenant which God made with Enoch, it being after the order of the Son of God; which order came not by man" (JST, Genesis 14:27–28). "From time to time," said the prophet, "these glad tidings were sounded in the ears of men in different ages. . . . Certainly God spoke to him [Abel]; . . . and if He did, would He not . . . deliver to him the *whole* plan of the Gospel? . . . And if Abel was taught of the coming of the Son of God, was he not taught also of His ordinances?"[159] Joseph explained to the brethren the ordinances and covenants

> on to the highest order of the Melchizedek Priesthood, setting forth the order pertaining to the Ancient of Days, and all those plans and principles by which anyone is enabled to secure the fullness of those blessings which have been prepared for the church of the First Born, and come up and abide in the presence of the Eloheim in

the eternal worlds. In this council was instituted the ancient Order of things for the first time in these last days.

All these teachings are given "knowing assuredly that all these things referred to in this council are always governed by the principle of revelation."[160] The cosmic aspect of these mysteries was not neglected for, as Joseph said, "The ancients . . . were [not] so ignorant of the system of heaven as many suppose."[161]

No one knew better than Joseph Smith that sacred things could be corrupted and changed, surviving in various parts of the worlds in different degrees of purity. Those traditions are to be held in respect; Joseph reprimanded those who mocked the "old Catholic Church, . . . worth more than all" by the richness of the elements of the history of the ancient order it has preserved.[162] "Much instruction has been given to man since the beginning which we do not possess now," he said. "Does it remain for a people who never had faith enough to call down one scrap of revelation from heaven . . . to say how much God has spoken and how much He has not spoken?"[163]

In support of Rigdon's claims to the presidency, John C. Bennett produced what he said was a revelation on the subject. It is an enlightening document by reason of the striking differences when compared to the manner and language of Joseph Smith; the work of one straining to be awesome and impressive. Bennett hails Joseph Smith as one to be "a great king and imperial primate over all Israel," with Hyrum and Sidney as "viceroys in the executive dominion," and "the key of conquest [to] be given to Sidney," in Joseph's "establishment of the Halcyon Order, which excelleth all things heretofore given unto men." Particularly interesting is Emma's role in a new "kingdom holding the new keys, . . . and her illuminati, and her princes, and

her dukes, and her mighty men . . . shall be decorated
with gems and costly array, with diadems and great
glory."[164]

Precisely because the earth is filled with apostate or
defective versions of the true order, a vital function of the
priesthood was the key to distinguishing among them.
"Joseph Smith taught that these ordinances would serve
as a standard by which the subcelestial impurities of surviving remnants of earlier Gospel dispensations could be
judged."[165] The employment of such keys, according to the
prophet, was in "certain signs and words by which false
spirits and personages may be detected from true."[166]

Mormonism is not a Hermetic movement nor a descendant from any older dispensation of the church
through horizontal succession. It is interesting that the
terms *vertical* and *horizontal* succession are now being used
by theologians to distinguish between two types of tradition, the one by revelation, the other by inheritance.[167]
A Yale professor has recently given expression to the frustration of the Doctors in trying to pin down Mormonism:
"The exact significance of this great story persistently es-
capes definition. . . . One cannot even be sure if the object
of our consideration is a sect, a mystery cult, a new religion,
a church, a people, a nation, or an American sub-culture.
. . . [The] Mormons . . . remain a people apart. . . . Their
inner intellectual and spiritual problems cannot easily be
shared with others."[168]

To justify the title of this talk a quotation from the Book
of Mormon will make the connection: "For he that diligently seeketh shall find; and the mysteries of God shall
be unfolded unto them, by the power of the Holy Ghost,
as well in these times as in times of old, and as well in
times of old as in times to come; wherefore, the course of
the Lord is one eternal round" (1 Nephi 10:19).

Notes

1. C. J. Jung, "Transformation Symbolism in the Mass," in Joseph Campbell, ed., *The Mysteries* (New York: Pantheon, 1955), 291.

2. Lord Raglan, *The Origins of Religion* (London: Watts, 1949), 54.

3. Ibid., 58.

4. Ibid., 67.

5. Ibid., 43.

6. Hugh W. Nibley, "The Hierocentric State," *WPQ* 4 (June 1951): 226; reprinted in *CWHN* 10:99.

7. Mircea Eliade, *Cosmos and History: The Myth of the Eternal Return* (New York: Princeton University Press, 1954), xiv.

8. Raglan, *Origins of Religion*, 47–48.

9. Eliade, *Cosmos and History*, xiv.

10. Ibid., 7.

11. Ibid., 78.

12. Karl Albert, "Kult und Metaphysik bei Platon," *Studi Storico-Religiosi* 5/1 (1981): 11.

13. Mircea Eliade, "Cosmogonic Myth and 'Sacred History,' " in *The Quest: History and Meaning in Religion* (Chicago: University of Chicago Press, 1969), 75–76.

14. Richard Muir, *History from the Air* (London: Joseph, 1983), 42. Cf. Aubrey Burl, *Prehistoric Avebury* (London: Yale University Press, 1979).

15. Muir, *History from the Air*, 50.

16. Ibid., 51.

17. Ibid., 58.

18. Ibid., 67.

19. Marija A. Gimbutas, *The Goddesses and Gods of Old Europe* (Berkeley: University of California Press, 1982), 11–18.

20. Ibid., 12.

21. Ibid., 238.

22. Ibid., 66.

23. Ibid., 228, 230.

24. Ibid., 235.

25. Ibid., 132.

26. Giorgio de Santillana, *Origins of Scientific Thought* (Chicago: University of Chicago Press, 1961), 13.

27. Ibid., 19–20.

28. Ibid., 17.

29. Nibley, "The World of the Jaredites," *IE* 53/54 (September

1951–July 1952); and "There Were Jaredites," *IE* 59/60 (January 1956–February 1957); reprinted in *CWHN* 5:172–84; 285–307; 380–94.

30. Cf. Sir Mortimer Wheeler, *Archaeology from the Earth* (London: Penguin, 1956).

31. De Santillana, *Origins of Scientific Thought*, 10.

32. Ibid., 19.

33. Heraclitus, fragment 115; for an English translation, see G. T. W. Patrick, tr., *Heraclitus of Ephesus* (Chicago: Argonaut, 1968), 111.

34. *JD* 6:283–84.

35. Ibid., 17:141.

36. Ibid., 10:2.

37. Ibid., 10:224.

38. Ibid., 9:190–91.

39. Ibid., 8:319.

40. Ibid.

41. De Santillana, *Origins of Scientific Thought*, passim.

42. Spencer W. Kimball, "Fundamental Principles to Ponder and Live," *Ensign* 8 (November 1978): 44–45; cf. Joseph F. Smith, *Gospel Doctrine* (Salt Lake City: Deseret Book, 1973), 265.

43. Spencer W. Kimball, "The False Gods We Worship," *Ensign* 6 (June 1976): 3–6.

44. The 1832 recital of the First Vision as dictated by Joseph Smith to Frederick G. Williams. See Dean C. Jessee, *The Personal Writings of Joseph Smith* (Salt Lake City: Deseret Book, 1984), 3–8; Milton V. Backman, *Joseph Smith's First Vision* (Salt Lake City: Bookcraft, 1971), Appendix A; cf. Dean C. Jessee, ed., "The Early Accounts of Joseph Smith's First Vision," *BYUS* 9 (1969): 280.

45. *TPJS*, 57.

46. Ibid., 58.

47. Ibid., 59.

48. Ibid., 137.

49. Ibid.

50. Charles Webster, "William Dell and the Idea of University," in Mukuláš Teich and Robert Young, eds., *Changing Perspectives in the History of Science: Essays in Honour of Joseph Needham* (London: Heinemann Educational Books, 1973), 117–18.

51. Phillipe Derchain, *Le Papyrus Salt 825* (Bruxelles: Palais des Académes, 1965), 60.

52. Ibid., 19.

53. Ibid., 10.

54. Albert, "Kult und Metaphysik bei Platon," 10.

55. Ibid.

56. Fabio Mora, "I 'silenzi erodotei,' " *Studi Storico-Religiosi* 5/2 (1981): 222.

57. Plato, *Phaedrus* 274E-275.

58. Plutarch, *Über Isis und Osiris*, ed. and tr. Theodor Hopfner, 2 vols. (Darmstadt: Wissenschaftliche Buchgesellschaft, 1967), 2:37, 244–45.

59. A. Fodor, "The Origins of the Arabic Legends of the Pyramids," *Acta Orientalia* (Budapest) 23 (1970): 336.

60. Günther Roeder, ed. and tr., *Urkunden zur Religion des alten Ägypten* (Jena: Diederich, 1915), 155–56.

61. Eric Hornung, *Das Totenbuch der Ägypter* (Zürich: Artemis, 1979), 26.

62. Ibid., 38.

63. Iamblichus of Chalcis, *On the Mysteries* VIII, 2.

64. Herodotus II, 81. Cf. Walter Wili, "The Orphic Mysteries and the Greek Spirit," in Campbell, *Mysteries*, 64–92.

65. Philippe Derchain, *Revue d'histoire des religions* 161 (1962): 301.

66. Jacob Burckhardt, cited in Wili, "Orphic Mysteries and the Greek Spirit," 2:78.

67. Ibid., 82–83.

68. Hans Leisegang, "The Mystery of the Serpent," in Campbell, *Mysteries*, 209–10.

69. Leucon Agathias, "La mystique grecque," in M. Davy, ed., *Encyclopédie des mystiques* (Paris: Laffont, 1972), 38.

70. Frederick C. Copleston, *The Philosophy of Greece and Rome*, 2 parts (Doubleday: Image, 1962).

71. Ibid., 2:230.

72. Ibid., 2:232.

73. Ibid., 2:329.

74. Ibid., 2:241.

75. Ibid., 2:229.

76. Omar Khayyam, *Rubaiyat* XXVII, tr. Edward Fitzgerald (New York: Avon, n.d.).

77. Plato, *Republic* X, 614B-621D.

78. Plato, *Crito* 49A-54E.

79. Cf. Hugh W. Nibley, "Goods of First and Second Intent," *CWHN* 9:524–53.

80. Copleston, *Philosophy of Greece and Rome*, 2:41.

81. Ibid., 2:123.

82. Ibid., 2:166.

83. Ibid., 2:167.

84. Ibid., 2:168.

85. Ibid., 2:197.

86. Ibid., 2:198.

87. Ibid., 2:201; cf. Josephus, *Antiquities of the Jews* XIII, 5, 9.

88. Copleston, *Philosophy of Greece and Rome*, 2:205.

89. Ibid., 2:215–16.

90. Ibid., 2:216.

91. *TPJS*, 300.

92. Plotinus, *Enneads* I, 6, 8 (56G) quoted in Copleston, *Philosophy of Greece and Rome*, 2:216.

93. Ibid., 2:216.

94. Ibid., 2:221.

95. Ibid.

96. Ibid., 2:227–28, 230.

97. Mircea Eliade, ed., *The Encyclopedia of Religion*, 16 vols. (New York: Macmillan, 1987), 6:295–96.

98. Ibid., 6:297.

99. Ibid., 6:297–99.

100. Ibid., 6:300.

101. Allen G. Debus, "The Medico-Chemical World of the Paracelsians," in Teich and Young, eds., *Changing Perspectives in the History of Science*, 87.

102. Morris Kline, *Mathematics and the Search for Knowledge* (New York: Oxford Unvirsity Press, 1985), 45.

103. Charles H. Dodd, *The Bible and the Greeks* (London: Hodder and Stoughton, 1964), 244.

104. Debus, "The Medico-Chemical World of the Paracelsians," in Teich and Young, eds., *Changing Perspectives in the History of Science*, 91.

105. Ibid., 98.

106. Walter Pagel, "The Spectre of Van Helmont and the Idea of Continuity in the History of Chemistry," in Teich and Young, eds., *Changing Perspectives in the History of Science*, 103.

107. Ibid., 107.

108. Ibid., 106.

109. P. M. Rattansi, cited in Mary Hesse, "Reasons and Evaluation in the History of Science," in ibid., 132.

110. See Seth Ward, cited in Hesse, "Reasons and Evaluation in the History of Science," in ibid., 140, n. 19.

111. P. M. Rattansi, "Some Evaluations of Reason in Sixteenth- and Seventeenth-Century Natural Philosophy," in ibid., 149.

112. Ibid., 152.
113. Ibid., 152–53.
114. Ibid., 153.
115. Ibid.
116. Shakespeare, *The Merchant of Venice*, act V, scene i, lines 63–65.
117. Rattansi, "Some Evaluations of Reason in Sixteenth- and Seventeenth-Century Natural Philosophy," in Teich and Young, eds., *Changing Perspectives in the History of Science*, 155.
118. Ibid.
119. John Maynard Keynes, *Collected Writings*, 29 vols. (London: Macmillan, 1972), 10:369.
120. Ibid., 10:368–69.
121. Ibid., 10:363–64, 366.
122. Rattansi, "Some Evaluations of Reason in Sixteenth- and Seventeenth-Century Natural Philosophy," in Teich and Young, eds., *Changing Perspectives in the History of Science*, 164.
123. Ibid., 165–66.
124. Karl-Wolfgang Troeger, *Mysterienglaube und Gnosis in Corpus Hermeticum XIII* (Berlin: Akademie-Verlag, 1971), 3.
125. Adolphe Franck, *The Kabbala* (New York: Bell, 1940), 164.
126. Alexander Altmann, "A Note on the Rabbinic Doctrine of Creation," *Journal of Jewish Studies* 7 (1965): 195.
127. J. van der Ploeg, "Psalm XIX and Some of Its Problems," *Ex Oriente Lux* 17 (1963): 109–201.
128. Nicholas Séd, "Une cosmologie juive du haut Moyen Age la *bĕraytā dī macaseh bĕrēšīt*," *Revue des études juives* 3 (1964): 269–70, 260.
129. J. Ruwet, "Les apocryphes dans les oeuvres d'Origène," *Biblica* 25 (1944): 334.
130. Origen, *Peri Archon (De Principiis)* II, 11, 7, in *PG* 11:246.
131. Ibid.
132. G. Florovsky, "Eschatology in the Patristic Age: An Introduction," in *Studia Patristica*, vol. II (*Texte und Untersuchungen zur Geschichte der altchristlichen Literatur* 64) (Berlin: Akademie-Verlag, 1957), 244.
133. Troeger, *Mysterienglaube und Gnosis in Corpus Hermeticum XIII*, 6–7.
134. Especially *Nag Hammadi Codex* VI, Tracts 6–8; for an English translation and comments on their Hermetic nature, see "The Discourse on the Eighth and Ninth" (VI, 6), "The Prayer of Thanksgiving" (VI, 7) and "Asclepius 21–29" (VI, 8).

135. *Jewish Encyclopedia,* Isidore Singer, ed., 12 vols. (New York: Funk and Wagnalls, 1906), 12:603, s.v. "Sefer Yetzirah."

136. Adolphus Woodford, "Freemasonry and Hermeticism," *Ars Quatour Coronatorum* 1 (1886): 41.

137. Ibid., 39.

138. Ibid., 41.

139. Ibid.

140. Ibid., 42.

141. Ibid., 43.

142. Ibid.

143. Ibid., 44.

144. Ibid., 43–45.

145. Albert G. Mackey, *Encyclopedia of Freemasonry,* 2 vols. (New York: Masonic History, 1920), 1:322.

146. Woodford, "Freemasonry and Hermeticism," 38.

147. Ibid.

148. Ibid.

149. E. L. Hawkins, "Freemasonry," in James Hastings, ed., *Encyclopedia of Religion and Ethics,* 13 vols. (New York: Scribners, 1951), 6:120.

150. See James Anderson, *The Constitutions of the Free-masons* (London: Hunter, 1723).

151. Albert G. Mackey, *A Manual of the Lodge* (New York: Macoy and Sickels, 1865), 68.

152. Adolphus Woodford, "Oration," *Ars Quatuor Coronatorum* 1 (1888): 6.

153. Ibid.

154. Samuel M. Jackson, ed., *The New Schaff-Herzog Encyclopedia of Religious Knowledge,* 13 vols. (Grand Rapids, MI: Baker, 1977), 4:380.

155. Hawkins, "Freemasonry," in *Hastings Encyclopedia of Religion and Ethics,* 6:118.

156. Woodford, "Oration," 5.

157. Andrew F. Ehat, "Joseph Smith's Introduction of the Temple Ordinance and the 1844 Mormon Succession Question," M.A. thesis, Brigham Young University, 1982, 142.

158. *TPJS,* 237.

159. Ibid., 58–59 (emphasis added).

160. *HC* 5:2.

161. *TPJS,* 59.

162. Ibid., 375.

163. Ibid., 61.

164. Ehat, "Joseph Smith's Introduction of the Temple Ordinance," 220–22, n. 660.

165. Ibid., 24.

166. *HC* 4:608.

167. Hugh W. Nibley, *Since Cumorah* (Salt Lake City: Deseret Book, 1970), 101–4; reprinted in *CWHN* 7:89–91.

168. Sydney E. Ahlstrom, *A Religious History of the American People* (New York: Yale University Press, 1972), 508.

Do Religion and
History Conflict?

A true philosopher can no more pass by the open door of a free discussion than an alcoholic can pass by the open door of a saloon. Since my hosts have been kind enough to invite me to say what I think, the highest compliment I can pay to their tolerance and liberality will be to do just that. This is not going to be a debate. I would be the most unteachable of mortals if at this stage of life I still believed that one could get anywhere arguing with a dialectician. One might as well attempt to pacify or intimidate a walrus by tossing sardines at him as to bate a philosopher with arguments. I have accepted your kind invitation because I think the subject is worth discussing.

"Do Religion and History Conflict?" Only a philosopher would word a question so strangely. If history and religion are different things, as the question implies, isn't comparing them like comparing a rose and a submarine, or might we not ask as well whether free trade and tap-dancing conflict? All things—whether ideas or concrete objects—compete for our attention, but that is plainly not the kind of conflict our questioner has in mind. Nor are we asked whether the laws of history and religion conflict. Such laws as we have in history—fundamental principles such as propounded by Thucydides or Buckle or Speng-

This was originally published in Great Issues Forum, *Series 2 (Religion), No. 5 (Salt Lake City: University of Utah, Extension Division, 1955), 22–39.*

ler — are simply generalizations based on insight and analogy: there is nothing rigorous or binding about them. Furthermore, your religion may conflict with my history and my religion with your history; but for that matter your religion and mine probably conflict, as do your history and mine.

Still, I think we can agree that the idea behind the question is clear: does the story of man's life as taken from the documents, that is, his history, resemble the life story of the race as taught by revelation, i.e., in holy scriptures? The question is valid for all Christian sects and for non-Christian religions as well. The alternative to the general question is a chaos of special problems. Every church comes before the world with certain basic historic propositions peculiar to itself. Every church may be judged by those propositions when they are clearly stated: if a group announces that the end of the world is going to come on a certain day or, like Prudentius, predicts victory in a particular battle as proof of its divine leadership, or claims like the Mormons that there once was a prophet named Lehi who did such and such, we can hold that church to account. Incidentally, it will not do to project those accepted propositions into inferences and corollaries of your own, and then criticize their supporters in the light of those inferences and corollaries. We must be very careful to determine exactly what is claimed, by exactly what particular group, and then to determine exactly what happened and is happening. At this point the discussion breaks up into thousands of special topics, none of which could be handled here tonight.

The religions of the world take their stand on history to a far greater extent than is commonly realized. Christianity is by nature apocalyptic — a definite concept of world history is implicit in its teachings, its scriptures are at least half history, and it rests its whole case in the last analysis on the fulfillment of prophecy. My own church by its very name takes a definite historical stand: these are the "last days," not the end of the world, but a time of continual crisis and mounting world conflict accompanying the "wasting away of the nations." I would like to spend all the time in an historical vindication of my religion: but no general conclusions can be drawn from one personal case. Something more general is indicated.

In civilized societies it is customary for educated people to carry around in their heads two images of the past, present, and future world — the one religious, the other secular. Here we have two drawings of the same landscape: are they identical, is there a general resemblance between them, or are they in hopeless conflict? If one has attended a liberal Sunday School, the two pictures will tend to co-incide because they have, conscientiously, been made to coincide; the same is true if one has been trained in a fundamentalist school or college. It is apparent that both pictures are highly adjustable — there is an orthodoxy and a heresy in history as well as religion. History is as much what a man believes as his religion is. History vindicates the proposition that God loves the Jews; with equal force, if you want it that way, it vindicates the proposition that he hates them. History has long been taken as a superbly convincing illustration of the working out of the principle of evolution in human affairs; today some scholars see in it a smashing refutation of any such idea. History is the story of man's progress or his frustration, depending on how you want to read it.

If we are to judge our two pictures on the basis of artistic merit, that is, of subjective appeal, we are under no obligation to declare either one the better picture, nor, on artistic grounds, is there any reason why they should look alike. If, on the other hand, we are judging for ac-curacy (and that is what is here clearly implied), there is no point in comparing the pictures with each other; we must instead compare both with the original model. At once the nature of tonight's loaded question becomes apparent. For the obvious intent of the question is to test religion's claims in the light of historical discovery, or as the newspaper phrased the question, "Can religion face its own history without flinching?" There is no hint that history might flinch in the face of religion (as some historians have): the question proposes a beauty contest in which one of the contestants has already been awarded the prize, a litigation in which the prosecuting attorney happens to be the judge. History is above the storm; the only question is, Can religion take it?

That won't do. We cannot assume at the outset that either picture is perfect. We have no right to treat "history" as the true and accurate image of things. Like science and religion, history must argue its case on evidence. This body is like a jury: every member must do his own thinking and make up his own mind (that is the beauty of these meetings, we have been told), but only after viewing all the evidence. This is a staggering assignment, but no one can evade it and still form an intelligent opinion. Professor W. S. McCulloch, the authority on the mechanics of the brain at the Massachusetts Institute of Technology, has written: "[Man's] brain corrupts the revelation of his senses. His output of information is but one part in a million of his input. He is a sink rather than a source of information. The creative flights of his imagination are but distortions of a fraction of his data."[1] In other words, we all receive information much better than we report it; so much so, that however bad the evidence may be, it is always better than any man's report of it. Every juryman must examine and, if you will, distort the data for himself, whether we are dealing with special or general problems of history. The prospect is terrifying—and it is the historian, not the prophet, who flinches.

What we are up against may be illustrated by the case of a speaker in this series who maintained that there can be no true religious knowledge because one can never produce reliable evidence for it. He was such a ferocious stickler for evidence (and in that I enthusiastically agreed with him) that when he said three or four times that the Egyptians in 5,000 years produced nothing but the sheerest nonsense in religion and insisted on using that supposed fact as evidence for his most questionable claim (i.e., that religious teachings need not be true to be valuable), I could not help asking myself on what evidence he could possibly rest such a statement. Five thousand years is no small slice of history, and the Egyptians have left us a very respectable heap of documents. I remembered that a severe and exacting Egyptologist, T. E. Peet, had written:

> As long as our ignorance is so great, our attitude towards criticism of these ancient literatures must be one of extreme humility. . . . Put an Egyptian [or Babylonian] story before a layman, even in a good translation. He is at once in a strange land. The similes are pointless and even grotesque for him, the characters are strangers, the background, the allusions, instead of delighting, only mystify and annoy. He lays it aside in disgust.[2]

Our speaker was properly disgusted with the Egyptians, but to charge them with uttering nothing but nonsense for 5,000 years really calls for a bit of proof.

At the first opportunity I hastened to the stacks of your excellent library, hoping to find treasures indeed, and there discovered just one Egyptian book—a religious work, incidentally, which I value very highly. I looked for other Oriental treasures, the heritage of great world civilizations—and found nothing! Surely, I thought, we can't talk about history intelligently and leave all that stuff out. But that is precisely what we do! And that raises the all-important question for the student of history: Is there not some way of obtaining a reliable impression of the past, or of building a plausible structure of history without having to examine all the evidence? The problem that concerns our historians today is that of reducing the bulk of evidence without reducing its value. The futility of the quest is a corollary of the oft-proved proposition that the quality of history is a function of its quantity: the more information we have, the better our picture, and the rule is in no wise vitiated by the fact that some information is more valuable than other information.

The historian's problem was correctly formulated by the scholars of the Renaissance and Reformation. These men suddenly had an enormous heap of documents dumped in their laps. They were tremendously excited about the new treasure and saw immediately that the whole pile would have to be gone through piece by piece and word by word: there could be no question of priority or selectivity or elimination, because there is no divination by which one can tell what is in a document before one has read it. This is a lesson which modern scholars have forgotten. The only legitimate question is: "By what method can one properly examine the greatest possible amount of material in a single lifetime?" The challenge has small appeal to a hurried and impatient generation like our own. We look for easier and quicker solutions, as did the Sophists of old. And like them we find those solutions in the endless discussions and expensive eyewash of the university. Consider what goes on in the history business.

1. First, the academic mind wants neatness, tidiness, simplicity, order. It is impatient to impress an order upon nature without waiting for the real order of nature to become apparent. Historical events occur in an atmosphere of perplexity. Whether we are dealing with unique events or characteristic and repeated ones, as in culture-history, we are given no respite from the unexpected: we never know what hit us. The historian must always step in and impose order after the event. He is like a general who, having all but lost his shirt in a campaign, blandly announces when it is all over, "We planned it that way!"

History is all hindsight; it is a sizing up, a way of looking at things. It is not what happened or how things really were, but an evaluation, an inference from what one happens to have seen of a few scanty bits of evidence preserved quite by accident. There is no such thing as a short, concise history of England, any more than there is an authentic three-minute version of Beethoven's Ninth Symphony. One might construct such a thing, and it might be a work of art in its own right, but it could only be a parody of the real thing—a pure fiction.

As I read the journal of Samuel Sewall, the letters of Cicero, the memoirs of Joinville or Froissart or Xenophon or Ibn Baṭṭūṭa, I cannot but feel myself getting involved in exciting and vivid situations that will forever be as much a part of my experience as, say, the invasion of Normandy (I still remember what I read in Normandy as vividly as what I saw there). But if I read a paragraph or a sentence or two about each of the above in a college textbook, I have really had no experience at all. Yet it is not in those great neglected writers that the most valuable evidence is found, but rather in such completely neglected trivia as letters, diaries, notebooks, ledgers, etc., which few historians and no others ever care to look at.

2. The modern college teaches us, if nothing else, to accept history on authority. Yet at the end of his life the great Eduard Meyer (who wrote a history of the Mormons, incidentally), marveled that he had always been most wrong where he thought he was most right, and vice versa. No man of our time had a broader view of world history than Professor Breasted, or was ever more dogmatically sure of himself or, in the light of subsequent discoveries, more completely wrong. To be open-minded in history one must be working constantly at one's own structure of history, not passively accepting any second-hand solution or textbook opinion that floats down from the shining heights, as crabs and mollusks in the depths gratefully

receive the dead and predigested matter that descends to them from luminous realms above. Everybody knows some history, nobody knows very much. Your *strengwissenschaftliche Geschichte* ("strictly scientific history") is nowhere to be found. Ranke tried for it, but I believe with the historian Frowde that our best historian was Shakespeare.

3. The insights of men like Taine, Mommsen, or Bury are not to be despised. Do not for a moment think that the only reliable evidence comes from brass instruments. But insight offers no escape from evidence. Insight requires in fact to be properly checked by the most exhaustive evidence of all—that which comes only by constant, intimate, lifelong familiarity with the sources. There is no more merit in armchair humanities than there is in armchair science: the learner must come to grips with the real thing at first hand; he must run the evidence to ground as in a laboratory and never be content with the fourth-hand hearsay of a textbook or the private evaluations of a translator.

4. The most popular attempt to grasp history at a gulp is the Cook's Tour, for which Mr. Toynbee's lumbering and laboring rubberneck bus is at present in great demand—though no one really seems to enjoy riding in it. Here the interest is in the monumental, the routine, the conventional, the accepted. The student is a tourist, a spectator, always detached, never allowing himself to become emotionally involved except at the prescribed stations where the guidebook instructs him to swoon. At best our college humanities are a sentimental journey, a scenic-postcard world of the obvious and theatrical: the Great Books, the Hundred Best Poems, the Greatest Works of the Greatest Minds, etc. What makes the study of history possible today I call the Gas Law of Learning, namely, that any amount of information, no matter how small, will fill any intellectual void no matter how large. It is as easy to write a history of the world after you have read ten books

as after you have read a thousand—far easier, in fact. This is the historian's dilemma: if his view is sweeping enough to be significant, it is bound to be inadequately documented; if it is adequately documented, it is bound to be trivial in scope. It is a cozy and reassuring thing for student and teacher alike to have our neat authoritarian College Outline Series Syllabi of Western Civilization, Surveys of Great Minds, and what not, to fall back on. But please don't point to these pedestrian exercises in skimming and sampling and try to tell me that they are a valid refutation of the prophets!

5. To handle problems requiring data beyond the capacity of students and educators impatient to shine, the ancient Sophists devised certain very effective discussion techniques. In these, the most important skill was that of presenting evidence by implication or inference only. Since it is quite impossible in a public discourse (or in print, for that matter) to put all one's evidence on display, one must be allowed on occasion to present one's knowledge merely by inference. The Sophists seized upon this welcome path of escape from drudgery, and by the arts of rhetoric made of it a broad highway to successful teaching careers. A limited use of jargon is indispensable in any field: having solved for "x," we do not have to derive "x" every time it is mentioned, but simply to indicate it by a symbol, such as those useful keywords commonly used to power historical discussions: the Medieval Mind, Sturm und Drang, the Frontier, Hellenism, the Enlightenment, Puritanism, the Primitive, Relativity, etc., each of which is supposed to set a whole chorus of bells chiming in our heads—the echoes of deep and thorough reading. But by a familiar process these labels are no mere labels anymore; they have become the whole substance of our knowledge. The student today has never solved for that "x" about which he talks so glibly—he has got its value from an answerbook; the cue word is not just a cue; it is now the whole play.

The stock charge against the philosophers in every age has been that they have made themselves experts in the manipulation of labels to the point where they live in a world of words. The art of implying the possession of certain knowledge without actually claiming it has become one of the great humanistic skills of our time, in Europe as well as America. Without it the teaching of history would be almost impossible.

My own self-confidence in sounding off on historical matters need not reflect any solid knowledge at all, but may well be the product of a careful grooming, a calculated window dressing. Today the typical academic historian does most of his training before a mirror. The modern world, like the ancient, is a world peopled largely by zombies. Occasions like this one tonight are not meant to teach but to impress. If it was knowledge we were after, we would all at this time be perusing the evidence, not listening to me.

The confusion of discussion-born ideas with evidence is the root of much trouble in education today. People wishing to be liberal demand that their ideas be given the authority of evidence with the general public and in the classroom. If we refuse to accept those ideas, however hackneyed and unobjectionable they may be, as legal tender in an economy where only evidence passes as such, they complain that their ideas are being held in contempt and that they are being persecuted — which is not true at all.

6. What about those great historical systems which the giants have erected from time to time — do not such give a faithful picture of the world? Alas, system is the death of history! The great historians have all been random readers. Werner Jaeger has said, "It must never be forgotten that it was the Greeks who created and elaborated not only the general ethical and political culture in which we have traced the origin of our own humanistic culture, but also

what is called practical education and is sometimes a competitor, sometimes an opponent of humanistic culture."[3] One builds systems by excluding as well as including. When you choose to build one structure rather than another you are not merely rearranging materials in new combinations, you are emphasizing some things at the expense of others. Excluding or suppressing evidence is dangerous business, and what makes it doubly dangerous is the way in which systems of history by their very exclusiveness convey a powerful and perfectly false sense of all-inclusiveness. The product of the System is the closed mind, the student who has taken the course and knows the answers, who has been systematically bereft of the most priceless possession of the inquiring mind—the sense of possibilities.

"The Bible excels in its suggestion of infinitude," said Whitehead and, as a friend describes it, "suddenly he stood and spoke with passionate intensity, *'Here we are with our finite beings and physical senses in the presence of a universe whose possibilities are infinite, and even though we may not apprehend them, those infinite possibilities are actualities.'* " Later he added, "I doubt if we get very far by the intellect alone. I doubt if intellect carries us very far."[4] The study of history in the schools today, with its "intellectual" orientation, effectively stifles that very sense of possibilities which it is the duty of history before all else to foster. For every door it opens, our modern education closes a thousand. We cannot insist too emphatically on the endless mass, variety, detail, and scope of historical evidence; every page of every text is a compact mass of a thousand clues, and every reading full of new and surprising discoveries. That is the essence of history, and the modern academic presentation completely effaces it. The modern scholar is eager to reach his conclusion, get his degree, and stop his investigations before there is any danger of running into contradictions. From a safe and settled position he wants only to discuss and discuss and discuss. The *via scholastica* is well marked: first one takes a sampling, merely a sampling, of the evidence; then as soon as possible one forms a theory (the less the evidence the more brilliant the theory); from then on the scholar spends his days defending his theory and mechanically fitting all subsequent evidence into the bed of Procrustes.

7. But surely there is a general overall picture of history, or some really basic points, upon which a massive consensus exists. Surely the verdict can be imparted to students in a few lessons, and it must be fairly reliable. There is a charming study by the Swede Olaf Linton on the basic certitudes of church history in the nineteenth and twentieth centuries—what he calls the Consensus with a capital "C." Mr. Linton shows us how the consensus changes with time and circumstances just as completely and just as surely as the fashions in women's hats. The Homeric question furnishes us with a good illustration of present-day consensus. What we call higher criticism is the application to the Bible of methods of textual criticism developed in the study of the Homeric problem. That problem is really far simpler than the biblical (there is hardly a book in the Bible that is not as mysterious as Homer), yet after 200 years of intensive investigation where do we stand? Listen to Professor Wade-Gery of Oxford: "Homer, who wrote the *Iliad* as I believe sometime in the eighth century, . . . lived (as I believe) in Chios, and knew the Eighth City of Troy. He was (as I also believe) a man of exceptional genius. . . . I feel sure that almost all which makes the *Iliad* a great poem is the poet's own creation."[5] And listen to Professor Whatmough of Harvard in the same issue of the same journal:

> Nothing is, or could be, more puerile than the notion that the *Iliad* could possibly have been composed by one man. . . . The complex descent (rather than "origin") of Homer's *Iliad* and *Odyssey* is as certain as anything can

be in this very uncertain world. . . . I know [of] no competent linguist . . . whose knowledge of Greek and Greek dialects I respect enough to quote his name, who holds any other opinion. . . . To use the term author or authorship . . . is simply to sin against the light.[6]

Note it well: "As certain as anything can be." Yet a host of big names are quite convinced of the opposite! The consensus has its fads and fashions like everything else.

As for the scientific consensus, with all its vaunted objectivity, let us hear Whitehead again:

In those years from the 1880s to the first war, who ever *dreamed* that the ideas and institutions which then looked so stable would be impermanent? . . . Fifty-seven years ago . . . I was a young man in the University of Cambridge. I was taught science and mathematics by brilliant men and I did well in them; since the turn of the century I have lived to see every one of the basic assumptions of both set aside; not, indeed, discarded, but of use as qualifying clauses instead of as major propositions; and all this in one life-span, the most fundamental assumptions of supposedly exact sciences set aside. And yet, in the face of that, the discoverers of the new hypotheses in science are declaring, *"Now at last, we have certitude"* — when some of the assumptions which we have seen upset had endured for more than twenty centuries.[7]

And but a few months ago Professor McCulloch wrote:

At last we are learning to admit ignorance, suspend judgment, and forego the *explicatio ignoti per ignotius* — "God" — which has proved as futile as it is profane. . . . So long as we, like good empiricists, remember that it is an act of faith to believe our senses, . . . and that our most respectable hypotheses are but guesses open to refutation, so long may we "rest assured that God has not given us over to thraldom under that mystery of iniquity, of sinful man aspiring into the place of God."[8]

I can answer the question "Do religion and history conflict?" for myself, but not for anyone else. At present, my religion and history do not conflict, as once they did. Well, you say, of course they agree because you make them agree. That is not entirely true. There are controls. Within the last three or four years leading Jewish and Christian scholars have been forced to relinquish a concept of history which they had painfully built up through the decades to an almost perfect consensus. Some of them put up a magnificent fight, but in the end the evidence was too strong, and one by one they gave in. It is a healthy sign when religion and history conflict: it means that they are not being bent wilfully to force them into agreement. In most historical fields the difficulty of the languages in which the sources are written is enough in itself to guarantee the minimum of intellectual integrity in the researcher: the documents simply refuse to speak unless one approaches them with a really open mind and is willing to swallow his pride and suppress self-will. In much the same way the rigorous demands of mathematics guarantee a measure of honesty in any scientist who is equipped to work in a field.

But unfortunately there are no such controls in those more socialized fields of learning which, for that very reason, have completely banished the older disciplines from our secondary schools and supplanted them at the university by pretentious techniques of discussion and pseudo-scientific "quantification of the obvious." In such an atmosphere it is futile to attempt a serious discussion of history.

I believe my history and religion agree in a way that is objective enough to justify my conviction that the agreement is not entirely the result of my own manipulating. But whether this agreement is significant or not must be decided by everyone for himself, on his own examination of the evidence. As to the general question, "When do we flinch?" the answer is: Wait until history comes up with all the answers, or with any answer we can be entirely sure of — then we will know whether to flinch or not. Meantime, it is the historian's duty (for it is he who appeals to an uncompromising objectivity) to flinch every time an answer of his proves defective — which is, roughly, on the hour every hour.

Does life on the moon resemble life on Mars? It is a good question, but premature. When I was a little boy we used to sit in a tent on hot summer afternoons and debate loudly and foolishly on just such lofty themes as this one. I think we all felt vaguely uncomfortable about the whole thing, and that made us all the more excitable, dogmatic, and short-tempered. The trouble was that we were not yet ready; we did not have the necessary knowledge. But when would we be ready? Are we ready yet? If not, we should stop playing this game of naughty boys behind the barn, smoking cornsilk and saying damn and hell to show how emancipated we are. It is much too easy to be a "swearing elder": knowledge is not so cheaply bought. We are not free to discuss any imaginable question simply because we say we are. I am not permitted to discuss botany with anybody, at any time or place; it is not the jealousy of a reactionary society or the dictates of a narrow church that cramp my style — I just don't happen to know anything about botany. Prejudice, says Haldane, consists in having an opinion before examining all the evidence. If anyone draws any conclusions but one here tonight, they must needs be prejudiced conclusions. If we have gathered here to read lectures to each other or to the Mormon Church, we might as well spare our breath; or if you are looking for a stick to beat the Church with, my advice is, leave history out of it — it will come apart in your hands. For our knowledge of the past is too trivial to serve as an effective instrument in real situations — that is why it is often appealed to but never actually used.

What do we have then? Well, I have a testimony: I may be ignorant, but I am not lost. Socrates counted a life well spent that ended only with the discovery that he knew nothing. That was not a figure of speech or a clever paradox: that was his solemn testimony delivered in the hour of his death. And if the most profitable activity of the mind is that which leads to the discovery of its own ignorance and ineptitude, we can all take heart in the thought that we have not entirely wasted our time in coming here tonight. At this point we can begin the study of the gospel; there is no further need for waiting around until "history" can make up its mind.

Notes

1. W. S. McCulloch, "Mysterium Iniquitatis of Sinful Man Aspiring in the Place of God," *Scientific Monthly* 80 (1955): 39.

2. T. E. Peet, *A Comparative Study of the Literatures of Egypt, Palestine, and Mesopotamia* (London: Schweich Lectures, 1931), 6, 12–13.

3. Werner Jaeger, *Paidea*, 3 vols. (New York: Oxford, 1945), 1:317.

4. Lucien Price, "To Live without Certitude: Dialogues of Whitehead," *Atlantic Monthly* 193 (March 1954): 58–59.

5. H. T. Wade-Gery, "What Happened in Pylos?" *American Journal of Archaeology* 52 (1948): 115–16.

6. Joshua Whatmough, "Hosper Homeros Phesi," *American Journal of Archaeology* 52 (1948): 45–46.

7. Price, "To Live without Certitude," 58; cf. Lucien Price, "Visit and Search: Dialogues of Whitehead," *Atlantic Monthly* 193 (May 1954): 53: "I had a good classical education, and when I went up to Cambridge early in the 1880's my mathematical training was continued under good teachers. Now nearly everything was supposed to be known about physics that could be known — except a few spots, such as electromagnetic phenomena which remained (or so it was thought) to be coordinated with the Newtonian principles. But, for the rest, physics was supposed to be nearly a closed subject. Those investigations to coordinate went on through the next dozen years. By the middle of the 1890's there were a few tremors, a slight shiver as of all not being quite secure, but no one sensed what was coming. By 1900 the Newtonian physics were demolished, done for! Still speaking personally, it had a profound effect on me; I have been fooled once, and I'll be damned if I'll be fooled again!"

8. McCulloch, "Mysterium Iniquitatis of Sinful Man," 36, 39.

Genesis of the Written Word

The most interesting thing about this article is that, within a month after it was printed, a cover story appeared in the prestigious journal Science *recounting the strange achievement of an Apache Indian by the name of Silas John, who not only claimed to have had a whole writing system revealed to him in a dream for holy purposes, but actually produced the system, which turns out to be a highly efficient one; an instant alphabet, not out of nothing, but out of a dream.[1] If it could happen in 1904 to a semi-literate Apache, could it not have happened earlier?*

Only such evidence could break the vicious circular argument which has long prevented serious investigation into the origins of writing. Many writers in scientific journals have recently deplored the way in which scientific conclusions reached long ago and held as unimpeachable truths turn students away from avenues of research which might well prove most fruitful. The evolutionary rule-of-thumb—convenient, satisfying, universal—is cited as the prime offender. Here is a test of how it works: Ask your students to write a paper on "A Day in the Life of a Primitive Man." None of them has ever seen a primitive man or ever will, but does that stop them? Before the question is on the board they are off and running and can go on writing at top speed indefinitely. They all know exactly how it should have been; evolution emancipated them from the drudgery of research. And in all of science

This was first delivered as the Commissioner's Lecture in 1972 and was published by BYU Press in 1973. It was later reprinted (without the complete footnotes) in New Era 3 *(September 1973): 38–50, and in* Nibley on the Timely and the Timeless *(Provo, Brigham Young University Religious Studies Center, 1978), 101–27, with the preface included above.*

there never was a more open-and-shut case than the origin of writing: intuitively we know it must have begun with pictures, and traditionally we know it can have developed in only one way—very slowly and gradually from simple to more complex forms, and all that. Some may elaborate on the theme with tree-alphabets, ogams, runes and (as we have) arrow-markings, but if there ever was a hypothesis which enjoyed complete and un-questioning obedience, the origin of writing has been it. Yet the discerning Kipling, taking a hard common-sense look at the official solution, found it simply absurd. It is the same hypothesis that we now dare to question, grateful for the support of the noble Silas John.

We have all grown up in a world nurtured on the comfortable Victorian doctrine of uniformitarianism, the idea that what happens in this world is all just more of the same: what lies ahead is pretty much what lies behind, for the same forces that are at work on the earth today were at work in the same manner, with the same intensity and the same effects at all times past and will go on op-erating inexorably and irresistibly in just the same way forever hereafter. There is no real cause for alarm in a world where everything is under control beneath the watchful eye of science, as evolution takes its undeviating forward course, steady, reliable, imperceptibly slow and gentle, and gratifyingly predictable. According to an eminent Brit-ish scholar of the 1920s,

> The skies as far as the utmost star are clear of any malignant Intelligences, and even the untoward acci-dents of life are due to causes comfortably imper-sonal. . . . The possibility that the Unknown contains Powers deliberately hostile to him is one the ordinary modern man can hardly entertain even in imagination.[2]

In such a world one needed no longer to run to God for comfort. The matter-of-fact, no-nonsense approach of science had since the days of the Miletian school and the ancient atomists banished all childish fears and consigned the horrendous and spectacular aspects of the human past and future to the realm of myth and fantasy.

Quite recently, however, scientists have noted with a shock that in looking forward not to the distant but to the immediate future what they discern is not just more of the same but something totally different, something for which they confess themselves entirely unprepared, since it is all entirely unexpected.[3] The idea that what lies ahead is by no means the simple and predictable projection of our knowledge of the present has, as John Lear points out, reconditioned our minds for another look at the past as well as the future. Since the past is wholly a construction of our own imaginations, we have always found there just what we expected to find, that is, more of the same. But now "future shock" has prepared us for "past shock," and we find ourselves almost forced to accept a view of the past that is utterly alien to anything in the experience of modern man.[4]

Antiquity of Writing

Joseph Smith as a prophet also looked both ahead and behind and came up with a picture of both worlds that violently shocked and offended his Victorian contemporaries. He presented his peculiar picture of the past in the most daring possible way, in the form of a number of books which he claimed to be of ancient origin, their contents given to him "by the Spirit." But his image of the future and the past was not conveyed in mystical utterances in the manner of Swedenborg, Jakob Boehme, or the "Urantia Volume," whose assertions may be tested only by waiting for history to catch up with them. His story was rather to be found in the pages of ancient books that purportedly existed and either still survived in the world or had left unmistakable marks behind them.

In the first lesson of the current Melchizedek Priesthood manual President Joseph Fielding Smith brings this formidable contribution to our attention:

> The Latter-day Saints are doubly blessed with the word of the Lord which has come to light through the restoration of the gospel. We have been given the records of the Nephites and the Jaredites. . . . The Lord restored much that had been originally revealed to Adam and Enoch and Abraham, . . . and it is to their condemnation when members of the Church do not take advantage of their opportunities to read, study, and learn what the records contain.[5]

Few people realize that in Joseph Smith's day *no* really ancient manuscripts were known. Egyptian and Babylonian could not be read; the Greek and Latin classics were the oldest literature available, preserved almost entirely in bad medieval copies no older than the Byzantine and Carolingian periods. The oldest text of the Hebrew Bible was the Ben Asher Codex from the ninth century A.D. Today we have whole libraries of documents more than 4,000 years old—not just their contents, but the actual writings themselves going back to the very beginnings of civilization. It is just as easy to dig back 6,000 years as it is to remove the dust of 5,000 years; and when we do so, what do we find in the way of written documents? Let us consider three main points: (1) what can be inferred from Joseph Smith's statements as to the nature of the oldest human records, (2) what the ancients themselves have to say about those records, and (3) what the actual condition of the records indicates.

First, if Joseph Smith is right, the written records should be as old as the human race itself, for, he tells us, "a book of remembrance was kept . . . in . . . the language of Adam" (Moses 6:7).[6] Now what do the ancients themselves have to say on the subject? Surprisingly, a great deal, of which we can give only a few quotations here.

According to them, the king had access to that divine book which was consulted at the time of the creation of the world: "I am a scribe of the god's book," says one of the earliest pharaohs, "who says what is and brings about what is not."[7] A later but still ancient (Thirteenth Dynasty) pharaoh recalls, "My heart yearned to behold the most ancient books of Atum. Open them before me for diligent searching, that I may know god as he really is!"[8] Over the lintel of the ancient library of the great temple at Edfu was a relief showing four kneeling figures giving praise to the heavenly book descending to earth; hieroglyphs above their heads show them to represent *Sia* and *Ḥw*, or the Divine Intelligence and the Divine Utterance (the Word) by which the world was created (fig. 59).[9] In Egypt every step of the founding of a new temple had to follow the prescriptions given in the heavenly book, since such a founding represented and dramatized the creation of the earth itself.

And what does the actual state of the documents attest? If writing evolved gradually and slowly as everything is supposed to have done, there should be a vast accumulation of transitional scribblings as countless crude and stumbling attempts at writing would leave their marks on stone, bone, clay, and wood over countless millennia of groping trial and error. Only there are no such accumulations of primitive writing anywhere. Primitive writing is as illusive as that primitive language, the existence of which has never been attested. And indeed the very nature of writing precludes anything in the way of a slow, gradual, step-by-step evolution: one either catches on to how it is done or one does not, and once one knows, the whole mystery lies revealed. All the evidence shows that that is the way it actually was. "Suddenly . . . graves in the predynastic cemeteries" display "the art of writing . . . with a fairly long period of development behind it," writes Engelbach. "In fact it was writing well past the stage of picture

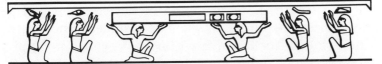

Figure 59. Two kneeling *Heh* gods representing "millions of years" support the scribal palette while four other gods representing all that is heard, seen, touched, and understood lift their arms in adoration.

Figure 60. On the famous slate palette (A), c. 2900 B.C., on which malachite was ground for eye makeup, much as ink was ground, the king's name, Narmer, is clearly legible. This Fifth Dynasty scribe (B) of "nimble fingers" has two extra reed pens behind his ear; the sign for scribe is written in front, showing the pen case and two cakes of red and black ink. Hundreds of seemingly crude ivory labels have been found on Old Kingdom stone jars (C). This one may refer to the heliacal rising of the star Sirius and the royal capital.

writing."[10] Both the long period of development and a primal picture writing must here be assumed, since there is no evidence for them. If writing did evolve in Egypt, the process took only "a few decades," after which the art remained unchanged "for thousands of years," according to Capart.[11] Alan Gardiner notes the same strange and paradoxical state of affairs: hieroglyphic "was a thing of rapid growth," but "once established remained immutable for fully 3,000 years."[12] So also A. Scharff assures us that with the First Dynasty "writing was introduced and perfected (*ausgebildet*) with astounding speed and detail."[13] "There is no evidence of a *gradual* development of script in Egypt," writes Elise Baumgartel,[14] and yet there is no evidence of that script anywhere else. There is something wrong with this evolutionary process by which one and the same people develop a system of writing almost overnight, and then refuse to budge an inch on the way of progress forever after. Stuart Piggott finds that *immediately* after "ambiguous stammerings . . . on the slate palettes . . . a rapid cursive form of writing with pen and ink" is in evidence.[15] Stranger still, on the most famous of those predynastic slate palettes with their ambiguous stammerings that suggest only the dawn of writing we see clearly depicted a king (Narmer) following behind an attendant (*ṭṭ*) who is carrying the classic two inkpots of the Egyptian scribe (fig. 60). The tombs of the First Dynasty "show that they had a well-developed written language, a knowledge of the preparation of papyrus."[16] Inscriptions found on tags and labels of First-Dynasty jars, often regarded because of their crudeness and brevity as primitive attempts at writing, are crude and brief because they were meant to be identification tags and nothing more—not literary compositions; actually, as Sethe points out, "they are written in a sophisticated cursive writing."[17] For though "hieroglyphics appear all at once in the world as an Egyptian

invention cir. 3000 B.C.," hieratic, the cursive writing of
the same symbols, was also in use just as early.[18]

Complexity of Nascent Languages

All of which is most retrograde to tenaciously held
theories of the evolution of writing in Egypt. But how about
the rest of the world? Wherever we look the earliest systems of writing are somehow connected with the Egyptian
and appear suddenly in the same paradoxical way. Though
there is "a prehistoric connection with Babylonian cuneiform" and Egyptian, according to Sethe,[19] and though J.
Friedrich has demonstrated the connection by an impressive catalogue of striking parallels,[20] the gap between the
two systems is still too wide to allow any thought of deriving the one from the other.[21] "The writing which appeared without antecedents at the beginning of the First
Dynasty (in Egypt) was by no means primitive," writes
Frankfort. "It has, in fact, a complex structure of . . .
precisely the same state of complexity which had been
reached in Mesopotamia. . . . To deny . . . that Egyptian
and Mesopotamian systems of writing are related amounts
to maintaining that Egypt invented independently a complex and very consistent system at the very moment of
being influenced in its art and architecture by Mesopotamia
where a precisely similar system had just been developed."[22] Not only are these two systems related, but they
show remarkable affinities to the earliest Chinese writing,[23]
as well as the Hittite, proto-Indian,[24] and proto-Elamitic
scripts.[25] P. Mordell insists that the Hebrew alphabet is
related to an Egyptian linear writing system, a real alphabet, which "evolved at a date when hieroglyphic writing
was unknown, then persisted with a strange vitality, and
was never absorbed or ousted."[26] This was that mysterious
prehistoric "Mediterranean" alphabet which is said to be
older than hieroglyphic,[27] and which suddenly spread all

over the Near East at the end of the second millennium B.C.[28]

"Evolved"? Many scholars have pointed out that the alphabet is the miracle of miracles, the greatest of all inventions, by which even the television and jet-planes pale in comparison, and, as such, a thing absolutely unique in time and place; they also agree that it was of Egyptian or West-Semitic origin.[29] It is also argued that by the very nature of the thing it can only have been the work of a single inventor.[30] "The gulf between the idea and the written word," writes H. Schmitt, "could only have been bridged once, by a miracle of invention."[31]

Dearth of Evolutionary Clues

Given the evolutionary hypothesis, any healthy normal growing boy can describe in convincing detail how long ago "the naive child of nature" everywhere drew crude pictures to convey his simple thoughts,[32] and how out of this the process moved "everywhere inexorably . . . towards the final stage, the alphabetic writing."[33] To save our eager high-school student from undue embarrassment, we have just quoted two eminent scholars. But if it really happened that way, then we would find traces of evolving writing "everywhere"; veritable middens of scratched rock and bones and shells would attest the universal groping toward the inexorable final stage over tens of thousands of years, while the clumsy transitional forms should outnumber proper writing by at least a million to one. However, the vast accumulations of attempts at writing simply do not exist; there is no evidence whatever of a worldwide groping towards the goal. Having made his lucid and logical statement, the author of our last quotation observes with perplexity that "it is surprising that the ultimate stage in evolution . . . was only achieved in a very few spots on the globe."[34] That is, we do not find a multiplicity of writing systems throughout the world; in fact when we come right down to it there seems to have been only one! We find "only a very few systems of writing," says David, ". . . and even these are so much alike and so closely related in time and space that their independence appears at least problematical."[35] The vast world-wide corpus of embryonic scribblings that should attest the long ages of slow transition from picture writing to true writing simply is not there, and the innumerable systems of writing which must have resulted from the basic psychological need of men everywhere to express themselves can be counted on the fingers, and most probably on the thumbs, of one hand.

Pictures Not Origin of Writing

People have always drawn pictures, but was that the origin of writing? Was there ever a real picture writing? E. Doblhofer defines "pictorial writing," which he says is "incredibly ancient," as "a series of images [which] can possibly be 'read' accurately by any spectator."[36] Kurt Sethe would agree: a "pure" picture writing is one which "could be read in any language at sight."[37] And right here the issue is settled: if there ever was a true picture writing it has not yet been discovered. Where on earth is a single inscription to which any and all beholders, scholars or laymen alike, regardless of their own language and culture, would give the identical interpretation? When Sethe sought for a true picture writing to illustrate the process by which hieroglyphic emerged, the only examples he could find in all the world were North American Indian petroglyphs, which no one can "read" or interpret to this day.[38] "True picturewriting," wrote Alan Gardiner, "makes excessive demand upon the skill and ingenuity of the writer, and its results are far from unambiguous."[39] It takes special skill, that is, to execute "true picturewriting" and special skill to read it: which is to say that it is not the simple and uninhibited drawing and viewing of pictures at all. Doblhofer himself confirms this when he assures us

that "the *most primitive* pictorial writings . . . translate . . .
abstract ideas with the aid of *symbolical signs*," for symbolical signs are not plain pictures but conventional devices
which must be learned; that is, even "the most primitive"
picture writing is not just picture writing as he defines it.[40]
In the very earliest Egyptian writing it is impossible to
interpret the pictures as such, and there is no evidence of
pictograms in Egypt at any time, according to Sethe.[41] Also,
we must not forget that along with the most "primitive"
Egyptian writing in prehistoric times we find a genuine
alphabetic writing flourishing most paradoxically.[42] Long
wrestling with the problem of deriving the alphabet from
a syllabic writing, that is, from a system in which the names
of things depicted supplied certain sound combinations,
has led to the general conclusion that syllabic writing was
"a blind alley which could not lead to alphabetic writing."[43]

Like the earliest Egyptian documents, the Babylonian
tablets bearing "the *oldest* written signs thus far known"
are highly stylized and cannot be read.[44] Granted they are
picture writing, no two scholars "read" them the same.
Mesopotamia offers to date the only chance of presenting
the evolutionary sequence of the development of writing
by a stratigraphic pattern. Only, alas, it doesn't work.
Though it is assumed, of course, that "the earliest examples
of writing in Mesopotamia are pictographs. . . . Very few
of these were actually excavated scientifically, so that, from
the chronological point of view, there is little help to be
obtained from stratigraphic connections," according to
Burton-Brown, who should also have pointed out that the
inscriptions which have been scientifically excavated have
a way of refuting the expected patterns, since some of the
most primitive writing is found in late strata and vice
versa.[45]

The paradox that anything as advanced and sophisticated as writing should come into the world full-blown
and all at once is invincibly repugnant to the evolutionary

way of thinking. Of recent years the anthropologists have taken a strong stand on the "tool" theory of civilization. The idea is that primitive hominids quite thoughtlessly and accidentally blundered on the use of this or that piece of wood, bone, or rock as a tool, and that "it was the success of the simplest tools that started the whole trend of human evolution and led to the civilizations of today."[46] It is the primitive tool, falling fortuitously into its hands, which draws mankind irresistibly forward to new levels of attainment, for "when men make a tool, they commit themselves, man depends upon his tools for his very humanity."[47] In a word, "social evolution is a consequence of technologic evolution."[48]

Some of the scientific speculators, however, take the opposite position, that man "has always had reservoirs of response far more than his devices (tools) asked of him," and that in "his attempts to transcend his biological limitations" his mind always runs ahead of his tools, not behind them.[49] When men need a tool they invent it, not the other way around.[50] Men themselves decide what tools they will have, so that one evolutionist notes with perplexity that "one of the most puzzling aspects of the culture" of the "Cavemen" is "their heavy dependence on tools whose use is now a complete mystery."[51] Carleton S. Coon observed that "for the simple reason that human beings are not equipped by nature to live without tools," we must suppose that they always had all the tools they needed for survival even in Pliocene.[52] Petrie, in a significant and neglected study, pointed out that instead of eagerly adopting a superior tool as soon as it was made known to them, human beings have shown "a resistance of almost 100 percent" to any new tool coming from the outside.[53] Though all the neighbors of the Egyptians knew about their superior axe forms for thousands of years, the only other ancient people to adopt them were of all things the South Americans.[54] Petrie knows of seventeen Egyptian tools and weapons, some of unsurpassed efficiency, which are over the centuries never found outside of Egypt, and, he observes, "the converse is equally true."[55]

Writing: A Gift from Heaven

Then whatever induced one people to adopt *writing* from another? The interesting thing here is that though the idea quickly caught on, each people in adopting it insisted on making it its own exclusive possession and devised from the first a native style that set it off from all the others. Both the popularity and the variety of ancient writing is to be explained by its religious nature. E. von Mülinen has noted that new scripts invariably appear as the vehicles of new religions,[56] while Jürgen Smolian points out that all of man's greatest inventions or discoveries seem to have the primary purpose of putting him into communication with the other world.[57] If Joseph Smith was right, books and writing are a gift to man from heaven, "for it was given unto as many as called upon God to write by the spirit of inspiration" (Moses 6:7). The art of writing was a special dispensation, an inestimable boon, enabling the righteous to retain the memory of divine visitations and communications ever fresh before them, and assisting them in coordinating their earthly activities with the heavenly order: "The *immediate* will of heaven is contained in the Scriptures," said the Prophet Joseph.[58]

The earliest records of the race have much to say "about the miracle of writing, which the Ancients regarded as a gift from heaven."[59] The Egyptians believed that writing was a sacred trust given to the king as "high-priest and scribe" to keep him and his people ever in touch with the mind and will of heaven.[60] Thus the *Book of the Foundation of Temples* was thought to have been sent down from heaven to the immortal genius Imhotep, the Vizier of King Djoser of the Third Dynasty and the greatest builder of all time (cf. fig. 51A, p. 390), after which the book "was taken

away to heaven at the time the gods left the earth," but
was sent down again by Imhotep at a later time, when he
"caused it to fall from heaven at the place north of Memphis" (cf. fig. 55, p. 413).[61] In Babylonia

> the King is the Sent One. He has ascended to heaven
> to receive . . . the tablets of destiny and to get his com-
> mission. Then he is sent out, i.e., he descends again. . . .
> And so the knowledge is communicated to the king, it
> is of a mysterious character, bearing upon the great mys-
> teries of heaven and earth, the hidden things, and is a
> revelation of the hidden knowledge by the gods (the
> god). Can we style it "primordial revelation "?[62]

The idea of a primordial revelation is that a complete
knowledge of the world from its beginning to its end is
already written down and has been vouchsafed to certain
chosen spirits from time to time, a doctrine familiar to
Latter-day Saints.[63] The heavenly origin of writing is constantly referred to anciently in the doctrine that writing
and the symbols of writing are derived from the starry
heavens (fig. 61). The Tablets of Destiny which contain all
knowledge and impart all authority "are the divination of
the world, the stars and constellations form the writing."[64]
As Clement of Alexandria observed, both in Egypt and
Chaldaea, "Writing and a knowledge of the heavens necessarily go together."[65] How this is can be seen if one
considers where all of the oldest writings of the race are
found.

If we turn from ancient doctrine to concrete discovery
we are soon made aware that the oldest writings are always
found in *temples*. "It is in these temples that we find the
first signs of writing. . . . The script appears from the first
as a system of conventional signs . . . such as might have
been introduced all at once. We are confronted with a true
invention, not with an adaption of pictorial art."[66] For
Egypt, Steindorff maintained that "the birthplace of this
'hieroglyphic system' of writing was the sacerdotal school

Figure 61. Many ancient cultures saw their letters in the stars of the heavens. Kircher shows us the four letters of the name of God יהוה as a constellation of stars (A), as well as the rest of the letters of the Hebrew alphabet in the stars of the Northern Hemisphere (B).

of Heliopolis."[67] In Babylonia, according to Hrozný, it was in the Uruk period, 3200 B.C., that "there originated . . . from the records of business transaction in the temple enclosure, the picture writing which in later times developed into cuneiform writing."[68] Though these symbols cannot be read (i.e., they were not picture writings, but "a collection of abstract tokens eked out with pictograms"),[69] it is apparent that they "were for the most part lists of commodities supplied to or delivered by officials and others concerned with the administration of the Temple."[70]

Here we have a combination of business and religion which has given rise to the discussion of the rivalry of *Kultschrift* (cultic or religious writing) and *Gebrauchschrift* (practical business writing). Actually no rivalry exists between them: the consensus is that the oldest written symbols are property marks, such as arrow markings and cattle brands (fig. 62), and in order to be respected as such they have to be sacrosanct, holy symbols duly registered in the temple.[71] If the oldest writing is used for business, it is always temple business, and the writing is also used for other — far more important — purposes. Examining the claims of the two, Helmut Arntz concluded that the holy or cultic writing has clear priority.[72] One can, like old Commodore Vanderbilt, carry on business in a state of total illiteracy, and indeed men of affairs have always viewed men of letters with suspicion: "Writing is an art despised by the Roman businessman," wrote Cornelius Nepos, "who have all their writing done for them by hirelings."[73] But one cannot carry on the holy business of the temple without the divine gift of writing.[74] "Hieroglyphic is correctly named," Sethe observed, being devised "only for the walls of temples. . . . It is a survival from prehistoric times."[75] It is no accident that temple architecture and writing appear suddenly together.[76] The *templum* is, as we have shown elsewhere, an observatory, where one takes one's bearings on the universe.[77] There the heavens are carefully

Figure 62. The Egyptians used copper cattle brands, such as these belonging to Pharaoh Amonhotep II, c. 1410 B.C., his government, and the "Beautiful House," or local temple.

Figure 63. The enthroned Ramses II is surrounded by the gods as they write his name on the leaves of the divine Ished tree behind him. Seshat and Thoth hold the palm rib symbol of "millions of years," from which hang the *heb-sed* hieroglyph (cf. fig. 48, p. 259). Even Amun-Re-Atum joins in the ceremony, while the common people under his throne rejoice at the establishment of the king's reign.

observed, and to be of value those observations must be recorded. Alphabet, calendar, and temple naturally go together, all devised for handling messages from the stars and planets.[78] "We may think of the stars as letters inscribed on the heavens," said Plotinus, and we may think of the heavens as a great book which men copy and project on tangible materials at the holy places.[79] Recent studies by Gerald Hawkins, Peter Tompkins, Giorgio de Santillana, and others have given vivid reality to the heretofore vaguely surmised existence of ritual complexes of great antiquity where men observed the heavens and acquired an astonishing amount of knowledge about them, which, in order to use, they faithfully committed to their books.

From first to last, ancient writing remains in the hands not of businessmen but of priests; it is a holy and a secret thing, imparted only to the elect and zealously withheld from all others. "He who divulges it," we read of a typical holy book, "dies a sudden death and an immediate cutting-off. Thou shalt keep very far away from it. It is to be read only by a scribe in the workshop, whose name has been duly registered in the House of Life. "[80] "Only the prophets may read and understand the holy books" is the rule.[81] Each system of writing itself is an effective seal on the holy books, a cryptogram, "a secret formula which the profane do not know."[82] The key to power and priesthood lies "in the midst of the Sea of Coptos, in a box of iron, the box of iron being (in) a box (of bronze, the box of bronze) in a box of kete-wood in a box of ivory and ebony, the box of ivory and ebony in a (box of silver, and the box) of silver in a box of gold, wherein is the book."[83] The idea of the holy book that is taken away from the earth and restored from time to time, or is handed down secretly from father to son for generations, or hidden up in the earth, preserved by ingenious methods of storage with precious imperishable materials, to be brought forth in a later and more righteous generation (i.e., Moses 1:41), is becoming increasingly familiar with the discovery and publication of ever more ancient apocryphal works, Jewish, Christian, and others.[84] But nowhere does the idea find clearer or completer expression than in the pages of the Book of Mormon and the Pearl of Great Price.

What is perhaps the oldest religious book known, the so-called Shabako Stone, instead of the primitive mumbo jumbo one might expect, contains a story strangely familiar to Latter-day Saints (cf. fig. 43, pp. 180–81). It is the text of a ritual drama enacted in the temple to celebrate the founding of the First Dynasty of Egypt, and it depicts the council in heaven, the creation of the world, the fall of man, and the means by which he may achieve resurrection and be reinstated in his primal glory. The book, on a scroll, was hidden up in the wall of that same temple of Ptah of Memphis, founded by Menes, the first Pharaoh, and was discovered by a later king, Shabako, who followed the same text in the rites establishing his own (Twenty-fifth) Dynasty.[85]

Another king reports that "when His Majesty settled the lands . . . he mounted the throne of Horus. . . . He spoke to his noble ones, the Smrw of his immediate presence, the faithful writers-down of the divine words, who were in charge of all the secrets."[86] Writing, here shared only with his intimates, is par excellence "the King's Secret," which gives him all advantage over his fellows and the ability to rule them. The technique of writing is the foundation of empire, for only the written document can overcome the limitations of space and carry a ruler's word and authority out of sight and beyond the hills, and even defeat the inroads of time on human memory by preserving the words of command and judgment for unlimited numbers of years.[87] The king describes himself as the mediator and scribe of the god in heaven in the administration of his empire: "I sit before him, I open his boxes, I break open his edicts, I seal his dispatches, I send out messengers."[88] In Mesopotamia also "the supreme sovereignty of the universe connected with the tablets of destiny is thus identical with the casting of the oracles of lots," the possession of which could give even a robber "possession of the rulership of the world."[89] The Pharaoh was authorized to rule only when "the master of the house of the divine books" had inscribed his royal names "on the true records deposited in the heavenly archives" (fig. 63).[90] The archives were known in Egypt as the House of Life (cf. fig. 1, p. 12), housing the writings upon which the life of all things ultimately depended.[91] It was a powerhouse humming with vital electricity, transmitting cosmic forces from heaven to earth, a place of deadly peril to any mortal not holding the necessary priestly credentials.[92] Wherever the heavenly book is mentioned, the heavenly scribe appears as king, priest, and mediator, in early Jewish and Christian as well as older traditions.[93] Pharaoh is preeminently "He who knows, being in possession of the divine book."[94] Like the Egyptian Thoth, the Babylonian Nabu, the prophet and scribe writes all things down in the "unalterable tablets" of destiny which determine all that happens upon the earth.[95] In the earthly as in the heavenly court, everything was written down, not only to follow the divine example but to coordinate earthly with celestial proceedings. In Persia, for example,

> the entire administration, as was customary from the earliest times in the Orient, was carried on by written documents, as it was in the courts of Egypt, Babylonia, and Assyria. . . . Everything is carefully written down; even in battle the King's secretary is beside him taking notes; every royal remark is written down and then gathered into "Daybooks" or "Memoranda books," such as have been found in the archives of Suza, Babylonia, Ecbatana, etc.[96]

The Myth of Irra, one of the oldest stories in existence, shows "that Mesopotamian theologians were not ignorant of the concept of a 'sacred book,' that is, of a divinely inspired, even dictated text, which contains the only correct and valid account of the 'story' of deity."[97] In Egypt it is "the King who is over the spirits, who unites hearts — so says He who is in charge of wisdom, being great, and who bears the god's book, even Sia ['the personification of intelligence and understanding' — Faulkner] who is at the right hand of Re."[98] The relief, mentioned above (cf. fig. 59, p. 455), from the temple library of Dendera shows us the scribe's palette, the Egyptian symbol of writing and all that it implies, descending from heaven; it is supported by two figures who strike the pose signifying "eternity" and who face each other, denoting "from eternity to eternity," while four other figures are in the attitude of adoration; hieroglyphic symbols above the head of each show them to represent the ear that hears, the eye that sees, the mind or intelligence (Sia) which conceives, and the word of power (Ḥw) which consummates the creation of all things.[99]

The books were consulted on every occasion: "Copy thy fathers who have gone before thee. . . . Behold, their words are recorded in writing. Open and read and copy."[100] When King Djoser away back in the Third Dynasty asked his all-wise minister Imhotep to explain a seven-years' famine, the latter "begged permission 'that I may enter into the Mansion of Life, and may open the books and may seek guidance from them.' "[101] Interestingly enough, the most important of all writings were genealogical records, and Gardiner concluded not only that the House of Life was, properly speaking, nothing more or less than the genealogical archives, but that the Great Pyramid itself was built to contain the royal genealogical records.[102] The astonishing mass and charge of ancient book making may be attributed to the basic doctrine that everything must be written down: "The Babylonian conception of Canonicity, . . . that the sum of revealed knowledge was given once for all by the antediluvian sages," necessarily posits the existence of the Primordial Book that contains everything that was, is, and is to come, and presents "a remarkable parallel to the Rabbinic view that God's revelation in its entirety is contained in the Torah," according to W. G. K. Lambert.[103]

Knowledge: A Gift from Heaven

This is consistent with the marvelous function of writing as the great synthesizer. To write is to synthesize. The basic idea of writing is that symbols represent sounds and that smaller units make up larger units — not compounds or composites, but true units. Thus a letter by itself is without significance; there must be a reference to something which goes beyond it — other letters making a word or a name. A single letter, heraldic mark, tally, crest, or *wasm* has no meaning without reference to the official heraldic list of such and the names they represent. The word in turn is also meaningless without reference to other words; even a one-word sentence such as "Alas!" takes its meaning from other unspoken words. The meaning of every sentence also depends on its larger context; even a short aphorism must be understood in its cultural context. For the ancients, any self-contained message was a book. They were not disturbed by the extreme brevity of many "books," because they regarded every book also as part of a larger context — for the Egyptians the "Hermetic" books. Every proper Arabic book, regardless of its subject, still opens with a paragraph praising God for his creation and the place in it which this particular writing occupies. Ancient records come to us not in single books but in whole libraries. These are not mere collections but organic entities, as the archaic Egyptian sign of the Book-lady Seshat attests: her seven-pointed star goes with her seven books, representing every department of human knowledge, being let down from the opened heavens (cf. fig. 46B, p. 229).[104]

The House of Life where the books were copied and studied had from the earliest times the aspect of a university, a super graduate-school;[105] "there it was that all questions relating to . . . learned matters were settled."[106] The place was always part of the temple, and the books contain the earliest poetry, for *poiēma* means "creation" and the business of the Muses at the temple was to sing the Creation song with the Morning stars;[107] naturally the hymn was sung to music, and some scholars would derive the first writing from musical notation.[108] It was performed in a sacred circle or chorus, so that poetry, music, and the dance go out to the world from the temple, called by the Greeks the museon, or shrine of the Muses (cf. fig. 6, p. 24). The creation hymn was part of the great dramatic presentation that took place yearly at the temple, dealing with the fall and redemption of man, represented by various forms of combat, making the place the scene of the ritual athletic contests sanctified throughout the world. The victor in the contest was the father of the race, the priest-king himself, whose triumphant procession, coronation, and marriage took place on the occasion, making this the seat and source of government (the king was always crowned in the temple rather than the palace).[109] Since the entire race was expected to be present for the event, a busy exchange of goods from various distant regions took place, the booths of pilgrims serving as the market booths for great fairs, while the necessity of converting various and bizarre forms of wealth into acceptable offerings for the temple led to an active banking and exchange in the temple courts; the earliest "money," from the shrine of Juno Moneta at Rome, is temple money (cf. fig. 7, p. 24). Since the place began as an observatory, and all things were tied to the calendar and the stars, mathematics flourished and astronomy was a Muse. History was another Muse, for the rites were meant for the dead as well as the living, and memorials to former great ones (believed to be in attendance) encouraged the production of a marvelous art of portraiture, of sculpture and painting, which would have flourished anyway as architectural adornments, since the design and measurements (the *middot*) of the temple structure itself as a sort of scale model of the universe and cosmic computer were all-important; the architecture of the hierocentric structure was of primary concern. And since from that central point all the earth was measured and all the lands distributed, geometry was essential: "In the Beginning the One God promised Horus that he should inherit the land of Egypt, which was written in the Books by order of the Lord of All. . . . At the Division of the Lands it was decreed in writing."[110]

The writings produced and copied in the House of Life were also discussed there, giving rise to philosophy, but concerned largely with cosmology and natural science. In short, there is no aspect of our civilization that does not have its rise in the temple, thanks to the power of the written word. In the all-embracing relationships of the Divine Book everything is relevant. Nothing is really dead or forgotten; every detail belongs in the picture, which would be incomplete without it. Lacking such a synthesizing principle, our present-day knowledge becomes ever more fragmented, and our universities and libraries crumble and disintegrate as they expand. Where the temple that gave it birth is missing, civilization itself becomes a hollow shell.

A Necessary Addition

In the short compass of a single lecture one always raises more questions than can be answered or discussed. The true origin of writing must remain, as Siegfried Schott observes, a subject of the purest speculation for a long time to come, and possibly forever.[111] The fact that all the scholars are merely guessing should not deter us from the fascinating game, for as Karl Popper puts it, it is only by guessing and discussing that any science makes any progress.

Some years ago there was a consensus among students that Egypt was the ultimate home of the alphabet. The decisive study was that of Kurt Sethe, who tried to follow a strictly evolutionary line, with writing evolving inevitably from everyday human needs throughout the world as if by natural law,[112] "gradually and imperceptibly," culminating in a full-blown alphabet in Egypt.[113] In the beginning, he avers, humans everywhere communicated by pictures, and to prove this he cites cases in which the white man astounded the Indians by communicating in writing without pictures; he then furnishes as a classical example of Indian picture writing the headstone of a famous chief on which three short vertical strokes represent three seriously wounded warriors while sixteen short horizontal strokes denote sixteen war-parties.[114] And this is picture writing? Well might the white man have been astounded that the Indians could thus communicate without letters. None, in fact, of the more than a dozen reproductions of Indian picture writing supplied by Sethe can be read as pictures, and Sethe himself concludes that all these examples are nothing but "mnemotechnical aids" to help the writer fix things in his own mind rather than convey them to others; most of the sketches are so reduced and stylized as to be entirely symbolic, with no attempt at realism, reduced cues that mean nothing to those who have not already experienced what they depict (fig. 64; cf. fig. 58, pp. 422–23).[115]

This, however, is not true picture writing, according to Sethe, that being a foolproof system in which "every single element of the thought process has its own picture."[116] But if Sethe's examples of primitive picture writing (of which he could find none in Egypt) were inadequate

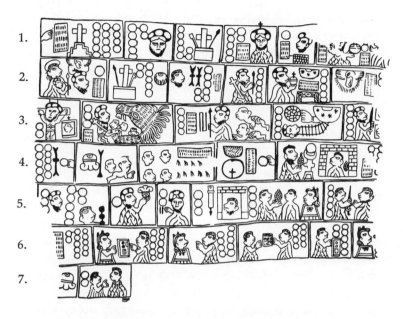

Figure 64. The famous Mexican Catechism might be deciphered by someone who had been told that it contains the catechism and the Ten Commandments (beginning on line 5, panel 2) and who also knew what the Ten Commandments were; but for any outsider the whole thing might as well be written in Chinese. For example, on line 3, panel 2, Christ delivers the righteous dead from the "jaws of hell" (cf. D&C 122:7).

Egyptian	Sinaitic	Phoenician	South Arabic	Greek
Ox		Aleph	Alf	Alpha
House		Beth	Bēt	Beta
Corner		Gimel	Gaml	Gamma

Figure 65. Sethe's "Evolutionary" Development of the Alphabet

and even irrelevant, his examples of true picture writing leave even more to be desired—there are none. All his evidence he must find embedded in later hieroglyphic writing.[117] In true picture writing, he says, every concept has its picture, so that the writing can be read by anybody anywhere in the world.[118] As an example he gives the sign of the cross, which accompanying a name signifies a dead person, forgetting that it only does so as a purely abstract and highly conventionalized symbol, and not as a picture.[119] But since "man thinks in words," according to Sethe, everywhere the true picture writing was "automatically" and "very early converted to phonetic writing."[120] But if men were thinking in words all the time they were drawing pictures, how long would it take them to associate the two? Why does there have to be a gap at all? The evolutionary rule requires it: true writing, being purely phonetic, must necessarily be the last step in the long evolutionary process.[121] Again the evidence is missing: all known picture writings in the Old World, according to Sethe, had already become phonetic scripts before their earliest appearance, so that we can only infer the existence of the previous primitive—and true picture writing—systems from indications discovered in the known systems.[122] The only clear evidence that Sethe can find for the evolutionary process is the existence of independent systems of writing, all of which, according to him, must have emerged in the same way from primitive picture writing; he lists ten such systems, of which only three had been deciphered in his time.[123] Since then the list has been extended, and in the process the independence of the various systems from each other has been brought under serious questioning. Since alphabetic writing is the ultimate perfection in the chain of evolution, it is disturbing that Sethe must conclude that the less efficient, clumsier, and more primitive syllabic writing was evolved from the more perfect alphabetic writing, and not the other way around.[124]

Sethe's thesis is that the Egyptians, beginning with a true picture writing containing "originally a countless multitude of symbols"[125] (which strangely enough have never turned up anywhere), through a series of inevitable and "purely mechanical" steps, "quite unconsciously and without intention" produced an alphabet of twenty-four letters, all consonants,[126] from which all the alphabets of the world were eventually derived.[127] The crucial step was the adoption of these characters to their own language by the Hebrews in Sinai—possibly by Moses himself.[128] For Sethe, the "missing link" was supplied by Petrie's discovery of the Siniatic script in 1905.[129] From first to last "the entire developmental process of writing from pictures to letters can be viewed in the framework of natural science" (fig. 65).[130]

To Sethe's famous study (based on a series of lectures, 1916–1934), Schott added an appendage in 1964. He notes that certain conclusions of Sethe are necessarily premature: the Sinai script has not yet been read with certainty.[131] And he cites the later study of Hans Bauer, who, while agreeing that "the Egyptian origin of alphabetic writing is by no means in doubt" and that "anything as rare and marvelous . . . can hardly have originated twice,"[132] sees the all-important transition to the standard Semitic alphabet taking place not in Sinai but in Canaan to the north.[133] The split between the northern and southern schools still maintains simply because of a lack of evidence.[134] Schott wonders if it is necessary to go through all that rigamarole about the various stages of picture writing, for which no rigorous test is possible.[135] If we are dealing with a "rare and marvelous" invention, where must we draw the line as to the inventor's inspiration—can he not have invented the whole thing? The trouble with the evolutionary concept in Egyptian writing, Schott observes, is that the process unfortunately runs backwards.[136] The only way to account for the total lack of evidence for all the necessary long transitional phases, according to Schott, is the assumption that everything in those days was written on perishable material, a proposition which he finds untenable.[137]

And this is where we come in—without apologies, since everything is pretty much up in the air, and there is much to be said that has not been said. Since it is admittedly poverty of evidence that leaves us all in a box canyon, one would think that the scholars, if only in desperation, would venture to consider all of the evidence and not only that which comes under the heading of natural science. With all other ways blocked, it might be a good idea to try some of the neglected passages and ask some of the unasked questions. Here are a few:

1. How are we to account for yawning gaps in the evolutionary record, the complete absence of those transitional documents which should, according to the theory, be exceedingly numerous?

2. What about the *sudden* emergence first of hieroglyphic writing and then of the Semitic alphabet, each in its perfectly developed form? Why in the case of admitted human inventions, the work of obvious genius, must we still assume long periods of gradual, accidental, unconscious development if no evidence for such development exists outside of the theory itself?

3. The oldest writing appears side by side with the oldest legends about writing. Wouldn't normal curiosity suggest a hearing of those legends? Greek tradition attributing the origin of the alphabet to Phoenicians has been thoroughly vindicated; no scholar denies that. Then why not examine other legends seriously, at least until something better turns up?

4. Why is it that the ancients are unanimous in attributing the origins of writing, including the alphabet, to a heavenly source?

5. Why are the earliest written documents always

found in temples? Why do they always deal with religious matters?

6. Whence the unfailing identification of reading and writing with divination, that is, with interpreting the will of heaven?

7. "There is in the very nature of writing something marvelous and mysterious, which at all times has exercised a powerful attraction on thoughtful minds," writes Sethe.[138] Why, then, does he insist that the first true writing, the process of an unconscious, mindless, "automatic" process "*can* contain only very trivial matters"?[139] Could anything so "*Wunderbares und Geheimnisvolles*" (wonderful and mysterious)[140] have been invented in a humdrum way for purely humdrum purposes?

8. The supernatural power of the written symbol is as old as the marking of arrows. How can one comprehend the nature of the earliest writing without considering the miraculous or magical powers it exercised over man and beast?[141]

9. The first writing appears full-blown with the founding of the First Dynasty of Egypt, and in a form far too well-knit and consistent to have evolved, according to Schott.[142] What is the significance of writing as "the King's secret," the indispensable implement to government and authority?

10. Why is writing always a mystery, a guild secret, a kingly and priestly monopoly? "The really marvelous things that writing does, the astounding feats of thought-stimulation, thought-preservation, and thought-transmission . . . are of no interest to practical people: business records, private letters, school exercises, and the like are periodically consigned to the incinerator by clerks and merchants to whom eternal preservation and limitless transmission mean nothing."[143] Why must the latter be given the credit for inventing writing?

Let these ten questions suffice to justify our own speculations. Schott rejects Sethe's main thesis, that the Egyptians had a true alphabet, on the grounds that they mingled their alphabetic signs with syllabic and picture writing (the ideograms or determinatives that come at the end of words; cf. fig. 44, p. 218). But whereas the scribes make constant use of the twenty-four letters or single-consonant symbols and could not write without them, they often omit the other signs and seem to be playing with them. Schott maintains that only the Phoenician genius suddenly realized the possibility of doing without the syllabic and pictographic elements entirely; yet for ages the Egyptian scribes freely dispensed with them, now in one word and now in another—they knew it could be done. Pictures? Hieratic is as old as hieroglyphic, yet it contains no recognizable pictures, and demotic is anything but picture writing. Why retain pictures in such systems, since no one can recognize them? To an Egyptian who spoke the language, the alphabetic signs would be enough, just as the same signs, without vowels, are quite adequate for the reading of Semitic languages. Granted that some of the other signs are necessary, why is the whole massive and awkward machinery of both picture writing and syllabic writing retained to clutter up an economical and efficient alphabet? I would like to suggest that those who employed the "holy engravings" (for that is what *hieroglyphic* means) had not only their own people in mind but were thinking of others as well. One need only think of countless early funeral-steles, consciously addressed to distant generations yet unborn. Without ideograms any learned Egyptian scribe could still read a text, but we today could never understand Egyptian without those pictures. Can it be that they are put in there for our benefit or the benefit of others like us? Likewise the eking out of the alphabetic signs with syllabic forms suggests a patient repetition and emphasis for the benefit of stumbling children. If Egyptian writing, because of its compound nature, is absolutely unique, perhaps its intention was also unique—to communicate more widely than the other languages. There is a good deal of evidence to support this theory, but we cannot go into it here. For many years learned men guessed at the meaning of hieroglyphics, and when some of them, like Horapollo, Kircher, or Seiffert, made some happy strikes, it was the pictographs that enabled them to do so and which could have put them on the right track had they properly pursued them. In the 1880s Egyptologists of a number of lands, under the leadership of Professor Samuel Birch of Oxford, collected and interpreted all the available hypocephali of that time, and came up with a surprising unity of views, based on the symbolism alone. Today, as many experts are pointing out, it is doubtful whether anyone really understands any Egyptian religious text; there is still a long way to go, though much progress has been made. But the point is that the evidence is all there before our eyes and that the Egyptians have perhaps consciously supplied us with an overload of material, a safety factor to make sure that in the end the message would get across.

As for the Semitic alphabet and our own, derived from the Egyptian and often called the greatest of all inventions, the most wonderful thing about it is that it seems to have been devised for the express purpose of recording the scriptures—our scriptures. The objection today to Sethe's suggestion that Moses himself may well have been the inventor is that the alphabet is older than Moses and seems to have been at home at an earlier time up north—in Canaan. Sethe does not apologize for citing a Jewish writer, Eupolemos, in support of the claims put in for Moses,[144] and so it seems only fair to point out that by far the overwhelming authority of Jewish tradition favors not Moses but Abraham as the inventor of the alphabet, though some say he inherited it from Enoch. Of recent years a number of new alphabets have turned up in the Near East, dating to 2000–1500 B.C. and all "clearly the inventions of individuals."[145] Well, why not? Once one knows it can be done, one is free to invent one's own alphabet; the Deseret Alphabet is an impressive demonstration of that (fig. 66).

Figure 66. A clever synthesis of several shorthand systems, the phonetic Deseret Alphabet of 1854 was intended to help teach English to children and immigrants. Here it is used on a gold coin of Zion.

But it would seem that "the Canaanitic alphabet, which has conquered the world," is the oldest of all, and as such is "a witness to the ancient origin of the Torah."[146] Some think it may be as old as or even older than hieroglyphic itself.[147]

By the most cautious estimate of the situation, it is safe to say that the scriptures are not to be taken lightly. When scholars who pride themselves on their freedom from any religious commitment are found seriously considering the genesis of the written word not only in holy writings but specifically in our own scriptures, it behooves us to pay attention. Whoever reads the Standard Works today has before him the words of God to men from the beginning, in witness of which the very letters on the page are but slightly conventionalized forms of the original symbols in which the message was conveyed. Merely as a cultural phenomenon the possibility is awe-inspiring, but that it should all go back to Israel and Egypt is too much to hope for. As members of the human race we are bound to approach the scriptures with new feelings of reverence and respect. They are the nearest approach and the best clue thus far discovered to the genesis of the written word.

Notes

1. This note appeared at the end of the *New Era* version, p. 50: Since these reflections first appeared in the Commissioner's Lecture Series, an important study on the subject has emerged in a feature article by K. H. Basso and Ned Anderson, "A Western Apache Writing System: The Symbols of Silas John," *Science* 180, no. 4090 (8 June 1973): 1013–22. The authors begin by deploring the strange indifference and neglect shown by scientists in the past toward the study of "so-called 'primitive' writing systems," as a result of which the present-day world is almost completely in the dark on the subject. "Under these circumstances," they write, "it is with considerable enthusiasm" that they call attention to an authentic Western Apache writing system that is still in use. The system is ingenious, original, and highly efficient, and is entirely the invention of one man, Silas John Edwards, who produced it in 1904, insisting that the whole thing was given to him in a "dream from God, . . . at one time in one dream," for the sole purpose of recording certain ritual prayers and ordinances that have since been faithfully perpetuated among his people. Since the value of the writing was the power to preserve the divine instructions unaltered through time, the knowledge of the system has been "restricted to a small band of elite ritual specialists" (1015). Of course, Silas John knew about alphabetic writing, yet his system is a "totally unique cultural form . . . among the significant intellectual achievements of an American Indian during the 20th century" (1013).

The thing to notice here is that Silas John was a plain, simple, but deeply religious Indian, while the system of writing he produced suddenly in 1904 was not only highly sophisticated but has proven perfectly functional. No long ages of evolution were necessary to its emergence; the thing was given, he always maintained, in a single vision, for the express purpose of instructing men in the will of heaven and keeping them faithfully observant of it; it has never been used for anything else. Here in a leading scientific journal is a scientific description of how a system of writing actually came into being among a "primitive" people, and it confirms our own suspicions at every point.

2. Edwyn Bevan, *Hellenism and Christianity* (London: Allen and Unwin, 1921), 81.

3. John Lear, "The Star-Fixed Ages of Man," *Saturday Review* 10 (January 1970): 99, speaking in particular of population and pollution problems.

4. "What is happening now is . . . an abandonment of Ren-

aissance-inspired approaches. . . . The new approach is quite different in spirit and in method. It begins with a clear acknowledgment of the impossibility of reconstructing the original order of things human," William D. Stahlman, "Global Myths Record Their Passage," in ibid., 101.

5. Joseph Fielding Smith, *Selections from Answers to Gospel Questions* (Salt Lake City: Deseret News, 1972), 4.

6. Early Jewish apocrypha emphasize the close association between Adam and the art of writing, a theme which cannot be handled in the scope of this paper. He is called "the four-lettered Adam" in the *Sibylline Oracles* 3:24, referring to the well-known Jewish doctrine that all things were created out of letters in the first place, the theme of the *Sefer Yetzira*.

7. Raymond O. Faulkner, *The Ancient Egyptian Pyramid Texts* (Oxford: Clarendon, 1969), no. 510:1146.

8. That this Atum is to be identified with Adam has been suggested by leading Egyptologists: Eugene Lefebure, "Le cham et l'adam égyptiens," *Biblical Archaeological Society Proceedings* 9 (1893): 174–81; Alexandre Moret, *Histoire de l'Orient*, 2 vols. (Paris: Presses universitaires, 1945), 1:209.

9. Jean Capart, "L'exaltation du Livre," *Chronique d'Egypte* 22 (1946): 25.

10. R. Englebach, "An Essay on the Advent of the Dynastic Race in Egypt and Its Consequences," *ASAE* 42 (1942): 197–98.

11. Jean Capart, "Thème religieux ou fantaisie," *Egyptian Religion* 1 (1933): 117.

12. Alan H. Gardiner, "The Nature and Development of the Egyptian Hieroglyphic Writing," *JEA* 2 (1915): 62.

13. Alexander Scharff and Anton Moortgat, *Aegypten und Vorderasien im Altertum* (Munich: Bruckmann, 1950), 22.

14. Elise Baumgartel, *Prehistoric Egypt* (London: Oxford University Press, 1947), 48.

15. Stuart Piggott, *The Dawn of Civilization* (New York: McGraw-Hill, 1961), 127.

16. Walter B. Emery, "The Tombs of the First Pharoahs," *Scientific American* 197 (July 1957): 112.

17. Kurt Sethe, *Vom Bilde zum Buchstaben: Die Entstehungsgeschichte der Schrift*, vol. 12 of *Untersuchungen zur Geschichte und Altertumskunde Aegyptens* (Hildesheim: Olms, 1964), 27–28.

18. Scharff and Moortgat, *Aegypten und Vorderasien im Altertum*, 46.

19. Sethe, *Vom Bilde zum Buchstaben*, 20.

20. Johannes Friedrich, "Schriftsysteme und Schrifterfind-ungen im alten Orient und bei modernen Naturvölkern," *Archiv Orientalni* 19 (1951): 251–52.

21. Henri Frankfort, *The Birth of Civilization in the Near East* (London: Williams and Norgate, 1954), 110.

22. Ibid., 106–7.

23. Antal Dávid, "Remarques sur l'origine de l'écriture sumér-ienne," *Archiv Orientalni* 18/2 (1950): 51–54.

24. Bedřich Hrozný, *Ancient History of Western Asia, India, and Crete* (New York: Philosophical Library, 1953), 116–17.

25. J. Jordan, " Ausgrabungen in Warka," *Archiv für Orientforschung* 6 (1930–31): 318.

26. Phineas Mordell, "The Origin of Letters and Numerals According to Sefer Yeṣirah," *JQR* 2 (1911–12): 575.

27. Émile Massoulard, *Préhistoire et Protohistoire d'Égypte* (Paris: Institut d'Ethnologie, 1950), 323–24.

28. Naphtali H. Tur-Sinai, "The Origin of the Alphabet," *JQR* 41 (1950–51): 296.

29. Sethe, *Vom Bilde zum Buchstaben,* 20; Friedrich, "Schriftsysteme und Schrifterfindungen," 259; Hrozný, *Ancient History of Western Asia,* 166–72, looks for the place of origin in northern Syria, northwestern Mesopotamia, or eastern Asia Minor.

30. Sethe, *Vom Bilde zum Buchstaben,* 45–47.

31. A. Schmitt, cited in Helmut Arntz, "Zur Geschichte der Schrift," *Zeitschrift der Deutschen Morgenländischen Gessellschaft* 97 (1947): 82–83.

32. Sethe, *Vom Bilde zum Buchstaben,* 10.

33. Ernst Doblhofer, *Voices in Stone,* tr. Mervyn Savill (New York: Viking, 1961), 33.

34. Ibid.

35. Dávid, "Remarques sur l'origine," 49.

36. Doblhofer, *Voices in Stone,* 22.

37. Sethe, *Vom Bilde zum Buchstaben,* 24–25.

38. Ibid., 9.

39. Gardiner, "Egyptian Hieroglyphic Writing," 64.

40. Doblhofer, *Voices in Stone,* 28 (emphasis added).

41. Sethe, *Vom Bilde zum Buchstaben,* 28.

42. Ibid., 18.

43. William F. Edgerton, "On the Theory of Writing," *JNES* 11 (1953): 287–90.

44. Heinrich J. Lanzen, "New Discoveries at Warka in Southern Iraq," *Archaeology* 17 (1964): 125.

45. T. Burton-Brown, *Studies in Third Millennium History* (London: Luzac, 1946), 66–67.

46. Sherwood L. Washburn, "Tools and Human Evolution," *Scientific American* 203 (September 1960): 63.

47. James K. Feibleman, "Philosophy of Tools," *Social Forces* 45 (1967): 331–37. See also Kenneth P. Oakley, "Dating the Emergence of Man," *Advancement of Science* 18 (1948): 422. Lewis Mumford, "Man the Finder," *Technology and Culture* 6 (1965): 375–81.

48. Leslie A. White, "Energy and the Evolution of Culture," *American Anthropologist* 45 (1943): 338, 347.

49. "Cybernation and Man," *Man on Earth* 1/4 (1965): 6.

50. Amélia Hertz, "L'histoire de l'outil en fer d'après les documents égyptiens hittites, et assyro-babyloniens," *L'Anthropologie* 35 (1925): 75–95.

51. Jean Hiernaux, "How Man Will Evolve," *Science Digest* 58 (August 1965): 93.

52. Carleton S. Coon, *The Story of Man* (New York: Knopf, 1962), 64. The Leakeys would concur with his verdict.

53. William F. Petrie, "History in Tools," *Smithsonian Institution Annual Report* (1918): 568.

54. Ibid., 568–69.

55. Ibid., 570.

56. E. von Mülinen, "Sprachen und Schriften des vorderen Orients im Verhältnis zu den Religionen und Kulturkreisen," *Zeitschrift des Deutschen-Palästina-Vereins* 47 (1924): 88, 90.

57. Jürgen Smolian, "Vehicula Religiosa: Wagen in Mythos, Ritus, Kultus und Mysterium," *Numen* 10 (1963): 203, citing as examples fire, wheels, wagons, architecture, and ships.

58. Joseph Fielding Smith, ed., *Teachings of the Prophet Joseph Smith* (Salt Lake City: Deseret Book, 1947), 54 (emphasis added).

59. Naphtali H. Tur-Sinai, "Šiṭir Šamê, die Himmelsschrift," *Archiv Orientalni* 17 (1949): 433.

60. Hermes Trismegistus, 1, cited in Theodor Hopfner, *Fontes Historiae Religionis Aegyptiacae* (Bonn: Marcus and Weber, 1922–24), 393.

61. Henri Brugsch, "Bau und Maasse des Tempels von Edfu," *Zeitschrift für ägyptische Sprache und Altertumskunde* 10 (1872): 3–4.

62. Geo Widengren, *The Ascension of the Apostle and the Heavenly Book* (Uppsala: Boktryckeri, 1950), 21.

63. Smith, *Selections from Answers to Gospel Questions*, 5; Moses 7:67.

64. Alfred Jeremias, *Das alte Testament im Lichte des alten Orients* (Leipzig: Hinrichs, 1916), 51.

65. Clement of Alexandria, *Stromata* V, 4, in *PG* 9:44.

66. Frankfort, *Birth of Civilization*, 55–56.

67. George Steindorff, *Egypt* (New York: Augustin, 1943), 24.

68. Hrozný, *Ancient History of Western Asia, India, and Crete*, 36–37.

69. Frankfort, *Birth of Civilization*, 56, n. 1.

70. Piggott, *Dawn of Civilization*, 90.

71. See Hugh W. Nibley, "The Arrow, the Hunter, and the State," *WPQ* 2/3 (1949): 329–39; reprinted in *CWHN* 10:2–15; Hugh W. Nibley, "Controlling the Past: Part V," *IE* 58 (May 1955): 307–8; reprinted in *CWHN* 4:245–47.

72. Arntz, "Zur Geschichte der Schrift," 76.

73. Cornelius Nepos, *On the Great Generals of Foreign Nations* XVIII, *Eumenes* I, 5.

74. Nibley, "Controlling the Past: Part V," 307–8; reprinted in *CWHN* 4:245–53.

75. Sethe, *Vom Bilde zum Buchstaben*, 20–21.

76. Siegfried Schott, *Mythe und Mythenbildung im alten Aegypten*, vol. 15 of *Untersuchungen zur Geschichte und Altertumskunde Aegyptens* (Leipzig: Hinrichs, 1945), 10–11.

77. See Hugh W. Nibley, "Tenting, Toll, and Taxing," *WPQ* 19 (December 1966): 603–7; reprinted in *CWHN* 10:41–43; see also Hugh W. Nibley, "The Hierocentric State," *WPQ* 4/2 (1951): 235–38; reprinted in *CWHN* 10:110–14.

78. Scharff and Moortgat, *Aegypten und Vorderasien im Altertum*, 3; there is a striking passage in Syncellus, cited in Hopfner, *Fontes Historiae Religionis Aegyptiacae*, 74.

79. Plotinus, *Enneads* II, 3, *On Whether the Stars Are Causes* 7.

80. Papyrus Salt 825A, in Alan H. Gardiner, "The House of Life," *JEA* 24 (1938): 167.

81. Heliodorus, *Aethiopica* (*Ethiopians*) II, 28, 2.

82. Étienne Drioton, *L'écriture énigmatique du livre du jour et de la nuit* (Cairo: l'Institut Français d'Archéologie Orientale, 1942), 86.

83. Francis L. Griffith, *Stories of the High Priests of Memphis* (Oxford: Clarendon, 1900), 21–22.

84. Leo Koep, *Das himmlische Buch in Antike und Christentum* (Bonn: Hanstein, 1952); Widengren, *Ascension of the Apostle and the Heavenly Book*.

85. Kurt H. Sethe, *Dramatische Texte zu altaegyptischen Mysterienspielen*, 2 vols. (Leipzig: Hinrichs, 1928), 1:5, 8.

86. Max Pieper, *Die grosse Inschrift des Königs Neferhotep* (Leipzig: Hinrichs, 1929), 6–11.

87. Moret, *Histoire de l'Orient,* 1:96–107.

88. Pyramid Text (PT) 309:490–91.

89. Widengren, *Ascension of the Apostle and the Heavenly Book,* 11, 10.

90. Alexandre Moret, *Du caractère religieux de la royauté pharaonique* (Paris: Leroux, 1902), 102.

91. Winfried Barta, "Bemerkungen zur Darstellung der Jahreszeiten im Grabe des Mrr-wj-k3.j," *Zeitschrift für ägyptische Sprache und Altertumskunde* 97 (1971): 7.

92. Gardiner, "The House of Life," 76.

93. Heinrich Zimmern, *Die Keilinschriften und das Alte Testament* (Berlin: Reuther & Richard, 1903), 405.

94. PT 250:267.

95. Bruno Meissner, *Babylonien und Assyrien,* 2 vols. (Heidelberg: Winter, 1927), 2:124–25.

96. Eduard Meyer, *Geschichte des Altertums,* 4 vols. (Stuttgart: Cotta, 1910–58), 1:42–44.

97. A. Leo Oppenheim, "Mesopotamian Mythology III," *Orientalia* 19 (1950): 155.

98. PT 250:267.

99. Capart, "L'exaltation du Livre," 25–27.

100. Alan H. Gardiner, "New Literary Works from Ancient Egypt," *JEA* 1 (1914): 25.

101. Gardiner, "The House of Life," 166.

102. Alan H. Gardiner, "The Secret Chambers of the Sanctuary of Thoth," *JEA* 11 (1925): 4.

103. W. K. G. Lambert, "Ancestors, Authors, and Canonicity," *Journal of Cuneiform Studies* 11 (1957): 9.

104. Heinrich Schäfer, "Mousa bei Horapollo II, 29 und die Göttin Šš3-t," *Zeitschrift für ägyptische Sprache und Altertumskunde* 42 (1905): 72–75.

105. Siegried Schott, in "Nachwort," to Sethe, *Vom Bilde zum Buchstaben,* 81.

106. Gardiner, "The House of Life," 159; cf. 174–79.

107. Walter Otto, *Die Musen und der göttliche Ursprung des Singens und Sagens* (Darmstadt: Wissenschaftliche Buchgesellschaft, 1961).

108. Fritz M. Heichelheim, "The Earliest Musical Notations of Mankind and the Invention of Our Alphabet," *Epigraphica rivista italiana di epigrafia* 12 (1950): 111–15.

109. We have treated the overall theme in "Hierocentric State," 226–53; in *CWHN* 10:99–147.

110. Siegfried Schott, *Das Buch vom Sieg über Seth* (Leipzig: Hinrichs, 1929), 16.

111. Schott, in "Nachwort," to Sethe, *Vom Bilde zum Buchstaben,* 83.

112. Sethe, *Vom Bilde zum Buchstaben,* 2–3; the only motivating force was immediate practical need, 41, 66.

113. Ibid., 32, speaking of Egyptian linear writing; ibid., 39, speaking of the Egyptian alphabet.

114. Ibid., 4–5; fig. 2.

115. Ibid., 6, 11, 14–17.

116. Ibid., 17.

117. Ibid., 18–19.

118. Ibid., 24–25.

119. Ibid., 25–26.

120. Ibid., 26.

121. Ibid., 27.

122. Ibid., 28.

123. Ibid., 20.

124. Ibid., 29.

125. Ibid., 34.

126. Ibid., 38.

127. Ibid., 45–63.

128. Ibid., 55–56.

129. Ibid., 57–59.

130. Ibid., 66.

131. Ibid., 73.

132. Bauer, *Alte Orient,* 12–13; citing Schott, in "Nachwort," to Sethe, *Vom Bilde zum Buchstaben,* 75.

133. Sethe, *Vom Bilde zum Buchstaben,* 74.

134. Ibid., 75.

135. Ibid., 76.

136. Ibid., 80.

137. Ibid., 81.

138. Ibid., 1.

139. Ibid., 73.

140. Ibid., 1.

141. See Nibley, "The Arrow, the Hunter, and the State," 328–44; in *CWHN* 10:1–32.

142. Schott, in Sethe, *Vom Bilde zum Buchstaben,* 81.

143. Nibley, "Controlling the Past: Part V," 307–8; reprinted in *CWHN* 4:245–47.

144. Sethe, *Vom Bilde zum Buchstaben,* 55.

145. Alfred Jirku, "Der Kult des Mondgottes im alter Palästina-

Syrien," *Zeitschrift der Deutschen Morgenländischen Gesellschaft* 100 (1950): 520.

146. Tur-Sinai, "The Origin of the Alphabet," 296.

147. Mordell, "Letters and Numerals According to Sefer Yeṣirah," 575.

Science Fiction and the Gospel

In the great fantasies of science fiction, the professor is almost always the central figure. That is natural, since the object is to tell a human story. There are very few science fiction stories in which the great professor is not the central figure, or at least one of the most important characters. The layman writer worships the great scientist as a superman. And scientists, writing scientifically, have been more than willing to go along. The scientists' descriptions of themselves are either hypercritical or very flattering, one or the other. Recently they have been extremely critical. Of course, they are the only ones who could be so, and science fiction is the only place they could get away with it. Some quite eminent scientists have been writing some scathing science fiction, in which they show up scientists. A layman couldn't do a thing like that; it would just be sour grapes. And where else could these men unburden themselves with impunity, except by putting their speeches in the mouths of other people, in fiction? That is very safe.

That is an interesting trend of our times. As Thomas Kuhn has recently shown, the history of science is actually fiction, deliberately contrived to make science look good.[1] The history of science itself is the foundation of science fiction. If every problem in science has a scientific solution

This address, given on February 13, 1969, was published in Benjamin Urrutia, ed., LDSF 2: Latter-day Science Fiction (Ludlow, MA: Parables, 1985), 5–28.

(that follows the Milesian school), then God isn't wanted in any solution. The original idea is that we can't bring God into the laboratory, we can't weigh him, we can't use him, so let's leave him out. He exists and all that, but we can't use him in our calculations. And before you know it, any problem can be solved without him, so he becomes an impediment: he becomes just so much useless baggage.

Science fiction uniformly describes life in worlds in which science is king—meaning the scientist is king. In this kind of world the dream of the Sophist is fulfilled, a world in which there is no room for any but one kind of thinking. This is the "one world" of John Dewey, which he carried to its logical conclusion. Richard McKenna, a scientist writing science fiction, recently said, "I am as positivistic a scientist as you will find. The students blush and hate me, but it is for their own good. Science is the only safe game, and it's safe only if kept pure."[2] The speaker here is, of all things, a geologist, whose business is to reconstruct the past; that is why he likes to write science fiction. Indeed, need we say that any reconstruction of the past is 100 percent pure imagination.

Speak of keeping science pure! Science fiction writers console the Western World by saying that everything happened before; they console the Western World with the image of the superscientist, who has become the figure of science fiction but never lived in real life, we find out now. He is calm, aloof, dedicated, unswayed, incorruptible, self-effacing, magisterial. Science is a superman, said Huxley; as far above the savage as the savage is above a blade of grass. Compare that with Claude Levi-Strauss's book *La Pensée sauvage* (*The Savage Mind*), which shows that it is a lucky anthropologist who can even equal the savages of many a tribe for sheer intellectual power and knowledge.[3] Yet the great science fiction by scientists deals with this theme, and the question is Should scientists rule the universe? Who else?

In Eric Temple Bell's *The Ultimate Catalyst*,[4] the pure-minded scientist does terrible things to a wicked dictator. This is all right, because he takes the scientific view. As an idealist, the scientist is a necessary enemy of all bad people. This is the Baconian image of the pure scientist. Another well-publicized story called "The Gostec and the Doshes," by J. M. Brewer, starts this way (and this is deadpan—he is quite serious): "Woleshensky [the great scientist] smiled indulgently. He towered in his chair as though in the infinite kindness of his vast mind there were room to understand and overlook all the foolish little foibles of all the weak little beings that call themselves men. A mathematical physicist lives in vast spaces." To him, human beings and their affairs do not loom very important. He is dead serious—we have a sort of superman here.[5] The nearest thing to him is the figure of Rutherford, as he is worshipfully described by C. P. Snow:

> The tone of science at Cambridge in 1932 was the tone of Rutherford. Magniloquently boastful, creatively confident, generous, argumentative, and full of hope. Science and Rutherford were on top of the world. Worldly success, he loved every minute of it: flattery, titles, the company of the high official world. He was also superbly and magnificently vain, as well as wise, and he enjoyed his own personality.[6]

Here, if ever, is the great, lovable scientist of science fiction. What more could one ask for than science on such a level? "He enjoyed a life of miraculous success," says Snow. But then, something strange follows. "But I am sure that even quite late in life he felt stabs of sickening insecurity." This is strange—"sickening insecurity" in this man, of all men.

Snow goes on to talk about other great Cambridge scientists. He says:

> Does anyone really imagine that Bertrand Russell, G. H. Hardy, Rutherford, Blackett, and the rest were

bemused by cheerfulness as they faced their own individual state? In the crowd, great—they were the leaders;
they were top men; they were worshipped. But, by themselves, they believed with the same certainty that they
believed in Rutherford's atom that they were going, after
this mortal life, into annihilation. Against this they had
only to offer the nature of scientific activity: its complete
success on its own terms. It itself is a source of happiness.
But it's whistling in the dark, when they're alone.

He gives some very interesting sketches of the very odd
way these people behave.

Only scientists dare criticize scientists as demigods,
and then only in science fiction, as we mentioned before.
J. B. S. Haldane, the great British biologist, in "The Gold
Makers," the only science fiction story he ever wrote,
shows that science as a key to power and gain is likely to
become a pawn to clever and unscrupulous men, that the
scientist really isn't ruling the roost at all, that he will be
victimized, just as sure as anything, and be used as a tool.
This becomes a theme of much science fiction, of course.[7]
Julian Huxley (the biologist), in the only science fiction he
ever wrote, a story called "The Tissue-Culture King," used
the theme of the superiority of the scientist over ordinary
people; with this superiority the scientist has the right to
meddle with all forms of life, including human.[8] In an
article in the *Saturday Evening Post*, a scientist says: "We
scientists have a right to play God." This is said by, of all
things, an anthropologist.[9] One has a right to play God,
or play Hamlet, or play the organ before the world only
if one has the capacity to do so. So the question is, Just
how godlike is this man's capacity? Many stories by scientists explode this myth of our great capacity, which we
pretend to have by hiding behind our specialties.

James McConnell, a psychologist, wrote a story, a very
good one, called "Learning Theory." It received a lot of
comment. A human scientist, a psychologist, thinks he's

pretty hot stuff; but there is a much smarter psychologist from the planet Uranus, who studies our human psychologist just as a bug under glass because as a man from the outer planet, he is so much more intelligent.[10] That's precisely the hypothesis. If we're the ones who know the answers, if we're the clever ones, the superior ones, we can cut up anybody we want. The psychologist from outer space puts the human psychologist in a maze situation that humiliates him, drives him crazy—which is what happens to poor rats when they are put in mazes. He removes the food from him, and so forth, just as you would treat a rat. What is more, and this is the irony of the story, this wise, wise man from the other planet completely misinterprets the behavior of the animal from earth. Of course the psychologist doesn't impute intelligence to the creature, or anything respectable; but he does have a theory to explain why the man in the maze does what he does. So the victim knows what it is like. Does a scientist have the right to play God? Yes. If one scientist is superior to another, he has the right to play God with the other one. But everybody knows a little bit about science; so where do we draw the line?

It is here that science fiction performs a useful function. We can carry the themes to their logical conclusions, to their *ad absurdum*, bearing in mind what they lead to. In "The Nobel Prize Winners," W. J. Gordon presents a very amusing story on this theme. On visiting a super research center, he explains, "If his picture of industrial research was true, what an indictment! . . . [The staff] never call each other anything but 'Doctor,' and they have an agreement about not showing each other up."[11] That is how scientists get away with projecting the image of superman: they agree that nobody will damage that image with the public. In Gordon's story, the character Dr. Fairly says, "The person they wanted to get rid of is the only man in the lab who really pushes his nose right down there and produces [the person who is running the laboratory]. But he isn't a guild member, no Ph.D., so they dared attack him. . . . The people were nice and clean in their lab smocks, very serious and busy-busy. . . . Over each door was the group name: Operations Research, Physics, Organic Chemistry, Inorganic Chemistry, Electrical Engineering, Mechanical Engineering—the works!" Hurlbet, the manager of the thing, says,

> "We keep the strains pure here—and you know what happened to the collie. Its nose got sharper and its head thinner till its brains were pushed out through its ears. A terrible, terrible thing. But what can I do? They've all got families to support. . . . The minute they're in a jam, my people scream for fancy instruments and tools, big enough to hide behind. . . . Don't laugh, . . . that's how we get the big government research jobs. Monumental cyclotrons and well-behaved, competent people to use them. God save us from competence! Isn't there one nut around? . . . [The board] asked me why I didn't have any great men around, . . . so I hired Cole and Hart, the Nobel Prize winners." I pointed out that Cole and Hart hadn't published anything in twenty years. "Of course not," said Hurlbet. "But look here. This lab is funded from the Defense Department—almost all of it, that is. You must show competence—not brillance. . . . Their degrees must appear on a laundry list of people who will make up the task force. The Defense Department loves the expression 'task force.' They eat it up. . . . Those two old Nobel-O-Rama gentlemen have put me over the top on contracts more than once. [It's the] Star system."[12]

In other words, he's telling us that the great scientists aren't all they're cracked up to be.

Norbert Wiener, in his story called "The Brain," points out that man's moral weakness is man's undoing.[13] The story is about a great brain surgeon who operates on a criminal who has offended him grievously. The man's brain was his moral weakness. He cuts his brain, making him incapable of the clever judgments necessary to carry out his criminal activities. Because of the brain, the criminal had been very smart. Does the doctor have a right to do that? If we become dependent on scientists, we are at their mercy. The doctor, as he is about to operate, says he doesn't like the idea at all: "It's an ugly business — I don't like it. Sometimes it cuts out a man's conscience, and pretty nearly every time it does eerie things to his judgment and personal balance." It is dangerous.

The writer says we feel free to exploit or destroy all other forms of life as we think fit. In contrast, we human beings act as if other living species, animals and plants, exist only for our convenience. We feel free to exploit or destroy them as we see fit. It is true that some sentimental laymen have moral qualms about vivisection, but no orthodox scientist would ever have any hesitation about an experiment involving mere animals. Do we have the right to play god?

There is a terrible story by H. G. Wells — the only one that ever kept me awake, because I was a little kid when I read it in *The Island of Doctor Moreau* — in which the very same thing happens. He cuts up animals and makes terrible creatures of them.[14] In another story by Fred Hoyle, called "The Black Cloud," we read: "It isn't so much the volume of talk that surprises me [among the scientists]. It's the number of mistakes they've made, how often things have turned out differently to what they've expected."[15] Hoyle mustn't let the outsiders in on that sort of thing, but it takes a scientist to get away with something like that. In the story called "The Miracle of the Broom Closet," Norbert Wiener brings in a little religion, which may have a very upsetting effect. He says, as a personal testimony, "In a long career extending over 40 years and three continents, I have never met the ideal scientist."[16] "To upset [a] scientific experiment at all requires a very small miracle indeed, and with a devout and faithful servant praying to Saint Sebastian in the direct presence of his arrows, what can one expect?" he explains.[17] These men are cutting quite near the edge. The scientist is not the tremendous, magisterial, powerful, and masterful image that was projected in the early science fiction.

And John R. Pierce, another scientist, an experimental psychologist, in a famous story called "John Sze's Future" (one of those "after the holocaust" stories), wrote: "In the world that the experimental psychologists had pulled together from the chaos of nuclear destruction, no one cared to speak the obscenity that physics had become."[18] Physics had become a dirty word, and because physical scientists were taboo, they were hiding under rocks and bridges. The only people who were really respected were psychologists, who were God. (I don't know how ironic Pierce intends this.) He relates,

> After the atomic blowup, . . . the experimental [psychology] men brought the remnants of the human race together. They founded our civilization; they evolved our culture. [No place for God in all this.] We live in a world in which orthodox scientists [a strange thing to say] refuse to see, or seeing, refuse to believe, that which is before their very eyes, . . . [that] a future that the openminded, the perceptive among us, have already foreseen, [is at hand].[19]

This is the way scientists talked about religion a very short time ago. Now it is the orthodox scientists whom Pierce jumps on, who refuse to see that which is before their very eyes. The dead hand of scientific orthodoxy cannot long delay the coming future. The dead hand of what? Scientific orthodoxy. The antidote to science is more science, but it is my science, Pierce insists. Get rid of those awful physicists; they are going to destroy us.

At the dawn of Western science, Heraclitus pointed out very clearly what many science fiction writers are now discovering: If the scientist is a faulty instrument—he is a human being after all—he will make mistakes, and the world he gives will be his own after all. The great scientist is not doing what he thinks he is doing—getting outside of the smoke-filled room. He is in it; that is when he is taking his measurements. We ring the changes on the same old bells, and every time we hit on a new combination, we gleefully announce that we have discovered a whole new set of bells. It sounds like it, but after a time, we begin to see that it is the same old belfry.

In his portrayal of the great mathematician G. H. Hardy, C. P. Snow says, "He could not endure having his photograph taken. . . . He would not have any looking glass in his rooms, not even a shaving mirror. When he went to a hotel, his first action was to cover all the looking-glasses with towels. . . . [Of] all mechanical contrivances including fountain pens, he had a deep distrust. . . . He [the great scientist] had a morbid suspicion of mechanical gadgets (he never used a watch), in particular of the telephone."[20] He hated all gadgets. His autobiography is "witty and sharp with intellectual high spirits: But it is also, in an understated stoical fashion, a passionate lament for creative powers that used to be and that will never come again." It is a book of such haunting sadness, because Hardy realizes "with the finality of truth, that he is absolutely finished."[21] Here again, we see these strangely acting men.

Notably, science fiction worships efficiency; it would promote in us bumbling amateurs the notion of the superiority of the scientific way over all other ways; the scientist doesn't guess, he knows. The scientific mind is direct, clear, intense, trenchant, clean; it is unhampered by any defects of wishful or mythical thinking, recognizes only facts, sees things always and only as they are. There are still people who talk that way: There is no assignment that science could not carry out. But who gives the assignments? This may be the point.

Nevertheless, the preoccupation with ways and means is another thing that science fiction has been helpful in explaining. Where does science lead us? Many years ago, the Edinburgh geographer Alfred McKinder (his student was Haushofer, Hitler's advisor) wrote a book on his geopolitics; it contains a marvelous section on ways and means. He claims the Germans always lose the war because they are so scientific. They know all about ways and means; they have everything figured out with the slide rule, everything to the sixth decimal place. They know just how it is. But they don't know exactly what they're after — they have just a vague idea of world conquest, so they always lose the war. By contrast, the British bungle along, and they really do bungle. Yet they conquered half the world with a mere task force, a mere token force, mere bluff, because they knew what they wanted. If you know what you want, you can always get it, McKinder argued. Bungle toward it, and you'll get it in the end. But if you just bog down in ways and means, you'll never get it. Science, he says, is preoccupation with *ways and means*, and, ironically, science fiction has been first to point that out.[22]

Recently (1969) in the *Christian Science Monitor*, W. H. Pickering, the director of the Jet Propulsion Lab at Caltech, said, "We are building communication systems very close to the ultimate you can ever get." We "can use more power, . . . [but] we are near the ultimate in performance."[23] *Ultimate* is a strong word. What happens to unending perfectability when we are already near the ultimate? Then comes the realization that perfectability lies in another direction, in another dimension. So "it's not a question of how difficult such exploration is." Ways and means isn't the problem. We'll always get the gadget if we know what we want.[24] He speaks of going even beyond the planets to the stars, the ultimate in human achievement, according to science fiction. But that isn't achievement at all, he explains. The question is whether or not what we're doing is worthwhile. The question is not the question of business, industry, and the military, as McKinder points out, but how to get a particular thing done. But what is it we are after, after all?

When William Morris's student rushed to him with the breathless news that the cable to India had been completed, Morris asked, "Young man, what message will it bear?" When Einstein heard that the atom bomb really worked, he grabbed his head and said, "Oy vey!" (Oh my, this is terrible!) He wasn't thrilled at all. Ted Serious today is causing a terrific rumpus everywhere; he's this guy who, when he gets drunk, can project images on film—sometimes he can't, sometimes he can. He has been tested—it seems that he can do it, all right. But the mere fact that he makes images appear on film is considered a wonder, and it is. But what images? Nobody cares.

British investigators, says Sir Oliver Lodge, are very firmly believed to receive spirit messages.[25] But what messages? Idiot gibberings and scribblings. The world makes a major measure over whether Joseph Smith really saw angels, possessed gold plates, or translated Egyptian, but they could not care less about what the angels, the plates, and the papyri have to say. For our age, the message is the medium, because we've run out of messages. A wise German scientist, writing very recently in a journal (which someone subscribed to for me some years ago, and is pretty good for popular people like me) called *Kosmos*, wrote a very good leading editorial. The theme is that nothing could be more foolish than for science to do or make something simply because it hasn't been done before and can be done now. A few years ago, this would have been thought rank heresy. But why do we need to make all these things? The important thing is, we know we can do it now. But why bother? It is like the hunter who has reached such a height of proficiency he now uses blanks, or doesn't use shells at all—he's not interested. It is really not sporting anymore, as long as he knows it can be done. A cobalt bomb can be made, but is that any reason for making it? We used to think, Oh yes, think of the wonderful things we can do.

This going forward without knowing where we're going, unable to think of any other goal but more power and more gain, and more gain for more power, is the way of insanity. Many stories point this out. From Tales of Ecstasy, then, science fiction quickly turned to Tales of Terror. Is there nothing in between? No, there isn't. Snow's scientists, great scientists, are manic depressive. They're either on top of the wave, or they're in the dumps, desperately haunted men, because you are either going somewhere, or you are going nowhere. If nowhere, no matter how great your eminence, how loud the shouting, it is but a brief, pathetic interlude, "One Moment in Annihilation's Waste. [You're not going anywhere.] One Moment, of the Well of Life to taste—the Stars are setting and the Caravan, starts for the Dawn of Nothing—Oh, make haste!"[26]

Groff Conklin, in his collection of works by great scientists, observes,

> Scientists on the whole are far too enthralled with their scientific work to want to go off on sidetrails that involve plot, characterization, and all that. . . . [But they have taken to writing science fiction for one reason: terror. They want to warn us. They want] to express moral or ethical points of view on science and its possible misuse. It is unfortunate that the stories . . . have been thought of by their readers as fantasies produced by great minds . . . rather than as the strong and pertinent warnings that they are on the dangers to certain applications of science or technology. It is also too bad that these men, once they have written their fictionalized danger signals, then ceased story writing entirely perhaps be-

cause they felt defeated by the lack of impact of their first efforts at education through fiction.[27]

The scientists think it their duty to the public, so they try their hand at it, but for some reason the stories don't cause the flurry they might, and so they fall over. But Conklin observes, "Almost all scientists who have dabbled in science fiction are modern scientists of the past twenty-five years [written in 1962]."[28] Then we have a little book that contains at least 75 percent of the science fiction written in English—by scientists. They're now writing to warn us. Science fiction has failed in the greatest promise of comfort and joy. Even the science fiction of H. G. Wells becomes fascinating only when he turns his attention to the sinister and appalling. The scientist becomes the mad scientist before you know it, as in *The War of the Worlds* and *The Island of Doctor Moreau*.[29] If science fiction can show us no convincing glories ahead, at least it can give us the comfort and warning, and it's a dismal message.

If John Jacob Astor could only think of aliens as inferior and dangerous, something to be met with guns, then combat is the theme; and of course it has remained that with Tarzan, and Doc Savage, and all the rest.[30] The alien is called the Bug-Eyed Monster, or BEM, in the school of science fiction writing, and it has the greatest appeal to adolescents; it once dominated the pulps. We are told it is now spurned by the better class of science fiction writers, but we mustn't believe it. The BEMs are in there as much as ever.

Thus, beginning with a great scientist of godlike knowledge and uprightness as central character, science fiction soon discovered chinks in the armor and ended up in very short order with the sinister figure of the mad scientist, either making a Frankenstein monster he can't control or deliberately perverting his knowledge for power. The mad scientist became a stock figure of the great scientist. He

passed away because he was altogether too fantastic, anyway.

A new book, *The Year 2000*, by Herman Kahn and Anthony Wiener, according to a reviewer, points out thousands of ways in which the world can go wrong, and the
very few ways in which it can go right. The chances of its
going right are extremely remote, according to these authors.[31] After all, how many wrong answers are there to
a problem? As many as you want. But how many right
ones? Very few. There are thousands of ways, the science
people point out to us now, in which the world can go
wrong, and only one way it can go right; there is the gospel.

Here are some of the new stories by scientists with the
end-of-the-world theme: in "Pilot Lights of the Apocalypse" (notice the common borrowing of biblical themes)
by Ridenour, the military controls the push buttons and
brings absolute disaster.[32] The militarists have the technique, they have the power, they have the ways and means
within their control by pushing the button; but they don't
really know what's going on. They don't know what's
beyond that, or what it is going to lead to. Another story,
by scientist Chandler Davis, is called "Last Year's Grave
Undug" and is also an after-the-holocaust story in which
the patrioteers have liquidated each other. The United
States invaded itself; everybody had haunting fears that
everybody else wasn't what he should be, and so they
wiped each other out.[33] A story by Leo Szilard (the famous
Hungarian all-around genius who died recently) called
"Report on Grand Central Terminal" features the deserted
earth: everything is wiped out, because the earth divided
into two factions (Shiz and Coriantumr), who extinguished
each other.[34] Another by Chandler Davis, called "Adrift
on the Policy Level," poses the question What can science
do? He says that science is the hard way — a matter of power
and salesmanship,[35] the same thing you deal with when
you're up against a corporation. Personality is the principal

asset of (rather than the path of becoming) scientists. The world of science is ruled by rhetoric; it is not the hardware that is important, but who controls it. The salesman is the one on top, Davis says.

"Nobody Bothers Gus," by Algis Budrys, is an alienation story in which the human race is described as *homo nondescriptus*.[36] The story deals with the idea of why humanity exists. If we don't know why, what's all the use of all these fancy, magnificent, shiny cities, materials, and everything else? The story concludes, What purpose did *homo nondescriptus* serve, and where was he going? We don't know.

And in "The Prize of Peril," Robert Sheckley, the most cynical and amusing of the present authors, tells a terrible story of total degeneration of society expressed in a TV gimmick in which scientists fight and exterminate each other.[37] In a story by Damon Knight, "The Handler," the look is everything.[38] Isaac Asimov, who dabbles in all sorts of things and writes a great deal of science fiction, features, in a story called "Dreaming Is a Private Thing," daydreaming as a highly paid profession. People have become too lazy to dream on their own, so specialists daydream; tracks are made, to be sold all around the country so people can have somebody to daydream for them.[39] Morganson, a psychologist, writes in "Coming-of-Age Day" of a compulsory sex gadget.[40] Lafferty in "Slow Tuesday Night" manipulates time *ad absurdum*.[41] These are all depressing stories.

An important theme is the victory of the robot—the ultimate in automation, regimentation, specialization, efficiency, and exploitation. The robot works for everybody. The robot does not, however, overpower suddenly. Humanity surrenders its functions gradually and willingly to the machine; this we read in countless robot stories—the favorite theme. The machine can move into a vacuum only after we have moved out; as soon as we have turned ourselves into robots, then we can be replaced by robots. When men use hardware to control the world, its resources, and other men, the hardware brings about destruction. Mormon 8 seems appropriate: "For behold, ye do love your . . . substance . . . more than ye love the poor" (Mormon 8:37). We love our expensive hardware, as described by Mormon, more than we esteem the inexpensive "live software." With what result? Again, the old science fiction theme — destruction: "Behold, the sword of vengeance hangeth over you; and the time soon cometh" (Mormon 8:41) — because you love your hardware, your substance, more than you love people.

Much is being written about the surrender to the specialization, to despiritualization. Martin Greenberg attributes the beginning of the robot to "R.U.R.," *Rustem's Universal Robots*, a play by Karel Capek. The robot is a creature that does work for a highly specialized job and nothing else; he becomes the worker, and then the thinker, and maybe even the feeler.[42] This is the favorite theme of stories today — robots that may have feelings. Do they or don't they? Greenberg explains, "The 'growth' of the robot continues until he ultimately achieves acceptance as an entity by his creators. The final phase in the inevitable ascent of 'man's servant,' is reached when man has disappeared and only a robotic civilization remains. A new cycle has begun, . . . when man is re-created by the beings he himself gave birth to."[43] Thus the machine takes the place not only of man, but of God. So we replace ourselves completely by robots; we do it ourselves. Nowadays, this is old stuff, or at least we are getting used to it. The Sutro Museum in San Francisco has a great collection of nineteenth-century clockwork people, just as impressive as real people, and they do all sorts of things. It is hard for us today to imagine the effect of clockwork man on eighteenth-century thinking, but it was great. Not only great but horrible. Ernst Theodor Amadeus Hoffman's *The Sand-*

man tells a story of a doll named Olympia,[44] just a pretty doll, but she was run by machinery. The doll became a monster as soon as it was accepted as a living thing. It is the same thing with the Golem: the Golem is just a machine that works; but when people regard the Golem as a personality, it becomes a horrible object.[45] The same theme occurs in the tales of Edgar Allen Poe, in Oscar Wilde's writings, and of course in Frankenstein. The monster is not a monster because of size. It doesn't have to be terrible-looking—the doll of Olympia was a beautiful object. It became a very terrible thing when people took it seriously.

Writing in the *Science Journal* in 1968, the editor says, There's no danger of machine personality devaluing human beings or that man "will suffer a loss of innocence if he comes to understand his own mental workings." The real danger, which is very serious, is "the programming of people to behave like computers."[46] Then he cites the case at the University of Michigan: students were conditioned to react to mere numbers with intense anxiety and other emotions, and to have programmed dreams. He continues, "If I were a parent of one of these students, I should be raising hell. . . . I am shocked that [the University of Michigan] tolerated this."[47]

In contrast, there is the case of the well-known Egyptian story. In the court of a pharaoh in the Old Kingdom, more than forty-five hundred years ago, was a magician who performed the favorite trick of Egyptian scientists, namely replacing the head of a decapitated goose or duck so that the bird could give a couple of quacks. It can actually be done and was considered a great thing. Someone in the court asked the magician whether the same could be done with a man, and the magician said it could. It was suggested that the act be tried on a criminal who was sentenced to be decapitated anyway, but the magician talked the pharaoh into abandoning the idea. He said that a man may have been condemned to death for crime, but it was his prerogative to die with dignity, to pay the price and no more.[48] Human beings are not to be subjected to this sort of thing, to be stooges for clever lab demonstrations. We've come a long way from the Old Kingdom of Egypt, where the pharaoh refused to let a condemned criminal serve as an experimental animal, to where this man says we have the right to play God and cut up anybody we feel like.

In Asimov's very popular story "Lenny," Susan Calvin says to Peter, "What's the use, you said, of a robot that was not designed for any job? Now I ask you — what's the use of a robot designed for only one job? It begins and ends in the same place." Lenny accidentally gets programmed the wrong way and begins to have human feelings.[49] This is the point. Asimov continues, "An industry tells us what it needs; a computer designs the brain; machinery forms the robot; and there it is, complete and done." But the same industry also wants the same type of man, one reliable as the robot to do certain things and nothing else.[50] And this is the theme, of course, of much thinking and writing; we just take the robot's place.

There are now (1968) 60,000 computers in the world (40,000 in the United States, 3,000 in the United Kingdom), all built within the last decade. Zera Colburn, who is *hexadactylous* (six fingers on both hands), extracted the cube root of 413,993,348,677 in five seconds: needless to say, in his head. Here is a real science fiction figure, a physical and mental freak. Is the world any better off because of him? (I don't mean to speak disrespectfully.) Socrates asks at the beginning of his famous discourse, "If every athlete in the world could run twice as fast as he does, lift twice as heavy a weight, jump twice as far, hit twice as hard, would the world be the least bit better off?" The world doesn't exist for specialists.

A favorite theme is the superior efficiency of the robot built by other robots, so programmed that any mistakes or malfunctions are automatically corrected. Machines are becoming more and more human, more refined, more complicated, more sensitive in their reactions, until they may even begin to feel emotions. Robert Bloch's story "Almost Human" is a good example of that. With human emotions and human sensibilities—human temper and tantrums, human fears and misgivings, and all the rest—come human fallibility; they are the very stuff of which human fallibility is made.[51] "Computers usually work with much greater accuracy than the human brain," says N. S. Sutherland, a British computer expert, "but if any element in a computer becomes faulty, then catastrophic errors occur."[52] A very good but terrifying story on this theme by Ron Goulart is called "Terminal." The robots get old, their relays wear out, wires get disconnected, and so forth, and then all hell breaks loose.[53] This is the point. But, says Sutherland, "in contrast to this, except in pathological conditions, the brain does not break down completely and, although much information processing is done rather inaccurately [to say the least], the result is almost never complete nonsense,"[54] whereas if one thing goes wrong with a machine the result is complete nonsense. In other words, the machine, while it functions, is an idiot savant (a person who can do fantastic things, but just those, and do them very well.) But if something goes wrong, as things do go wrong, in the material as well as the spiritual world, all is lost.

Incidentally, a whole issue of the *Science Journal* is devoted to intelligent machines; the editor writes, "I believe diversity is rewarding in itself and deplore the way in which the world is tending to a single universal culture . . . [which used to be thought a great blessing; when I was in high school, this was the thing they looked forward to—a great, universal single culture, and not even a very admirable one]. I regard respect for life as the touchstone of ethics." Then he notes the 240 species of animals now threatened with extinction.[55] The gospel applies here too, because "God has commanded that all forms of life should multiply and fulfill the measure of their creation, that every form of life might have joy therein." How very different this is from coming out and saying, "You just specialize and do this, or do that."

Another award goes to Jack Vance, who wrote an exciting story, but the usual thing: "The Mechs of Revolt." Although it is a new story, you would think it was written forty years ago. The Mech-brain (that is, the mechanical man) is from another world (though we've made Mech-brains work for us here). The Mech-brain falls shortest in its lack of emotional color: one Mech is precisely like another. They serve us efficiently because they think nothing about their condition. They neither loved us nor hated us, nor do they now. Why did they revolt? For a familiar reason. The answer is just as unoriginal as the question: because they do not like to be serving somebody else all the time, and because the world is too small for two races — one exploits the other. And this is supposed to be original science fiction.

One of my children has the psychology book *Psychology: The Science of Behavior*, by A. A. Branca. On the flyleaf and covers are three photographs of a rat in a box.[56] (Never mind that the poor rat is almost certainly crazy, driven insane by the ways of science. A good recent article on that subject claims that these animals are not living under normal conditions, and they soon lose their balance; a creature in a maze is not a normal creature at all.) In the inky tracks that show the rat's wanderings in the box, our school children are told, are a sure index to the workings of the mind. The genius of behaviorism was to discover that overt behavior is the only kind we can study; therefore, to all intents and purposes, overt behavior is the complete disclosure of the mind at work. It is the story of the lost keys. We look in a certain place, not because we think we lost them there, but because conditions for looking there are much more convenient and comfortable than elsewhere. We search for the mind in a rat maze because it is easy to make mazes and put rats in them. But psychology, being the science of behavior, is the equivalent to religion being the study of bells and steeples, or patriotism being the study of firecrackers. Only the external aspects of the thing can be studied. Therefore, for the sake of convenience, we assume that only the external aspects exist, and of course this leads to trouble.

A big issue today, being discussed a great deal, is Do computers think? I won't go into that, but recently a German science journal, in an editorial, asked the question (which has started a furor), "Does a tea-strainer think?" A tea-strainer has one simple task to perform, and it is a task that requires making a decision. It must remove the leaves from the tea and let the liquid pass through. In this act of selectivity, the editor points out, the tea-strainer does just what a computer does. So if a computer thinks, so does a tea-strainer. The response from the readers, many of them scientists, was spirited. Most of the contributors vigorously defended the proposition that a tea-strainer does think. Some felt that the effect of this doctrine was not to exalt the tea-strainer as a thinker, but to debase the mind of man as an automaton. Others replied heatedly that that simply showed their pride, arrogance, and pigheadedness. They would not admit that a tea-strainer thinketh as a man thinketh because they didn't want to believe it.

Marvin Minsky, an electrical engineer at M.I.T., says, "Our pious skeptics told us that machines could never sense things. Now that machines can see [he doesn't put *see* in quotes, he just assumes that machines see] complex shapes, our skeptics tell us that we can never know that they sense things. Do not be bullied by authoritative pronouncements about what machines will never do. Such statements are based on pride, not fact."[57] How neatly the issue is drawn here. André Maurois actually wrote a science fiction story, based on the stubborn insistence of scientist friends of his who observed the social instinct behavior of insects and animals and maintained that the creatures do not think.[58] They admit that insect and animal behavior shows all the outward signs of intelligence and that they sometimes display amazing problem-solving capacities. Scientists admit that, but they insist that no intelligence whatever is involved, taking the position of Bertrand Russell that "animals behave in a manner showing the rightness of views of the man who observes them," not the animal itself.[59] The rightness of their behavior and the correctness of their response is appreciated by the beholder, but the actors themselves are completely unaware of what they are doing.

These same scientists who unhesitatingly and emphatically insist that animals do not think, in spite of the clear thought patterns implied in their behavior, insist just as unhesitatingly and emphatically that machines do think, because of the thought patterns implied by their behavior. The electric eye that opens the door for you at the supermarket is able to think. In the best Watsonian sense, it gives a useful, sensible response to a definite stimulus. And what is thought, but a matter of response to stimulus? But the dog, who gives you a resentful, guilty look and scurries out of your way at the supermarket, doesn't think at all. He seems to be aware he's not welcome in the store, but that's only your impression of the way he behaves. So the electric eye, which opens the door, is thinking, but the dog has no thought at all. The question is just a matter of opinion and interpretation.

Exactly the same sort of yea and nay was reached with the argument of the stars. The Sophists said, "Look, the stars are just moving up there; that proves there's no God." Aristotle looked at the same stars moving and said, "That proves there is a God. I don't need any more argument." The very same evidence, but two different conclusions.

And it is the same way here. You see a response to a stimulus; that proves thought, because it was an intelligent response. The tea-strainer took out the tea leaves, as it is supposed to.

"There's a real possibility," writes Sutherland, "that we may one day be able to design a machine that is more intelligent than ourselves, . . . a species of superior intelligence to replace ourselves as lords of the Earth. The species could also of course be morally much superior to ourselves."[60] Here we see the enormity—or rather perversion—of a misconception. According to the early Christian idea of the ancient law of liberty, a gadget programmed in a way that avoided any behavior that might be called immoral would not be a morally superior being at all. When Simon Magus asked Peter, "Could not God have made us all good so that we could not do anything else but be virtuous?"[61] (Satan wanted to program everybody to be virtuous and nothing else; St. Augustine later asked the same question in anguish), Peter replied,

> That's a foolish question, for if he made us unchangeably and immovably inclined to good, we wouldn't really be good at all, since we couldn't really be anything else. And it would be no merit on our part that we were good, nor could we be given credit for doing what we did by necessity of nature. How can you call any act good that is not performed intentionally?[62]

Of course that is the answer to this idea that we could make a machine morally superior to ourselves because we program it not to do certain naughty things. Would you call that a moral machine? What an enormous gulf between this type of thinking and the gospel!

Incidentally, in the same issue in which Minsky let out that blast about our pride, an article by J. N. Holmes says, "As recently as April of this year Professor D. B. Fry of University College, London, said he thought [a machine which can understand normal, fluent, human speech] might never be possible."[63] A crew has been working on that a long time. And talking about Aldous, the machine at the University of Texas which reacts, which seems to have emotions, which reacts with fear, anger or attraction, reminds us (and this should be emphasized, but it is diligently deemphasized by most of us) that Aldous is only a model of personality, not the thing itself. Thus when I speak of Aldous's fear, I refer to a numerical variable in the program that takes on different forms to represent different degrees of fear. The model or computer does not *feel* (and Aldous underlines that) any more than a molecular model of plastic balls and wooden dowels will enter into a real chemical combination. The introspection routine in Aldous can report on certain of its states because it was constructed to do so. It is not a pipeline to some ghostly inner world of the computer. This argument goes on, as a theme of many science fiction stories today.

Frank George, who is in charge of the program in England for computers, says, All this simulates emotion, "sometimes deceptively like the real thing. . . . If you build imitation human responses into a machine, then you've cheated; you haven't done anything really interesting, however practical."[64] It is precisely this dissimulation that is the satanic part of the machine. So we want to watch that we don't get programmed.

The basic characteristic of science fiction is its unoriginality. It is, as Judith Merril says, a commentary on present conditions, what will happen if things continue in the same course they are now in.[65] As such, it can perform a valuable critical function. The stock themes of science fiction are "the wonderful journey," including time travel; "the wonderful invention," including the time machine; "the end of the world," especially today, after the atom bomb, after the holocaust; then the beginning of the new world; "big and little," we mentioned before—mere size; "the con-

quest" —the war of the worlds, galactic empires; strange
visitors, including the Bug-Eyed Monsters, and including
visitors better than people on our world. "The duel" is a
great favorite today—the magnificent fighting machines
dueling to the last survivor, lights out. Other great themes
today include "the breakdown" of the machine, including
the revolt of the robots; "strange worlds," usually pure
description, far-future or far away in distance, and man
coping with the challenge of strange environments; "boy
meets girl" (humanity is the same in all environments);
"man meets rival"; and "alienation."

Every one of these themes is biblical; and often the
authors use biblical terms in their titles, showing where
the titles came from. Science fiction writers, with the ad-
vantages of modern science, presume to describe and interpret more accurately than the scriptures, and the result is
rather pathetic. Brian Wilson Aldiss, who is editing the
stuff in the latest anthologies, claims that writers are running out of ideas; they have nothing to offer anymore. The
once-daring assumptions are no longer daring; they are
clichés. Originally, science fiction stories had bold and imaginative thinking behind them; now they merely anni-
hilate thinking.[66] In the last issue of *Kosmos* (the journal I
get—but don't think I'm quite the scientist just because I
get a German science journal), the leading article by Professor Werner Braunbek was entitled "1968 brachte keine
Revolutionen in der Physik."[67] Compared with 1957, 1958,
and 1960, it *was* quite barren. Aldiss goes on:

> In the science fiction we are getting today, we can't
> find any good stuff. The decay of language that always
> goes hand in hand with the decay of ideas is what we
> find. There is no science here, no imagination. Spaceship
> tales, robot tales, invention tales, these old themes roll
> forth, clad in dead language. Guys still fight over the
> last oxygen cylinder on Mars. The great big, wonderful
> world of Western technology is rolling on, but nothing
> is being done about it.

Isn't it because the great big, wonderful world of Western technology itself is plainly going nowhere? Science fiction, after all, is simply reacting to the emptiness of the material it depends on. The antics of Tarzan and Fu Manchu are almost perfectly representative of the type of science fiction appearing in the contemporary catalogs: the super-brain and super-brawn of man outcalculates, outwits, outcomputes hordes of robots and other monsters, mechanical or organic, and it is all on the level of naked power, right out of the worlds of the Djins of the *1001 Nights*. Isn't that the world we live in already? This is the science fiction that appeals to us most; so we get the apocalyptic stories. No matter how negative science fiction has become, it still can't be original. The worst you can think of happening has already happened.

It really does seem that the effect of every major scientific discovery has been to make men lose their balance, giving them a sense of dependence on anything but themselves. A wonderful passage from Socrates says, "When I was a kid and went to school, science knew all the answers. We knew that the brain was the center of everything, and we were on top of the world. We were just too cocky for anything." Plutarch talks about the same thing. He says the new physics taught people "to despise all the superstitious fears which the awe-inspiring signs in the heavens arouse in the minds of those who are ignorant of the real cause of things."[68] From then on, the Sophists carried the ball as ardent debunkers of all that was not science. The Milesian school claimed again and again to have discovered the basic principles and elements of all existence. In launching the program of modern science, Bacon announced that if he could just enjoy one season of uninterrupted work he would be able to embrace all knowledge in a single system. Newton's discoveries were held to answer all the essential problems of cosmology for all times. By a simple rule of thumb, Darwin explained

forever the origin of all forms of life. Freud, by a single
stroke, solved all our psychological problems. Grimm's law
explained the nature of all languages. The computers finally can solve all problems of any kind. As Whitehead
reminds us, it seems with every breakthrough that this is
the immediate response. It's always the same old story:
"Now at last we have certitude!"[69] Even though we had it
before, again and again and again, and it turned out to be
wrong—no, at last we do have it. The most wonderful
machines have already been invented long ago. We think
of computers as intelligent entities because we're not used
to living with them. That is all. When a punched card or
magnetized tape is stored away, we think of it as memory,
because of the novelty of the thing. We don't think a book
remembers, even when it can be arranged to be opened
automatically at a given item of information by pressing a
button, like an address finder. Isn't that memory? No, we
say, that isn't memory at all. We've been living with that.
But once upon a time people thought it was. There was a
time when people thought the book was actually a thinking
machine; it would think for you. They thought it such a
miracle they couldn't get over it. It took them a long time
to get used to it. And then they realized that the book
wasn't actually thinking or remembering. It was just *you*
operating *it*. Yet those who didn't understand how it
worked really believed that the written page was a thinking, living entity, just as we now think that the computer
has a memory.

Plato (in talking about the Egyptians) tells a wonderful
story about this. When Hermes, who was Thoth in Egyptian, discovered writing, he went to Ammon, the father
of the gods, in great excitement. "I have discovered a device that will infinitely project the power of the human
mind—writing." Of course, it is a tremendous invention;
it beats anything else one can imagine. But Hermes was
wrong, as Ammon immediately pointed out. Writing will

not aid men's mental powers, Ammon said, but cripple
them. It will seriously damage both their power to think
and to remember.[70]

In the end, no gadget makes us better off. This may
sound strange, but if we think of it, the purpose of every
gadget is to liquidate itself. As it is improved more and
more, it becomes progressively reduced in size, complexity, cost, and rarity, until in the end the best transportation
is that which requires no gadget at all. Gigantic trans-
formers, cables, wheels, rails, enormous computers filling
whole buildings, ponderous weapons, monstrous machines — all those belong to the essentially barbaric world.

The ultimate achievement is to do what we want to do
without depending on gadgets. The best gadget is no
gadget. There are some stories on that. But on this idea of
futility, the hero, in a story by Chad Oliver, says, "I sometimes think there's nothing as dull as constant, everlasting
change. . . . The devil of it is, there's just plain nothing
new under the sun, to coin an inspired phrase."[71] There's
nothing behind the door, just more of the same. That's
what the writers are telling us now. Fritz Leiber, who has
written a lot of junk, writes a story called "Marianna"
whose closing line is, "Annihilation brings unutterable relief."[72] This idea, a favorite theme of Heinlein, is that when
we've solved all our problems, when we've licked the biological problems, when we've even solved the problems
of death, then what do we do? We sit round bored to tears,
yearning for death, because we have nothing to live for
anyway. Without the gospel, life is completely hollow.

There are more stories on this theme. In one called
"Traveller's Rest," by David Masson, there is a perennial
war going on all the time. Ordinary people bother little
about the war; their spare mental energies are spent in a
vast selection of play and ploys: making, representing,
creating, relishing, criticizing, theorizing, discussing, arranging, organizing, cooperating. That sounds like living.

But it is all busywork, meaningless in the end, futile.[73] In a story by Arthur C. Clarke, who has written much, called "At the End of the Orbit,"[74] the theme is clear. Boy meets girl in a sputnik background. In one by William Morrison, called "A Feast of Demons," people can make themselves get younger and older all they want;[75] it is terrible, because nobody dies. Our old friend Isaac Asimov comes back again in the story "The Eyes Do More Than See."[76] The main character, Ames, hopes to manipulate matter before the assembled energy beings who have so drearily waited over the eons for something new. He flees back across the galaxies on the energy track of Brock, back to the endless doom of life. The energy beings can no longer weep for the fragile beauty of the bodies they had once given them a trillion years ago. The worlds lose all significance; there is nothing behind the door. We go back to "the endless doom of life," doomed to more of the same. So when we go out in space, what do we find? Just more of the same we find here, and it is not as good. What a disillusionment.

The splendors and high hopes soon shot their bolt and fizzled, because they had nowhere to go. Science without religion, like philosophy without religion, has nothing to feed on. "All [true] science," says Karl Popper, "is cosmology";[77] and all cosmology is eschatology: "It is my contention that any branch of human thought without religion soon withers and dies of anemia." In the symposium "Life in Other Worlds," sponsored by the Seagram Whiskey Company,[78] such scientists as G. B. Kistiakowsky, Donald N. Michael, Harlow Shapley, Otto Struve, and Arnold Toynbee went out of their way to show something that had nothing to do with the case, namely that the existence of life on other worlds is at last the definite, final proof that we need to rule God out of the picture. The immediate effect of scientific discovery was a sense of emancipation; we are now on our own. At last man can throw off the shackles of the past. God was all right for our ancestors, but we certainly don't need him in our calculations. Man is, at last, the master. A great deal of scientific experience, as well as science fiction, has shown that that is the way to madness.

So science fiction is a faith-promoting discipline after all. It is a wasteland, a heap of slag, as far as the eye can see — joyless, endless, monotonous, repetitive, empty but cluttered, a haunted universe. When we think that the project started out as a joyful and confident search for the best world or worlds the human mind could conceive and bring into existence, and after generations of untrammeled and soaring imagination, this desolate city dump is what we have come up with — well, it shows how far we can get without the gospel.

My time is up, and I should be entertaining questions, but I have some ancient texts that beat all science fiction hollow. I will read a sample of each: the *Berlin Manuscript* (*Kephalaia*),[79] the newly discovered *Apocalypse of Abraham*,[80] some from the *Clementine Recognitions*,[81] and one from the *Ginza*, that is, early Christian Mandaean.[82] Some of these are very good, and they are good science fiction, too. I keep the translation quite literal, as literal as possible, but of course I load the dice all along, you can well imagine. The Lord is talking to the apostles, in a very early Christian document (first or early second century): "This earth is littered with remnants of other worlds which have been mixed up in earth fire in places where it is still impossible for plants to take root." There are desolate places on the earth — forms and stages of creation. "But what about the material that is still out there in orbit?" the apostles ask the Lord. He replies, "They still surround the earth in the sky, but they are not brought down into the common crucible." The word used is *trench* — there exists a sort of circulating trench; and as matter is required, it is drawn off from this, being purified by the circular motion. Further, "It's first poured down upon the earth, and then swept together and thrown into a pit, a sort of crucible. This is so that the fumes [this is a passage nobody understands] can mount up and mingle with yet more elements which are to descend" — in some kind of feedback process. Then he says, "There are space waters out there, too, but they have to be purified of certain poisoned elements of outer darkness."

The idea that things coming from outer space are poisoned and must be decontaminated before they can be used in this earth recurs constantly in these old documents. Great advantage came to the earth when these fragments, or vehicles, were scrapped in the heavens. They were turned into junk, because they were the remnants of other worlds, to be used again. They were swept up from earth and cast out to circulate among the worlds in various disposal areas, where they would follow certain laws that would get them in motion again.

The Father emptied the three vehicles or vessels; the word used here means elements — namely, water, dark heavy matter, and fire — necessary heavenly ingredients used in all these processes.[83] He empties them together in dumps at the edge of the firmament, or else pours them out upon the earth. After that, they will be swept away from the earth to some other place. Each is a deposit of stuff being poured out in a particular place, where it is to be kept until it will be needed, again clothed with the forms — the three forms of wind, water, and fire — which are the three great forces of metamorphosis and erosion that make a world when they are used in a solid body; then, the father says, we start making a world with it.

This is how the earth was established. The sons of light came down in ships and purified the light and removed the slag from the *apporoia* — the scum that is poured off is the slag, the stuff that melts. It is taken to a dump, where there are five types of depositories, from which five elements come as they are necessarily used, some being used more than others.

What we call elements, however, is the energy which is in all things. In the womb of the earth the elements are gathered, fused, and poured out. It is an amazing picture of a physical process of creation, of which we get dim visions. Of course you may protest, "That is certainly a mess"; and it certainly is. But it is the sort of thing Isaac Asimov gives, and is as good as any science fiction you get today, considering its date.

Here is an interesting description from the *Apocalypse of Abraham*. Abraham is taken on a wonderful journey (just as much science fiction begins with the wonderful journey). The whole field of testamentary literature and testaments has seen many discoveries recently, and we learn that any prophet you can name, and any apostle, has a testament; and that testament always ends with a great trip, a guided tour through the universe. (The prophet or apostle usually gets in a vessel of some sort, in which he travels around, inspecting things). Guided by an angel, Abraham passes with violent winds to heaven above the firmament (cf. fig. 49, p. 278). He sees an indescribably mighty light, and within the light there is a vast, seething fire; and within the fire is a great host of moving, changing forms—moving within each other—of mighty forms that exchange with each other and constantly change their forms, as they go and come and alter themselves. They seem to call out to each other, in strange, confused noises.[84]

Abraham asks the angel, "What is this all about? Why have you brought me here? I can't see anything. I don't know what is going on. I've become weak. I think I am out of my mind." The angel answers, "Stay close to me and don't be afraid." The angel is beginning to shake, though. He himself is seeing too much. Then they are wrapped in fire and hear a voice and a mighty rushing of waters. Abraham wants to fall down on his face and worship. But there is no more earth under their feet and nothing to fall on. They're just there, suspended.[85]

Abraham cries out with all his voice, and the angel cries at the same time, "Oh God! Oh, thou who hast brought order into this terrible confusion, into the great confusion of the universe, and hast renewed the worlds of the righteous."[86] There is a power that actually can master these terrible forces whose simple contemplation is absolutely appalling. This is what the great Catholic scholar, Pierre Teilhard de Chardin, a paleontologist who just died, says: man is the most refined being there is. He is much more complicated, in chemistry and everything else; he is far more complicated than a star, even a giant star, or a star system, or a galaxy. This must be the end product of the thing—to be organized and controlled, to be able to carry on like this, with all these terrible forces unleashed all around. This appalling performance is the story of Abraham, who sees it all and says there is a God who can actually bring a world out of such chaos where the righteous can dwell. This is quite an idea.

In one of the very early Christian writings, the *Clementine Recognitions* (the earliest Christian writing we have after the New Testament), we learn the legitimate questions that interested the early Christians, questions to which the church would ordinarily say, "You're not supposed to ask that."[87] Clement said he had been to the university, and the professors couldn't answer his questions; the only person who could answer them was Peter. Clement's questions were "Is there a preexistence? Is there life after death? If we live after, will we remember this life? Why don't we remember the premortal existence? When was the world created? What existed before that? If the world was created, will it pass away? And then what? Will we feel things we cannot feel now?" Clement says he could not shake from his mind the *immortalitatis cupido*, the desire to go on living. It was such questions, he said, that led him to seek the true light.[88] Notice these are primarily scientific questions, but they are actually the basic religious questions, too. The scientists say this doesn't have anything to do with religion; we say that it does.

Clement complained that the Doctors could not give him any answers, only a lot of clever talk, but nothing else. When he was young, the pagan philosophers had scared him out of his wits with stories of hellfire. That came from pagan schools; Clement never learned that hellfire from the Christians. Finally he went to Palestine, where he met Peter at a conference of the church. When he put these questions to Peter straight, he got his answers. "Is the soul mortal or immortal? Was the world created? Why? Can it be dissolved? Will another world take its place? Will there be something better after it? Or will there be anything at all after this world?" Then Peter explained to him how it is, adding that it *is* important to find answers to these things. The important questions are, first of all, what came first? What was the immediate, direct cause of anything, if anything? By whom, through whom, and for whom were things created? Of one, two, or many substances? How many substances are there? Did these substances themselves come out of nothing, or out of something? Is there any virtue? The answers that Peter gives to these legitimate questions are very interesting.[89]

Here's an interesting theme from the early Mandaean Christian writings on other worlds. Those in other worlds move with great, almost instantaneous, speed, as quickly as human thought. In a single hour they reach a distant place. Their motion, however, is calm and effortless, like the rays of the sun passing between heaven and earth.[90] The Father ordered *Hibel Ziwa* (Abel) to make a world and to place Adam and Eve in it. Then the three angels of glory and light would come down and instruct them and keep them company. God said to the pure Sent One, who was to lead this delegation, "Go call Adam and Eve and all their posterity, and teach them concerning everything about the king of light and the worlds of light. Be friendly with Adam, and give him company, you and the two angels that will be with you, and warn him against Satan." The three angels are also instructed to go down and teach Adam the law of chastity. Adam was also told, "We will also send helpers to those of your progeny who seek further light and knowledge from us." This was the principle given them.[91]

There is also a lot to say on the practice of beings visiting other worlds. The Evil One complains about it. Another version says that God sent down the Sent One to help Adam and Eve get back to his presence, where they had come from. He spread a table for them, instructing them there. And then the Evil Ones complained, saying, "The children of men have taken over the earth. They are strangers who speak the language of those three men who visited them. They have accepted the teachings of the three men, and rejected us and our own world, so they plot against us, and they say that Mandadihaya [teacher of life] is coming to give them aid and support. . . . These three men are in this world, but they are not men. They are beings of light and glory. They are trespassing on our territory. They have come to this little *Enosh*, this little man who is helpless and alone in the world, to instruct him and to give him an advantage over us."[92] Thus, the evil beings complain.

This is the very stuff you read about in science fiction all the time, written up beautifully in these old sources, and there is much of it: ships with ropes of light, with crews clothed in light, laden with treasure; going from one world to another, the Evil Ones waylay and pirate it. In the *Psalms of Thomas*, a recent discovery, but a very old text, the Evil One in his ship comes out of I do not know where, and he hijacks the cargo, dividing up the treasure among the worlds over which he rules[93] — the galactic empire motif. He plants precious plants in those worlds, the plants he had stolen. He fixes precious stones in their firmaments, and they glory in their stolen finery. God, on finding out about it, sends a messenger to get back all the stolen things and replant the plants in their proper worlds, for which they had been intended in the first place; and all this is described in very physical terms.

Then he says, "Prepare your people to receive, reclaim, and disinfect all these things they have stolen from us, so that we can put them in the worlds for which they were designated."[94] This messenger is Rezin, the son of light himself, a real person. So Rezin goes and gets the things, and puts them in the worlds where they belong.

Many Coptic documents treat these themes. Note how realistic this example is: From the place of your inheritance, the Lord explains, the sun will look like a little, tiny grain of flour; that is how far away it is from this sun. The distance between the others worlds is vast, their size is enormous, and there is a hierarchy among them. Every one of these worlds is ruled on a single pattern, however, though no two of them are alike. There is always a governing body of twelve, wherever you go. Every *topos* (place) has twelve rulers over each part.[95] Each world, whether it is awaiting occupants — or those who have not yet found their place, who have not yet been assigned — or whether it is already occupied, is governed by the same plan. Every kingdom requires a space; so we have to go down and find a space to build a kingdom. "My father laid his hand upon my head, gave me the name of *Hibbel Yabbah*, and created for me a world, containing ten thousand worlds of light with 360 mighty inner Jordans, and every one of these had 360,000 *Uthras*, and every *skina* had 360,000 *skinas*, and every world was different." Then follow descriptions of these various things.

We read in the *Manichaean Psalmbook* that a thousand thousand mysteries and myriad myriad planets, each with its own mysteries, preceded this world. During Yahweh's great discussions of the new creations that were to take place, he sent down envoys to report to him how things were going. They did not send all the *Uthras*, nor did they teach them all the worlds, and this is the usual order; it says, "Uthra after Uthra will reach thee, will take thee by the right hand, and will show thee worlds" and dwellings and treasure houses, and so forth.

The *Ascension of Isaiah* describes one thing the devils don't know about. They are banished to particular places, and they are not aware of how much really goes on — they miss all the show. The devils exclaim, "We are alone, and there are none besides us." They suffer the same illusion that the human race has suffered for a long time.[96]

I see that the time's nearly gone, and I've almost forgotten to bear my testimony! I can't stop without that. What else is there but the gospel, brothers and sisters? If I didn't believe it, I'd jolly well have to, but I don't believe it for that reason. I believe it because it is true, and I hope we all get testimonies of the gospel. In the name of Jesus Christ, amen.

Notes

1. Thomas S. Kuhn, *The Structure of Scientific Revolutions* (Chicago: University of Chicago Press, 1962), 1.
2. Richard McKenna, "The Secret Place," in Brian W. Aldiss, ed., *Nebula Award Stories: Number Two* (New York: Pocket, 1969), 15.
3. Claude Levi-Strauss, *The Savage Mind* (London: Weidenfeld and Nicolson, 1962).
4. Eric T. Bell, "The Ultimate Catalyst," in Groff Conklin, ed., *Great Science Fiction by Scientists* (New York: Collier, 1962), 35–59.
5. Miles J. Breuer, "The Gostec and the Doshes, " in ibid., 63.
6. [Nibley cites C. P. Snow a number of times in this volume, but we have been unable to locate the source.]
7. J. B. S. Haldane, "The Gold Makers," in Conklin, ed., *Great Science Fiction by Scientists*, 125.
8. Julian Huxley, "The Tissue Culture King," in ibid., 147.
9. Edmund R. Leach, "We Scientists Have the Right to Play God," *Saturday Evening Post* (16 November 1968): 16.

10. James McConnell, "Learning Theory," in Conklin, ed., *Great Science Fiction by Scientists*, 227.

11. W. J. J. Gordon, "The Nobel Prize Winners," in Judith Merril, ed., *The 9th Annual of the Year's Best SF* (New York: Simon and Schuster, 1964), 253–67.

12. Ibid., 258–59.

13. Norbert Wiener, "The Brain," in Conklin, ed., *Great Science Fiction by Scientists*, 299.

14. H. G. Wells, *The Island of Dr. Moreau* in *Seven Famous Novels by H. G. Wells* (New York: Knopf, 1934), 69–157.

15. Fred Hoyle, "The Black Cloud," in Frederik Pohl, ed., *The Expert Dreamers* (New York: Doubleday, 1962), 149.

16. Norbert Wiener, "The Miracle of the Broom Closet," in ibid., 183.

17. Ibid., 189.

18. John R. Pierce, "John Sze's Future," in Conklin, ed., *Great Science Fiction by Scientists*, 260.

19. Ibid., 262, 265.

20. See the foreword by C. P. Snow, in G. H. Hardy, *A Mathematician's Apology* (London: Cambridge University Press, 1973), 15–16, 32, 48.

21. Ibid., 50–51.

22. Karl Haushofer, *Leben und Werk* (Rhein: Boldt, 1979), 483–645.

23. Interview with William H. Pickering by Robert C. Cowen, "Tantalizing Invitation to the Solar System," *Christian Science Monitor* (3 February 1969): 9.

24. Ibid.

25. Sir Oliver Lodge, *The Survival of Man* (London: Methuen, 1910), 253, 321–22, 333.

26. Omar Khayyam, *Rubaiyat XXXVIII*, tr. Edward Fitzgerald (Great Britain: Harrop, 1985).

27. Conklin, *Great Science Fiction by Scientists*, 9–10.

28. Ibid., 10–11.

29. Both *The War of the Worlds* and *The Island of Dr. Moreau* are contained in Wells, *Seven Famous Novels by H. G. Wells*.

30. John Jacob Astor, *A Journey in Other Worlds* (New York: Appleton, 1898).

31. Herman Kahn and Anthony J. Wiener, *The Year 2000: A Framework for Speculation on the Next Thirty-Three Years* (New York: Macmillan, 1967).

32. Louis N. Ridenour, "Pilot Lights of the Apocalypse," in Conklin, ed., *Great Science Fiction by Scientists*, 281.

33. Chandler Davis, "Last Year's Grave Undug," in ibid., 103.

34. Leo Szilard, "Grand Central Terminal," in ibid., 291.

35. Chandler Davis, "Adrift on Policy Level," in Pohl, ed., *The Expert Dreamers*, 125.

36. Algis Budrys, "Nobody Bothers Gus," in Judith Merril, ed., *SF: The Best of the Best* (New York: Delacorte, 1967), 310.

37. Robert Sheckley, "The Prize of Peril," in ibid., 325.

38. Damon Knight, "The Handler," in ibid., 344.

39. Isaac Asimov, "Dreaming Is a Private Thing," in ibid., 398.

40. A. K. Jorgensson, "Coming-of-Age Day," in Judith Merril, ed., *11th Annual Edition: The Year's Best S-F* (New York: Delacorte, 1966), 53–65.

41. R. A. Lafferty, "Slow Tuesday Night," in ibid., 34–41.

42. Martin H. Greenberg, ed., *The Robot and the Man* (New York: Gnome, 1953), v-vii.

43. Ibid.; cf. Isaac Asimov, "The Last Question," in *The Best of Isaac Asimov* (New York: Doubleday, 1974), 157–69.

44. Ernst Theodor Amadeus Hoffman, "The Sandman," in *Tales of Hoffman* (Middlesex, England: Penguin, 1982).

45. Arram Davidson, "The Golem," in Merril, ed., *SF: The Best of the Best*, 349.

46. Gordon R. Taylor, "Focus," *Science Journal* 4 (June 1968): 31–32.

47. Ibid.

48. See "King Cheops and the Magicians," 8, 10–9, 1, in William K. Simpson, *The Literature of Ancient Egypt* (London: Yale University Press, 1973), 24.

49. Isaac Asimov, "Lenny," in Pohl, ed., *The Expert Dreamers*, 62; reprinted in Isaac Asimov, *The Rest of the Robots* (New York: Doubleday, 1964), 111–26.

50. Ibid.

51. Robert Bloch, "Almost Human," *Fantastic Adventures* (June 1943): 185, under the pseudonym Tarleton Fiske; cf. Leo Margulies and Oscar J. Friend, eds., *My Best Science Fiction Story* (New York: Merlin, 1949), 66.

52. N. S. Sutherland, "Machines Like Men," *Science Journal* 4 (October 1968): 47.

53. R. Goulart, "Terminal," in Merril, ed., *11th Annual Edition: The Year's Best S-F*, 174–83.

54. Sutherland, "Machines Like Men," 47.

55. Gordon R. Taylor, "Focus," *Science Journal* 4 (May 1968): 35.

56. Albert A. Branca, *Psychology: The Science of Behavior* (Boston: Allyn and Bacon, 1968).

57. Marvin Minsky, "Machines Are More Than They Seem," *Science Journal* 4 (October 1968): 3.

58. André Maurois, "The Earth Dwellers," in Judith Merril, ed., *The Year's Best SF*, 9th ed. (New York: Simon and Schuster, 1964), 229–51.

59. Ibid., 252.

60. Sutherland, "Machines Like Men," 48.

61. *Clementine Recognitions* III, 26, in *PG* 1:1294.

62. Ibid., in *PG* 1:1294–95.

63. J. N. Holmes, "Machines That Talk," *Science Journal* 4 (October 1968): 80.

64. Frank George, "Towards Machine Intelligence," *Science Journal* 4 (September 1968): 82.

65. Judith Merril, ed., *SF12* (New York: Delacorte, 1968), 9–11.

66. Brian Aldiss, "Afterword: Knights of the Paper Spaceship," in Harry Harrison and Brian W. Aldiss, eds., *Best SF: 1967* (New York: Berkley Medallion, 1968), 241.

67. Werner Braunbek, "1968 brachte keine Revolutionen in der Physik," *Kosmos* 12 (December 1968): 490–92.

68. Plutarch, *Pericles* VI, 1.

69. Lucien Price, "To Live without Certitude," *Atlantic Monthly* 193 (March 1974): 58.

70. Plato, *Phaedrus* 274C–275A.

71. Chad Oliver, "The Mother of Necessity," in Conklin, ed., *Great Science Fiction by Scientists*, 245.

72. Fritz Leiber, "Marianna," in Merril, ed., *SF: The Best of the Best*, 255.

73. David Masson, "Traveller's Rest," in Merril, ed., *11th Annual Edition: The Year's Best S-F*, 358–75.

74. Arthur C. Clarke, "At the End of the Orbit," in Pohl, ed., *The Expert Dreamers*, 1.

75. William Morrison, "A Feast of Demons," in ibid., 25.

76. Isaac Asimov, "The Eyes Do More Than See," in Merril, ed., *11th Annual Edition: The Year's Best S-F*, 214–17.

77. Karl Popper, *Conjectures and Refutations* (New York: Harper and Row, 1968), 136.

78. Life in Other Worlds Symposium, sponsored by the Seagram Whiskey Company, March 1, 1961.

79. Carl Schmidt, ed, *Kephalaia*, 2 vols. (Stuttgart: Kohlhammer, 1940), vol. 1.

80. *Apocalypse of Abraham* 15:1–17:7, in *OTP* 1:696–97.

81. *Clementine Recognitions* I, 1–14, in *PG* 1:1207.

82. Mark Lidzbarski, *Ginza: Der Schatz oder das grosse Buch der Mandäer* (Göttingen: Vandenhoeck and Ruprecht, 1925).

83. *Psalms of the Bema* CCXXII, 16–19, in C. R. C. Allberry, ed., *A Manichaean Psalm Book* II (Stuttgart: Kohlhammer, 1938), 9.

84. *Apocalypse of Abraham* 15:3–7, in *OTP* 1:696.

85. *Apocalypse of Abraham* 16:1–17:5, in ibid., 1:696–97.

86. *Apocalypse of Abraham* 17:17, in ibid., 1:697.

87. *Clementine Recognitions* I, 1–3, 11–19, in *PG* 1:1207–16.

88. Ibid., I, 2, in *PG* 1:1207.

89. Ibid., I, 14, in *PG* 1:1214.

90. Cf. Lidzbarski, *Ginza*, 13; Ethel S. Drower, *One Thousand and One Questions* (Berlin: Akademie, 1960), 164, 192.

91. Lidzbarski, *Ginza*, 13, 42.

92. Ibid., 263–64.

93. *Psalms of Thomas* 3:1–15, 18–32, 35, in Allberry, *A Manichaean Psalm Book* II, 207–11; cf. Hugh W. Nibley, "Treasures in the Heavens: Some Early Christian Insights into the Organizing of Worlds," *DJMT* 8/3–4 (Autumn/Winter 1974): 76–98; reprinted in *Nibley on the Timely and the Timeless* (Provo: Religious Studies Center, 1978), 49–84; and *CWHN* 1:176, 195–96.

94. Schmidt, *Kephalaia*, 1:109, 111–14, 177.

95. *Pistis Sophia* II, 84, in Carl Schmidt, ed., *Pistis Sophia* (Leiden: Brill, 1978), 186–88.

96. *Martyrdom and Ascension of Isaiah* 10:11–14, in *OTP* 2:173.

The Best Possible Test

What Brother Bush has given us in this excellent study is not a history of the Negro policy in the Church, but of the explanations for it. The "attitudes" shift in "a complex evolutionary pattern," as he puts it, while noting in his concluding sentence that from first to last there has been no weakening of "the belief that the policy is justified."[1] That is why this indispensable study seems strangely irrelevant the more one reads it. It is an interesting chapter in the history of thought, showing how the leaders of the Church have from time to time come up with various explanations for limitations placed on the activity of the Negro in the Church. To engage in such mental exercises has been not only their prerogative but their duty. When faced with such a problem, the command is, "You must study it out in your mind," then, when you have gone as far as you can, you must ask God not to confirm your solution but to let you know whether it is right or not: "Then you must ask me if it be right, and if it is right I will cause that your bosom shall burn within you; therefore you shall feel that it is right" (D&C 9:7–8). This is exactly what the brethren have done; not only Oliver Cowdery (to whom the order was first addressed) but all the great patriarchs and prophets from Adam down have had to exercise their own minds to full capacity in earnest seeking (Abraham 2:12),

---

This was originally published in Dialogue: A Journal of Mormon Thought *8 (1973): 73–77, five years before the June 8, 1978, revelation on priesthood.*

until God has finally deigned "after many days" (Moses 5:6) to give them an answer. No matter how satisfied they may have been with their own conclusions, they have had to have them checked upstairs, and the answer comes with absolute certainty: "You shall *feel* that it is right" (D&C 9:8). Nothing could be more penetrating and final, but how can you explain your feeling to others? Simply by telling them how to go about getting the same feeling.

This, of course, does not satisfy the world; it has always put the prophets in bad with the rest of mankind and has repeatedly put the Mormons in an awkward position, individually and collectively. For every individual must solve the "Negro Question" for himself. The late President Joseph Fielding Smith in the current Melchizedek Priesthood manual repeats the words of earlier leaders when he writes, "It is the duty of every male member of the Church to know the truth, for each is entitled to the guidance of the Holy Ghost. . . . Each member of the Church should be so well versed [in the Standard Works] that he, or she, would be able to discern whether or not any doctrine taught conforms to the revealed word of the Lord. Moreover, the members of the Church are entitled . . . to have the spirit of discernment."[2]

This not only guarantees that every worthy member, if he puts his mind to it, can know the answers for himself just as surely as the prophet does, but throws the floor open to discussion when President Smith adds that members are "under obligation to accept the teachings of the authorities . . . unless they can discover in them some conflict with the revelations and commandments the Lord has given."[3] Hence, though the mind of the Lord is confirmed by an imponderable feeling, one is required, before asking of the Lord and receiving that feeling, to exercise his own wits to the fullest, so that there must be place for the fullest discussion and explanation in the light of the scriptures or any other relevant information.

More than an explanation for the world, such discussion is really a heart-searching and a test for the Latterday Saints themselves. Nothing could be easier than to join in the chants of unison that proclaim the perfect equality of all men in all things that are fashionable at the moment; that way we could proclaim our idealism to the world while continuing, like the rest of the world, to treat our fellowman much as we always have. As C. S. Lewis used to point out, the test of the Christian is not to conform with the commandments and accept teachings which are perfectly right and sensible to any normal way of thinking; if the gospel consisted only of such convenient and unobjectionable things, we could be quite sure that we were making it up ourselves. It is the very contrariness and even absurdity of the Christian teachings that provide, for him, the highest proof of their divinity — this is not man's doing. In the efforts of every president of the Church to explain our position to the world, as presented in Dr. Bush's study, we see the admission that this thing is not the invention of those men — they are embarrassed by it, and they all pass the acid test for honesty when they refuse to put their own opinions forth as revelation — which in their case would have been an easy thing to do. They are all sure that the policy is right, but none claims to give definitive rational or scriptural justification for it, though they are not backward in putting forth suggestions and speculations. This puts the Mormons in an embarrassing position, and why not? The Lord has often pushed the Saints into the water to make them swim, and when our own indolence, which is nothing less than disobedience, gets us into a jam, he lets us stew in our own juice until we do something about it. The most impressive lesson of Bush's paper is how little we know about these things — and how little we have *tried* to know. The man Adam is expected to seek for *greater* light and knowledge, ever seeking "for the blessings of the fathers, . . . desiring also to be one who possessed great knowledge" (Abraham 1:2). This seeking must go on: "Wherefore murmur ye, because that ye shall receive more of my word? . . . My work is not yet finished; neither shall it be until the end of man" (2 Nephi 29:8–9). On the other hand, nothing displeases God more than to have his people "seek for power, and authority, and riches" (3 Nephi 6:15). It is God who gives us the answers, but only after we have been looking for them for quite a while—and what the Saints have been seeking is not light and knowledge, but those other forbidden things.

In searching for the answers, we must consult our feelings as well as our reason, for the heart has its reasons, and it is our noble feelings and impulses that will not let us rest until God has given us the feeling of what is right. Charity does not split hairs or dogmatize, and charity comes first. So I ask myself, first of all, is this policy a humane and generous thing? Am I not turning my back on my brother in not sharing the work of the priesthood with him? Not at all! There is a vast amount of work going on in the Church all the time, all directed by the priesthood, but not necessarily carried out by it. To be engaged in any of these jobs is to be engaged in one and the same work; and can the eye say to the hand, I have no need of thee? Thinking I might be slipping into easy rationalization, I consider my own case. I have always been furiously active in the Church, but I have also been a nonconformist and have never held any *office* of rank in anything; I have undertaken many assignments given me by the leaders, and much of the work has been anonymous: no rank, no recognition, no anything. While I have been commended for some things, they were never the things which I considered most important—that was entirely a little understanding between me and my Heavenly Father, which I have thoroughly enjoyed, though no one else knows anything about it.

Interestingly enough, this is the case not only with an

occasional oddball, but with *all* holders of the priesthood. Men can confer the powers of the priesthood upon others, it is true (D&C 121:37), but only God can validate that ordination, which in most cases he does *not* recognize: "Hence many are called, but few are chosen" (D&C 121:40). And he has been kind enough to tell us why: "And why are they not chosen? Because their hearts are set so much upon the things of this world, and aspire to the honors of men" (D&C 121:34–35). It so happens that "almost all men, as soon as they get a little authority . . . will immediately begin to exercise unrighteous dominion" (D&C 121:39), and the exercise of the powers of heaven "in any degree of unrighteousness" invalidates the priesthood—"Amen to the priesthood or the authority of that man" (D&C 121:37). What supreme irony! The withholding of the priesthood is supposed to be an unkind act because it deprives a fellow man of a thing of social value, a measure of status and dignity in the Church. Yet the moment I even *think* of my priesthood as a status symbol or a mark of superiority, it becomes a mere hollow pretense. At the slightest hint of gloating or self-congratulation, the priesthood holder is instantly and automatically unfrocked. What is the priesthood on this earth? Brigham Young called it "an onerous duty,"[4] a load to be borne, work to be done and nothing more—the glory comes hereafter. One cannot give orders by the priesthood, for it operates "only by persuasion" (D&C 121:41); Christ commanded the spirits and they obeyed him; he commanded the elements and they obeyed him. But men he would not command, and he rebuked the apostles at Capernaum for suggesting it. "How often would I have gathered thy children together . . . and *ye* would not!" (Matthew 23:37). Only "if ye *love* me, keep my commandments" (John 14:15). There is nothing here resembling earthly authority.

But whether it is worth anything or not, am I not by the mere act of withholding something guilty of an offensive gesture, a denial of rights, an act of rejection, of implied superiority? Certainly, in the world, if both of us are thinking in worldly terms, but not in the kingdom. I would rather be a doorkeeper in the house of the Lord than mingle with the top brass in the tents of the wicked (cf. Psalms 84:10). If we think in terms of rank and honor, we share the folly of those early councils of the Church which, with all the logic in the world, declared it the height of blasphemy and an insufferable affront to Jesus to place him second to the Father. Seeing all things in the setting of the empire, as we do of a status and success-oriented society, they were completely blinded to reality. Is the Son jealous of the Father's superior rank, or is the Father disturbed by the aspirations of the Son? Nothing sounds more brutal and direct than Brigham Young's "The Negro should serve!"⁵ But what is so bad about serving in the light of the gospel? "The Son of Man came not to be ministered unto, but to minister" (Mark 10:45), "meek and lowly" (Matthew 11:29), a man of sorrows and acquainted with grief, despised and rejected (Isaiah 53:3). Need we go on? His true followers will take up the same cross: "In the world ye shall have tribulation" (John 15:33), for "if the world hate you, ye know that it hated me" (John 15:18). The greater the tribulation here, the greater the glory hereafter, while he who is exalted in this world shall be abased in the next. If we really took the Lord's teachings seriously, we would be envious of the Negroes.

But do we take them seriously? Have we really searched the scriptures? Consider a few. First the terrible warning: "Whosoever slayeth Cain, vengeance shall be taken on him sevenfold. And the Lord set a mark upon Cain, lest any finding him should kill him" (Genesis 4:15). The mark on Cain is for his protection, and as a warning to all the rest of us—hands off! If Cain must be punished, God does not solicit our services for the job: "Behold, the judgments of God will overtake the wicked; and it is *by the wicked* that the wicked are punished" (Mormon 4:5). Next, in all the talk about the sin of Cain, we hear no mention of his motivation, which lies at the root of sin. Lamech, too, committed murder, but his sin was not as reprehensible as that of Cain, who "slew his brother Abel, for the sake of getting gain" (Moses 5:50). Cain was carrying out a systematic operation which he learned from Satan, and which he calls "this great secret, that I may murder and get gain" (Moses 5:31), and in this he "gloried, . . . saying: I am free; surely the flocks of my brother falleth into my hands" (Moses 5:33). Cain was "master of that great secret" of converting life into property in which the mighty have prospered ever since his day. Do we ever take this lesson to heart?

Again, our scriptures tell us that all little children are pure and innocent by nature, and as such are saved in the celestial kingdom of God, and declare the contrary teaching of the world to be particularly devilish (Moroni 8:5–22). Now the vast majority of Negroes who have lived on the earth have died as little children; the celestial kingdom will be full of them, while, as we have indicated, there may be very few present-day priesthood holders among them. Has this been duly noted? It has been maintained that because of the curse of Cain the Negro should never be allowed to vote; but our scriptures tell us that that race is peculiarly fitted for government: "Now the first government of Egypt was established by Pharaoh . . . after the manner of the government of Ham. . . . Pharaoh, being a righteous man, established his kingdom and judged his people wisely and justly all his days. . . . Noah, his father, . . . blessed him with the blessings of the earth, and with the blessings of wisdom, but cursed him as pertaining to the Priesthood" (Abraham 1:25–26). Now we have seen that the priesthood does not entail authority to give orders to men, whose absolute free agency it rigorously respects. Where order must be given, a just and righteous man, blessed with

wisdom and earthly knowledge, is just what we need—
would we had such leaders today!

The hardest thing in the world for men to learn is "this
one lesson—that the rights of the priesthood are insepar-
ably connected with the powers of heaven" (D&C 121:35–
36). They are God's alone to give and take away, and no
one will dispute his right to do as he pleases with his own.
So now the whole issue boils down to asking whether it
is really God and not man who has ordered this thing.
Members and nonmembers alike who up until now have
laughed at the thought of asking such a question are suddenly exercised by it. And so it gives me great pleasure to
be in a position to answer the question with an unequivocal
affirmative: it is indeed the Lord's doing. How do I know
it? By revelation—which I am in no position to bestow
upon others; this goes only for myself. And that makes
the "Negro Question" as unreal as the "Mormon Question" which kept the nation in an uproar for many years.
Left to myself, the last thing in the world I would do would
be to advocate polygamy or impose any limitations whatever on the Negro—and I have often heard the brethren
express themselves to the same effect. When the Lord told
Joseph Smith that he couldn't always tell his friends from
his enemies or the wicked from the righteous, what was
left for him to do? "Therefore I say unto you, hold your
peace until I shall see fit to make all things known unto
the world concerning the matter" (D&C 10:37). Granted
that this puts us, as it put the prophet, in an uncomfortable
and even dangerous position, still it provides the best possible test for our faith, our hope, and above all our charity.

Notes

1. Lester E. Bush, "Mormonism's Negro Doctrine: An Historical
Overview," *Dialogue: A Journal of Mormon Thought* 8 (Spring 1973):
48–49.

2. Selections from *Answers to Gospel Questions*, taken from the
writings of Joseph Fielding Smith, *A Course of Study for the Melchizedek*

Priesthood Quorums of the Church of Jesus Christ of Latter-day Saints 1972–73 (Salt Lake City: Deseret Book, 1972), 190–91.

3. Ibid., 191.

4. *Times and Seasons* 1 (1839): 13.

5. Fred C. Collier, ed., *The Teachings of President Brigham Young,* 7 vols. (Salt Lake City: Collier, 1987), 3:49.

Some Notes on Cultural
Diversity in the
Universal Church

Is there a gospel culture? We begin with the idea: Is there a gospel community or society? There clearly is. Zion has always been described as a city, an organized society, set apart from the world. If the community preserves its integrity for any length of time, it is bound to emerge as a separate culture. The earliest reference to the culture I have in mind is Israel as the "peculiar people." Moses and Aaron disengaged the children of Israel from the culture of Egypt, the most distinctive culture of its time. The Lord tells them: "Ye have seen what I did unto the Egyptians, and how I bare you on eagles' wings, and brought you unto myself. Now therefore, if ye will obey my voice indeed, and keep my covenant, then ye shall be a peculiar treasure unto me above all people" (Exodus 19:4–5). The King James Version uses "peculiar treasure" for *sǝgullāh*, a word meaning "set apart," "sealed," "removed from the rest of the world." Exodus continues: "And ye shall be unto me a kingdom of priests, and an holy nation" (Exodus 19:6). A distinctive culture begins there. The cultural franchise is set down in Deuteronomy. In the light of recent

This response to a paper read by Noel B. Reynolds entitled "Cultural Diversity in the Universal Church" was part of the symposium on the "Expanding Church" held during the centennial celebration of Brigham Young University. It was originally published as "Comments" in F. LaMond Tullis, ed., Mormonism, a Faith for All Cultures (Provo: BYU Press, 1978), 22–28.

541

documentary discoveries the true nature of that culture is beginning to appear, presenting ever closer resemblances to the picture Joseph Smith has given us of ancient Israel and early Christianity.

The Mormon basic concept is that we are God's spirit children; that idea separates us from the world: "Ye are the children [of Jehovah Elohim] of the Lord your God." Hence, "ye shall not cut yourselves, nor make any baldness between your eyes," etc. (Deuteronomy 14:1–2). Awareness of their heavenly parentage sets Israel apart *culturally* as well as doctrinally.

Their ordinances set them apart too. Every ancient civilization is hierocentric; it is the temple that sets it apart from the rest of the world. And so we read in the 135th Psalm of praises to the Lord, to the name of the Lord and to the servants of the Lord standing "in the house of the Lord [the temple], in the courts of the house of our God" (Psalm 135:2). "Praise the Lord; for the Lord is good: sing praises unto his name; for it is pleasant. For the Lord hath chosen Jacob unto himself, and Israel for his peculiar treasure [for his *sǝgullāh* again]" (Psalm 135:3–4).

In his letter to Titus (2:12–14), Paul translates *sǝgullāh* by a very interesting word that Aristotle uses also: *periousios*. It means a peculiar treasure.

The saints are to deny "ungodliness and worldly lusts" to become "a peculiar people." The word here rendered "peculiar," *periousios*, designates that part of any wealth that is set aside or reserved in a separate account, not part of the common deposit, a peculiar treasure, something special and set apart to be of value in times of dire need. When the going is bad, this is where we will go for our salvation. Paul continues: "zealous of good works" (Titus 2:14). It is specifically their good works that set the saints apart.

What is the gospel culture composed of? Everything good. Like patriotism, it is more inclusive than exclusive.

Its peculiarity, its *səgullāh,* is a seal set upon whatever it finds desirable, rendering that thing also peculiar. It is the combination, the structure, that is peculiar, not the separate elements. Our Thirteenth Article of Faith sums it up beautifully: we accept everything we put our stamp on. Can anything be more universally appealing, more desirable for the whole human race, than being honest, true, chaste, benevolent, virtuous (that's inner culture acceptable to any society), and in doing good to all men? Moreover, we *seek* after every good thing; we are in the market for everything good. Articles six (dealing with organization, the same organization as the primitive church), seven (dealing with the spiritual gifts that set the Mormons apart from the rest of the world at this time), and ten, especially (looking forward to another kind of secular environment)—all have very strong cultural implications. "We believe in the literal gathering of Israel [the same thing we have already been referring to] and in the restoration of the Ten Tribes; that Zion (the New Jerusalem) will be built upon the American continent; that Christ will reign personally upon the earth; and, that the earth will be renewed and receive its paradisiacal glory" (Tenth Article of Faith). We shall see all these things. These are very special things.

So we believe there is a culture here, a single culture peculiar to Mormons. Brigham Young expressed it well when he said, "We have commenced to organize, I will say partially, in the Holy Order that God has established for his people in all ages of the world when he has had a kingdom upon the earth. We may call it the Order of Enoch, the Order of Joseph, the Order of Peter, or Abraham, or Moses, and then go back to Noah," always the same order.[1] It is essentially the same culture, we shall see.

Brigham continues: "We will organize as far as we have the privilege . . . under the laws of the land,"[2] that is, under its restraining influence, its alien culture. We have to defer to it because we are dependent on it, and without those laws we would not even be allowed to exist at all. The gospel would never have emerged. "Many branches of industry have been organized here to help sustain each other, to labor for the good of all, and to establish cooperation in the midst of the Church in this place."[3] The concept is of an ongoing culture that had in each dispensation been restored — not the teachings alone, but celestial manners, morals, and environment.

Now, not only is there a single, central celestial culture reserved for the saints, but such a culture has also served as the model for the greatest peaks of human civilization as a whole. Those "Golden Ages," all too few and far between, which have illuminated the long night of history have, I believe, all drawn their nourishment from the memories of lost Zions. Whenever Homer speaks of anything virtuous, lovely, or of good report, he invariably compares it with a heavenly model; whether it is an individual, some godlike hero, a society like the Phaeacians, a dream, or a landscape; it is always compared with some heavenly ideal. Hundreds of graffiti made by the Egyptian pilgrims to holy shrines describe the temples on which they scratch their names as places that make them think they are in heaven. How often the art of the Chinese (flowing robes amid the clouds) refers to its celestial counterparts; the people see themselves as a culture blessed and set apart, frankly styling themselves "the celestials." The brief splendor of Arabic Spain left behind the haunting image of a paradise on earth, just as the Gothic glories of the Middle Ages coming through Byzantium from the court of Persia transmit the heavenly visions of the Asiatics. The Egyptian court was also another heaven on earth, though its real glory was confined to an early dynasty.

There have been but few such golden moments in history; their flourishing has been all too brief. But they do seem to follow a common pattern. "We are trying to be the image of those who live in heaven; we are trying to pattern after them, to look like them, to walk and talk like them, to deal like them, and build up the kingdom of heaven as they have done," said Brigham Young.[4] Another celestial culture. God has already supplied us with the necessary materials and plans; indeed, the stage has been set for Zion from the beginning. "Heaven," said President Joseph F. Smith, "was the prototype of the beautiful creation when it came from the hand of the creator and was pronounced good."[5] We have a good start.

The clearest evidence that the great cultures of the world were inspired by a common model is their common dependence on one special institution—the temple. Ancient civilizations were what Eric Burrows called "hierocentric" in nature, that is, all their activities and thoughts were centered around the single sacred point, which was marked in every case by the temple and its ordinances.[6] But even apart from that, if we compare the moment of fulfillment of these great cultures such as those of Greece, Persia, China, Arabic Spain, or Egypt, we find the external manifestations are strangely alike. They all sought the heavenly. So it is with us. Brigham Young was the first person to speak in tongues in this dispensation (1832).[7] When he did so in the presence of Joseph Smith, the Prophet declared it to be the pure Adamic Tongue.[8] It was the language of our father Adam, walking in Eden, and the time will come again when the Lord brings again Zion, the likeness of Zion and Enoch; this people will then all speak the language that Brigham Young spoke. A single language, someday, and a single culture, all based on a heavenly model.

I am going to read from an old book of Adam, a Syriac text[9] originally published in 1815, translated into French in 1856, and long forgotten, describing an ancient writer's idea of what the civilization of Enoch was like. For him it is a common culture scattered among countless worlds.

He tells us what life is like on these worlds. His description is noteworthy because while writers of every age have found the description of hell only too easy, they become lost and unconvincing as soon as they attempt to depict what heaven is really like; that is a task that daunts Dante himself. But this old Christian writer, who has Mandaean connections, tells us that Zion is a place "without discord or dissent," where angels wise and gentle, without malice or deceit, come and go on cheerful assignments. There is a perfect agreement among the worlds, each having its particular glory, and all the inhabitants share their knowledge freely with each other. The worlds averaged one million *parasangs* (a *parasang* is about four miles) apart, and through the people's common knowledge and their common God, the Lord, they share a common glory. They are all incorruptible, without death. They do not grow old or wear out. Their nature is unfailing. They cannot be numbered, and their number is unchanging.[10] Each of the worlds is a Zion, though each is different, for, most delightful of all, there is not monotony; there is a single universal culture which, as described in our own scriptures, "shall come forth out of all the creations which I have made" (Moses 7:64) — the culture of Zion. Yet variety (as Brigham Young often noted) was the very keynote to that culture.

But the text describes Zion in negative terms, which are indeed the only terms in which it can be described to people living in another world. Thus in 4 Nephi the only way to tell us benighted people what was going on is to say what was not going on: "There was no contention among all the people, in all the land . . . and there were no envyings, nor strifes, nor tumults, nor whoredoms, nor lyings, nor murders, nor any manner of lasciviousness; and surely there could not be a happier people" (4 Nephi 1:13, 16). Not surprisingly, therefore, we are told in this old Adam text that each of these worlds is a Zion, having no law courts, no hungry or thirsty, no cold nor heat, no aged or fear, no war, no slavery, no harmful creatures or plants.[11] How boring it all seems to primitives like us! We already possess the technical know-how to achieve something very near to this, but who wants it? "Magnificent buildings beside tranquil seas, . . . flowing springs of life-giving water, . . . everything vibrates with joy; the wants of the people are few, they move about through the air by the power of flight."[12] They are not overly concerned with technology because their technological knowledge has taken them far beyond our clumsy contraptions. "They are at home with the firmaments, . . . with the 'Jordans' [a special term referring to ordinances], with groves, with kings, with spirits; their beauty is within them and shines out as if they were pure crystal. Force flows through them from the King as they persevere in prayer and song."[13] (It was a demanding thing; the celestial spirits had to work at it—"Force flows through them from the King as they persevere in prayer and song.") They study and meditate constantly. "They exhale a fragrance of divine happiness; . . . each is more remarkable than the other, each more illustrious."[14]

Such a world, we are told, is only congenial "to the spirits of good men"; it is a life for the wise and prudent, for the families of Abel, Seth, and Enoch.[15] This state of things is scattered throughout the universe, according to our old Adam text; and the various colonies, in spite of the vast differences between them, are quite aware of each other.[16] In something the same way, the fabulous dream-like cultures of which we have spoken, in spite of their wide spacing in time, were quite aware of each other's existence. Thus Professor Werner Jaeger pointed out that both Plato and Aristotle were devoted followers of Zoroaster.[17] Buddhism, as we know, moved from India to become the religion of distant China. The world of Lehi was one of widely shared cultures. Buddha, Confucius,

Lao-Tzu, Mahavira, Zarathustra, Pythagoras, and An-
thales were all contemporaries of Lehi at that magic moment in history which Karl Jaspers calls the "axial [pivotal]
period," that is, the moment when the civilization of the
whole world turned on its axis as a new order of the spirit
succeeded the old sacral kingship.[18] That was the time
when the seven wise men would come together from time
to time from the ends of the earth to share their knowledge
and wisdom at the Feast of the Seven Sages, knitting all
the world together in a common cultural heritage.

Let me conclude with some quotations from the prophets of the restoration:

> The Lord spake unto Enoch [Joseph Smith, Jun.],
> saying: Hearken unto me, saith the Lord your God, . . .
> who have assembled yourselves together; . . . it must
> needs be that there be an organization of my people
> . . . in the land of Zion—[or in other words, the city of
> Enoch (Joseph)], for a permanent and everlasting estab-
> lishment and order unto my church, . . . that you may
> be equal in the bonds of heavenly things, yea, and
> earthly things also, for the obtaining of heavenly things.
> (D&C 78:1–5)

Such passages plainly look to the distinctive culture being
"of one heart and one mind" (Moses 7:18), setting them
apart from all the others. "We are following," said Brigham
Young, "the customs of Enoch and the holy fathers, and
for this we are looked upon as not being fit for society.
We are not adapted to the society of the wicked."[19] The
strong word that Brother Reynolds has used here today is
that we are subversive to certain cultures. Brigham says
much the same thing: "We are looked upon as not being
fit for society. We are not adapted to the society of the
wicked and do not wish to mingle with them."[20]

What I wish to indicate, very briefly then, is that behind
all this there is a culture of Zion, a culture that has the
virtue of being an eternal one, yet never boring, never

monotonous. It is something toward which we should be striving. There are cultural images here, and there is a cultural reality, and we move into it by faith and prayer. It is not a pure figment of the imagination, because every time the human cultures have reached a real peak they have been infatuated with this idea, and have been convinced that they were imitating the heavenly model and doing the best they could. There *is* a gospel culture.

Notes

1. *JD* 17:113.
2. Ibid.
3. Ibid.
4. Ibid., 9:170.
5. Ibid., 23:175.
6. Eric Burrows, "Some Cosmological Patterns in Babylonian Religion," in Samuel H. Hooke, *The Labyrinth* (London: SPCK, 1935), 46; cf., Hugh W. Nibley, "The Hierocentric State," *WPQ* 4 (June 1951): 226–53; reprinted in *CWHN* 10:99–147.
7. *HC* 1:279.
8. Ibid.
9. "Le Code Nazaréen (or the Livre d'Adam)" in J.-P. Migne, ed., *Dictionnaire des Apocryphes*, 2 vols. (Paris: Migne, 1856), 1:25–28. All subsequent references to the Syriac text are referenced to this volume.
10. Ibid., 1:27.
11. Ibid.
12. Ibid., 1:27–28.
13. Ibid., 1:28.
14. Ibid.
15. Ibid.
16. Ibid., 1:26–27.
17. Werner Jaeger, *Aristotle* (London: Oxford University Press, 1948), 132–36.
18. Karl Jaspers, *The Origin and Goal of History* (New Haven, CT: Yale University Press, 1953), 1–21.
19. *JD* 10:306.
20. Ibid.

From the Earth upon
Which Thou Standest

A vital preliminary to Joseph Smith's First Vision was another vision that prepared the way:

> For I looked upon the sun the glorious luminary of the earth and also the moon rolling in their magesty through the heavens and also the Stars Shining in their courses and the earth also upon which I stood and the beast of the field and the fowls of heaven and the fish of the waters and also man walking forth upon the face of the earth in magesty and in the Strength of beauty . . . and . . . my heart exclaimed all these bear testimony and bespeak an omnipotent and omnipreasant . . . being. . . . [I also] pondered . . . the sittuation of the world of mankind the contentions and divi[si]ons the wicke[d]ness and abominations and the darkness which pervaded the minds of mankind [sic].[1]

Here we have two worlds: the world of the artist and that of the businessman. The Lord himself drew the clear distinction. Telling of "a certain man," i.e., the Lord, who had prepared a feast of delights but the invited guests excused themselves because they had really important business to attend to: "I have bought a piece of ground, and I must needs go and see it. . . . Another said, I have bought five yoke of oxen, . . . I pray thee have me ex-

---

This essay originally appeared in Wulf Barsch, Looking toward Home *(Salt Lake City: privately printed, 1985), 10–13. The volume consists of a collection of Barsch's paintings.*

cused" (Luke 14:18–19). Admittedly important business deals; yet the rejected host was angry and did not excuse them — "None of those men which were bidden shall taste of my supper" (Luke 14:24).

From the first, God prepared the earth with an eye to making it "most glorious and beautiful" for us, with special care to giving "variety and beauty to the scene." To this the artist calls our attention; and if we reject God's proffered bounty, we offend him — "Deny not the gifts of God"! is the impassioned plea of Moroni to our generation at the end of the Book of Mormon (Moroni 10:8).[2] For "in nothing doth man offend God, or against none is his wrath kindled, save those who confess not his hand in all things" (D&C 59:21). Specifically, "all things which come of the earth . . . are made for the benefit and the use of man, both to please the eye and to gladden the heart; yea, for food and for raiment, for taste and for smell, to strengthen the body and to enliven the soul" (D&C 59:18–19). The pleasing of the eye comes first, the gladdening of the heart next; only then come the food and clothing, and that for the benefit of the fine senses of taste and smell, with not a word about efficiency and convenience but with special attention to the enlivening of the *soul*. In his great Bicentennial message, President Kimball deplored the sad ascendancy in our society of the business mentality over the contemplation of the beauty around us. "This is a marvelous earth on which we find ourselves," he wrote, for heaven is a state of the environment as well as a state of mind, and the one begets the other.[3] As heaven takes form around the Saints, so steadily and inevitably the acquisitive society becomes enwrapped in an obnoxious, brutalizing, poisonous ambience of mind and body. The command is that "Zion must increase in beauty, and in holiness . . . and put on her beautiful garments" (D&C 82:14), placed in direct contrast to "the mammon of unrighteousness," which seeks for gain (D&C 82:22).

In the Old Testament, the *piqqeaḥ* (seer) is one whose eyes God has opened, so that he can see what others do not see—it is really there, but uninspired minds do not perceive it. When the eyes of Adam and Eve were opened, they beheld what they could not see before (Genesis 3:7). Abraham tells how God "put his hand upon mine eyes, and I saw those things which his hands had made, which were many" (Abraham 3:12). It was so with his wife Hagar, when "God opened her eyes, and she saw a well of water"—which had been there all the time (Genesis 21:19). There is no such vision for those not in tune with the Spirit: "They have eyes but do not see, ears but do not hear!" (cf. Isaiah 6:9–10; Matthew 13:13–14).

In Wulf Barsch's paintings (fig. 67) there is a sense of deep concern, an ominous and brooding feeling of admonition and warning.[4] This I find disquieting until I remember that that is exactly the effect the reading of the scriptures has on me. The pictures do not tell a story—there is nothing trivial, contrived, clever, or cute about them; they seem more like a solemn summing-up, with something of both suspense and finality about them. For Plato true art must have *spoudaiotēs,* usually rendered "high seriousness."[5] Its opposite is blasphemy; which does not mean thundering denunciation, solemn deprecation, or consuming wrath, but the very opposite—it means not taking holy things seriously, being too stupid or insensitive (*blax* means both) to value anything beyond the business of business.

Was there ever an artist less inclined to show off than Wulf Barsch? He does not hesitate to try again and again to get through to us, not seeking novelty, but fighting for expression and perfectly willing to stay with a problem. It is that, I suppose, that gives his work the sense of deep sincerity that demands to be taken seriously. Strangely enough, with all his moving solemnity, I find some of his things intensely romantic. The constant dialogue of the

Figure 67. Wulf Barsch, "The greater light to rule the day—the lesser light to rule the night"

poplar and the palm is right out of the most ancient traditions of romantic poetry, whether Barsch is aware of it or not, with echoes from the Patriarchal romances of Genesis. The poplar is the tree of the pioneers, marking their farms on all the benches and valleys from the red sands of Moencopi to the plains of Alberta. It is becoming rare as business supplants the noble windbreaks with billboards. And the palm evokes the wandering tribes of Israel (the palms of California are never convincing), for it is their hope and succor in the desert.

Notes

1. The 1832 recital of the First Vision as dictated by Joseph Smith to Frederick G. Williams. See Dean C. Jessee, *The Personal Writings of Joseph Smith* (Salt Lake City: Deseret Book, 1984), 5; appendix A in Milton V. Backman, *Joseph Smith's First Vision* (Salt Lake City: Bookcraft, 1971); cf. Dean C. Jessee, "The Early Accounts of Joseph Smith's First Vision," *BYU Studies* 9 (1969): 280.

2. Cf. Hugh W. Nibley, "Deny Not the Gifts of God," in *Approaching Zion*, *CWHN* 9 (Salt Lake City: Deseret Book and F.A.R.M.S., 1989), 118–48.

3. Spencer W. Kimball, "The False Gods We Worship," *Ensign* 6 (June 1976): 3.

4. For a further example of Wulf Barsch's paintings, see the frontispiece in the first volume of John M. Lundquist and Stephen D. Ricks, eds., *By Study and Also by Faith: Essays in Honor of Hugh W. Nibley*, 2 vols. (Salt Lake City: Deseret Book and F.A.R.M.S., 1990).

5. Plato, *Definitiones* 412E. See Ioannes Burnet, *Platonis Opera* (London: Oxford University Press, 1976), 534.

Foreword to
Eugene England's Book

At last a Latter-day Saint book that really says something! Carrying the momentum of *Dialogues with Myself* into fields where no one else is walking, Eugene England has given us some stereoscopic views that take us out of our intellectual flatland and find us room to turn around in, breathe deeply, and do some exploring.

The Church, we have been told, has at times been "under condemnation." But how could the gospel be under condemnation? Unthinkable—they are not the same thing at all, right? Wrong, and England will show you just how wrong and misleading that assumption can be. The gospel and the Church: we call one the *plan* and the other the *work*. The plan looks to the eternities and must necessarily be perfect; but the *work is right here and is anything but the finished product.* Yet the two are inseparable! "To bring to pass the immortality and eternal life of man" is the *plan;* to carry it out, *"this* is my *work* and my glory"— the glory is in the work. We are permitted to take part in the work, to participate like eager but bungling children in the kitchen or the shop—dropping things, doing it all wrong, quarreling, getting in each other's way, trying the patience of indulgent elders. What a headache! Yet such is the best and happiest arrangement for all concerned,

This foreword appears in Eugene England, Why the Church Is as True as the Gospel *(Salt Lake City: Bookcraft, 1986), vii–viii.*

everybody having a wonderful time—and it is found only in the restored Church, where the plan and the work are equally exhilarating and equally sacred. England shows us for the first time what a truly astounding phenomenon the Latter-day Saint Church is, "as true as—that is, as effective for salvation as—the gospel."

Yet the plan does not suffer fools gladly. If its object is perfection—eternal progression, no less—nothing could be more retrograde to it than the easy self-congratulation, shallow learning, vanity of office, quest for wealth and recognition, the futile ambition and careerism that characterize our present society. England calls upon the singular eloquence of Brigham Young and Spencer W. Kimball to affirm the values on which the Church was founded. That means seeking and finding, never hesitating to question, for there are answers awaiting those who question. We are here to take advantage of all the facilities provided, and the early Saints knew that the treasures of the race, especially Shakespeare, were not to be neglected. Professor England bids us carry on the careful study which hard necessity denied our yearning ancestors. It is the schoolmen and the fundamentalists who stop the process with final answers, satisfied with what they have. Too often the mere fact that the teaching and history of the Church raise unanswered questions is taken as proof positive that something is seriously wrong. And it *is* wrong if we ever stop seeking. The author understands perfectly well the position of the disillusioned and the paradoxes of a world where evil is suffered to exist. Who else would head a chapter "The Trouble with Excellence"? England does not apologize for preaching when that cuts through the underbrush, and he spares the tenderest plants while vigorously raking out a lot of dead stuff.

But it is the stereo effect, bringing a third dimension into bold relief, at which Eugene England excels. The cumulative effect as one reads along is the emergence of a perfectly matter-of-fact realization that the other world does exist. He takes you there with people whose stories would be quite incredible were their deeds not equally incredible and undeniable. You must discover for yourself some of those electrifying insights that shock with originality and unexpectedness. (Hint: Look for Eden!)

Illustration Sources

Except where noted, the illustrations have been drawn for this volume by Michael Lyon (ML), Tyler Moulton (TM), Mark Clifford (MC), and Nathan Pinnock (NP).

Frontispiece. Perspective rendering in ink and water-color by William Ward, c. 1850. Courtesy of the Church Museum of History and Art.

Figure 1, p. 12. (A) Osiris temple, Alan H. Gardiner, "The House of Life," *Journal of Egyptian Archaeology* 24 (1938): 169, fig. 2; (B) Osiris seed bed, redrawn (ML) from Howard Carter, *The Tomb of Tutankhamen* (New York: Dutton, 1954), 175.

Figure 2, pp. 16–17. (A) Salt Lake Temple, inscription plaque, Big Dipper, redrawn (ML) from photographs, computer-assisted design courtesy of John Hamer; (B) moon-stone plan, redrawn (ML) from photograph of original, lettering enlarged for legibility; (C) Nauvoo and Salt Lake Temple elevation detail, redrawn (ML) from original plans by William Weeks and Truman Angell. Egyptian hieroglyphs from Alan H. Gardiner, *Egyptian Grammar* (London: Oxford University Press, 1957), 486–89, N8, N14, N27.

Figure 3, p. 18. (A) Dendera zodiac, redrawn, slightly restored (ML) from Champollion, *Monuments de l'Égypte,* 4 vols. (Paris: Didot, 1845), 4: pl. CCCXLIX (bis); (B) Fore-leg, redrawn (ML) from Otto Neugebauer, *Egyptian Astronomical Texts,* 4 vols. (London: Brown University Press, 1960), 1: pl. 8; (C) rotating Forelegs, redrawn (ML) from ibid., 3: pl. 24.

Figure 4, p. 20. (A) Roman augur, drawn (ML) from

description in Varro, *De Lingua Latina* VII, 6–11. He gives the augural prayer designating specific trees as markers of the right and left divisions, all under the blue, concave hemisphere of the heavens; (B) Teotihuacán map, redrawn (ML) from E. C. Krupp, *Echoes of the Ancient Skies* (New York: Harper and Row, 1983), 279.

Figure 5, p. 21. (A) Stonehenge, Phase III, c. 2100 B.C., drawn (ML) from a photograph of a model, courtesy of James Fleugel, and description in Christopher Chippindale, *Stonehenge Complete* (Ithaca, NY: Cornell University Press, 1932), 266. (B) Karnak sun room, reconstructed (ML) from description and photographs in Louis-A. Christophe, "Ramsès IV et la 'Salle des fêtes' de Thoutmosis III à Karnak," *ASAE* 52 (1952): 254–58, pl. 1.

Figure 6, p. 24. Nine Muses, redrawn (TM) from Pierre Grimal, *The Dictionary of Classical Mythology* (Paris: Presses universitaire de France, 1951; English ed. 1985), 298.

Figure 7, p. 24. Coin, redrawn (TM) from ibid., 295.

Figure 8, p. 24. (A) Bust of Idu, redrawn (TM) from William Kelly Simpson, *The Mastabas of Qar and Idu* (Boston: Museum of Fine Arts, 1976), pl. XXIXc; (B) Roman couple, redrawn (TM) from Albert Kuhn, *Roma* (Cologne: Waldshut, 1912), 171, fig. 199.

Figure 9, pp. 36–37. LDS temples, redrawn (NP) from various photographs and drawings. Concerning Nauvoo temple orientation, see Joseph Smith, *HC* 6:197: "I have seen in vision the splendid appearance of that building illuminated, and will have it built according to the pattern shown me."

Figure 10, pp. 50–51. (A) Tabernacle, drawn (ML) from descriptions in Exodus 25–57, 36–38; (B) Solomon's Temple, drawn (ML) from description in 2 Chronicles 3–5 and various sources; (C) Herod's Temple, redrawn (ML) from Charles J. Melchior, Marquis de Vögue, *Le Temple de Jerusalem* (Paris: Noblet & Baudry, 1864); (D) pomegranate, redrawn (ML) from Nahman Avigad, "The Inscribed Pomegranate from the 'House of the Lord'," *Biblical Archaeologist* 53/3 (September 1990): 160; (E) bowl, redrawn (ML) from Yigael Yadin, *Hazor*, 4 vols. (Jerusalem: Magnes, 1961), 3–4: pl. CCCLVIII.

Figure 11, p. 53. (A, B) Temple plan, redrawn (ML) from Yigael Yadin, *The Temple Scroll* (New York: Random House, 1985), 142–43.

Figure 12, p. 62. Temple sign, redrawn (ML) from J. Boudet, *Jerusalem, A History* (New York: Putnam, 1965), 112.

Figure 13, p. 68. "The Mass of St. Giles," National Gallery, London, redrawn (ML).

Figure 14, p. 92. Praying Christian, *Papyrus Erzherzog Rainer: Führer durch die Ausstellung*(Vienna: Hölder, 1894), 93, where it is called "Betender Christ" while Fernand Cabrol and Henri Leclerq, eds., *Reliquiae Liturgicae Vestustissimae, Monumenta Ecclesiae Liturgicae* I (Paris: Firmin-Didot, 1913), cxl, describes it as "Chrétien en priéres."

Figure 15, p. 94. Justinian and Maximianus, northwest wall mosaic in the apse of San Vitale, Ravenna, from J. G. Davies, *A New Dictionary of the Liturgy and Worship* (London: SCM, 1986), 523.

Figure 16, p. 95. Henry V and Pope Paschal II, MS painting in *Ekkehardi Historia* fol. 83 in the possession of Corpus Christi College, Cambridge, redrawn (ML) from *Encyclopedia Britannica* (Chicago: Encyclopedia Britannica, 1987), 5:848; quotations from *Encyclopedia Americana* (Danbury, CT: Grolier, 1989), 8:60, citing the Catholic Press, Chicago, IL.

Figure 17, pp. 98–99. High Priest's vestments, redrawn and modified (ML) from Moshe Levine, *Melekhet ha-Mishkan: Tabnit ha-Mishkan ve-Kelav* (Tel Aviv: Melekhet ha-Mishkan, 1968), 124–41.

Figure 18, p. 100. (A) Heracles, slightly restored (ML) from Philip Brize, *Mitteilungen des Deutschen Archäologischen Instituts, Athenische Abteilung* 100 (1985), pl. 16; (B) Heracles and Menerva, redrawn (TM), from *LIMC* vol. 5, pt. 2, p. 170, Hercle 1133.

Figure 19, p. 101. (A) Egyptian priest bronze, redrawn (ML) from Günther Hölbl, *Zeugnisse Ägyptischer Religions-vorstellungen für Ephesus* (Leiden: Brill, 1978), pl. III; (B) Khufu-khaf and Nefert-kau, redrawn (ML) from William K. Simpson, *The Mastabas of Kawab, Khafkhufu I and II* (Boston: Museum of Fine Arts, 1978), fig. 33; R. Engelbach, "The Sign S̱t̲," *ASAE* 29 (1929), 33–39. Quotation from Wolfhart Westendorf, *Painting, Sculpture and Architecture of Ancient Egypt* (New York: Abrams, 1968), 49; (C) Egyptian priest, redrawn (ML) from Nina M. Cummings Davies, *Ancient Egyptian Paintings* (Chicago: University of Chicago Press, 1936), pl. LXXXVIII.

Figure 20, p. 104. (A) Ivory pharaoh, redrawn (ML) from S. R. K. Glanville, "An Archaic Statuette from Abydos," *Journal of Egyptian Archaeology* 17 (1931): 65–66; (B) seated figure, redrawn (MC) from Massimo Pallottino, *Art of the Etruscans* (New York: Thames and Hudson, 1955), pl. 23; (C) bronze statuette from Gaul, Orleans Museum, redrawn (ML) from Francois Boucher, *20,000 Years of Fashion* (New York: Abrams, 1967), 141, fig. 216.

Figure 21, p. 105. (A) Sumerian priest, redrawn (ML) from Piérre Amiet, *Art of the Ancient Near East* (New York: Abrams, 1980), 357, fig. 234; (B) stele of Gudea, Berlin Staatliche Museen, Ägyptisches Museum, redrawn (ML) from André Parrot, *Sumer und Akkad* (Munich: Beck, 1983), 242; concerning ephod and *kaunakēs*, see Heinz E. Kiewe, *The Sacred History of Knitting* (Oxford: Hallprint, 1967).

Figure 22, p. 106. (A) Cupped hand incense burner, redrawn (ML) from F. Ll. Griffith, *Beni Hasan* (London: Egypt Exploration Fund, 1900), pt. IV, pl. XVII; (B) steatite incense burner, redrawn (ML) from Herbert G. May, *Material Remains of the Megiddo Cult* (Chicago: University of Chicago Press, 1935), pl. XVII.

Figure 23, p. 107. Mantle with *gammadia*, redrawn (ML)

from Yigael Yadin, *The Finds of the Bar Kokhba Period in the Cave of the Letters* (Jerusalem: Israel Exploration Society, 1963), 238, fig. 78.

Figure 24, p. 108. Christ and the miracle of the loaves and fishes, mosaic cycle on nave, Sant' Apollinare Nuovo, Ravenna, redrawn (ML) from color photograph in Helen Gardner, *Art through the Ages*, 6th ed. (New York: Harcourt, Brace, Jovanovich, 1975), pl. 7–2.

Figure 25, p. 109. Abraham presiding at the sacrifice of the firstborn, redrawn (ML) from color photograph on postcard; concerning restorations of the mosaic, see Friederich Deichmann, *Ravenna* (Wiesbaden: Steiner, 1969), fig. 287.

Figure 26, p. 110. (A) Moses before the Tabernacle, Dura Europos Synagogue, redrawn (ML) from Erwin Goodenough, *Jewish Symbols in the Greco-Roman Period*, 12 vols. (New York: Pantheon Books, 1954), vol. 11, ill. 331; (B) Egyptian burial shroud, Berlin Staatliche Museen, Ägyptisches Museum, redrawn (ML) from Cyril Aldred, *L'Égypte du crépuscule* (Paris: Gallimard, 1980), frontispiece.

Figure 27, pp. 12–13. (A,B,C) Amulets and mummy, redrawn (ML) from W. M. Flinders Petrie, *Amulets* (London: Constable, 1914), pl. LI, 12, p. 16, nos. 36–37; (D) Sennedjem level, drawn (ML) from Lisa Sabbahy, *Ramses II Exhibition Catalog* (Provo, UT: BYU Press, 1985), 58; (E) amulet list, redrawn (MC) from Auguste Mariette, *Dendéra* (Paris: Librairie A. Franck, 1870), vol. 4, pl. 87.

Figure 28, pp. 114–15. Fan Yen-Shih tomb, reconstructed (ML) from Sir Aurel Stein, *Innermost Asia*, 3 vols. (Oxford: Clarendon, 1928), 2:663–66; 3: plan 34, Astana IX.2; veil, redrawn (ML) from ibid., pl. CIX.

Figure 29, p. 116. Gallus, Peiresc copy of the Roman calendar of 354, slightly restored (ML) from Tonio Hölscher, *Victoria Romana* (Mainz am Rhein: Verlag von Zabern, 1967), pl. 4, 2.

Figure 30, p. 125. (A) Athena and *aegis*, marble statue

from Herculaneum, redrawn (TM) from *LIMC* vol. 2, pt. 2, p. 723, Athena 171; (B) Odysseus, vase painting, slightly restored (ML) from Denyse Le Lasseur, *Les Déesses armées* (Paris: Hachette, 1919), 141.

Figure 31, p. 127. Muslim in white robes, redrawn (ML) from *Encyclopedia Britannica*, 15th ed., (1974–87), 6:251.

Figure 32, p. 142. (A) Camel shrine, from Sir Richard Burton, *A Personal Narrative of a Pilgrimage to al-Medinah and Meccah*, 2 vols. (London: Tylston and Eduards, 1893), 1:233; (B) *haūdaj*, redrawn (ML) from Thierry Mauger, *Bedouins of Arabia* (Paris: Souffles, 1988), 107.

Figure 33, p. 143. (A) Osiris, gold bas-relief, Cairo Museum, from Alexandre Piankoff, *The Shrines of Tutankhamun* (New York: Pantheon, 1955), fig. 41; (B) Celtic horse, Museo Archaeologico Madrid, redrawn (ML) from Roger Cook, *Tree of Life* (New York: Thames & Hudson, 1974), 86, fig. 54; (C) Swedish altar from Balkaakra, redrawn (ML) from Felix Guirand, *Mythologie Géneral* (Paris: Larousse, 1935), 223; (D) Kogi calendar model, *pispiska*, redrawn (ML) from Gerardo Reichel-Solmatoff, "Templos Kogi," *Revista Columbiana de Antropologica* 19 (1975): 242; (E) Hindu sun temple, redrawn (ML) from Lucille Schulberg, *Historic India* (New York: Time-Life Books, 1968), 106–7.

Figure 34, p. 146. (A) royal tomb, redrawn (ML) from Edward Bacon, *The Great Archaeologists* (London: Secker & Warburg, 1976), 250; (B) Sanchi stupa, redrawn (ML) from Henry Millon, *Key Monuments of the History of Architecture* (New York: Abrams, 1965), 162; (C) Ezekiel's chariot, Bear's Bible, seventeenth century, English, slightly restored (ML) from Alan Unterman, *Dictionary of Jewish Lore and Legend* (London: Thames and Hudson, 1991), 199; (D) Pantheon, redrawn (ML) from Anne MacGregor, *Domes: A Project Book* (New York: Lothrop, Lee & Shepard, 1981), 18–19.

Figure 35, p. 147. (A) Dome of the Rock, redrawn (ML) from John J. Norwich, *Great Architecture of the World* (New York: Bonanza Books, 1975), 132; (B) tomb of Christ, from

Fernand Cabrol and Henri Leclerq, *Dictionnaire d'archéologie chrétienne et de liturgie*, 15 vols. (Paris: Letouzey, 1907), vol. 1, pt. 3, col. 2929, fig. 988; (C) tourist map, redrawn (ML) from Desmond Stewart, *Mecca* (New York: Newsweek, 1980), 20; (D) Great Mosque, modified and redrawn (ML) from ibid., 166.

Figure 36, p. 148. (A) Ark of the Covenant, reconstruction (ML) based on Exodus 25:10–22, and Werner Keller, *The Bible as History* (New York: Murrow, 1956), 134; (B) Egyptian ark, Karnak, Pylon VII, redrawn and slightly restored (ML) from *Lepsius Denkmaler*, III, 14; (C) Abydos ark, slightly restored (ML) from Herbert Winlock, *Bas-Reliefs from the Temple of Ramses I at Abydos* (New York: Metropolitan Museum of Art, 1921), pl. 1.

Figure 37, pp. 150–51. (A) obelisks of Senwsret I, reconstruction (ML) of vanished temple to north of remaining right-hand obelisk. R. Engelbach, "The Direction of the Inscriptions on Obelisks," *ASAE* 29 (1929): 28; quotation from Maqrīzī al-Khiṭaṭ (Beirut: Dar Sader, reprint of Bulaq edition), 1:230, line 2; translation courtesy of Dr. William Hamblin; concerning lampstands, cf. W. Robertson Smith, *Religion of the Semites* (Edinburgh: Adam and Charles Black, 1889), 468, and W. F. Albright, "Two Cressets from Marisa and the Pillars of Jachin and Boaz," *Bulletin of the American Schools of Oriental Research* 85 (February 1942): 18–27; (B) temple model from Idalium, Cyprus, redrawn (ML) from Goodenough, *Jewish Symbols*, vol. 4, ill. 25; (C) Cyzicus coin, redrawn (ML) from Martin Price, *Coins and Their Cities* (Detroit: Wayne State University Press, 1977), 110, fig. 201; (D) Kogi sun temple, reconstruction (ML) from descriptions and diagrams in Gerardo Reichel-Dolmatoff, "The Loom of Life," *Journal of Latin American Lore* 4/1 (1978): 16–19; cf. fig. 33D; (E) Torah shrine, redrawn (ML) from Kurt Weitzmann, *Age of Spirituality* (Princeton: Metropolitan Museum of Art, 1979), 372; (F) baptismal font, redrawn (ML) from ibid., 648; (G) spiral column, redrawn (ML) from

Michael Grant, ed., *Greece and Rome: The Birth of Western Civilization* (London: Thames and Hudson, 1986), 21; (H) "square knot" column, redrawn (ML) from Frederic van der Meer, *Atlas of the Early Christian World* (London: Nelson, 1958), fig. 248; these columns inspired numerous imitations, e.g., the Cathedral at Trento, Italy, and Wurzburg Cathedral; (I) Charles I pillars, redrawn (ML) from Ottfried Neubecker, *Heraldry, Sources, Symbols and Meaning* (London, McGraw Hill, 1976), 211–12; concerning the dollar sign, see Harwood Frost, *Evolution of the Dollar* (Chicago: privately published, 1927), 61–64; (J) columned niche, redrawn (ML) from Boudet, *Jerusalem, A History*, 219; (K) silver Torah plaque, redrawn (ML) from Goodenough, *Jewish Symbols*, vol. 7, ill. 89.

Figure 38, pp. 154–55. (A) butter paddle, redrawn (ML) from Aylward M. Blackman, "The Porridge Stirrer as an Egyptian Hieroglyph," *Man* (1909): 168; (B) Pakastani butter churn, redrawn (ML) from Najma Jusuf, "How We Live in Pakistan," *Junior Scholastic* (9 February 1970): 12; J. D. McGuire, "A Study of the Primitive Methods of Drilling," *Annual Report of the U.S. National Museum* (1894): 714; (C) marble image of divine butter churn, "Samudra Mutu," from McGuire, "A Study of the Primitive Methods of Drilling," 742, fig. 177; (D) Angkor Thom, redrawn (ML) from Miloslav Krása, *The Temples of Angkor* (London: Wingate, 1963), 103; (E) Shinto priest, redrawn (ML) from Floyd H. Ross, *Shinto: The Way of Japan* (Boston: Beacon Press, 1965), 63; (F) German need fire, from Paul Herrmann, *Altdeutsche Kultgebräuche* (Jena: Diederichs, 1928), 35.

Figure 39, p. 160. (A) pillar omphalos, amphora, *LIMC* vol. 3, pt. 2, p. 599, Erinys 51; (B) Delphi omphalos, redrawn (ML) from photograph, Delphi Museum; (C) Nubian omphalos, redrawn (ML) from F. Ll. Griffith, "An Omphalos from Napata," *Journal of Egyptian Archaeology* 3 (1916): 255; (D) Pompeian omphalos, House of the Vettii, redrawn (ML) from *LIMC* vol. 2, pt. 2, p. 327, Apollo 356;

(E) Orphic bowl, redrawn (ML) from R. Delbrueck and W. Vollgraff, "An Orphic Bowl," *Journal of Hellenic Studies* 54 (1934): 129–39, pl. III.

Figure 40, p. 163. (A) ziggurat, redrawn (ML) from André Parrot, *The Tower of Babel* (New York: Philosophical Library, 1955), 39; S. Mayassis, *Mystères et initiations* (Athens: Bibliothèque d'Archéologie Orientale d'Athènes, 1961), 63, describes the ziggurat at Borsippa and its seven colored levels related to the planets; (B) planisphere, from L. W. King, *Cuneiform Texts from Babylonian Tablets in the British Museum*, Part XXXIII (London: British Museum, 1912), pl. 10.

Figure 41, pp. 166–67. (A) Avebury, redrawn (ML) from Alan Sorrell's reconstruction in Aubrey Burl, *Prehistoric Avebury* (New Haven & London: Yale University Press, 1979), 231, fig. 100; (B) Silbury Hill, redrawn (ML) from ibid., 129, fig. 56; (C) beehive tomb, Ile Longue, Brittany, redrawn (ML) from W. Müller, *Der heilige Stadt* (Stuttgart: Kohlhammer, 1961), 224; (D) Medamud mound, redrawn (ML) from Alexander Badawy, *A History of Egyptian Architecture*, 3 vols. (Berkeley: University of California Press, 1954), 1:116; (E) Osiris mound, British Museum Papyrus 1008, redrawn (ML) from Andrzej Niwiński, *Theban Funerary Papyri* (Freiburg, Switzerland: Universitäts-Verlag, 1989), pl. 29a; (F) Osiris mound with trees, stone sarcophagus, Museum of Marseilles, redrawn (ML) from Robert Lawlor, *Sacred Geometry* (London: Thames and Hudson, 1982), 60; (G) Step Pyramid, redrawn (ML) from Jean-Philippe Lauer, *Les pyramides de Sakkarah* (Cairo: IFAO, 1977), fig. 6; (H) Pyramid of Unas, redrawn (ML) from Alexandre Piankoff, *The Pyramid of Unas* (Princeton: Princeton University Press, 1968), pl. 1, foldout B.

Figure 42, p. 168. Hopewell mound, High Bank Works, 5 miles south of Chillicothe, Ohio, redrawn (ML) from Ray Hively and Robert Horn, "Hopewellian Geometry and Astronomy at High Bank," *Archaeoastronomy* 7 (1984): S94, fig. 7.

Figure 43, pp. 180–81. Shabako Stone, black granite, .92 x 1.3 m, British Museum No. 498, James H. Breasted, "The Philosophy of a Memphite Priest," *Zeitschrift für Ägyptische Sprache* 39 (1901): pl. 1.

Figure 44, p. 218. Ammon, from *Hieratische Papyrus aus den Königlichen Museen zu Berlin* (Leipzig: Hinrichs'sche Buchhandlung, 1905), P3056, 30–31, line 1; Wilhelm Spiegelberg, *Mythus vom Sonnenauge* (Strassburg: Schultz, 1917), 72, 53.

Figure 45, p. 222. Skyscraper, redrawn (TM) from Thierry Mauger, *Bedouins of Arabia* (Paris, Souffles, 1988), fig. 45. Concerning the king's tower, see Harlan B. Clark, "Yemen," *National Geographic* 92/5 (November 1947): 660.

Figure 46, p. 229. (A) Stellar observation, redrawn (ML) from I. E. S. Edwards, *Pyramids of Egypt*, rev. ed. (Middlesex: Penguin, 1985), 247, fig. 56; (B) rope-stretching ceremony, shrine of Hatshepsut, Karnak, redrawn (ML) from Isha Schwaller de Lubicz, *Her-Bak, Egyptian Initiate* (Rochester, VT: Inner Traditions, 1967), 187, fig.31.

Figure 47, p. 239. Three men in white, Dura Europos Synagogue, redrawn (ML) from Goodenough, *Jewish Symbols*, vol. 11, ill. 334.

Figure 48, p. 259. *Heb-sed* pavilion, Cairo Museum, redrawn, slightly restored (ML) from Vagn Poulsen, *Egyptian Art* (Greenwich, CT: New York Graphic Society, 1968), 82, and Lucie Lamy, *Egyptian Mysteries* (New York: Crossroad, 1981), 77.

Figure 49, p. 278. Abraham and the angel, Gustav Davidson, *A Dictionary of Angels* (New York: Free Press, 1967), 317, citing *Apocalypse of Abraham* (St. Petersburg: Slavonic Church Publication, 1891).

Figure 50, p. 300. Mandaean handclasp, from E. S. Drower, "Mandaean Writings," *Iraq* 1/2 (November 1934): 173.

Figure 51, p. 390. (A) Imhotep, Late Period, Cairo Museum, redrawn (ML) from Manfred Lurker, *Gods and Symbols of Ancient Egypt* (London: Thames & Hudson, 1980), 70; (B) Hermes Trismegistus, redrawn (ML) from Eric Iversen, *The Myth of Egypt and Its Hieroglyphs* (Copenhagen: Gec Gad, 1961), pl. IX.2.

Figure 52, p. 398. Dr. Faustus summoning the devil, redrawn (ML) from woodcut in Christopher Marlowe, *The Tragicall Historie of the Life and Death of Dr. Faustus* (1631), title page.

Figure 53, p. 400. Collapsing world mountain, Buddhist cave temple, c. A.D. 700, Kizil, Sinkian, China, redrawn and slightly restored (ML) from Albert Gruenwedel, *Altbuddhistische Kultstaetten in Chinesisch-Turkestan* (Berlin: Reimer, 1912), 46, fig. 92.

Figure 54, p. 404. Phanes within the zodiac, redrawn (ML) from *LIMC* vol. 1, pt. 2, p. 314, Aion 17.

Figure 55, p. 413. Kepler's model, from Giorgio de Santillana and Hertha von Dechend, *Hamlet's Mill* (Boston: Gambit, 1969), opp. 222, from Johannes Kepler, *Mysterium Cosmographicum* (1621).

Figure 56, p. 414. Newton's diagram, redrawn (ML) from Malcolm W. Browne, "In Alchemists' Notes, Clues to Modern Chemistry," *New York Times Science*, 10 April 1990, B9.

Figure 57, pp. 416–17. Cabalistic tree of life, from Athanasius Kircher, *Oedipus Aegyptiacus*, 3 vols. in 4 (Rome: Mascardi, 1652–54), 2:288.

Figure 58, pp. 422–23. Masonic monitor , slightly restored (ML) from James Hardie, *The New Free-Mason's Monitor; or, Masonic Guide* (New York, 1818), frontispiece.

Figure 59, p. 455. Library lintel, redrawn (ML) from Jean Capart, "L'exaltation du livre," *Chronique d'Égypte* 22 (1946): 25, fig. 1.

Figure 60, p. 455. (A) Narmer's palette, from Walter B. Emery, *Archaic Egypt* (Baltimore, MD: Penguin, 1961), 45;

(B) standing scribe, redrawn (ML) from Heinrich Schäfer, *Principles of Egyptian Art* (Oxford: Clarendon, 1974), pl. 23; (C) ivory tablet, Philadelphia University Museum, redrawn (ML) from W. M. Flinders Petrie, *The Royal Tombs of the Earliest Dynasties* (London and Boston: Egypt Exploration Fund, 1901), pl. V.1; concerning Sirius, see L. van der Waerden, "Babylonian Astronomy II," *Journal of Near Eastern Studies* 8 (1949): 7.

Figure 61, p. 464. Hebrew letter constellations, from Kircher, *Oedipus Aegyptiacus*, 2:268, 3:217–18.

Figure 62, p. 466. Egyptian cattle brands, Tomb of Userhet, redrawn (ML) from Walter Wreszinski, *Atlas zur altaegyptischen Kulturgeschichte* (Leipzig: Hinrichs'sche Buchhandlung, 1923), vol. 1, pt. 2, pl. 187; tomb of Kenamen, redrawn (ML) from William K. Simpson, *Egypt's Golden Age*, Exhibition Catalogue (Boston: Museum of Fine Arts, Boston, 1982), 49, fig. 20.

Figure 63, p. 466. The gods writing pharaoh's name on Ished leaves, Ramesseum, slightly restored (ML) from Champollion, *Monuments*, vol. 4, pl. CCCXXXIV.

Figure 64, p. 475. The Mexican Catechism, from Kurt Sethe, *Vom Bilde zum Buchstaben: Die Enstehungsgeschichte der Schrift* (*Untersuchungen zur Geschichte und Altertumskunde Aegyptens* 12) (Hildesheim: Olms, 1964), 9. fig. 12.

Figure 65, p. 475. Sethe's "evolutionary" development of the alphabet, redrawn (ML) from ibid., 58, fig. 24.

Figure 66, p. 482. Deseret alphabet on an 1860 gold coin, redrawn (ML) from a color postcard.

Figure 67, p. 553. "The greater light to rule the day—the lesser light to rule the night," Wulf Barsch, 1991, oil on gessoed paper, 35 x 24 1/2 inches, painted especially for this volume, courtesy of the artist.

Index of Passages

571

Index of Subjects

Aaron, 55–57, 97

Abraham: sacrifice of, 59; connection of temple with, 77–78; transformation of star shown to, 277, 279, 522–23; was instructed by angel, 301; prayer offered by, 307; ordinances given to, 317–18

Adam, 77; garment of, 124, 125, 127–32; Satan refuses to worship, 195–96; is visited by "Sent Ones," 299–303; journey home of, after death, 304–5; role of, in creation, 306; prayer offered by, 306–7; ordinances given to, 307–8

Ahlstrom, G. A., 47

Albert, Karl, 381, 399–400

Aldiss, Brian Wilson, 515

Alexandria, university of, 269–70, 276

Alphabet: Egypt as home of, 474, 477; Semitic, 481–82. *See also* Writing

Altmann, Alexander, 417

Anaxagoras, 351

Angel: visit of, to Zacharias, 42–43; seen by Mary, 43; Abraham taught by, 301, 522–23; appearance of, causes fear, 388

Animals: sacrifice of, 54–58; resurrection of, 320–21

Anna, 44

Apocalypse of Abraham, 35, 38, 317–18, 522–23

Apocalyptic imagery, 235–37

Apocrypha: knowledge of gospel expanded by, 179; premortal existence expounded in, 186–92, 369; doctrine of Two Ways in, 195–99, 220; were outlawed by American Bible Society, 258–59; multiple worlds mentioned in, 285–86, 290–92; mention of prayer circles in, 313–16; passages from, likened to science fiction, 520–27. *See also* Apocrypha and Book of Mormon, parallel images in

Apocrypha and Book of Mormon, parallel images in: desert imagery, 220–21; plan of salvation, 223–32; heavenly treasures, 233–35; apocalyptic statements, 235–37; filthy and pure waters, 239–41; "looking beyond the mark," 241–43; flight into wilderness, 243–44; tree of life, 244; prophet Zenos/Zenez, 244–51; doctrine of

585

Redeemer, 252; likening
scriptures to selves, 252–55;
righteous designated as
poor, 253–54; ritual war, 255;
kings and covenants, 255–58
Apostasy, 395–97
Apostles, twelve, of Christ: in
prayer circle, 22, 96, 309,
313–16; ordinances revealed
to, 28, 295–96, 309–11; as
"Sent Ones," 299, 303
Aquinas, Thomas, 294, 362
Architecture of temple, circle
and square in, 145, 149
Aristides, 200, 275, 357
Aristophanes, 391
Ark of the covenant, 145
Asimov, Isaac, 508, 519
Assembly, New Year's, 153,
156–62
Athanasius, 227, 292
At-one-ment, yearning for,
379, 381–82, 399–400, 404–5
Atonement of Christ: decay
reversed by, 10; infinite
nature of, 10
Augustine, 47, 149, 152, 316,
361, 370
Avebury, 162–69, 382

Babel, tower of, 13
Babylonians: fear of chaos
among, 13; creation hymn
of, 161; search of, for lost
knowledge, 215
Bank: system of, rooted in
temple, 23; as rival of
temple, 33–34
Barnabas, 349–50
Barsch, Wulf, 552–54
Bauer, Hans, 477
Behaviorism, 510–11

Bell, Eric Temple, 493
Benjamin, King, 256–58
Bennett, John C., 425–26
Bernhardt, J. K., 256
Blacks, Church policy
regarding, 532–39
Blood, symbolism of, 55, 57–58
Book of Life, 158, 214–15
Book of Mormon, 212–14; olive
culture in, 251–52;
supported by Dead Sea
Scrolls, 325. See also
Apocrypha and Book of
Mormon, parallel images in
Book of the Dead, 402
Borel, P., 365
Bousset, W., 362
Brain: computer cannot
replace, 7–8; lack of
evolutionary need for, 340–
41
Brandon, S., 45–46
Brewer, J. M., 493
Bruno, Giordano, 365
Building: temple as,
importance attached to, 29–
32; great and spacious,
imagery of, 221, 223
Bultmann, Rudolph, 362
Burckhardt, Jacob, 403
Burl, Aubrey, 164–65
Bush, Lester E., 532–39
Business: serious education
supplanted by, 391–92, 395;
writing systems associated
with, 465; rejecting gospel in
favor of, 550–51

Cabalism, 274, 415, 417
Cain, 221, 223, 537–38
Calder, Nigel, 1–2, 7
Catullus, 341–42